THE AGE OF
THE DEMOCRATIC REVOLUTION

THE STRUGGLE

The Age of the
Democratic Revolution

A POLITICAL HISTORY OF
EUROPE AND AMERICA, 1760-1800

★ ★

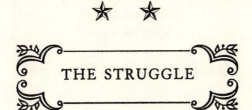

THE STRUGGLE

BY R. R. PALMER

PRINCETON, NEW JERSEY

PRINCETON UNIVERSITY PRESS

L.C. Card: 59-10068

S.B.N. 691-00570-2

First Princeton Paperback Printing, 1970

Printed in the United States of America
by Princeton University Press, Princeton, New Jersey

★ PREFACE ★

THIS book describes the confrontation that took place in Europe and America at the time of the French Revolution and the wars that accompanied it. Though it can be read independently, the book is a sequel to one published in 1959 under the same title, but subtitled "The Challenge," as the present one is subtitled "The Struggle." The connecting thought is that in the years from about 1760 to 1791 or 1792, the period of the earlier volume, revolutionary movements against aristocratic forms of society made themselves evident in many countries, but that except in America they were either crushed or, as in France and Poland in 1791, were of very doubtful success, so that a "challenge" had been issued which awaited resolution by further "struggle." The present volume traces the fortunes of both revolution and counter-revolution to about the year 1800. By that time, it is argued, although counter-revolutionary or aristocratic forces had prevailed in some countries, the new or democratic view had established itself, in a way less than ideal, against attempts of its adversaries to put it down.

The reader can judge whether "democratic revolution" is an appropriate term for the transformations here recounted. Reasons for using it are given at the outset of the earlier volume, and will be apparent at many places in the present one. I have tried to take note of criticisms raised against the plan of the work after publication of the first volume. Some have thought that my interpretations are too purely political, and give inadequate attention to social or economic realities. Others, doubting the feasibility of a comparative view of so many countries, have stressed the distinctive peculiarity of the situation in England, France, or America. Many have questioned whether there was any real revolution except the actual French Revolution, which, they fear, is minimized when seen as part of a wider revolutionary disturbance. Here also it is for the reader to judge; but I do not think I have slighted the national peculiarity of any country, and I do not see how anyone, upon reading the present volume, can think the importance of the French Revolution to be understated.

It has been difficult or impossible to find, in English, any account of certain areas of Europe at this time, and notably of the Batavian, Cisalpine, and Helvetic Republics. I have therefore adopted a regional arrangement, hoping to give a concrete picture of each of these revolutionary states in turn, as well as of Britain and Ireland, Poland and

Eastern Europe, Germany and America—and of course France. At the same time I have tried to avoid a merely country-by-country treatment, and to set forth a chronological narrative of events on the wider stage of Western Civilization. It is hoped that this broader view will be apparent, not only in Chapters I, XI and XVII, where it is most explicitly aimed at, but also in the way in which more geographically localized chapters are put into relation to each other.

My obligations are numerous. I am indebted to younger colleagues, who, as assistants, have read for me in languages that I do not know: Messrs. Jeffry Kaplow and William Blackwell in Russian, Peter Kenez in Hungarian, Andre Michalski in Polish, and H. A. Barton in Swedish. I wish I had been able to make better use, in a fuller treatment of Latin America, of the help given me by my friends, Professor and Mrs. Stanley J. Stein, in Spanish and Portuguese. For permission to reproduce, with adaptations, the contents of three articles of which I am the author, I am indebted to the editors of the *Journal of Modern History, French Historical Studies,* and the *Proceedings of the American Philosophical Society.* Mrs. Louis Gantz of Princeton has done most of the typing, Professor Stanley E. Howard of Princeton has assisted with the proofs, and Mrs. Leon Gottfried of St. Louis has prepared the index.

For the freedom given in the use of my own time I should like to thank the Rockefeller Foundation, which has generously supported this volume as it did its predecessor. Without the Princeton University Library, in which most of the research was done, the book would probably never have been written. As so often in the past, I am under a great obligation to the officers and staff of the Princeton University Press, and notably to its Director, Mr. Herbert S. Bailey, Jr., and its Managing Editor, Miss Miriam Brokaw. Most of all, most lastingly and most deeply, I am indebted to Princeton University itself, which over a period of many years made possible the conditions for the writing of this and other books. In particular, I must gladly acknowledge the aid received from the Council of the Humanities at Princeton, and from the Benjamin D. Shreve Fellowship awarded by the Department of History there.

For all such help I express my thanks, the more feelingly since I am no longer at Princeton, and have now completed a work that has occupied me, with interruptions, for fourteen years. *Forsan et haec olim meminisse iuvabit!*

R. R. PALMER

Washington University
St. Louis, Mo.
May 1964

★ CONTENTS ★

CONTENTS

MAPS

THE AGE OF THE DEMOCRATIC REVOLUTION

Every European is today part of this last struggle of civilization. . . . The Revolution being cosmopolitan, so to speak, ceases to belong exclusively to the French.—J. MALLET DU PAN, Brussels, August 1793

THE ISSUES AND THE ADVERSARIES

"WHAT had *liberty* and the *rights of man* to do with this second revolution?" Noah Webster posed the question in a tract on the French Revolution published in New York at the height of the Reign of Terror. By the second revolution he meant the events in France in the summer of 1792. Later historians have also used the term "second revolution" for these events—the popular upheaval in Paris which led to the attack on the Tuileries on August 10, the dethronement, humiliation, and subsequent death of Louis XVI, the collapse of the first constitution of the Revolution, the deportation of priests, the September Massacres, the mounting violence, the streaming of French armies across the frontiers into neighboring countries, and the famous decree of November by which the French Republic offered "aid and fraternity to all peoples wishing to recover their liberty."

A methodical man, author of children's spelling books, eventually to be famous as a maker of dictionaries, Webster admitted that he had welcomed the French Revolution of 1789. He had seen in it the same objectives as the Americans had sought in 1776. But the developments since 1792 went beyond anything he could approve. They showed a "wild enthusiasm," a "political insanity." In American politics he had become rather conservative; at least he was now a staunch Federalist. He could hardly share the enthusiasm for France which American democrats continued to feel. But he was far from taking part in the unqualified denunciation that was the stock in trade of Federalist polemics. He was willing to admit, as news of the guillotinings was brought by successive vessels into American seaports, that not all the relevant facts might be known. The French, he thought, were excited because foreign powers had tried to intervene in their affairs. "Perhaps other circumstances, not known in this country, may serve to palliate the apparent cruelty of the ruling faction." Like a Jeffersonian republican, Webster remarked that the French were at war with "a vile league of tyrants." Personally, he hoped and believed that they would be victorious.[1]

Noah Webster never did understand the French Revolution of 1792, or the relation of the ensuing violence to "liberty" and the "rights of man." It is a question that will always be open to discussion. But he put his finger on part of the answer when he pointed to the war. In April 1792 France had declared war on the "King of Hungary and Bohemia," that is the House of Austria or Hapsburg, which, since it possessed most of Belgium, was the most important of the powers that adjoined the French frontiers. By the following summer the French were also at war with the kingdoms of Prussia and Sardinia, and by 1793 with Great Britain, the Dutch Republic, and the Bourbon Monarchy of Spain.

The war revolutionized the Revolution, in the words of Professor Marcel Reinhard of the Sorbonne, making it more drastic at home and more powerful in its effects abroad. With the war, a specifically French Revolution was merged into a more general Revolution of Western Civilization.[2]

In an earlier volume I have tried to explain how revolution or serious political protest had broken out in many countries—in preceding years—at Geneva in Switzerland in 1768, in the American Revolution in the 1770's, in the discontents of Ireland, in the reform movement in Britain, among the Dutch and the Belgians in the 1780's, in Poland and to an extent in Hungary between 1788 and 1791, and not least in France in 1789. It was argued in that volume that except in America these movements had not succeeded. By the year 1791 the established interests had triumphantly prevailed in Britain, Ireland, Holland, Belgium, Hungary, and Geneva; the Polish revolution was in process of liquidation; and in France the Constitution of 1791 was by no means generally accepted, nor had the dispossessed interests by any means admitted defeat or even the necessity of compromise. Everywhere a "democratic" revolution had challenged the aristocracies, patriciates, oligarchies, and privileged orders. But nothing was settled. "Only a challenge had been issued to the old order; the real struggle was yet to come." With these closing words of the earlier book the present one may open.[3]

[1] Noah Webster, *The Revolution in France Considered in Its Progress and Effects* (New York, 1794), 3-4, 38, 70.
[2] See Jacques Godechot, *La grande nation: l'expansion révolutionnaire de la France*, 2 vols. (Paris, 1956).
[3] *Age of the Democratic Revolution: A Political History of Europe and America, 1760-1800.* Vol. 1, *The Challenge* (Princeton, 1959), 364-70, 502. This volume will henceforth be cited as *Age*, 1.

The struggle worked itself out in conjunction with the war. The forces that had opposed democratizing changes in their own countries for twenty years now opposed the France of the Revolution. Those who for a generation had hoped to open up their own societies looked with more favor on developments in France. The war that began in April 1792, and that lasted essentially, though with intermissions and shifts of alliances, until the second exile of Napoleon in 1815, was not simply a war between "France" and "Europe." "France" had its friends in all countries, and "Europe" its well-wishers within the boundaries of France. Despite occasional appearances, or stated war aims, the war became an ideological conflict between new and old—between "democratic" and "aristocratic" forms of society in the sense explained in the preceding volume.

It is a complex story, in which not everything can be told. Something must be said of a dozen European countries and of America. In the following pages the method will vary from the expository to the impressionistic. Let us begin with a tale of two cities, involving ceremonial events in Frankfurt and Paris on July 14, 1792. It was, of course, Bastille Day, but it was also the date of the imperial coronation of Francis II, a young man of twenty-four who proved to be the last Holy Roman Emperor.

Bastille Day, 1792

"Those concerned seem to attach importance to the appropriateness of the day, in crowning the Emperor on the very day of the anniversary of the taking of the Bastille, that is in choosing for the destruction of the Revolution in France the very day on which it began." It was the Abbé Maury, cardinal designate, papal nuncio at Frankfurt, who thus reported to the Curia a few days before the coronation. Or, as the correspondent of the *Leyden Gazette* remarked, writing from Frankfurt, "The date of this solemnity did not pass unnoticed, being the very day of another at Paris with the honors inverted."[4]

The free city of Frankfurt had for centuries been the site of the imperial coronation. Most of the old city was destroyed by bombing in 1944. Into its now vanished hive of crooked streets, churches, and public buildings, in July 1792, there converged a variety of great or important persons in whom the Old Order was ostentatiously represented.

[4] J. S. Maury, *Correspondance diplomatique et Mémoires inédits*, 2 vols. (Paris, 1891), 1, 68; *Gazette de Leyde* for July 27, 1792.

There were the young Emperor Francis and his wife. There was the brother of the French king, the Count of Artois, leader of the most irreconcilable of the French émigrés, expecting to return momentarily to France now that the Allied armies were about to invade it. With him were three generations of the princely house of Condé, and Marshals de Broglie and de Castries. Calonne, Louis XVI's reforming minister of 1786, was in close attendance; as "prime minister of the emigration" he expected to be prime minister of the new government which the Allied victory would make possible in France.

The three ecclesiastical Electors of the Holy Roman Empire were present for the coronation in person. So was Prince Esterhazy, the great Hungarian magnate. The Swedish count Axel de Fersen was there, the secret correspondent and personal devotee of Marie Antoinette, whom he had tried and failed to spirit out of France a year before. He had just received another note from her, in cypher, telling how Lafayette and other French generals meant to get the king out of Paris within the next few days. The Swiss Mallet du Pan was among those present; he had lived for years in Paris, and brought secret messages from Louis XVI himself. He made little impression, since he was lacking in rank for the circles now assembled in Frankfurt, and his political opinions, like those that he conveyed from Louis XVI, were brushed aside as too conciliatory toward the Revolution. The Abbé Maury represented the Pope. He had sat for two years in the Constituent Assembly, where he had been one of the chief spokesmen against the early phase of the Revolution. He now anticipated an early restoration of the French church and clergy.

Representing the younger generation, apart from the Emperor himself, were Prince Augustus Frederick, the sixth son of King George III of England, who had come down from his studies at Göttingen, and the young Klemens von Metternich, who had recently, as a student at Strasbourg, had a chance to see something of the French Revolution at first hand. His father, newly appointed imperial minister for the Belgian provinces, was grappling with the problem of bringing the Belgian revolutionaries of 1789 under control. It was at Frankfurt in 1792 that Francis II and the younger Metternich first met. They were to know each other well in later years, cooperating at the interminable task of putting down revolution, a task which in Metternich's case would last until 1848.

The city was full of excitement. Prussian troops kept passing through on the way to France. Three regiments marched through the streets, pausing stiffly before the Emperor's lodgings, during the days of the celebration. It was uncertain whether they could arrive in time. The Emperor expressed concern that harm might befall his aunt, Marie Antoinette, during the Bastille Day demonstrations in Paris. The date provoked apprehension for Frankfurt also, since the city was full of newspapers and pamphlets brought in from Strasbourg, written in German and extolling the new order in France. It was possible that there might be manifestations of sympathy for France among the townspeople. Internal security was turned over to the Austrian General Brentano, who used reliable troops, and took care to close the city gates on July 14. It was reassuring to learn at this moment that the Erfurt Academy of Sciences was offering a prize of one hundred thalers, to be given for "the best popular writing in which the German people are instructed in the advantages of the Constitution of their own country, and warned against the evils to which exaggerated ideas of unlimited liberty and idealistic equality may lead."[5]

The Emperor arrived on July 11, incognito, but with a train of forty carriages, already chosen by the imperial electors, as a Hamburg paper expressed it, "to the supreme headship of the German empire, the first of the human race . . . to celebrate the thousandth year of the Roman emperorship, and in another eight short years to begin a new millennium of the Roman-German empire."[6]

The coronation was staged in keeping with the Golden Bull of 1356, but with more than the usual solemnity in view of the seriousness of the times. Maury told the Pope that he wept with emotion, and that the Archbishop of Mainz had employed the Roman pontifical service. Francis took the oath in a firm voice. The gorgeous procession then left the cathedral in the rain, amid cheers of undampened enthusiasm, to the discharge of cannon and peal of bells, with the Emperor wearing the six-pound crown, and bearing the orb and scepter. Goldpieces were thrown to the multitude, and red and white wine flowed from certain fountains.

That night Prince Esterhazy gave a ball. Young Metternich opened the dance with the Princess of Mecklenburg, the future Queen Louise

---

[5] *Hamburgische unparteischen Correspondent* for July 20, 1792.

[6] *Politisches Journal* (Hamburg, 1792), ii, 767. Details on July 14 at Frankfurt are taken from reports in these two Hamburg periodicals, from the memoirs of Maury, studies of Metternich, Calonne, Mallet du Pan, and Fersen; and from I. Kracauer, "Frankfurt und die französiche Revolution, 1789-92," in *Archiv für Frankfurts Geschichte und Kunst*, 3rd ser. ix (1907), 211-97.

of Prussia. Nineteen years old, he had been designated for the coronation as Master of Ceremonies of the Catholic Westphalian Imperial Princely Bench. At this ball Esterhazy spent ten thousand guilders on the illuminations alone. A few years later Gouverneur Morris was told in Vienna that Esterhazy had spent eighty thousand English pounds in six weeks at Frankfurt in 1792, so that, although the wealthiest subject in Europe, his estate was in the hands of its creditors. The American Morris took this as a sign of the "feudal system" in its decline.[7]

The Prussian troops continued to pass through the city, and the Emperor and his advisors, Maury, the French émigrés, and various others moved on to Mainz, there to take counsel with the King of Prussia on their joint policies toward France. They considered a manifesto to the city of Paris, of which more will be said.

In Paris the proceedings of July 14 showed "the honors inverted." Since 1790 the anniversary of the Bastille had been the day of the *fédération*, on which patriotic delegations from various communities met together regionally, and also at a national level in Paris, to "federate" with each other, that is to pledge themselves to each other and to the new constitution in support of the new order in France. Organized by the political clubs which had sprung up everywhere, these exchanges of delegates were a means by which men who had had no chance for political experience before 1789 acquired a sense of political awareness and participation, felt themselves to constitute a "nation" by the use of their own free will, or to act collectively, as they saw it, as a free and sovereign people. The federation of 1792 was the first since the beginning of the war. The war had gone badly, the Prussians were approaching, the king was distrusted, and the émigrés announced with loud menaces their imminent return. The Assembly had passed a decree of national emergency, *la patrie en danger*. Bells clanged in Paris as in Frankfurt, but they were bells of alarm, the tocsin.

The men who converged on Paris to celebrate July 14 were therefore very different from those who converged upon Frankfurt for the same day. They were the patriots and superpatriots sent in from the provinces, or rather by the authorities of the new "departments" into which the provinces had been reorganized. By half-dozens or by hundreds they dribbled into the capital, where they joined with one another and with the Parisians in a great surge of national and revolutionary feeling, to defend the Revolution against all who might threaten it—the foreign

[7] *Diary and Letters of Gouverneur Morris*, 2 vols. (New York, 1888), II, 248.

powers, the émigrés, the aristocrats, the French king and queen—against all who might be suspected of treachery, or who merely by moderation might open the way to the enemy. Some of the congregating provincials arrived too late for the actual day. Among these were several hundred from Marseilles, who on July 14 were somewhere in central France on a twenty-seven-day walk from Marseilles to Paris. As they trudged through the countryside they chanted Rouget de Lisle's new war song, since known as the Marseillaise. Its refrain leaped from town to town: *Aux armes, citoyens, Formez vos bataillons*!

The observance in Paris took place at the Champs de Mars, the open area now graced by the Eiffel Tower, then lying on the outskirts of the city. The Ecole Militaire was there then, as today; from one of its balconies Marie Antoinette and the court looked down upon the proceedings. Sixty or a hundred thousand people filled the space, some in the uniforms of the National Guard and keeping casual military formations, others in the ordinary clothing of the various social classes of Paris, individuals, families, children in holiday mood to see a bit of pageantry and public festivity. Along the edge of the crowd was a series of tents, one for each of the eighty-three departments, each with its name in a tricolor decoration. Near the Seine, about where the Eiffel Tower now stands, was a temporary structure put up for the occasion, some twenty feet high, with a curved flight of steps and adorned with classical urns, and at the top an oblong block on which a copy of the constitution rested. This was the Altar of the Country, *l'autel de la patrie*. Near it stood a "genealogical tree," a sapling already felled and placed here for the day, with a pile of kindling at its base. From its branches hung escutcheons, coats of arms, and coronets of various descriptions, the apparatus of "counts and barons, but not of kings," as one Paris newspaper reported, "blue ribbons, gold chains, ermine mantles, parchment titles and all the baubles of the former nobility."[8]

The much buffeted Louis XVI still occupied his shaken throne, and he led the procession, consisting of his own guard, and of members of the Assembly and various civic magistrates, from the Ecole Militaire the length of the Champs de Mars, through the crowds and through the massed pikes and bayonets of the citizens in arms, to the Altar of the Country at the other end. Here he mounted the steps and renewed his oath to the constitution, which he was of course known to have re-

---

[8] *Révolutions de Paris*, Nos. 157 and 158, pp. 81-82, 97-106. Details on July 14 at Paris are taken from this journal, and from A. Mathiez, *Le Dix-Aout* (Paris, 1931) and *La Révolution et les étrangers* (Paris, 1918).

pudiated at the time of the flight to Varennes. The genealogical tree was then ignited. The emblems of aristocracy went up in smoke. The French people thus published their counter-threat to the French émigrés, and their defiance to Europe.

In Paris as in Frankfurt there were a good many foreigners on July 14, though except for occasional appearances at the Jacobin club, or at the bar of the Assembly, they played no public role. Some were individual travelers, sympathizers with the Revolution, such as James Watt, Jr., son of the inventor of the steam engine, who was there partly out of curiosity and partly as a salesman for his father's industrial products. Others were political exiles, émigrés of an opposite character to those who attended Prince Esterhazy's ball—refugees from the counter-revolution at Geneva, Belgian "democrats" who had fled from the Austrian restoration of 1790, and, above all, the Dutch refugees from the Orange restoration of 1787, of whom thousands had come to France and an unknown number were in Paris. Each of these groups hoped to advance its own cause by the war. As the Count of Artois hoped to re-enter France in the wake of the Prussians and Austrians, so these émigrés in Paris hoped that with French victories they might return to resume their interrupted efforts in their own countries. As the Prince of Condé formed a military unit of French émigrés, "Condé's army," to serve alongside the Austrians, so these other émigrés worked to form auxiliary units of their own nationalities to fight alongside the French. Thus arose Belgian, Dutch, and other "legions," of which more is said in the next chapter.

Ideological War

The war was an ideological war, but anyone who tried to see it as a straight clash between Revolution and Counter-Revolution would soon become confused. Partisans of the Revolution differed violently with each other, as did their opponents. For contemporaries, as for historians, the Revolution might refer to specific events, like the capture of the Bastille, or to a vast personified force, or to an abstract cause for which the French or others might be fighting. It could mean taking titles away from dukes, or giving bread to the poor. It could mean the teachings of Jesus, or of Voltaire. It could be for constitutional kings or no kings, for nations or for mankind. There were not two sides, but a dozen, or a hundred.

"The war of democracy is giving way to the war of intrigue," reported Maury to Rome in August.[9] He meant that when the war had begun, in April, the French had launched it as a crusade, a holy war of liberty against tyrants, in the cause of all peoples against all kings, but that now that the French were worsted, and initiative was passing to the two chief Allies, the various interests that hoped to profit from a French defeat were mainly engrossed in trying to outwit each other. The French émigrés, led by Artois and Calonne, meant to use the Allies to recover their own lost position in France, their manorial estates, and their former perquisites of nobility. Fersen was genuinely concerned for Marie Antoinette, but the émigrés cared little for Louis XVI, whom they regarded as a dupe of the Revolution. Louis XVI had an equally low opinion of the émigrés. Maury hoped to use the Allies to put the French Catholic Church back on its old foundation, and to regain Avignon for the Pope, who had lost it when it was merged into France without his consent, by a plebiscite in 1791. The rulers of Austria and Prussia cared nothing about restoring the French émigrés. If they hoped to assure the personal safety of Louis XVI and Marie Antoinette, and to uphold the dignity of royalty in a general way, they had no program for the internal rearrangement of France, and preferred if anything that the French monarchy should remain weakened by insoluble problems. They cared nothing about the state of the Catholic Church in France—the Prussians were Protestants, and the Austrian government had been anti-Catholic and anti-papal for a decade. It was of no concern to the Powers whether the Pope got back his territory of Avignon, except insofar as by the return of Avignon France might be weakened, and other territorial cessions facilitated. The French émigrés likewise were not noted for churchly devotion; a few became more seriously religious in adversity, but as the Abbé Leflon has remarked, a historian at the Catholic Institute in Paris, the émigrés used religion to beautify their more worldly aims. Pope Pius VI, and the best of the French émigré bishops, did not confuse political or material restitution to the émigrés with the requirements of religion.

The Allies of 1792 were not, by policy or intent, conducting a war for religion or Christianity or the French émigrés, or Louis XVI, or restoration of the Old Regime. As hostilities proceeded, the Austrians developed certain territorial ambitions, hoping to make gains at French expense in Alsace or along the Belgian border. The miniature King

[9] *Mémoires*, I, 89.

of Sardinia had entered the war with similar aims. The Prussians wondered why they were in this queer war at all, since Austria rather than France had been the chief Prussian enemy for generations. For many of the King of Prussia's advisers, and for some in Austria, the whole French adventure was a diversion if not an error, and the important front lay in Poland, where it was expedient to make a quick end to the Polish revolution. Either a successful Polish revival leading to a lasting and independent Polish state, or a collapse in which Poland should be absorbed or dominated by Russia, would be equally distasteful to the courts of Berlin and Vienna. The two German powers therefore held many of their best troops for use on their eastern borders, believing in any case that no full-scale military effort would be necessary against a France weakened by internal anarchy. As for the powers still neutral in 1792, they hoped and expected to remain so. Neither the British nor the Dutch government had any intention of going to war to effect counter-revolution in France. Catherine II, the Russian tsarina, sent money to the French émigrés, and urged on the Prussians and Austrians against the French Jacobins. She refrained from taking part herself. She said that she would "fight Jacobinism, and beat it in Poland."

As for the French, though they talked of the *guerre universelle* of all peoples against all tyrants, they had really gone to war for less cosmopolitan purposes, less to liberate humanity than to serve certain purposes of their own domestic politics. An intense war spirit had arisen in the six months before April 1792. It had been fomented by threats of foreign intervention. In August 1791, by his Declaration of Pillnitz, the then Emperor, Leopold II, had announced that under certain conditions the European powers might collectively take military action against the Revolution in France. The Declaration was qualified and Leopold did not yet think collective intervention likely. He had issued his statement to quiet the importunities of the French émigrés, and in a vague hope of doing something useful for the French king and queen. The émigrés seized on the declaration to intimidate the Revolutionary leaders in Paris. However interpreted. the Declaration naturally caused alarm and indignation in France.

Various groups in France, as the year 1791 passed into 1792, came to feel that a short decisive foreign war would advance their own domestic interests. Each hoped by war to get rid of its adversaries. For the firebrands of the Jacobin Club, a war would make it possible for traitors to the Revolution to be exposed, it would sort out the true and the false patriots, and under conditions of military emergency would allow the use of strong measures by which the Revolution could be carried further. For the liberal or constitutional monarchists, called the Feuillants, the moderates of this stage of the Revolution, a war would consolidate opinion throughout the country, reduce internal dissension, make it possible to suppress radicalism, add to the stature of the executive, and oblige the Assembly to accept the lead of the king and his ministers. For the extreme right, those opposed even to moderate revolution, who had always believed or had come to believe that everything since 1789 was a mistake, a short and sharp war would reveal the chaos and incompetence of the new government, and after a victory by one or more foreign powers, which in these circumstances could not be regarded as enemies of France, the Jacobins and Feuillants and all involved since 1789 in the Revolution would be swept aside, and the true France, the historic France, would be put back together.

Leopold died in March 1792. During the winter he had become more positively inclined toward intervention. In any case his son Francis was closer than his father to those conservative forces in the Hapsburg empire which had opposed the reforming spirit of both Leopold and his predecessor Joseph. These were the people most eager for war with France, which would have the advantage of destroying the center of Revolution, from which certain citizens of Vienna, and everywhere else, were getting dangerous ideas.

In Paris, both the Jacobin Club and the Legislative Assembly resounded with speeches demanding war. Only Robespierre and a handful of others spoke against it almost to the end. Robespierre, at the Jacobins, scoffed at the rhapsodies of Brissot, who said that war would produce a kind of world revolution, in which the peoples everywhere would rise against their governments in sympathy for France and for the cause of freedom. To Robespierre such talk was extravagant ("No one loves armed missionaries") and dangerous for the future of liberty in France: "To want to give liberty to others before conquering it ourselves is to assure our own enslavement and that of the whole world."[10]

The vote on war came in the Assembly on April 20, with only one recorded speech against it, by an obscure deputy named Bequet, a political moderate, who insisted that the war was not inevitable, that Austria did not wish to fight, being mainly concerned with Poland

---

[10] Bouloiseau, Lefebvre, and Soboul, eds., *Oeuvres de Maximilien Robespierre,* VIII (1953), 81-82, speech at Jacobin Club, Jan. 2, 1792.

and more afraid of Russia than of France. Bequet predicted much of what was to follow, saying that if the French entered Belgium to fight the Austrians, and if they threatened Holland, the British would come in and France would face a coalition of all Europe. He was answered by an array of Jacobin luminaries and spellbinders, Brissot, Condorcet, Vergniaud, Bazire, Guadet (the "Girondins" of later historians) who insisted that the war was necessary and right, that it was not a war of "nation against nation," and added the theory (which came to be the "democratic" theory of war) that they had no quarrel with any people, but only with kings and their henchmen. With seven negative votes, war was declared on the King of Hungary and Bohemia.

It was not the purpose of the French to revolutionize other countries by the war, nor of the Allies to bring about counter-revolution in France. It was not in this sense of war-aims that the war was ideological. It became an ideological war, and remained so, because the war came upon a world already divided by serious cleavages. These were the cleavages, of varying depth in different countries but found almost everywhere, described in Volume I.

Given the fact of war, each of the belligerents looked for sympathizers within its enemy's territory. Thus each expected to weaken its adversary. The Allies found their natural friends in France among the more intense royalists and political Catholics. The French enjoyed the favor of persons already discontented with conditions in their own countries. Sometimes these internally alienated groups actively collaborated with the enemies of their governments, as when royalists in France conspired with foreign agents for the invasion of France, or when Dutch democrats, before 1795, entered into understandings with the French for the invasion of Holland. More often it was not by such "treason" (a term always relative to accepted legality) that these internal divisions made themselves felt, so much as by apathy or uncooperativeness with the demands of governments. The war against France was not popular among the burghers of Berlin. Many middleclass people in Vienna, as in Paris, disliked the Emperor's Declaration of Pillnitz in 1791, and showed no enthusiasm for the war in 1792. When Britain and Holland became involved in the war in 1793, the anti-war feeling in both countries was very strong. In France, so far as the war was expected really to defeat the enemy, the royalists, clericals, and other conservatives had the least interest in its vigorous prosecution.

Hence, again given the war as a fact, and independently of original wish or intention, each government made ringing appeals to those of its own subjects who were already inclined to support it. Each government indeed became more dependent than ever on those classes of the population to which it owed its strength. The class complexion of the regime in each country was accentuated. Each government touted and publicized the advantages of the constitution and way of life which it presumably defended. The Hapsburg government, to carry on the war, had increasingly to agree with the landlord and noble interests which it had itself so stoutly resisted in the days of Joseph II. In Germany, the Academy of Erfurt, as already mentioned, hoped to teach the people the peculiar advantages of the *Vaterländische Verfassung*, or "national constitution"; even though no one quite knew what it was, it must be worth fighting for when one was fighting the French. In England the spokesmen of government, to justify the war and recruit support, became more emphatic than ever in praise of the glories of the British Constitution, by which the existing peculiarities of Lords and Commons were principally to be understood. In liberal language, "reform" became impossible; it had, of course, been equally impossible before the war.

This self-praise in each country of its own institutions is not to be taken as a sign of national solidarity. It is evidence rather of internal division and an attempt at persuasion. The secure and the confident do not need such reminders of their own worth. In France, under stress of war, the government, or groups of men who in the turmoil of revolution were attempting to function as a government, tried to appeal to the mass of the population to sustain the military effort. Former nobles, aristocrats, Rome-minded clergy, and people of inherited wealth or position being in these circumstances the least reliable, the government made concession after concession to the more numerous and popular ranks who must man its armies. The leaders of Revolution became dependent on the most committed, most intense, and most activist revolutionaries. They had also to persuade the masses that the Revolution was to their advantage. In this sense, as will be seen in more detail, while the war made other countries more aristocratic in official doctrine, it made the French Revolution more democratic than intended in 1789. Somewhat the same, on a smaller scale, had happened in America in 1775 and 1776, when the members of colonial assemblies, facing war with Britain and needing soldiers, had extended the suffrage or taken other steps toward "equality," and introduced into

American political life a habit of praising the virtues of the common man.

If the war became ideological because each party expected its enemy to be handicapped by internal dissension, and because each made itself agreeable to those classes within its own borders from which it could expect the most enthusiastic support, it became ideological in a third sense also, having to do with revolutionary expansion. Neither France nor Britain or the Coalition entered the war for the purpose of spreading its own ideas. Such, however, was one of the earliest consequences. Each belligerent, when in the course of hostilities it found itself in occupation of enemy territory, like the French in Belgium at the end of 1792, or at Milan in 1796, or like the Austrians in French Flanders in 1793, or the British in Corsica in 1794, naturally favored its own supporters among the local population, and proceeded to organize public authority according to its own principles and through the medium of its own adherents. The British, with certain Corsicans, set up a "Kingdom of Corsica" in 1794, supposedly modelled on Great Britain. But after 1794 the fortunes of war favored the French. The result was a revolution in political geography signified by the contrast between the two maps on pages 18 and 19. By 1799 there existed a cordon of sister-republics, brought into being by collaboration between native revolutionaries and the French government or armies—the Dutch or Batavian Republic of 1795, the Cisalpine and Ligurian Republics set up in Italy in 1796-1797, the Helvetic Republic in Switzerland in 1798, the Roman and Neapolitan Republics in Italy in 1798-1799. There were Irishmen in France and Ireland who would have been delighted to create a Hibernian Republic, independent of Britain, if the French had been able to land and maintain themselves in that island.

The Adversaries

It is necessary and possible to generalize on the matter of who favored, and who opposed, in various countries, a more or less successful preservation of the Revolution in France. The Revolution itself could be variously understood. There were not two "sides." The interests of monarchy, nobility, social classes, churches, religious minorities, national groups, internal factiousness, inter-state rivalries, boundary questions, coalition politics, and much else were too conflicting to produce a simple duality. Yet the war introduced a kind of two-sidedness. It polarized the issues. Some expected to gain, others to lose, by a French victory. Which were which? In such matters much depended on personal temperaments, and much on the play of events and circumstances in which an individual might be caught up. We find no absolute or one-to-one correlations between sympathy for the French Revolution and any social or political category of persons. Any kind of person *might* have "Jacobin" inclinations. Any kind *might* detest the Revolution and all its works. Prince Henry of Prussia, Frederick the Great's brother, was a "Jacobin." So were several members of the English House of Lords. Cardinal Maury was a shoemaker's son, and an extreme conservative. In America the notable anti-Jacobin, Fisher Ames, was offset by his brother Dr. Nathaniel Ames, one of the most convinced "Jacobins" in Massachusetts. But though an individual could be anything, certain statistical correlations are evident.

In simple and obvious terms, those who enjoyed high status under the old or existing order were mainly anti-French. These included the nobilities and patriciates and social élites of various countries. Governing élites, everywhere closely allied to social élites, were generally in the same category: the parliamentary class in Great Britain, the regent class in the Dutch Netherlands, members of governing councils in Geneva or Bern, men who before 1789 had held seats in the French parlements, those in general who belonged to the "constituted bodies" as described in the earlier volume were overwhelmingly hostile to the principles of the Revolution. Those on the other hand who had served government in the role of experts, or as career officials, or as ministers to "enlightened monarchs" with reforming programs that clashed with feudal or ecclesiastical or localistic urban interests, were more likely to turn up as revolutionary sympathizers in the 1790's; there were many such cases in the Italian states, and some in the Austrian empire. Town notables such as burgomasters and councillors in various countries, given the municipal arrangements of Europe before the revolutionary era, enjoyed high and usually inherited status, and were generally anti-French. Persons deriving status or material and psychological satisfaction from historic craft and mercantile gilds were conservative. Those living from forms of property-right that the Revolution threatened were naturally opposed to it; these were mostly the European landowners possessing manorial estates, receiving manorial or seignieurial rents, with a perpetual family interest protected by various equivalents of primogeniture and entail. Those drawing income and prestige from various public emoluments, the rich sinecures of England and the numerous "offices" available in the Dutch, Swiss,

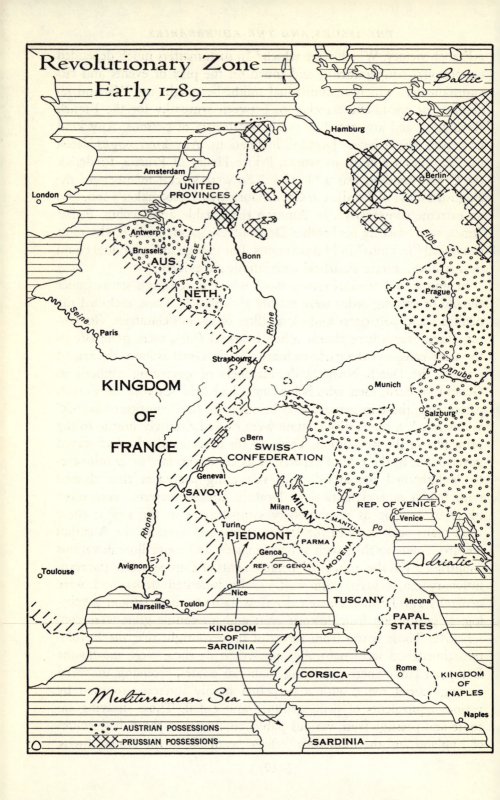

Revolutionary Zone
Early 1789

Baltic

Hamburg

Berlin

Amsterdam

London

UNITED
PROVINCES

Antwerp

Brussels

AUS.

LIEGE

Bonn

NETH.

Elbe

Prague

Seine

Paris

Strasbourg

Rhine

Danube

KINGDOM

OF

FRANCE

Munich

Salzburg

Bern

SWISS
CONFEDERATION

Geneva

SAVOY

Milan

MILAN

MANTUA

REP. OF VENICE

Po

Venice

Rhone

Turin

PIEDMONT

PARMA

MODENA

Adriatic

Toulouse

Avignon

Genoa

REP. OF GENOA

Marseille

Toulon

Nice

KINGDOM
OF
SARDINIA

TUSCANY

Ancona

PAPAL
STATES

Rome

KINGDOM
OF
NAPLES

CORSICA

Mediterranean Sea

SARDINIA

Naples

AUSTRIAN POSSESSIONS
PRUSSIAN POSSESSIONS

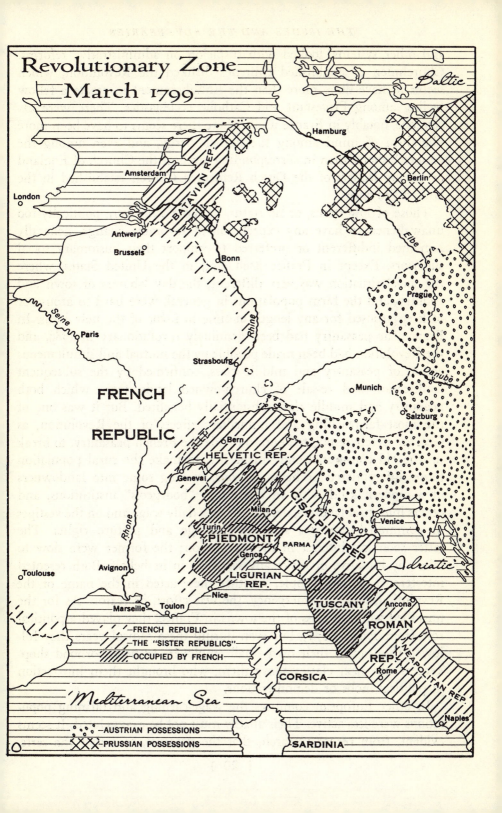

Revolutionary Zone
March 1799

Baltic

Hamburg

Amsterdam

London

BATAVIAN REP.

Berlin

Antwerp

Brussels

Bonn

Elbe

Prague

Seine

Paris

Rhine

Strasbourg

Danube

Munich

FRENCH

Salzburg

REPUBLIC

Bern

HELVETIC REP.

Geneva

CISALPINE REP.

Milan

Venice

Turin

Po

PIEDMONT

PARMA

Adriatic

Genoa

Toulouse

Avignon

Rhone

LIGURIAN
REP.

Nice

TUSCANY

Ancona

Marseille   Toulon

——FRENCH REPUBLIC——
///——THE "SISTER REPUBLICS"——
////——OCCUPIED BY FRENCH——

ROMAN

NEAPOLITAN REP.

REP.

Rome

CORSICA

Naples

Mediterranean Sea

∘∘∘——AUSTRIAN POSSESSIONS——
XXX——PRUSSIAN POSSESSIONS——   SARDINIA

and other systems, looked with suspicion on administrative reforms. Churchmen of established churches disliked the Revolution, which seems to have done more than the Enlightenment to create a fellow feeling among Protestant and Catholic ecclesiastics. There were exceptions, notably in France itself, where there seems to have been more liberalism of mind among the higher clergy, and even among the émigré bishops, than in corresponding levels of the Church of England or among leaders of the Dutch Reformed Church established in the United Provinces.

Those of low status, or no status, or those who were politically too unawakened to have any expectation of favorable change, generally remained indifferent or preferred to support their customary social superiors. Except in France itself, and in the United States, where the social situation was very different, the day laborers of town and country, and the farm populations in general, were hard to arouse or to keep aroused for any length of time in favor of the new ideas. In France the peasantry had been genuinely revolutionary in 1789, and the Revolution had been made possible by the mutual and simultaneous action of peasantry and middle class, confirmed by the subsequent confiscation and re-sale of church-owned lands, from which both peasantry and middle class substantially benefited. But it was one of the most far-reaching and immediate effects of the Revolution, as Georges Lefebvre pointed out, to divide the French peasantry, to break up the old communal and village life, to make the rural population more differentiated or heterogeneous, turning some into landowners of a modern kind with an interest in "bourgeois" institutions, and others into rural laborers, dependent on a daily wage and on the vestiges of communal practices such as gleanage and pasture rights. The latter soon lost interest in the Revolution; the former were slow to take any initiative or make any sacrifices in its behalf. Both resented interference by city people, whether these acted in the name of the Revolution, national emergency, the war effort, or reason. As for the unskilled working class of the towns in France, they played a political role from 1792 to 1795, but even during these radical years they followed the lead of their own small employers or neighborhood shopkeepers, the next classes above them, who brought them into action in political mobs or demonstrations.

In other European countries the wage-earning and farming populations were less active. Their apathy must not be exaggerated. It seems evident, from recent research, that the peasants, or rather the serfs, of Bohemia and Hungary knew and talked a good deal more of the French Revolution than historians have generally supposed. They had their own grievances, and their own frustrations when the reforms of Joseph II were blocked by the serf-owning landlords. Elsewhere the weight of the peasantry, on balance, turned against the Revolution. Sometimes, as in Belgium, the Catholicism of the farm population was outraged. Sometimes, as in southern Italy, what seemed to be a religious movement, an outburst of rural fanaticism or superstition, carried with it a well-grounded and accurate social protest, in the belief that the revolutionary intellectuals of the south-Italian cities neither knew nor cared about the real needs of the rural masses. In any case, sympathy for the new order everywhere varied in direct proportion to communications, to the contact between town and country, the state of the roads, the reading of newspapers, the frequency of inns and of travelers, the habit of small farmers selling their own produce in a market. Rural communities that had the least contact with the outside world were least interested in a new legal or political order.

The most depressed workers in the cities could usually be counted on for support by the existing governments and established upper classes. Among the Dutch, the populace was more uncritically loyal to the House of Orange than the middle classes. In England, the most dependent workers, those below the level of the skilled trades or self-employment, could be rallied by the squires and gentry in defense of church and king. They could become as nervous over Unitarianism as over Catholicism. They produced the mass following in the wholesale Birmingham riots of 1791, in which Joseph Priestley's home and scientific instruments were destroyed.

It was among persons of intermediate status, or whose status was indeterminate or changing within the categories of the older society, that most Revolutionary leaders or sympathizers with the Revolution were to be found. Lawyers were divided, largely according to the nature of their clients and habitual practice. Lawyers whose cases came mainly from church bodies or great landowners were conservative. So were those schooled in the intricacies of "feudal" law, or those in countries, like England, where legal doctrines put heavy emphasis on the inheritance of a complex legal tradition. Lawyers who served small clients or new forms of business enterprise, or those who thought that rationality and justice in the law should prevail over its customary or mysterious aspects, were more receptive to the Revolutionary message. Persons with some legal education, but with no practice or settled careers, were of course among the first to plunge into revolutionary and reformist movements.

In the other professions there was much sympathy with the Revolution. Attitudes of reform-minded career servants of enlightened monarchy have been already noted. Doctors were also susceptible. Probably because medicine was as closely related as any profession to science, and touched also on the humanitarianism of the Enlightenment, its practitioners were impatient of much in the old order of society and ideas. It was not surprising that Dr. Nathaniel Ames should be the "Jacobin" of his family, while Fisher Ames became the High Federalist. The guillotine itself had been promoted by a leading French medical man, Dr. Guillotin, who favored it as a scientific and humanitarian innovation, preferable on these grounds to the older techniques of execution. Men with an interest in science, engineering, mining, road building, and other such modern undertakings were also amenable to new ideas. Teaching was undeveloped as a profession. Individual cases could be cited; Fouché, for example, was a physics teacher in a secondary school before the Revolution. In the English universities, which were Church of England institutions, and in the French universities which the Revolution abolished, there were not many incumbents against whom revolutionary sympathies could be charged. But in the universities of Holland, Switzerland, Germany, Poland, and Italy professors of "Jacobin" inclinations could readily be found.

Student radicalism was no more than embryonic. There was unrest among students at the University of Jena when Fichte was professor there; and at Princeton, New Jersey, when the college burned in 1802, the president attributed the disaster to years of "Jacobinical" agitation among the students. The young William Wordsworth, planning to edit a political journal in 1794, observed to his collaborator that he wanted no misunderstanding of his ideas: he was "of that odious class of men called democrats"; he disapproved of "hereditary distinctions and privileged orders of every species"; he was therefore "not amongst the admirers of the British Constitution." They would naturally, in their proposed review, he said, deplore the current atrocities in France, but would often speak favorably of the Revolution. They could expect to find no friendly readers among partisans of the war, but might attract a few Dissenters and students at Oxford and Cambridge.[11] The experiment was never tried.

In all European countries, before the 1790's, there was an established

---

[11] W. Knight, *Letters of the Wordsworth Family*, 3 vols. (London, 1907), I, 66, 70, 75.

or officially recognized church, in which membership was necessary for the enjoyment of full political rights. Persons outside such a church, or those of its own members who strongly desired to reform it, were more than ordinarily liable to the appeal of the Revolution. In Italy there were many Catholics who thought the Church unnecessarily wealthy, too little truly Christian, and too much influenced by Rome; they were called "Jansenists," and when revolution came to Italy in 1796 the Italian Jansenists were among its sponsors. Jansenism, Gallicanism, anti-papalism, and church-reformism had also been important in France in bringing on the first ecclesiastical legislation of the Revolution. French Protestants divided after 1789 into many camps, and did not noticeably differ from Catholics of similar social condition in their political behavior; but the Protestants owed full equality of rights to the Revolution, and there were few absolute or total counter-revolutionaries among French Protestants. In the Dutch Republic the large Roman Catholic minority, and the Protestant sectaries, who though tolerated remained in an inferior social status with a second-class citizenship, furnished many recruits to the Batavian revolution. In England there was a high correlation between Dissent and a proclivity to "French ideas." In Ireland both the Presbyterians and the Catholics remained outside the Anglican establishment; the Catholic authorities tended to be cautious, knowing the vulnerability of their flocks; the Presbyterians were active in protest movements, and notably pro-French. Jews also found the promise of the equality of rights in the program of the Revolution. Jewish communities as such, where they existed in strength, as at Amsterdam, Frankfurt, Venice, and Rome, played a passive role; but individual Jews who had grown away from institutional Jewry, and become active in trade or letters or social life, were highly receptive to the new forms of state and society. In Poland an organized Jewish battalion defended the revolution at Warsaw in 1794.

In an occupational analysis, the rank and file of support for the new order, or for "French" ideas, came from the levels above the lowest class, and below the well-to-do and the prominent, from the pre-industrial world of the self-respecting and more or less literate workingmen, those in the skilled trades, the retail shops, or the kind of manufacturing establishments in which an employer worked alongside a dozen men whom he knew personally and in whose work he shared. These were the people who, in an actual revolution, furnished the bulk of the insurrectionary crowds in the cities of France or Holland. People of similar social station made up most of the membership of the London Corresponding Society and the political clubs of the English Midlands and of Scotland. Often they received direction from "intellectuals," or lawyers not too fully employed, or persons who for one reason or another did not have to work for a living, *fils de famille*, strays from the aristocracy, or sometimes men of actual means. Thus in Paris the wealthy brewer Santerre, the lawyer Danton, the doctor Marat, became in various ways spokesmen, or attempted to be such, for a revolutionary following made up of the working class.

The working class world, at its upper levels, through the owners of middle-sized manufacturing enterprises, touched on the world of merchants and large-scale commercial entrepreneurs, the "middle class" properly so called. The business or commercial class enjoyed an intermediate status; its members might be wealthy, economically powerful, and respected as useful and important members of the community, while remaining on the fringes of political life, and either not received at all in the choicest society, or received with a certain condescension. Many of the business groups were also outside the officially preferred churches, Dissenters in England, or Protestant but not Dutch Reformed in the Netherlands, or Protestant in some of the French provincial towns, or occasionally Jews. The business classes took a great variety of attitudes to the Revolution. At the most radical moment, in France in 1793 and 1794, business men in general came under suspicion, and those of all countries disapproved of the Terror. Even in 1794, however, much depended on political circumstance: of two Dutch financial men then in Paris, one, Kock, became involved in French politics and was executed; the other Abbema, accepted and worked for the Revolutionary government. He was questioned during the Terror, but was acquitted and came through unscathed.

On the whole, the European business class produced a large number of sympathizers for the Revolution, though not for its most radical aspects. Even in England, where the government had long favored commercial interests, many of the business leaders viewed the French Revolution with tolerance and hoped for a Parliamentary Reform in which commercial wealth would be represented, and Dissenters should obtain fuller recognition. At Manchester, where the textile manufacture was being industrialized, and the population had risen to 70,000, the chief "radical" was the civic and business leader, Thomas Walker. The *Manchester Herald* excused the September Massacres in Paris, and denounced the rising cry for a war with France. Both partners in the famous firm of Boulton and Watt, the makers of steam-engines, favored "democratic" ideas, though Watt sometimes thought his son in Paris went too far. Men of this kind regarded the English aristocracy as idlers. They were shocked and disgusted by the Birmingham riots, in which persons with new ideas had been set upon by ignorant ruffians with the collusion of the justices of the peace and the gentry. Watt wrote to the eminent chemist, Joseph Black, that Birmingham was divided between "aristocrates" and "democrates" (since the words were new in English he used the French spelling); the "aristocrates" relied on the mob, the "democrates" really wanted orderly and reasonable government, and would not object to a real aristocracy of which they might be members.[12]

In Holland the regent families were largely business men themselves, and the conflict at its upper levels was in part between politically privileged and unprivileged commercial interests. The ties with England, and fear of competition from a Belgium under French influence, deterred many from sympathy with change. Nevertheless, important mercantile and banking houses supported the Dutch Revolution of 1795, and at the most radical moment of the Batavian Republic, the spring of 1798, various millionaires were at the head of its affairs. In Belgium it was the most forward-looking business interests that favored the opening of the Scheldt river and annexation to France, in which they saw a widening of their markets and operations. In northern Italy the business classes generally favored the Cisalpine and Ligurian republics, and even showed an interest in a more comprehensive unification of Italy in which their trading area could be enlarged.

Seldom did business men take any initiative in bringing on revolution. Very commonly they accepted it, benefited from it, and supported it once it was an accomplished fact. The Revolutionary changes, in France and in the sister-republics, as later under the Napoleonic empire, had much to offer the most active commercial interests. The dissolution of gilds, while damaging to small or traditional or purely local activities, favored the manufacturers of new products and those seeking to operate

[12] For the Watts and Boultons, fathers and sons, see Eric Robinson, "An English Jacobin: James Watt, Jr.," in *Cambridge Historical Journal* xi (1955), 349-55; for Manchester, Leon S. Marshall, *Development of Public Opinion in Manchester, 1780-1820* (Syracuse, 1946); for continental business men, J. Godechot, "The Business Classes and the Revolution outside France," in *American Historical Review*, LXIV (1958), 1-13. Much detail on financial men of various nationalities in Paris during the Revolution, including those whose names occur in the present pages, such as Walckiers, Abbema, Kock, and Clavière, can be found in J. Bouchary, *Les manieurs d'argent à Paris à la fin du dix-huitième siècle*, 3 vols. (Paris, 1939-1943).

in a market of national or international scope. It was useful to get rid of provincial tariffs, and river and road tolls, and to replace the endless archaic peculiarities of boroughs and towns with a more uniform plan of municipal government. It was useful to have uniform and easily calculable weights and measures, and a sound decimal currency which after 1796 was free from paper inflation. Law courts, legal definitions, and legal proceedings had advantages for business over those of former regimes. Former church lands could be, and were, bought up by business men, in Belgium and northern Italy as in France. Land thus acquired could be used to raise capital for productive investment through new laws of mortgage loans. In the eyes of the law, commercial men of variant religion were no longer social deviates, and well-to-do merchants or bankers were in theory the social equals of former aristocrats. In addition, many merchants, contractors, and bankers profited from the immediate situation, through services of supply to the French armies during the war.

In the United States, thanks to peculiarities of its history, the division of opinion on the French Revolution, while very heated, followed somewhat different lines. The United States was a new country, only a few generations removed from the original settlement. It had no real problem of feudal survivals or of ecclesiastical power. Its people had never been brought, like those of various European countries, to accept subordination to a central or national government. It already had more "equality," and more "liberty," than any part of Europe. Though not backward, it was economically undeveloped, compared to England or Holland or many parts of France. Towns were very small compared to those of Europe. Most people lived in the country. Landownership was widespread, and there was only one kind of landed property. Some owned more, some less, and some none; but such differences were quantitative, not qualitative: there were no lords, manors, or seigneurial encumbrances on the plain farmer's land, except to a certain degree in New York.

On the whole, therefore, and allowing for qualifications and anomalies, a paradoxical situation existed when comparison is made to Europe. The most outspokenly pro-French, or democratically minded persons, were to be found among Southern landed gentry and the more remote farmers living toward the Western frontier, the very kinds of people who in Europe were the least attracted to the Revolution. The most outspokenly anti-French, and least cordial to self-consciously democratic movements, were likely to be found among the business interests of the seaboard towns, or the settled New England farmers living relatively close to the main channels of trade, the very kinds of people who in Europe were likely to regard the Revolution with favor, or to be involved in it themselves.

The truth seems to be that the "democrats" in America were conservative in terms of the American scene, however responsive to the revolutionary movement in Europe, wanting to preserve the simpler equalities of an earlier day, the agrarian self-sufficiency, and the liberty which meant the virtual absence of centralized government; and that the opposite party, the Federalists, were the party of change in terms of the American scene, however much they sympathized with conservatism in Europe, because they wanted to develop banking, credit, reliable currency, commercial investment, and domestic and foreign trade, and also to build up a more powerful and centralized national government, all of which were newer in America than in Western Europe. In Europe, in France, Switzerland, Holland, and Italy, the democratic movement always sought a unitary, homogeneous, and juridically centralized republic. This was because in Europe the aristocratic interests were strongly rooted in the historic localisms of manor and town. In America the democratic movement was suspicious of centralized, homogeneous, or unitary government, and strongly insistent on local liberties and state rights. This was because a democratic outlook in America had been rooted locally from the beginning among yeoman farmers, and those larger Southern farmers and slaveowners who functioned as gentry. In Europe a democratic movement required a strong central government to overcome adversaries. In America a democratic movement could be content to leave well enough alone. In Europe the term "federalism," which became current in several countries in the 1790's, signified decentralization and fragmentation of power. It was viewed by democrats as a cloak for social reaction, behind which local privileged interest might take refuge. In America Federalism meant the concentration and unification of public power; democrats feared that it might be despotic, but it was certainly less reactionary than "federalism" in Europe.

The paradoxes in the American relation to Europe will be among the topics pursued in the following pages.

Shades of Doctrine

By 1792 there were five recognizable shades in the spectrum of opinion generated by the Revolution. They had an existence of their own apart from the categories of people who might adopt them. The same person during the decade might change his hue.

At the extreme Right was the idea that the good society was what had existed before 1789. In this view everything that had happened since June of that year should be undone. It was positively desirable to have a society of legal estates, with an acknowledged hierarchy of unequal or dissimilar rights, an honoring of the aristocratic virtues, corporate and concrete liberties (or privileges) for particular groups, a monarch surrounded by worthy advisers but not responsible to them, and a form of government and authority closely related to one specific church. French members of the school have been recently described in a work by Paul Beik.[13] The Savoyard Joseph de Maistre was one of the principal theorists. Edmund Burke was the most eloquent philosopher of this school; he had developed his ideas in opposition to Parliamentary Reform in England some years before, and elaborated them as a critique of the French Revolution, on which he wrote his *Reflections* in 1790.[14] In general, in this view, any deliberate, planned, or rational and conscious remaking of institutions was difficult, impossible or delusive; societies must change if at all by an imperceptible organic growth; custom, tradition, and habit must determine the content of law. Each country in this respect must follow its own peculiarity or national spirit. "Reason" was not to be trusted. There were no "rights of man" but only rights of Englishmen or other such actual communities. The French Revolution, according to this doctrine, was really un-French, inhuman, and contrary to the structure of the universe and the will of God. The extreme French émigrés, so far as they had any philosophy, agreed with this one. The future Louis XVIII, who became claimant to the French throne in 1795, was also of this school in the 1790's, though not in 1814.

Next came a more conciliatory form of conservatism, favored by men who had taken part in the Revolution of 1789, but who had by 1792 joined the emigration. In this group was J. J. Mounier, who had sponsored the Tennis Court Oath and the Declaration of Rights, and favored, in 1789, a constitution in which the king should have an absolute veto and the assembly be in two houses. In the same group

[13] Paul Beik, *The French Revolution Seen from the Right. Transactions of the American Philosophical Society*, new ser. XLVI, Part 1 (Philadelphia, 1956).

[14] On Burke see *Age*, 1, 308-17. Malouet (see below) remarked in late 1792, that "M. Burke avait toutes les idées d'un aristocrate francais," and that "les Anglais en général, sont disposés à croire que le commerce du monde et la liberté sont deux choses qui leur appartiennent exclusivement." P. V. Malouet, *Mémoires*, 2 vols. (Paris, 1874), II, 260-61.

were the Swiss Mallet du Pan, P. V. Malouet, who had been intendant of the navy before the Revolution, and a number of others who formed a colony of liberal émigrés in London in the later 1790's. They were in touch also with the more liberal of the émigré clergy, especially Boisgelin, Fontanges, and Champion de Cicé, the archbishops respectively of Aix, Toulouse, and Bordeaux. As these men saw it, the Old Regime required modernization. Total restoration was neither possible nor desirable. They accepted the replacement in France of the Three Orders—clergy, nobles, and Third Estate—by a more modern representative system of which individual citizenship and property should be the basis. They favored a clearly ordered constitutional monarchy. To them the most unmanageable obstacle was the Extreme Right, whose obstinacy, they felt, by alarming the French people, threw France upon the mercy of the Left. They believed that political action and forms of government could be and must be rationally directed. They were too much interested in practical politics, and in intelligent action, to accept a kind of vegetable theory of merely organic social development. These constitutionalist or liberal émigrés, or conservatives as distinguished from outright reactionaries, anticipated better than any other group the actual settlement of 1814. As political analysts, since they were detached from the excited ideologies of Right or Left, they probably would have a strong appeal to many twentieth-century American readers, to whom, however, they remain almost unknown. Their trouble was that, however intelligent, they had no following.

Next, and in the middle of the present spectrum, came those constitutionalists, or moderate revolutionaries, who remained active in France at the beginning of 1792. They were called Feuillants in the party language of the day. Afraid of popular radicalism, they were concerned for order and property, and willing to cling to the person, symbol, and authority of Louis XVI, however much his attachment to the Revolution might be questioned, lest the country slide into republicanism. Mirabeau might have been of this group had he lived. By the middle of 1792 they had the cooperation of Lafayette, who in June left his war-time command in the field and returned to Paris, hoping to suppress Jacobin radicalism, and to remove Louis XVI from the city, so that, from a point in the provinces, the somewhat patrician forces of orderly revolution could take a stand. In opinion, this group was not very different from the liberal émigrés, but its members remained involved in French politics; some perished in the Terror, but others emerged among the leaders of the Directory, when a constitutional republic was set up on a constitutional monarchist model.

To the left of this constitutionalism stood the ideas of the Jacobins, by far the best known and most famous of all elements in the Revolution. Found everywhere in France, the Jacobins took their name from the Jacobin Club of Paris, as it was commonly called, its actual name before 1792 being the Society of Friends of the Constitution, and after 1792 the Society of Friends of Liberty and Equality. There was nothing secret or conspiratorial or even very well organized about the Jacobin Club, or the thousands of provincial clubs with which it exchanged correspondence and delegations. They publicized themselves as much as possible. They generally said what they thought and believed what they said, being naive rather than devious. They gloried in the name of "Jacobin," until the club was closed late in 1794; but the use of the term by conservatives, both in and out of France, and the equating of the Revolution itself with "Jacobinism," was usually highly inaccurate and intended to be disparaging. The Jacobins were overwhelmingly Frenchmen of the middle class, men of some schooling or professional standing or assured income or moderate property-holding before the Revolution, aroused by the ideas of the Enlightenment, acrimoniously hostile to the nobility, dubious of the church, intolerant of opposition, believers in the close imminence of a better and freer world, and absolutely dedicated to the great principles of the Revolution, in whose defense they could be ruthless. Distrust of the upper classes, in the conditions of 1791 and 1792, converted the Jacobins to republicanism. They also had come to accept political democracy in the sense of universal suffrage, which a few like Robespierre had urged from the beginning. Though great talkers, they were also men of action. They lacked patience for the hesitant, the moderate, the procrastinating, and the indecisive. Such qualities aroused their suspicions. They were combative personalities, more than willing to knock down and drag out the upholders of royal courts and ornamental nobilities. They welcomed war in 1792. Though middle-class, they were not above working with mobs, and could rally the common people against common enemies by promises and concessions. Their club was the Mother Society, and they regarded themselves as the orthodox of the Revolution; the Feuillants had originated in a split in the club in 1791, and after Brissot and his followers left the club in October 1792 the Brissotins, or Girondists, were at a great political disadvantage. But

Gironde, Mountain, Brissotins, Robespierrists, and Dantonists were really all Jacobins.[15]

At the extreme Left was the popular revolutionism so brilliantly described in a recent book by Albert Soboul.[16] It was most especially voiced by the *sans-culottes* of Paris between 1792 and 1794. The sans-culottes, who took this name in derision for the knee-breeches or *culottes* of the middle and upper classes, which they neither wore nor owned, were the activists and militants among the really plain people of Paris. More will be said of them shortly. They were small people unavoidably engrossed in immediate matters. They, and their wives and children, were the ones that went hungry if bread was unobtainable or too highly priced. No Jacobin, in the strict sense, was ever really uncertain about his next meal. The sans-culottes lived with this elemental problem. They rioted for bread. For them, the Revolution would miscarry if it did not alleviate the economic and social condition of the common man. Constitutions and legislative debates seemed to them remote and unrealistic. They believed in direct action, and in direct democracy. They met locally, face to face, in neighborhood clubs, with like-minded acquaintances who lived in the same streets. By the sovereignty of the people they meant what they could do themselves. They distrusted representative and parliamentary institutions. No mere delegate could long retain their confidence. To them it seemed that all persons in the upper classes had to be closely watched, and among the "upper" classes they included the gentlemen who paid dues to the Jacobin Club.

It was the self-assertion of these sans-culottes that made the "second" revolution of 1792.

Meanwhile the Prussians continued their march toward the French frontiers. The letters of Malouet to Mallet du Pan in June and July of 1792 had a prophetic ring. It will be remembered that they were both conservatively liberal émigrés. Of course, remarked Malouet, the Powers have no plan or intention of counter-revolution. But when the Count of Artois and his retinue return, "they will make the king do what suits them." There is talk of a threatening manifesto to the city of Paris. What madness! And Malouet gave a kind of answer to Noah Webster's question: "Do these people suppose that they can easily wipe out, like an idle fable, that Declaration of Rights by which the French are so intoxicated?"[17]

---

[15] See Crane Brinton, *The Jacobins: an Essay in the New History* (New York, 1930), which stresses their middle-class and radically ideological qualities.

[16] See below, pp. 46-49.   [17] *Mémoires*, II, 341-42, 354-55.

THE REVOLUTIONIZING OF THE
REVOLUTION

*The arms of the French are all the more danger-
ous since the poison of their maxims is diffused
everywhere, and by preceding their armies con-
tributes to their success. The people imagine that
their poverty will be relieved by such doctrines.
. . . It is above all worthy of remark, how even the
lowest class of the people . . . now turn their attention to the present war, and reason in their own
way about the motives that have brought it on. . . .
The French Revolution is gradually bringing
another equally dangerous revolution in the universal way of thinking.*—DANIEL DOLFIN, Venetian
Ambassador at Vienna, reporting to the government of Venice, 1793

THE REVOLUTIONIZING OF THE
REVOLUTION

IN 1792 the Revolution became a thing in itself, an uncontrollable force that might eventually spend itself but which no one could direct or guide. The governments set up in Paris in the following years—the Convention, the Committee of Public Safety, the Thermidorians, the Directory, however they might differ, whether "Jacobin" or "anti-Jacobin" in their composition—all alike faced the problem of holding together against forces more revolutionary than themselves. Two such forces may be distinguished for analytical purposes. There was a popular upheaval, an upsurge from below, *sans-culottisme*. This occurred only in France; there were revolutions outside of France, but they were not *sans-culotte* revolutions. Secondly, there was the "international" revolutionary agitation, which was not international in any strict sense, but only concurrent within the boundaries of various states as then organized. From the French point of view these were the "foreign" revolutionaries or sympathizers. The most radical of the "foreign" revolutionaries, whether we think of those who congregated in Paris or those who in greater numbers remained in their own countries, were seldom more than advanced political democrats.

Repeatedly, however, from 1792 to 1799, these two forces tended to converge into one force of *révolution à outrance*. Between the French popular revolutionism and international revolutionism there was an affinity. In France, the vanguard in 1792 meant the Jacobins; in 1794 it meant what Robespierre called the Ultras; in the following years it was what the Thermidorians and the Directory called the "anarchists," among whom the Babouvists of 1796 may be especially distinguished, though few in number; in 1799 it was the neo-Jacobins or "true republicans." In each case there was some kind of sympathetic relationship between French extremists and non-French revolutionary leaders. *Révolution à outrance* had two meanings: destruction of the Old

Regime anywhere and everywhere, and, in France, attack on a merely. middle- or upper-class revolution.

The two repeatedly came together in common opposition to the French government of the moment, because every group among the French revolutionary leadership, as soon as it felt itself to be established in a position of government, resisted the more vehement demands both for popular revolution and for international revolution. Or, at the most, in certain conjunctures, as in the latter part of 1792, or at times in later years, the men trying to govern France might use the language of social or international revolutionism as a means to an end, to protect themselves and the specifically French Revolution, as they understood it, at moments when Counter-Revolution seemed the more imminent danger.

The "Second" French Revolution

How we judge the "second" revolution in France depends entirely on our judgment of the strength and chances, in 1792, of a Counter-Revolution aiming at integral restoration, with accompanying repression and punishment of those implicated in subversion of the Old Order. Since the event did not happen, historians must remain as uncertain as contemporaries were on its likelihood. It is a fact, however, that the Counter-Revolutionary leaders expected an early success in the summer of 1792.

At Mainz, a few days after the coronation at Frankfurt, there was a grand confabulation on the political steps with which the military intervention should be accompanied. No significant resistance was anticipated. The two crowned heads of Prussia and Austria, the various French princes, the Fersens, the Esterhazys, the Metternichs, and the Maurys were in a mood of confidence. France, in their opinion, was in the hands of a few adventurers from whom all decent people wished to be liberated. It was decided to issue a manifesto. Mallet du Pan, expressing the preference of Louis XVI, submitted the draft of a relatively moderate text. It was rejected. Another was adopted; coming by way of an intermediary named Limon, and Count Axel de Fersen, it expressed the views of Marie Antoinette. The queen, increasingly desperate in Paris, wounded and frightened by a series of popular insults, too proud to let herself be "saved" by Lafayette (he was too "revolutionary"), and at her wits' end when both blandishments and actual bribery of Revolutionary leaders produced no results, had concluded that the only salvation for herself, her family, her husband, and the world lay in a resounding ultimatum that might restrain the fury of the Parisians until help arrived.

At Mainz therefore a menacing announcement was drawn up. The two rulers decided not to issue it in their own names, but to have it signed by their military commander, the Duke of Brunswick. Readers of the preceding volume may recall, as more than a historical curiosity, that this same Duke of Brunswick had issued a manifesto to the city of Amsterdam five years before. At that time the Prussian forces had pushed through to Amsterdam without difficulty, and the Dutch Patriot revolution had been stamped out.

The Brunswick Manifesto was addressed to the city of Paris—just as Counter-Revolutionary Russian troops were entering the city of Warsaw. It invited all good Frenchmen to return to their "former fidelity," and required "the city of Paris and all its inhabitants, without distinction . . . to submit at once and without delay to the king." "If any force or insult is used against the Palace of the Tuileries, if the least violence or the least outrage is done to Their Majesties . . ." the Allied Powers would "exact an exemplary and forever memorable vengeance by delivering the city of Paris to military execution and total subversion, and the rebels who are guilty of such outrages to the punishments they will have deserved." No one knew exactly what "military execution and total subversion" might mean, but the words had an ominous sound. Thousands of copies of the Manifesto were printed and circulated in all directions. Switzerland was "inundated with copies," according to a report from the French minister early in August, and on August 3 the text was published in the Paris *Moniteur*.[1]

Paris still had newspapers of every political stripe, and those hostile to the Revolution expressed hearty joy. One predicted the return of the émigrés within the month. Another announced that patriots would soon be chained in pairs to sweep the streets, under German overseers being trained for the purpose. Marie Antoinette received word to prepare rooms at the Tuileries for the Duke of Brunswick, and to be thinking about a list of suitable cabinet ministers for her husband

---

[1] For the text of the Manifesto see the *Moniteur*, August 3. The role of Fersen and Marie Antoinette, though generally known, is clarified and emphasized in a doctoral dissertation at Princeton University by H. A. Barton, "Count Axel von Fersen: a Political Biography to 1800." See also Delbeke, "Le Manifeste de Brunswick," in *La franc-maçonnerie et la Révolution française et autres essais sur le dix-huitième siècle* (Antwerp, 1938), 97-136. For circulation in Switzerland see J. B. Kaulek, *Papiers de Barthélemy, ambassadeur français en Suisse 1792-97*, 6 vols. (Paris, 1886-1910), I, 233.

under the new conditions. Calonne, as "prime minister of the emigration," began to arrange the collection of taxes in France to support a restored royal regime. Members of the former parlements who had emigrated prepared to annul the actions of the Revolutionary assemblies. The abbé Maury rejoiced that "armed force will decide. . . . The problem will soon be resolved."[2]

The Paris thus ordered into submissiveness by an international ultimatum, a royalist and aristocratic pronouncement largely inspired by the French queen, was the city that had just celebrated the Federation of July 14. It was full of *fédérés*, or high-pressure patriots sent in from the departments. Parading about the streets, falling into tavern brawls with aristocrats, sitting in at meetings of the patriotic clubs, the *fédérés* gave the Parisians the sense that throughout all France these were men who were on their side. They were, in the words of Albert Mathiez, the yeast in the revolutionary dough of the summer of 1792, though the substance of this dough was furnished by ordinary inhabitants of the city. The agitation of the *fédérés* made the upheaval seem more national and less purely Parisian than that of the first Bastille Day in 1789.

The effect of the manifesto was precisely the opposite of its purpose. It led within a week to the attack on the Tuileries which it so explicitly forbade. With the usual aid of organizers hard to identify, the insurrection was generated at the popular level of the "sections" of the city, the forty-eight neighborhood subdivisions of the municipality as set up in 1790. During the summer of 1792 these sections underwent small internal revolutions. Since 1790, and by the constitution of 1789-1791, it was the "active" citizens who had the right to attend the section assemblies, where votes were taken and public business discussed. Now a great many "passive" citizens began to take part in these neighborhood meetings also, especially in the populous quarters where the "active" citizens were themselves men of small means, shopkeepers, master-craftsmen, and the like, who, alarmed by the political and military crisis, welcomed or solicited the influx of neighbors and employees only slightly below them on the socio-economic scale.

The militant *sectionnaires* of the less fashionable parts of the city had lost all confidence in the various constituted authorities. The king and queen were suspected, correctly, of collusion with the invaders. In the army, the enlisted ranks were full of enthusiasm but weakened by revolutionary disorganization; most of the officers were ex-nobles;

[2] A. Mathiez, *Le Dix-août* (Paris, 1931), 68-69; Maury, *Mémoires*, I, 93.

and the troops were in retreat. Lafayette, commanding on the frontier, had left his post on a political errand to Paris, intending to take the king and queen under his protection and to rally the constitutionalists against radicalism. The *sectionnaires* replied with charges of military dictatorship. The Legislative Assembly was paralyzed; its Feuillant and Jacobin members feared and detested each other; it could take no action, but only called for calm and legality, and by a vote of 406 to 224 it absolved Lafayette of any misconduct. The enraged *sectionnaires* called the Assembly "corrupt."

The sections began to act as little independent republics. There was no armed force in the city to hold them down. Apart from the Swiss Guard at the palace, the only armed force consisted of the National Guard of the sections themselves, each of which had a battalion formed of its own residents. The National Guardsmen of the popular quarters greatly outnumbered those of the upper-class quarters which were more favorable to the king.

Various of the sections demanded the dethronement of Louis XVI, "as the first link in the chain of Counter-Revolution."[3] On July 31 the Monconseil section announced that it no longer recognized him. Plans for insurrection went ahead without attempt at concealment. The red flag made a brief first appearance as a Revolutionary symbol during these preparations, originating as a grim political joke. By an earlier provision of the Revolution, a large red flag was used as a sign of martial law, displayed by the authorities as a warning that they were about to fire on civilians. It had been so employed a year before, when, in the "Massacre of the Champs de Mars," the authorities had broken up a republican demonstration. In July 1792 the Jacobin journalist Carra, turning the tables, procured a red flag on which he had sewn in black letters: "Martial Law of the Sovereign People against Rebellion by the Executive Power."[4]

This political theory of insurrection was elaborated by Robespierre. As a former Constituent, ineligible at the time of the election, he was not a member of the Legislative Assembly. He was thus in a better position to yield to the demand for its replacement, and to formulate a program and offer a leadership for the section pressures. He did so in a series of speeches at the Paris Jacobin Club. To the negative insistence upon dethronement he added two positive aims: There should be a National Convention, and in election of deputies the suffrage should be universal for all adult males.

---

[3] Mathiez, *op.cit.*, 75, quoting a section petition of August 3.　　　　　[4] *Ibid.*, 61.

Thus the second French Revolution adopted for its justification the essential revolutionary theory of the whole revolutionary era. Against a constitution that proved to be an embarrassment the revolutionaries of 1792, like those in America in the 1770's, offered the doctrine of the people as a constituent power. They undercut existing authorities with the claim of popular sovereignty. The authorities now undercut were those which the Revolution of 1789 and the constitution of 1789-1791 had created: Louis XVI in his legal role as constitutional monarch, and the Legislative Assembly as the elected body of deputies. Both, in the circumstances brought on by war, were easy for radicals to discredit, and difficult for moderates convincingly to defend. Both could be accused of helplessness if not downright collusion in the face of invasion. Against Counter-Revolution both seemed a frail defense. As Robespierre put it, since the executive and the legislature were equally rotten, both should be regenerated by the people. They were legally washed away by the appeal to a new Convention.

This new Convention, far more than the first Constituent Assembly, would have that fullness of constituent power which the abbé Sieyès had described in 1789. It could, in principle, create organs of government freely. It would not have to accept a ready-made king as its executive as in 1789. It would be a true image of the people of France. Where half the members of the first Constituent had come originally from the nobility and the clergy, the Convention would suffer from no such distortion. Even the vestiges of the former estates now disappeared. Events of 1792 had discredited the upper classes in the eyes of the lower. Leadership structures were in ruins, habits of deference had been broken. Universal suffrage in election of the Convention was the result. Some demanded it as a thing good in itself, or in the belief that the less favored classes of society would benefit. Others accepted it as a necessity or an expedient, to placate the popular agitators, or in the belief that all should vote because no particular group could be trusted.

In terms of social identity, the first revolution had put into power, or left in it, persons who before the revolution had been of some importance: Louis XVI himself, carried over as constitutional ruler and chief executive, important members of the nobility such as Lafayette and Talleyrand, and well-to-do or otherwise prominent members of the bourgeoisie, from whom some of the first Jacobins had been recruited. The Revolution of 1792 rose from deeper depths in the population. With it, classes hitherto not heard from in European politics, except episodically on days of riot or insurrection, made their influence felt as a continuing source of power. They were not the "dregs," as they seemed to some more highly placed. They were the small people in plain occupations, the *menu peuple*, the butcher, the baker, and the candlestick maker together with those Jacobins who would work with them.

Men of this kind attacked the Tuileries Palace on August 10, with cries of "Down with the fat-head!" (*le gros cochon*), by which they meant Louis XVI. The palace was defended only by the Swiss Guard and a few gentlemen in waiting. The king and queen fled to the Legislative Assembly, which gave them refuge in the stenographer's box and continued in session, listening to irrelevant speeches, waiting with inert dignity to see how events would turn out. After several hours the king ordered his defenders to cease fire. No one knows how many were killed, since there never was any official inquiry. There were some six hundred casualties among the defenders, mostly killed, some massacred after the end of the fighting. The attackers had over three hundred killed and wounded, among whom there were men from forty-two of the forty-eight Paris sections and from nineteen of the eighty-three departments. The *fédérés* from Marseilles alone lost twenty-four killed. Parts of the palace caught fire, and Marie-Antoinette's books were thrown out the window, but there was little actual pillage; a few thieves were put to death on the spot, and patriotic prowlers who came upon jewelry or other valuables ceremoniously deposited them at the bar of the Assembly. It was a purely political riot.

Delegates from the sections, who had formed an association of their own some days before to prepare the insurrection, now took over from the municipal authorities as the government of the city. Thus originated the revolutionary Commune of Paris, which became a rival power to the Convention, while remaining highly responsive to the radicalism welling up from the sections.

The Commune imprisoned Louis XVI and his family in the Temple, a grim building dating back to the medieval Templars. Lafayette tried to lead his army to Paris to interfere, but his men would not follow him. To the radicals he was now clearly a "traitor." He gave himself up to the Austrians, who shut him up in a Silesian castle as a prisoner of war and dangerous revolutionary.

The Legislative Assembly meekly accepted the accomplished fact. It declared the king dethroned, set up a provisional executive council, and authorized elections for a convention. While thus preparing for its own liquidation, it meanwhile enacted a number of significant measures, in which the nature of this "second" revolution was made more manifest. The Revolution was reaching the point where its most zealous supporters were to be found in the lesser ranks of society. It was necessary to make a popular appeal, to get the bulk of the country to accept the new order in Paris and to recruit strength for the war. Universal suffrage was one such step. It was now also, after August 10, that "feudalism" was at last "abolished." In 1789 the abolition of the most important seigneurial dues had been made subject to compensation. The compensation was now done away with, and the peasant landowner was now fully free from the manorial lord. The significance of this development, brought on by the violent eruption of 1792, is more evident when we remember that elsewhere in Europe, as the agrarian problem came to be dealt with in the following century, the former lords received compensation and so remained economically stronger than in France. After August 10 the landed property of émigrés, which had been confiscated during the preceding months against the king's resistance, was put on public sale in small lots so that peasants and other small purchasers might obtain it, in twenty-year installments without interest if they chose.

Priests were associated in the minds of patriots with the Counter-Revolution, both rightly and wrongly in individual cases. On August 11 the Assembly closed the remaining monasteries. It forbade priests to wear clerical costume in public, required them to accept the new laws of civil marriage and divorce, and imposed upon them, as upon others, a new oath of fidelity "to liberty and equality." Though the Pope never officially forbade this oath, many clergy refused to take it. Shoals of priests were ordered deported.

On August 30 Paris learned of the surrender of Longwy and the siege of Verdun, so that the Prussians were known to be within the frontiers. The city was in turmoil, with authority in collapse. To political excitement and anger were added the fears and hatreds induced by military emergency. There were over two thousand persons in the Paris prisons, most of them for ordinary crimes or offenses, but including several hundred "politicals." Word circulated in the heated atmosphere of the city that the prisoners were in secret contact with the enemy and the émigrés. It was said that the worst enemies were not at the border but in Paris itself. A few activists took matters into their own hands, with no attempt on the part of the Commune to prevent them. For several days, in an orgy of what in America would be called lynchings, and with the callous brutality and atrociousness that later characterized American lynch mobs, these bands of marauders, for whom violence was now a patriotic act, burst into the prisons and put to death some 1,300 inmates after pretended trials in the streets. These September Massacres were an indiscriminate butchery; over two hundred priests and aristocrats perished, but most of the victims were ordinary prisoners of the kind that any prison in any city might contain. Respectable people, however pained, thought it wise at the moment not to be too critical. It might be dangerous not to condone them. And it was no time to complain about excessive zeal.

The same atmosphere that produced and excused the September Massacres surrounded the elections. Voters assembled locally in thousands of primary assemblies to choose electors who convened at regional levels to designate members of the Convention. There seem to be no good estimates of the proportion of adult men who participated. There is no reason to suppose it to have been especially small. The country was aroused by the invasion, and politicized by three years of revolution. Provincials might dislike Paris, but they hardly depended on it for their ideas. There was more indigenous vitality in the provinces than in later times, under different conditions of transport and communication. Every town—and there were over seventy of them with populations of over 10,000—had its own revolution, its own newspapers and journalists, its own political club, its own factions and quarrels. Even small villages were involved. Everywhere there were farm people and townspeople who were committed to the Revolution, and who could not take the risk of seeing it undone. They were men who had either accepted local or municipal office under it, or talked rather volubly in public, or given offense to cleric or noble, or spent their money to purchase land or buildings that had formerly belonged to the church. The local political clubs, following the lead of the Paris Jacobins, saw to it that the primary assemblies were filled by as many good patriots as possible, while taking steps to keep "uncivic" persons away. Since these steps involved actual danger to those excluded, the election was no model of democratic propriety. The Convention when elected, was "democratic" in principle, but not in practice. It represented the revolutionary element in the population, not France as a whole. By its later actions it alienated much of the support with which it began.

The French republican historian, Aulard, writing in the 1890's, thought that the Convention well represented the France of 1792. Opponents of the Revolution, in France and elsewhere, then and since, have seen in it the representative only of a Jacobin minority. In recent times it has been called a minority government also by writers of the Left, who relish the idea that vigorous élites are the real authors of revolutions. Actually the question seems irrelevant. Majorities and minorities exist only where men can be counted, pro or con, on specific questions or candidates. To be for or against so vast and undefinable a thing as the Revolution was highly unspecific. There was no majority and minority on such a question. All sorts of people who favored something in the Revolution probably put in an appearance in the voting assemblies. The convention was as representative as any conceivable assembly in France in 1792 could have been. Any assembly in which all the divisions in the country were exactly reflected could never have functioned as a parliamentary body at all. The Convention did not function well, but it did function, too effectively indeed for the taste of those who most despised it.

It first met on September 20, 1792. Avoiding a direct proclamation, it resolved two days later that September 22, 1792, was the first day of French Republic.

At the same time the French met the Prussians at Valmy, fifty miles within the French frontier, and after a brief engagement the Duke of Brunswick retreated. Elation on one side was matched by consternation on the other.

Popular Revolutionism

The Revolution was revolutionized in 1792, as already remarked, by the infusion of popular and international revolutionism. Let us look more closely at each of these in turn.

Popular revolutionism is taken to mean the rebelliousness and state of mind of persons who, in occupational or income levels and hence in their mode of life, stood below the professional, business and property-owning classes. The French language distinguished them as *peuple* as opposed to *bourgeoisie*. Class analysis has often been attempted with categories derived from Marxism. But the best recent Marxist historians, in France and elsewhere, insist that the popular elements in the French Revolution were not proletarians in a Marxist sense. Class and class-consciousness were nevertheless very important.

If we wish a "model" as an aid in seeing the class conflicts, none is more appropriate, or more readily understandable, than that of a large transatlantic ocean liner of the twentieth century, with its distinction of passengers into First, Cabin, and Third or Tourist Class. The model reminds us, first of all, of a truth relevant to the eighteenth century, that the classes lived in considerable ignorance of each other. To the First Class passenger on the sun-deck or in spacious lounges, the daily shipboard life and the exact differences between Cabin and Tourist may be rather hazy. In the Cabin or "middle" class there may be people who would prefer to travel First if they could afford it, others who think the First stuffy, pretentious, and over-privileged in the amount of space it enjoys on the ship. The Tourist or "popular" class is made up of people of more limited means, with a sprinkling of college professors and "intellectuals" who are there by necessity or by choice. The people in Tourist Class are not the rabble, nor paupers, nor idlers, nor chronically unemployed, nor afflicted with any higher proportion than other classes of the criminally inclined. They have a general idea of the boat as a whole, and they have a destination in view. The more intimate details of the rest of the ship, however, remain something of a mystery to them. They know that it is very commodious, but have seen nothing of it except possibly a few public rooms. Normally they accept their cramped quarters as in the ordinary scheme of things.

Comes a revolution; the command of the ship breaks down. The Tourist Class swarm over the ship; this is the Revolution of 1792. The First are appalled, crying "mob rule"; some take to the life-boats (emigrate), others try to sit inconspicuously in their staterooms, some resist, and a small handful pitch in with the insurgents. The Cabin Class is torn both ways; some join with the First, but a good many during the melée join forces with the Tourist. The Tourist insurgents cannot themselves manage the boat, nor bring it to the destination to which they themselves wish to go. Problems of management and destination are not especially on their minds. They do not wish to eat in the First Class dining salon, where they would only be ill at ease. But they have the idea that dining facilities and other amenities might be apportioned somewhat more equally.

The popular element in the French Revolution did not do very much writing, so that in the absence of documents it has not been seen very distinctly by historians. Some years ago, in a book by an American, the mood of Paris in 1789 was reconstructed through popular songs, sung in the streets, market-places, and cafés. It showed a genuine surge of political feeling among an array of people from engravers to fishwives.[5] The Revolution, among its other innovations, saw the beginnings of a popular journalism. But the papers directed to a mass audience, such as

[5] Cornwell Rogers, *The Spirit of Revolution in 1789* (Princeton, 1949).

those of Hébert or Marat, were written by men originating in the middle class, who had aims of their own, and who sometimes adopted an air of exaggerated vulgarity. Recently a number of studies, based on sources such as police records and the surviving papers of the sections of Paris, have been made in France, England, and East Germany. It is at last possible to draw a picture of the *menu peuple* in the French Revolution, those who drove through the Revolution of 1792, and continued to press upon French governments thereafter. The most important of these writers is Albert Soboul of Paris, from whom the following description is mainly drawn.[6]

In the years from 1792 to 1795 the more aggressive and class-conscious of these small people proudly called themselves sans-culottes, spurning the knee-breeches of their social superiors; and the term *sans-culottisme* can be understood to mean the aroused and politically active state of these people during the two or three years that it lasted.

These sans-culottes were in effect popular democrats. In the crisis and breakdown of 1792 they represented an enormous wave of citizen self-help. They applied the great concepts of liberty, equality, and the sovereignty of the people to themselves and to the concrete circumstances with which they were personally familiar. They believed that they themselves were sovereign, in face-to-face contact in their section meetings; and that distant elected persons were only their delegates, often not to be trusted. They favored what a later generation in America would know as the referendum and recall. "Consent of the people" meant their consent in their own assemblies. The right to bear arms meant that they should carry pikes in their own streets. The judgment of the people meant that they should denounce their own neighbors for suspicious behavior or unsuitable sentiments, and that their own committees should put them under arrest. They resisted attempts at control of their activities by the Convention and its Committee of Public Safety in 1793.

If they thus presumed to exercise sovereignty, they accepted the corresponding responsibilities; they were ready to give their time, to act

[6] A. Soboul, *Les sans-culottes parisiens en l'an II* (Paris, 1958). See also R. C. Cobb, "Quelques aspects de la mentalité révolutionnaire, avril 1793–Thermidor an II," in *Revue d'histoire moderne et contemporaine*, VI (1959), 81-120. Both these works refer to a period slightly later than the one discussed here, but apply in general to late 1792. See my article discussing these and other writings, "Popular Democracy in the French Revolution," in *French Historical Studies*, I (1960), 445-69. Cobb's full work has also now appeared: *Les armées révolutionnaires: instrument de la Terreur dans les départements, avril 1793–floréal an II*, 2 vols. (Paris, 1963).

and to fight. The younger ones were gradually absorbed into the army. They spent long hours at meetings, and in the work of committees, or on the exposure of suspects, or on errands and missions and patrols about the city, or in exchange of delegations with sister groups, or in semi-military formations in which men from the city went into rural areas to procure food from the peasants, or bring patriotic pressure to bear in other communities.

Shopkeepers, retail merchants, traders, artisans, small manufacturers, hired laborers, porters, water-carriers, waiters in cafés, janitors in buildings, barbers, wig-makers, stonemasons, and makers of ladies' hats, they were the people of Paris without the frosting—and generally without the dregs, since the vagrant, the shiftless, and the delinquent did not become true sans-culottes. Some lived by a daily wage, some by the sale of articles of their own production, some by the proceeds of retail shopkeeping, and a few indeed by the income of their capital. Among men arrested in 1795 as dangerous sans-culottes were a dyer with a fortune of 21,600 livres, and others owning workshops that employed sixty men. No less than 1,311 individual *sectionnaires* of the height of the Terror have been identified and socially classified by Soboul. Of those in the section committees, that is the leaders, over half were shopkeepers, another tenth were of liberal professions, and still another tenth lived from property or small incomes of their own. Of ordinary *sectionnaires*, not members of committees, over half were shopkeepers, and a fifth were wage-employees.

They burned with a new sense of equality, which Soboul finds to be their main characteristic. They wanted respect and recognition. They "no longer accepted a subordinate position in social relations." On holidays they flocked to the fashionable boulevards which in the past they had avoided. "Citizens of poor outward appearance," in the words of an approving contemporary, "who in former times would not have dared to show themselves in these places reserved for more elegant company, were going for walks along with the rich, and holding their heads as high."[7]

They could not bear arrogance and disdain. Irony and elaborate speech aroused their hostility. All above their own level they came to regard as "aristocrats." "Gentlemen" (*les honnêtes gens*) became a term to be used with sarcasm. A certain goldsmith said he wished people with lace cuffs and hair-powder were dead. They made a virtue of their

[7] Soboul, *op.cit.*, 408, 660.

long trousers, and a vice of breeches, and at the height of excitement they advertised a few other peculiarities of dress, such as the red or "Phrygian" cap. Since the difference between *vous* and *tu* was a genteel affectation, used to connote class relations, they favored honest *tutoiment* by all persons—like the Quakers in the use of English a century before. Their mood was one of tense expectation of better things. The world would be better after the war, if the enemy were defeated. The Revolution opened a new era for the common man. The imminent possibility of this new era made strenuous exertion urgently necessary and worth while. Those who opposed it were selfish and evil. Their tricks must be exposed. The hour for the vengeance of ages had arrived. In the popular outlook there was much that was naive and credulously suspicious. It was easy to believe in any plot or in prison conspiracies, or that the common people might be betrayed by seeming friends among politicians. It was easy to be sarcastic about religion, or rough with priests, especially those who became nervous at the thought of equality, or refused civic oaths, or talked too much about social order and rewards in an afterlife.

These popular democrats had no developed economic ideas, but they took a negative attitude toward the wealthy, and while not objecting to private property believed that a more equal division of it was desirable. It is notable also, and more new, that Soboul finds in the documents repeated demands for public schools, more education for all, and vocational training. In general, in economic ideas, the popular democrats looked backward rather than forward. They came to demand more "equality of enjoyments," but never thought in terms of higher production or rising material standard of living. Though perhaps as much as half the Paris working class were wage-earners, attitudes were shaped by the artisan-shopkeeping outlook. The sans-culottes favored small property, small business, small employers, small workshops. They objected to business men, big merchants, financiers, commercial capital, and stock companies. They wished to preserve an older economic system against new forces by which they felt threatened.

Unprogressive in economic ideas, they were opposed to the actual course of economic development, whether it be called bourgeois capitalism, industrialism, or modernization. An American is bound to feel that these French popular democrats had something in common with their contemporaries the Jeffersonian democrats, and with the later Jacksonians, except that the French popular democrats were typically not agrarians, and were prepared to see power in the hands of the state.

Their ideal was "a community of independent producers among whom the State, by its laws, should assure an approximate equality."[8]

Such were the attitudes and ideals, and the popular democrats were highly political, as shown notably on August 10, 1792. More often, however, it was hunger and the fear of hunger that aroused them to take part in demonstrations and make demands on the public authorities. The price of bread, even in normal times, in the amount needed for a man with a wife and three children, was half as much as the daily wage of common labor. A rise in its price brought disaster. At times, from 1793 to 1795, there was positive scarcity, to the point where bread and other foodstuffs became unobtainable at any price. The effects became grimmer as one descended the income scale. The fear of hunger colored all sans-culotte politics. It motivated their demands on the Convention to obtain price controls, or repression of hoarding and profiteering; it made the popular democrats favor the bourgeois leaders who were willing at least temporarily to agree with them, and force the expulsion of those who did not; it made them hate the "rich" and the "aristocrats" because they ate better, or abhor and fear them, in the belief that the rich might use popular starvation for their own political advantage. The economic class issue was not at all between labor and capital, but between those who in times of scarcity either did or did not face the possibility of actual hunger for themselves and their children.

Violence, which has seemed to some an essential characteristic of the Paris populace during the Revolution, seems to Soboul a natural by-product of real events. Violence, *exaltation terroriste, buveurs de sang* there were. The *Septembriseurs* were drawn from sans-culotte ranks. But overwhelmingly the sans-culottes were not violent men—or women. They were "often rough men, without education, their souls inflamed by poverty."[9] Their violence was rarely wanton. It had an understandable aim. It was directed against the use of force by the counter-revolution. There was fear, but it was well-grounded fear. The idea of an aristocratic conspiracy was not baseless. There was the crisis of war and civil war, betrayal and secret conspiracy and the fear of the unknown. The guillotine in 1793 was welcomed and idealized; it was the "popular ax," the "scythe of equality," and it was believed to promote the supply of bread.

In the face of this uncouth manifestation of true popular revolution the Jacobins divided. The Jacobins, in the strict sense of those who belonged to the Jacobin Club, were, it must be repeated, almost all

[8] *Ibid.*, 473.   [9] *Ibid.*, 577.

drawn from the middle class, and had at least had enough education to make a speech in public, or even refer to the progress of humanity, the Greeks and Romans, and the famous authors of the Enlightenment. Some could not manage to adjust to dealing with irate tradespeople, or worse. They in turn came to be detested by the sans-culottes. This was the group of Jacobins who came to be called Girondins—Brissot, Cordorcet, Vergniaud, the Rolands, and others—for whom the Revolution of 1792 was the beginning of the end. Others made the adjustment with more success, including men like Danton, a bit plebeian himself, or like Robespierre, who managed to go along with the popular upsurge without sacrifice of his own meticulous habits. These were the kinds of Jacobins known in 1793 and 1794 as the Mountain.

But the Jacobins of the Mountain were never free agents. With many sans-culotte ideas, for a time at least, they genuinely agreed. They had little alternative, if they were to try to govern. They worked under enormous popular pressure. It was their dilemma that they had to yield to and use this popular zeal, but also to bring it under control.

International Revolutionism

The French popular democrats, or sans-culottes, were usually friendly to foreigners whom they saw personally, even to prisoners of war interned in French villages, but they knew little of foreign countries, which they believed to differ from France in being peopled mostly by slaves. They were suspicious of foreigners in the abstract. French popular revolutionism and international revolutionism were entirely distinct.

Agitation within the several countries will be described in succeeding chapters. At present, the problem is to see international revolutionism as it presented itself in France in 1792. Three preliminary observations may be made.

First, French historians, including those most sympathetic to the Revolution, have generally set a low estimate on the degree of genuine Revolutionary activity in the 1790's outside of France itself. For Albert Mathiez the presence of foreign zealots in Paris was a kind of illegitimate interference with the French Revolution, one of the many nuisances with which Robespierre had to deal.[10] Few Frenchmen have been attracted to the subject. Not until the work of Professor Godechot of Toulouse, published in 1956, had a French scholar given a full account

---

[10] A. Mathiez, *La Révolution et les étrangers* (Paris, 1918).

of international revolutionism as a whole in the 1790's.[11] In countries with a stable history in the past century, such as England and Holland, there has been little incentive to study, still less to emphasize, their native "Jacobins" of that time.

Secondly, it is true that these radicals or revolutionaries in other countries accomplished nothing except in conjunction with the French armies. Revolutions failed where they were attempted without French military support, as in Poland and Ireland. They succeeded where, and as long as, they could make use of French power, as in the Netherlands and Italy. This fact has lent weight to the line of thought under the first point, suggesting that the non-French revolutionaries were insignificant or ephemeral groups, mere immediate by-products of French invasion. It was the purpose of the preceding volume, by describing conditions in Europe for a generation before 1792, to prepare the reader of the present volume for a rejection of this idea.

Thirdly, the reader must put out of mind a good deal that will be suggested to him by twentieth-century international communism. There was never any concerted international organization directed from Paris or anywhere else. There was not even a French propaganda office trying to reach sympathizers in other countries. We find, indeed, as early as June 1790, counter-revolutionary allegations that such a "propaganda" existed. The word itself was then new, and usually found in the French form, *propagande*; it was used almost exclusively by conservatives, and what it meant was not the publicity or the open promotion of ideas that the word now suggests, but secret conspiracy and subversion. A letter written on July 31, 1790, from Turin, where the Count of Artois and other émigrés were assembled, mentioned a society called the *De propaganda Libertate*, a term obviously modeled on the *De propaganda Fide* of the Catholic Church.[12] About the same time, both from Turin and from Coblenz, another émigré center, the Emperor Leopold II heard that "a democratic party" in Paris had set up a clandestine *club de propagande* to bring about revolution in other countries.[13] The conservative Hamburg *Politisches Journal* and Girtan-

[11] J. Godechot, *La Grande Nation: l'expansion révolutionnaire de la France dans le monde, 1789-99*, 2 vols. (Paris, 1956). There have been, however, some excellent French studies of single foreign countries at the time of the Revolution, such as Droz on Germany, Fabre on Poland, or Dufourq on Rome, cited in relevant chapters below.

[12] Pia Onnis Rosa, "Filippo Buonarroti nel Risorgimento italiano," in *Rassegna storica del Risorgimento*, XLIX (1962), 31, notes 1 and 2.

[13] E. Wangermann, *From Joseph II to the Jacobin Trials: Government Policy and Public Opinion in the Habsburg Dominions in the Period of the French Revolution* (Oxford, 1959), 62.

ner's *Historische Nachrichten* gave further currency to the story and to the word.[14] Count Axel de Fersen, in March 1791, told the King of Sweden of "the Propaganda, that infernal abyss of secret agents everywhere."[15] Where the Turin report had attributed the "propaganda" in part to French Protestants, Fersen now also included the "Jew Ephraim." Later, on July 15, he recorded in his diary a report that the Propaganda had burned the Arsenal at Amsterdam. "If this should not be true," he added, "it would at least be useful to spread the story."[16] Meanwhile the British envoy at the Hague, Lord Auckland, sent Lord Grenville a paper obtained "on good authority" describing the "Society of the Propagande," whose aim was to produce revolution not only in France and Holland but in the "whole world." The society was now said, in May 1791, to consist of 5,000 members who paid dues of four louis a year, and 50,000 who paid nothing but were organized "in every country to spread this so-called philosophical enlightenment."[17] The idea found favor among opponents of the French Revolution: at Philadelphia, in 1796, William Cobbett talked of "the Propagande at Paris," and the Scottish Robison, in a book of 1797 of which more will be said, believed that the "propaganda" had been secretly at work since 1790.[18] What historians have somewhat uncritically called the two Propaganda Decrees of 1792 became for Robison a kind of climax and main argument of his book.

Nevertheless, there was no such Society of the Propaganda. Not only was there no such organization, but the whole thing was an invention of the counter-revolution, going back to a document fabricated by the Comte d'Antraigues, and designed to persuade the European governments to intervene in France against the Revolution.[19]

---

[14] *Politisches Journal*, Hamburg, Aug. 1790, 833-40; Sept., 963-65; Oct., 1,087-91; *Historische Nachrichten*, Hanover, III, 3.

[15] R. Klinckowstrom, *Le comte de Fersen et la cour de France*, 2 vols. (Paris, 1877), I, 87.

[16] Fersen's *Dagbok*, 4 vols. (Stockholm, 1925), under date of July 15, 1791. I am indebted for this item to the dissertation by H. A. Barton mentioned above in note 1.

[17] Great Britain: Historical Manuscripts Commission, *The Manuscripts of J. B. Fortescue Preserved at Dropmore*, 10 vols. (London, 1892-1927), II, 69-70, 117, 342, 358.

[18] W. Cobbett, *History of the American Jacobins Commonly Denominated Democrats* (Philadelphia, 1796), 7; J. Robison, *Proofs of a Conspiracy Against All the Religions and Governments of Europe, Carried on in the Secret Meetings of Freemasons, Illuminati and Reading Societies* (Edinburgh, 1797), but see the New York edition, 1798, 317-23.

[19] J. Feldmann, "Le 'discours de Duport' et la propagande révolutionnaire en Suisse," in *AHRF*, No. 138 (1955), 55-58; and *id.*, *Propaganda und Diplomatie: eine Studie über die Beziehungen Frankreichs zu den eidgenössischen Orten vom Beginn der fr. Rev. bis zum sturz der Girondisten* (Zurich, 1957). To the statement that the word "propaganda" was used exclusively by conservatives I know at present of only one

The "foreign" revolutionaries, in short, were not at all the victims or targets of any secret propaganda conducted by the French government, or by any organized association operating with its knowledge or its official or financial support. Their problem, on the contrary, was to get the French government to take them seriously. At most, there were *ad hoc* or temporary arrangements: thus Dumouriez, when foreign minister in 1792, had a secret fund for use in Belgium after the war began, or generals in the field might have talks with local collaborators, or the French government might send out a spy on a special mission, as it sent William Jackson to Ireland in 1794.

On the other hand, the "international" revolutionaries could readily share in many "French" ideas. They could count on a certain cosmopolitanism of the eighteenth century. Social and class relationships, and problems of church and state, had a certain resemblance throughout much of Europe. In many places, as in Belgium and Italy, governments rested on no basis of national loyalty or cohesion, and in other places, such as the Rhineland, Central Europe, and even the Dutch provinces, national loyalty as a political sentiment was unformed. French was the international language. Its literature had long been internationally read. The journalists of the French Revolution had a ready-made international audience among educated people. The relatively staid *Moniteur*, with its reports of debates in the French assembly or Jacobin Club, had an international circulation, despite attempts to keep it out. The radical journalist Carra, a very secondary figure in the French Revolution, became a name dreaded in Russia and South America when copies of his paper were discovered in those countries.

The Masonic lodges also provided a kind of international network of like-minded people. Their existence facilitated the circulation of ideas. But the lodges took no orders from any headquarters, their members never acted as a group, and their very taste for elaborate mystification made them innocuous if not ridiculous in real political life. Probably the reading clubs which sprang up in many European cities after about 1770, for the joint purchase and discussion of newspapers and books, were more important than Freemasonry as nurseries of pro-Revolutionary feeling. Nothing more conspiratorial than the Free-

exception, the ultra-revolutionary "Propaganda" suppressed by Saint-Just in Alsace in 1794. (See my *Twelve Who Ruled: the Committee of Public Safety in the French Revolution* [Princeton, 1941], 187-190.) It would not be unreasonable as a hypothesis to suppose that this ultra-revolutionary "propaganda" was somehow related in its origin to counter-revolutionary activity, somewhat in the manner suspected by Robespierre; see below, p. 120.

masons has ever been discovered. Belief in a concerted, secret, underground international revolutionary movement, as developed by the French Barruel and the Scotch Robison, and advanced in America by Jedidiah Morse, is an item not in the history of fact but in the history of counter-revolutionary polemics.[20]

The French Jacobins of 1792, among whom a few individuals like Robespierre were the exception, developed a psychology of world-revolution because they felt so insecure at home. They demanded war at a time when they considered their own king a traitor, when the Assembly was mortally divided, the generals unpredictable, and the country struggling to live under new laws on which the ink was scarcely dry. Brissot argued, before war was declared, that it would be short and easy because peoples everywhere would rise in a massive sympathy with France. Many believed, or said they believed, that that other land of liberty, the United States of America, in memory of French aid fifteen years before, and in common opposition to tyrants, would rush immediately into the struggle. On April 20, the very day on which the Assembly passed the declaration of war, an enthusiast at the Jacobin Club jumped up to cry to a screaming audience, "Washington is at Sea!"[21]

On August 26, 1792, the Assembly took one of the more extraordinary steps of the Revolution, decreeing honorary French citizenship for seventeen foreigners of varying eminence, as "men who in various countries have brought reason to its present maturity."[22] Coming at this moment it can be understood as a gesture of defiance. With the Prussians approaching, bringing the émigrés in their train, with Louis XVI unseated, and Paris quaking beneath them, with the Assembly itself now marked for an early disappearance, the harassed legislators made common cause with a wide assortment of benefactors of the human race. If on nothing else, they could agree on a list of notable foreigners. The list itself is a subject of curiosity. The poet, M. J.

[20] The literature on Freemasonry is large and disputatious. See Gaston Martin, *La franc-maçonnerie française et la préparation de la Révolution* (Paris, 1926); B. Fay, *Revolution and Freemasonry 1680-1800* (Boston, 1935), translated from the French; with a new edition (Paris, 1961). For the "plot" theory of international revolution as advanced by Barruel, see Chapter VIII below; by Robison, Chapters V and XV; by Morse, Chapter XVI. The plot theory was refuted by J. J. Mounier, *De l'influence attribuée aux philosophes et aux illuminés sur la Révolution de France* (Tübingen, 1801).

[21] A. Aulard, *Société des Jacobins*, 6 vols. (Paris, 1889-1897), III, for April 20, 1792. See also Lucy M. Gidney, *L'influence des Etats-Unis d'Amérique sur Brissot, Condorcet et Mme. Roland* (Paris, 1930).

[22] See the debates in the Moniteur; I am also indebted to a seminar paper by my student, Mr. J. E. Seigel, "The Honorary Citizens of France: August 26, 1792."

Chénier, first proposed fourteen names, of which the Assembly adopted eight: Thomas Paine, James Madison, Joseph Priestley, James Mackintosh (known for his reply to Burke), William Wilberforce (the anti-slavery leader), the Italian economist Gorani, and the German and Swiss educators, Campe and Pestalozzi. To these, after discussion, the Assembly added Jeremy Bentham, Thomas Clarkson (another anti-slavery Englishman), David Williams (a minor British "radical"), Thaddeus Kosciuszko, Klopstock the German poet, George Washington, Alexander Hamilton, the Dutch Cornelius de Pauw and his nephew J. B. Cloots, called Anacharsis Cloots, a rich baron from the duchy of Cleves, near the Dutch frontier, who had been in Paris for several years, gathering a circle of miscellaneous foreign radicals about him. The American Joel Barlow, in addition, was given honorary citizenship in the following February.

It may seem a mystery how the name of Alexander Hamilton ever got on this list, and even more of a mystery why Thomas Jefferson was omitted, since he was better known in Paris than almost anyone whose name was adopted, having spent five years in France before September 1789. On reflection, there is perhaps no mystery at all. Perhaps the Assembly, less erratic than it seems, understood the qualifications of Hamilton and Jefferson for honorary French citizenship, as of 1792, better than modern Americans who look back through various veils of illusion. If the deputies knew that Hamilton mixed in banking and commercial circles they need not have been deterred; after all, the Belgian banker Walkiers, and the Dutch bankers Abbema and Kock, were at this very moment, as refugees from their own countries, pleading with the French to assist them in revolutions in Belgium and Holland. As for Jefferson, when in France he had been close to Lafayette; and Lafayette, unable to reverse the events in Paris, had only a week before surrendered voluntarily to the Austrians. It made sense for the French in August 1792 to suppose that Hamilton might be better disposed than Jefferson to the Revolution. Events in the United States had not yet gone far enough to teach them the contrary. In any case, it was chiefly as authors of the *Federalist*, recently translated into French, that Hamilton and Madison were included.

Priestley, Paine, and Cloots, since they now enjoyed citizenship, were elected in several departments to be members of the coming Convention. Priestley declined, prudently emigrating to the United States instead. Paine and Cloots both sat in the convention. Paine found his political friends among people like Condorcet and Brissot, with whom he shared the idea of universal revolution. Cloots continued to associate with the Dutch and other revolutionary exiles, and with radical journalists like Hébert, who held no national office, and who continued to demand war upon tyrants wherever found. Both 'the Brissot group and the Hébert group, the two spearheads in French politics of international revolutionism, were eventually outmaneuvered by Robespierre, who had Paine imprisoned and Cloots executed in 1793-1794.

The "legions" of various national groups, organized in 1792, allow another insight into the international revolutionary spirit. Refugees from abroad asked to form military units to fight alongside the French. Hardly had the war begun, in April, when the French Assembly, foreseeing an advance into the Austrian Netherlands, authorized a Belgian-Liégeois Legion, to which it granted six million livres. Two such legions were formed. They both fought with Dumouriez, and accompanied him on his entry into Brussels in November 1792. A Dutch or Batavian legion was authorized in July. Within the next few weeks, under similar pressure of foreign revolutionaries in Paris, other similar "legions" were organized: an Allobrogian Legion for Savoyards and Swiss, and a Germanic Legion which had a thousand men by the end of 1792. There was even a shadowy English Legion, raised by John Oswald, who was killed in the Vendée in 1793. A proposal by an Italian named l'Aurora to set up an Italian Legion was rejected by the Convention in February 1793.[23]

At the same time, on the remote borders of civilization, in Kentucky, "at the falls of the Ohio" (i.e. Louisville), George Rogers Clark penned an unsolicited letter to the French minister at Philadelphia.[24] He asserted that if the French gave a little secret assistance, he could raise a party of some 1,500 men to liberate Louisiana and New Mexico from the rule of tyrants. When Edmond Genet arrived as French minister shortly thereafter, he set about forming "legions" in America, and

[23] On the "legions" see A. Mathiez, *La Révolution et les étrangers*, pp. 65-68, who however sees them from a French point of view, and does not mention the Italian proposal, or Genet's activities in America. On the idea of an Italian Legion there is some reference in R. Soriga, *L'idea nazionale italiana del secolo XVIII all'unificazione* (Modena, 1941), 166. More will be found on the Belgian Legion in S. Tassier, *Histoire de la Belgique sous l'occupation française en 1792 et 1793* (Brussels, 1934), 42, 52-53; on the Batavian Legion in H. Colenbrander, *Gedenkstukken der algemeene geschiedenis van Nederland*, I. *Nederland en de Revolutie, 1789-95*, I, 35-41, 74, 79, etc. There was also a Polish Legion in 1796-1799; see below, pp. 268, 379.

[24] *Report of the American Historical Association for 1896*, "Correspondence of Clark and Genet," 967-71.

commissioned Clark as a brigadier-general in the French Republican army.

It is important to realize that in this formation of legions, the demands of foreign revolutionaries and French military requirements were at least as important as a Jacobin crusade to overturn the world. Once the war began, the French Assembly had no difficulty in recognizing a Belgian Legion, because Belgium was a Hapsburg country, in which military operations were to be conducted. The Allobrogian Legion was intended mainly for Savoyards after the king of Sardinia, to whom Savoy belonged, became a belligerent. Genet's legions on the American frontier were obviously of a different kind; they were not intended to revolutionize the United States, nor were they composed of revolutionaries in exile. They were intended, by operations in Florida, Louisiana, or Canada, to cause trouble to the powers in possession of these regions, namely Spain and Britain, after France was at war with them also.

More difficulties attended the formation of the Batavian Legion. Of the various revolutionary agitations in Europe before the French upheaval, the Dutch Patriot movement had been the strongest. The provinces of Holland and Utrecht especially were full of former Patriots who looked forward to the return of their friends among the Dutch exiles. These exiles saw in the war between France and Austria a chance to advance the Dutch Revolution. They found it hard to persuade the French Jacobins, who, for all their crusading mentality, did not wish the Dutch and British governments to be drawn into the war. Dumouriez, when still foreign minister, wrote the French minister at the Hague, five days after the declaration of war against Austria, that it was in France's interest to have as few enemies as possible, and for the Dutch government to remain neutral. Since, however, the Dutch government was very hostile to the French Revolution (which was true), he, de Maulde at the Hague, should keep up secret contact with Dutch Patriots; if the Dutch government departed from neutrality, then de Maulde should come out more openly, "to accelerate a change in the Form of Government for which [Dutch] opinion seems to be entirely prepared." Meanwhile it was Brissot, the most voluble of the French world-revolutionaries, who thought Dumouriez went too far. The Dutch exiles in Paris complained of opposition to them at the Jacobin Club. Late in July, the French Assembly at last authorized a Dutch Legion, at first calling it the Free Foreign Legion to prevent trouble with the Dutch government. The Dutch exiles called it the Batavian Legion, after the Latin name for Holland. Not until October were its officers really named. It was then organized on a basis of 2,822 men, 500 horse, and two companies of artillery, under an administrative committee of the Dutch exiles. The Batavian Legion fought with Dumouriez in Belgium, and was naturally impatient to push on into the United Provinces.[25]

The early weeks of the National Convention saw a remarkable upturn in the military fortunes of the newborn Republic. The hopes of the Counter-Revolution, so confidently expressed at Frankfurt on July 14, were completely crushed for the time being; indeed the French general Custine occupied Frankfurt itself in October. Other columns entered Savoy, where many of the French-speaking population favored annexation. The turning point came with the battle of Jemappes, near Mons in Belgium, where the Austrians retreated before Dumouriez' army of 40,000 ragged republicans. Poorly clothed, poorly supplied, spontaneous and undisciplined, a true revolutionary horde, spurning all military proprieties, they overwhelmed the enemy by sheer numbers, while bellowing the Marseillaise. The French spread throughout Belgium. The Belgian and Dutch revolutionaries were delighted. Success breeds enthusiasm, and in England the sympathy for the French Revolution among the popular classes, undeterred by the dethronement of Louis XVI or the September Massacres, reached a new height of excitement. English political clubs sent congratulations to the French Convention. In the English militia companies, not only the soldiers but even some of the officers contributed sums of money to buy muskets and shoes for the triumphant sans-culottes. There was a banquet on November 18 of the English-speaking residents of Paris, presided over by Harfurd Stone, an English business man who owned an ammonia plant in France, and attended by various English and Irish, including Lord Edward Fitzgerald and Arthur Dillon, the latter a general in the French army. They drafted a statement to the French Convention, which received one from the London Constitutional Society on the same day.

The French government and army had an international coloring. They were dominated at the moment by the Brissot group. Brissot, having traveled in the United States in former years, and having been at Geneva during the troubles of 1782, considered himself well informed on international revolution. Clavière, the finance minister, was

---

[25] Colenbrander, *Gedenkstukken*, I, 38-45.

an exile from the Geneva counter-revolution. Lebrun, the foreign minister, had spent years as an editor in Liége, and was closely involved with the Belgians. Dumouriez was the friend and patron of Lebrun. His second-in-command in Belgium was the Venezuelan, Miranda, who already had plans for revolution in South America. Other generals in Dumouriez' army were the New Yorker, John Eustace, the Swiss A. E. La Harpe, exiled by the Bern authorities on the charge of revolutionary activity at Lausanne, and a number of officers of Irish birth or connections.

In Savoy, in the county of Nice, at the city of Mainz and in the towns of the Austrian Netherlands, as the French arrived, local patriots came forward to ask for French protection. They declared that they lived in fear of counter-revolutionary reprisals. Their case came before the Convention, where hesitation at premature action was expressed, but which enacted as a temporary measure, pending further review of the question of occupied territories during the war, the famous decree of November 19, 1792, "according aid and fraternity to all peoples wishing to recover their liberty." Lebrun, as foreign minister, tried to explain in England and Switzerland that the decree had no application to neutrals. But conservatives took the decree as a challenge, and to French sympathizers in all countries it brought a thrill.

The idea of the sovereignty of the people, used in August to sweep out the government in France itself, was now used abroad for a similar purpose. Juridically, it was the essence of the Revolution, since it denied the claims of governments over their own populations. It also set up a new principle of international law. The idea was that peoples could no longer be transferred by arrangements of governments as set forth in treaties, or be subject to any government except by their own consent. A year before, at Avignon, in defiance of the existing ruler, the Pope, the population had been joined to France after a plebiscite. The same was now done in Savoy, and was soon done in Belgium.

As always, however, the simple explanation of ideology, or revolutionary enthusiasm, or political theory must be kept in perspective and received with some reservation. The Convention debated the annexation of Savoy on November 27. The debate was perfectly rational. The Abbé Grégoire, who led it, reviewed the arguments, pro and con, remarking that not all peoples were equally suited for freedom or were developing at the same historical pace. He concluded, however, that in time of war, if the French found a sentiment for union among an adjoining people of their own language and kindred they could not well ignore them, or leave them as a source of strength for an enemy king who wished the ruin of France. He added that Savoy had enough resources in its own wealth, population, and church lands that might be resold, to finance its own share in the French war-effort against the Counter-Revolution. The Convention then admitted Savoy as an eighty-fourth department, Mont Blanc—the present French departments of Savoie and Haute Savoie.

There were some enthusiasts, to be sure, for whom no Revolutionary emancipation seemed too far-fetched—notably Brissot, for whose long career as a pre-Revolutionary intellectual the present moment came as a supreme climax. Locked as we are, he said on November 26, in a death struggle with the "Germanic colossus," we "cannot be at ease until Europe, and all Europe, is in flames." He demanded the Rhine frontier, and hoped through Miranda, and a Spaniard named Marchena, to drive the Bourbons out of Spain. He had the idea also that Spanish America could be liberated, if Miranda recruited some 6,000 mulattoes in Haiti (to whom the Revolution had given civil rights) and reinforced them with volunteers from the United States. He rejoiced in "upheavals of the globe, these great revolutions that we are called upon to make."[26]

The American Joel Barlow was another. Lately in London he had written his *Advice to the Privileged Orders*, which the British government found only slightly less subversive than Paine's *Rights of Man*. He had come to Paris as one of the delegates bringing greetings from the London Society for Constitutional Information. After the annexation of Savoy, when the Abbé Grégoire went on a tour to the new eighty-fourth department he took the Connecticut Yankee with him. Barlow was led to believe that Savoy might elect him as one of its deputies to the Convention. He was not elected; he was not yet a French citizen. In the Alpine majesty of Savoy his thoughts turned to plain little Connecticut. He wrote his mock-epic on corn-meal mush, *Hasty Pudding*, at an inn in Chambéry. He also wrote on a more pressing topic, *A Letter addressed to the People of Piedmont*, published in French at Grenoble, in Italian at Nice. The latter edition was so thoroughly suppressed by the King of Sardinia that no known copy is in existence. Barlow advised the Italians to join in the general rev-

[26] J. P. Brissot, *Correspondance et papiers* (Paris, 1912), 304, 313-16.

olution. "Italy must be free . . . Italy is destined to form one great republic."[27]

Condorcet meanwhile penned his *Avis aux Bataves*, urging the Dutch to revolt. The Dutch exile, Kock, translated it. He and others, after Jemappes, had set up a kind of government in exile, the Batavian Revolutionary Committee. Word came from Amsterdam that the patriots were ready to rise, but would do so only after the arrival of the French army, not before. Even Brissot hesitated to invade the Dutch provinces after the victory in Belgium, knowing that invasion would bring both the Dutch and British governments into the war. A group of Dutch revolutionaries appeared at the Jacobin Club in December. They met with considerable skepticism from Robespierre and others.[28]

"Why don't the Batavian patriots make their own revolution," someone asked at the Jacobin Club, "since they have the money and means of their own? Or why don't they offer a hundred millions to the French nation to enable us to do it?"[29]

This picture should be kept in mind, since it was to be reproduced many times in the following years, in connection with Italy as well as Holland. It is a picture in which revolutionaries from other countries importune the French, and the French are themselves divided, some urging the "foreign" revolutionaries to revolt, some favoring positive French assistance, others expressing contempt for these ineffectual malcontents or unwillingness to spend French blood and treasurer for their liberation.

These various points of view came momentarily together when the Convention, on December 15, issued its famous decree on policy to be pursued in occupied countries during the war. This decree represented the definitive action foreseen in the decree of November 19. The two together have been commonly called the Propaganda Decrees, though mere propaganda was hardly their purpose. More will be said of the decree of December 15 in the next chapter. Its most immediate purpose was to arrange for supply of the French armies in Belgium. French generals in the field were therefore directed to seize the revenues of enemies of the Republic, that is to say, of the enemy governments, the noble and feudal classes, and the church. The decree was

---

[27] J. Woodress, *A Yankee's Odyssey: the Life of Joel Barlow* (Philadelphia and New York, 1958), 134-35.

[28] Colenbrander, *Gedenkstukken*, I, 79-84, 92-96, 196.

[29] *Ibid.*, 81 n. Colenbrander gives no source, and the sentences are not in Aulard's *Jacobins*, but are characteristic of what was then being said in other speeches printed by Aulard.

explained in the Convention by Cambon, who was no ideological hot-head, but simply a revolutionary of the workhorse or practical type. "We must," he said, "declare ourselves to represent revolutionary power in the countries we enter." After a careful exposition of the practical circumstances he launched the phrase in which international revolution and popular revolution, at least in appearance, seemed to be joined: *Guerre aux châteaux, paix aux chaumières!*—war on the castles and manor houses, peace to the cottages and cabins. The enemies of the Revolution were to pay for its triumph.

Whatever the intent, the war had in fact become ideological, with partisans on each side urging an international effort to destroy the other. Within a week the Abbé Grégoire and the Count de Fersen used the same word to explain what their side must do—*étouffer*, or smother, its opponent. "When my neighbor keeps a nest of vipers," said the mild and humanitarian priest on November 27, "I have the right to smother them lest I become their victim." And the sensitive and refined Swedish count, writing at Aachen on November 19, and observing that the German Rhineland re-echoed with praise of French liberty and equality, observed that unless the European powers banded together "to stop the evil by smothering it, they would all be its victims." He added that "there will then be no more kings or nobility, and all countries will experience the horrors of which France is now the victim, and to preserve an existence and a livelihood, we shall all have to turn into Jacobins."[30]

Of this atmosphere of world upheaval, at the close of 1792, there is another piece of evidence in which American readers should take a particular interest: the career of Edmond Genet, always called Citizen Genet in American history, since he so shocked the Federalists and pleased the democrats as French minister to the United States for a few months in 1793.

It was in Russia that Genet first acted as an international firebrand, but the earliest influence of this kind upon him had come rather from the American Revolution. Of noble family, a brother of Mme. de Campan, one of Marie Antoinette's ladies in waiting, he had worked during the American war in the French Foreign Office under his father, who was chief of the interpreters' bureau. He knew six languages at the age of fifteen. He assisted his father and Benjamin Franklin in obtaining favorable publicity for the United States. As a youth

---

[30] Grégoire in the *Moniteur*, November 27, 1792 (*réimpression*, xiv, 587); R. Klinckowström, ii, 392.

he met such other notables as John Adams, Joseph Priestley, James Watt, and Matthew Boulton. In 1788 he was sent to the French embassy at St. Petersburg. Here he strongly favored the French Revolution of 1789 and the new constitutional monarchy, as did his superior the ambassador, the Count de Ségur. They both boldly defended events in France from the aspersions of émigrés who turned up in Russia. In 1790 Ségur went home, and Genet became chargé. He thought he saw signs in Russia that the liberating new modern spirit would soon be felt. The court nobles seemed to be full of it; they were fascinated when Ségur showed them his American Order of Cincinnatus, and expressed great interest in France. The two Grand Dukes, Alexander and Constantine, were considered to be sympathetic. They were still under the care of their Swiss tutor, F. C. La Harpe, who was instilling in them the ideas of the Western Enlightenment, and whose first cousin was a general in the French army. The great Russian landowner Stroganov, said to own 10,000 serfs, when in Paris with his French tutor, had even been a registered member of the Jacobin Club. Genet expected something to happen in Russia, without knowing what: a palace revolution, a guards' revolt, a move patronized by the Grand Dukes, a serf uprising, or a Cossack rebellion.

After the interception of Louis XVI at Varennes in 1791, Catherine II forbade Genet to appear at her court and imposed censorship on news from France. Genet continued to justify the French Revolution in an increasingly hostile environment. More determined than ever he took to hiring spies, and on July 19, 1792, was ordered out of Russia.[31]

Returning to France in October, he mixed with people like Condorcet, Brissot, Paine, the Rolands, Dumouriez and Lebrun. He was almost immediately appointed minister to the Hague, to which however he never went. The Dutch exiles, preparing their plans for revolution, were told by Lebrun to maintain secret contact with Genet in Paris. Genet therefore spent several weeks in close touch with real revolutionaries who expected at any moment to return to Holland. On October 28, meeting with the Batavian Revolutionary Committee, he expressed "entire approval" of its plans and organization. He was then sent on a brief mission to the republic of Geneva, where the old conflict between democratic and patrician parties was brought to a crisis by the operation of French armies in neighboring Savoy. At

[31] For Genet in Russia I am indebted to my former student, Mr. W. L. Blackwell, who has examined Russian as well as French sources.

Geneva Genet was thought very conciliatory. Late in November he was appointed minister to the United States.[32]

When he arrived in America, in April 1793, he therefore brought with him a sense of the supra-national conflict of 1792, at a time when in Paris itself it was already abating. For Genet it was not new to be hailed by foreign democrats as their champion, or to have them request French sponsorship for special military formations. He thought he understood, from experience, the real significance of the emerging Federalists and Republicans in America; and he had reason to believe that governments hostile to the French Revolution did not really represent their own peoples.

Let us summarize this chapter, and venture one new thought. The French Revolution was revolutionized in 1792 by the war, through the simultaneous eruption of popular and of international revolutionism. Some of the constructive efforts of the Revolution of 1789, notably the constitutional monarchy, were swept aside. In this crisis of invasion and imminent counter-revolution, the "people" took over in default of everyone else. Given the fact of war, the leaders of the Revolution in France made concessions to more popular elements. And given the fact of war, the potential revolutionaries of other countries hoped for French aid. The French Revolution could no longer be a mainly middle-class or an exclusively French affair.

The Jacobins in France—that is, the predominantly middle-class revolutionaries who had some capacity for leadership and for government—reacted to popular and to international revolutionism in various ways. The idea of world revolution was no mere "Girondist" crusade or propagandistic dream. People of all kinds, as someone said in 1793, wanted to strangle the last king in the entrails of the last priest. But there is some evidence to suggest that some Jacobins saw popular and international revolutionism as alternatives. Those who could work most effectively with popular revolution in France, those who could go along with the lower classes of their own country, were the least inclined to befriend the revolutionists from foreign parts. These included men like Robespierre, who were to govern France during the Terror. Those Jacobins, on the other hand, who saw in popular revolutionism an outburst of anarchy, who shrank from involvement with the lower

---

[32] For Genet and the Dutch, see Colenbrander, *Gedenkstukken*, I, 44, 184-91; at Geneva, H. Fazy, *Genève de 1788 à 1792: la fin d'un régime* (Geneva, 1917), 478-81; in Russia, Chapter v below; in the United States, Chapter xvi.

classes of France and Paris, were more likely to lend a sympathetic ear to revolutionaries from Belgium or Holland, who were after all middle-class persons like themselves, and usually spoke excellent French. As Brissot wrote to Dumouriez in November: it is your glorious destiny to plant the tree of liberty everywhere, carrying pamphlets in German on your bayonets, while we languish at home watching the anarchists by whom we are surrounded.[33] And Dumouriez, the victor of Jemappes, the hero of the international revolution, reached the point where he meant to use his prestige and his power, won in Belgium, to bring the "anarchists" in France under control. This is one of the themes of the next chapter.

[33] Brissot, *Correspondance*, 314.

LIBERATION AND ANNEXATION:

1792-1793

Sir: The democratic government of France is said to have invented a new system of foreign politics, under the names of proselytism *and* fraternization. *My present letter . . . will show that* an internal interference *with foreign states, and the* annexation of dominion to dominion *for purposes of aggrandizement are among the most inveterate and predominant principles of long established governments. These principles, therefore, only appear novel and odious in France because novel and despised persons there* openly *adopted them.*—BENJAMIN VAUGHAN to the editor of the *Morning Chronicle*, London, May 16, 1793

LIBERATION AND ANNEXATION:
1792-1793

THE YEAR 1793 was one of great successes for the Counter-Revolution, especially in Belgium and Poland, the two theaters in which the forces of a democratic revolution most conspicuously failed to maintain themselves. For a while it seemed that the same would be true in France.

In 1792 the French army occupied Belgium, and the Russian army, closely followed by the Prussian, occupied Poland. In both cases the entering powers announced themselves as liberators, and were welcomed as such by certain elements in the population. The French in Belgium within a few weeks passed to a policy of annexation. The Russians and Prussians had annexationist designs on Poland from the beginning. The French were soon driven out, but returned in 1794, so that Belgium remained incorporated into France for twenty years. The Russian and Prussian monarchies never gave up what they took of Poland in 1793, except that for a few years the Prussian segment belonged to Napoleon's Grand Duchy of Warsaw. Only with the destruction of the Russian and Prussian monarchies themselves, in 1918, were the annexations of 1793 undone, and then only in part. The territory taken by Catherine II in this "second" partition of Poland, involving White Russia and the Ukraine, has remained in the Soviet Union.

It is the purpose of this chapter, under the formal parallel of liberation and annexation, to trace the realities which these terms represented in 1792-1793—that is, to show who was liberated from what, or how and why annexed—and to indicate also the impact of these events on the further radicalizing of the Revolution in France itself.

The Storm in the Low Countries

The contacts of French and Belgians in the winter of 1792-1793 form a prelude in which many themes of later years are already sounded.

Problems later raised in the "sister republics" were already prefigured. With allowance for differences, there is still a distinguishable pattern. Populations greet the arrival of the French with enthusiasm, set about introducing liberty and equality, and hope to enjoy an independent republic. They want the French to protect them against their own old regimes, but are unwilling or unable to share in the war effort against the Coalition, and object to French exploitation of their resources for this purpose. They become disillusioned with the French, who in turn become contemptuous of them. Some become more dependent on the French, even subservient, than they originally meant to be. Others of those who originally hailed the invaders, or were at least willing to accept them, begin to regret the disappearance of the old order, while still others remain revolutionary in spirit while turning anti-French. There was also for the French government the problem of control over military command, the fear that a successful French general in the field, enjoying the prestige of sensational victory, and building a base for himself in an occupied country, through keeping control of its resources in his own hands, and directing the loyalties of local sympathizers to himself, might become independent of the government in Paris that he was supposed to serve, overshadow his own civilian superiors, and emerge as a military dictator over the Revolution. This was what General Bonaparte did in Italy a few years later. It was what General Dumouriez dreamed of doing in Belgium.

It was only in a rough geographical sense that the French invaded "Belgium."[1] There was strictly speaking no such country, but only ten provinces belonging to the Austrian monarchy (of which Brabant, Flanders, Hainault, Namur, and Luxembourg were the most important), virtually cut in two by the large Bishopric of Liége, an inde-

[1] For the following account of Belgium, and of the views of the French and of Dumouriez with respect to it, I follow the thoroughly documented and admirably thought out work of Suzanne Tassier [Mme. G. Charlier], *Histoire de la Belgique sous l'occupation française en 1792 et 1793* (Brussels, 1934). There are also about a hundred relevant pages in the first volume of [Baron] Paul Verhaegen, *La Belgique sous la domination française, 1792-1814*, 5 vols. (Brussels, 1922-1935), and other older works. Verhaegen's book, actually written before the First World War, has a definite nineteenth-century tone. That is, it simply assumes that the revolutionaries of the 1790's were mistaken (Rousseau was a "dreamer," etc.), and its author closely identifies himself with the Belgian Statists, in whom he sees the true embodiment of Belgian character, nationality, and interests. Except upon episodic facts, Tassier and Verhaegen profoundly disagree, but Miss Tassier's work is so good, and coincides so fully with all that I have been able to learn, that I have made no attempt to split the difference, but have simply agreed with Miss Tassier. For an account of the Belgian revolution of 1789-1790, see *Age*, I, 341-57.

pendent member-state of the Holy Roman Empire. There had been no national government or institutions embracing these provinces as a whole, except what the Hapsburg monarchy had supplied as a superstructure, until the Belgian revolution of 1789, in which the United Belgian States had asserted their independence from Austria. The anti-Austrian movement was made up of two groups with diametrically opposed intentions. One, the Estates party, consisted of those who objected to Austrian reforms in the 1780's, and wished to preserve the historic identity of the several provinces unimpaired. This meant preserving the position of the great abbots, who led the regular clergy and controlled much of the land, of the nobility with its seignieurial and political rights, and of certain burgesses of old-fashioned type, gildmasters, burgomasters, and councillors in those towns which enjoyed representation in provincial bodies. Few groups in Europe were more conservative and even traditionalistic than the Belgian Statists, whose "revolution" was entirely exhausted in revolt against the Austrian crown. The men of the other party called themselves Democrats, and were termed Vonckists by their opponents. They wished in the Revolution of 1789, while getting rid of the Austrian overlordship, to introduce internal changes also, by which the special political role of great prelates and nobles should be reduced, and more of a place marked out for middle-class people, beyond the sphere of town and gild localism as inherited from the Middle Ages.

It is a disputed question whether there was any Belgian nationality at this time. Both parties were anti-foreign and anti-Austrian. The Estates party felt a kind of cultural nationalism, setting a high value on the rich heritage of town and province in the old Low Countries. The Democrats moved more toward the modern conception of a political nation, with a degree of equality of rights and opportunity for participation in public life for all residents of the area. The two were too divided to create any workable government. Provincial, town, and class barriers were stronger than all-Belgian national ties. The two parties together drove out the Austrians in 1789; the Statists then in 1790 suppressed and drove out the Democrats, of whom thousands fled to France; the Austrians then at the end of 1790 put down the Statists, many of whom fled to England or Holland. The years 1791 and 1792 are known in Belgian history as the first Austrian restoration.

A shaky regime confronted Revolutionary France when war began. The Austrian officials enjoyed little useful support. The native Belgian leaders were in exile, and those who remained at home were disaffected, and secretly in touch with one or the other of the two opposing émigré camps. The Antwerp bankers refused the war loan of 1792. There were anti-Austrian demonstrations in various towns, and some young men went off to join the Belgian Legion in France. Paine's *Rights of Man* circulated in French and Flemish. The populace, as in most countries of Western Europe outside France, tended to uphold their existing superiors. But in Belgium, more than in most countries, the rural and urban masses were amenable to direction by monks and abbots, and the great abbots strongly disliked the secularist and reforming governments of Joseph II and Leopold II, against which they had in fact led the Statist party in the Revolution of 1789. The situation was so confused, and the dislike of Austrian church policy so intense, that some of the Belgian upper clergy, even after the September Massacres and the expulsion of priests from France, expressed a preference for the French over the Austrians. There were cases in which ignorant peasants believed that the French were coming to avenge true religion.

Where the Estates party adhered to the Old Regime, the Democrats stood for the New Order. They were clearly a middle-class group, drawing their strength from financial and commercial men of the newer type, who could not operate within the old town and gild limits, and they were reinforced by the younger generation in general, by lawyers of various kinds, by a few individual noblemen, and by doctors, intellectuals, and journalists who were impressed by the ideas of the Enlightenment. The spectacle of the French Revolution made the Statists more wedded than ever to ancestral ways. The Democrats, on the other hand, thanks to their treatment in 1790 at the hands of the Statists, and to disillusionment at the Austrian restoration, and in some cases to inspiration from the French Revolution, were less inclined in 1792 than in 1789 to be content with moderate counsels. The sight of foppish French émigrés congregating in Brussels—"powdered abbés flitting about with lorgnettes"—made many Belgians into Democrats.[2] Others were converted to enlightened ideas by a criminal case at Antwerp in the summer of 1792, when a young man was put to the torture four times, against the protests of his mother, until he admitted that he worshipped the devil. The Belgians live in fear of "hunger and hell," wrote a disdainful Frenchman.[3] The Dutch also thought them backward. The Belgian Democrats hoped to rectify this situation.

[2] Tassier, *op.cit.*, 78, 73 n.   [3] *Ibid.*, 61.

Many Belgians, of both parties, therefore saw in the war another chance—their second chance, the first having failed in 1790—to set up an independent Belgian republic. Events of 1790 had shown that the Belgians could not live politically with each other. As the Poles could only live under a king who was not one of themselves, so the Belgians (it is the Belgian historian, Suzanne Tassier, who says so) needed a dominant personality from outside. They needed someone identified with neither party, and whom both could accept. This outside personality was furnished by Dumouriez. They took hope also in the fact that after the August revolution the French foreign minister was practically a Belgian, Lebrun, who though of French birth had lived for years in Liége, and was in fact a refugee from the Liége revolution of 1789. Events in the Bishopric of Liége in 1789 had been if anything more turbulent than in the Austrian provinces; the rebels, wishing to be rid of the rule of the bishop, favored a merger in a Belgian national state, and so agreed with the Democrats of Brabant, Flanders, Luxembourg, and the other Austrian territories. Lebrun, a young man, was very much under the influence of Dumouriez, who had befriended him upon his arrival in Paris. Dumouriez, over fifty, was a thorough product of the Old Regime, and is more appreciated by Belgian historians than by the French, who see him either as the adventurer of 1792 or the traitor of 1793.[4] An age that saw one French general become king of Sweden might have seen another end up as a prince of Belgium.

Dumouriez defeated the Austrians at Jemappes on November 6, and entered Brussels soon thereafter, with the Belgian legions riding at his side, amid the cheers of those who came out to welcome him. At this moment the French had no plan of annexation. Brissot, Condorcet, Lebrun, Robespierre, and Dumouriez himself, in both public and private statements, expressed a preference for an independent republic. Dumouriez had already matured a private policy of his own. He hoped, after the war and revolution were over, to retire as a kind of stadholder or protector of a Belgian republic, which should serve as a barrier between France and the German states, and be guaranteed by international treaties (as in fact happened in the 1830's) in the status of a neutral country which foreign armies might not invade or cross.

As the French occupied Belgium, Dumouriez therefore tried to make himself agreeable both to the Statists and to the Democrats. It was his idea that the Belgians should create a government and an army of

----

[4] *Ibid.*, 34.

their own, to carry through the liberation from Austria. The Paris authorities shared this idea at first. Within a few days of Jemappes, local elections were held throughout Belgium, conducted largely by returning exiles, that is by the most advanced and indeed vengeful of the Belgian Democrats expelled by the Statists in 1790. The electoral assemblies received guidance from political clubs, which now sprang up everywhere, called, like the French Jacobins, the Friends of Liberty and Equality. At Namur the members were mainly the larger merchants called *négociants*. At Bruges a lively club developed out of the old literary society. At Louvain, a Catholic center, the members were mainly French soldiers. There were large clubs at Ghent and Liége. The one at Brussels began in November with five hundred members—lawyers, doctors, business men, and Belgian military officers—but its numbers fell off very rapidly. The clubs and assemblies together chose "provisional representatives" whose duty was to work locally with the French military authorities.

As the Democrats thus began to dominate the new political organization rising in Belgium, Dumouriez tried to hold them in check, knowing that an exclusively Democratic victory would antagonize the Statists, and counting on support from both parties to further his own plans. The Belgian Democrats, to win mass support, made public promises to abolish manorial dues and tithes, and shift the tax burden from ordinary consumers' goods on to the incomes of the well-to-do. Meanwhile some of Dumouriez' own subordinate generals, to supply their troops, began confiscations and direct requisitions on their own authority upon the inhabitants. To all these developments Dumouriez objected.

It was his plan, in structural matters, to wait for the assembling of a Belgian Convention, which should not represent the Three Estates as such, but be chosen by universal suffrage in which men of all parties could cast a vote. Such a Convention would have, as in France, the power to write a constitution, to decide upon forms of government and reforms, and to raise a Belgian army. Meanwhile, in the supply of his troops, he tried to shield the Belgians from the direct impact of French or revolutionary demands. For the purchase of food, fuel, bedding, horses, hay, and other requirements, he thought it best to deal with Belgian business men himself, and to pay them in hard currency, not the paper money which the Revolution had brought into circulation in France. In this way the Belgian business classes might be attached to the new regime. To pay the contractors, he hoped to obtain a loan of several millions from the Belgian clergy, who controlled a large share of the wealth of the country, and would presumably be willing to pay for liberation from Austria. If they were to make such a loan, however, they must be assured in the possession of their incomes from tithes and manorial dues. They expected protection, also, against the rampant anti-clericalism brought in by French soldiers and Belgian exiles. Dumouriez, in having to protect the church, if only for financial reasons, departed widely from the views of the men now in power in Paris.

He showed signs also, like Bonaparte in Italy in 1796, of developing a foreign policy of his own. Dutch as well as Belgian exiles were with him on the campaign.[5] The Batavian Legion soon reached the Dutch frontier, which it was eager to cross. Schemes were in the air for a combined Dutch-Belgian republic, of all seventeen Netherlands provinces, an idea that Dumouriez toyed with for a while, though he soon gave it up. He did propose, however, the invasion of the United Provinces, not to liberate the Dutch, but rather with the thought that these provinces could be returned to the House of Orange at a peace conference in return for international recognition of a Belgian republic. (Here Bonaparte's treatment of Venice will suggest itself.) The Convention forbade Dumouriez to enter Dutch territory. It ordered him to pursue the Austrians into Germany instead. He refused, saying his troops were tired. The Convention became suspicious. The Dutch patriots also were alarmed. They feared that France, Austria, and Britain might agree to an independent Belgium, and the war be over, before their own aims were achieved.

In Belgium, Dumouriez' program met with difficulties from the start. While affronting the Democrats, it reckoned also without the actual Statist aspirations. Immediately after Jemappes the Belgian émigrés in England were heard from. Their leader there was Van der Noot, the anti-Austrian hero of 1789. Van der Noot now proposed to Dumouriez and the French, while thanking them for the liberation of Belgium, that an independent federal republic be set up, to be composed of the ten provinces each with its historic constitution (clergy, nobles, and privileged towns), with a kind of stadholder or president to be chosen from the ruling family of England, Holland, or Prussia. Neither Dumouriez, nor the French, nor the Belgian Democrats could of course tolerate such a solution, which would not only leave Belgium

---

[5] For Dumouriez and the Dutch during the Belgian campaign see H. T. Colenbrander, *Gedenkstukken der algemeene geschiedenis van Nederland*, I, 34-124, 176-295.

in the hands of their class enemies, but probably make it a protector-
ate of Great Britain.

Lebrun, in reply, took a step that proved to be a turning point in the
war. He persuaded a not very reluctant Convention to declare the river
Scheldt open to international navigation. The significance of this move
was far-reaching. For well over a century the Scheldt had been closed
by international treaties. Attempts in the past to open it by international negotiation had always failed. The decay of Antwerp, and suppression of long-distance commerce in Belgium, were considered by
the Dutch and the English to be essential to their own commercial
superiority. The British and Dutch would always oppose the opening
of the Scheldt. To the prelates, nobles, and gildmasters of the Statist
party it made no difference. It was the enterprising and modern-
minded among the Belgian business interests that wanted Antwerp
opened to the world. These men included many who tended to sympathize with the Democrats and the French. Lebrun opened the
Scheldt in order to hold them to the side of France. He did it also to
embarrass the Belgian exiles in England, who if they accepted the
opening of the Scheldt would embroil themselves with the British
government, and if they rejected it might be exposed to the Belgians
as British tools.

By English historians, the opening of the Scheldt is generally attributed to French ambitions, and given as a main cause driving
England into the war. By French historians it is given as a sign either
of French Revolutionary crusading or of French economic expansion-
ism. Lebrun, however, who was a former Belgian revolutionary himself, seems to have been actuated mainly by the need of favoring
revolution in Belgium.[6] It is a case in which the international revolution reacted violently upon the French Revolution proper, for with the
opening of the Scheldt, in November 1792, both the Dutch and British
governments began to think war with France unavoidable. It was only
a matter of timing, wrote Van de Spiegel on December 1.

Dumouriez' original plans soon proved unworkable. The Democrats
strained at the leash. The Statists were unreconciled. The clergy,
though some made the attempt, produced no adequate loan. Dumouriez had no money, and was unable even to begin to raise a
Belgian army. Disorder reigned in the French army, where many of
the patriot soldiers either deserted, taking their equipment with them,
or simply lost their blankets, shoes, or firearms. To save time, and get

[6] On the opening of the Scheldt see Tassier, 117-18; Colenbrander, 194-95, 198, 238.

supplies, Dumouriez made some very disadvantageous bargains with get-rich-quick operators and speculators, both French and Belgian. He met with increasing objection in Paris to his direct dealings with Belgian contractors. There was fear in Paris that, by such close arrangements between Dumouriez and the Belgians, the commanding general would become altogether too independent. Meanwhile the French soldiers in Belgium were going unsupplied. And the wealth of Belgium was going untapped, because Dumouriez, thinking of a future peaceable principality for himself, hoped to mollify the monks and abbots, the tithe-owners and the manor-owners, who were sworn enemies of the French Revolution.

Since he could not get the Belgians to do anything effective in liberating themselves, through providing a Belgian administration, funds, or army, Dumouriez found himself increasingly in the position of using his French soldiers to create a Belgian republic for himself. It was this that the French Convention objected to. And it is against this background that the famous decree of the Convention of December 15, the so-called second Propaganda Decree, must be understood.

"The more successful a general is," said Cambon in the Convention as early as November 22, "and the more he has a hold on public opinion, the more important it is that he should not have the management of finances, but be subjected to strict rules; I propose therefore that the army supply commissioners should be under the surveillance of the Minister of War, and the control of metallic currency under the surveillance of the national Treasury."[7] And the Convention, which had so recently offered "aid and fraternity to all peoples wishing to recover their liberty," took the matter-of-fact line that France should not pay for this aid. The Bourbons in former times had given away millions in *louis d'ors* to subsidize their international ventures. The British government, between 1793 and 1815, gave away £57,000,000 to keep Continental armies in the field against the Revolution and Napoleon. The governments issuing from the French Revolution were not so generous. For one thing, they lacked the money. In any case, it is doubtful whether any government, bourgeois or democratic, claiming responsibility to the people, could in the eighteenth century have given away such sums for foreign aid.

Cambon estimated that the war was costing some hundred million livres a month, of which the large portion expended beyond the French frontiers had to be paid in gold or silver on ruinously un-

---

[7] Tassier, 155.

favorable terms. "There is everlasting talk that we are carrying liberty to our neighbors. What we are carrying to them is our hard currency and our food supplies; they don't want our assignats."[8]

Clearly Belgium could not be abandoned in wartime to the enemies of France—to Austria, or the Statists. Just as clearly France would not pay for its liberation. The solution was obvious, and painless both to France and to the Belgian friends of France. The enemy governments and privileged classes should pay. Crown domains, public revenues, church lands, the property of other old-regime corporate bodies, tithes, seigneurial dues—all of which had been appropriated in France by the Revolution—should now be appropriated by *pouvoir révolutionnaire* in Belgium also. *Guerre aux châteaux, paix aux chaumières*!

The decree of December 15 began as follows:[9]

"I. In countries which are or will be occupied by the armies of the French Republic, the generals will immediately proclaim, in the name of the French nation, the abolition of existing taxes and revenues, of the tithe, of feudal dues both fixed and occasional, of servitude both real and personal, of exclusive hunting rights, nobility and all privileges in general. They will declare to the people that they bring peace, aid, fraternity, liberty and equality.

"II. They will proclaim the sovereignty of the people and suppression of all existing authorities; they will immediately convoke the people in primary or communal assemblies, to create and organize a provisional administration."

The following articles specified that officers of the old government should be excluded from the first election, and that property of the "prince" (meaning in Belgium the Hapsburgs, but the decree applied to all occupied countries), the local ruling bodies, and the church, should be confiscated. Against this property, assignats should be issued, to be used as money.

The decree stupefied all concerned. For Dumouriez, it meant the ruin of his plans. He rushed to Paris to obtain its repeal, but only aroused further suspicion of his motives. For the Statists, it killed such slight tendencies to reach an understanding with the Democrats as may have existed. Even now, at the end of December, there was some bare possibility of a Belgian republic. The French had too low an

---

[8] Cambon on December 9, *Moniteur, réimpression*, XIV, 703.

[9] *Moniteur, réimpression*, XIV, 755. On international law at the time as it pertained to conquest and annexation see J. Basdevant, *La Rév. fr. et le droit de guerre continentale* (Paris, 1901), 185-97.

opinion of the Belgians to be altogether eager to live with them in the same body politic, and might still have settled for a program in which, while making use of Belgian resources during the war, they obtained a theoretically independent but not unfriendly buffer republic on their borders. Probably a mutual toleration of Statists and Democrats was impossible anyway. Miss Tassier has observed that there could be no viable Belgian state until one of the two parties was defeated, and that the break-up of the Statists during the twenty years of French rule after 1794 was prerequisite to the independent Belgium of 1830.[10] In any event, the Statists at the end of 1792 were intransigent. Elections for the Belgian Convention took place in Brussels on December 29. It was in such a Convention that any hope for a Belgian republic would have to rest. The Statist party, led by gildmasters and priests (although only 3,000 voted in a population of 80,000), completely swamped the Brussels section assemblies, which voted overwhelmingly to uphold the Joyous Entry of 1355, the Three Estates, and the Apostolic and Roman Catholic Religion.[11]

The Democrats also were dismayed by the December decree. Among the Dutch Patriots, including those with Dumouriez and those in Holland, it became an overriding concern, from that day forward, that when revolution came in the United Provinces the terms of the decree of December 15 must be avoided. The Belgian Democrats were forced into painful decisions. Some drew back. Others, already too far committed, or determined to advance their principles at any cost, were obliged to follow French policy wherever it might lead.

It must be understood that the Belgian Democrats, though relatively not numerous, genuinely shared in the revolutionary spirit of the age, and were distributed through most parts of the country. Under French auspices, they agitated in their clubs and municipal assemblies. They had become more radical and more anti-clerical than in 1789. At quaint little Bruges they smashed up noble emblems, and demanded the abolition of servants' livery. "It is unfortunate enough," they said, "that a servant should have to wait on a fool or a crazy woman, without being excluded from society, the theater and public balls by these humiliating outward signs."[12] They fumed against privilege, declaring that the only source of true nobility was virtue. A certain Dr. Defrenne demanded that the Cardinal Archbishop of Malines give up his title

---

[10] Her final conclusion, 328.

[11] On this critical question of whether the intransigence of the Statists was the final obstacle to a Belgian republic, contrast Tassier, 168-72 with Verhaegen, I, 124.

[12] Tassier, 218-19.

of Eminence, as "contrary to Christian humility." A certain Verplancke (as if reviving the Protestantism stamped out two centuries before) announced that "priests were made for the people, not the people for the priests," and that the people should "feed but not fatten them."[13] Everywhere there were demands for the confiscation of church property, and contrasts were drawn between the opulence of monks and abbots and the poverty of Jesus and the first apostles.

Men who had publicly taken such positions had no hope except in the French. But the Belgian Democrats could not govern the country, nor even exercise much influence within it. They were too few, or too lacking in standing, or too much merely intellectual radicals or enthusiasts. Some began to see no safety for themselves, or hope for realization of their ideas, except by incorporation into the French Republic. And the governing group in Paris came to feel—no doubt rightly enough at this moment, with the trial of Louis XVI going on, and his death imminent—that an independent Belgium would be dominated by the enemies of France and of the Revolution.

Requests for annexation came in from Liége. The Democrats were stronger in Liége than almost anywhere in the Austrian provinces, since the city of Liége was of some economic importance, and so had a considerable population of business men and industrial workmen. The territory of the bishopric comprised about a fifth of present-day Belgium. The inhabitants, having thrown off the temporal power of the bishop, had little sense of forming a state of their own, and no feeling of political kinship to their neighbors in the Austrian provinces. They could consider union with France without violating a national consciousness which they did not have. The aristocratic and Statist Triumph in the election of December 29 at Brussels made many Liégeois very cool toward the idea of joining a Belgian republic. At Spa, Stavelot, the city of Liége, and elsewhere, local assemblies petitioned for annexation to France. Voting was by acclamation, and under strong pressure from the most radically minded, but the numbers present in the assemblies were proportionately higher than in the Statist elections at Brussels.[14] Requests for annexation came in also from the clubs at Ghent and Mons in January 1793.

French policy therefore entered a third phase. There had been a first stage in which an independent Belgian republic was contemplated,

[13] *Ibid.*
[14] For the rather unsatisfactory figures see Tassier, 261-62 for Liége, and 170 for Brussels.

with matters left largely to Dumouriez. There had been a second stage in which a program of revolutionary confiscation was adopted, for the period of wartime occupation, and arising from fear of Dumouriez and from the needs of military supply. In the third stage it seemed that there could be no assurance of French interests in Belgium except by permanent annexation. The convocation of the primary assemblies throughout Belgium, anticipated since November, took place in February 1793. It is difficult to make any estimate of their tendency. Neither Belgian nor French historians have claimed that the proportion of voters really favoring annexation was very high. For modern Belgians it is a source of national embarrassment that any significant numbers voted for union with France at all. The matter is confused by the fact that Miss Tassier, while insisting that only a small minority favored annexation, offers figures which seem really to indicate the contrary. She seems to have made the error, common enough, but surprising in so exact a worker, of comparing the number of votes, not with the number of adult males, but with figures for total population in which women and children are included.[15]

For the election in each primary assembly a French commissioner or general would set a day and place, to which men over twenty-one from surrounding villages would repair. The French official was present, but the assembly chose its own chairman, usually a local lawyer or other radical Democrat. Club members made speeches, urging that for safety against the Austrians, or against counter-revolutionary reprisals, there was no protection except in union with the mighty Republic. Someone usually called for a vote by acclamation, and so it would be ruled; but figures for a minority as well as the majority were often recorded.

It is a curious fact that the farm population, in many regions, attended the assemblies in larger numbers than inhabitants in the towns. The best explanation is that the French and Democratic propaganda

[15] Tassier, 305-308. For example, she says that at Couvin, "la réunion à la France ne fut voulue que par une minorité," and tabulates the figures for twenty communes in Couvin, with the following totals:

Population	9,523
Voters	1,855
For annexation	1,747
Against annexation	108
Citizens taking the oath to Liberty and Equality	1,366

The real elements of doubt are in the accuracy of the figures as reported, and in what voters had in mind in declaring their votes in the assemblies.

consisted in more than words—that the abolition of tithes and seigneurial dues appealed strongly to the peasants. That peasants voted as requested under these circumstances is not surprising; they undoubtedly had a hazy idea of what they were doing, and in accepting the benefits had no particular thought of any legal obligation which French citizenship, especially in time of war, might impose upon them. If they at first favored the new order, taking the gains it offered, and then soon lost interest, or turned furiously against it on other grounds (religion, conscription, or price controls) they would only be behaving like many peasants in France itself.

In any event, in February 1793, France annexed Belgium, on the advanced principles of the Revolution which were then dominant, abolishing tithes and dues without compensation, encouraging an extreme anti-clericalism, favoring the most radical of the Belgian Democrats. The old Austrian provinces and Liége were to dissolve, and be reorganized as *départements*. Belgians were to be in principle not subjects, but equal citizens of the French Republic. They were to use *assignats*, and pay war costs, drawing on the wealth of former privileged classes, just as the French did in France itself.

These events in Belgium were watched by the Dutch with a mixture of excitement and chagrin. They wanted no December decree, and no annexation. But the Patriots did want some kind of a revolution, to undo the Orange counter-revolution of 1787. Those in Amsterdam, Utrecht, and other cities became very restless. They knew from experience that there could be no Dutch revolution without French aid. Who were these Patriots? To the British ambassador at The Hague they were "noisy and impudent" persons who sat in alehouses and "obscure clubs" engaging in seditious talk. To the representative of the French Republic they were mostly rich men and bankers, who were indeed boycotting the Orange war loan, but on whom in the end the French could not really rely.[16] Estimates of a social level, it would seem, depend largely on the social level from which perception takes place. And it appears that among the Patriots there were men of many kinds, who sat both in banks and in taverns.

The French government, as already noted, long resisted the appeal of Dutch émigrés for an invasion of the United Provinces. But after

---

[16] Auckland to Grenville, The Hague, June 12, 1792, in Great Britain: Historical Manuscripts Commission, *The Manuscripts of J. B. Fortescue preserved at Dropmore*, 10 vols. (London, 1892-1927), II, 279; Auckland to Grenville, November 12, 1792, in Colenbrander, *Gedenkstukken*, I, 286; Noël to Lebrun, Amsterdam, January 14, 1793, *ibid.*, 254, 261.

the opening of the Scheldt, and with the execution of Louis XVI, on January 21, 1793, the Convention accepted war with the British and Dutch as inevitable. On January 31 Lebrun instructed Dumouriez to occupy Maastricht. Within a few days, by its own declaration, France was at war with the British and Dutch governments, which joined with Austria and Prussia in the First Coalition.

French and Dutch now crossed the Belgian-Dutch frontier. The exiles brought with them a plan for revolution, complete with primary assemblies representing the sovereignty of the people, and the banker Abbema and the nobleman Capellen van de Marsch prepared a draft constitution, in which a new government was derived from *Vrijheid en Gelijkheit,* that is Liberty and Equality.[17]

But the Dutch revolutionary exiles now had disillusionments in their turn. They expected, upon re-entering their own country, to take over administrative positions themselves. They wanted to bring into being, through clubs and elections, a native Dutch organization to deal with the French in matters of military housing and supply. They thought that the Dutch people, in meeting these legitimate French needs, should be allowed to deal with their own Dutch leaders. The French saw it otherwise. French generals levied direct requisitions on the population in the neighborhood of Breda. The Dutch émigrés protested. A committee of them, led by Johan Valckenaer, a former law professor in Friesland, who was to be one of the most notable of the Dutch democrats of the following years, waited upon Cambon on February 15. They asked that the decree of December 15 be not applied, and that the French accept instead a revolutionary Batavian republic. Cambon refused.[18] He remarked that since the Dutch had had their own Protestant revolution in the sixteenth century, the Reformed Church possessed little property of its own, and that both the Dutch clergy and the House of Orange were already on a kind of salaried basis, so that there was little wealth in Holland of the sort that qualified for confiscation. The existing tax-structure and public revenues should therefore be maintained. But the French should control the use of them during the military occupation. At most the taxes on bread and beer should be abolished as a gesture to the Dutch populace. It was not a program with much revolutionary appeal. But the men in the French government were not enthusiasts for a Dutch revolution. It was

[17] Colenbrander, I, 106-11.
[18] Colenbrander, *Gedenkstukken,* 105; *Bataafsche Republiek* (Amsterdam, 1908), 25-26.

radicals outside the government, like Marat, who demanded a true revolutionizing of the United Provinces. It was at this time also that the Dutch émigrés in Paris founded a journal, *Le Batave*, which, somewhat following the line of Hébert's *Père Duchesne* without the vulgarity, remained for several years one of the chief organs of advanced doctrine. Pressures of popular and of international revolution thus converged against those in power.

The December decree was to be applied, at least in the sense that the French would keep the sources and channels of Dutch wealth under their own control. Serious conflict between the French and Dutch could be foreseen.

Dumouriez became increasingly desperate. Not only had the French Convention taken the management of affairs out of his hands, but the Austrians began a counter-offensive, reoccupying Maastricht and Liége. Insurrection against the French spread through Belgium, redoubled in vehemence by the expectation of the Austrian return. The French, fearing the worst, now began to loot the country in earnest. They and their Belgian supporters plundered and desecrated the churches, regarding the clergy as the most implacable of their enemies. Priests said that anyone shooting a Frenchman would go to heaven. There were murders on both sides.

Hastily returning from Holland to Belgium, Dumouriez tried to check the violence and the outrages. He denounced the radicals, ordered agents of the Convention out of the country, and tried to appease the clergy, still pursuing the idea of a middle way, to lay a broad base on which his Belgian republic could be built. He was in extreme need of a personal military victory. Only by another great battle, as at Jemappes, could he dominate the Belgian Statists and Democrats, and stand up against the French Convention.

On March 18 he accepted battle with the Austrians at Neerwinden. But this time he lost. He made an unauthorized armistice with the Prince of Coburg.

Everything must now be settled in Paris. The Convention, for months, had had good reason to distrust his intentions. His political friends in France—Lebrun, Brissot, and others—were getting increasingly into trouble. Some of them had shown hesitation at the execution of the king; and Robespierre, leading the emerging group called the Mountain, had in fact used the king's trial to discredit them, to expose them as political irresponsibles who, having started the war, could not wage it in the true interests of France, of the new France which the

Revolution was to create, and in which the demands of popular revolutionaries must somehow be satisfied.

Dumouriez therefore loudly denounced the radicalism reigning at Paris. He became a "moderate." Despairing of the republic, he even saw himself as a "General Monk," in the image of the English Cromwellian who had paved the way for the restoration of King Charles II. He openly tried to persuade his army to follow him to Paris to put down the Jacobins. The troops refused. It seemed that the rank and file, given the choices, still favored the Revolution. There was clearly now nothing left for Dumouriez in France but the guillotine.

He therefore gave himself up to the Austrians, like Lafayette before him. The Austrian army, crossing into France, laid siege to Condé and Valenciennes.

The defection of Dumouriez produced violent repercussions in Paris. If Dumouriez was a traitor, it seemed that anyone might be. No one could tell whom to trust. The Brissot group, having touted Dumouriez as their great general and genius, was hopelessly compromised. The Jacobins, tearing each other to pieces, were harried by the sans-culottes. Thousands of Dutch and Belgian revolutionaries flocked back into France and Paris, there to add to the recrimination and the confusion. There were food riots in the city. Journalists screamed their denunciations. Insurrection brewed in the Vendée. In the preceding fall there had been moments of hope and elation; with Jemappes the crisis of the summer of 1792 seemed to have lifted. Now matters were worse than ever. Dumouriez had proved as bad as Lafayette; the enemy armies were again on French soil. The stage was being set for the Terror.

To many on the side of the Counter-Revolution, however, watching these same events, it seemed that the stage was being set for a drama more to their liking. The defection of the most spectacular Republican general suggested that the Republic must be nearing its end. The feuds among the Jacobins were taken as a sign of anarchy, showing that the whole foolish experiment was about to fall to pieces. The abbé Maury was so certain of an imminent counter-revolution that he feared he could not reach Rome in time to lay plans for a restoration of the French clergy. The Count de Fersen was appointed Swedish minister to the court of Louis XVII. There was, of course, no such court; but observers in Sweden and elsewhere thought there soon would be.

In Holland, the Orange regime felt the pleasures of a narrow escape. In Belgium the returning Austrians, to consolidate their second restoration, persecuted the Democrats and made all possible concessions to the Statists. The Monarchy, which had been so aggressively enlightened under Joseph, and more moderately so under Leopold, had fought a losing battle in Vienna, and now met complete defeat in Brussels. The elder Metternich, representing the Hapsburgs, agreed to the most reactionary demands of the Belgian privileged classes, who insisted on going back to the state of affairs, not before 1792, or 1789, but before 1780, to the good old quiet days under Maria Theresa. The historic constitutions and liberties of towns and provinces were solemnly reaffirmed. The Three Estates would rule again. The abbots and the town notables had their way. Tithes and seigneurial dues were restored, as before the late disturbance.

The Submersion of Poland

While the French liberated and then annexed Belgium in the name of the Revolution, the Russian and Prussian monarchies liberated and then annexed large parts of Poland, using the argument that Eastern Europe must be saved from revolutionary infection. The validity of this argument must be examined. It is not that anyone is now much concerned over the degree of honesty or hypocrisy in the cabinets of Berlin and St. Petersburg. The question is whether the new Polish regime, against which the Eastern monarchies intervened, did in fact represent a "revolution" of any significant kind. The view taken here is that it did, and that the allegations of the neighboring monarchies were not mistaken. There are two collateral questions: first, to what extent the territorial ambitions of the powers that took part in the Second Partition were infused with an ideology of social conservatism; and second, to what extent the intervention in Poland and France, which began simultaneously in the spring of 1792, represented two branches of a single movement of European scope, designed to put down a newly emerging and in some sense "democratic" order.

The Poland of the eighteenth century was described in the first volume of the present book.[19] Very different from France, it was a

---

[19] *Age*, I, 412-29. The present section draws on B. Lesnodorski, *Polscy Jakobini* (Warsaw, 1960), summarized for me by Mr. André Michalski; R. H. Lord, *Second Partition of Poland* (Cambridge, Mass., 1915); H. de Montfort, *Le drame de la Pologne: Kosciuszko* (Paris, 1945); Jan Wasicki, *Konfederacja Targowicka* (Poznan, 1952), with an eight-page résumé in French; and a very useful collection of documents in French, edited by K. Lutostanski, *Les partages de la Pologne et la lutte pour l'indépendance* (Paris, 1918). It is the plan of the present book to present the Second Partition in connection with Belgium, and the Third Partition in connection with Eastern Europe as a whole in Chapter v.

country of a kind admired in America a half-century later by John C. Calhoun, since it was dominated by owners of rural estates who elected their king, and kept the central government remote and weak. Within the frontiers after the First Partition (shown on the accompanying map) only about 40 per cent of the population was actually Polish in language. In the eastern region (in what are now White Russia and the Ukraine) many of the landowners were Polish, while the general population was not. It has been recently estimated that, of true ethnic Poles, as many as 25 percent may have been "noble."[20] These nobles predominated the more easily because the burgher class was relatively weak and the peasants were serfs—"subjects" of their lords. Numerous changes, which left the peasants still in serfdom, had been introduced by the Four Years' Diet. They were embodied in the Constitution of May 3, 1791, of which the king himself, Stanislas Poniatowski, was the main author.

It came to be widely asserted, in 1791 and 1792, by persons of most opposite opinions, that there was nothing really "revolutionary" about the new order in Poland. The French Jacobins ridiculed the Polish Constitution for being so favorable to gentry and nobles. Edmund Burke elaborately praised it for the same reasons, the better to discredit the French. Even the Polish authors of the new constitution, including King Stanislas, in the hope of protecting themselves from foreign intervention and internal revolt, explicitly, emphatically, and repeatedly disavowed any similarity in their work to French Jacobinism and democracy.

Nevertheless the Constitution implied changes which were revolutionary for Eastern Europe. Since it was introduced by the king and his co-workers, it was not brought into being by revolutionary violence from below. Since it preserved the pre-eminence of the middle ranks of a serf-owning noble class, it was neither "bourgeois" nor "democratic." It was anti-aristocratic, however, in reducing the powers of the great Polish magnates, and in strengthening the powers of the crown, which it made hereditary instead of elective, and it granted rights to the burgher class, rights which might seem little enough in France, but were without parallel in Eastern Europe. Townspeople in Poland (unless they were Jews) received the right to purchase rural or noble land, to own serfs and whole villages, to be army officers except in the cavalry, to govern themselves in their towns by new electoral procedures, to be secure from arbitrary imprisonment, to be elevated to

[20] Lesnodorski, *Jakobini*, 92.

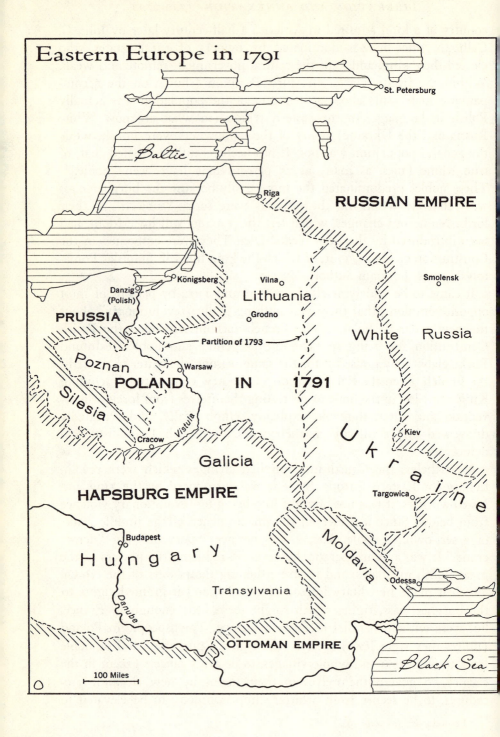

Eastern Europe in 1791

St. Petersburg

Baltic

RUSSIAN EMPIRE

Riga

Smolensk

Königsberg   Vilna

Danzig   Lithuania
(Polish)   Grodno

PRUSSIA   White   Russia

Partition of 1793

Poznan   Warsaw

POLAND   IN   1791

Silesia

Vistula   Kiev

Cracow

Galicia

HAPSBURG EMPIRE   Targowica

Budapest

Hungary   Moldavia

Transylvania   Odessa

Danube

OTTOMAN EMPIRE   Black Sea

100 Miles

noble status on relatively liberal terms, and to take part in a national assembly or diet, which was still thought of as a body suited only for landed gentry, but in which burgher representatives were admitted as observers with restricted voting rights.

Such changes were sweeping enough to create opposition, especially among some of the greatest magnates, and among the small, landless, or "barefoot" nobility, the *golota,* who supplied the personal followings on which the importance of the magnates rested. These groups denounced the new order as a "revolution." They considered themselves to be counter-revolutionary in the good sense which the word enjoyed among European conservatives. They were strongest in the eastern parts of what was then Poland, that is in Lithuania, White Russia, and the Ukraine. Their aim, at first, was to turn Poland into a federation of agrarian or gentry republics, in which monarchy would be elective and very weak, or even abolished. Their leader was Felix Potocki, who had been known a few years before as an enlightened and philanthropic grandee. He was a great builder of churches and palaces, as well as an old-fashioned patriot, who had given millions of his own money to build up a Polish army. His ideal of a good society was one that would exist by the benefactions of men like himself. He registered a formal protest against the constitution of 1791, tried without success to persuade the Emperor Leopold II to intervene in Poland for the defense of its ancient liberties, and then in March 1792 went off to St. Petersburg, where Potemkin was one of his friends, to seek Russian help.

It is important to contrast what the neighboring powers, Austria, Prussia, and Russia, thought about the new Polish constitution at the time of its promulgation in the spring of 1791, with what they said about it, or conceivably even thought about it, a year later when military intervention began.

In the spring of 1791 the prevailing view in Berlin, Vienna, and St. Petersburg was that the new Polish constitution, far from being anarchic, would make Poland into a stronger and more viable country. Leopold II spoke of the new order in Poland with approval. The octogenarian diplomat, Kaunitz, thought that the Polish crown, now made hereditary, "would find in a free bourgeoisie as well as in the peasant class a means of gradually limiting the power of the great houses" whose rivalries had kept Poland in turmoil.[21] The Austrians regarded this prospect of a stronger Poland as desirable. Prussians and Russians made a similar diagnosis of fact, but found the fact unpleas-

[21] Lutostanski, *Les partages,* 117.

ant. The Prussian minister, Hertzberg, wrote confidentially in May 1791 to his envoy in Warsaw that by its "revolution" (as he called it) Poland "received a constitution more firm and better organized than the English." He feared that such a Poland would be dangerous to Prussia, since it might take back the losses of the First Partition. How, he asked, could Prussia defend its exposed frontier "against a numerous and well-governed nation?"[22] And the Empress Catherine, in her zeal for the traditional liberties of Poland, feared in the new Polish government not its anarchy but its despotism.[23]

Hardly was the new Polish constitution proclaimed when a variety of developments raised up new alarms. Political clubs multiplied rapidly in Warsaw and other cities, representing the heightening of political consciousness and participation under the new regime. Free, open, busy, and extensive discussion of public matters was not welcomed by the three eastern monarchies in their part of the world. The Polish clubs, it was therefore alleged, were but the surface manifestation of an international network of secret societies. It may in fact have been true that Poles made some attempts at propagandizing for liberty within Russia at this time.[24] News arrived also of the arrest of Louis XVI at Varennes, to the great consternation of royal courts. In July 1791 the first French ambassador to Poland in twenty years arrived in Warsaw. A former marquis, now an ardent revolutionary, named Descorches, he mixed actively in the Polish clubs; in any case, his very presence, after so long an interval, suggested to neighboring powers the possibility of an alliance between the two revolutionary countries. At the same time Edmond Genet was shocking the Russian upper classes in St. Petersburg, where he was French chargé d'affaires; and a colony of French émigrés added their own contribution. One of them, Count Valentin Esterhazy, in April 1792, passed on a mixture of true and false information to his wife: the King of Sweden had been murdered by Jacobins; French democrats were being rounded up in St. Petersburg and sent to Siberia, the proliferation of clubs in Poland was "opening Russian eyes on the tendency of that impious and regicide sect"; and it was feared in Russia that "the fire will start up in this

---

[22] *Ibid.*, 115.
[23] Lord, *Second Partition*, 244-47.
[24] Lesnodorski describes attempts at propaganda in Russia, 274, and gives an account of the clubs in 1791 and 1792 on 131-47. He quotes, 146, a contemporary diarist for the beginning of 1792: "clubs of servants are being organized, in which the people are informed of events in France and the Declaration of the Rights of Man is read in translation, with other things relating to the freeing of the serfs."

country." Esterhazy, however, writing on the eve of military intervention in France and Poland, was confident that "the counter-revolution is inevitable."[25] The Russian army moved into Poland in May 1792.

The Russians in invading Poland were able to make common cause with the Polish counter-revolutionaries, as the French in invading the Austrian Netherlands were able to make common cause with the Belgian democrats. The Russian use of an internal Polish party, in fact, was more palpable and direct. The French Revolutionary government did not, in the spring of 1792, before the war began and hostilities opened in Belgium, take concerted action with refugee Belgian democrats in Paris to prepare a ringing democratic manifesto calling for liberation of their country. This is precisely what the Empress Catherine did with the Polish noblemen in St. Petersburg. Poles and Russians in the tsarist capital, on April 27, 1792, signed a document in which their ideas were combined. It presented a long indictment of the now year-old new order in Poland. To make its publication coincide with the Russian invasion, already in preparation, the document was given a suppositious date and place—May 14, at Targowica, a village in the Ukraine a hundred miles south of Kiev, on the Polish-Russian frontier as it then was, but within Poland.

The Act of Targowica is one of the more interesting declarations of the European counter-revolution, if only because of its purely nobilitarian and agrarian-gentry character.[26] The fact that it was immediately translated into German and Dutch and issued as a pamphlet under the title of *The Spirit of a Truly Free Government*, suggests that there were elements in Western Europe that found its doctrine relevant and congenial.[27]

[25] E. Daudet, ed., *Lettres du comte Valentin Esterhazy à sa femme* (Paris, 1907), 422-26. For Genet in Russia see above, pp. 63-64.

[26] The text of the Act of Targowica was published in French in Comte d'Angeberg (pseud. for L. Chodzko), *Recueil des traités, conventions et actes diplomatiques concernant la Pologne, 1762-1862* (Paris, 1863), 262-74. The issue for interpretation is between the view expressed by Lord, *Second Partition*, 274-76, that the Targowicans were a small and insignificant handful of Poles whom Catherine II was able to exploit for the aggrandizement of Russia, and the view set forth in the French summary of Wasicki, *Konfederacja targowicka*, 185-92, that the Targowicans were those among magnates and lesser gentry, significantly numerous but by no means "all" of these classes, who were willing forcibly to oppose the Polish revolution and constitution of 1791. The latter view is followed here; it is favored by recent Polish and French writers, and coincides with what one expects to find in revolutionary situations.

[27] *Der Geist einer wahrhaft freien Regierung, gegründet auf der Targowiczer Conföderation*, Hamburg, n.d.; *De Geest eener waarlijk vrije regeering, door de tegenconfederatie von Targowitz, naar eene Hoogduitsche overzetting uit het Poolsch vertaald*, "in Vriesland," n.d.

The Act opposes those twin enemies of effectual aristocracy: monarchy and democracy. It reaffirms as an ancient Polish principle the "liberty and equality of all nobles," demands that *gentilhommes non-possessionés*, i.e., the "barefoot" *golota*, be restored to their former dignity, denounces the institution of hereditary monarchy as despotic, and declares that ambitious men have "everywhere sown the seeds of democratic ideas." To have brought "the hitherto peaceful towns" into the political order is "to drag the whole nation into slavery." The constitution of 1791 is due to a "plot." It is an "audacious crime" against the spirit of our ancestors, presenting the "fatal examples of Paris as models to our Polish cities." The new order arouses "hatred against the rich," because it deprives the great lords of "the support of gentlemen." The signers solemnly swear to destroy the new constitution, and express their confidence that the great Catherine will preserve the liberties, independence, and territory of the Republic of Poland intact.

The Russian invasion met with little resistance. With the rural population in a state of serfdom, and the burghers only barely and timidly emerging into public life, the leaders of the Polish revolution could not rally an adequate following. There was no *levée en masse* in Poland in 1792. King Stanislas, the leader of the patriot group—in an action that has been much criticized, since his emigration, flight, or death would have preserved his dignity and served the new order better—capitulated to the Russians, made his peace with the dissident Poles, and adhered to the Act of Targowica. He signed his acceptance on July 24, as the Russians approached Warsaw. It was the day before the Brunswick Manifesto against the city of Paris.

The constitution which the king now repudiated was notable for its moderation and intricate compromise. It had even been lauded by Edmund Burke. Compromise, however, was no more palatable to the Targowicans and the Russians than extremism would have been. The king was obliged to humble himself. He was required to endorse the commonplaces of the European counter-revolution—to confess that he had been "seduced by new and bold maxims," that he now understood that "only the government as established by our ancestors can eternize the duration and glory of Poland," and to agree upon the "terrible disasters" that ensued "whenever a nation, instead of correcting the defects of its former government, endeavors totally to overthrow it."[28]

[28] This "confession" extorted from King Stanislas was published in the *Annual Register for 1792*; see also Angeberg, 295-96.

With the Russians occupying most of the country and the Targowica party coming into control, the governments of Austria and Prussia in the summer of 1792 each signed an agreement with the Russian Empress, committing themselves to uphold the former constitution of Poland, as arranged in 1773 after the First Partition. Thus the new order in Poland was suppressed and the focus of revolutionary agitation in Eastern Europe brought presumably under control. It is conceivable that Catherine II might have been satisfied with a plan that left Poland undividedly under her own influence. But both Prussia and Austria now had reason to urge a further dismemberment.

For the Austrians, who a year before had favored the prospect of a strengthened and independent Poland, the situation was entirely changed, not only by the death of Leopold II, and not only by the Russian occupation of Poland, but by the war against France, which in the summer of 1792 the Austrians expected to be short and successful. The Vienna cabinet revived its plan for the annexation of the territories of the house of Bavaria. The Elector of Bavaria could be readily compensated by a transfer of his throne to Brussels; that is, the Austrians would give him their ten Netherlands provinces in exchange for his various south German holdings. But it could not be expected that Prussia and Russia would consent, without corresponding gains for themselves, to the substantial growth of the Hapsburg monarchy as a German power. Kaunitz therefore changed his mind on Poland, and accepted the principle that, to enable Austria to acquire Bavaria, Prussia and Russia must be allowed to take portions of Poland. A few months later, after Dumouriez' victories, and the renewal of revolutionary activity in Belgium, when it seemed that the Hapsburgs might be unable to retain their Netherlands provinces, and might have to forego the Bavarian exchange, the availability of territory in Poland became a matter of more poignant concern. Even at best, after the defeat of Dumouriez at Neerwinden, it seemed that the effort necessary for retaining Belgium might be too great. It would be still more troublesome for Austria to acquire territory, such as Alsace, from France itself. It was now clear that Prussia and Russia were about to engage in a second partition of Poland. It now seemed unfair to the Austrians, a year after the three monarchies had entered upon their operations against the revolutionary contagion, that Austria should have to work so hard for its reward, while Prussia and Russia enjoyed the advantage of a more facile self-enrichment. To quote one of the more candid expressions of the older diplomacy (so often admired for its "style"), the Austrians protested that "the indemnities and compensations due to the Emperor should have to wait upon conquests to be made against France, conquests in which, so to speak, every inch must be bought at the price of blood and at the immense cost of a ruinous war, while the acquisitions of the two Courts in Poland have been accompanied by no danger and have met with no resistance."[29] Austria, in short, desired an easier dividend. Finding France too strong, it would prefer to join in an expropriation of the weak.

As for the Prussians, they had long aspired to the annexation of the city of Danzig, and of the area called Great Poland or Poznan, which reached westward as a triangular salient between Silesia and Prussia proper. While the Russians occupied Poland, the Prussians were involved as allies of the Austrians in the war against France. The conjuncture was unfortunate for the court of Berlin, which, after its disconcerting experience with the French at Valmy, notified the court of Vienna that it would abandon the French war unless compensated by territory in Poland. In January 1793 the Prussian army crossed the Polish frontier. The governments of Prussia and Russia immediately began to negotiate their territorial demands upon Poland—the "second" partition—expecting to exclude Austria, as they in fact succeeded in doing.

It was to combat "the spirit of French democratism" that the king of Prussia sent his army into Poland.[30] He feared the "maneuvers of Jacobin emissaries" both in Poland and in his own adjoining states. Where formerly there had been a fear that the Poles might govern themselves only too well, it was now feared that they could not govern themselves at all. Anarchy and the poisonous influence of secret societies were seen as menaces to neighboring countries. The Poles were not even credited with having their own revolution; they were said to be merely the dupes and victims of French subversives. In January 1793 the Prussian and Russian rulers signed a kind of holy alliance; at least it was drawn up "in the name of the Most Holy and Indivisible Trinity." The two powers declared that they must protect themselves against the "imminent and universal danger" presented by the "progress and extension" of the French Revolution. They would therefore each annex certain specified territories in Poland, in return for which

---

[29] Lutostanski, 152.

[30] The declaration of the king of Prussia on the entrance of his troops into Poland in January 1793 was widely published at the time, e.g. in the Paris *Moniteur* and in the *Annual Register*. The same is true of various Russian declarations of 1792 and 1793.

the king of Prussia agreed to remain at war "against the French rebels."[31]

The experience of the Targowica Poles was not unlike that of the Belgian democrats. They had been liberated from domestic despotism by a foreign army. Supposedly they had come, with foreign aid, into power in their own country. They had expected to enjoy an independent republic, constructed according to their own political philosophy and befriended by an ideologically sympathetic neighbor. To be annexed to this mammoth neighbor was no part of their original design. They were surprised and dismayed at the new turn of affairs. They were also divided; for, as in Belgium some of the democrats concluded that their own security, and the security of their principles, would be better assured by incorporation into France, so some of the Targowicans came to feel that their control of their serfs, and their preferred agrarian and social system, would be better guaranteed by membership in the Russian Empire. As the French promised the Belgians all the rights of citizens in the French Republic, so Catherine II promised the Poles, in the territories she annexed, "all the rights, liberties and privileges which our older Russian subjects enjoy."[32] In Poland as in Belgium there were elections superintended by an occupying power. The Russian General Ingelström, in May of 1793 (and one thinks of Belgium in February) gave instructions for the local assemblies to elect certain acceptable Poles whose names were on lists which he submitted, and promised to supply either money or detachments of Russian soldiers in such amounts as might be required. The local assemblies chose deputies to a new national gathering, the Diet of Grodno. This diet, according to the Russians, really represented the "general will of the better people and of the Nation."[33] The diet, under irresistible Russian pressure, ceded large tracts of White Russia and the Ukraine to the Russian Empire. Soon thereafter it ceded Danzig and Great Poland to Prussia.

In 1793 the central part of Poland still remained technically independent, and here the Targowicans were briefly allowed to maintain a republic to their own liking. The Diet of Grodno enacted a new constitution. It followed lines which in Poland were staunchly conservative. With a few exceptions—neither the *liberum veto* nor the nobleman's right of life and death over his serf was restored—the residual Polish state was to be much as in the 1770's. Kings were again to be elected

[31] Lutostanski, 140-43.
[32] *Ibid.*, 180, 223.
[33] *Ibid.*, 159.

by nobles. Attempts to strengthen the central government and to give representation to townspeople were abandoned. The work of the Four Years' Diet was swept away.

It has often been said, even by the best of historians, that the counter-revolutionary professions of the partitioning powers were a mere pretense to cover up crude aggression. It has been thought that, since the French and Polish revolutions were not alike, the loudly publicized need of suppressing "Jacobinism" in both countries was nothing but an "insidious theory."[34] On the whole, the view that still prevails of the Second Partition (which, as Robert Lord said, was the true *finis Poloniae*) was set by a historiography that antedates 1914 and the modern revolutionary age. In the older diplomatic histories, often written with a belief in the primacy of foreign over internal politics, the expansion of the Great Powers of Europe seemed more real and important than unsuccessful revolutions or the fears that they engendered. Older histories of a liberal tendency, on the other hand, were perhaps too ready to dismiss the claims of monarchical diplomats as merely empty or "cynical." In either case the phenomena of revolution in Poland, of discontents in other parts of Eastern Europe, and hence of the genuine counter-revolutionary intentions of the three Eastern monarchies, may be excessively discounted.

The question in the summer of 1793 was whether France would go the way of Poland. It was a question not so much of partition (though talk of carving up French territory was heard) as of the imposition under foreign auspices of a form of government approximating the old regime. The powers of the First Coalition, together with Russia, after the defection of Dumouriez, the Austrian reconquest of Belgium, the insurrection in the Véndée, and the beginning of the invasion of France, believed that they would soon put an end to the revolutionary disturbance in Western Europe, as they had seemingly done in the East.

In the East, they still had the rebellion led by Kosciuszko to contend with. In the West, they still had to face the France of the Committee of Public Safety.

[34] Lord, 281, 504.

THE SURVIVAL OF THE REVOLUTION
IN FRANCE

The theory of revolutionary government is as new as the revolution that has produced it. It cannot be found in the books of political writers, by whom this revolution was not foreseen. . . .

The aim of constitutional government is to preserve the commonwealth; of revolutionary government, to found it. . . .

Under the constitutional regime it is almost enough to protect the individual against the abuse of public authority. Under the revolutionary regime the public authority must defend itself against factions that attack it.

Revolutionary government owes good citizens the whole protection of the nation. To enemies of the people it owes nothing but death.—MAXIMILIEN ROBESPIERRE, December 1793

THE SURVIVAL OF THE REVOLUTION
IN FRANCE

EVERYTHING now depended on what happened in France. The revolution in Poland had been stopped. Belgian democrats had again scurried out of their country, where the Statists came to terms with the Austrians. The Dutch émigrés had their expectations suddenly dashed, and the Dutch patriots at home, sadly disappointed, were reduced to passively awaiting a change in the fortunes of war which would bring in the French as liberators. In Ireland, Wolfe Tone privately remarked in March 1793 that ten thousand French troops in Ireland would effect Irish deliverance from Great Britain. In Britain the radical feeling was less subversive, but reformist and radical groups, of various descriptions, were dismayed and outraged by the war in which the British government was now engaged. In every country where the government was at war with the French Republic in 1793—in Britain and Ireland, in the United Provinces and in Belgium restored to the Emperor, in the Austrian Monarchy, the small German states and the Prussian kingdom, in the Italian kingdom of Sardinia (the one exception may be Spain)—there were groups of people, more than individual dreamers, whose sympathies lay in varying degree with the declared enemy.

Feeling ran high in neutral countries. In the United States the emerging Republicans repeatedly said, in the large language of the day, that the cause of the French Republic was the cause of the human race. There were even Federalists, like Noah Webster, who could not bring themselves to desire victory for the Coalition. On the other side of Europe, in Russia, where Catherine II and the upper classes were now hysterically fearful of France, they were afraid also of malcontents among their own people, especially among the "low-born intelligentsia," or persons who did not belong to the nobility but had acquired some knowledge of the world. "I venture to predict," said a worried writer of 1793, "that the agitation in France will have many unhappy consequences for these wondrous lands"—i.e., Russia.[1]

Wherever the French Revolution had been heard of there were men who wished it not to fail. Their concern was not only for France but for the future of some kind of democratization in their own countries.

For those, on the other hand, who hoped to see the whole Revolution undone, these same first months of 1793 saw a revival of the exciting expectations of a year before. In the execution of Louis XVI they saw a sign of desperation, the act of a handful of cornered regicides who had turned all decent men against them. To the outside world no one could seem more revolutionary than Dumouriez. Yet Dumouriez had repudiated the Revolution, declaring that it had collapsed into anarchy. The Republic seemed a sinking ship, crazed, in addition, by mutiny in its own crew.

The king's death was received with mixed feelings. Catherine II became ill. Pope Pius VI was genuinely concerned. He declared after much thought, as his personal opinion, that Louis XVI had died a martyr to the Catholic faith, for whom canonization proceedings might some day be in order. For a precedent he looked back, not to Charles I of England, where the analogy was clear enough to more secular minds in all camps, but to the Catholic Mary Queen of Scots, who had been considered a true martyr by Benedict XIV. The French Convention, according to Pius VI, was no better than the dreadful Elizabeth of England. Both, in his view, had been swayed by bad books and "factious, Calvinistical men."[2]

A week after Louis' death his brother, the Count of Provence, took the title of Regent and issued a proclamation, declaring his intention to restore the "ancient constitution" of France. No European power recognized him. The powers at war with France did not wish it to have a government that they need respect. Nor were leading French émigrés and noblemen in a mood to subordinate themselves to the monarchy. When a rumor spread after the king's death of a plot to assassinate his two brothers, the Prince of Condé, a leading émigré (and himself a Bourbon) put it off with a joke: "Be assured, Princes without armies,

---

[1] For Wolfe Tone see his *Life* (Washington, 1826), I, 108; for Noah Webster, pp. 3-4 above; for the Russians, M. M. Shtrange, *Russkoye Obshchestvo i Frantsuzkaya Revolyutsiya* (Russian Society and the French Revolution, 1789-1794) (Moscow, 1956), 146. I am indebted to Dr. W. L. Blackwell for summarizing this Russian book.

[2] A. Theiner, *Documents inédits relatifs aux affaires religieuses de la France, extraits des archives secrètes du Vatican* (Paris, 1857), I, 177-91.

Bourbons not surrounded by a nobility, are such nonentities as hardly to be worth the honors of assassination."[3]

Beyond an Allied military victory, and restoration of the French throne, what the aristocratic French émigrés and conservative church-men hoped for, and what the revolutionary element in France with good reason feared, was restoration of the nobility and the church. It would not be a mere restoration of their persons, but restoration of social bodies with something of the old powers and privileges, and the old forms of wealth and income.

The Pope asked Maury to draft memoranda on the steps to be taken, now that the Revolution seemed to be nearing its end. The memoranda do not show what the Pope would have actually done, but they do show what the most conservative of the French clergy wanted in 1793, and the pressures to which the Pope would be subjected by his own most loyal supporters. Here is what Maury advised: the Pope should excommunicate all French constitutional clergy and depose recalci-trant bishops. A restored king should crush the Gallicanism of the restored Parlements. Toleration of Protestants should be withdrawn, and Jansenism and Freemasonry extirpated. Bad books should be cen-sored, education supervised by bishops, and school-teaching turned over to priests. All remarriages of so-called divorced persons should be declared void. Religious orders should be re-established, with vows permitted at age sixteen. And all their former property should be re-turned to ecclesiastical owners, subject, however (it was Maury's one concession), to taxation by the restored king.[4]

In a few places the probable consequences of Counter-Revolution became concretely evident at the time. After defeating Dumouriez at Neerwinden, the Austrians crossed the border and occupied the regions about Valenciennes and Lille. They remained there about a year, and what happened is significant in suggesting what might have happened in the rest of France if the armed forces of the Coalition had obtained a clear victory. The occupying administration set up by the Austrians was not reactionary in principle. It tried to be moderate with the local people involved in the Revolution, those who had accepted office under the new municipalities, or purchased land formerly belonging to church bodies or to émigrés. But under the Austrian administration, local malcontents emerged from obscurity, and French churchmen,

[3] E. Daudet, *Coblentz 1789-1793* (Paris, 1890), 297.
[4] "Memoire de Maury . . . sur les déterminations du Pape envers l'église de France" (Rome, June 23, 1793), in Theiner, I, 381-420.

nobles, and émigrés swarmed into the occupied area, despite Austrian efforts to keep them out. Where the Austrians, for example, at Valenciennes, authorized only six persons to reside as actual returned émigrés from the locality, the Valenciennes municipality, now in the hands of French counter-revolutionaries, authorized over two hundred. The Austrians, naturally enough, gradually and under pressure came to favor their own supporters. Tithes and seigneurial dues were declared collectible, former landowners re-established themselves, and townsmen and villagers who had accepted office under the Revolution, since 1789, were branded as menaces to society.[5]

Somewhat similarly, when the British occupied Corsica in 1794, and remained for two years, setting up an Anglo-Corsican kingdom, the attempts of the British viceroy at moderation were repeatedly frustrated; and Corsica, which had belonged to France for twenty-five years, exhibited what might have happened in France if the Counter-Revolution had succeeded at this time.[6]

Rebellion broke out in western France, beginning in the Vendée, in March 1793. Led by disaffected seigneurs, in touch with the émigrés and the British government, it appealed to peasant grievances against the Revolutionary church policy and military conscription. It spread most rapidly in rural areas, since the towns, even the small ones, characteristically remained as isolated and besieged pockets adhering to the new order. The leaders of the rebellion attempted to set up a civil authority over such territories as they were able to control. This authority restored the church tithe, re-established the royal courts as before 1789, and declared all sales of former church and émigré property null and void.[7]

The issue, for France and the world in 1793, was not whether one band of Jacobins should chase out another, but whether Revolution or Counter-Revolution should prevail.

Gouvernement révolutionnaire

It was true that France at the moment suffered from anarchy, and that what it needed was government. "Anarchy" is hardly too strong a word. Ministers and ministries remained in existence, but decisions

[5] Georges Lefebvre, *Les paysans du Nord pendant la Révolution française* (Bari, 1959), 572-76; but for this purpose the first edition (Paris, 1924) is better, including note 1 to Book II, chap. 5, omitted in the reissue.
[6] See Chapter IX below.
[7] For a good summary see J. Godechot, *La Contre-révolution* (Paris, 1961), 235.

lay with committees of the Convention, which consisted of 750 men from the middle classes assembled under chaotic conditions, and enjoying neither confidence in each other, nor the prestige of an acknowledged authority, nor habits of obedience on the part of the population. Organs of local government, as set up in 1790 and 1791, had not had time to consolidate. Tax reforms of the early years of the Revolution had also been caught unfinished by the war and the upheaval of 1792. Taxes, like much else, existed mainly in principle. There were no regular revenues, so that the Convention depended on paper money. Army reforms, begun early in the Revolution, had also been far from complete; the country went to war with its armies commanded largely by officers of the Old Regime; and as the revolutionary spirit mounted into 1793, the officers increasingly lost respect for the civilians in Paris who claimed to govern. Dumouriez was only the most spectacular case.

Impotence in what would normally be considered the government was matched by an intense political liveliness among the "governed." It was a question whether the country could be governed at all, except by dictatorship, whether a revolutionary dictatorship such as soon developed, or the dictatorship of a restored king, such as the moderate Mounier, writing in exile, had recommended in 1792. The French people in 1793 were too highly politicized, too spontaneously active, too disillusioned with persons in public office (not without reason), to accept orders from any political heights. When they said the people were sovereign, they meant it literally, and they meant themselves. Middle class citizens, associated in the Paris Jacobin club and in similar clubs in the provinces, and acting on their own initiative, tried somehow to keep going, coordinate, and dominate the shattered apparatus of state, from the National Convention down to the village communes. Citizens of more modest station were aroused in the popular revolutionism described in Chapter II above. They met in lesser clubs, like the Paris Cordeliers, or in the face-to-face groups of immediate neighbors, as in the section assemblies of Paris and other large cities. They too, at the local level, helped to carry on the business of government.

The people were not only sovereign but *debout*, "on their feet," to use the expression of the time. Popular leaders called for a *levée en masse*, or general "rising." The term *levée en masse* has become frozen to signify the universal military service of the Revolution, a conscription conducted by government and designed to expel foreign invaders.

It is true that the military *levée en masse* would not have been very effective if it had not been converted into an organized raising and equipping of troops by a government. But in its origin the term meant much more. A "mass rising," in 1793, could be a general rising of the people for any purpose, with or without the assistance of official persons who did not command much public confidence. It could be a swarming of citizen soldiers to defy the regular armies of Prussia and Austria. It could be a rising of the sections of Paris against the Convention or some of its members. It could be an armed insurrection or an unarmed demonstration in the streets. It could be the wandering of a band of sans-culottes from one part of France to another, self-organized as an *armée révolutionnaire*, in pursuit of aristocrats or in search of food. There was something inherently anarchic in the whole idea.

Out of this anarchy there arose, however, by gradual stages, the *gouvernement révolutionnaire*, confirmed by the Convention in a famous decree of October 10, 1793, declaring "the government of France revolutionary until the peace." It began with an at first little noticed provision, when on April 6, the day after Dumouriez' final defection, the Convention authorized a special Committee of Public Safety, which in six months became the keystone of the *gouvernement révolutionnaire*. It was this government, which lasted until the death of Robespierre, and which Napoleon once called the only serïous government in France in the decade after 1789, that turned the tide of foreign invasion, carried on the Terror, protected the country from both anarchy and counter-revolution, and initiated the military offensive which was to revolutionize Holland and Italy and shake the established order of Europe.

For the purposes of this book, it is of especial interest to trace the relations of this Revolutionary Government with popular revolutionism and with international revolutionism. Pressures generated by both these movements helped to bring the Revolutionary Government into being. Once established, it sought to subordinate both movements to itself.

Between the two, as noted in an earlier chapter, there was often a certain affinity. It was not that the popular spokesmen in Paris cared much about revolution in foreign countries. Still less, in general, did the foreign revolutionaries understand or know much about the demands of the most advanced revolutionaries in Paris. Usually, however, both had much to complain of at the hands of the French revolutionary authorities. In March and April 1793 the Brissot-Dumouriez group, despite Dumouriez' disaffection, was still preponderant in the committees of the Convention. The international revolutionaries blamed them for the defeats and failures in Belgium and Holland. (Much less concern was expressed for Poland, although Kosciuszko was in Paris at this very time to solicit aid.) The popular revolutionaries were annoyed by the defeats also, which were bringing the enemy within the gates, and in addition they suffered the effects of food shortage and inflation. An extreme crisis of confidence in the political realm coincided with an extreme economic crisis. In the inflamed psychology of the moment, both crises were blamed on the same people. Suspicion was rampant. The guilty must be investigated and pursued. In March the Convention created a new special court for this purpose, the Revolutionary Tribunal, in which the civil liberties and legal reforms introduced by the Revolution could be suspended.

An enlightening history of the Revolution in France could be written in terms of the paper money alone, the *assignats*. For the political and social consolidation of the Revolution the program proved highly successful. In the absence of gold coinage (which was hoarded, or taken out of the country by émigrés, or used in connection with foreign payments), the paper money enabled the successive Revolutionary governing groups to finance their operations. It also provided the mechanism for the transfer of former church, crown, and émigré real estate to new owners, blending the upper levels of the peasantry, the bourgeoisie, and many ex-nobles into a numerous property-owning class of modern type, which had a material interest in the preservation of the Revolutionary innovations.

But the costs of war led to a rapid printing of assignats, which steadily lost value, especially since the future of the régime that printed them was highly uncertain. The decline was precipitous in the first half of 1793, when the assignats fell to only a fourth the value of gold. There were also positive scarcities. As causes of scarcity, to the normal effects of war and mobilization, and unwillingness of farmers to part with their produce for paper money, was added a general breakdown in commercial distribution in the confusion of revolutionary conditions. Prices soared. Bakeshops and grocers' shops were often found empty by women who had waited for hours to obtain a day's supply.

There were therefore demands for price controls, and for measures against hoarding and profiteering. By attributing these demands specifically to the working class, and resistance to them to the bourgeoisie, various historians have seen this period of the Revolution as characterized chiefly by a class conflict, of a kind that relates it to the socialisms of the twentieth century.[8] It is true that the Brissot group, setting the tone in the Convention, objected to economic controls. They had fallen into an attitude of negativism and helplessness toward everything that had happened since the preceding August. The idea of price control was not in itself very radical. The monarchy had practiced it before 1789, and even the weakly organized American states, during the American Revolution, had made similar attempts in the face of inflation. So bourgeois a figure as Alexander Hamilton, in 1778, had been as incensed at profiteering as a Paris sansculotte of 1793. But what for Hamilton and middle-class people was a matter for moral indignation, was for the working people of Paris a matter of life and death. The sections of Paris seethed with protest. There developed a great *poussée populaire*, as Albert Soboul calls it, a rising tide of the popular democracy described above in Chapter II, against the "corrupt" element in the Convention.

Early in April the Section Halle au Blé circulated among the other sections of the city a proposed petition to the Convention. Halle au Blé was not a poor section; indeed, it had the fewest "indigent" of any of the forty-eight.[9] It demanded action against hoarders, speculators, and monopolists. Still more vehemently, it accused the Convention of endless talk and insidious treachery. The proof lay in Dumouriez'

---

[8] Notably Albert Mathiez in various writings; and with a significantly different emphasis, in that they see a sharp opposition between the popular revolutionaries and the middle-class Jacobins of the Mountain, Albert Soboul, *Les Sans-culottes parisiens de l'An II: mouvement populaire et gouvernement révolutionnaire, 2 juin 1793-9 thermidor An II* (Paris, 1958), and the more narrowly conceived G. Rudé, *The Crowd in the French Revolution* (Oxford, 1959). See also M. J. Sydenham, *The Girondins* (London, 1961), which is wholly different in purpose and inspiration from the Left-oriented works of Soboul and Rudé, but is more consistent with them in its findings than with Mathiez. Sydenham argues that the existence of the Girondins, as a set group or party, is a myth; that the "Girondins" can hardly be distinguished from members of the Convention as a whole, and that the name came to be attached during the political strife, and then by historians, to those persons in the Convention who called attention to themselves by outspoken opposition to Robespierrists and the sans-culottes. This view is consistent with the view of Soboul and Rudé that the sans-culottes, or popular democrats, in their demands for price controls, etc., found virtually the whole Convention and the whole Jacobin Club hesitant and unsympathetic.

[9] Soboul, 1091. The petition was printed in the *Moniteur, réimpression*, XVI, 100.

whole record in Belgium. If the Convention had not protected Dumouriez and his accomplices, so ran the indictment, "the Belgians and Liégeois would not today accuse France of having aided them only to turn them over in chains to their tyrants. It is with this that all Europe reproaches you, and posterity will do the same." The petition demanded the arrest of certain Brissotins, i.e., a purge of the Convention.

Robespierre defended the petition at the Jacobin Club and in the Convention. He paid little attention to the economic demands. It was treason that he scented, and for proof he pointed to the betrayal of the international revolution. He now sympathized with the *patriotes bataves* and the *braves Liégeois*. Why had not Dumouriez pursued and destroyed the Prussians after Valmy? Why had the Belgian Democrats been blocked by him at every turn? Why had he not sooner and more vigorously carried the war into Holland? (Readers of the last chapter will have an answer.) Had he seriously invaded Holland, France would now have the use of Dutch wealth and shipping, so that England would be ruined, and "the revolution of Europe would be assured." (This had been precisely the argument of the Dutch émigrés in December and January, which Robespierre himself had then opposed.) But no, the Brissot-Dumouriez group had never favored international revolution. They had disapproved of the annexation of Savoy and Belgium, betrayed the Dutch, tried "to halt the progress of our revolution in neighboring countries." In addition, they were suspiciously close to their friend Philippe Egalité, the *ci-devant* Duke of Orleans. Why had this person's son (the future King Louis-Philippe, who later boasted of having fought at Valmy) been commissioned as a lieutenant-general at the age of nineteen? What kind of officers were in this republican army anyway? Brissot, according to Robespierre, now really wanted to make peace with the foreign powers, with a restoration of monarchy in the Orleans line.[10]

Anyone living in the democratized twentieth century knows that there can be no public talk of peace in time of war. There could be no talk of peace for Robespierre, especially if it meant a relapse into monarchy. He demanded the death penalty for anyone suggesting compromise with the enemy. This proposal, amended in the Convention by Danton, who favored private overtures to the enemy, turned into a well-known decree, by which France was supposed (at least by his-

---

[10] Speeches of April 3 and 10, 1793, Robespierre, *Oeuvres*, IX: *Discours*, IV (Paris, 1958), 357-68, 376-416.

torians) to "renounce" the two Propaganda Decrees of 1792, which, as already explained, were not really "propaganda" decrees at all. The Convention now declared that it would not interfere with the government of other powers, but that these powers must not interfere in the affairs of France and its constitution; and that anyone favoring compromise with the enemy should be put to death, *unless* the enemy, in advance, recognized "the sovereignty, independence, indivisibility and unity of the Republic, founded on liberty and equality."[11] This left matters not actually much changed, since the powers had not yet made clear any such bland intentions.

Meanwhile the Convention, an incredible body, at war with all Europe, with its commanding general in Belgium proved disloyal, with peasants in armed rebellion in the West, with the currency out of control, the economy collapsing, and the popular agitation in the Paris sections boiling over, found moments to engage in its theoretically principal business, to "constitute" a regular government through a new written constitution and declaration of rights. The committee on the constitution was dominated by Condorcet and other Brissotins or Girondists. There was much on which they did not disagree with the Mountain, notably universal suffrage, universal schooling, public relief to the needy, and other attributes of a democratic state. Robespierre, however, was convinced that the Girondists were unfit to govern. He made an issue over their proposed Declaration of Rights. On April 24 he submitted and explained to the Convention a draft Declaration of his own. Though never adopted, it is a key document to the understanding of his thinking and his tactics.[12]

For one thing, where the Girondist draft would limit resistance to government to "legal" channels, Robespierre was more indulgent to the right of insurrection. This meant, in the political realities of the moment, that Robespierre supported the dynamism of the sans-culottes

[11] *Moniteur*, XVI, 143.

[12] *Oeuvres*, IX, 459-75, with the valuable editors' notes. This speech of Robespierre's has always been a favorite with those publishing collections of his speeches, on which curious observations can be made: *The Speeches of Maximilien Robespierre* in the *Voices of Revolt* series (New York, International Publishers, 1927) simply deletes Robespierre's remarks that "equality of wealth is a chimera," and that "it is more important to make poverty honorable than to proscribe opulence." On the other hand, *Robespierre: pages choisies des grands républicains* (Paris, 1907), published for patriotic purposes, simply omits this "social-democratic" speech altogether. It was this sort of thing that understandably annoyed Albert Mathiez. Mathiez, however, in expounding this speech, always emphasized its social democracy while saying little of its international revolutionism, which Mathiez preferred to attribute to the "Girondins."

in the Paris sections against the convention. Not yet in power himself, he was more sympathetic to "direct democracy" than he would be later.

He also called for the addition of two groups of new articles to the Declaration of Rights. The first group, composed of five articles, referred to the right of property, and touched on the ideology of popular revolution. The second group, in four articles, referred to international fraternization, and touched on the matter of international revolutionism.

Robespierre, like the popular democrats, favored a degree of economic equality which he never specified, but which fell short of the equality of incomes that Babeuf demanded three years later. "Equality of wealth is a chimera," he said, "necessary neither to private happiness nor to the public welfare." But "the world hardly needed a revolution to learn that extreme disproportion of wealth is the source of many evils." He proposed, therefore, to lay it down as a principle that property right was a creation of law, not of nature apart from law, and that, like liberty, it was inseparable from considerations of ethics, and found its limits where it touched on the rights of others. He also proposed a progressive income tax. Brissot objected, and praise for Robespierre on this score has come more from posterity than from his contemporaries. Since there was no discussion of actual rates, it is hard to estimate the social significance of Robespierre's idea of a progressive tax. He himself soon changed his mind, coming to believe that in a democratic society it was better for men of small means to carry a proportionate share of the costs, lest the well-to-do, by supplying the money, make themselves too indispensable to the state. That he was something of a social as well as a political democrat there can be no doubt.

He appealed also to the force of world revolution, which he now blamed the Girondists for ignoring. He scorned the argument that to stir up the peoples might aggravate the trouble with kings. "I confess that this inconvenience does not frighten me." The kings were already combined against France and against liberty everywhere. "All men of all countries are brothers." They should lend mutual aid as if they were citizens of a single state. The oppressor of one nation is the enemy of all. "Kings, aristocrats and tyrants, of every description, are slaves in revolt against the sovereign of the earth, which is the human race, and against the legislator of the world, which is nature." "Verbiage pretending to profundity," said Brissot, who had done as much as anyone to introduce such language into French politics since 1789.

In time of war and defeat, against the Brissotins in the Convention, and against the cosmopolitan forces of Counter-Revolution, Robespierre was willing to ally himself with two spirits that have never since been quite conjured away: those of mass upheaval and world revolution.

The Paris sections exploded in May. The Convention enacted controls on the retail price of bread. Agitation continued, sponsored by Jacobins of the Mountain. On May 31 a rising of *sectionnaires* captured the city government, and on June 2 eighty thousand armed sans-culottes besieged the Convention, demanding the arrest of twenty-two of its members. Defenseless and divided, the Convention yielded. Brissot and his friends were arrested (or fled, like Condorcet), to be disposed of by the Revolutionary Tribunal. The same kind of popular rising which by overthrowing the monarchy in 1792 had brought the Convention into being now threatened the Convention itself in 1793. It remained to be seen whether the Jacobins of the Mountain could avoid the fate of those of the "Gironde."

A constitution was thrown together in a few days. Full of elaborately democratic provisions, it came to be known as the Constitution of the Year I—that is, the first year of the Republic. The primary assemblies, throughout the country, ratified it with a vote reported as 1,801,918 to 11,610, out of some seven million adult men over 21. (Neither the French constitution of 1789-1791, nor the American federal constitution of 1787, had even been offered for direct popular ratification at all.) The Convention, given the facts of war and revolution, made no move to put the constitution into effect, seeming rather to envisage its own indefinite continuation. It appears that the mass of sans-culottes and *sectionnaires* accepted this decision, seeing in the Convention, now purged of its Girondist leadership, a necessary center and symbol of government in time of emergency. Immediately, however, voices were heard demanding the introduction of constitutional government. They came from journalists and militants, like Hébert, who were not members of the Convention and who really meant, not constitutionality, but the dissolution of the Convention and overthrow of Robespierre. Robespierre coined the term "ultra-revolutionary" to describe these men. In the logic of revolution, as he understood it, ultra-revolution came to be an insidious form of counter-revolution. Was he merely setting himself up as a norm? Was he simply identifying his own purposes with "the Revolution"? Was he only resisting the fate he had meted out to Brissot? It does not seem so. To purge the Convention was one thing; to dissolve it, another. The logic of revolution is not altogether weird or subjective, and demands for dissolution of the Convention in 1793, as voiced on the Left, would produce exactly what the most unregenerate conservatives throughout Europe most desired. It can be considered as certain that France could not be governed in 1793 by liberal or democratic constitutional means. To disband the Convention could only perpetuate anarchy. In that case a monarchist restoration, even if it masked a clerico-aristocratic dictatorship, would be welcomed.

That Robespierre could now detect "ultras" was a sign that he was turning from insurrectionism to *gouvernement révolutionnaire*, and that he himself had a hand in this incipient government. In July the Convention elected him to its Committee of Public Safety. But matters had never been worse for the Convention than in this summer of 1793. Marat was assassinated in his bath. He was the second member of the Convention to be assassinated since January. The great provincial cities, Lyon, Marseille, Bordeaux, where the expulsion of the Girondists angered the urban bourgeoisie, denounced the anarchy in Paris and defied the authority of the Convention. This "federalist" rebellion was of course a sign of anarchy in itself, and was abetted by the secret maneuvers of true counter-revolutionaries and foreign agents. At the end of August the royalists at Toulon threw the city open to the British and surrendered the fleet. Edmund Burke demanded that the Allies, now that they had a foothold in southern France, recognize a royal government and make clear their common cause with the émigrés—the true people of France, as he called them (estimating their number at 70,000), the revolutionaries being "robbers" who had driven them from the house.[13] The powers did not take his advice. They wished a free hand in what seemed an imminent victory.

In Paris the sans-culottes again invaded the Convention on September 4. The Revolutionary Government was the outcome. It rested on a compromise between the popular democrats of the sections and the middle-class Jacobins of the Mountain in the Convention. The Convention saved itself from further purging or dissolution, but only by accepting the demands of the populace, in which hysteria, suspicion, fear, revenge, resolution, and patriotic defiance were mixed together.

---

[13] "Policy of the Allies," (1793) in Burke, *Writings and Speeches*, 12 vols. (Boston, 1901), IV, 446.

The Convention authorized a *levée en masse* to enlarge the army. It consented reluctantly to a semi-military *armée révolutionnaire* to patrol the country. It enacted the General Maximum, a system of nation-wide price controls on a wide range of consumers' goods. It promised to rid the army of unreliable officers. It passed a draconian Law of Suspects, and enlarged the Revolutionary Tribunal. The Terror began in earnest, as the Brissotins, Marie Antoinette, and various unsuccessful generals went to the guillotine. A Republican Calendar was adopted, marking the end of the Christian Era, and the beginning of the movement known as Dechristianization. In this, as in some other measures, it was only a small minority that called for such extreme action. But it was dangerous and impossible at such a time, opening the way to suspicion and denunciation, for anyone to question the demands of the most intransigently patriotic.

On the other hand, the government began to govern. The Committee of Public Safety received larger powers. Its membership settled at twelve, who remained the same twelve individuals from September 1793 to July 1794.[14] They included Robespierre, Saint-Just, Couthon, Barère, and Lazare Carnot. The Committee of General Security obtained wide powers of political police, and gradually subordinated the local and largely spontaneous "surveillance committees" to itself. The government was declared "revolutionary until the peace." That is, the question of constitutionality was suspended for the duration. Members of the Convention, despatched to the provinces, to insurgent areas, and to the armies, reported directly to the Committee of Public Safety. This network of *représentants en mission* coordinated and enforced national policy, and worked to assure some measure of uniform loyalty to the Revolution. In December the ruling Committee received powers of appointment and removal of local office-holders throughout the country. A Subsistence Commission, building on the price-controls, and working under the ruling Committee, developed an elaborate system of requisitions, priorities, and currency regulations. The value of the assignat was held steady. The armies were supplied, while Carnot supervised their mobilization and training. By the end of 1793 the Vendéan rebellion was neutralized, the federalist rebellions suppressed, and the British ejected from Toulon. By the spring of 1794 an army of almost a million men faced the foreign enemy. It was the

---

[14] The Revolutionary Government is the subject of my book of 1941, reprinted in 1958 with a slightly different subtitle, *Twelve Who Ruled: the Committee of Public Safety during the French Revolution* (Princeton, 1958).

first mass or "democratic" army, or at least the first above the level of casual militia, possessed of a modern kind of national consciousness, with its morale heightened by political attitudes in the common soldiers, its higher ranks filled with men promoted from the ranks on grounds of "merit," and prepared to act, by its training, equipment, and discipline, in a great war among the old military powers of Europe. Eight marshals of Napoleon's empire, in addition to Bonaparte himself, were promoted to the rank of general officer at this time.

By the spring of 1794 the French armies resumed the offensive. In June they won the battle of Fleurus, and the Austrians abandoned Belgium. In the Dutch cities the potential revolutionaries took hope again. The Poles, with Kosciuszko, again attempted revolution. Its outcome was uncertain. But in France it was clear, by mid-1794, that the Republic had survived.

It survived at a certain cost, or on certain terms. Much happened in France during the climactic Year Two of the republican calendar. Within the larger framework of the general eighteenth century revolution, and indeed of the subsequent history of modern times, it is illuminating to see two of these developments in some detail. First, the Revolutionary Government reacted strongly against popular and international revolution, exhibiting what, in the jargon, might be called "bourgeois" and "nationalist" inclinations. Second, in the extreme emotional stimulation, the Revolution, as understood by Robespierre, became the means to call a new world into being, and turned into something like a religion.

Reaction against Popular
and International Revolutionism

The Revolutionary Government, representing re-established authority, turned at once against the self-generating dynamism of the popular democrats. Events now in truth followed the lines of a classical tragedy, as seen so clearly by Albert Soboul. The Revolutionary Government crushed the very spirit which had brought it into being. The popular democrats, or sans-culottes, "had demanded a government strong enough to crush the aristocracy; they did not realize that this government, if it was to conquer, would have to force them to obey."[15]

[15] Soboul, *Sans-culottes parisiens,* 1026. The following pages draw heavily on this book; see also Soboul's "Robespierre et la formation du gouvernement révolutionnaire, 27 juillet-10 octobre, 1793" in *Revue d'histoire moderne et contemporaine* v (Oct-Dec. 1958), 283-94.

The Paris sections had met *en permanence* since July 25, 1792. In September 1793 they were limited by the Committee of Public Safety to two meetings a week. They had originally elected their own committees, which concerned themselves with searches, arrests, identity cards, ration cards, patrols, and political agitation in their neighborhoods. By the spring of 1794 the ruling Committee appointed the members of these committees. The committee members, originally unpaid, began to receive five francs a day for their services; they developed increasingly the mentality of small public job-holders, dutifully carrying out instructions from on high. The section assemblies long practiced open voting. The ruling Committee imposed secret voting, which reduced the influence of the most militant.

Many demands were never granted. It was a favorite idea of the popular democrats that public employments should go to worthy family men and elderly patriots of limited means. The ruling Committee never accepted any such principle. The popular democrats, and their journalistic spokesmen, inveighed against big business men and wholesale traders, who were accused of withholding goods from the market. The Committee of Public Safety protected them, needing the services of men whose operations were above the shopkeeping level. "Profit" had an evil sound to the sans-culottes; the Committee accepted it as a necessity of the economic system, and allowed for it in its scales of administered prices. There were requests for more free time and easier conditions for workmen in the arms manufactories. The Revolutionary Government adopted a stern code of labor discipline. There were demands for rent controls, which the government never conceded, believing that the price controls were only a temporary wartime expedient, and fearing that rent controls might become permanent if incorporated in leases. The sections and the Commune resisted and evaded the legislation setting ceilings on wages. The Committee of Public Safety tried to enforce it, knowing that otherwise the price controls would not work at all. By a politically somewhat inept measure, on July 23, 1794, which aimed at enforcing the already legalized wage scales, but which had the effect of abruptly cutting wages in half for many workers, the Committee alienated popular sympathy at the very moment when the Convention was conspiring to overthrow Robespierre.

Independent Revolutionary activists, or persons outside the government who identified themselves with the cause of the needy, now received short shrift. The government proposed to attend to the needy itself, and denounced such agitators as *enragés*. Such was Jacques Roux, a priest who had become a vehement popular spokesman; he was put in prison, where he committed suicide. An organization of Revolutionary Women, who continued to complain of high prices and shortages, was broken up.

The last weeks of 1793 saw the outburst of Dechristianization. It developed independently in various parts of France, but in Paris, where the mass of sans-culottes seem to have been indifferent to it, it was brought on by certain prominent figures in the sections and in the Commune. It appealed most strongly to intellectuals of various types, such as the poet Fabre d'Eglantine, who coined the names for the months in the Republican Calendar, and the printer and bookseller Momoro, a chief sponsor of the Worship of Reason as conducted in a grand festival at Notre Dame in November. The Committee of Public Safety, while embarrassed at seeming to defend priestcraft and superstition, regarded such anti-Christian demonstrations as highly impolitic. Robespierre called them "philosophical masquerades."

Robespierre himself, so long as the Brissot group had been in power, had been indulgent to the claims of the Paris sections to a direct and immediate sovereign liberty of their own. He had been tolerant of insurrectionism, and would not confine the right of resistance to "legal" channels. Now, as spokesman for the Revolutionary Government, he adopted a different tone. In a great speech of February 5, 1794 in the Convention, he took care to offer definitions of "true" democracy, which he said the Revolutionary Government meant to introduce, as distinct from the mistaken democracy with which plausible agitators tried to confuse the people.

"Democracy," he said, "is not a state in which the people, continually assembled, itself directs public affairs; still less is it a state in which a hundred thousand fragments of the people, by contradictory, hasty and isolated measures, should decide on the destiny of society as a whole. Such a government has never existed, and if it did could do nothing but throw the people back into despotism."

This was an admonition to the Paris sections and corresponding local bodies throughout the country.

"Democracy is a state in which the sovereign people, guided by laws of its own making, does for itself what it can do well, and by its delegates what it cannot."[16]

This was a vindication of delegated authority, or of the powers which

---

[16] C. Vellay, ed., *Discours et rapports de Robespierre* (Paris, 1908), 324-28.

a representative democracy should confer on its government. It must be remembered that the idea of representative democracy was still new and unformulated in Europe, since "democracy" had hitherto meant a direct democracy feasible in very small states, and since representative institutions, as they had come down from the Middle Ages, were linked closely to ideas of social rank and estate.

Robespierre went on to remark, reminding his hearers of the war, that the military strength of a democracy lay in the fact that all citizens felt that they fought in their own interest—and that France was the first "true democracy" granting a full equality of rights. "That, in my opinion, is the real reason why the tyrants allied against the Republic will be defeated."

There were some who could be electrified by such doctrine, others to whom it seemed remote and unreal. There were some, among the ordinary people, who hoped for more material benefits from the Revolution. The Committee of Public Safety devised a new program looking toward an equalization of wealth: property was now to be confiscated from "suspects" (not only from émigrés and the church as hitherto), and transferred gratis to "indigent patriots" (not sold to new buyers, as in the past). This measure failed in its purpose. It made no dramatic impact on the sans-culottes, who saw nothing new in confiscations from enemies of the state. In any case the real poor people of the city, whose problems were food shortage and poor housing, had little to gain from the problematic future ownership of land, most of it agricultural.

Unrest continued in the Paris sections. Militants resented the loss of initiative. There was talk of another insurrection or "rising," or vast popular demonstration against the Convention, such as had ousted the Brissotins on June 2.

There were "ultras" of another kind against whom the Revolutionary Government also turned. These were the foreign revolutionaries and ideologists who abounded in Paris, who preached universal revolution, and whose real aim was to use France to liberate their own countries or "the world." During the Year II, among the most authentic Jacobins, there was a strong nationalist reaction against revolutionary cosmopolitanism. The men in the Revolutionary Government, while hopeful for revolution elsewhere, turned to the idea, in modern terms, of revolution in one country first. This had always been Robespierre's real conviction, suspended only in moments of rhetoric or during the contest with Brissot. It was clear, in the supreme hour of need for the Republic in

France, that no other people would lend any useful assistance. There was apathy, and even public protest against the war, in England, Holland, Belgium, the Rhineland, and elsewhere. Nowhere, except in far-off Poland, was there any revolt against a government with which France was at war. There was no revolution in aid of France. It was perfectly evident that the foreign revolutionaries were entirely dependent on the French. The French were indeed the only people in the whole period (the Americans having been no exception) who carried out a revolution, and defeated a counter-revolution, entirely with their own resources. The fact offers some explanation of the intensity of the Terror, and of why the Terror occurred only in France.

The French Jacobins, these being the facts, developed a scorn for the revolutionaries of other countries, whom they accused of lacking the vigor or courage to stage a revolution of their own. On September 15, 1793, as the Revolutionary Government was taking form, the Convention, on initiative of the Committee of Public Safety, in effect rescinded the decree of the preceding November promising "aid and fraternity to peoples wishing to recover their liberty." French generals in the field should have nothing to do with revolutionaries in Belgium or elsewhere. "Renouncing henceforth all philanthropic ideas adopted by the French people with a view to making foreign nations alive to the value and advantages of liberty, French generals shall conduct themselves toward the enemies of France in the same manner as the Allied powers conduct themselves toward it; they shall observe, toward countries and individuals subjected by French arms, the ordinary laws of war." They should therefore disarm the inhabitants, take hostages, and exploit the local resources, keeping such exploitation under control of the French army and government. It was the policy, which had so dismayed the Dutch and Belgian revolutionaries in Dumouriez' time, of treating occupied areas as conquered country.[17]

The foreign revolutionaries in Paris were a miscellaneous lot. Since they lived in an atmosphere of secrecy and intrigue, most of them on the fringes of politics, they remain one of the mysteries of the French Revolution. The personal relationships between the two kinds of "ultras," the foreigners and the spokesmen of popular revolution, remain very unclear.[18]

[17] Mavidal, et al., *Archives parlementaires 1787-1801* (Paris, 1909), vol. 74, p. 231; A. Aulard, *Recueil des actes du Comité de salut public* (Paris, 1893), vi, 553-54.

[18] Soboul, interested in the popular revolutionaries but not in the international revolutionaries, believes (*Sans-culottes parisiens,* 779-885) that there was no political or ideological connection between the two groups, and that the governing committees

Anacharsis Cloots, for example, who may well have been mad, had at first called himself the *orateur du genre humain*, and now called himself the *orateur des sans-culottes*. He was in touch with the revolutionaries in Holland, and with the ambiguous Chevalier d'Eon in London. An extreme sponsor of radical Dechristianization, he presented the Convention, as an insult to Christianity, with a copy of his *Certainty of the Proofs of Mohammedanism*. He was hardly a man of the people; rich and titled by origin, he wrote laughingly to his brother that he had bought one of the confiscated estates near Paris, and was living well "for a sans-culotte." To his constituents (he was a member of the Convention) he expressed "bourgeois equality" with fatuous complacency: "all being equal before the law, if some are wealthy, others industrious, all have their qualities."[19] He urged them to forget their own disagreements in a campaign against *la tyrannie européenne*.

The Dutch banker, Kock, lived in a fine house at Passy with nine children, a private preceptor, numerous servants, and facilities for entertainment. Hébert and other radicals from the Paris Commune and government bureaus were among his most frequent guests. It has been argued that they had no common political interests, and that the gatherings were purely for relaxation; but this seems unlikely, since Mme Kock complained that Mme Hébert talked too much politics, and Kock, who had been a member of the Batavian Revolutionary Committee since 1792, signed a petition of this committee to the Committee of Public Safety, on March 9, 1794, urging the French to invade and revolutionize Holland.[20] What Kock and Hébert had in common was a dislike of the personnel and policies of the Revolutionary Government of the Year II. They both accused it of "moderatism."

Cloots, Kock, and other Dutch émigrés supported a paper in Paris,

---

threw the two together under a common indictment, so as to discredit the popular revolutionaries with a stigma of "conspiracy" and of association with foreigners. This view seems to arise from Soboul's unwillingness to understand Robespierre's conception of "ultras" except in a context of class conflict. On the intricacies of the foreign revolutionaries not much has been accomplished since the monographs of Mathiez over forty years ago, except for sporadic and sometimes excellent pieces of specialized research, such as those of General Herlaut, including his *Autour d'Hébert: Deux témoins de la Terreur, le citoyen Dubuisson, le ci-devant baron de Haindel* (Paris, 1958).

[19] A. Tuetey, *Répertoire général des sources manuscrites de l'histoire de Paris pendant la Révolution* (Paris, 1912), x, No. 2482. Much else on Cloots, Proli, Kock, and others may be found here, and in the preface to Volume xi.

[20] Colenbrander, *Gedenkstukken der algemeene geschiedenis van Nederland van 1795 tot 1840* (The Hague, 1905) i, 337. On Kock see also Tuetey, *op.cit.*, and pp. 24 and 61 above.

Le Batave. It lasted under different titles for over three years, and is among the rarest, in libraries today, of all French Revolutionary journals that had so long a life. In general, it closely followed the line of Hébert's *Père Duchesne*. It lauded the Worship of Reason in Paris, and gave admiring publicity to the most violent episodes of the Terror. It was full of reports on revolutionaries in Holland and various other countries, whom it presented as oppressed patriots eagerly awaiting the moment of liberation.

There was also the Batavian Legion. Or rather, at the end of 1793, there were apparently two organizations by this name.[21] One was in the field with the French army, as in 1792. The other, which remained closer to Paris, was composed of nondescripts and persons without visible means of support, recruited from half a dozen nationalities, but including Frenchmen also. One of these was "Gracchus" Babeuf, who, between periods in prison on ordinary criminal charges, kept away starvation by briefly joining the Batavian Legion at the end of 1793.

The other "legions" and émigré groups, founded in 1792, were leading a troubled existence. The United Belgians carried on in rooms supplied by the Paris Commune. They feared infiltration by other Belgians who were really Austrian spies, and indeed the émigré groups were natural places of concealment for the agents of governments with which France was at war.

Among Belgians in Paris, the most notable was a man named Proly.[22] He was supposed to be the cousin of Cloots and the illegitimate son of Prince Kaunitz by a Belgian mother. Once rich, though no longer so in 1793, he had been active among the Belgian Democrats of 1789. He had edited a paper called *Le Cosmopolite* in Paris in 1792. He had served Dumouriez as a financial middleman in Belgium in January 1793, and had something to do at that time with a bold scheme to ruin the Bank of England, through counterfeit banknotes to be circulated through Amsterdam Jews during the proposed invasion of Holland. It seems altogether possible that, to protect Belgium from exploitation by the French, Proly had had some share in Dumouriez' secret plans for a separate Belgian republic. Proly was a mysterious person, who in 1793

---

[21] *Le Batave*, No. 265, Nov. 7, 1793. On Babeuf's membership in the Batavian Legion, see M. Dommanget, *Sylvain Maréchal: l'homme sans Dieu* (Paris, 1950), 303. On the dissolution of the legions, and arrest of foreigners, see Mathiez, *La Révolution et les étrangers* (Paris, 1918), 168-188.

[22] On Proly see Tuetey, *op.cit.*, Mathiez, "Vonck et Proli," in *Annales historiques de la Révolution française*, 11 (1925), 58-66; and the writings of Suzanne Tassier on Belgium, mentioned in the preceding chapter.

divided his time between the Stock Exchange and the Commune. It is understandable that Robespierre should have suspected him, however falsely, of being an Austrian spy.

Among other foreigners in the city was Thomas Paine, now under suspicion for his English birth, his itinerant past, his world-revolutionism, and his friendship with Brissotins now deceased. There was an innocuous Italian named Pio, who had a job at the Foreign Office.[23] Considering how important the Italian revolutionaries became in 1796, their absence from Paris in 1793-94 is remarkable.

Robespierre became convinced of the existence of a vast Foreign Conspiracy, composed of all kinds of "ultras," both of the popular and international kind, preaching the *révolution à outrance*, insatiable activists, enemies of all government and all religion, working in collusion with old Brissotins, "moderates" and accomplices of Dumouriez, reinforced by super-Terrorists who feared that the Revolutionary Government would repudiate them, joined by grafters and common cheats who feared exposure, and driven frantically onward by the machinations of true counter-revolutionaries, royalist agents, clandestine clergy, and foreign spies who wished to throw the Republic into chaos so that monarchy and aristocracy could be restored.[24] There was no such "conspiracy." It is true, however, that men of the most varied stripe wished the destruction of the government. It puts Robespierre's "foreign conspiracy" in an intelligible light to observe that a certain royalist spy in Paris, who had an unknown but profitable access to the secrets of the Committee of Public Safety, came to much the same conclusion—namely that "Hébertists," foreigners, and spies were somehow involved with one another to overthrow the ruling Committee—and so reported to Lord Grenville in England.[25]

The Committee of Public Safety struck at all its enemies together, "amalgamating" them, as it said in its instructions to the Revolutionary Tribunal. The ensuing trials of Germinal (March 1794) marked a dramatic end to popular and international revolutionism as they had

[23] Mathiez, "Le Chevalier Pio," *Annales révolutionnaires*, XI (1919), 94-104.

[24] "Rapport écrit de la main de Robespierre sur la faction de l'étranger" in *Pièces trouvées dans les papiers de Robespierre et complices: affaire Chabot, faction Proly* (Paris, Imprimerie Nationale, Brumaire III), 90-99, which Mathiez seems to have accepted as genuine.

[25] The reference is to the Dropmore Spy on whose "bulletins" much has recently been written. For a résumé see Godechot, *Contre-révolution*, 186-190. For the bulletins themselves see Great Britain: Historical Manuscripts Commission, *The Manuscripts of J. B. Fortescue Preserved at Dropmore* (London, 1894), vols. II and III, and for the spy's fantastic reports on "foreign conspiracy" see II, 548-63.

taken form in the summer of 1792. They were purely political trials, victories of one group of men over others, justified only by emergency and the "public good," and with no pretense that either the charges, the evidence, the procedure, or the decisions would meet ordinary criteria of law.

The guillotining of Hébert, Momoro, and others, for whom the epithet "Hébertist" was invented, coming after so much else in the way of political and administrative subordination, reduced the spontaneous revolutionary enthusiasm of the common people of Paris, who from now on, like ordinary people in most countries, either accepted the decisions of government, or became politically apathetic, or, if rebellious, could hardly form more than small and sectarian movements.

Cloots and Paine were expelled from the Convention. Cloots was guillotined; Paine sat for months in prison. Proly and some of his French associates, on the charge of implication with Dumouriez' defection, went to the guillotine. Kock was arrested a week after signing the Batavian petition to the Committee of Public Safety. He was guillotined as a friend of Hébert. Another signer, van Hooff, was imprisoned but survived. The Batavian Revolutionary Committee and the other émigré organizations disappeared. The Batavian, Belgian, Germanic, and Allobrogian "legions" were dissolved. In the pursuit of foreigners three Irish-born generals in the French army, Arthur Dillon, Thomas Ward, and James O'Moran, went under the "popular axe." The Prince of Hesse, another foreign general in the French Revolutionary Army, went to prison. Various insignificant foreigners were rounded up, like the Italian Pio, and a man named Dengs, whose father was French Canadian.

It may be added, as a commentary on the use of such tactics in politics, that Robespierre, when his turn came a few months later, was likewise charged with implication in foreign conspiracy and world-revolutionism. The case concerned the Englishman, Benjamin Vaughan. A member of Parliament, one of the Earl of Lansdowne's radical friends, Vaughan had defended France in the pages of the *Morning Chronicle*. In 1794 the French sent William Jackson to Ireland on a secret mission; the British discovered the plot, Wolfe Tone fled to America, and Benjamin Vaughan to France. Robespierre protected Vaughan as he passed through France in May. Vaughan then wrote to Robespierre from Geneva, urging that France invite the revolutionaries of Belgium, Holland, and the German Rhineland to form a great federation, with universal suffrage and a Congress, so that "nine million men," paying their own war costs, could ally with France against tyrants. This letter reached Paris on 9 Thermidor, the day of Robespierre's fall, and was opened at the Committee of Public Safety by Barère and Billaud-Varenne. They seized on it as evidence to prove that Robespierre was conspiring with William Pitt against the Republic.[26]

The point at present, however, is that at the height of the Revolutionary Government, in the months between the trials of Germinal and the death of Robespierre, during which the French armies resumed the offensive and again overflowed into adjoining countries, the mood was somewhat different from what it had been during the abortive victories of Dumouriez a year and a half before. The same cry was heard again: *Guerre aux châteaux, paix aux chaumières*! Its impact was as revolutionary as ever. Governments and privileged classes might be undermined—not, however, as enemies of the human race, nor as enemies of their own peoples, but because they were at war with the French Republic. The men ruling France had no confidence, and little interest, in the potential revolutionaries of foreign parts. Indeed their attitude was one of contempt.

The Committee of Public Safety had its representatives with all the armies, who plied it with reports and questions. On the Italian front, the French occupied Oneglia in the kingdom of Sardinia. Italian patriots flocked about the two Italian-speaking French agents, Saliceti and Buonarroti. The Paris government cared nothing about them.[27] At Geneva there was an entirely separate little disturbance arising from indigenous causes; the Genevese, setting up a Revolutionary Tribunal of their own, executed fourteen persons, in July 1794, who had been involved in the Geneva counter-revolution of 1782. The French agent, observing it from Grenoble, was extremely skeptical of this "hypocritical" revolution.[28] In Belgium, as the French re-entered it, the French agent held aloof from the returning Belgian refugees. They were concerned, he reported to Paris, only with their own interests and their own vengeance.[29] The Dutch problem was more difficult, because the

[26] Mathiez, "Robespierre et Benjamin Vaughan" in *Annales révolutionnaires* (Jan. 1917), 1-11; Vaughan, *Letters on the Subject of the Concert of Princes and the Dismemberment of Poland and France* (London, 1793). Vaughan lived from 1796 to 1835 in the United States, where he received honorary degrees from Harvard and Bowdoin, to both of which he left many books.

[27] Aulard, *Recueil des actes du Comité de salut public, avec la correspondance des représentants en mission* (Paris, 1899-1904), XII, XIII, XIV, XV, where the various reports of Saliceti and the younger Robespierre make no mention of the Italian refugees or patriots, although corresponding reports from the *Armée du Nord* make frequent reference to the analogous Dutch patriots.

[28] *Ibid.*, XV, 433.

[29] *Ibid.*, XV, 295, 361, 386, 409.

Dutch revolutionary movement, since the early 1780's, had been the strongest of all those outside France itself. The French civilian representative attached to the Army of the North was beset by Dutch patriots. The Dutch émigré general Daendels offered to make a secret trip to Amsterdam to produce revolution there at once. The French agent asked for instructions. The Committee of Public Safety gave Delphic answers. It would welcome a revolution in Holland, but not start one. It might sponsor a Dutch revolution, or it might not. It must be remembered that the Dutch revolutionaries were thinking only of their own country. And as Carnot said, "We who are French must think of our own."[30]

As for Poland, the French had no contact with it, military or diplomatic. They would of course welcome Kosciuszko's rebellion as a diversion against the Coalition. But they neither would nor could do anything about it. In May 1794 a German Protestant pastor, Karl Held, appeared in Paris, sent by a secret "Jacobin" group in Vienna, which had contacts with the insurgent Poles. The Committee of Public Safety rebuffed his approaches and put him under arrest.[31]

The mood of 1794 was realistic, ruthless, disengaged from cosmopolitan ideological sympathies, military in motive, revolutionary in the sense of securing the Revolution in France. It is a question how different it had really been in 1792. Even then, at the time of the so-called Propaganda Decrees, there had been, as was seen in the last chapter, a good deal of realistic consideration of similar problems. It has been customary for historians to see three phases in the spread of revolution during the wars of the 1790's: a "Girondist" phase of supposedly eager and indiscriminate idealistic crusading in 1792, a sterner "Jacobin" phase of triumphant republicanism in 1794, and a cynical phase under the Directory from 1795 to 1799, characterized by manipulation of satellite republics. It is doubtful whether these phases ever really existed, with enough distinctness to aid in an understanding of what happened. The problems throughout were much the same. Since the problems were difficult, recurrent, and real, answers naturally varied from person to person and from time to time.

[30] *Ibid.*, xiv, 712; xv, 292, 383. See also xv, 261-67, for a general memorandum of the Committee of Public Safety, dated July 18, 1794, on policies to be adopted in occupied territories. Also Lazare Carnot, "Vues proposées au Comité de salut public . . . ," July 16, 1794, in *Correspondance generale de Carnot* (Paris, 1907), 496-502; Colenbrander, *Gedenkstukken*, I, 336-37.

[31] France: Commission des archives diplomatiques, *Instructions données aux ambassadeurs: Pologne* (Paris, 1888), ii, 328-30. On Held's mission see below, p. 165.

The Moral Republic

The purpose of the Revolutionary Government was not merely to defend the state but to found it, not only to win a war but to introduce a new and better society. That was what made it a revolutionary and not merely an emergency regime. In its vivid sense of a new world coming, its "eschatology," the Revolution became a kind of religion. The substance of things hoped for, or new world as now desired, was one in which human dignity would rest on a foundation of fellow citizenship, freedom, and equality of status and respect. The picture had been drawn eloquently by Rousseau. It occupied the minds of many. Consider these statements by two "founders":

"A constitution founded on these principles introduces knowledge among the people, and inspires them with a conscious dignity becoming free men; a general emulation takes place, which causes good humor, sociability and good manners to be general. That elevation of sentiment inspired by such a government makes the common people brave and enterprising. That ambition which is inspired by it makes them sober, industrious and frugal. You will find among them some elegance, perhaps, but more solidity; a little pleasure, but a great deal of business; some politeness, but more civility. If you compare such a country with the regions of domination, whether monarchical or aristocratical, you will fancy yourself in Arcadia or Elysium."

The other said:

"We want an order of things . . . in which the arts are an adornment to the liberty that ennobles them, and commerce the source of wealth for the public and not of monstrous opulence for a few families. . . . In our country we desire morality instead of selfishness, honesty and not mere 'honor,' principle and not mere custom, duty and not mere propriety, the sway of reason rather than the tyranny of fashion, a scorn for vice and not a contempt for the unfortunate . . . good men instead of good company, merit in place of intrigue, talent in place of mere cleverness, truth and not show, the charm of happiness and not the boredom of pleasure . . . in short the virtues and miracles of a republic and not the vices and absurdities of a monarchy."

The first was written by John Adams in 1776, the second by Maximilien Robespierre in 1794. The pictures in their minds were much alike. Both thought that a properly drafted constitution (producing what Robespierre, but not Adams, called a "democracy") would do much to bring such a world about.[32]

The difference was not so much in the main idea as in the action that they were prepared to take. Adams already lived in a kind of Arcadia, as contrasted, at least, with Europe. Robespierre did not. No doubt Adams had a saving grace of skepticism that would have held him back from Robespierre's course, but it is intriguing to speculate on whether John Adams, an impatient, irritable, easily frustrated but very determined man, with no very high opinion of his contemporaries, was not the one among the American founders who, under pressures such as those in France, could have most easily turned into a "Jacobin."

Robespierre, in the speech in which he defined democracy, coupled Virtue and Terror. It was clear enough what the Terror meant. It was very much a fact of political life in February 1794. It had risen gradually, from the street murders of July 1789, through the gruesome lynchings of September 1792, through the frenzies of suspicion that came with Dumouriez' defection and led to the creation of the Revolutionary Tribunal, on through the executions of the Brissotins and the queen. As in much else, so here, what began as popular clamor and violence ended up as a weapon in the hands of the government. The Terror had become an instrument of state. There had been genuine public revulsion against the Brissotins and the king and queen. There was no such popular demand for the deaths of the Hébertists, nor of the Dantonists a few weeks later, nor of the victims of the climactic "great" Terror of June and July 1794. These were devised by the government itself, which manufactured the necessary demand. Acts of government, also, were the death sentences meted out by revolutionary courts in punishment for rebellion in the Vendée and at Lyon and other federalist cities. These sentences, in retribution for armed rebellion, made up almost two-thirds of all deliberate executions during the Terror. More conservative governments, if equally frightened, might have done the same. There is little evidence that the Terror was used as a weapon of class war: three-fifths of those executed were peasants and workingmen, and only eight percent were noble. All told, about 17,000 were condemned to death.[33] The figure can be made to look small by application

[32] Adams, "Thoughts on Government," in *Works*, 10 vols. (Boston, 1851), IV, 199; Robespierre, "Rapport sur les principes de morale politique qui doivent guider la Convention," February 5, 1794, in C. Vellay, *Discours et rapports de Robespierre* (Paris, 1908), 325-26.
[33] D. Greer, *The Incidence of the Terror during the French Revolution* (Cambridge, Mass., 1935).

of twentieth-century standards, but such a well-publicized holocaust (there was no secrecy because there was no shame) had been unknown in western Europe since the wars of religion, and broke upon men of the humane eighteenth century with peculiar horror.

To Robespierre, a humane man himself, such violence was intolerable unless it had a strong ethical justification. It is sometimes argued that Robespierre, and others like him, ended up by killing people because they began with a visionary idea of an impossible future world—that fanaticism leads to murder. The opposite may be at least as true of real human psychology: that fanaticism itself is bred by events, or that Robespierre and others, caught up in events, and having accepted a series of decisions each more ruthless than the last, dwelt at length on the better world they hoped to create—if only to transform their own doubts or guilt feelings into a state of mind with which they could live. It is hard to explain otherwise the intensity of the feelings, since the idea of a moral republic, as a flat thing itself, was common enough to many people who did not become so excited. The French Revolution, by 1794, had in fact been so vast, so soul-shaking, so ferocious, and so pitilessly demanding of sacrifice, that it would seem to have been totally unsuccessful unless it was followed by an incomparably better world.

For moral as well as for practical reasons, for Robespierre, the Terror was unacceptable without Virtue. "If the mainspring of popular government in time of peace is virtue, the mainspring of popular government in time of revolution is both *virtue and terror*: virtue, without which terror is evil; terror, without which virtue is helpless. Terror is nothing but justice, prompt, severe and inflexible; it is therefore an emanation of virtue." It was also the "principle of democracy applied to the pressing needs of the country."[34]

It was the equation of Virtue and Terror that many persons then and since have found especially nauseous, and which does indeed distinguish the Terror of the French Revolution from other general liquidations in history. There seemed something insufferably hypocritical about it. To which a good Jacobin would reply that much hypocrisy has been expended on less defensible causes.

And what was this Virtue—the "virtue" which without terror was helpless? In part it meant only common honesty, the avoidance, for example, of the corruption and thieving in which a few members of the

[34] Robespierre in Vellay, *Discours*, 332.

Convention were implicated when the East India Company was dissolved. In part it meant a kind of austerity, a willingness to go without coffee or new shoes when such items were in short supply, and a belief that the sacrifices imposed by public emergency should be equally shared. It meant also patriotism or good citizenship, a subordination of private to public good, a willingness to do one's part, whether by serving in the army or by scraping saltpeter in caves. It required a suspension of factiousness and complaining, at least for "the duration." It forbade profiteering and dabbling in the black market. And it included all those qualities that were believed to be permanently necessary to a wholesome commonwealth in the future. The good citizen, in the good republic, would put behind him the false values of the immediate past, care nothing for social rank, detest everything ornamental, frivolous or rococo, live contentedly at his business and in his family, spurn riches as a snare, be free from consuming ambition, guard his civic and political freedom, accept other men as his equals and delight in a classless society.

Robespierre was not so simple as to suppose these qualities easy or "natural." Like everyone else in his day, he believed religion to be necessary to society. For the kind of society he had in mind the authorities of the Christian churches had ceased to offer much support. It was commonly believed, on all sides, that religions had been "invented." Moses and Numa Pompilius had been notably successful in this respect. In founding a religion they had each also founded a polity and a people. The Revolutionary Government would therefore invent a religion of its own. Prompted by Robespierre, the Convention decreed, on May 7, 1794, that "the French people recognizes the Supreme Being and the immortality of the soul."[35]

Thus originated the famous Worship of the Supreme Being, best known for the mammoth celebration held in Paris on June 8. Though arising from the same sources as the Worship of Reason of the preceding winter, it differed from the latter, in Robespierre's mind, in being less aggressively anti-Christian. It was his hope that all good citizens, whatever private religious views they might entertain, could publicly unite in religious services so comprehensive, so tolerant, so

[35] See, besides the decree, Robespierre's speech in its support, "Sur les rapports des idées religieuses et morales avec les principes republicains et sur les fêtes nationales," May 7, 1794, in Vellay, *Discours*, 347-75. The decree itself appears on 375-78. For the idea of "inventing" a religion, and for the whole present discussion, see M. Reinhard, *Religion, Revolution et Contre-Revolution*, Centre de Documentation Universitaire, Paris, 1960. The question of religion and revolution is also taken up in Chapter XI below.

lacking in dogmatism, so irenical and so useful. As the "decadary cult," celebrating republican or civic religion on each *décadi*, or "Sunday" of the republican calendar, the observances originating in the worship of the Supreme Being lingered on for several years. Contrary to Robespierre's hope, they never enjoyed any mass following, and by attracting mainly the anti-Christians remained as a divisive force in the republic.

There was a genuine religious feeling in the new cult, but it was a religion that was overwhelmingly ethical. There was a sense of man's place in the universe, but a much stronger sense of his proper role and attitudes in society. As Robespierre explained it (not unlike Burke), the individual reason could be frail and misleading. It was too involved with self-centered emotions. "Human authority can always be attacked by human pride." The inadequacy of human authority is therefore "supplemented by the religious sense, by which the soul is impressed with the idea of a sanction given to moral principles by a power superior to man."[36] The value and even the truth of religion were seen in the moral principles and public conduct which religion instilled. This being the end of the eighteenth century, the publicists of the opposition did not argue very differently. For Joseph de Maistre, as for Edmund Burke, the importance of religion lay in the inculcation of moral principles, that is, in a doctrine of attitudes and duties towards one's fellow man, and one's own place in society. The clash was less between religion and irreligion than between the cults, respectively, of an idealized aristocratic and an idealized democratic world.

The Year II reached a culmination on 20 Prairial, or June 8, 1794. It was the day of the Festival of the Supreme Being. Robespierre, just elected for the two-week term as president of the Convention, officiated as a kind of priest of the Republic as tens or hundreds of thousands watched. The victories at the front, the coming of summer, the recollection of a terrible danger that had been survived, gave a joyousness to the occasion. For Robespierre, very likely, it was the climax of his own life and the day of foundation of a new world. Even Mallet du Pan, a realistic observer, when he read the reports in the Paris papers, believed that Robespierre had successfully healed the wounds of the past years and might consolidate the new state.

Events proved otherwise. The Law of 22 Prairial gave freer rein to the Revolutionary Tribunal. Most of those executed in Paris died in

---

[36] Vellay, *Discours*, 361.

June and July of 1794. The Terror had got out of control, or at least it bore less relation to outer realities, and was carried on by the relentless will of a few individual men. Everything was now centralized in the government, even the definition of religion and virtue. Virtue itself came to mean harmlessness to the government. As Robespierre himself had said, human authority was attacked by human pride. Never had he been so inquisitorial, so implacably suspicious, as in these last few weeks.

If he had no longer objective grounds to fear for the Republic, he had good reason to be fearful for himself. By his preaching of virtue, and hieratic performance on June 8, he made enemies among his own colleagues. Old Voltaireans sneered at the new Rousseau. So strict a state could have no lasting appeal for the mass of actual Frenchmen—or of actual human beings. Some were guilty of offenses, of super-terrorism in the provinces, or political or money-making intrigues, for which it was evident that Robespierre questioned their virtue, and contemplated their demise. He had sent Danton to death, and some of his associates, to hold some kind of middle ground after the death of the Hébertists. But in attacking the Dantonists he had attacked the Convention itself. He had violated the body which he himself had always held up as the only symbol of legitimate power.

The restoration of public authority, the achievements of the Revolutionary Government, the tremendous year which had assured the survival of the Revolution, and which seemed to promise the foundation of a moral and democratic republic, thus ended up in an unedifying spectacle, in which the issue was to see which handful of men would get rid of the other first. By a palace revolution, a mere conspiracy in the Convention, Robespierre was outlawed on 9 Thermidor of the second year of the Republic, and died the next day.

The Meaning of Thermidor

Thermidor has become a byword for the reaction in which revolution ends. Many older histories of the French Revolution terminate here. For a long time Robespierre was taken to represent the most advanced point of the Revolution. He was not exactly *ne plus ultra*, but the "ultras" beyond him did not reflect the "true" movement. With his death came a "bourgeois" reaction, or at least a long, sordid, and uninspiring period until the appearance, or "advent," of Bonaparte. In more recent times, as the world has changed, it has been increasingly seen that Robespierre was by no means the furthest Left among authentic voices of the Revolution. There was a whole movement of popular excitement among the common people, largely autonomous and spontaneous, without which the Revolution could never have succeeded, or taken the course that it took. The popular movement was indeed crushed after Thermidor. But even before Thermidor it had been crushed, or at least mortally weakened. Popular revolutionism reached its height late in 1793. It was checked, disciplined, and calmed down by the Revolutionary Government itself, following the lead of Robespierre.

The French Revolution was by no means ended at Thermidor. The Revolution survived, but at a certain cost and on certain conditions. One of these was the supremacy of middle-class attitudes. Only the bourgeoisie, outside the aristocracy, was capable at the time of carrying on public business. A revolution, to be successful, was bound to be "bourgeois." This did not mean merely a triumph for a pre-existing bourgeoisie, for indeed many of the old-fashioned *bourgeois* were severely mauled. It meant that a wide variety of people, from government personnel to schoolteachers and landowning farmers, came to share in the advantages of a "bourgeois" society. It carried with it, however, the estrangement, not only of aristocrats, but of the economically most depressed classes and their spokesmen. It prepared the way for an accentuated class conflict after 1830, when the middle and the lower classes, looking back, glorified the Revolution for very different reasons.

The survival of the Revolution in 1794 was purchased also at great cost to the republican idealism for which Robespierre had stood. The Republic after 1794—if not as "cynical" as conservatives, radicals, and high-minded altruists have agreed in alleging—was above all else a government among governments.

If a certain idealism was lost, a powerful image had been created, the vision of a Revolution militant and victorious, of Liberty and Equality marching irresistibly forward. "The Convention," as Alexis de Tocqueville once said in the 1850's, "which did so much harm to contemporaries by its fury, has done everlasting harm by its examples. It created the politics of the *impossible*, turned madness into a theory, and blind audacity into a cult."[37] The Convention was not really so mad or so blind. If it was the Convention that accepted and conducted

[37] A fragment from Tocqueville's unfinished volume on the Revolution, published by J. P. Mayer, ed., *Oeuvres complètes* (Paris, 1951-   ), II, part 2, p. 255.

the Terror, it was also the Convention that called the Terror to a halt. The Convention checkmated the counter-revolution, but the price paid was to turn revolution into a highly charged social myth, which would animate revolution-makers of the future. Revolution became a kind of miracle for the correction of social ills. The Convention even created, for future use, the idea of *gouvernement révolutionnaire*: the theory of a revolutionary dictatorship, exercising special or emergency powers under no controls, as a "temporary" device for the introduction of constitutional government or a new peaceable and secure form of society. That Robespierre and the Revolutionary Government of 1793-1794 genuinely intended their powers to be temporary, "until the peace," cannot be doubted. There was no hypocrisy in this respect. But it seems likely also, as matters actually worked out, that there could have been no transition to constitutional liberties as long as Robespierre lived.

Thermidor in a way was a positive vindication of the Revolution. The basically liberal and constitutionalist ideas of the whole revolutionary era reasserted themselves. For the adherents of monarchy and aristocracy, the Reign of Terror had in fact been a piece of remarkable good fortune. It "proved" what they wanted to know—that a republic, in a large, powerful, and civilized country, was an impossible, anarchic, dictatorial, and bloodthirsty kind of regime. A republic in France that could function without Terror was not exactly what conservative Europe wanted. As the American writer, W. E. B. DuBois, once remarked of South Carolina during Reconstruction: "If there was one thing that South Carolina feared more than bad Negro government, it was good Negro government."[38] Somewhat the same holds for conservative Europe and republican France. If there was one thing that conservatives, at least of the unregenerate kind, wanted less than the Republic with the Terror, it was the Republic without the Terror.

For friends of the French Revolution, in Europe and America, the relaxation of dictatorship and the closing down of the guillotine brought relief. Freed after Thermidor of the incubus of political bloodshed, the Republic became an inspiration for analogous developments in other countries.

[38] *Black Reconstruction in America* (New York, 1935), 428.

VICTORIES OF THE COUNTER-REVOLUTION

IN EASTERN EUROPE

Quis scopus revolutionis Polonicae? . . . *The aristocrats expect an aristocracy to result, the wiser and more enlightened expect a future democracy, the populace and poorer people . . . will seize the land. My own belief is that the beginning was a cloak for the aristocracy, but that the end will be a democracy.*—A HUNGARIAN PATRIOT on the Polish Revolution, 1794

The Russian tsarina, rightly and for the good of Russia and the deliverance of the entire North from the ulcer of French corruption, had to take arms for the pacification of the wanton Warsaw horde established by the French tyrants.—CATHERINE II to Marshal Suvorov, 1794

Hope, for a season, bade the world farewell,
And Freedom shriek'd—as KOSCIUSZKO *fell!*
   —THOMAS CAMPBELL, Edinburgh, 1799

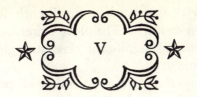

VICTORIES OF THE COUNTER-REVOLUTION
IN EASTERN EUROPE

THE YEAR that saw the survival of the Revolution in France saw its extinction in Poland. The same months in which it became clear that structural changes would spread to Belgium and Holland saw the stamping out of "Jacobinism" in Austria and in Hungary. The present chapter is designed to describe—not the failure of revolution in Eastern Europe, since, except in Poland, no revolution was attempted— but the triumph and strengthening of counter-revolutionary forces in Eastern Europe at this time. These were the forces, agrarian and conservatively aristocratic, which had already largely destroyed the work of Joseph II in the Hapsburg empire, and combined to annihilate the Polish constitution of 1791.

The Problem of Eastern Europe

There are at least two reasons why it is especially difficult for an outsider to reach a firm judgment on the state of Eastern Europe in the 1790's. One is a technical or historiographical reason. Since 1945, both in Russia and in Eastern Germany and the other "people's democracies," there has been a strong movement of revisionism among historical scholars, who have generally operated, or attempted or claimed to operate, within Marxist or "scientific" historical categories. It is stated that bourgeois historiography has been in error on the matter of revolutionary or potentially revolutionary sentiment in Russia and Eastern Europe at the time of the French Revolution. It is held that bourgeois historians—that is, those of Russia, Poland, or Hungary of an older day, and those of the West even now—have through a natural bias underestimated the degree of discontent and rebelliousness in Eastern Europe in the 1790's, that they have focused their attention too much on the upper classes and have minimized the extent to which the lower classes were interested in the French Revolution and dissatisfied in their own countries. The older writers are said to have been blind to the elements of significant class struggle which existed in Eastern Europe before 1800.[1]

The new tendency, therefore, is to collect all possible evidence for revolutionary inclination or class consciousness at a popular level, in which a long background for "people's democracy" in Eastern Europe may be found. The dangers in this tendency are apparent, and the ideological interest is as clear in the case of the new writers as in that of the bourgeois historians. For a Westerner, the evidence is hard to examine because the difficulties presented by the languages are formidable. And yet, while remaining on guard, and pending further elucidation, an American may especially have reason, on somewhat *a priori* grounds, to suppose that the critique made by recent East European historians may have some validity. It is now commonly thought in America, for example, that European university professors in general, and historians in particular, have until recently most often been recruited from the well-established and relatively affluent levels of society. It is increasingly realized, also, how in American historical thinking such matters as Negro dissatisfaction or former slave rebellions long tended to disappear from view. If a Russian historian, such as M. M. Shtrange, tells us that bourgeois historiography has minimized the

[1] Such is the tenor of M. Shtrange, *Russkoye Obshchestvo i Frantsuzkaya Revolyutsiya* (Moscow, 1956), Fr. trans. (note the French transliteration, Strange) *La Révolution française et la société russe* (Moscow, 1960); B. Lesnodorski, in *La Pologne au Xe Congrès International des Sciences Historiques à Rome* (Warsaw, 1955), 212, and the same author in very measured terms in *Polscy Jakobini* (Warsaw, 1960), with a summary in French; A. Korta, "Hugues Kołłątaj et les problèmes sociaux et politiques de la seconde moitié du 18ᵉ siècle," in *Przeglad historyczny*, XLII (1951), which contains several articles on the subject with French summaries; K. Benda, "Les Jacobins hongrois," in *Annales historiques de la Révolution française* (1959), No. 155, 38-60, but apparently less is claimed for revolutionism in Hungary in Benda's introduction to his edition of the sources, *A magyar jakobinusok iratai*, 3 vols. (Budapest, 1952-1957); K. Mejdricka, "Les paysans tchèques et la Révolution française," in *AHRF* (1958), No. 154, 64-74; S. Vianu, "Quelques aspects de l'influence exercée par la pensée progressiste russe sur la société roumaine de la fin du 18ᵉ siècle," in *Nouvelles études d'histoire présentées au Xe Congrès des sciences historiques* (Rome, 1955), 285-97; H. Voegt, *Die deutsche jakobinische Literatur und Publizistik, 1789-1800* (Berlin [East Berlin], 1955); and articles on numerous countries assembled in W. Markov, ed., *Maximilien Robespierre 1758-1794: Beiträge zu seinem 200 Gebürtstag* (Berlin [East Berlin], 1958). I should like to acknowledge the criticisms made of some of my previous writings by Shtrange and Lesnodorski, and make clear that I have no knowledge of East European languages, being indebted to Messrs. Jeffry Kaplow and William Blackwell for digests of work in Russian (including Shtrange's book before its appearance in French), to Mr. André Michalski for a long digest of Lesnodorski's *Polscy Jakobini*, of which a French translation is reported to be underway, and to Mr. Peter Kenez for reading works in Hungarian.

extent of serf uprisings and lower-class discontent there is no inherent reason to disbelieve him.

The other reason why it is difficult to deal with Eastern Europe is that as a cultural area it is impossible to define. Especially in the eighteenth century there were strong ties, reaching the point of close personal' acquaintance and even frequent intermarriage, between the upper classes of Russia and Poland on the one hand and Germany and France on the other. German reached far to the east as a language of business, and French as a language of business, government, diplomacy, and polite intercourse. Books and periodicals in both languages conveyed news and works of literary and intellectual content far into the Eastern plains. Politically, the same government in Vienna ruled over Germans, Slavs, and Hungarians, and the same government in Berlin over Germans and Slavs, even before the Second Partition of Poland, effected in 1793. It must be remembered also that, before the great demographic changes of the nineteenth century, when rural migrants poured into the cities in all areas of Western Civilization, the cities of Eastern Europe were often of different nationality from their surrounding country. If Helsinki was Swedish, and Bucharest partly Greek, most of these urban islands were predominantly German. Thus Riga, Prague, and even Budapest (or rather Buda, which was called Ofen in German) were essentially German colonies of many generations of settlement, maintaining cultural contacts with Germany rather than with the non-German populations within which they were located. Even at Warsaw, Moscow, and St. Petersburg many foreigners could be found both in the government and in the merchant communities.

In basic social structure, eastern Germany merged into Eastern Europe without identifiable boundary. East of the Elbe river the peasantry was unfree. The fact was politically significant, not so much for the weakening of the peasantry, as for the enormous power that it gave the landowning class. The landowner also in a sense owned his tenants, who were subject to his local surveillance and jurisdiction, provided him with labor services which were not compensated in wages, and could neither leave the estate, nor marry, nor enter upon a new occupation without his consent. Increasingly, and notably in Russia, the lords put their laboring people into various new industries and skilled trades, even in distant cities, or in mines, allowing them to receive wages upon the remittance of a fee to their masters. These institutions, which had various legal names, but are called "serfdom" by historians, bore a strong resemblance to the slavery and plantation system of the American South.

The resulting ascendancy of a landowning gentry was made even more marked in Eastern Europe than in the Southern United States by a number of other considerations. Only "nobles" could own rural estates and serfs; or, conversely, all persons qualified to own them were considered "noble." Nobles formed a larger proportion of the population than in Western Europe, a fact which carried with it numerous corollaries; the noble estate included both great magnates and a mass of lesser gentry; the latter were not considered by West European noblemen as their equals; and in Eastern Europe the noble class greatly outweighed and overshadowed the bourgeoisie. Town and country lived under separate legal institutions. Townspeople, nobles, and peasants possessed different kinds of property and different rights, and were subject to different taxes and obligations. A certain qualitative difference between town and country, characteristic of all Europe before the "bourgeois" revolution, was especially accentuated everywhere in Eastern Europe by these fundamental social and legal arrangements. Where, in addition, town and country were also of different language, the difference or indeed the antagonism became even more pronounced. Nobility, peasantry, and bourgeoisie constituted different social classes of an obvious kind—known to all, self-perpetuating, each living to itself, and unchangeable. There was little basis for cooperation or even communication between them. The possibility of change in a West-European direction, "revolutionary" or otherwise, was not very great in a world where gentleman and burgher were strangers to each other, yet both regarded the peasant as a kind of brute.

Perhaps because of the lack of homogeneity within the society, or the presence of deep estrangements, two other kinds of people took on attributes of a social class—kinds not unknown in the West but with their peculiarities heightened in the East—the bureaucracy and the intelligentsia. Both were mainly recruited from the nobility, but occasionally from townsmen. Except within the shrinking confines of Poland, where the reverse was true, the East European monarchies were highly bureaucratic. The Romanov, Hapsburg, and Hohenzollern systems had been put together, partly indeed by war, but largely by élites of government officials, who characteristically had no local roots, were intolerant of local interests, and felt that progress was to be accomplished by working against, not with, the natural inclinations of the peoples over whom they were placed. Since local interests almost always meant the interests of serf-owning nobles, who were usually very impatient of government, this bureaucratic attitude was not without foundation. Educated circles shared in the same psychology. Heavily dependent on foreign books, especially French, to some degree English (and in the Slavic world German books had the same effect), conscious of a certain superiority of other countries over their own (or consciously concerned to deny it), troubled in their own sense of rootedness or identity, lacking respect for their own people and their own society, sometimes working as employees of government, sometimes outside the government but very critical of its operations, these educated circles of Eastern Europe were developing into the group for which Russians in the following century coined the word *intelligentsia*. Bureaucracy and intelligentsia were alike in that they drew their strength not from below but from above or from outside; not from having a mass of followers but from representing authority, the authority of a monarch, or of a doctrine. Both had the psychology of an élite or a vanguard; they knew better than anyone else what was good for the country, and were not disinclined to impose their ideas.

The conflict in Eastern Europe was not between social classes. Or, at least, social classes were not the protagonists. The pattern of a conflict between bourgeoisie and aristocracy, or between new men and old hereditary corporate groups, a pattern that can be seen roughly to fit in Western Europe, is hard to detect in Germany at the close of the eighteenth century, and invisible further east. Burghers and peasants were too weak to engage in any protracted struggle. Measures taken in their behalf were taken by others.

The conflict was between monarchy, bureaucracy, or the intelligentsia on the one hand, and the conservative interests of the serf-owning nobilities on the other. In Eastern Europe, as elsewhere, there was a clash between what may be called democratic and aristocratic principles. These terms themselves were sometimes used. But in Eastern Europe the democratic principle (as in the West, only more so) stressed the equalization of rights more than the liberty of self-government. The democratic principle in Eastern Europe was characteristically upheld, so far as it was upheld at all, by monarchy and its bureaucratic servants or by the intelligentsia either in or out of the government.

Twice, before 1793, there had seemed almost to be a "revolution" in Eastern Europe. The reign of Joseph II in the Hapsburg empire had signalized one such occasion, the Polish constitution of 1791 the other.[2]

---

[2] See *Age*, I, 373-435.

Joseph's attempted reforms had implied a revolution from above; the work of the Four Years' Diet in Poland represented more of a movement from below. But both were revolutionary in their assault on the powers and privileges of the landowning magnates, both involved a strengthening of monarchical government, and both sought to broaden the rights and opportunities of certain disadvantaged categories of people, notably burghers and Protestants, and in the case of Joseph II even the serfs, and even the Jews. Both had failed. In both cases (in the Polish case with Russian and Prussian intervention) the forces of agrarian noble conservatism, allied with certain ecclesiastical powers, had proved stronger than the sponsors of innovation.

The continuation of this story is the theme of the present chapter.

The Impact of the Western Revolution in Russia

Russia in the eighteenth century, behind the facade of its tsarist autocracy, was a country of chronic instability and violence, whose history was a series of palace revolutions and assassinations at the upper level, and of bizarre pretenders and peasant revolts among the common people. The horrors of the Pugachev rebellion of 1773 were not soon forgotten. The better to keep control, the Empress Catherine had issued her Charter of Nobility in 1785, which codified and extended certain liberties of the nobles, including the liberty for them to do as they liked with their serfs. It was precisely at this time that serfdom reached its high (or low) point in Russia. Discontent continued in both the servile and the courtly classes: Catherine's son, Paul I, was assassinated in a palace revolution in 1801, and no less than 278 serf rebellions have been counted for the years 1796 to 1798 alone.[3] The two facts were not unconnected, since Paul, unlike his mother, had shown signs of trying to conciliate the peasants and of opposing the nobles.

With or without events in the West these discords would have continued in Russia. The question is whether they in any way resembled those of Central or Western Europe, and whether a knowledge of the European Enlightenment and the French Revolution acted as a new cause of dissatisfaction, and contributed to a clearer formulation of goals. The best answer seems to be a cautious and indefinite affirmative. Assassination of rulers by noble coteries seems less peculiarly Muscovite when we recall the death of Gustavus III of Sweden in 1792. Noble self-assertiveness, carrying with it a demand for more aristocratic privi-

[3] Shtrange, *Rev. fr. et société russe*, 208. Most of the present section is drawn from Shtrange.

lege, seems quite foreign to the French Revolution, unless we believe, with Mathiez and Lefebvre, that such an aristocratic resurgence was part and parcel, at the beginning, of the French Revolution itself. A rebellion of Russian serfs—desperate, elemental, and negative, stirred up by religious eccentrics and Old Believers, often led by a strange meteoric personage who claimed to be the true tsar and father of his people, and receiving no aid or sympathy from the city-dwellers—was not much like the French peasant uprising of 1789. When we are told that Russian serf uprisings resembled the revolution of the French bourgeoisie in that both were directed against "feudalism,"[4] it is easy to retort that "feudalism" in such a statement has no meaning except in Marxian dialectic. Yet there is a touch of truth in the observation that both French bourgeois and Russian serf opposed a privileged class which was of military and agrarian origin.

In Russia as elsewhere, though starting from a lower base, there was a rapid development of communications in the latter part of the eighteenth century, both within the empire and with Europe. Thirty newspapers and magazines were published in 1789. The censorship sometimes forced them to use guarded language in reporting on the French Revolution; if one read that there had recently been a great change in Paris fashions, one knew that some great political event had occurred. Despite all the difficulties, new papers were also founded, including the *Political Journal* established in 1790. In it one could read, for example, that in 1789 "there originated in Europe the beginning of a new era for mankind," and that this epoch, unparalleled since the Crusades, was "the epoch of adjustment of the position of the so-called lower estates."[5]

With the usual channels for public opinion obstructed by government, and in an atmosphere where knowledge was expected to be the possession of a special few, there developed in Russia, through contacts with Germany and central Europe, a taste for secret and mysterious "enlightenment" or "illumination," the reverse of the publicized and rational Enlightenment that the French *philosophes* preferred. There was a fear of "Martinists," followers of the French writer Saint-Martin, a kind of pietist in religion, some of whose admirers combined an earthly reformism with a peculiar religiosity. Freemasonry spread, and by the 1770's there were three large Masonic lodges in Moscow. A German, a certain Professor Schwarz of the University of Moscow,

[4] *Ibid.*, 209.
[5] Quoted by A. Kaganova, "Frantzuskaya Bourzhuasnaya Revolutziya . . ." in *Voprosi istorii* (1947) No. 7, p. 89.

introduced Rosicrucianism, which in Russia more than elsewhere soon turned into a secret movement for social reform. The Scottish chemist, John Robison, mixed in Masonic circles in St. Petersburg in the 1770's. He found Russian Masonry very different from the British in its commitment to a kind of world salvationism. One night, at midnight, according to Robison's own account, a strange Russian gave him custody of a locked box full of Masonic papers, and thereupon disappeared. Years later he opened it in Edinburgh; and it was from the contents of this box, and from reading the *Neueste Religionsbegebenheiten* published in Germany, that he learned of the Masonic plot for world revolution whose details he purported to reveal, in 1797, in his *Proofs of a Conspiracy against all the religions and governments of Europe, carried on in the secret meetings of Freemasons, Illuminati and reading societies.*[6] Thus Russia in its turn exerted an influence in Western Europe.

It was in the Russian higher classes and literary circles that the impact of the French Revolution was most evident. So much has always been well known. The same circles had shown enthusiasm for the American Revolution also. Alexander Radishchev, when he published his *Voyage from St. Petersburg to Moscow* in 1790, included parts of the ode to liberty that he had written on America several years before; and the whole book was so outspoken in its picture of the brutalities that occurred under serfdom, and so unfavorable to Russian institutions of government, that Radishchev was exiled to Siberia, and is still regarded as the first modern Russian revolutionary. N. I. Novikov was active both in Masonry and in more public ways, editing journals for popular education, such as the *Village Inhabitant*, and helping to organize a public library in Moscow and a school for translators of foreign books. Censored in 1785, obliged to see his school closed in 1787, he was sentenced to fifteen years in prison in 1792. N. M. Karamzin was somewhat exceptional in that, after long travels in Europe, he began after returning home to publish idealized pictures of rural life and serfdom in Russia, for which, however, he was much criticized by more progressive members of the nobility.

Among the high-born who took a positive attitude to new ideas, if not to popular revolution, the most notable were Catherine II's two grandsons, the future tsar Alexander I and his brother Constantine.

---

[6] 4th ed. (Edinburgh, 1798), 1-4. Whatever judgment may be made of his political opinions, Robison was a man of good repute and a credible witness on matters of his own biography, except as his memory may have betrayed him after so many years.

These two young men, at the ages of fifteen and thirteen, were heard to discourse on the abuses of "feudalism"; their tutor, the Swiss La Harpe, was ordered out of the country in 1794, and soon thereafter began to figure in the revolution in Switzerland.[7] Among the nobility, the best known in this connection is Count Stroganov, one of the largest serf-owners in the empire, who as a young man went to Paris with his French tutor, Gilbert Romme. Stroganov belonged to the Paris Jacobin club in 1790, and after Stroganov's return to Russia Romme became a member of the National Convention, where he spoke up in favor of Condorcet's project for public education. When in 1801 Stroganov became one of the circle of reformers about Tsar Alexander I he had not forgotten Romme and Condorcet; and the five new Russian universities created in 1804 embodied Condorcet's ideas.[8] La Harpe also paid a visit to his former pupil in 1801; he now offered the experience of a Swiss revolutionary to the new Tsar who hoped to revolutionize his empire from above.

The penetration of French and revolutionary ideas into the Russian lower classes is insisted on by M. M. Shtrange, the most recent authority on the subject. It must be remembered that "lower" in Russian usage meant anything lower than the nobility; and the "low-born" intelligentsia were mainly middle-class people, though the number of educated and even intellectual serfs (usually belonging to humane families like the Stroganovs), while not large, was increasing. The evidence for this deeper social penetration of the new ideas is to be found in detailed examination of provincial periodicals, in police records on the circulation of forbidden materials, in the surviving caricatures and engravings showing sympathy for the French or dislike of aristocrats, in booksellers' catalogues, and in the perusal of books and pamphlets that have been forgotten because their authors were neither literary nor famous. For example, about 1793 a manuscript pamphlet circulated surreptitiously in Western Russia, called the *Gospel to the Russian Israel*. It declared for the rights of man, questioned the rights of property and of noble distinctions, urged that "all the Russian and Slavic peoples" should be freed from serfdom, and proposed that "all gentry, lords, counts and princes should be universally destroyed."[9] As already men-

---

[7] On La Harpe and Alexander see two articles by L. Mongeon in *Revue historique vaudoise* (1938), 83-102, 129-45.

[8] G. Vernadsky, "Reforms under Czar Alexander I: French and American Influences," in *Review of Politics* (1947), 47-52.

[9] Shtrange, *Rev. fr. et soc. russe*, 196-97.

tioned, some 278 peasant uprisings were recorded officially in thirty-two *guberniyas* of the empire in the later 1790's.

This new insistence, in Soviet historical writing, on the penetration of French, Western, and revolutionary ideas into relatively popular levels tends to confirm, curiously enough, the observations made at the time by the French diplomatic observer, the much decried Edmond Genet. Genet, as French *chargé* and a nobleman himself, mixed readily in Russian court circles, though barred officially from Catherine's presence after the episode of Varennes, and ordered out of Russia in the summer of 1792. Genet was an enthusiast, but not a fool; he saw that all the talk of "liberty" that he heard among the Russian nobility might mean no more than the traditional palace revolution, and that many excited Russian aristocrats admired the Polish revolution more than the French, being more interested in powers for themselves than in rights for others. But Genet thought also, like Professor Shtrange, that the peasants were very restless, and that the growth of schools and of reading habits had created a class of people who "devour the news from France which is published fairly accurately in the Russian magazines." (He was writing in 1791, before the censorship tightened.) "There exists in this empire," reported Genet, "a real germ of democracy."[10] Argument will fall on the dimensions of this "germ."

Further evidence, more open to question, of the spread of unsettling ideas to lower and wider classes of people is furnished by the chorus of conservative writings that pointed to it with alarm. In this flood of literature (as in the corresponding literature of other countries) it was said that cities are parasitic, that city people are dangerous to society because peculiarly susceptible to delusions of equality, that the poor oppose the rich because of envy, and that partisans of new ideas are a half-educated rabble composed of cobblers and lawyers—all of whom looked alike from a social point of view sufficiently elevated. In a book published at St. Petersburg in 1793, called *Thoughts of an Impartial Citizen on the Stormy Changes in France*, concern is especially expressed that the "low-born" intelligentsia are a danger to Russia, since they agitate the whole "third estate." The author sees a danger of international revolution: "The moral epidemic of our present century may have a more rapid success than the plague that ruined Constantinople, and quarantine will be necessary."[11]

[10] Genet to Montmorin, St. Petersburg, Nov. 8, 1791, in *Recueil des instructions données aux ambassadeurs et ministres de France . . . Russie* (Paris, 1890), II, 518-19.
[11] Shtrange, 170-71. Where the French translation reads *classe intellectuelle roturière* I follow my assistant, Mr. Blackwell, in his rendering, "low-born intelligentsia."

Quarantine, indeed, became the watchword. Against what disease? It may be thought, since there was no real possibility of revolution in Russia, and no organized group working for it in any practical way, that the counter-excitement among Russian conservative interests was an outburst of hypocrisy and hysteria. It may be supposed that the idea of quarantine was misconceived, unless we see what it was really directed against. It was really directed against even moderate change— against even partial breaches in the system of serfdom, of noble ascendancy and of a conception of monarchy by which the monarchy should exist to protect these elements in the Russian way of life. Russians who favored even piecemeal changes usually favored the French Revolution. Those who opposed such changes not only opposed the French Revolution, but equated liberalization with revolution and idealized the existing order. They became fearful of secret societies, which did in fact exist and a few of which were subversive, and even were afraid of the public expression of thought, of discussion and disagreement, of news, facts, events in the outside world or contacts with it. The impact of the French Revolution in the 1790's, which in the United States helped to form merely a two-party system, laid the basis in Russia for both revolutionary and counter-revolutionary traditions.

Anti-revolutionism gathered strength and took many forms. Radishchev and Novikov were arrested. Genet and La Harpe were expelled. The assassination of the King of Sweden was attributed to Jacobin plotters. The stories and the theories of French émigrés congregating in St. Petersburg were accepted and publicized. Police action against secret societies and Masonic lodges became more intense; the arrests reached their height between 1793 and 1796. Censorship became more strict, and foreign books and periodicals were banned; the result was a greater circulation of an underground literature of disaffection, both native and foreign.

In the spring of 1792 St. Petersburg was gripped by the fear of an international revolutionary plot against all nobility and all monarchs, a plot in which Jacobins, Freemasons, Martinists, and devotees of occult societies everywhere were said to be involved, and of which the recent deaths of Gustavus III and Leopold II, the continuing revolution in Poland, and the French declaration of war upon Austria were supposed to be evidence. It was reported also that a Frenchman was heading for St. Petersburg with designs on the "health" of the empress.[12] It was at

---

[12] Shtrange, 125ff. It is a matter for conjecture why Shtrange, in describing this scare of April and May 1792, refrains from observing that it was exactly simultaneous with the Russian invasion of Poland.

this time that Catherine II sent her army into Poland. She "would fight Jacobinism and beat it in Poland," according to her own comment to Baron Grimm.[13] The ensuing Second Partition, and the replacement of the Polish constitution of 1791 by the counter-revolutionary constitution of 1793, have been described.

Poland, however, continued to be a center of infection from the point of view of East European conservatism. Indeed, what is generally called the "insurrection" led by Kosciuszko, in 1794, threatened to become more of a "revolution" than anything that Eastern Europe had thus far seen.

The Abortive Polish Revolution of 1794

After the Second Partition the core of the old Poland, a region extending several hundred miles east from Warsaw and Cracow, was still left in existence as a supposedly independent state. Internally it was dominated by the counter-revolutionary party of Targowican Poles. The Russian army remained in occupation at Warsaw under General Ingelström. The new Poland was bound to Russia by a new treaty, which gave the right of entry to Russian troops, and allowed the Russian Empress "any degree of useful influence" that she might require.[14]

The treaty in a rough way resembled the agreements demanded by the French from their satellite republics after 1795. There was a significant difference in the relationship, however, suggesting a difference in the confidence felt by the greater power in its adherents. The French repeatedly urged the Batavian, the Cisalpine, and the Helvetic republics to maintain armed forces of their own. The Russians immediately

[13] Quoted by Lesnodorski, *Pologne au Xe Congrès*, 216.

[14] The treaty is printed in Comte d'Angeberg (pseud. for L. Chodzko), *Recueil des traités, conventions et actes diplomatiques concernant la Pologne, 1762-1862* (Paris, 1862), 347-53. This collection is valuable also for including documents of importance for internal Polish affairs. See also the twenty-four documents printed as an appendix to Zajazek, *Histoire de la Révolution de Pologne par un témoin oculaire* (Paris, 1797). Zajazek (pseud. for Zajoncek) was one of Kosciuszko's chief military subordinates, and was a general in the French army from 1797 to 1814; he served under Bonaparte in Italy and in Egypt and was wounded at Smolensk and at the Beresina in 1812. The present section draws mainly on the important book of B. Lesnodorski, *Polscy Jakobini* (Warsaw, 1960), summarized in detail for me by Mr. André Michalski, and also on H. de Montfort, *Le drame de la Pologne: Kosciuszko, 1764-1817* (Paris, 1945). See also J. Grossbart, "La presse polonaise et la Révolution française," in *AHRF* (1937), 127-50, 241-56; (1938), 234-66. Many documents of the insurrection of 1794 have been published by the Polish Academy of Sciences, unfortunately for foreigners all in Polish: *Akty Powstania Kosciuszki*, 3 vols. (Cracow, 1918-1955). A recent historiographical survey of the whole period 1764-1795 is available in French: B. Lesnodorski, "Le siècle des lumières en Pólogne: l'état des recherches dans le domaine de l'histoire politique, des institutions et des idées," in *Acta Poloniae historica*, IV (1961), 147-74.

began to impose a reduction of the Polish army. Even the Targowicans, the original pro-Russian group, objected to the new situation. They had anticipated neither the Second Partition nor the continued Russian control over what was left of the Polish state, and were increasingly ready, therefore, to take sides with those who had opposed Russia all along.

Many leaders of the defeated party, those who had produced and vainly defended the Constitution of 1791, fled from the country when the Russians came in. An important colony of émigrés formed at Dresden around Ignace Potocki and Hugo Kollontay. The latter, who has been called the Polish Robespierre, had long been active in the Polish Enlightenment and the Four Years' Diet; although himself born into the lesser gentry, he had been among the most vehement in insisting on rights for the burghers in 1791, and was even known to favor an eventual emancipation of the serfs. Other émigrés went to France, among them Thaddeus Kosciuszko. A professional soldier, Kosciuszko had spent seven years in the War of American Independence, after which he returned to Poland and played a secondary military role against the Russian invasion of 1792. He reached Paris in January 1793, at the moment of the execution of Louis XVI. In the following months, with the defection of Dumouriez and the Austrian invasion of France, he was unable to get more than verbal expressions of French sympathy. In fact, by its decrees of April and September the National Convention, as already explained, disavowed any program of "world revolution" that might be read into the so-called Propaganda Decrees of 1792. The fact that the Poles planned to avoid an attack upon Austria, since it had had no part in the Second Partition, made their enterprise of less interest to the French, for whom Austria was at the moment the most dangerous of their enemies.

Throughout 1793, with no loss of time, under the noses of the occupying authorities, a Polish resistance movement formed against them. It arose spontaneously in many places, in secret meetings of angry gentry in country houses, and in the clubs and discussion groups which still existed in Warsaw, where men of noble and burgher status could meet together. The Masonic lodges now proved convenient for this purpose also. The various groups established contact with each other and with the émigrés. Together they began to prepare an armed insurrection, for which they chose Kosciuszko as the leader.

General Ingelström, the Russian commander in Warsaw, obtaining a fragmentary knowledge of the conspiracy, attributed it to French machinations. He made some arrests and ordered the immediate disbandment of certain Polish regiments. The conspirators could wait no longer; they were counting on the organized Polish armed forces to take the first step in revolt; they were obliged to act before their plans were fully laid. Kosciuszko reached Poland early in 1794; and after an uprising at Cracow he was able to defeat a force of Russians at the neighboring village of Raclawice. Upon news of this victory, in April, revolts broke out elsewhere. At Vilna the movement was very strong. The leader, Jasinski, became the best known of Lithuanian "Jacobins," and in their act of adherence to Kosciuszko several hundred citizens of Vilna pledged their "lives and fortunes" to recover "the rights of liberty and equality."[15] The most decisive events occurred in Warsaw. In this city of over 100,000 inhabitants thousands of civilians joined with soldiers in assaults on the Russian troops, making the situation so intolerable for them that Ingelström left the city.

The question now faced by the leaders of the movement, as later by historians in their interpretation of it, was whether it was to be thought of as a war of independence or as a revolution. For Kosciuszko, the problem was to obtain maximum unity among Poles, to give the mass of the people something to fight for. He believed from the beginning that this meant the abolition of serfdom. But abolition of serfdom would offend many estate-owners, whose courage, military experience, and dedication to independence were also needed. If "unity" included the lower classes, the upper class would become disunited. If independence could be obtained only by revolution, some would lose interest in independence. And Polish historians have apparently been divided by the same issues, some preferring to see in the movement of 1794 little more than a national uprising against foreigners, while others find in it, in addition, an attempt to deal with class antagonisms, including serfdom, in Poland.[16]

In a rebellion against foreigners even the disillusioned Targowicans could now take part. Mainly, however, the division was within the ranks of the anti-Russians of 1792, those who had been the constitutionalists of 1791 and the mild "revolutionaries" of the Four Years' Diet. The Right in this group, in 1794, meant those who wished in getting rid of the Russians simply to restore and maintain the constitution of 1791. The Left were those who believed that, if anything at all

[15] Angeberg, 373.
[16] Lesnodorski, 28-86, gives an excellent account of the historiography, including a comment on the work of Jacques Godechot and myself, 83.

were now to be accomplished, much more than what the constitution had envisaged would have to be done. These were the Polish "Jacobins." Since no Pole applied the word "Jacobin" to himself, the term is something of a misnomer, or a mere historian's expression taken over from counter-revolutionary polemics; but we may conclude, with Lesnodorski, that, since many kinds of people called themselves "patriots," and since there did exist a category of militant patriots who resembled those of Western Europe, the word "Jacobin" can be conveniently used as a name for them.[17]

The leader of the Right was none other than the king himself, the pathetic Stanislas Poniatowski, the patriot-king who had virtually written the constitution of 1791, and then been obliged under the most humiliating circumstances to disown it. After the revolt in Warsaw, Stanislas came out openly for the insurrection, hoping both to moderate it and to give it strength by contributing his prestige, which, however dulled, was still royal. Actually, since he had capitulated once before, in July 1792, his return to the patriot ranks inspired little confidence, and indeed aroused typical Jacobin fears of aristocratic conspiracy and royal betrayal. With the king stood various conservative nobles and well-to-do Warsaw burghers, who were ardently anti-Russian, but feared the effects of upheaval among the Polish masses. Friends of the lower classes reciprocated their distrust.

Most of the Polish Jacobins were of the class called noble in Eastern Europe: that is, they came from the middling and lesser landowning families, or from families that enjoyed noble status, but owned no land. Army officers, government employees, lawyers, university people, and others of the professions and the intelligentsia were overwhelmingly of this noble class, and many were "Jacobins" in 1794. Burghers were less numerous in Poland, and not all burghers in the Polish cities were actually Poles; but the Polish bourgeoisie had received important advantages from the Statute of Cities of 1791, which was part of the Constitution of the Third of May, so that the extinction of these gains, in the reaction of 1792 and 1793, left many burghers in a belligerent and angry mood, in which an aggressive Jacobinism was easily generated. The working classes took part only sporadically. On several occasions, in Warsaw, artisans, journeymen, and small shopkeepers demonstrated or fought in the streets, but they neither developed the

---

[17] Lesnodorski, 7-27, has a full discussion of the term "Jacobin" as used in Poland, and an extensive treatment (239-61) of the changing meanings of other words in the Polish language (such as "revolution," "citizen," "people," etc.), summarized below.

organized means of action, nor enjoyed the sustained influence of the French sans-culottes whom as a class they resembled. The peasants contributed no initiatives of their own. We are warned by Lesnodorski against recent tendencies to exaggerate the plebeian element in Polish Jacobinism.[18]

After the Warsaw uprising a club was formed in the city, whose official name was Citizens Offering Aid and Service to the National Magistrates for the Welfare of the Country. Composed of leading patriots in the capital, it revived the club that had been active in 1791 and had disappeared in 1792-1793. It was, in fact, the "Jacobin" club, consciously modeling itself on the club in Paris which was then at its height. It conceived its function to be the surveillance of the new government, and the stimulation of political interest among the people. Moderate patriots feared that the club, by seeking retribution against Targowicans and traitors, would sow division among those now willing to fight against Russia. The king asked Kosciuszko, as recognized dictator, to disband it. It is significant that Kosciuszko concluded that he could not do so, that no dampening of the most ardent spirits was advisable in the circumstances, that what the country needed was precisely the excitement and determination that the club attempted to arouse.[19]

The abundant symbolism of the movement gives evidence of its numerical strength, of the emotional force behind it, and of its affinity to the upheaval in Western Europe. Altars of the fatherland were built, Phrygian caps were worn, and the all-seeing eye of Providence was represented in pictures. Civic hymns were composed and sung. There were new military and marching songs, but the present Polish national anthem, as will be seen, appeared two years later among the Polish Legion in Italy. The *Marseillaise* and the *Ça ira* were translated. Prints and caricatures likewise carried the message to those unable to read. In recent years a good deal of Polish Jacobin poetry has been rediscovered, published, commented on, and admired at least for its political content. One such poem, a *Catechism of Man*, expressed the attitude both to France and to the revolutionary triad:

> France is our example,
> France will be our help;
> Let cries of Liberty and Equality
> Resound everywhere.

[18] Lesnodorski, 27. [19] *Ibid.*, 165-81.

Let us follow in her footsteps . . .
Let the nobles and lords disappear
Who would deny Fraternity to the people.[20]

Further symptoms of a deeper development may be seen in the changes of meaning of certain Polish words, changes such as were occurring in the West European languages also. In the older usage the Polish word for "citizen" (*obywatel*) had referred to nobles only, others being called "inhabitants." A different connotation had been implicit in the constitution of 1791, but it was only in 1794 that "citizen" was applied to virtually everyone. Formerly the "nation" had meant the gentry who sat in provincial diets and took part in political life. Townsmen and serfs had formed no part of this nation; the idea of burghers in the diet, in 1791, had come to many "gentlemen" literally as a shock. Now the "nation" came to signify the Polish people, defined not by linguistic or cultural lines, but as a civic community of harmoniously cooperating classes living under the same laws. The old expression, *pospolite ruszenie*, which had formerly meant the general call to arms of all nobles, now came to mean the *levée en masse*, or mass rising of the people. Such words as "people," "liberty," etc., underwent similar modifications. In this semantic transition, it was the Jacobins who used such words in their most extended and modern sense.

The impression can be ventured, for what it is worth, that "Jacobinism" or the democratic excitement in some parts of Poland, including Warsaw, though much briefer if only because soon repressed, compared in intensity with what happened in Holland beginning in 1795, and with what happened in northern Italy beginning in 1796. In some ways its intensity was greater. The Poles, in driving out the Russians and upsetting the Polish regime which the Russians sponsored, were the only people in Europe who effected so much of a revolution without French help. A furious vindictiveness against "traitors" showed itself also, when a mob broke into a Warsaw prison and hanged eight of the prisoners, six of whom had in fact collaborated with the Russians, including the prince-bishop of Vilna. Since Polish Jacobinism was simultaneous with the triumph in France of the *gouvernement révolutionnaire*, that is, since it came before Thermidor, much sympathy was expressed in Poland for Robespierre and for the Terror, mat-

[20] *Ibid.*, 256, translated by A. Michalski.

ters which the post-Thermidorian Dutch, Italian, Swiss, and other democrats generally avoided as an embarrassment.

The requirements of a war against foreigners, with the need for a maximization of manpower, advanced the principle of equality in a way that was by no means unique for Poland. In France, it had been the war of 1792 that radicalized the Revolution, and the need of raising a citizen army that forced the leadership to make concessions to the lower classes; in America, in 1775, the upper-class colonial leaders, finding themselves at war with Britain, took steps to popularize their cause; and one recalls that few things have done as much for racial equality in the United States as the wars of the twentieth century. "We want to move the whole nation," wrote a Polish diarist of the time, "and therefore an equal freedom is necessary for all classes of people."[21]

In Poland the main problem was serfdom. Kosciuszko, as military commander of the insurrection, vested in fact with the powers of a dictator, had to choose between Right and Left among his supporters— between a Right which said that peasant emancipation would create anarchy at an inopportune moment, and that the peasant question should be regulated after independence was won; and a Left which said that more equal rights for the peasant would never be granted at all after the crisis was passed, and that, in any case, independence could not be won unless the mass of the population was given reason to fight for it. Kosciuszko chose for the Left, pressed by such Jacobin advisers as Kollontay. On May 7, he issued, at his camp at Polaniec, the most memorable document of the abortive Polish revolution of 1794.

The Polaniec Proclamation, though it declared the serfs free, was nevertheless a compromise, by which it was hoped that serf-owners could maintain their zeal for the national movement. It called for a unity of all the people of Poland, blaming the long record of past disunity on the intrigues of foreign courts. If this was an exaggeration, it spared the sensibilities of the Polish nobles. "It is this day and this moment that we must seize with enthusiasm. The enemy deploys all his forces to make us fail. . . . Against this horde of frightened slaves we must set the imposing mass of free men. Victory, we may be sure, will go to those who fight in their own cause." Robespierre had said the same, in effect, on the preceding February 5.[22]

Kosciuszko therefore declared as follows:

"1. The people [including the peasants], by virtue of the law, enjoy the protection of the national government.

[21] *Ibid.*, 218.   [22] The Polaniec Proclamation is printed in Angeberg, 373-79.

"2. Every peasant is free in his person, and may live where he pleases"—but must report his movements to the public authorities.

"3. The days of labor owed by peasants to proprietors are reduced and regulated"—in a complex way, with peasants owing six days a week now obliged only for four, and so in proportion for those owing less. . . .

"5. Men who have been called up in the general levy [the *pospolite ruszenie* mentioned above] are exempted from labor service while under arms; they will not be obligated to it again until they return home."

Much else followed, including appeals to the peasants to continue faithfully at their labors, so that agricultural production could be maintained during the struggle. For the landlords it was revolutionary thus to emancipate their serfs. It was of revolutionary import however considered. If carried through, and reinforced by the rest of the Jacobin program, it might radically transform not only the labor arrangements but many aspects of class status and human relations in Poland. But for the peasants, or those of them who gave it thought, the proclamation seemed grudging and hedged about. It lacked the ringing appeal of true revolutionary declarations. It was too calculated and practical to fire anyone with a passion for combat and sacrifice, too tepid to ignite any mass upheaval.

Fighting against the Russians, and also the Prussians, begun in April, continued into the autumn. Only in a few localities did the peasantry take part. Nothing was created (nor could it have been in the circumstances) like the French citizen army which at the same moment was pushing the forces of the First Coalition back across the Rhine. Tens of thousands took to arms. But the insurrection remained mainly an operation conducted by nobles (it must be remembered that they formed a large proportion of the population) with support from the middle classes, with many Catholic clergy of the lower grades lending aid, and with some participation by non-Polish elements, including the Jews, who were exceptionally numerous in Poland. In the defense of Praga, across the river from Warsaw, a Jewish battalion took part, commanded by a Jewish merchant named Berek Joselewicz, who fled later to the Polish Legion in Italy, and died in 1809 in the service of Napoleon's Grand Duchy of Warsaw. There were many cases in Italy, Holland, and elsewhere of individual Jews favoring the new political order, but Poland seems to offer the only case of an organized Jewish body, and an armed one at that, acting in support of the eighteenth-century revolution.

The Poles made attempts to propagandize in neighboring countries. The Polish Jacobins, like those of France in 1792, entertained a generous hope for the liberation of mankind. They drew confidence in the strength of their own cause by identifying it with both the French and the American revolutions, as in the *Civic Sermons* of a certain priest, Father Florian Jelsky.[23] Kosciuszko himself, who was not a Jacobin but inclined in that direction, believed that the liberation of Russia might be a necessary prerequisite to freedom in Poland. Emissaries were sent to Hungary, where opposition to the Hapsburgs was chronic, and where a Jacobin conspiracy was discovered in July 1794. Revolutionary literature was translated into Russian and German, and used to subvert the enemy armies. The national insurrection, and the revolutionary agitation which accompanied it, communicated itself to the former parts of Poland which the Russian and Prussian monarchies were barely beginning to organize after the Second Partition. Unrest spread even to Silesia, which had belonged to Prussia for fifty years.

There can be no doubt that Poland was a menace to the three eastern monarchies as they then existed, more of a menace even than distant France. Even a restored Constitution of 1791 might cause restlessness in Breslau, Lemberg, or Prague. A successfully established civil community on a Jacobin model might have less appeal; but the mere mention of the abolition of serfdom was enough to annoy landlords all over Eastern Europe; it might set a bad example for peasants everywhere, and remind those of Bohemia and Hungary of what they had won and lost under Joseph II; it might even infect the enlisted ranks of the Austrian, Prussian, and Russian armies. The governments of these empires were not mistaken in the belief that the new Poland was a country they could not live with, at least without some modification in their own.

The denunciations of Jacobinism in Poland were no mere high-sounding justifications for territorial ambition. They did indeed serve that purpose. But when we find the rulers of Russia and Prussia expressing their dread of Jacobinism in Poland, not only in public to the world at large, or to the British government, but privately to their own confidential and trusted servants, we have more reason to accept such sentiments as genuine. "I feel keenly," wrote the King of Prussia to his ambassador at Vienna, referring to the insurrection in Poland,

[23] Lesnodorski, 210, 278.

"how essential it is to crush in its germ this new and dangerous revolution, which touches so closely on my own states, and which is also the work of that diabolical sect against which a majority of the powers have combined their efforts."[24] And Catherine II wrote to Marshal Suvorov that, "for the good of Russia and the entire North [as much of Eastern Europe was then called] she had to take arms against the wanton Warsaw horde established by French tyrants."[25]

The military power of the Russians and Prussians soon prevailed. In October Kosciuszko lost the battle of Maciejowice. He was taken prisoner, but soon managed to flee with his friend Niemcewicz to America, where Niemcewicz lived for years with an American wife in New Jersey. Hugo Kollontay, after desperate last-minute efforts to arouse the peasants by adding redistribution of land to emancipation, was also captured, and spent several years in prison in Austria.

Suvorov, fresh from the wars against the Turks, on November 3 occupied Praga, a suburb of Warsaw, and, though the battle and the whole war were decided, allowed his troops to slaughter six thousand civilians crowded against the river in full sight of the inhabitants of the capital. Polish nationalists long remembered this dénouement as a "massacre." On the same day the claimant to the throne of France, Louis XVIII, having received news at Verona of Kosciuszko's defeat by the Russian General Fersen, wrote humorously to a feminine correspondent: "I should like to establish a chair for professors of anti-republicanism in some university, and make this General Fersen the first incumbent."[26] The three monarchies moved in and effectuated the Third Partition. That was the end of Poland, and of revolutionary threats in Eastern Europe—for a long time.

The failure of the Polish effort in 1794 has been attributed to many causes, of which the overwhelming might and the mutual rivalries of the surrounding powers would not be the least. The misfortune of Poland, however, lay in its internal divisions, which no institutional superstructure had been devised to overcome. There were ethnic divisions, whereby in large parts of the country only the ruling nobles were Polish, divisions and rivalries within the large and scattered Polish nobility, divisions between classes, and especially between free men and serfs. Given these circumstances, it was probably true that national

[24] Quoted by Lesnodorski in *Pologne au Xe Congrès*, 216.
[25] Quoted by P. K. Alefirenko in *Istoricheskiye Zapiski* (1947), 236.
[26] See Montfort, *Drame de la Pologne*, p. 246 for the slaughter at Praga, and p. 242 for Louis XVIII's letter. General Fersen, of the nobility of the Baltic provinces of Russia, was unrelated to Axel de Fersen.

independence could not be maintained without some kind of internal revolution. But the same internal divisions made successful revolution impossible. It was the tragedy of the Poles, in the 1790's, that, to exist as a state at all, they had to challenge, without hope of success, the social order of Eastern Europe.

It is well to give attention to what succeeded, rather than to what failed. The three eastern monarchies, in annexing their several portions of Poland, established a mutual interest in the continuing repression of revolution. They committed their own survival to the exclusion of "Western" ideas. In the long run, they only became the more susceptible to collapse in the twentieth century. In the short run, certain features of the European scene that are often dated from the Congress of Vienna can be more justly dated from the 1790's. In a way not true of preceding centuries, a chasm between Eastern and Western Europe had opened up—between a West that had been animated by "Jacobinism" and an East which, in repressing Jacobinism so successfully, became timorous and immobile, fearful of the future, and afraid of the modern world. This development was furthered by what happened in the Hapsburg empire.

Agitations in the Hapsburg Empire

It has often been observed, since Pascal's remark on Cleopatra's nose, that in human affairs, unlike the world of physical objects, causes and effects and other relationships may be fantastically disproportionate. The reminder is useful in approaching the Danubian countries. In Vienna and its appertaining duchies, and in the Kingdoms of Hungary and Bohemia, we enter a world with a character its own, in which, if a select few responded to the music of Mozart, the surrounding atmosphere was a kind conveyed in later times by the ideas of Graustark, Dracula, and the Orient Express. In the division between noble landowner and agricultural serf, the empire resembled other parts of Eastern Europe, but Italian connections were strong (Leopold II had spent most of his life as grand duke of Tuscany, where his son Francis II had grown up), and above all it was the German influence that predominated. The higher government was more German than anything else, and the towns also were mainly German, from Bohemia through Hungary into the elbow of Transylvania, where Klausenburg (the modern Cluj) and Kronstadt (the modern Brasov) remained German after a period of settlement longer than the entire history of the United

States. Neither the Czechs nor the Hungarians had yet developed a literary language, and they depended on German; but the Hungarian nobles, many of whom knew little else, actually spoke and wrote Latin as a common medium of expression, like the Poles a generation or two before. It was a world in which German Masonic lodges became even more occult and mysterious, where popular religion tended to weirdness and disguised Jesuits could really exist, where hidden revolutionaries conspired with a minimum of political purpose, and a truly secret police pursued its habits of intrigue. It was a region not easy to understand for anyone accustomed to French rationality or Anglo-Saxon common sense.[27]

Three points must be made. First, there was a good deal of basic disaffection in these Hapsburg countries in the 1790's. Second, Jacobin conspiracies were formed in Vienna and Hungary in 1794. Third, it was an extreme form of socio-political conservatism that won out. The three stood in no proportionate relationship to each other. The Jacobin conspiracies were fairly insignificant. Contrived by handfuls of intelligentsia, they were far from reflecting the broad discontents that were real enough. Among historians there have been attempts, on the Left, to set up the Jacobins of 1794 as spokesmen of a latent revolutionism, or predecessors of the revolution of the twentieth century, and, on the Right, to suggest that because the conspiracies were small and ineffectual there was little real dissatisfaction in the empire. The repressiveness that came to prevail was also out of proportion to any danger posed by the Jacobin plots. It might logically seem, therefore, that the repressiveness was hypocritical or hysterical, or that the social order of the Hapsburg empire was threatened by nothing at all. None of these allegations seems to be true. Pascal's principle of disproportion may save us from the errors of misplaced logic.

What happened was a continuation, very much accentuated by the war against France, of the conflict described in the first volume of this book, between the attempted revolution from above under Joseph II and the aristocratic counter-attack that gathered strength during the reign of his brother, Leopold II.

[27] For the Hapsburg empire see, in addition to items by Benda and Mejdricka in note 1 of the present chapter, E. Wangermann, *From Joseph II to the Jacobin Trials: Government Policy and Public Opinion in the Habsburg Dominions in the Period of the French Revolution* (Oxford, 1959); Denis Silagi, *Ungarn und der geheime Mitarbeiterkreis Kaiser Leopolds II* (Munich, 1960) and *id., Jakobiner in der Habsburger-Monarchie: ein Beitrag zur Geschichte des aufgeklärten Absolutismus in Österreich* (Vienna and Munich, 1962); and parts of F. Valjavec, *Die Entstehung der politischen Strömungen in Deutschland, 1770-1815* (Munich, 1951).

Dissatisfaction was to be found among both burghers and peasants. The nobles also had their grievances against a government that had undertaken so many reforms, especially in Hungary, where the lesser Magyar nobility had developed a strong nationalistic feeling against the Hapsburg court. A further source of unrest lay in the Protestant minorities of Hungary and Bohemia, which had been reduced to inferior status by the Catholic triumphs of the Counter Reformation; in Hungary the Protestants might be relatively enlightened burghers, but in Bohemia they included many rude country people subject to queer notions of what happened in the outside world.

There had been a mass peasant rebellion in Hungary as recently as 1790 and in Bohemia as recently as 1775.[28] Government and landowners rightly feared renewed outbreaks. For the most part the middle class townspeople, radically set apart from the peasants by language and culture, and debarred from common interests with them because unable to own rural land, were as horrified as their social superiors by such nameless stirrings of thousands of Calibans. The peasants, however, were not totally isolated. In Hungary there is evidence that Leopold II himself stirred up rural protest, as part of his campaign against the Magyar nobles. News of the French Revolution reached the villages. As elsewhere, priests or tavern-keepers read aloud from newspapers to their illiterate neighbors. What the peasants talked about was less the declared principles of the new France than the fact that in France peasants had revolted, and that seigneurial dues and tithes had been done away with. Peasants of the Hapsburg countries had been made conscious of their even heavier burdens, especially the labor service or *robot* that might be as much as six days a week, by the attempts of Maria Theresa and Joseph II to bring it under regulation. They knew about Joseph II's granting of personal freedom. Agrarian discontent was directed against immediate and visible targets—nobles, burghers, churchmen, and Jews—but seldom against the Emperor, who was seen as the loving father of his people. The feeling was confused and amorphous; after the war began it was said that the French would come someday, bringing liberation; but there were also Biblical prophecies and visions to the same effect; and it was thought also, in some quarters,

[28] For the Hungarian peasant rising of 1790 see *Age*, I, 392-93. The present paragraph draws on K. Mejdricka's two articles, "Les paysans tchèques et la Révolution française" in *Annales hist. de la Rev. fr.*, No. 154 (1958), 64-74, and "Die Jakobiner in der tschechischen öffentlichen Meinung" in W. Markov, *Robespierre* (Berlin, 1958), 423-39, and on F. Kutnar, "La critique de la Rev. fr. dans les brochures tchèques d'alors," in *Le Monde slave*, I (1935), 131-58.

that Joseph II was not really dead, and would return. The peasants objected both to conscription and to the war against France. There was a near revolt in 1797, when a group led by Protestant sectaries conspired to evade military service; in this case, somewhat exceptionally, a Slovakian burgher named Michal Blazek was involved, and was found to have Latin and Hungarian pamphlets originating with the Hungarian Jacobins in his possession. The peasants expected more from the Directory than from previous French regimes, being more aware of its military successes than of its "bourgeois" character. The Austrian general, the Archduke Charles, sojourning on his Bohemian estates in 1800, declared that nine-tenths of the people wanted the French to arrive. "In the country they all say: let them come and we will kill the lords and pay no more. In the towns they all say: let them come and occupy Vienna so that we can have peace."[29] In the following years there continued to be sympathy for Napoleon, who, according to some, was really the avenging son of Joseph II.

In Bohemia practically everyone of the literate classes was afraid of the peasants, and an active counter-revolutionary literature developed, replete with the niceties of argument of Edmund Burke, whose *Reflections* were read in Gentz's German translation. Existing society was said to be natural, necessary, and organic, and the ideas of the French Revolution were described as abstract and mechanical. The Revolution itself was attributed to ambitious upstarts, and to the machinations of secret societies. A certain Cornova, who was both an ex-Jesuit and a Freemason, wrote a history of insurrection in Bohemia to show how all classes suffered alike. Peasants were wrong to be so chronically discontented, said a theology professor at Prague, because they had the happiness of living close to nature. They were mistaken, said a writer named Vivak, in expecting anything of the French, who, if they came, would bring nothing but desolation, barbarity, and atrocity. The frequency with which these writings justified the *robot*, as a mere legitimate return on property, suggests how heavily it was under fire.

The Czech national revival was then barely beginning, and its spokesmen feared that disputes over social problems would interfere with the national movement. One of its leaders, V. M. Kramerius, edited the first successful popular journal in the Czech language. He gave detailed attention to the French Revolution, but his purpose was to present it as sinister and destructive. He made no mention of the abolition of seigneurial dues, but dwelt on the downtrodden state of peasants in

[29] Quoted by Mejdricka in *AHRF, loc.cit.*, 72.

France, besides whom, he declared, the Bohemian peasant lived as a veritable "count." He developed a kind of demographic theory of the Revolution: France in the eighteenth century had become overpopulated; and its National Assembly, having purposely decided to conquer territory in Europe, had invented slogans of liberty and equality to soften up neighboring peoples for subjugation.[30]

The upper classes of the towns had reasons for looking on events in France with favor. In Hungary they were very weak. In Bohemia their voice was muted by ethnic fears and problems; but it seems significant that the only literate Bohemian known to have strongly sympathized with the French Revolution was a banker, J. F. Opiz, who in his private correspondence expressed the hope that the French would defeat the Coalition and justified the Reign of Terror.[31] In the solidly German areas the position of the burghers was less precarious. A certain political consciousness developed at Vienna. It included a class consciousness, which the program of Joseph II had done much to arouse. Mozart thought himself as good as any count, and he approved of the social message of Beaumarchais' *Marriage of Figaro* when he set it to music. As early as 1790 his librettist, da Ponte, was ordered out of the country, with a number of other Italians and Frenchmen, whose views were thought unsuitable by the police. The governments of Joseph and Leopold, the examples of "enlightened despotism" *par excellence*, intended to keep careful rein over the privileged classes and so were willing to equalize the status of peasants and burghers within certain limits; but it was no part of their program to do away with nobility itself, and still less to surrender any authority. Non-nobles, however, especially among intellectuals, journalists, and government officials in the capital, were beginning to outgrow the mere paternalism of enlightened despotism, to demand more latitude for expression, discussion, and debate, more freedom from censorship and from guidance by the police, more opportunity in their careers and even more of a role in decisions affecting taxation, foreign policy, and war. The idea got abroad that absolutism should be checked, not merely by the privileged classes, the nobility, and the prelates—the old idea in the Hapsburg empire as elsewhere—but also by persons of suitable substance who did not happen to belong to the aristocracy.[32]

---

[30] On Kramerius see Mejdricka in Markov, *Robespierre*, 426-30, and Kutnar, 135.

[31] Mejdricka in Markov, 435-38.

[32] Wangermann, *From Joseph II to the Jacobin Trials*, 5-35. For the state of political feeling in Vienna see also W. C. Langsam, "Emperor Francis II and the Austrian 'Jacobins,'" in *American Historical Review*, L (1945), 471-90.

It was discontent among nobles that any monarchy viewed with really serious concern. Leopold II, on coming to the throne in 1790, had found the nobilities of his duchies and kingdoms in a state of rebellion, in consequence of Joseph's reforms of serfdom and his movements toward equality of legal penalties and taxation. The years beginning with 1790 were a time of revival of the traditional constitutionalism, that is, of the powers of the diets as against the ruler. These diets were bodies of nobles. In part because of religious troubles two centuries before, and in part because of agrarian predominance in the society, the burghers had long ago been excluded. In the diet of Bohemia no city was represented except Prague. In the lower house of the Hungarian parliament only one person represented all the towns of Hungary. In the estates of Styria one person spoke for all the towns of that duchy, and cast one vote. In such conditions even the Polish constitution of 1791 might seem attractive to the bourgeoisie. The Styrian burghers were the most successful in their protests, because they were able in a measure to make common cause with the peasantry; and they could do this the more readily because the duchy was ethnically homogeneous, town and country alike being German. In Styria, Leopold ordered the representation of the Third Estate raised from one to ten. On the whole, the revival of the diets marked a victory for aristocratic counter-revolution in the Hapsburg empire.[33]

On the aims and personality of Leopold II there has been much discussion, because he made it a matter of policy to be devious. The best explanation is that he continued to represent, like his brother Joseph, the idea of revolution from above.[34] As Emperor, he favored for the whole empire the kind of modernization for which he had worked for many years as Grand Duke of Tuscany, and was therefore in conflict with the aristocratic, privileged, ecclesiastical, and particularistic forces in his dominions. But his position was complicated by the fact that he came into conflict with "democratic" forces also. It was not only that political journalism and criticism of government were developing in Vienna. There seemed also to be an international secret democratic conspiracy against all kings, himself included. In June 1790, as already noted in Chapter II, Leopold received word from the elder Metternich at Coblenz, a gathering-place of French émigrés, that a *club de propa-*

[33] *Age*, I, 384-97.
[34] Here I follow D. Silagi (note 27 above) and A. Wandruszka, "Die Persönlichkeit Kaiser Leopolds II," in *Historische Zeitschrift*, Vol. 192 (1961), 295-317; Wangermann and certain writers of the Left are less inclined to credit Leopold's commitment to a "democratic" revolution from above against the *Ständestaat*.

gande was at work in Paris to bring about revolution in other countries. The idea of a great secret international Jacobin conspiracy began to spread. It had been launched by a fabrication of the royalist Comte d'Antraigues. Even the astute Leopold II, with his supposed Italian cunning, did not altogether see to the bottom of these intrigues, or perceive that the idea of a great democratic conspiracy was actually only another weapon in the hands of his real adversaries, the aristocratic and privileged classes. He began to take steps for a quarantine against the revolutionary contagion. In his Declaration of Pillnitz he spoke of intervention in France under certain conditions. This trend of his policy met with opposition among his own subjects. In Austria as elsewhere many enlightened middle-class people, not to mention the peasants, disapproved of interference with the French Revolution, and of the war against it which might result.

Leopold, beset on all sides, both by aristocrats and by democrats, built up his own network of secret agents. It was largely from the personnel of this network that both the Austrian and the Hungarian "Jacobins" were to arise.[35] In part the secret police watched over democrats; they censored newspapers, and expelled troublesome foreigners like da Ponte. Mainly, however, under Leopold as under Joseph, the secret police was an agency of the enlightened and reforming state. The weakness of enlightened despotism was that its reforms could be carried through only by bureaucrats; and that the bureaucrats were overwhelmingly drawn from the very privileged classes whose privileges enlightened despotism sought to reduce. Bureaucrats and officials were therefore often slow in the carrying out of their orders. The main task of Leopold's secret police was the surveillance of the bureaucracy itself.

The point is illustrated by Leopold's dealings with L. A. Hoffmann, editor of the *Wiener Zeitschrift*.[36] Hoffmann knew a great deal about the more recondite branches of Masonry, including its offshoot the Illuminati, who had been defunct for several years. Their machinations, he claimed, were the true cause of the French Revolution. He was willing enough, however, to see such methods employed to advance the Revolution from Above. Under Leopold's instructions, he began in 1791 to organize an Association with a hierarchy of four levels of secrecy. The lowest "secret" was to combat the French Revolution, to inculcate obedience in the people, and obtain "a more secure balance

[35] This point, though not unknown before, is developed with new evidence, and with a new fullness and significance, in the two books by Silagi mentioned in note 27 above.

[36] Silagi, *Ungarn*, 108-16, 128-31.

between moderate monarchism and democratism." The next higher secret was to oppose "aristocratism" so far as it obstructed the plans of the government. The "highest secret" was to bring the crown prince, Francis II, to these views; and the top secret of all, the *allergeheimster Zweck*, was to exert an influence on foreign states. In the whole program, and especially in the idea of propagandizing in foreign countries, Leopold and Hoffmann proposed to do precisely what they imputed (perhaps "projected" is the modern psychologist's term) to the leaders of the Revolution in France. It was the second level of secrecy that was closest to Leopold's continuing interests—the campaign against "aristocratism" within his own empire. He hoped to strengthen the bureaucracy whose inadequacy had caused the failure of Joseph's plans; to infiltrate the government service with secret members of his Association, men known only to each other, a disciplined elite with shared ideas, responding to confidential directives, inspecting, reporting on, and driving forward the ordinary employees of government; working, in short, for a Revolution from Above, and in effect realizing what the Illuminati had vainly dreamed of. Hoffmann managed to recruit various persons for the Association, including several professors and a Hanoverian doctor, J. G. R. Zimmermann, who was a personal physician to the King of England. But Leopold died before the Association could be really formed, and with his death it was forgotten.

Meanwhile the ordinary police pursued similar aims. If by "Jacobins" in Austria and Hungary are meant the conspirators of 1794, then the most notable of them originated in the secret police under Leopold II in 1790 and 1791, and not merely because of a taste for conspiratorial action, but because there was in fact an affinity between the Revolution from Above and straight revolutionism, or between enlightened despotism and "Jacobinism," in that both found their enemies in the nobility and in the prelates of the church. It was possible, therefore, for a man of some principle both to work for the police under Leopold and to conspire against his successor. But among those whose services the police accepted were also various opportunists and adventurers. The most extreme of these was Ignaz Martinovics, who ended his life as the chief Hungarian Jacobin.

Both the actual facts of Martinovics' career, and the wild imaginings which he declared to be true, suggest a wonderland in which the difference between probable and improbable has disappeared.[37] Born

---

[37] On Martinovics see Silagi, *Jakobiner*, 65-86 ff.; but I am especially indebted to an unpublished senior thesis at Princeton University, by Peter Kenez, "The Con-

in Hungary of Serbian background, trained for the church but a declared atheist, at one time the friend of the Polish patriot Ignace Potocki, for several years professor of natural sciences at Lemberg, by his own avowal a philosopher of international repute, but pronounced incompetent by the faculty at Budapest after deliberate consideration, Martinovics was pretty clearly a megalomaniac and pathological liar, who in 1791 began to work for the Vienna police. He became the panegyrist of Leopold II, and, as such, in denouncing the resistance of privileged bodies, could even say a good word for the French Revolution;[38] but mostly he spied on the disaffected Hungarian nobles, and submitted reports on revolutionary conspirators. In these reports, unlike those of the Abbé Barruel a few years later drawn from somewhat similar sources, numerous Jesuits and high-churchmen were as dangerous as Freemasons and Illuminati. The Belgian van Eupen, for example, a canon of the cathedral at Antwerp, was a real person and a real intriguer, one of the Statist party in the Austrian Netherlands, and a confirmed clerical reactionary. His name haunts Martinovics' pages as that of an incorrigible revolutionary, endlessly scheming against the Hapsburgs Joseph and Leopold. It is doubtful that Leopold's police believed much of the phantasmagoria that Martinovics submitted to them. Who could believe, even in Europe in 1792, that a combination of Jesuit theocrats, Illuminati, Freemasons, the Abbé Maury, itinerant Poles, and subversive Americans was at work to overthrow kings, priests, and aristocrats, turn the Holy Roman Empire into a republic, give all Europeans equal access to India, introduce Cagliostro's projects at Rome, where the papacy would disappear, and "put all states on the footing of North America"?[39]

The Jacobin Conspiracies at Vienna and in Hungary, 1794

Leopold II died in March 1792. His successor, Francis II, though more conservative and aristocratic in his sympathies than his father,

spiracy of the Intellectuals: the Hungarian Jacobin Movement" (1960), which draws on the documents published by K. Benda, *A magyar jakobinus mozgalom iratai*, 3 vols. (Budapest, 1952-1957). This work is edited in Hungarian, but many of the documents are in German and Latin.

[38] "Oratio pro Leopoldo II," Benda, 1, 559. Here *tota Europa* admires the "metamorphosis" in France against "magnates and monopolists," but about the same time (Benda, 575), Martinovicz expressed to Leopold the more characteristic attitude of supporters of enlightened absolutism: "The Americans and the French made good laws through bloody upheavals, but Your Majesty, without any revolution, has made laws which the learned world marvels at, and humanity adores."

[39] Martinovicz' reports to the police chief Gotthardhi, Benda, 1, 440-507 and 787-89. The quotation is from 788.

was a young man of more straightforward personal character, and dis-approved of using police spies in the same way. War with France began in the following month. The war was not popular in many middle-class and intellectual quarters. To support it, Francis II had to rely on the aristocracy of his empire. Anti-French and anti-Revolutionary propa-ganda increased. Men who had worked for Leopold's police found themselves distrusted, rejected, or unemployed. In addition, as con-cessions to the aristocracy and to political churchmen multiplied, and as a clamorous conservative ideology became dominant, people who supported the progressive programs of Joseph and Leopold—the so-called Josephinists of Austrian history—became increasingly frustrated. Two years passed, and in the spring of 1794 the French armies were victorious in Belgium, and the Poles under Kosciuszko seemed on the point of victory also. It was in these circumstances of frustration sud-denly buoyed up by hope that the Jacobin conspiracies took form in Vienna and Hungary.

The Vienna conspiracy amounted to very little. The accomplices had casual contacts with the burghers of Styria but none with the peasantry or with the simultaneous conspiracy in Budapest. Nor did they have any ties with France. No Frenchman was ever found in any contact with either the Austrian or the Hungarian "Jacobins."

At Vienna the conspiracy began when an emissary of Kosciuszko, Count Soltyk, came to Austria to seek support for the Poles. He met a Protestant pastor named Held, who introduced him to a former army officer named Hebenstreit. Hebenstreit had worked for the police under Leopold, and was at odds with the reigning society at Vienna. He in fact hoped that the French would win the war. He was also something of an inventor, who had developed a new contrivance for defense against cavalry. He put his idea at the disposal of Soltyk, who sent it on to Kosciuszko, and who also, at Hebenstreit's insistence, provided the money for Held to make a secret trip to Paris to offer this military invention to the French. Held made the trip, successfully passing through the enemy lines and reaching Paris; but the Committee of Public Safety, far from welcoming either the invention or the ap-proaches of an Austrian revolutionary society, put Held under arrest as a suspicious enemy alien. Meanwhile, in Vienna, his associates met in small discussion groups and circulated literature hardly aimed at the lower classes, since Paine's *Rights of Man* was passed around in French, and one of Hebenstreit's contributions, a long poem called *Homo hominibus*, was written in Latin. More popular pamphlets were composed by Andreas Riedel, former professor of mathematics, former tutor to Francis II, and former agent of Leopold's police.[40]

The conspiracy in Hungary had more roots. Here, as in Poland, a national feeling gave body to a potential movement of political revolution. The small nobles or gentry were especially restless, regarding the higher and more cosmopolitan aristocracy, the magnates and prelates, as sold out to the court of Vienna. They blamed the Hapsburg government for its trend to centralization and Germanization, and above all for its attempts to interfere with their free control over their serfs. The makings existed here for a national revolution of marked conservative and agrarian social content.

There were also smaller groups, with very different objectives, who favored reform and Westernization in Hungary. Intellectuals, lawyers, government employees, they regarded the Magyar nobility as backward and narrowly selfish; most of them were themselves nobles (since the noble class in Hungary was far more numerous than the burghers), but some were from the towns, and some were Protestants. (The names are known of about 700 Hungarian Protestants who attended German and Swiss universities in the half-century after 1750.) In the 1780's these men supported Joseph II, and from 1790 to 1792 some of them worked for the government or the secret police under Leopold. The accession of Francis II, and the beginning of war with France, for the first time estranged many of them from the authorities at Vienna. Some were not estranged, but remained faithful to the idea of imperial centralization; this was especially true of non-Magyars such as Samuel Kohlmayer, a lawyer from an old German burgher family in Pest. Kohlmayer disliked the Magyar nobility, suspected Hungarian nationalism, joined Leopold's secret police, wanted immediate abolition of serfdom, and was generally more radical than those who turned Jacobin. Ethnic Hungarians who shared Kohlmayer's anti-aristocratic views found it easier to cut the tie with Vienna. For example, Kohlmayer's friend, Joseph Hajnoczy, the son of a Calvinist minister, was able, thanks to Joseph II's policies, to become the first non-noble to hold the office of vice-sheriff in a Hungarian county. He lost it in the aristocratic reaction after Joseph's death, which was unfavorable both to non-nobles and to Protestant.. He became the

---

[40] Wangermann, 132-38. For an unflattering picture of the personalities involved see also Silagi, *Jakobiner*, 161 ff. Excerpts from three of Riedel's writings are published in the appendix to Valjavec, *Entstehung*.

leading non-noble among the Hungarian Jacobins, most of whom, as already said, were of the noble or gentry class themselves.

To a larger mass of Hungarian nobles, who were hostile to the Hapsburg dynasty anyway, were therefore added smaller circles who turned against it because they opposed the increasingly aristocratic trend of its policies. Together they formed an incipient party of Hungarian revolution and independence. They expressed their feelings in clubs and reading societies, and in demonstrations of enthusiasm for France and its revolution. They read and translated the Paris *Moniteur.* They sang the *Ça ira* and translated the Marseillaise into Latin, Hungarian, and Slovakian.[41] Ferenc Szentmarjay, well known as one of the creators of the Hungarian written language, made the first Hungarian translation of Rousseau's *Social Contract* (which had been known in Latin before); in doing so, he designed the modern Hungarian terms for *citoyen, peuple, souveraineté, égalité,* etc. Revolutionary tracts appeared in Serbo-Croatian, and at the University of Zagreb the students affected short Jacobin haircuts and planted a liberty tree in 1794 at the time of the French victories, nailing the words "Liberty and Equality" to its trunk. When French prisoners of war were brought to Hungary for internment, Hungarian sympathizers flocked to meet them. Szentmarjay traveled fifty miles to see these Frenchmen, embraced a few of them, it is said, with tears in his eyes, and obtained from them a small tricolor which he kept as a kind of idol, allowing others to see it only if they would kneel before it in reverence.

For the Vienna government these widespread agitations, at the least, were a serious handicap to its war effort, and, at the most, a threat to the continuation of Hungary in the Hapsburg empire. The police therefore infiltrated the excited Francophiles. Among their operatives was Martinovics, who managed to retain his position after Leopold's death. It is clear from the documents published by Kalman Benda that Martinovics, in 1793, was a double or triple agent. He simultaneously spied and reported for the police, and moved as a comrade among the revolutionary group, or rather the two groups, the conservative and nationalist nobles, and the more radical political ideologists. In 1794, as his position with the police became more uncertain, and with what seemed to be the great revolutionary victories in France and Poland, Martinovics went over, at least temporarily, to the revolution in Hungary. Making use of a genuine movement that he had in no sense created, and taking advantage of men like Hajnoczy and Szentmarjay,

[41] Benda, I, 1,049-54.

men of far more character and principle than himself, he began to organize an actual rebellion against Vienna. He impressed his Hungarian friends, most of whom were fairly unsophisticated, by boasting of his important connections in France with the Committee of Public Safety. Actually he had no such connections. The revolutionary government in France had nothing to do with the projected revolution in Hungary.

Facing the fact that there were two kinds of potential revolutionaries in Hungary, the nationalist aristocratic and the equalitarian Jacobin, Martinovics brought to the problem a simple solution. He organized not one secret society but two: one for the nobles, and one for persons who did not believe in nobility. The former he called the Society of the Reformers of Hungary; the latter, the Society of Liberty and Equality. As a revolutionary tactician, he devised an expedient unparalleled in the eighteenth century for its "realism," except in the plans of Babeuf: one society should have no inkling of the other's existence; its members, having joined in the revolution and served their purpose, should later simply be liquidated. It was the noble society of Reformers who were thus marked in Martinovics' plan for extinction. When Hajnoczy and some of the democrats protested, they were told that such methods were necessary. The idea was not new to Martinovics in 1794; in his wild fabrications, he had accused the Jesuits of a similar manipulation three years before.

For each society he wrote a separate call to arms, or a kind of prospectus in question-and-answer form which he entitled a "catechism."[42] Both breathed a savage hatred of kings and priests, but it is the differences that are of most interest, and which serve to identify the two kinds of revolutionary spirit in Hungary. The tone of the catechism addressed to the noble Reformers was that of long-standing national opposition to the Hapsburgs, reinforced by the more recent note of a highly inflamed resistance to the innovations of the tyrant, Joseph II. The nobles were led to expect a future aristocratic republic without king or taxes, in which "equality" meant the equality of gentry with great magnates, who together would remain the sole owners of rural land, after acquiring all the properties of the church, and would continue to enjoy the forced labor of their peasants under the "feudal system." In this catechism the war with France was deplored because

[42] These are translated in full by R. R. Palmer and Peter Kenez, "Two Documents of the Hungarian Revolutionary Movement of 1794," in *Journal of Central European Affairs*, xx (1961), 423-42. The original texts, in Latin and Hungarian respectively, are in Benda, I, 1,002-36.

it had let democratic ideas seep into Hungary, and because, if the French won, "nobility perishes." The catechism written for the Society of Liberty and Equality was of a contrary tenor. Addressed to men without experience or institutional connection with each other, widely departing from the traditions of the Hungarian diet and constitution, it moved on a level of high-flying philosophy, elucidating the nature of "man" and "reason"; but it also denounced the evils of serfdom, it referred to the "feudal system" as "awful," and it expressed contempt for all nobles, who were portrayed as brutal and vicious. France was pointed to as a model to emulate.

Both catechisms issued a ringing summons to rebellion. For the democratic Society for Liberty and Equality the call was "To arms, citizens! Let us swear freedom or death!" Such was the formula of the French Revolution. But for the noble Society of Reformers, the appeal was more dignified, in its modernized Latin, and perhaps less likely to stir up revolutionary fanaticism: *Ad arma, cives patriae nobiles et ignobiles!*

Armed with these catechisms, and with other similar literature, Martinovics and his followers set about recruiting for the two societies, and within a few weeks may have obtained two or three hundred members in various parts of the country. Given the prevalence of discontent, it seems likely that, had there been more time, a much larger number might have been brought in. The police, however, learned of Held's mission to Paris, and arrested various members of the Vienna conspiracy. Martinovics, in Vienna at the time, was also taken into custody, and whether because he thought the secret was known, or because he still hoped to ingratiate himself as a police agent, revealed the identity of the chief Hungarian Jacobins. The movement in Hungary was thus stopped sooner than it might otherwise have been.

Neither conspiracy, as an organized bid for revolution, posed any serious threat to the government. Both vividly illustrated, if anything, the impossibility of any groundswell of revolution in the Hapsburg countries, where social classes and ethnic groups were too separated to allow for common action, nobles and burghers had few shared ideas, and few educated persons could establish any contact with the peasants. Serious disaffection existed—noble complaint at the reforms of enlightened despotism, middle-class annoyance that these reforms had been compromised or abandoned, peasant resentment against poverty and servitude, all compounded by the unpopularity of the war—but on this sizeable body of discontent the "Jacobin" conspiracies were no more than tiny specks. Denis Silagi insists, indeed, that the two conspiracies, far from being the products of revolutionary ferment, or forerunners of a later liberal movement, were only the last erratic episodes of enlightened despotism in its decline, manned as they were by former servants of Leopold's police, and using the same kind of mysterious apparatus that Leopold himself had employed.

The discovery of actual Jacobin plotters nevertheless contributed greatly to the growing counter-revolutionary mentality in the Austrian empire, a mentality which had arisen, not from the fear of Austrian Jacobins, nor even from opposition to the French Revolution, but some ten years before in the aristocratic and ecclesiastical resistance to Joseph II. The Jacobin trials could be taken (like the English state trials of 1794) as evidence of conservative fears, but the Austrian and Hungarian Jacobins, unlike those of England, were in fact guilty as charged: Held had offered aid to the enemy, and the Hungarians had plotted armed insurrection, in time of war. The trials were secret, but not egregiously unfair. Two Austrians and eighteen Hungarians were executed, and others condemned to prison.

The need of supporting an unpopular war led not only to a dramatization of the Jacobin menace, but to repression of all groups or shades of opinion that might be critical of the government. The continuing unpopularity of the war is attested by many sources (such as the statement of the Archduke Charles quoted above), and is especially emphasized by one recent student of the subject, Ernst Wangermann, who remarks that the Hapsburg government could not carry on the war after 1795 except with financial aid from Great Britain; that in 1796 the chancellor, Thugut, feared the peace sentiment in Vienna more than Bonaparte's successes in Italy; and that when the French broke into the empire in 1797, reaching as far as Leoben in Styria, they met with no popular opposition. The Austrian government, the only important Continental state remaining at war with France after 1795, was obliged to resort to more stringent controls over its own people. The war therefore, in Wangermann's view, was the "gravedigger of enlightened despotism in Austria," and marked the true beginning of the Vormärz.[43] In addition, the government had to deal with what happened in Poland, kill off the sympathy for Kosciuszko, disparage the Polish constitution of 1791, discredit the Polish moves toward abolition

---

[43] Wangermann, 107, 169. Silagi, *Jakobiner*, 200-201, sees less of a "turning point" than Wangermann in the Jacobin trials, but there is not much disagreement between them on the depth and scope of the reaction.

of serfdom—and justify the Third Partition. The French Revolution was denounced because it succeeded; the Polish, because it failed.

The rising tide of counter-revolutionary activity was not peculiar to the Hapsburg empire. Those who pressed for it pointed to the example of England, where the formation of voluntary associations against "levellers and republicans," and the suspension of *habeas corpus*, were seen as desirable models. But matters went further than in England, if only because Austrian bureaucrats were more expert and professional than English squires, and the Catholic prelates in Austria less easygoing than those of the Church of England. Church and State, recently estranged in the Hapsburg empire, joined hands for mutual protection. There was great alarm over professors, who, in truth, had proved to be less content than those of Oxford or Cambridge. The bishops extended their influence over the schools. Experiments in rural education were given up, lest peasants by learning too much become discontented with their station. The censorship clamped down, the police became more potent, more omnipresent, more unchecked by liberal protest. A police power originally designed to facilitate progress was now used to restrain it. On recommendation of the police, in 1794, measures were even initiated to prevent economic expansion, to discourage the growth of cities and the building of new manufacturing plants, since both the business and the industrial laboring classes were feared as sources of disaffection. The Josephinists were reduced to silence; and the Austrian monarchy, so recently an exemplar of fast-moving modern enlightenment, entered upon the course that would make it, until 1848, what impatient liberals called the China of Europe.

An Addendum on Southeast Europe

There is room for only a few words on Southeast Europe beyond the Hapsburg borders, that is, on Rumania, Greece, and the Balkan countries, all of which, except the Dalmatian coast, then lay within the Ottoman Empire. Even the Moslem parts of that empire felt an immediate impact of the French Revolution.[44] Newspapers were published in French at Constantinople, for the use of the foreign commercial and diplomatic colony there, but various Turks were able to read in them the

[44] B. Lewis, "The Impact of the French Revolution on Turkey," in *Journal of World History*, 1 (1953), 105-25; L. LaGarde, "Note sur les journaux français de Constantinople à l'époque révolutionnaire," in *Journal asiatique*, vol. 236 (1948), 271-76; E. de Marcère, *Une ambassade à Constantinople: La politique orientale de la Révolution française*, 2 vols. (Paris, 1927); and, for Egypt, J. Godechot, *La Grande Nation: l'expansion révolutionnaire de la France dans le monde, 1789-99*, 2 vols. (Paris, 1956).

news from Paris; and the French invasion of Egypt in 1798 not only brought in new ideas but produced an emergency which forced the issue of Westernizing reform upon the imperial government. It is said that the French Revolution was the first European event to make a positive impression upon Islam, precisely because it did not come to the Moslems as a Christian movement, of a kind which their religion would require them to oppose.

The Christian peoples of the European parts of the empire were subject to many diverse influences. In part these were internal, as when, with the growth of trade in the eighteenth century, Greek and Serbian traveling merchants developed a network of habitual contacts throughout the Balkans, Hungary, and Rumania. Along these lines of exchange new ideas traveled also, and by the end of the century a kind of revolution of knowledge and communications had occurred, from which the political movements of the following generation were to come.[45] External influences were miscellaneous. Recently, in the Rumanian People's Republic, historians have tried to show that there was a Russian progressive influence at this time. In Moldavia, Russian soldiers during the Russo-Turkish war smuggled in manuscript copies of Radishchev's *Voyage from St. Petersburg to Moscow*, which, it is said, were openly sold in Jassy.[46] There were German influences also. In the last decades of the century over a hundred Christian Balkan merchants went annually to the Leipzig fair. Colonies of South Slavs and Greeks in Vienna made that city a cultural center for their peoples under Ottoman rule. The first Greek and Serbian newspapers were published at Vienna in 1790 and 1791; in 1792 Francis II gave his consent to a new project for a paper in the Cyrillic alphabet, on condition that it emphasize only the evils in the French and Belgian revolutions. For Rumanians and Greeks the contacts with France were important. The first Rumanian newspaper, *Courier de Moldavie*, was published in French and Rumanian in 1790; it lasted less than a year but printed news of the French Revolution.

[45] See the long and remarkably illuminating article by T. Stoianovich, "The Conquering Balkan Orthodox Merchant," in *Journal of Economic History*, xx (1960), 234-313; L. Stavrianos, "Antecedents to the Balkan Revolutions of the Nineteenth Century," in *Journal of Modern History*, xxix (1957), 335-48, and id., *The Balkans since 1453* (New York, 1958). I am indebted also for much information to Professor Peter Sugar of the University of Washington, Seattle.
[46] S. Vianu, "Quelques aspects de l'influence exercée par la pensée progressiste russe sur la société roumaine de la fin du 18e siècle," in Academie de la République populaire roumaine, *Nouvelles études d'histoire présentées au Xe Congrès des sciences historiques, Rome 1955* (Bucharest, 1955), 285-97. The article shows more French influence than Russian.

Events, as such, were not yet of much importance, and those of political significance occurred on the Hapsburg side of the border. A congress of Serbs met in southern Hungary in 1790. The excitement in Croatia over the French Revolution has already been mentioned. The Vlachs of Transylvania (the Rumanian-speaking people, mostly peasants, among whom Magyar landowners and German burghers lived), obtaining assistance from one of the modern-minded Austrian officials, presented a petition to the Emperor and to the Diet of Transylvania in 1791. Called the *Supplex libellus Valachorum*, it requested equality for the Vlachs with the Magyars and "Saxons," or Transylvanian Germans. It asked for representation of Vlachs in the diet, and revealed a knowledge of the French Revolution in proposing an administrative reorganization into territorial "departments," which should be named after mountains and rivers, so that old memories might be lost.[47] The Diet of Transylvania, however, was composed of Magyar landlords. Leopold soon died, Francis succeeded, and war with France began. Nothing was done on the Vlach petition. Of the Transylvanian Vlachs it may be said that they, too, succumbed to the general counter-revolution in Eastern Europe.

It was among the Greeks that the beginnings of political action were most evident. The word then had a wide reference, including, in addition to Greeks living in Greece, persons throughout Rumania, the Balkan peninsula, and Asia Minor who were Greek in religion and language. The Greeks had connections both with central Europe and with France. Adamantios Korais went as a medical student from Smyrna to France shortly before the Revolution; he remained in France for many years, and became known as the father of the Greek cultural revival. His more active compatriot, Rhigas Velestinlis, organized a conspiracy in Vienna. His dream, in effect, was to convert the Ottoman Empire into a Greek one, undoing the Turkish conquest of 1453. He was impressed by the Cisalpine and Ligurian republics, formed in northern Italy under French auspices in 1797. In that year the French also occupied the Ionian Islands, only a few miles from the coast of mainland Greece itself. A secret assembly of Greeks from many parts of the Hellenic world met in the Peloponnesus; it began to plan revolution against the Sultan, and requested aid from the French army. Meanwhile Rhigas, in Vienna, wrote songs and pamphlets for a Greek revolution, including a proposed constitution modeled on the French.

[47] N. Iorga, *Histoire des Roumains de Transylvanie et de Hongrie*, 2 vols. (Bucharest, 1915), ii, 216-25; E. Pascu, "Mémoires et protestations des Roumains de Transylvanie et de Hongrie de 1791 à 1892," in *Revue de Transylvanie*, v (1939), 326-36.

The Austrian police discovered him and several companions, and turned them over to the Turkish authorities, by whom they were executed in 1798 at Belgrade.[48]

Polish patriots, after Kosciuszko's defeat, scattered in a diaspora into many countries. Thousands went to France and Italy, where they formed a Polish Legion that was attached to the French army. Other thousands took refuge in the Rumanian principalities of Moldavia and Wallachia. They sought Turkish and French aid for an armed return to Poland. The French sent a special agent to Wallachia and Moldavia, a Greek named Constantine Stamati, who like Korais had come to France as a medical student and become infused with the spirit of the Revolution. Stamati wrote pamphlets to arouse the Greeks to revolution, and also worked with the Poles, hoping that a great Polish revival would undermine the Hapsburg government, with which France was still at war.[49]

The Polish exiles in Paris, having in mind their armed countrymen in Italy and Wallacho-Moldavia, submitted an ambitious proposal to the Directory in April 1797. Not only, they argued, would the restoration of Poland be of strategic value to France, but "the evident protection which France is giving to the newly born republics in Italy suggests that, if the Carinthians, Croatians, Slavonians, Hungarians, and Galicians will only follow the example of the Lombards in throwing off the yoke of the House of Austria, their insurrections will suit the French system of government in many ways."[50] When Bonaparte invaded the Austrian empire from Venetia, Dumbrowski, the commander of the Polish Legion, was with him, urging him to cut through the Hapsburg dominions, rekindle the embers of revolution in Hungary, join with the Poles on the lower Danube, crush the Hapsburgs, and restore Poland.

Bonaparte, however, signed a truce with Austria at Leoben. So the dream of revolution in Eastern Europe faded away.

[48] A. Descalakis, *Rhigas Velestinlis: la Révolution française et les préludes de l'indépendance hellénique* (Paris, 1937), id., *Les oeuvres de Rhigas Velestinlis* (Paris, 1937). On Rhigas' proposed constitution see also Chapter XI below.

[49] On the Poles: L. Chodzko, *Histoire des légions polonaises en Italie sous le commandement du général Dumbrowski*, 2 vols. (Paris, 1829); M. Oginski, *Mémoires*, 4 vols. (Paris, 1826-1827). On Stamati as a Greek patriot and as a French agent, J. Lair and E. Legrand, *Correspondances de Paris, Vienne, Berlin, Varsovie, Constantinople* (Paris, 1872); Descalakis, *Rhigas*; E. Lebel, *La France et les principautés danubiennes du 16e siècle à la chute de Napoléon I* (Paris, 1955).

[50] Chodzko, II, 331-34; Angeberg [i.e., Chodzko], *Recueil*, 424.

THE BATAVIAN REPUBLIC

Is the seven-headed monster of the Union of Utrecht not a mere combination of special interests?

It is more than time to put an end to this ruinous situation, so that a political system can be built upon new ground in the Netherlands, securing the unity and indivisibility of all the various pieces of territory in the Republic. A National Assembly, a legal code founded on natural right, guaranteeing to each inhabitant his place as a citizen and member of society, are the only means of saving the Netherlands.

Without the National Convention our country will never be confirmed in its right to be One and Indivisible.—DECLARATION OF THE CENTRAL CONFERENCE OF PATRIOTIC SOCIETIES meeting at The Hague, September, 1795

VI

THE BATAVIAN REPUBLIC

AT THE very moment when the Old Order entrenched itself in Eastern Europe it began to crumble in the West. As the "Jacobins" of Poland, Hungary, and Vienna were put down, the friends of revolution from Italy to Ireland took hope from the victories of the French armies. The end of the Terror, following the death of Robespierre, persuaded most friends of France in other countries that the Revolution would succeed.

By the summer of 1794 the French were everywhere on the offensive, crossing the Pyrenees into Catalonia, occupying Oneglia on the Italian Riviera, overrunning the German Rhineland and Belgium, and penetrating the Dutch territory south of the Rhine delta, which they crossed in January 1795. The French government took a reserved attitude toward revolutionary sympathizers in these countries. They had done nothing to assist the French Republic when it seemed to be losing, and the Committee of Public Safety, with the tide now turned, viewed them with a skepticism mixed with scorn. The French authorities and the foreign revolutionaries were willing to use each other—each for their own ends. Idealism existed, but it too was something to be used.

It was the weakness of the governments of the Coalition that brought their ruin, as much as the power generated in France in the Year II, and more than the strength of revolutionary agitation within their respective borders. With their trained armies in headlong retreat, the governments tried to appeal to their civilian populations. In Catalonia, the Rhineland, the Austrian and the Dutch Netherlands, the year 1794 saw attempts to invoke a mass rising against the French invaders. The conservative powers in desperation proclaimed the *levée en masse* for their own purposes.

The Emperor called for a "general arming" in Belgium. "Religion, constitution, property, the sovereign who wears you in his heart . . . these are the watchwords that will organize you." He added that service would be neither long nor difficult. The Prince of Orange appealed to the Dutch: "I call upon you. . . . Here are arms and powder. . . . Take them! . . . Soldiers, citizens and peasants, let us all unanimously assemble!" He added that no one need leave his own province. The Prince of Coburg, commanding the Austrian army, tried to rally the Rhineland Germans: "Rise then, German friends and brothers! Procure us subsistence. . . . Share with us your savings. . . . Employ the treasures of your churches. . . . Arm yourselves, valorous men! Rise by thousands!" And in Catalonia, in default of action by the Madrid government, local leaders issued an appeal for men and money: "Catalans, your country is in danger!"[1]

All these appeals came to nothing, except in Spain. Catalonia, indeed, seems to have been the one part of Europe where a general rising took place successfully for strictly conservative purposes. Here the issue was mainly religion. The French republicans were portrayed as fiends and monsters, and the Catalans went beyond the requirements of Christianity in defense of Holy Church. French generals found the mutilated dead bodies of their men with the genitals stuffed in the mouth.[2]

Further north the call was a total failure. In part, the governments were afraid of their own peoples. The King of Prussia feared that the arming of peasants would ruin both the regular army and the "constitution of the empire." In Holland it was feared that the Dutch farmers, if armed, would turn upon their supposed allies, the British army in disorderly retreat. The call failed also because it could inspire no idealism or sacrifice. Property, constitution, and the father-image of a benign ruler could hardly stir people as civilized as the Dutch, Belgians, and Rhinelanders; such a watchword lacked the ringing echoes of the French *levée* of 1793: "The French people risen against tyrants!" The citizens (who were not really "citizens") were told that the task would be easy; they did not believe it, and they did not care. Governments, in the political structure of the Old Regime, did not have enough moral, psychological, or social *rapport* with their own peoples to make a strong stand in adversity against the Revolution. In any case, in 1794, they were beaten, bewildered, and in disarray. The mass rising in France had succeeded because a revolutionary government simultaneously arose to carry it out, to channel, organize, equip, discipline, and direct the excited

[1] On the appeals for a mass rising in the Austrian and Dutch Netherlands and in the Rhineland see the *Annual Register for 1794* (London, 1799), 59, 204, 212-14, 232. Colenbrander, *Gedenkstukken der algemeene geschiedenis van Nederland* (The Hague, 1905), I, 470-72, 504, 547, 577, contains details on the attempt and failure of a mass rising in the United Provinces. For Catalonia, see A. Ossorio y Gallardo, *Historia del pensamiento politico catalan durante la guerra de Espana con la Republica francese*, 1793-1795 (Barcelona, 1913), 162-72.

[2] Ossorio y Gallardo, 153.

feelings of the country. The Houses of Hapsburg and Orange, in the breakdown of 1794, had nothing to offer even at this purely practical level.

The French therefore met with little resistance. The Coalition broke up in 1795. The Prince of Orange fled to England, and the pro-French Dutch came into power. The King of Prussia made peace, and all the German states north of the Main River, under Prussian leadership, were declared neutral. The Bourbon king of Spain recognized and signed a treaty with the regicide Republic. The British army withdrew from the Continent, to which it did not return except for sporadic raids until 1799. After the treaties of Basel, in 1795, France remained at war only with Britain at sea, and on land only with Sardinia and Austria, with which hostilities fell into abeyance until reactivated by Bonaparte in north Italy in the following year.

Meanwhile the French prepared to re-annex Belgium. There was no talk this time, as in 1792, of a separate Belgian Republic. Belgium would simply be consolidated with France, and the Belgians assimilated as French citizens, somewhat as the segments of Poland were to be consolidated or assimilated to the three East-European monarchies. To military and strategic arguments, made important by the war, were added commercial considerations arising from the century-old mercantile rivalry between France and England. The idea of Napoleon's Continental System, of a Continent to be economically dominated by France, and closed to England, was beginning to take form. Numerous Belgians of the business classes, long stultified by the old provincialisms, were more than willing to enter into this arrangement.[3]

As for the Rhineland, after initial uncertainties, the French eventually decided to annex it also.

Among the Dutch there was a true revolution, of which the result was the Batavian Republic, the first and the most important of the "satellite" or "sister" republics created under French auspices. The Batavian Republic was important not only in itself but more broadly. It was hoped, by enemies of Great Britain, that the alliance of the French and Batavian Republics, controlling the whole coast without interruption from the Frisian Islands to the Pyrenees, and using the extensive shipping, banking, and other resources of the two together, would form an invincible combination against British trade and sea power. And when Italian, Swiss, German, or Irish revolutionaries

---

[3] On the willingness of Belgian business men see above, pp. 25 and 80.

wished to explain to the French what they wanted in the following years, they often named the Batavian Republic as their model.

Of the Batavian Republic it may also be remarked, as a suggestion of its intrinsic significance, that it was the first to use the words "Liberty, Equality, Fraternity" as an official motto. It is well known that these three words, used thus together, have been the motto of republican France, but this usage in France dates only from the Second Republic of 1848. In documents of the First Republic we find *Liberté* and *Egalité* printed officially on the top, and *Salut et fraternité* used as a complimentary close at the bottom, but we never find the three key words as an official triad. For a time, in 1793, the departmental authorities of Paris invited citizens to paint on the façades of buildings a formula which included the words *Liberté, egalité, fraternité ou la mort*. After Thermidor the citizens were invited to efface them. It was not by any wish of the French government that the Dutch in 1795 adopted so dangerous a slogan. There was more of a mood of revolutionary defiance among the Dutch at this time than among the now somewhat jaded French. The Batavian Republic (dropping the reference to death) printed officially, as a heading to its first proclamation, simply the three words, "Liberty, Equality, Fraternity."[4]

The Dutch Revolution of 1794-1795

The Dutch Revolution of 1794-1795 was a continuation, with differences, of the Patriot movement of the 1780's, in which an attempted revolution had been stopped by a combination of British diplomacy and the Prussian army. Britain and Prussia had "guaranteed" the restored Orange regime of William V in 1788. It was this regime with which France went to war in February 1793, a regime, as Pieter Geyl has said, "in which William V stood apart from the nation with his following of oligarchs and preachers," and in whose war with France the Dutch people generally felt no concern.[5] The "preachers" were the clergy of the Dutch Reformed Church, which was established with

---

[4] See A. Aulard, "Liberté, Egalité, Fraternité" in *Etudes et leçons* (Paris, 1910) VI, 1-31, but Aulard did not know of the use of the triad in Holland. For this see the *Proclamatie van der Nationale Vergadering*, 15 vols. (The Hague, 1795 ff.); the journal edited in Paris by persons with Dutch connections, *Le Batave*, the issues for February 19 and 25, 1795, and other dates; a Dutch newspaper, the *Binnenlandsche bataafsche Courant*, which appeared in 1795, and carried "Gelykheid, Vryheid, Broederschap" at its masthead; and J. Hazeu, *Historie der omwentelingen in vaderlandsche gesprekken voor kinderen* (Amsterdam, 1796), in which the three key words are explained at length to children.

[5] *Age*, I, 340, n. 25.

certain privileges, in that no other worship was legally allowed to be public, no other church could ring bells, and members of no other church could hold important office in the government, army, navy, Bank of Amsterdam, or East India Company. The "oligarchs,". in Geyl's phrase, were the hereditary "regent" families, Reformed in religion, who occupied all the positions of power or prominence. Each of the many towns and each of the seven provinces had a limited number of such local dynasties. For example, thirty-six regents composed the governing council of Amsterdam, a city of 200,000, the largest in Western Europe except for London and Paris. The Amsterdam council was highly typical of those "constituted bodies" against which, according to the argument of the preceding volume, the democratic revolution of the eighteenth century was most essentially directed. They sat for life and chose their own successors. They controlled the Amsterdam delegation in the Estates of Holland, and, through Holland, influenced the Estates General of the Union.

The Union meant the Union of Utrecht, formed in 1572 during the war of independence against Spain, and consisting of a league of the pre-existing towns, provinces, and miscellaneous districts that had taken shape in the Middle Ages, and whose medieval liberties, privileges, and autonomies persisted in the eighteenth century as inherited rights. The Estates General, though supposedly sovereign, had little power, could act on most matters only if the seven provinces were unanimous, and had to operate through a network of boards, colleges, councils, and committees among which authority had purposely been divided. A "stadtholder," or chief executive and military commander, had the task of making all this complex machinery function. The stadtholderate had become hereditary in the House of Orange, which had repeatedly intermarried with the British royal family, so that the old Dutch republic had the next thing to a king. The House of Orange, like all good monarchies, enjoyed much traditional support among the lower classes and had long seen the aristocratic regents as its chief political rivals. But William V in 1788, like Louis XVI in 1789, had become fatally identified with the cause of the privileged orders.

The system left a good many people in the position of outsiders. Persons not regents were referred to as "burghers" or "inhabitants," and were expected to have nothing to do with public or great affairs. There was no Dutch citizenship, and according to Colenbrander hardly any Dutch nation in a political sense before 1795. The lowest classes, their levels of expectation not yet raised, had little sense of exclusion, and generally felt a continuing warmth to the Orange regime. But the United Provinces, though small in size (with a population of only two million), were the wealthiest country in Europe, probably even more so than England, so that persons above the "lowest" classes were exceedingly numerous. Those of the shopkeeping and artisan levels had become very restless. Many of the outsiders were established merchants and bankers. Some were actually rich. In addition, defining the in- and out-groups in another dimension, was the difference of religion, which was the more significant since the Dutch were less homogeneous in their churchmanship than almost any other European political community. About forty percent were not Reformed. Most of these were Roman Catholic, but there were many Mennonites and other Protestant dissenters, and the Amsterdam Jewish group was the most important in Western Europe. All these people had long been peaceably tolerated, and many were affluent, but they possessed, and had come to feel, an inferior status.

It was the memory of 1787 that made the difference in the 1790's. The Patriots had been suppressed with no pretence of tact or conciliation. There was much resentment against England, by whose exertions the Patriot movement had been so recently crushed, and which also annoyed some of the mercantile interests by its old habit of appropriating the Dutch overseas possessions. As recently as the treaty of 1783, concluding the War of American Independence, in which Amsterdam and the Patriots had befriended the Americans, the British had taken the Dutch post of Negapatam in India. The callous restoration of 1787 had also had the effect of making many of the Dutch more radical. Those who emigrated had learned much from the French Revolution; some, like Conradus Kock, had died in it. But disappointed Patriots who stayed discreetly at home also underwent a change of mind. In the Patriot movement, before 1787, the dominant feeling had been for "restoration" of an older and freer Dutch constitution. A few years later, thanks both to unpleasant experiences at home and to the spectacle of the French Revolution, the restless elements took a more forward-looking and comprehensive view. As with the Americans in the 1770's their focus changed from the Ancient Constitution to the Rights of Man.

The Dutch revolutionaries were therefore a composite group, hardly to be understood in terms of socio-economic classes, except that neither the very poor, nor the most self-consciously aristocratic, were to be found among them. Since they reflected a wide social spectrum, from

Catholic to Calvinist, and from journeymen barrel-makers to modern-minded individuals of the old families, contrary reports could both be true. Thus an Englishman could see them as tavern loungers, and a Frenchman as disaffected financiers. Sometimes the class-consciousness of their enemies could make absurd mistakes.[6] For example, the British secret agent, Robert Barclay, reporting to George Canning on conditions in Holland shortly after the revolution, commented on the appointment of the new Batavian minister to Denmark. He was, said Barclay, "the son of a shopkeeper and clerk to a parish church of the town," who certainly would "not be received as a person agreeable to his Danish Majesty." Actually the man in question, one Christiaan Huygens, was the son and grandson of East India Company officials, had been in the foreign service before 1795, was received by the Majesty of Denmark, and ennobled by King William I of the Netherlands after 1814.

It is well to take note of these later careers in understanding the revolutionaries of 1795. They show that the Dutch "Jacobins" (like many of the French Jacobins in the true sense of the word) were by no means revolutionaries merely by temperament, nor by lifelong commitment, nor as a permanent occupation or concern, but might be men of substantial abilities and position who turned temporarily very radical in dealing with real problems and real events. Some took part in, and were accepted by, every regime for over thirty years. The career of Isaac J. A. Gogel is illuminating in this respect. Born in 1765, the son of a German officer in the Dutch service, and hence not of old regent background, Gogel was employed before the Revolution in one of the Amsterdam commercial houses. He was a true subversive in 1794. With his government at war with the French, he wrote to the French, at the height of the Terror in France, to urge them to invade Holland, to bring in a ready-made constitution, abolishing the privileges, gilds, provinces, corporations, monopolies, magistracies, and law courts of the existing Dutch regime, and enforced by a temporary *gouvernement révolutionnaire*, a revolutionary tribunal and guillotine. In 1795, after the Dutch Revolution, Gogel became president of the radical club in Amsterdam, the *Een-en Ondeelbarheid* or One and Indivisible Club. He wanted the Batavian Republic to assume and consolidate the various provincial debts, and indeed to wipe out the provinces themselves. (One is reminded of Alexander Hamilton in America.) He was finance

[6] Above, p. 82; and for Barclay's letter, Colenbrander, II, 368, with Colenbrander's note on Huygens.

minister during the radical phase of 1798, again under the "second" Batavian Republic, and again under King Louis Bonaparte in the days of the Napoleonic Kingdom of Holland. When Napoleon, in 1810, simply annexed Holland to France, he made Gogel his superintendent of Dutch finances. After Napoleon's fall, Gogel went into private business. But King William I of the Netherlands named him to his council of State.[7] Such were the tolerance of Dutch politics and the calibre of some of its "Jacobins" during this turbulent generation.

In 1794, before the French invasion, and in eager expectation of their arrival, the political or "Jacobin" clubs in the Dutch cities became very active.[8] In June there were 34 clubs in Amsterdam and 12 in Utrecht, organized in small neighborhood units. There were probably some 5,000 or 6,000 members at Amsterdam, 800 at Utrecht, 300 or 400 at Leiden and at Haarlem, representing from 4 to 12 percent of the adult males. The clubs at this moment were known collectively as the Leather Apron, and were composed largely of tradesmen. Publicly, before the revolution, they called themselves "reading societies." They read and discussed the news from France, and such books as Paine's *Rights of Man* and the Dutch Pieter Paulus' *Menschenvriend*. They also secretly stored up arms, exchanged delegations with each other, and maintained communication with the French and the Dutch émigrés. Since the break-up of the old Batavian Revolutionary Committee in Paris, in connection with Robespierre's liquidation of the "foreign conspiracy," the most prominent of the émigrés was H. A. Daendels, a former brick manufacturer, doctor of law, Patriot of 1787, and officer of the Batavian Legion, who in March 1794 became a general in the French army.

On the night of July 31, with the French now in North Brabant, a great assemblage of the Dutch clubs from all seven provinces met at Amsterdam. It authorized Gogel and Irhoven van Dam to proceed secretly to the French headquarters, to learn the terms on which the Dutch, if they opened their gates, would be spared the fate of a "conquered province" which they thought was being meted out to Belgium.

The French reiterated the view they had adopted since the beginning of the campaign: they would treat the Dutch as allies if they first staged their own revolution. The Dutch were a little discouraged. Revolution

---

[7] *Nieuw nederlandsch biografisch woordenboek*, VII, 480. Gogel's letter to the French commissioner with the Army of the North, dated February 21, 1794, is printed in Colenbrander, I, 378-81.

[8] See my article, "Much in Little: the Dutch Revolution of 1795" in *Journal of Modern History*, Vol. 26 (March 1954), 15-35, from which several paragraphs in the following pages are reproduced with permission of the editors.

was risky with the stadtholder's government still in existence. There was also fear of popular violence. "Nothing is easier," wrote Gogel to the French, "than for us to raise up popular disturbances, but we want no revolution unless we can protect our fellow citizens from murder and pillage."[9]

The relative moderation of the Batavian Revolution, or its weakness, as one may choose to call it, was thus manifest from the beginning. The Dutch revolutionists could enjoy sweeping change, without the accompanying "horrors," as Gogel called them, because they were willing to rely, and could rely, on the French army both to overthrow the Orange regime and to prevent insurrectionary violence.

The country fell into dissolution as the French advanced. The government could get nothing done. Sporadic attempts at a mass rising failed. Nothing was offered to arouse popular loyalty. "His Highness," wrote the pensionary van de Spiegel, must "keep the republic what it now is, and yield as little to aristocracy as to democracy." He talked a little like Robespierre, but did nothing. Force must be used, he said, "to impose on the evil and sustain the good." When wealthy people refused taxes and loans to the expiring state, or shifted their investments to England, he remarked that stringent measures should be taken, "in order to leave the Hopes and other overgrown capitalists of this country no other chance of saving their property than in giving, or at least lending, part of it to supply the wants of the government." But nothing happened. The country could not exert itself. Perhaps van de Spiegel was right in observing that the Dutch enjoyed too high a standard of living to meet such an emergency.[10]

The British army, feebly commanded by the duke of York, behaved very badly on its retreat through the Netherlands, whereas the incoming French, under firm discipline, made a good impression. Such is the unanimous testimony of Orangist and hence Anglophile sources and of the Prussian representative at The Hague.[11] Peasants, if armed, preferred to fight the British; the city of Delft refused to receive British wounded. One Orangist complained that French intrigues had done less than British pillaging to alienate the Dutch people. All agreed that the duke of York was incompetent. All the old fear and dislike of the British was awakened. Even Orangists, who had owed their position since 1787 to British support, were troubled and divided. Some

[9] Colenbrander, I, 413.
[10] *Ibid.*, I, 401, 476.
[11] *Ibid.*, I, 473, 503, 505, 525-26, 562, 565, 572.

believed, as did the Patriots, that Britain was dangerous as either friend or foe.

The revolutionary clubs speeded up their preparations in proportion to the approach of Daendels, the émigrés and the French. Committees made ready to move in and replace existing officials in the various town halls. Soldiers in the garrisons were won over. Plans were laid to assemble insurrectionary crowds. At Utrecht, a city of some fifteen thousand, two thousand persons were in the "secret" for yielding the place to the French, and the garrison of twenty-eight hundred expressed its disinclination to resist.[12]

By keeping their troops under discipline, and holding their official demands to a minimum, stipulating only that the Prince of Orange must go, and the Dutch enter the war against England, the French reassured the numerous moderate element, who were relieved to learn that *la guillotine, réquisition, assignats, égalité, etc.* need not be expected.[13] The French thus built on the broadest possible basis of pro-French feeling. Moderates agreed with radicals; burgomasters sat down with incendiaries. Riots in Amsterdam and elsewhere unseated the authorities. Revolutionary committees installed local provisional governments. The French cavalry rode into Amsterdam on the ice, and in January 1795 the Batavian Republic was proclaimed.

For two years the French, although they were in military occupation, interfered relatively little in internal Dutch affairs.[14] The French aim was to use Holland in the war against Great Britain. This aim did not constitute forcible interference, since many Dutch were in favor of it. Nevertheless, when the terms of the treaty between the French and Batavian republics became known (the treaty of The Hague of May 1795), many in the Netherlands were disappointed. The Batavian Republic was required not only to declare war on England but to maintain a French occupying army at Dutch expense, to accept French paper money, to cede Flushing and the mouth of the Scheldt to France enlarged by Belgium, and to pay an indemnity of 100,000,000 florins.

This was severe treatment for an alleged ally. It was not severe enough to alienate Dutch revolutionaries from France, since they saw no alternative except capitulation to England and the House of Orange. Containing as it did, however, elements of both ruthlessness and

---

[12] *Ibid.*, 412.

[13] *Ibid.*, 583. An Orangist testimony, van Citters to van Nagel, Jan. 29, 1795.

[14] Colenbrander, *Bataafsche republiek* (Amsterdam, 1908), 79; P. Geyl, *Patriotten en N.S.B.ers* (Amsterdam, 1946), 27, 30.

deception, it gave serious offense to a great many of the most advanced Batavian democrats. One of these was Jakob Blauw, one of the negotiators from whom the treaty was extorted. He formed a deep dislike not for the French Revolution but for the French government, and seems to have been somehow involved in the Babeuf conspiracy against it a year later.

The relation of the French and the Batavian Republics, if such a figure may be allowed, was in no sense a rape, since the Batavians were more than willing to enter upon it. It rested on comparable revolutionary sentiment in both countries, but it was less a love match than a marriage of convenience.

As the Batavian Republic was proclaimed, William V retired to England. Here one of his first actions was to authorize British occupation of all Dutch colonies at the Cape of Good Hope and in the East and West Indies. Few Dutchmen believed that the British would ever give them all back. With war now declared, within a few months the British had captured some 85,000,000 florins' worth of Dutch shipping. They also naturally suspended payment on the huge British debts owed to Dutch creditors remaining in Holland.

It would be a difficult problem to compute whether the Dutch in these years lost more to the French or to the British. The question was rather, for the Dutch, what they preferred to pay for. For a price, one could have British assistance toward restoration of the Old Order, or French support for the Batavian Republic.

The Frustration of the Conciliators

Most of the Dutch, in all probability, wanted neither the Old Order nor the New—neither the confused and ineffectual old confederated republic with its more recent adornment of a hereditary stadtholdership, nor the up-to-date republic on the French model in which the separate identity of the provinces and the inheritance of office would disappear. Nowhere did the middle extend more widely or moderation run deeper than among the Dutch. There were important patricians who saw the need of change. Some favored simply a modernization of the Union of Utrecht. Others, of whom G. K. van Hogendorp became the most important, had firmly believed, since long before the revolution of 1795, that political life should be opened up and broader elements in the population be admitted to a liberalized citizenship. One of the most intelligent conservatives in the Europe of his generation, Hogendorp had detected a conflict between "aristocrats" and "democrats" in his own country as early as 1786. He had then advised the House of Orange to lean to the "democrats." He had seen the same conflict agitating "all nations" in 1791.[15] He knew that revolutionary discontent in the Dutch Netherlands was no mere contagion from France. Ejected from office in 1795 (he was of a long line of Rotterdam regents), he neither emigrated, nor took to arms, nor secluded himself on his estates, as a French nobleman might have done. As an aristocratic "bourgeois," he turned to private business to build up the family fortunes. In 1814 he became the chief author of the constitution of the Netherlands monarchy.

The party of conciliation was strengthened by another fact unusual at the time. The Heir Apparent was himself a conciliator. The Hereditary Prince, as he was called, the son of the stadtholder William V, was a young man of twenty-three in 1795, and in 1814, accepting Hogendorp's constitution, he became the first King of the Netherlands as William I. In the 1790's, Hogendorp and the Hereditary Prince resembled in their ideas the circle of liberal or liberally conservative French émigrés that gathered about Malouet in London. In both cases it was their program, more than any one else's, that was to be embodied in the settlement of 1814. Meanwhile, however, they met only with frustration.

William V, after leaving Holland at the time of the Batavian Revolution, lived in England until his death. Hardly had he reached England when he began to receive approaches from certain moderates, men who had accepted the revolution but soon became alarmed by the radicalism of the clubs or annoyed by the demands of the French. Some of these men were old regents and Patriots of 1787. To their overtures William V responded with delight. He would now, eight years later, compromise with those whom he had found intolerable in 1787. But there could be no compromise with the Batavian Revolution. "The present day democrats and their whole faction can never receive any consideration from us."[16]

Other loyal Orangists approached the Hereditary Prince. They believed that there was a genuine Dutch revolution with which an understanding must be made. They were not democrats; what they wanted was an accommodation between the Orangists and the former

[15] On Hogendorp see *Age*, I, 2, 335, and the *Nieuw nederlandsch biografish woordenboek*, II, 587-93.
[16] Colenbrander, *Gedenkstukken*, II, 831.

Patriots of 1787 against "the unfortunate system of democracy that prevails today." Yet action was necessary. As an émigré named d'Yvoy wrote to the prince from Hamburg: "I believe it impossible for things to remain on their old footing. . . . What we need is not the triumph of a party, but a means of uniting parties, which we shall not have until the different sovereignties in the state are formed into a single body. The whole machine is too broken down to be cured by palliatives. We need an extraordinary remedy, a new order, a general recasting, a completely new administration, which, while injuring no individual, can arouse enthusiasm for the re-establishment of order and the public credit, by giving more consideration to some people and more part in the government to others. . . ." In this very accurate diagnosis he suggested England as his model, but what he described was what most Batavians hoped to achieve.[17]

Another Orangist, van Lampsins, submitted long reports to the Hereditary Prince after a secret visit to Holland. He thought counter-revolution impossible. He found no one outside the Batavian government itself complaining of dependency upon France. He believed that Orange and British agents were supporting "aristocracy in a few provinces like Zeeland and Friesland only by all sorts of artifices," while in Holland and Utrecht, the principal provinces, "democracy is making rapid progress." The democrats and lesser people, suspicious of old regents and oligarchs, were, it seemed to him, natural allies for the House of Orange. He proposed, therefore, that "the self-respect of the patriots of 1795 and the democrats should be saved" by a few concessions. In addition to trifles, such as abolition of hunting rights, these concessions should include the admission of the whole burgher class and of Catholics and minority Protestants to positions in most offices of state, and to the managing boards of the Bank of Amsterdam and the East India Company.[18] Van Lampsins' belief that the Reformed Religion should nevertheless remain established, with the highest political office limited to its adherents, was enough to keep his program, as of 1795, in the "moderate" category.

The Hereditary Prince, persuaded of the wisdom of such advice, repeatedly took up the matter with his father.[19] William V, however, could not be moved. He was much influenced by his wife, a Prussian princess, who, as the heroine of counter-revolution in 1787, had shown that she was not a woman to put up with radical impudence. William V

[17] d'Yvoy to the Hereditary Prince, July 17, 1795, in Colenbrander, I, 841.
[18] Colenbrander, II, 839-41, 873, 924-25.
[19] Ibid., 893-908, 961-65.

was willing to throw himself humbly on England and Prussia, though the Prussian king, having just made peace with France, showed little inclination to aid his embarrassed sister. Frederick William II, indeed, determined to keep north Germany neutral, even broke up the gathering of two thousand armed Dutch émigrés at Osnabrück. It was therefore without much chance of success that the exiled stadtholder, in May 1795, entreated his brother-in-law "to restore the constitution which Your Majesty and His Britannic Majesty deigned to guarantee in 1788."[20]

"I persist," wrote William V to his son in September 1796, "in the idea I have always had, that I cannot accept the stadholderate unless the [old] constitution is re-established." The Batavian ideas were to him French ideas, and there could be no question of adopting "the French system and the ideas of equality and abolition of nobility, hereditary honors and offices and the dominant position of the Reformed religion." In June 1797: "Privileges of provinces, towns and *corps des nobles* must be restored. . . . I will not accept any such position as president of a Congress, Executive Power or Directory, or even constitutional King." In July 1797: "I am positively decided not to return on any conditions founded on the democratic basis of alleged rights of man and equality." In short, William V would not compromise with the Revolution. Among his other reasons, he knew that Louis XVI had tried such a compromise, and come to a bad end.[21]

The situation was complicated by the British occupation of the Dutch colonial empire, which William V had sanctioned on his arrival in England. On the face of it, the British were occupying the colonies to keep them out of the hands of the French, or to protect the colonials of European origin, such as those at the Cape of Good Hope, from the influence of revolutionary ideas. But there were few even among William V's advisers who believed that Britain would ever restore Ceylon and the Cape to any Dutch government.[22] William V's own followers, and his own son, were dismayed at his willingness to protect his own interests at the expense of the Dutch empire. As for the Dutch remaining in Holland, the fear of losing their empire to Britain was one of the most powerful and realistic sentiments that held them in a half-willing and half-reluctant alliance with France.

[20] *Ibid.*, 827.
[21] *Ibid.*, 936, 948, 950, 971.
[22] *Ibid.*, 909, 980, 988-89. It was rumored that the British might offer St. Helena to the Dutch in compensation. As it turned out, the British never returned Ceylon, but returned the Cape in 1802, reoccupying it in 1806, and thereafter holding it.

In 1797 the British and French governments were engaged in serious peace talks, conducted for the British by the Earl of Malmesbury, the very man who had outwitted the Dutch Patriots and restored the Orange dynasty in 1787. So successful were French military operations on the Continent, and so difficult were conditions for the British at home, that Malmesbury recommended, and Pitt had almost agreed, that Britain should sign a treaty. By this treaty it would recognize both the French and Batavian Republics and the French annexation of Belgium—in return for retaining those of the Dutch colonies which it most desired, Ceylon and the Cape of Good Hope. Reports of these discussions leaked out, and the Dutch, both the Batavians and the émigrés, were indignant.

The Hereditary Prince, who by now was living in Germany, believed that his father could no longer remain with dignity in England. His father thought otherwise. The British had "saved" him in 1787. No one but the British could "save" him again. In his mind there was simply nothing that anyone could do about British intentions. As the Princess of Orange wrote in explanation to her son: "No one will make a man budge for us without British money."[23]

The Hereditary Prince suggested to his father that he might do as well, for Dutch interests, by approaches to France as by relying on England. William V stuck to his opinion. He was more outraged that the French had annexed Flushing and Maastricht, than that the British should take Ceylon and South Africa.

As events proceeded, to be explained later, the British gave up their momentary inclination to accept the Batavian Republic, and turned increasingly to a positive insistence upon an Orange restoration in Holland (as upon a Bourbon restoration in France) as the most likely means to obtain a durable peace that would be satisfactory to England. Late in 1798, through the United States ministers at The Hague and London, William Vans Murray and Rufus King, a group of moderate democrats and Orangists in Holland opened negotiations with Orangists in London. They had in mind some kind of arrangement from which the Orange family might be excluded as, indeed, it had been excluded twice before since the seventeenth century. These talks col-

[23] *Ibid.*, 896 n. 1, 900, 908, 986. On February 16, 1795, the British had authorized up to £30,000 (330,000 Dutch guilders) for underground purposes in the Batavian Republic. Grenville to Bentinck, in *Papers of J. B. Fortescue preserved at Dropmore*, III, 20. At least £70,000 had been spent to overthrow the Dutch Patriots in 1787, *Age*, I, 337.

lapsed when the British insisted on an Orange restoration.[24] In 1799 the British and Russians, as will be seen, invaded Holland, in the mistaken belief that the Dutch people would greet them as liberators and welcome the Orange family and the émigrés. They were soon expelled.

The obstinacy of William V, and the unwillingness of the British government to make any plain promise of return of the Dutch colonies (or its inability to do so, given the state of British public opinion and the attitudes in Parliament), actually worked to the advantage of the French and of the more ardent Batavian democrats. It was one of the fears of the French that the British, by promising return of the Dutch colonies, or resumption of payments to Dutch creditors, would build up an Anglophile party in the Batavian Republic. This did not happen. As for the Batavian moderates, they found that they could reach no understanding with the exiled stadholder. It remained to be seen whether there could be any agreement between the moderates and the more radical democrats.

Federalists and Democrats

The internal history of the Batavian Republic remained a stalemate for three years, from January 1795 to January 1798, during which it had no constituted or settled government, even on paper.

The French government, when its forces entered Holland in January 1795, six months after Thermidor, by no means represented the most radical or the most democratic opinion to be found in Europe. Still dangerously revolutionary in the eyes of European conservatives, the governments of the later Convention and of the Directory came to seem reactionary to the democrats, who were now called "anarchists" by French officials. The words sans-culotte and "Jacobin" now had a bad connotation to those in power in France. In the spring of 1795, in what was known as the Prairial uprising, the Convention defended itself against a renewal of popular violence only by extremely repressive action against the common people of Paris. In the spring of 1796 the Directory discovered the conspiracy of Babeuf, and arrested its leaders.

The French were afraid of the Dutch democrats, whom they described as *véritables sans-culottes*, and who were in fact not altogether dissimilar to their famous counterparts in Paris a year or two before. The Dutch democrats, issuing from the "Leather Apron" mentioned above, were composed of artisans and mechanics, shopkeepers and inn-

---

[24] Grenville to Rufus King, November 6, 1798, in *Papers of J. B. Fortescue preserved at Dropmore*, IV, 365.

keepers, grocers and printers' devils, organized in clubs, and especially strong in the towns of Holland and Utrecht. To very conservative people, like William V, it might seem that the Dutch were infected by the French, but in fact, by a curious inversion, it was now the French who feared infection by the Dutch. French soldiers in the Dutch provinces were under orders to keep away from the Dutch clubs.

The Dutch popular democrats had as their leaders various men of higher economic status who, like the French Mountain in 1793, were willing to make common cause with them, the better to oppose the exiled Stadtholder's party, or to resist those who might attempt a compromise with the Orange family and the British. Among these leaders were Gogel, the financial expert mentioned above; Jakob Blauw, the Batavian envoy in Paris also already mentioned; Pieter Vreede, a wealthy cloth merchant, former Patriot, and friend of John Adams in 1780; and Johan Valckenaer, sometime professor of law, who had spent the years from 1787 to 1794 largely in France. The French, despite their apprehensions, were drawn to work with these men, not so much because of close ideological sympathy, as because these were the men most committed to the Revolution, and hence most likely to manage Dutch resources in a way useful to France in the common war against England.

All issues in the Batavian Republic came together into one—whether the new republic should be a unitary or a federal state. The bitterness of this conflict amazed even the French, though they had faced something like it in their own revolution. As a Dutchman explained to Noël, the French emissary at The Hague: "There had been less of a gulf to fill between monarchism and republicanism in France than exists here between federalism and unity."[25] The formal difference reflected social realities. Democrats were unitarists, conservatives were federalists, in an almost perfect correlation. The democratic clubs called themselves societies of *Een-en Ondeelbarheit*, Unity and Indivisibility, with reference to internal not external problems. Noël caught on quickly, "It is obvious," he wrote home, "that the families which, under the monstrous system of sovereignty for each province, each town, were able to perpetuate themselves in offices which became hereditary for them, are not inclined to fuse all these sovereignties into one."[26]

Federalism or decentralization, the letting of each town and province alone, thus came to stand for "feudalism," for the old patriciates and

[25] Colenbrander, II, 60.
[26] *Ibid.*, 13. See also 27, 510-11.

oligarchies, with closed magistracies and self-perpetuating councils, for the corporative and ecclesiastical society, the *Ständestaat*, and also for the clumsy and slow-moving administrative machinery which even conservatives admitted to require some reform. The unitary, solid state, in which the old entities should be abolished, meant uniform rights for all persons considered as individuals, and it meant the sovereignty of the people one and indivisible, which in turn was a legalistic way of saying that neither family, nor church, nor estate, nor town council, nor provincial assembly possessed any public power in its own right.

There was also the matter of the public debt of the province of Holland. For two centuries Holland had kept the confederation going by its own inordinate contributions. Its debt was enormous, larger than the debt of the Bourbon monarchy in 1789. In a unitary state this debt would become the debt of a so-called "Batavian nation"—an uninviting prospect outside Holland, especially among the squires of the inland provinces, who had never much approved the financial and maritime activities of the Hollanders anyway.

For a whole year, throughout 1795, it was impossible even to convene a National Convention or constitution-drafting body, since there was no agreement on how such a Convention should be formed. Conservatives wished to retain the form of the estates general, that is, to represent the seven provinces (as the Philadelphia Convention of 1787 represented the thirteen states) so that persons who enjoyed importance at the existing provincial levels would be present in the new Constituent Assembly. This arrangement was not generally favored in Holland, which had half the population of the Union. Radicals and Hollanders insisted upon a true national convention, representing, and elected by, individual voters throughout the republic. The clubs kept up constant pressures, staging demonstrations, issuing broadsides, interviewing officials, and convening tumultuous assemblies of delegates from many cities. Noël was more afraid of them than the Dutch upper-class revolutionists were. The latter, following the usual dynamic of revolution, made use of popular impatience so long as they needed it. The "people" were encouraged to hope for more. By October four provinces—Holland, Utrecht, Gelderland, and Overyssel—had consented to the election of a convention. A small Jacobin revolution then took place in Friesland, where Orange and British agents worked busily but in vain in the opposite direction. Friesland now favored the National Convention.

The Convention was elected in February 1796. For this purpose the seven provinces, and the two areas (Drenthe and North Brabant) which had never been admitted to provincial rights and powers, were dissolved and re-arranged into 124 equal electoral districts. All adult males were entitled to vote, except paupers. An oath, however, was required. One had to subscribe, before voting, to the belief that "all hereditary offices and dignities" were illegal and that the supremacy of the governed was the only lawful source of public authority.

The Convention, so elected, gave a broad hearing to many talents and interests. There were the usual professors and lawyers, merchants from old Amsterdam families, clergymen both Protestant and Catholic, persons socially unknown and of small incomes, and five noblemen, two of whom were Catholic. At the same time, because of the electoral process, important actual forces were underrepresented, as in all revolutions. Strict Orangists were excluded by the oath; and the smaller provinces had far fewer delegates than they had been accustomed to in the old estates general. For example, of 124 members, only 5 came from Zeeland.

The Convention, meeting on March 1, fell into acrimonious disagreement, despite the underrepresentation of upholders of the Old Regime, on the same unitary-versus-federalist question that had so long delayed its election. The clubs renewed their agitation, to persuade federalists to yield to unitary democrats in the Convention. Of the disturbances which took place in various towns, the most serious was the revolt of certain Amsterdam cannoneers, a National Guard unit which, on May 10, invaded and menaced the municipal authorities of that city.

The revolt of the Amsterdam cannoneers was simultaneous with the conspiracy of Babeuf, who was arrested in Paris on the same day, and it came very soon after the attempt of certain Italians, taking advantage of Bonaparte's victories, to set up a republic at Alba in the Kingdom of Sardinia. It is a question, therefore, whether some kind of concerted international revolutionary action was underway. More will be said later of the Babeuf affair. Contemporaries widely believed, though without much evidence, that the uprising in Amsterdam was somehow connected with the Babeuf plot.[27] It was known that Valckenaer, who as

[27] Bielfeld to Frederick William II, The Hague, May 19, 1796, in Colenbrander, II, 273; newsletter of Bosset to the Court of Prussia, June 3, 1796, *ibid.*, 275; van Lampsins to the Hereditary Prince, June 1796, *ibid.*, 927; Noël to Delacroix, May 19, 1796, *ibid.*, 52-53. See also J. Godechot, "Unità batava e unità italiana all'epoca del Direttorio" in *Archivio storico italiano*, Vol. 113 (1955), 347-48, and A. Saitta, *Filippo Buonarroti* (Rome, 1950), I, 30-32, II, 26-32, where additional letters of Noël to Delacroix are printed.

a former émigré had a wide acquaintance among revolutionaries of various nationalities, had made a trip from Leyden to Amsterdam with a French Jacobin, Ysabeau, a few days before the Amsterdam revolt. When Noël, in agreement with the Batavian government, called in French troops to preserve order in Amsterdam, Valckenaer was among those who objected to such intervention. It was rumored that he had paid 7,000 guilders to the cannoneers to instigate insurrection. It was not known, but was stated over thirty years later by Philip Buonarroti, in his history of the Babeuf conspiracy, that the Babouvists had received a donation of 240 francs from the envoy of an allied republic in Paris, who would seem to have been Jakob Blauw. The Paris police, when they arrested the Babouvists, found various writings on revolution in Belgium and the Rhineland in their possession.

On May 27 Valckenaer left Holland for Paris, presumably on his way to Spain, to which he had been appointed as Batavian minister several weeks before. On June 12 the French Directory decided to order Valckenaer out of Paris as an undesirable, and to apply to the Batavian Republic for the recall of Blauw as minister to France and of Valckenaer as minister to Spain. Valckenaer, however, did proceed to Spain; the Batavians were not wholly subservient. Blauw was recalled, but was immediately sent to Turin as Batavian minister to the North Italian states.

What do these facts add up to as evidence of an international revolutionary conspiracy in the spring of 1796? Italian and French historians have puzzled over the problem, in which the Dutch have taken less interest.[28] It seems likely enough that among Dutch, Italian, and French revolutionaries, of the type feared as "ultra" or "anarchist" by the Directory, there was a considerable mutual acquaintance, and that they shared in many of the same ideas. All thought the Directory too timid, too tepid, too inclined to put the interests of France first, and too likely to make peace with England and Austria before their own aims were accomplished. It is now widely thought that the famous "communism" of Babeuf was limited to a small circle within his movement, and that all kinds of persons discontented with the Directory on other grounds— popular democrats and international revolutionaries—gave his group

[28] Godechot and Saitta, while not affirming a connection between Babouvists and Dutch democrats, think that it would have been characteristic of the Babeuf movement, and that it was probable enough to alarm the French Government. P. Geyl, *Geschiedenis van nederlandse stam* (Amsterdam and Antwerp, 1959), III, 395-99, believes the connection highly unlikely, but emphasizes the cannoneers' revolt as a step in differentiating radicals and moderates among the Batavian revolutionaries.

such strength as it had. The involvement of Dutch and Italians with Babeuf would offer no evidence whatsoever that they were more than advanced political democrats, as we know Blauw and Valckenaer to have been.

It is certain that the Babeuf group, through Buonarroti, was engaged in concerted action to bring about revolution in Italy. That they would have liked to drive forward the revolution in Holland is equally beyond doubt. But the evidence seems to be against any equally concerted action by the Dutch. Valckenaer, it would seem, if knowingly involved with the Babouvists, would hardly have chosen a moment two weeks after their arrest to stop in Paris on his way to Spain. Valckenaer also, at the time, denied the reports that he had paid money to the Amsterdam cannoneers; and while the denial proves nothing, the tone of the private letters in which Vreede, Schimmelpenninck, and Valckenaer discussed the rumor suggests that it was really a false charge, or at least that the radical democrat, Vreede, had no knowledge of any such fact. As for Blauw, recalled from Paris, he went to Turin. But at Turin, during the remainder of 1796 and 1797, while he continued to dislike the French Directory, he did not befriend the Italian revolutionaries nor favor the establishment of the Cisalpine Republic. He preferred to leave North Italy under Austrian influence, the better to persuade the Austrians to recognize the Batavian Republic and give up their claims in Belgium, where the Batavians did not want them.[29] Blauw, in short, proved to be less an international revolutionary than a Dutch one.

The disturbances of May 1796 at Amsterdam and in other cities soon subsided, thanks in part to the French army. Though the French were apprehensive about anarchists, the foreign minister, Charles Delacroix, instructed Noël to continue to work for a centralized and unitary government in the Batavian Republic. Only a strong central government, he remarked, could both keep "anarchists" under control and subdue the British and Orange sympathizers.[30] The French were impatient of Dutch delay, but still refrained from imposing a form of

[29] For the correspondence of Valckenaer, Vreede, and Schimmelpenninck, see Colenbrander, ii, 502-506. For Blauw's mission to Italy and opinions there see G. W. Vreede, *Nederlandsche diplomatie* (Utrecht, 1863), iv, 248-50, 264-75, where Blauw's reports of 1796-1797 to the Batavian committee on foreign affairs are excerpted. Neither Godechot nor Saitta, in noting the possibility of connection between Dutch democrats and Babouvists, has dealt with these aspects of the evidence. It seems significant also that *Le Batave*, the radical democratic paper published in Paris by persons with Dutch connections, having suspended publication on March 11, 1796, resumed it on May 11, the day after the arrest of Babeuf. Resumption on May 11 would be highly unlikely if the editors of *Le Batave* had any conscious connection with the Babouvists.
[30] Delacroix to Noël, May 24, 1796, Colenbrander, ii, 54.

government, believing that a government agreed upon by the Dutch, if only the strict Orangists were excluded, would be the most likely to employ the Dutch wealth and fleet to mutual advantage.

After much backing and filling, amending and patching, the Dutch Convention submitted an admittedly compromise constitution to the voters in August 1797. Its most sweeping single innovation was the disestablishment of the Reformed Church. Catholics, Jews, and minority Protestants all received equal political rights. Most of the Jews, including the rabbis, lacked enthusiasm for this "French" idea. They lived apart, unused to politics, in a corporate body of their own, and they felt a loyalty to the traditional Dutch Republic to whose protection they had in fact owed so much for two hundred years. But there were also in Holland a great many modernized Jews who received their new status with pleasure, and who even had some of the Dutch legislation translated into Hebrew.[31] Noël and the leading Dutch democrats insisted on this equality of civic rights for Jews. At a crude or immediate level the matter had little importance, even in Holland, where the Jews were exceptionally numerous; but at a more general or "abstract" level there was no better way of affirming the difference between an old regime and a state issuing from the eighteenth-century revolution.

Many Dutch leaders, as well as Noël and Delacroix, hoped desperately for approval of the constitution in August 1797. They felt that any constituted government was better than none. Nevertheless the Dutch voters rejected the constitution overwhelmingly, by a vote of 108,761 to 27,955. It clearly failed because it was too much of a compromise. It satisfied no party of any strength. It was rejected in every province. In populous Holland and Utrecht, where unitary democrats were strong, it was the democrats who voted against it; in the eastern or land provinces, the federalists and conservatives. Both parties hoped to do better on a new draft.

Thus in August 1797, almost three years after the revolution, the Batavian Republic still had no government. The old order had collapsed, leaving only a vacuum. The revolutionaries in the broad sense of the word—men of all political stripes who were willing to take the antihereditary oath—were unable to agree and unwilling to compromise.

[31] For this apparently unknown fact I am indebted to Professor Jacob R. Marcus of the Hebrew Union College in Cincinnati. For Noël's insistence on equality of rights for Jews see Colenbrander, II, 50, 56, 60, 65, 67.

The Coup d'Etat of January 22, 1798:
Dutch Democracy at Its Height

At this point it is necessary to anticipate developments that will be further explained in a later place. The fate of the Batavian Republic, at the time of the rejection of the constitution in August 1797, depended on events of an all-European scope.

The summer of 1797, throughout Europe, was a time of reviving counter-revolutionary expectations. Elections in France, in the spring of 1797, had produced a majority of the "royalist" or peace party in the French legislative chambers. If this group got control of the French government, reaction could be expected in France, and the spread of revolution in Italy under Bonaparte could be stopped. Dutch conservatives took hope in the rejection of the Dutch constitution. It was known that French *émigrés*, royalists, Orange emissaries, spies, and British agents were everywhere active. Rightist coups were expected.

What happened, however, was the French coup d'état of Fructidor, on September 4, 1797. Republicans in France combined with Bonaparte to suppress counter-revolution. They purged the French chambers and Directory, thus for a time giving encouragement to the democratic left. The Dutch democrats were delighted. As one of them wrote to Valckenaer in Spain, "If the plans of the [French] royalists had only succeeded, how fast Father William [i.e., William V] would have been with his! We have been finding this citizen's agents all over the country. Six of them were arrested yesterday in this city." Or as Robert Barclay, the British secret agent at The Hague, described the reassertion of revolutionism to the British foreign secretary, Lord Grenville: "The same ill temper that prevails in France is attempted to be raised in every shape in the minds of the unfortunate inhabitants of this country, and in order to effect this, My lord, more speedily, the moderate and respectable persons comprising the municipalities of the towns and villages have already been changed to make way for the most violent, and of course the vilest and most ignorant among the people."[32]

After rejecting the constitution, the Dutch elected a new convention to draft another. Moderates were weaker, and democrats stronger, than in the first; but still no majority could be formed to agree upon anything. On October 11 came the battle of Camperdown. The Dutch fleet was defeated by the British. For the first time in history a Dutch admiral was taken captive. This turn of events discredited the provi-

[32] *Ibid.*, 132, 396, 538.

sional governing committees. Patriots believed that moderates in the government had deliberately ordered out the fleet before it was ready and before the time called for in the Franco-Batavian war plan, in order to avoid making a true contribution to the impending invasion of Ireland. The cry was renewed for a unitary and effectual government that would not mismanage the navy.

The Dutch clubs and other radicals demanded a Dutch Fructidor.[33] They asked for the recall of Noël, who they said had mixed too much with "aristocrats." The French post-Fructidorian government, having broken off peace talks with England, was committed to a renewal of hostilities and preparing to invade the British Isles. It was losing patience with the interminable Dutch indecision and prepared to support any strong government that would act as an ally. The Fructidor turnover brought Talleyrand to the foreign ministry, while his predecessor, Delacroix, went to Holland to replace Noël. Delacroix was an old Jacobin, who had voted for the death of Louis XVI; he was a man of experience and ability, who had been chief assistant to Turgot years before, and was to end his life as one of Napoleon's prefects. According to his present instructions, his first duty was to get a workable constitution adopted in the Netherlands; the matter should preferably be left to the Dutch, and honest elections were to be desired, but if necessary to get a decision, the elections might be "fixed."[34]

Dutch historians seem to differ in judging what followed. For Pieter Geyl, the French interference was very high-handed, and the Dutch democrats who demanded it went far beyond the bounds of political common sense. To Professor Geyl it seems that the moderates in the Dutch Convention were on their way to accepting a compromise with the democrats. For H. Brugmans, the Dutch moderates had an opportunity to work with Delacroix, but failed to use it; it was the democrats who, impatient at the long deadlock of parliamentary methods, were eager to take direct action, and it was therefore the democrats with whom Delacroix worked.[35]

Delacroix brought with him a draft constitution, put together by both French and Dutch hands, and retouched in Paris by Merlin de Douai

[33] Notes to Barras, Talleyrand, etc., *ibid.*, 548-52; The Amsterdam Club to Vreede, December 1797, *ibid.*, 563; "Observations sur l'état actuel de la République batave," December 17, 1797, *ibid.*, 567-71; Lestevenon to Valckenaer, Jan. 9, 1798, *ibid.*, 582-84.
[34] *Ibid.*, 140-45.
[35] Geyl, *Geschiedenis*, III, 478-81; Brugmans, *Geschiednis van Nederland* (Amsterdam, 1937), VI, 327. See also Geyl's "The Batavian Revolution, 1795-98," translated in his *Encounters in History* (New York, 1961), 226-41.

and Barras. This constitution, or something like it, he had to get accepted by the Dutch convention, which therefore had to be purged. Forty-nine members of the stalemated convention—about a third of the whole—reached an understanding with him. They submitted to him a long document, entitled "Constitutional points agreed upon," and listing the articles of a "democratic, representative constitution." They agreed to exclude forcibly those of their fellow-members "in known opposition to the principles here announced."[36]

It is a fact of interest, for Americans, that one of these forty-nine democrats bore the name of Roosevelt—or rather of F. A. van Rosevelt-Cateau. Not much is known of him, but he had recently written a pamphlet in which the words Liberty, Equality, Fraternity, and the Year III of Batavian Freedom were liberally sprinkled. Six months later he was briefly imprisoned as one of the "chief anarchists" in the country, defended by a few who objected to such abuse of language, and released.

The coup d'état took place on January 22, 1798. Twenty-two members were driven from the assembly. The re-formed constitutional committee considered Delacroix's draft, which it felt no obligation to accept blindly. In fact, it did not find the draft democratic enough. Small Holland now gave revolutionary lessons to its mighty neighbor. The Dutch, as the committee explained to Delacroix, were "capable of a greater measure of democracy than would be suitable for the French." They proposed more direct election by original voters (i.e., less power to electoral colleges), procedures for amendment by popular initiative, and modification of the bicameral provision to keep aristocrats from dominating the upper chamber. Delacroix accepted these suggestions.[37]

The resulting constitution, agreed to by the purged convention, was unitary and democratic. It extinguished the old provinces and replaced them with eight "departments" of equal population, whose frontiers bore no relation to the old provincial borders. It granted manhood suffrage except to persons receiving public relief. It consolidated the debt and the revenues. It abolished all guilds, monopolies, and other barriers to the circulation of persons and goods, and it completed the disestablishment of the Reformed religion. It provided for a bicameral legislature and for a collegiate executive of five directors to supervise the ministries, as in France.

This constitution, submitted for popular ratification in April 1798,

---

[36] Colenbrander, II, 171-77.
[37] *Ibid.*, 190-94. For a French translation of the constitution see D. R. C. Verhagen, *L'influence de la Révolution française sur la première Constitution hollandaise du 23 avril 1798* (Utrecht, 1949), 59-99.

was overwhelmingly adopted by a vote of 165,520 to 11,597. Pressure was brought at the polls, where the anti-heredity oath was again exacted, so that conscientious Orangists were excluded. The best evidence that the constitution suited a great majority of the Dutch people is the fact that, when the democrats themselves were driven from power, their democratic constitution was retained. It remained in effect until replaced by the Bonapartist constitution of 1801, which modified only a few of its principles. Unity, consolidation, equality of civil rights, and religious disestablishment remained permanent. As the Dutch say of their work of 1798, they took the medicine but threw away the bottle.

It was the behavior of the democrats rather than their constitution that led to further discord. They did nothing really drastic; there was no attempt at social revolution, general confiscation, or terror. They did, however, take steps to secure themselves in power. There was a general scramble for office; the unitary central government, using its newly acquired powers, put all sorts of democrats into local jobs. It was called a purge but was not altogether different from the American practice of "rotation." What was more serious, and justified only by the familiar argument of defense against reaction, the Dutch democrats also tried to purge the voters, by excluding political rivals from the polls. It was of course true that British and Orange agents were trying to subvert the new regime.

There was an upsurge of popular democratic excitement in which ideas like those of the Paris sans-culottes or American democrats were expressed. An example is offered by a certain obscure Lucas Butot. He was a warehouse keeper by vocation and a Catholic. He was also a member of the secret committee of the One and Indivisible Club at the time of the coup of January 22, and thereafter was employed by the government to conduct local purges. He thought that all, including the poorest, should vote, except for known Orangists and persons holding foreign investments, unless these were in France. He thus aimed at Dutch capitalists, who held a good deal of wealth in England. The state, in his opinion, should ignore all religious cults, and no clergy should be paid from the public purse. Merit should be the only qualification for civil and military office. Officeholders should be modestly paid ("a man can live well in the Batavian Republic on 3,000 guilders a year"); and public offices or jobs should not be held by persons drawing income from their own property or business, but be reserved for those who needed them to live. Such persons, he believed, would in any case discharge the duties better. Modest payment of officeholders, added Butot, would make the effects of bribery immediately visible. The money saved on officeholders and clergy should be put into the fleet, to aid France in the joint war against Britain.[38]

The inrush of really plain people, with popular ideas, created general consternation, even among upper-class persons known for democratic opinions. How much the efficiency of government really suffered is endlessly debatable. Delacroix stoutly defended it, as did many others; but it would seem in the nature of the case that efficiency was not such a government's strongest point. Democrats fell out with one another. "True" democrats denounced "false" ones. Gogel, the radical democrat, finance minister under the new constitution, complained that all sorts of people—druggists, organists, notaries' clerks, and policemen—were trying to tell the government what to do.[39] People began to send anonymous letters to Talleyrand in Paris, describing the horrors in Holland; Talleyrand sent them back for comment to Delacroix, who was able to expose many gross misrepresentations. To refute the allegation, for example, that the country was ruled by riffraff and fortune-hunters he reviewed the five-man Directory: "As to the dilapidation of their fortunes, this is perhaps a matter on which a republican should keep silence, but I will reply: Pieter Vreede is a millionaire, head of one of the finest manufactories in the republic. Van Langen is hardly less rich; he enjoys large credit, and does an extensive business with Spain. Fynje was on the old East Indies Commission, with a 12,000 guilder salary. This is not rich for this country, but his affairs are in good order. The same can be said for Fokker and Wildrik, who enjoy a comfort in this country that would be called wealth in ours."[40]

It is probably true that the Dutch regime set up on January 22 did not offer a basis on which the politically significant classes could reach stable agreement. The men who controlled the Dutch finances and the Dutch navy withheld their support. The French government still wanted an effectual ally. Delacroix, the old Jacobin, earnestly defended the military usefulness of the Dutch regime to France. Where the preceding Dutch rulers had done nothing but get the fleet knocked to pieces at Camperdown, the present Dutch government, he wrote in May 1798, maintained twelve ships of the line and transport for 15,000 troops and had assembled 230 vessels at Dunkirk to embark the right wing of the French *Armée d'Angleterre*.[41]

[38] Colenbrander, II, 709-10.
[39] *Ibid.*, 761-62; see also 796, n. 2, and 807, n. 1.
[40] *Ibid.*, 203, n. 2.
[41] *Ibid.*, 218, n. 2.

But, unknown to Delacroix, in May Bonaparte sailed for Egypt to assail Britain in the East. The French, while still needing Dutch power in northern waters, postponed the invasion of the British Isles. In May, also, the French government veered in an antidemocratic direction; the French elections of 1798, having shown a revival of democratic agitation, were quashed by the so-called coup d'état of Floréal. Talleyrand and the French Directors allowed Gogel, Daendels, and other Dutch leaders, in agreement with the French military commander in Holland, to form a conspiracy against Delacroix and the existing Dutch regime. Dutch politics, if not dictated, were certainly shaped by the French: the Dutch Fructidor was followed by the Dutch Floréal, which, in turn, foreshadowed the French Brumaire.

On June 12, 1798, by a second coup d'état, General Daendels arrested the leading members of the Batavian government and dissolved the chambers. Delacroix left Holland a week later. He submitted to Talleyrand a final report on his mission, justifying his own and the Dutch democrats' actions. The coup of June 12 looked to him like military dictatorship. "May the excessive ease with which it was carried out not persuade some obscure centurion that to win all he need only dare all!"[42]

After Daendels' coup d'état, matters quieted down. There was very little punishment or retribution, and an increasing willingness of men of various parties to work together. The next test came with the Anglo-Russian invasion a year later, of which more will be said.

A Word on the Dutch of South Africa

When the British occupied Cape Town in June 1795 they believed themselves to be surrounded by "Jacobins."[43] There had in fact been a rebellion against the Dutch East India Company, to which the colony had belonged as a way-station on the route to Ceylon and Java. This rebellion had occurred in February, at the time of the Batavian Revolution in the home country. The European population in the Cape

[42] *Ibid.*, 245.

[43] Dundas to Grenville, November 16, 1794, in *Papers of J. B. Fortescue Preserved at Dropmore*, II, 645; G. E. Cory, *Rise of South Africa*, 5 vols. (London, 1910), I, 35-86; G. M. Theal, *History of South Africa Since 1795*, 5 vols. (London, 4th ed., 1915), I, 1-70; C. de Kiewiet, *History of South Africa* (Oxford, 1941), 30-31; John Barrow, *An Account of Travels into the Interior of Southern Africa in the Years 1797 and 1798* (New York, 1802); Lady Anne Barnard, *South Africa a Century Ago, 1797-1801* (Cape Town and Oxford, 1926); J. S. Marais, *Maynier and the First Boer Republic* (Cape Town, 1944); J. P. van der Merwe, *Die Kaap onder die Bataafse Republiek 1803-1806* (Amsterdam, 1926).

Colony, some 20,000 in number, and not yet extending very far from Cape Town, was almost exclusively made up of Dutch people some three or four generations removed from the homeland. Politically it was divided; some favored the Company and the Orange regime in the Netherlands, some had favored the Patriots and now sympathized with the Batavians, and a great many, living widely dispersed on huge tracts of land on which they raised cattle, were unconcerned with events in Europe or even at Cape Town, wishing mainly and somewhat obstinately to be let alone. Nevertheless, when the British arrived, certain symbols of the European revolution were current. There were people who wore tricolor cockades (in protest against the Orange cockades of Company officials), or who called themselves "citizens," or spoke of Liberty, Equality, and Fraternity.

The handful of English who occupied the Cape were naturally of the classes, back in England, which produced naval and army officers, as well as colonial administrators and empire-builders, the very kinds of Englishmen who were most nervous about "Jacobins" in England, and not very congenial to such plain people as the South African Dutch. The British occupation introduced a kind of modernization, and it is from 1795 that the modern history of South Africa has been generally dated. Some of the stuffiness and narrowness of the Dutch Company, against which the South Africans had protested, was done away with. A freer internal and external trade replaced the old monopoly of the Company. But the British were not welcomed, and probably the South Africans, as between the two, would have preferred occupation by the French.

It seems likely that the British authorities may have created as many "Jacobins" as they discovered. Burghers and officials were required, against their will, to take an oath to King George III. They were disappointed when a Dutch fleet, sent by the Batavian Republic to relieve them, was defeated by the British off Walvis Bay. Nor were they pleased when another Dutch relief ship, sent from Java, was captured by a stratagem in which a British warship pretended to be an American merchant vessel. It was not very edifying when, after a mutiny in the British South African squadron, twenty-three of the sailors were brought ashore at Cape Town (alleged to be "blind agents of French miscreants") and three of them were executed. Censorship at the Cape had never been so severe. The official salary scales were a source of discontent. The Dutch head of the high court at Cape Town received £400 a year, while the Earl of McCartney, the governor, drew £10,000 a year plus a table allowance of £2,000, and ten British officials together drew £23,000, which was equal to the total revenue of the colony in 1796. The British did not much associate with the local Dutch, as may be seen from the letters of Lady Anne Barnard. She had persuaded Pitt's government to give her husband some kind of position, which, to her dismay, proved to be the secretaryship of the Cape colony, paying £3,100 a year, or the equivalent of 35,000 Dutch guilders. She complained that the Cape burghers did not seek acquaintance with the English. "As for the young Dutchmen, I hardly saw any," she said after two months, ". . . perhaps they are altogether Jacobin."[44]

On the frontier, some two hundred miles east of Cape Town, at Graaf Reinet, where the Dutch and Bantu cattle-herders had recently begun to come into collision, there had long been dissatisfaction on the part of the settlers with the government at the Cape. Dutch officers of the Company, in the interests of a compact and peaceable colony, designed primarily as a service station for the Eastern trade, had long attempted to restrain this migration and the accompanying clashes between the Dutch and the Africans. The frontier Boers had always resisted, demanding the freedom to take up apparently unoccupied land, and to handle their labor problem in their own way, which meant in effect, though not exactly in law, the enslavement of African tribesmen. Rebelling first against the Dutch Company, and then holding aloof from the British, they set up a somewhat shadowy Republic of Graaf Reinet, often called the First Boer Republic, since it antedated the Transvaal by half a century. Another small republic was proclaimed at Swellendam.

It is perhaps unseemly for an American, having in mind conditions in the United States at this same time, to question the democratic principles of slaveholders, or the ideas of liberty and equality to be found among frontiersmen bent on acquiring land in conflict with an indigenous population. The language of the French and Batavian republics was heard on the South African frontier, as on the American. "Citizens" talked of "liberty and equality" and of the "sovereignty of the people." The republic of Graaf Reinet had a "convention." It is hard to estimate the depth of conviction which such language represented. The republics of Graaf Reinet and Swellendam, mere associations of a few hundreds of Dutch families out of touch with the world, were hardly viable as political entities in any case, and soon disappeared. Their political doctrine, such as it was, seems to have served a quite specific negative

[44] Barnard, xxiv and 8.

purpose—to keep outsiders, whether Orange Dutch, Batavian, or British, from interfering with them in matters of land or labor.[45] Probably there was more sympathy with the Batavian and European revolutions among the Dutch in and near Cape Town than in the two "republics."

The British in 1802, by the Treaty of Amiens, handed over the Cape Colony to the Batavian Republic, which held and administered it for four years. In 1806, with the renewal of war, the British returned, this time to remain permanently. In 1806 they met with considerable resistance, where they had found virtually none in 1795. There is this much evidence that the South African Dutch favored the changes brought about by the Batavian revolution.

Developments within South Africa, with its mere 20,000 whites, were of no more than incidental significance on the larger stage, except as a reminder of geographically remote repercussions of movements stirring the world of western civilization. External implications were more important. The British occupation of the Dutch colonies, made possible by the Batavian revolution, had many international and worldwide ramifications.

Noël, as French envoy at The Hague, in January 1796 sent an interesting letter to the French foreign minister, Delacroix.[46] The Batavian Republic, he said, naturally wished French aid in getting back the Cape. The Cape was the key to India. If the British, having the Cape and Ceylon, should succeed in the conquest of India, they would gain "much more than they lost in the American Revolution." The French should therefore send agents to India to persuade "Tippu-Saib" (the sultan of Mysore) to ally with France and Holland. "It is in India that the strongest blows against British power must be delivered." So the idea now arose, as some might say, of exporting "Jacobinism" to India.

[45] This is the view of Marais, vi and 90. The British General Craig believed the two republics to be "infected with the rankest poison of Jacobinism." Cory, 1, 63.
[46] Colenbrander, 11, 29.

THE FRENCH DIRECTORY: MIRAGE
OF THE MODERATES

The French government is now concerned with a problem of interest to all nations. How does one come out of a regime of violence after having once been in it? How get back on the road of justice and moderation once it has been left?—THE COUNT DE MONTLOSIER, London, 1796

VII

THE FRENCH DIRECTORY: MIRAGE
OF THE MODERATES

AFTER Robespierre's death, as the Terror came to an end, and the political and emotional crisis of the Year II receded, the question that a great many Frenchmen put to themselves both in France and in the emigration, and a question to which observers throughout Europe and America awaited the answer, was whether some kind of moderate or constitutional regime would be durably established. The next four years, punctuated toward their end by the coups d'état of Fructidor and Floréal, were to show that constitutional quietude was still far away.

The difficulty was that not everyone agreed on what either moderation or justice should consist in. Justice, for some, required the punishment of all revolutionaries and their sympathizers. For others, it meant a continuing battle against kings, priests, aristocrats, and the comfortable middle classes. Both groups saw in "moderation" a mere tactic of the opposition, and moderates as the dupes of the opposite extreme. Compromise for them meant the surrender of principle. It meant truckling with an enemy that could never be trusted, and had no real intention of compromise.

In any case, what was "moderation"? Did it mean merely the absence of spectacular violence, with no more busy public guillotines and forced liquidations and purges? Was a regime moderate because it managed to exist without such exhibitions of ruthlessness? What if it persisted in an obstinate violation of the Christian religion, of the rights of the French king, nobility, and former property-owners, or of the authority of foreign governments over their own peoples? Such were the questions asked on the Right. What if the regime, however decorous and constitutional, violated the rights and the needs of the common people of the working classes, harrying and insulting the very patriots who had saved the Revolution in '92 and '93? Such were the questions asked on the Left.

After Thermidor

It has already been remarked that for extreme conservatives the French Republic after Thermidor was even less welcome than the Republic of the Terror, since as long as the Terror lasted the republican government was discredited in principle and seemed to be destroying itself in practice. At the other extreme also, among the fiery activists, the post-Thermidorian republic was repugnant because it seemed to betray the glorious promise of the Year II. The *purs* of both sides combined to see in the post-Thermidorian republic a scene of peculiar corruption and cynicism. Later on it became the habit of all partisans of Napoleon to throw a bad light on the republic which he had supplanted. All who felt strongly felt a preference for something else. No one loved the Thermidorians and the Directory.

The stereotypes of corruption and cynicism were greatly exaggerated. It has been concluded by one scholar that, of all the men in the higher positions under the Directory, that is, the thirteen who served as Directors and the others who acted as ministers, only three are known to have been financially corrupt: Barras, Talleyrand, and Fouché; and it is added (as if in defence of the French bourgeoisie) that the two former were ex-nobles by origin, and Fouché an ex-priest.[1] A number of contractors and generals, including Bonaparte, made fortunes in the occupied countries during the wars, and in Paris there was more minor graft than there ought to have been, as when a bureaucrat accepted money to remove someone's name from the official lists of émigrés. As for the making of fortunes in occupied countries, the British were doing the same by not wholly dissimilar methods in their conquests in India during these same years, without incurring the shocked indignation of Europeans. As for the minor graft, such commonplace misconduct was hardly enough to meet the ideological requirements of the stereotype, since it did not prove, especially in the eighteenth century, that the Directory was especially shameless or disgraceful. Other profits were made from the purchase and sale of confiscated lands, or from business ventures that took on new life after the year of the Terror. Many kinds of people thus quietly added to their fortunes, including such diverse characters as the social philosopher Saint-Simon and the honest Yankee Joel Barlow.

In the more conspicuous circles of Paris there was a debasement of moral tone. Some of the new rich, and some who felt they had had a

[1] A. Meynier, *Les coups d'état du Directoire*, 3 vols. (Paris, 1927), II, 168-78.

narrow escape in surviving the Terror, many of them persons who had never shared either in the idealism of the Revolution or in the refinements of the Old Regime, now found it safe and clever to make a joke about "virtue," wear exaggerated dress, chase after absurd luxuries, and otherwise make a show of their wealth and superiority. There was a certain amount of political hooliganism, led especially by young men of good family, the *jeunesse dorée*. Their importance should not be overstated. As a British spy reported in 1795: "The famous youth of Paris is only a conglomeration of scamps and elegant rascals, of whom this city always has a fortunate abundance. The body of them, so to speak, numbers four or five hundred." Gathering in cafes, they wear what they think is English costume, but is "really only a ridiculous caricature." Sometimes they are joined by ruffians from the public markets and by swarms of draft-dodgers. "These gentry police the theaters, and if an actor is thought tainted with Jacobinism, he dares not appear." The author of this report advised the British Foreign Office not to be misled by French foolishness. Hacking down liberty trees and stamping on the tricolor did not mean that the country had rejected the Revolution.[2]

The trouble with the stereotype, apart from its inaccuracy, is that it diverts attention from the problem of real interest, the political problem of introducing a moderate regime after a period of drastic action and feverish excitement. By a "moderate" regime is here meant, not merely one that preferred to avoid obvious violence, but in a more objective sense a regime that occupied an intermediate position on the spectrum of political beliefs.

This spectrum, it may be recalled from an earlier page, while of course having its nuances, consisted essentially in five distinguishable shades. At the Right was the extreme royalism of monarchical absolutism. Next came the idea of some kind of liberal, constitutional, and modernized monarchy. Then came constitutional republicanism. To the left of it was the doctrine of those republicans who were less insistent on constitutional forms, more dedicated to equality and fraternity, more militant in temper, and more hostile to all vestiges of the former social order in France. The Jacobinism of 1792-1794 had fallen at this place in the spectrum, but even at that time most Jacobins had looked forward to constitutional republicanism as their goal, so that after 1795 many Jacobins had "evolved," as the phrase was, a bit rightwards into the

[2] Great Britain, Historical Manuscripts Commission, *Report on the Papers of J. B. Fortescue Preserved at Dropmore*, 10 vols. (London, 1892-1927), III, 63-64.

constitutional category. Others, unsatisfied with the new constitution after 1795, may be thought of as straight political democrats. To their left, and the furthest left on the spectrum, carrying on the tone of the popular revolutionism of 1792-1793, and attracting a few former Jacobins, was the doctrine of those for whom political democracy should merge into a kind of social democracy, with some degree of equality in wealth and income.

The post-Robespierrist Convention, continuing the reaction against popular revolutionism which the Revolutionary Government had itself initiated, ran into increasing trouble with the popular classes of Paris, whose elementary needs for warmth and sustenance in the terrible winter of 1794-1795 went neglected and unsupplied. Invaded by angry crowds, the Convention reacted with vehemence, and in the ensuing repression alienated the most active popular revolutionaries from the "bourgeois" republic. Scrapping the constitution hastily adopted and ratified in the summer of 1793, but never put into effect (the Constitution of the Year I), the Convention drafted another, the Constitution of the Year III or 1795. The universal manhood suffrage and elements of direct democracy that had characterized the earlier constitution were abandoned, but the new one preserved the basic changes brought by the Revolution.

The Directory

In its actual terms, or formal provisions, the Constitution of the Year III, was about as much or as little "democratic" as the first constitution of 1789-1791.[3] The number of citizens who might qualify to vote in primary assemblies (men of twenty-one or older, paying an annual property tax equivalent to three days wages for common labor), and the number of those who might legally qualify to sit in the electoral assemblies of the departments (proprietors and tenants defined at exactly the levels of 1791) must if anything have been a trifle larger in 1795 than in 1791. It was provided that a literacy restriction should go into effect in the future (and when operating, this provision would greatly reduce the electorate under conditions then existing); but on the other hand, any young man who had fought in a military campaign had the right to vote whether he paid a tax or not. The primary assemblies

[3] For the text of the Constitution in English see John H. Stewart, *Documentary Survey of the French Revolution* (New York, 1951), 572-612; see also *Age*, 1, 522-28, Appendix v, " 'Democratic' and 'Bourgeois' characteristics in the French constitution of 1791."

of original voters, which in 1791 had chosen one "elector" for every hundred citizens, in 1795 chose only one for every two hundred. Hence, though millions were legally eligible, the number of electors actually chosen, meeting and functioning in the departmental assemblies at any one time during the Directory, was probably in the neighborhood of 30,000, fewer than under the constitutional monarchy as set up in 1789-1791. The Directory was a "bourgeois republic" in the sense that, in fact, a few hundred locally prominent persons in each department (though subject to annual re-election as electors) kept matters pretty much in their own hands. The accentuation of class fears during the Revolution made these prominent persons, or bourgeoisie, the more determined to stay in power. The decline of political interest and spontaneous activity since the first years of the Revolution also had the effect of leaving the field more open to the upper middle class. But the Constitution of the Year III was such that a more broadly based democratic movement could legally take place under it.

The Constitution created a legislative body in two Councils, the Elders and the Five Hundred, whose members were elected by the electors in the departmental assemblies. It set up the usual ministries of foreign affairs, finance, etc. As a supervisory board above the ministers, it provided an Executive Directory of five Directors, one to be elected each year by the legislature. This collegiate executive, elected by the legislature, was of course designed, in keeping with Republican principles of the day, to avoid the danger of dictatorship or despotism, of which all constitutionalists were much afraid.

By special provision, in effect until the election foreseen for the spring of 1797, two-thirds of the first members of the two legislative chambers were required to be former members of the Convention. The members of the post-Robespierrist Convention saw no other way of assuring not only their personal security but the continuity of republican institutions than by thus perpetuating themselves at least temporarily in office. But in so doing they made a great many enemies, who attempted in October 1795 (Vendémiaire of the Year IV) to block the two-thirds decree or indeed to stop the introduction of the republican constitution itself. This uprising of Vendémiaire was led by royalists and anti-republicans, against whom the outgoing Convention used the services of a young general then in the city, Napoleon Bonaparte, who fired his "whiff of grapeshot" on this occasion. The Directory (as the whole regime came to be called) thereupon established itself. It had been dependent on military protection for its very birth. And from the beginning a good deal of the activity in politics (for it was at first sufficiently liberal to allow "politics") was aimed at the election scheduled for March 1797, at which time the two-thirds rule would not obtain, so that persons opposed to the whole system might be elected to the two chambers.

The Directory looked like a government, and indeed was one, the first constitutional republican government on modern principles that France or Europe had seen. It was meant to be of moderate or intermediate political color. But from the beginning there was a certain lack of substance in the Directory, which was indeed something of a mirage, because so many of the real forces and realities of political life lay outside it, distributed elsewhere along the spectrum. If the Directory failed, as it did, the failure was due in part to the war, yet in other political conditions peace might have been made. It was due partly to economic troubles and inflation, yet inflation was brought under control; and partly to religious troubles and conflict with the Church, yet these were less irreconcilable than they seemed later in retrospect. It was not due to the incompetence of the men in power, who were by no means incompetent, nor to faults in the constitution, which under more favorable conditions might have been made to work or been modified into something workable.

The difficulty was that the Directory occupied too narrow a band in the spectrum. It was never able to broaden its base. Not even all moderates could agree on it. There were too many people who refused to accept it with any finality—Frenchmen who saw in it only an interim arrangement preceding one more to their liking, whether more royal or more democratic; and foreign powers, at war with it, which hoped and expected that if they waited long enough this republican experiment would collapse and be forgotten.

Never during its four-year life was the Directory able to formulate a clear program or policy, either on internal problems or on questions of war and peace and revolutionary movements in other countries. Five in number at any given moment, the Directors were a changing body, one being replaced each year constitutionally, with additional replacements through irregularities in September 1797 and June 1799, so that thirteen persons, all told, served as Directors. Only one was in office throughout, namely Barras; but Barras was never as influential as some of his colleagues, especially Reubell, who was in office for over three years and had the main voice in foreign policy, and LaRévellière-Lépeaux, who lasted over three years and was mainly interested in the propagation of natural religion. No combination of five incumbents ever agreed even within itself, and the Directors were often also at odds with the two legislative chambers. Far from being a disciplined committee intent on world revolution or anything else, the French executive presented itself to the world as irresolute, vacillating, and unpredictable, at the mercy of events, improvising its policies to keep abreast of accomplished facts. It shifted with developments that it could not control: conspiracies, intrigues, and elections at home; the victories and the independent actions of its generals in the field; the demands and disturbances of revolutionaries in other countries.

If not always moderate in its actions, the Directory remained essentially moderate in its preferred position, and in any case lived in nervous apprehension of the extremes. The "first" Directory, until the coup d'état of Fructidor (1797), was a predominantly liberal government, allowing much latitude to the press and to the embryonic manifestation of political parties. The "second" Directory, from Fructidor to Brumaire, was more arbitrary and dictatorial. Throughout, as Marcel Reinhard has said, the Directory "was falsified by its own principle."[4] Claiming to represent the sovereignty of the people it could not let the people alone, since the "people," when not hostile, were largely indifferent to the men now trying to govern the country. Claiming to be a constitutional government, it could not protect the constitution except by use of unconstitutional methods. It was an awkward fact, for a government that would have preferred to be moderate, that the majority of the population, especially the rural people, had relapsed into a non-political apathy, content to enjoy the gains derived from the Revolution but no longer excited by them, while the minorities that remained most politically sensitive and alert, both the Right and the Left, made no virtue of moderation and were untroubled by constitutional scruples.

The Directory therefore followed a zig-zag or see-saw policy, *la politique de la bascule*. It was buffeted repeatedly between Right and Left, between "royalism" and "democracy." Alarmed by signs of activity on one of these sides, the moderates of the Directory would try to make common cause with moderates inclining to the opposite side, until, given such encouragement, the second side became active to the point of threatening to dominate, setting up another alarm in which the trend started in the other direction.

[4] M. Reinhard, *Le Departement de la Sarthe sous le régime Directorial* (Saint Brieuc, s.d.), 629-31.

Of the real condition of the French people during these constitutional and political vicissitudes it is hard to speak. Marcel Reinhard concludes that the country was better off at the end of the Directory than at its beginning: the scarcities of 1795 had been overcome, a more stable currency had been introduced, schools and law-courts and regular procedures of administration and taxation had been put into operation, people were normally at work in the shops and on the farms. The "anarchy" under the Directory, according to Reinhard, came more at its beginning than at its end.

Contemporaries were very much interested in the true state of a country that had passed through so tremendous a revolution. Their judgments were widely different, but the difference was not due to impediments in the way of observation. No curtain screened France from the outside world. Travelers of all nationalities, except the British and Austrians with whom France remained at war, were free to travel in the new republic. An abundant press appeared in a language that was no barrier to international understanding. Differences among observers tended to reflect their own predilections. The American Jeffersonian, James Monroe, who was in France as American minister from August 1794 to December 1796, was favorably impressed. But the Massachusetts Federalist, Fisher Ames, called France "that open hell in which we see their state of torment."[5] A large sector of British opinion, strongly influenced by French émigrés, was also very unfavorable.

Late in 1796 the King of Prussia, having now been neutral for over a year, sent a special observer, D. T. Bayard, to give him an accurate and secret description. Bayard reported that he was surprised, after reading so many newspaper declamations, to find prosperity instead of revolutionary ruins. Trade was resuming with Holland and Spain. In the cities, he said, there were a good many men who thought conditions had been better in the days of Robespierre. In the country he saw well-clothed peasants with teams of horses, industriously tilling fields where the titles to property were still unsettled. There was plenty to eat in rural areas, he found; and the country people had benefited from the abolition of manorial dues and the Revolutionary reforms in taxation. They would accept the government if it made no demands upon them. In general, according to Bayard, people thought better of the new constitution than of the character of the men in office. There

---

[5] Monroe's letters and reports in *Writings* (New York, 1899), II, and see below, pp. 267, 532-33; Fisher Ames, "Laocöon," written in 1799, *Works*, 2 vols. (Boston, 1854), II, 112.

were also, he warned his royal employer, in France as in other countries, especially among intellectuals, numerous cosmopolitan philanthropists, or *républicanisateurs* who wanted to transform all Europe.[6]

In short, the weakness of the Directory was not so much economic or social or administrative as it was political. And the failure in these years to find an acceptable solution to the problems of the French Revolution was of such importance, for France and for the world, both then and subsequently, that a closer examination must be made, first of the moderates, then of the two extremes.

The Sources of Moderate Strength

The sources from which a moderate solution might have been drawn were numerous and significant. They existed all over Europe. In no country of the Coalition had the war against revolutionary France enjoyed much popular support. None of the Coalition governments had gone to war for the express purpose of putting down the Revolution, and as their territorial and other aims were made difficult by the French resistance, there was a general inclination to call a halt. Older issues of international politics reasserted themselves. In Spain, the dislike of the French Republic was eclipsed by fear of the expansion of British power in Latin America and the Mediterranean. In Prussia, the main danger was seen in the growth of Austrian power in Germany. Both Prussia and Spain made peace with France in 1795. Spain in the next year even signed an alliance with the Republic. Prussia embarked on a policy of neutralism that lasted for eleven years. The King of Prussia accepted the Batavian revolution as he did the French. No government except the British objected with any vigor to the French incorporation of Belgium. The Austrians were willing enough to be rid of their former Austrian Netherlands if compensated elsewhere. Dutch affairs, after the Batavian revolution, were in the hands of men who, while lacking enthusiasm for the French control of Belgium, saw in Great Britain the principal menace both to the new regime in Holland and to the preservation of the Dutch colonial empire.

It was Britain that kept the war going against France. For this fact various reasons can be seen. Though England was by no means the most conservative country in Europe, it was a country in which the virtues of an aristocratic society had been elaborated explicitly, and in which conservatism had become something of a philosophy of history

[6] P. Bailleu, *Preussen und Frankreich von 1795 bis 1807*, 2 vols. (Leipzig, 1881-1887), I, 91-101.

and of society. Some Englishmen, in their way, in arguing against the American revolution, or against reform of the British and Irish Houses of Commons or the granting of equal civic rights to Dissenters, had made an ideology of conservatism even before the Revolution in France. Englishmen of this same kind, in 1795 and 1796, preferred to see in the war with France a great ideological struggle. They found "Jacobins" everywhere, even in South Africa and India, and to Morton Eden, the British envoy at Vienna, it seemed that even the Austrian chancellor, Thugut, who was certainly very much opposed to the French Revolution, was a "Jacobin" because insufficiently energetic against France.

England also at this time, with the industrial revolution setting in, was in a phase of rapid growth in its trade and overseas empire. For this reason also it could not readily accept peace with France, especially with a France that had been its chief commercial competitor for a hundred years, and which if successful might close the Continent to British exports. It is certainly too much to see in the Anglo-French war of the 1790's an essentially commercial conflict waged in the respective interests of French and British merchants.[7] Too much else was at stake. But the fact that Britain was not in a passive or defensive phase, but was on the contrary highly dynamic, had important and somewhat paradoxical consequences.

On the one hand, it kept the hostilities going. The British could afford abundant outlays of money. By 1797, some eighty thousand pounds sterling had been paid to the royalists of northern France alone, to foment resistance against the Paris government.[8] As early as the end of 1794 the British treasury had paid £1,225,000 to Prussia, over a million to the smaller German states, and £350,000 to Sardinia, to keep them in the field against France. In 1795 and 1796, through guarantees of loans on which in the end it had to pay, the British government contributed over five millions to Austria.[9] But the Austrians, thus enabled to remain in the war after the other Continental states had left it, were badly defeated in north Italy by the French. This defeat opened

---

[7] As in E. Dejoint, *La politique économique du Directoire* (Paris, 1951).

[8] Windham's report to Pitt, *Dropmore papers*, III, 363. Windham remarked that the French royalists could not exist as a party without British money. The Princess of Orange had said the same of the Dutch Orangists, p. 191 above.

[9] Great Britain, House of Commons, *Sessional Papers for 1900*, Vol. XLVII, No. 180, "Loans and advances to foreign states since 1792"; J. H. Clapham, "Loans and Subsidies in Time of War," *Economic Journal*, XXVII (1917), 495-501. In 1796 an offer of £300,000 was made to Russia, for operations in the Rhineland or Holland, but it was refused. In 1799-1800 the British granted almost £3,500,000 to finance the Second Coalition.

the way to the indigenous forces of revolution in Italy. The Italian revolutions of 1796 and 1797, accompanied as they were by French predominance, and coming in addition to similar developments in Holland and Belgium, greatly reduced the chances for any moderate settlement of Europe's problems.

On the other hand, the dynamism of the British was certainly one of the factors (along with the partition of Poland and the unexpected strength shown by the French themselves) by which the military effort against France was greatly weakened. In some ways, the British could more effectively have led an anti-French and anti-Revolutionary alliance had their own aims been more disinterested. It was the well-grounded fear, derived from experience, felt in Holland and Spain, that the British would seize upon opportunities to acquire their colonies, or to impose undesirable trading advantages, that did as much as anything else to throw Holland and Spain—Holland with revolution, Spain without it—into alliance with the French Republic. Throughout the Continent there was a latent antipathy to England. The French could exploit it but did not have to create it, since it had accompanied the phenomenal rise of Britain and British sea power in the eighteenth century, been confirmed in the Seven Years' War, and somewhat glamorized by the American struggle for independence.

Even in England, however, there were important voices on the side of moderation. Pitt's government had no patience with French republicanism, but it refrained from recognizing the Count of Provence as Louis XVIII, and tried to persuade him of the advantages of constitutional monarchy. Of the English popular radicals, who were more sympathetic to French republicanism, more will be said in a later chapter. In the governing classes there were a good many men of political sagacity and fair-mindedness. Many of these men believed— and it was one of the signs of a "moderate" as distinguished from a *pur*—that the troubles in France could be largely attributed to the extremism of the Right. The Earl of McCartney, for example, before going to South Africa (where his sojourn was noted in the last chapter) was assigned as an unofficial British representative to the "court" of "Louis XVIII," which in 1796 gathered at a hotel in Verona. McCartney did not like what he saw there of the French émigré noblemen. "It is amusing to hear them discourse," he said, "on the former happiness of *all* social classes in France; they cannot conceive that the lower classes should have had aspirations to improve themselves, or that men of talent, without other advantages of fortune, should have any right or claim to positions of distinction."[10] William Wickham, the British agent in Switzerland, lost all respect for the future Louis XVIII and Charles X. "When one has observed them as closely and as often behind the scenes as I have," he wrote in 1796, "one is tempted to believe that God Almighty has willed this appalling revolution, among other aims, for their personal correction."[11] Lady Elliot, the wife of Sir Gilbert Elliot, was astonished that the French émigrés insisted on getting back their position and possessions as a matter of right. "I fear that great troubles are in store for France," she said in 1794.[12]

To men and women of this kind the extreme conservatives in England were no better. Late in 1796 Pitt sent the Earl of Malmesbury to France to enter upon talks to end the war. Edmund Burke, frightened and angry, penned his *Letters on a Regicide Peace*, in which he denounced the very thought of peace or compromise as outrageous and immoral. The Revolution in France was a "system of robbery." "It *must* be destroyed, or it will destroy all Europe." What the twentieth century would call "co-existence" seemed to Burke impossible. "With this republic, nothing independent can co-exist."[13] Burke's was not however the voice of all Britain. He was answered by Thomas Erskine in a widely read pamphlet.

Erskine, a brother of the eleventh Earl of Buchan, was an eminent lawyer, who had successfully defended the English "Jacobins" in the state trials of 1794. He believed that the French Revolution had been thrown onto a radical course by the Allied intervention of 1792. He saw the origin of an excessive British conservatism in the fears of republicanism raised by the American Revolution, not the French. He thought, in 1797, that the French Directory should be recognized by Britain, that it was "fit," as he put it ironically, "to be received into the holy communion of the robbers and despoilers of Poland." Pitt's government, he insisted, in remaining at war with France, pursued no attainable objective, and in fact, "while railing at home against republican theorists," was actually, since the French continued to win, contributing to the republicanization of Europe.[14]

[10] Quoted by A. Lebon, *L'Angleterre et l'émigration française* (Paris, 1882), xxiii.
[11] Quoted by G. Walter, *Le comte de Provence, frère du roi, "régent" de France, roi des émigrés* (Paris, 1950).
[12] *The Life and Letters of Sir Gilbert Elliot first Earl of Minto*, 3 vols. (London, 1874), II, 230.
[13] Edmund Burke, *Letters . . . on the Proposals for Peace with the Regicide Directory of France*. Letter II "On the genius and character of the French Revolution as it regards other nations," *Works* (Boston, 1877), v, 377.
[14] T. Erskine, *A View of the Causes and Consequences of the Present War with*

Burke's *Regicide peace* went through about a dozen pamphlet editions, Erskine's *View of the causes and consequences of the present war with France* through thirty-five. In later times, for whatever reason, it was Burke's effort that was remembered, and Erskine's forgotten.

Nor, despite all the provocations, were spokesmen for compromise absent from the Roman Catholic Church. Both Popes of the period offered gestures of conciliation. Pius VI, to be sure, had little sympathy or understanding for the Revolution. Nevertheless, when the Count of Provence, on assuming the title of King of France, hoped for the Pope's endorsement, Pius VI refused to give it. His Holiness, while expressing great personal sympathy in this awkward situation, replied that only the Almighty "will decide between you and the French people, whether they ought to be republicans, or be subject to a king." He hoped and believed that the new republican regime in France was superseding the "barbarous system of terror."[15] In the next year, 1796, in response to approaches by the Directory, Pius VI prepared a conciliatory letter, *Pastoralis sollicitudo*, recommending to French Catholics the acceptance of the republican order.[16] It was never published, largely because the French constitutional clergy, issuing from the Revolution, feared that reconciliation would work to their disadvantage. Pius VI was also the first Pope to grant full diplomatic honors to an envoy from a power not Catholic in principle, when he received Joseph Bonaparte as representative of the French Republic after the Treaty of Tolentino; and the modern period of papal affairs, in which no distinction is made diplo-

---

France (London, 1797), to which there were numerous replies, notably John Gifford, *A Letter to the Hon. Thomas Erskine* . . . (London, 1797, at least eleven editions), where Gifford insists on a French design of conquest since 1791, the danger of Jacobin conspiracy in England, and British need for a Belgium independent of France.

[15] The quotations are from a letter said to be from Pius VI to Louis XVIII, published in English in the *Annual Register for 1795* (London, 1800). I have been unable to locate any better source or authority, but see J. Gendry, *Pie VI, sa vie, son pontificat*, 2 vols. (Paris, 1907), II, 243, n. 4. The Pope also intimated that Louis XVIII might accept a "heroic sacrifice which is worthy to be made by a soul like yours in favor of the repose of human kind." It is understandable that later royalists and ultramontanes might not wish to publicize such a letter.

[16] E. E. Y. Hales, *Revolution and Papacy: 1769-1846* (New York, 1960), 89; L. von Pastor, *History of the Popes from the Close of the Middle Ages* (Eng. trans. London, 40 vols., 1890-1953), XL, 303-05; A. Latreille, *L'église catholique et la Révolution française*, 2 vols. (Paris, 1946), I, 231-33; J. Leflon, *Histoire de l'église*, vol. 20, *La Crise révolutionnaire 1789-1846* (Paris, 1949), 142-44; M. Reinhard, *Religion, Révolution et Contre-révolution* (Paris, Centre de documentation universitaire, photo-duplicated, 1950's), 242-43. Hales is a British, Pastor a German, and the others French Roman Catholic historians. Their views may be contrasted with the more common belief of recent American Catholic writers in an essential incompatibility between the principles of the Church and the Revolution.

matically between Christian and non-Christian states, is dated precisely from this year 1797.[17] In that year the man who soon became Pius VII (and was to sign the Concordat of 1801), Barnaba Chiaramonti, then bishop of Imola, near Bologna, declared his sympathies with the Italian revolution, consented to work with the French, and accepted the Cisalpine Republic.[18]

The French clergy made notable efforts to dissociate religion from politics. The constitutional clergy in France, after 1795, were no longer paid by the state nor considered established by it, and while generally remaining committed to the Revolution were absorbed in religious reconstruction in the ruins that followed the Dechristianization. Clergy both in France and in the emigration resisted the overtures of Louis XVIII. The Abbé Emery, head of the seminary of Saint-Sulpice in Paris, evaded the approaches of royalists. Even the émigré bishops, all of whom were monarchists by personal preference and belief, refused on various occasions to set up committees at the request of Louis XVIII, or take other joint action in which it should seem to be taught, as official Catholic doctrine, that Christianity had any intrinsic attachment to monarchy. In short, political Catholicism of the kind taught by some clerics and by such laymen as Joseph de Maistre—the doctrine of the "throne and the altar"—seems to have drawn little support from the most qualified spokesman for Catholicism at this time. This too, in later times, was easily forgotten.[19]

Indeed, less was heard from the Protestant clergy than from the Catholic in the way of tolerance for the new order. The various established churches of the Protestant world remained very conservative, or inclined to moralizing outbursts against the French Directory and the Batavian revolution. One has the impression (more investigation would be in order) that neither the Dutch Reformed pastors, nor the Anglican episcopate, nor the Puritan pontiffs of New England showed much tendency to moderation on these subjects. The minority churches, which might be more likely to do so (and whose importance in the Dutch revolution has been seen), lacked the organization through which public statements attracting public attention might be made.[20]

[17] R. A. Graham, *Vatican Diplomacy* (Princeton, 1959), 41.
[18] J. Leflon, *Pie VII, des abbayes bénédictines à la papauté* (Paris, 1958).
[19] P. de la Gorce, *Histoire religieuse de la Révolution française* (5 vols., Paris, 1912-1931), v, 270-79, and works cited in preceding notes.
[20] Being negative, this statement on Protestantism is hard to document. Note the impatience of Erskine, *View of the Causes . . .* (p. 55), where the war, he observes, "is said to save religion and its holy altars from profanation and annihilation. Of all the pretences by which the abused zeal of the people of England has been hurried on

Among the hundred thousand French émigrés there were some who were moderate, and who are best represented by a group settled in London. This group included P. V. Malouet, who had been a naval official before 1789 and had signed the Oath of the Tennis Court; the Marquis de Lally-Tollendal, who had been a leading liberal nobleman in the Constituent Assembly; the Marquis de Bouillé, a professional army officer, who had tried to save Louis XVI at the time of Varennes; the Count de Montlosier, a conservative of 1789 who had now become more pliable; the publicist Mallet du Pan and his son, Louis Mallet; the three archbishops of Aix, Bordeaux, and Toulouse; and, in 1796, Calonne, the reforming minister of 1786-1787, who had moved away from his absolutist views. All regarded the Terror with horrified aversion, all considered the extreme revolutionaries to be no better than criminals, and all believed that the Revolution was a destructive menace to all Europe. What made them moderate was their conviction that mere reaction was impossible; that the new property owners and other beneficiaries of the Revolution must be dealt with on some basis of compromise; and that the future government of France must be constitutional, allowing for a modern form of elected representatives, and taking account of the principles enunciated in the revolutionary declarations of rights. They shared also in a kind of theory of the French Revolution, which they did not attribute to the *philosophes*, or to conspiracy, propaganda, or "abstract ideas," believing, instead, that it had arisen from actual and weighty causes and moved forward by real considerations of politics. They did not think, as the extreme Right did, that the whole Revolution was a fateful force, in which small initial concessions had led on inevitably to convulsions of violence and fanaticism. That the Revolution had become violent and fanatical they agreed, but for this development they blamed the unyielding obstinacy of the extreme conservative opposition, which, they thought, gave the mass of Frenchmen no effective choice. Frenchmen in France, according to this view, were thrown on the mercy of revolutionary extremists, seeing no other defense for even moderate gains of the Revolution, so long as they believed, or were told by reactionary publicists, that any restoration meant a total and punitive restoration of the Old Order. These moderate or liberal-conservative émigrés therefore detested the

to a blind support of ministers, this alarm for the Christian religion is the most impudent and preposterous. . . . Who ever heard of the Christianity of the French court and its surrounding nobles?"

royalist *purs*, in whom they saw, after the Terror, the main obstacle to conciliatory arrangements.[21]

Agreeing in so much, the moderates of the emigration could not agree on what attitude to take toward the Directory. Many of them published books or pamphlets on the question. Calonne thought no peace possible with the republic; for him nothing would do except constitutional monarchy, with the institution of nobility recognized.[22] Mallet du Pan, in 1796, considered the Directory to be a vulgar democracy, hardly less ruthless than the government of the Terror.[23] Except that he now seemed to disapprove of everyone equally, from Right to Left, Mallet du Pan had lost most of his earlier "moderation." He now insisted that any acceptance of equality must lead to equality of wealth. This was of course the view of Babeuf and shows the convergence of extremes against a merely "bourgeois" republic. Malouet thought Mallet du Pan's tract of 1796 unconstructively angry and doctrinaire.[24]

His son Louis Mallet, along with Malouet, Montlosier, and Lally-Tollendal, were more willing to compromise. Disgusted with the two Bourbon princes, despising and despised by the "aristocrats" of the emigration, they were ready to believe that life in France under the Directory was possible for civilized men, while suspecting that at some future time, without much other change, the five Directors might simply be replaced by a king. From them, almost jointly (since they knew and talked with each other in London) there issued two pamphlets, one by Montlosier addressed mainly to the émigrés, and one by Lally-Tollendal addressed to the "sane" element among republicans in France.

Montlosier appealed to his fellow émigrés to give up their narrow

[21] The best source is P. V. Malouet, *Mémoires*, 2 vols. (Paris, 1874), containing correspondence with and references to the others named in this paragraph.

[22] C. A. de Calonne, *Tableau de l'Europe en novembre 1795* (London, 1796), published in English as *The Political State of Europe at the Beginning of 1796; or Considerations on the Most Effectual Means of Procuring a Solid and Permanent Peace* (London, 1796).

[23] J. Mallet du Pan, *Correspondance politique pour servir à l'histoire du républicanisme français* (Hamburg, 1796). The most recent of many works on Mallet du Pan is by N. Matteucci, *Jacques Mallet du Pan* (Naples, 1957), emphasizing his "moderation" and hostility to the extreme Right, which were more in evidence in the *Considerations* of 1793 than in later writings.

[24] Malouet, 466-68. It is significant of the difference between them that Malouet thought of settling in the United States, Mallet du Pan in Russia (422-23). Malouet thought that Britain's colonial ambitions were among the main obstacles to peace, and that France therefore should simply declare its own colonies independent; this plan, he said, would please the United States (413, 424, 438, 452).

and self-righteous royalist orthodoxy. It seemed to him incredible that, when a revolutionary leader became disillusioned with the Revolution, they ridiculed and spurned him instead of welcoming him as an ally. He himself, he complained, called an "aristocrat" in Paris, was ostracized as a "democrat" in London. The émigrés would never return to France until they co-operated with people different from themselves. "What are we to think of a party which, to prepare for a great conquest, instead of enlarging itself seeks only to diminish itself ... which has no projects but only memories, and marches forward while not ceasing to look behind!" What are we to think of people for whom "it is not enough to be pure, but necessary to be pure in their own fashion, pure as of a certain date in the past?" We are told that everyone in France is cursing the Revolution. This is both true and false. France today is a new amalgam in which we must find our place. If we want a king, he must be the king of all France. "Nothing can efface from French soil the imprint of its revolution." But Montlosier's arguments had little effect on those whom he most wished to persuade.[25]

Lally-Tollendal published his *Défense des émigrés adressée au peuple français* in both London and Paris (where the press was at the time quite free) at the turn of the year 1796-1797. His intention was to influence the coming French elections, in which, without any "two-thirds rule," a third of the members of the two chambers were to be chosen. Moderates in all camps were optimistic. In France there was a strong desire for peace, which it seemed might be more easily obtainable with a constitutional monarchy than with a republican government. Moderates in France, while adhering to the principles of 1789, and believing that events since 1792 had been at worst a piece of criminal excess and at best a necessity now happily over, were in a mood to make any compromises with the monarchy and the emigration that they could consider reasonable and safe. Among the five Directors themselves, Lazare Carnot, a mainstay of the Revolutionary Government three years before, but now a Jacobin *évolué*, inclined to this opinion. Among the generals, Pichegru, whose victories had brought the Batavian Republic into being, and who still commanded the French Army of the North, was actually engaged in secret correspondence with agents of Louis XVIII. England and France were carrying on serious peace talks. The moderate émigrés in London took heart; they followed developments in France very closely, and believed that the conciliatory

---

[25] Montlosier, *Des effets de la violence et de la modération dans les affaires de la France* (London, 1796), 2, 18, 42.

views of Thomas Erskine and Charles James Fox were gaining ground in England.

Lally-Tollendal's arguments were highly realistic, and aimed straight at the political center. He made no plea for restoration of either the monarchy or the church. Do not believe, he told his readers, the propaganda of those who say that return of the émigrés means the return of privilege and feudal rights. There is only one difference between us— property. By some compromise, the émigrés must receive back some of the property they have lost, and the present possessors of émigré property must give up some of what they now hold. No questions need be asked about former properties of the church. A union of old and new proprietors should be formed, of constitutionalists both monarchist and republican, but without regard to Louis XVIII or the *ancien régime*, while on the other hand presenting a strong front against the *Jacobins prolétaires*.[26] This was a reference to Babeuf's "communist" conspiracy discovered in 1796. In short, Lally-Tollendal proposed a bargain. The extremes of Right and Left would be ignored. Decent Frenchmen would defend themselves against both Bourbons and Babouvists. The still insecure property titles of beneficiaries of the Revolution would be confirmed, and the émigrés languishing in exile would come home.

The elections held throughout France in March 1797 proved to be an overwhelming repudiation of the Directory, and a victory, presumably, for the party of compromise settlement, stabilization, and peace. To pursue the question of the failure of moderation in the First Republic we must now look at the two extremes.

[26] *Défense*, part ii, 170. *Prolétaires* was one of the new words given currency by the Revolution; its association with "Jacobins" was mere name-calling, since the Jacobins were seldom proletarians.

THE FRENCH DIRECTORY BETWEEN
EXTREMES

[*The Extreme Right*] *There has been formed in Europe a league of fools and fanatics, who, if they could, would forbid man the faculty to think or see. The sight of a book makes them shudder; because enlightenment has been abused, they would exterminate all those they suppose enlightened. . . . Persuaded that without men of intelligence there would have been no revolution, they hope to reverse it with imbeciles. . . .*

[*The Extreme Left*] *Europe today excludes any possibility of democracy, direct or representative; to try the experiment is not to recast the state but to destroy it. . . . Do you wish a republic of equals amid the inequalities which the public services, inheritances, marriage, industry and commerce have introduced into society? You will have to overthrow property.*—MALLET DU PAN, 1796

THE FRENCH DIRECTORY BETWEEN
EXTREMES
Democracy and Communism

As ONE moved from the center in a leftward direction, one at first entered a territory that was not very radical, peopled by men who can be called "democrats" in the ordinary American sense, though they were more likely to call themselves "true republicans" or "good patriots." They accepted the constitution and saw no further need of violent insurrection, but they feared that the new national government might go too far in an understanding with émigrés or refractory clergy, or that the governing groups in Paris did not hold to the great principles of Liberty and Equality as firmly as they themselves did. Some now owned pieces of former church or émigré property, in amounts either large or small. Some, without having been terrorists themselves, had praised the Terror in its day or been busy and useful as local administrators for the Revolutionary Government. They feared that in a White Terror, of which there had already been enough painful examples, or even in a more moderate reaction against persons supposed to be dangerous, they themselves might sooner or later be engulfed. Of similar views were many shopkeepers, recently prospering farmers, ex-soldiers, young men just beginning to imagine their futures, Julien Sorels of one kind and another who disliked the notables of the newly emerging social establishment, and for whom, therefore, equality represented a value still to be achieved. Disapproving and aloof, the "pures" of the Republic, fearful of being tainted by compromise, never ready to admit that the Revolution had quite achieved its aim, they were often called *exclusifs* by the more complacent official republicans.

It is impossible to estimate the number of persons of this kind in France in 1796. Probably it was large, perhaps as large as any group that had a definite political consciousness. Their relative strength varied greatly from place to place. A good deal is known about the city of Toulouse, one of the most "Jacobin" cities of France, where the "Jacobins" controlled the municipality and won all the elections under the Directory. In this city of 60,000 (or some 15,000 grown men) there were about 1,500 persons sufficiently animated in their politics to be called Jacobins. They were recruited from the same social levels as the true Jacobins before 1794: that is, from all levels except the former nobility and the most depressed segments of the working class. They included well-to-do merchants, lawyers, doctors, teachers, members of learned academies, manufacturers, artisans, shopkeepers, and proprietors of small businesses. They kept their own firebrands under control, so as to give no excuse for counter-revolutionary reprisals, and if they were conscious of having allied with lower-class sans-culottes in the Year II they were now willing to forget any such troublesome connections. They were political or middle-class democrats. Tenacious of their own property, they were hostile to the rich. Civilized themselves, they were scornful of high society. They were out of sympathy with the reigning republicans, those who dominated in the departmental electoral assemblies and in Paris, because the reigning republicans had a low opinion of them. One has the impression that here if anywhere, among democrats of this kind, were the materials from which a law-abiding opposition to government, and a regime of competing political parties, might have been made, if only the Directory itself had been more tolerant of such opposition, and other circumstances had been more propitious.[1]

There was, however, no visible boundary, at any fixed point, between these political democrats and other democrats further to the Left, though in the end the differences were clear enough. Political democrats, critical of the Directory but loyal to it, continued to use the language of the Revolution and enjoyed reading radical newspapers. Sober citizens, with no intention of acting upon or even agreeing with their contents, subscribed to journals that ferociously denounced kings, aristocrats, leagues of tyrants, the clergy, the English, and the rich. Among the numerous radical papers that sprouted up at the end of 1795 was the *Tribun du peuple*, by a then obscure journalist who called himself "Gracchus" Babeuf.

[1] J. Beyssi, "Le parti jacobin à Toulouse sous le Directoire," in *Annales historiques de la Révolution française*, Nos. 117, 118 (1950), 28-54, 109-33. For enlightening accounts of democrats of this kind see also the second volume of A. Meynier, *Les coups d'état du Directoire*, 3 vols. (Paris, 1927), and relevant parts of M. Reinhard, *Le Département de la Sarthe sous le régime Directorial* (Saint-Brieuc, no date).

The *Tribun du peuple*, of which about 2,000 copies were printed, was sold both in the streets of Paris and by subscription, and had a national circulation. A surviving list of 590 subscribers has been analyzed. Of these subscribers, 238 were in the departments and 345 were in Paris. In the departments a majority of the subscribers were people in the more comfortable social positions—the big merchants called *négotiants*, engineers, lawyers, doctors, public officials, army officers, and the like. In Paris a majority of the subscribers were artisans and small shopkeepers, such as house-painters, wine-merchants, and proprietors of cafes—the kind of people who had been sans-culottes and section committeemen in the Year II. Vehement revolutionism, it is clear from these lists, was relished by a precarious combination of provincial bourgeoisie and Parisian populace. All kinds of persons read Babeuf.[2]

Further to the Left than most readers of political papers was a much smaller category of activists for whom political agitation had become a habit, and who, having called attention to themselves by leadership in the Paris sections after August 1792, or in the Parisian *armée révolutionnaire* of 1793, or in other ways, were now regularly watched by the police. From the police records of the Directory it appears that there were some 200 or 250 such men whom the police repeatedly arrested and re-arrested between 1795 and 1800, simply on general grounds of their past records, as a preventive measure to stop insurrectionary turbulence before it could flare up. By arresting, questioning, confining, liberating, and again arresting these same individuals, the police of the Directory, in the words of R. C. Cobb, "decapitated the democratic movement," so that there was no successful popular uprising between 1795 and 1830. From this same category of small-scale militants much of the secondary leadership in the Babeuf conspiracy was recruited.[3]

With Babeuf and with his co-worker Philippe Buonarroti, a French citizen of Italian birth, and with their Conspiracy of Equals of 1796, we reach the extreme Left of the French Revolution.[4] The bare facts of the

[2] A. Soboul, "Personnel sectionnaire et personnel babouviste," in *AHRF*, No. 162 (1960), 438-46.
[3] R. C. Cobb, "Notes sur la répression contre le personnel sans-culotte de 1795 à 1801," in *AHRF*, No. 134 (1954), 23-49.
[4] The literature is large, and the subject has attracted increasing historical interest in recent years in many countries. The basic documents are the proceedings at the High Court at Vendôme, with speeches and papers submitted in evidence, published by the Directory under various titles in 1797. They have become very rare, but six volumes of them are at the Princeton University Library. Important also as a source is Filippo Buonarroti, *La conspiration pour l'Egalité dite de Babeuf*, 2 vols. (Brussels, 1828), reprinted with a preface by Georges Lefebvre, 2 vols. (Paris, 1957); Eng. trans. by Bronterre O'Brien (London, 1836). For current work see *AHRF*, No. 162 (Oct.-

conspiracy are briefly told. Babeuf and Buonarroti met in 1795 in a Paris prison, where they were confined by the Thermidorian Convention, along with others who were regarded as dangerous or who had been active during the Terror. In October 1795, when the Directory took over from the Convention, it did so against the royalist opposition shown in the Vendémiaire uprising and the attempted Anglo-royalist invasion of western France, and so made a bid for support on the Left, and released these political prisoners. These men, as soon as liberated, began to publish journals like the *Tribun du peuple*, and to gather in an assembly called the Pantheon Club, of which Buonarroti was president for a time, and which had about 2,000 members. The authorities closed the Pantheon Club on February 28, 1796. The officer who enforced its closing was none other than Bonaparte, who, having put down the royalists in October, now did the same to the republican extremists, after which he went off to his military campaign in north Italy. The ardent spirits of the Pantheon Club, thus repressed, began to plot revolution. An inner circle composed of Babeuf, Buonarroti, and five others formed themselves into a secret insurrectionary committee. They worked through an outer circle of "revolutionary agents" who were unknown to each other, and each of whom was to recruit followers, among civilians and in the army, who were prepared to receive orders on the day of insurrection. The evidence is uncertain as to whether they intended to put the five Directors to death. One of the inner circle, Sylvain Maréchal, composed a Manifesto of the Equals, a powerful statement of an ongoing revolution in which property should be abolished; but the group never formally approved it, nor was it published at the time. What was published, or placarded about the city, was an *Analyse de la doctrine de Babeuf*, a declaration in twelve brief articles, very emphatic in its demand for equality of wealth, education,

---

Dec. 1960) where the whole issue is devoted to Babeuf in honor of the bicentennial of his birth. It is introduced by an extensive bibliographical survey by J. Godechot, "Les travaux recents sur Babeuf," and contains articles by French, Italian, Norwegian, East German, and Russian historians. See also A. Galante Garrone, *Buonarroti e Babeuf* (Turin, 1948), and S. Bernstein, *Buonarroti* (Paris, 1949). Babeuf's writings are most easily consulted in M. Dommanget, *Pages choisies de Babeuf* (Paris, 1935); for Buonarroti's writings of 1795-1796 see A. Saitta, *Filippo Buonarroti*, 2 vols. (Rome, 1950). Where Godechot holds that the recent interest in Babouvism reflects the movement of historical science, Elizabeth Eisenstein in *The First Professional Revolutionist: Filippo Michele Buonarroti* (Cambridge, Mass., 1959), relates it to ideological interests of the modern Left. That the Left may be "scientific," and that agreement is possible, is evident from the fact that my own indebtedness at this point is chiefly to Saitta. Saitta emphasizes the differences between the real situation of 1796 and Buonarroti's recollections as published in his book of 1828.

and happiness, but not explicitly proposing the abolition of private property, and ending up with a demand for the Constitution of the Year I.[5] Probably the inner circle intended, after the insurrection, to govern as a revolutionary dictatorship, on the model of the Revolutionary Government of the Year II, and following the principles enunciated by Robespierre, by which a temporary dictatorship held power for a transitional period until the old order was liquidated and the new one established.

The police, through an informant, broke up the conspiracy on May 10, 1796, a few days before the day set for insurrection. At the ensuing trial Babeuf and one other were condemned to death, and Buonarroti and others sent to prison.

The Conspiracy of Equals has always been looked back on with respectful interest by partisans of the modern Left, as the first manifestation of the revolutionary movement of the nineteenth and twentieth centuries. How far the Conspiracy was "communistic" remains uncertain, though Babeuf and Maréchal, as individuals, had ideas which are accepted by modern Communists as in effect communistic. But even the inner leadership had diverse aims, and the whole movement was so secret and so short-lived that the secondary organizers, not to mention the ordinary followers, never knew who the leaders were or what their purposes might be. Not much was said at the trial about "communism" or the abolition of property. The charge was subversion of the government and constitution. Babeuf, at his trial, therefore said little of private property or its abolition, denied that there had been any conspiracy except insofar as the whole Enlightenment had been a "conspiracy" for human freedom, and insisted repeatedly that he had been no more than secretary to a peaceable Society of Democrats.[6] At no time did Babeuf ever use the word "communism," which was still unknown to the French language; but he did, both before and after

---

[5] Most historians have used the text of the *Analyse* as published by Buonarroti in 1828 with amplifications. A version of the 1796 text was published by V. Advielle, *Histoire de Gracchus Babeuf et du Babouvisme*, 2 vols. (Paris, 1884), I, 207-208. For the importance of using the 1796 text see Saitta, I, 28, 262-63. The exact place of Maréchal's *Manifeste des Egaux* in the conspiracy has long been debated, and various explanations have been given for the refusal of the insurrectionary committee to adopt it: that these "communists" would not accept the barbarous phrase, *perissent les arts*; that they wished not to frighten the straight democrats among their allies; and, third, that for most of the committee "communism" and abolition of property were not of central importance to their program anyway. Saitta inclines to the third explanation; M. Dommanget to the first in *Sylvain Maréchal, l'égalitaire, "l'homme sans Dieu"* (Paris, 1950), 322.

[6] Babeuf's final speech was published by Advielle, *Histoire*, II, 1-322.

his arrest, make frequent use of the words "democrat" and "democracy." In fact, of all groups in France during the Revolution, it was the Babouvists, far more than Robespierre, who most often used the word "democracy" to describe a desirable state of society. Much of the interest in the whole affair lies in the relationship between "democracy" and "communism" in this early stage of their history. In the case of Babeuf personally and a few others, we can also see how "democracy" was already used as a screen behind which a "communist" program might be advanced.

The Conspiracy of Equals was a joining together of men who genuinely believed that they were furthering the cause of democracy or equality, though they understood it in different senses. It carried on the popular revolutionism of 1792-1794, with a touch of international revolutionism in the person of Buonarroti and possibly the Dutch Blauw;[7] and it gathered to itself a great variety of people who, for one reason or another, domestic or international, thought the Directory too bourgeois, too compromising, or too timid. Anyone having any touch with the conspiracy knew at least that insurrection was contemplated, so that all were further to the Left than the regular democrats such as those just described at Toulouse.

The actual relationship between elements in the movement is suggested by Albert Soboul, the great authority on the Paris sans-culottes, an admirer of Babeuf, and an eminent representative of the best Marxist historiography. "In the center," he says, "appears the directing group, resting on a small number of tested militants; then the fringe of sympathizers, 'patriots' and 'democrats,' kept outside the secret, and who seem not to have shared in the new revolutionary ideal; finally the popular masses themselves who were to be led. One of the essential problems of revolutionary practice posed for the Conspirators was that of their relationship to the popular masses by way of the sympathizers, who were the framework (*cadres*) not so much of the Conspiracy as of the revolutionary movement that was to follow the seizure of power." It is Soboul's belief, which seems to be well founded, that the "popular mass" in the movement (who may have numbered several thousands) clung to the sans-culotte ideas of the Year II, but that the ideas of the inner circle had undergone a "sudden mutation," which was "the first form of the revolutionary ideology of the new society born of the [French] Revolution itself."[8]

---

[7] But for the evidence against the intriguing hypothesis of a Dutch connection, suggested by Godechot and Saitta, see above, pp. 195-97.

[8] Soboul, *AHRF*, No. 162, 455-56.

Thus Soboul connects certain subsequent features of Marxism with a group of men in 1796 to most of whom such ideas were entirely foreign. The great majority of persons in contact with the Babouvist movement were excited by ideas of direct democracy, popular democracy, busy and spontaneous local activity, the massive rising of the people, with an insistence on a degree of equality of respect, of dignity, of education and material level of life, but with a strong emphasis on small private property, small private enterprise and private workshops, by which small men could preserve their individual independence. The inner circle, however, by a "sudden mutation," had passed beyond this somewhat pettifogging equalitarianism to envision a truly socialist or communist world. The inner circle, who already perceived or anticipated the "new revolutionary ideal," kept its views concealed from the mass of "democrats" whom it intended to lead or manipulate. One is reminded of the manipulations of Martinovics in Hungary.

By the "sudden mutation" is meant also that the Babouvist inner circle was no mere continuation of Robespierrism. Here the views of Soboul must be supplemented by the more refined analysis of Armando Saitta, the authority on Buonarroti. Saitta notes that two kinds of revolutionaries of the Year II came together to form the Conspiracy of Equals of the Year IV.[9] One group was typified by Buonarroti, who had been a staunch Robespierrist in 1793-1794, had worked for the Revolutionary Government, and remained faithful to Robespierre even after Thermidor; his belief in equality had a strong moral and religious tone, he was a fervent Rousseauist, and he strongly supported the Worship of the Supreme Being. He wanted to revolutionize or democratize Italy, his own native country, and joined the Conspiracy of Equals with that purpose in mind, believing that only by a revival of truly revolutionary forces in France could the right kind of popular revolution come in Italy, without exploitation by the French Directory and the French armies. Over thirty years later, in the book which he published in 1828 and which made the Babeuf conspiracy famous, Buonar-

[9] Saitta, *AHRF*, No. 162, 427-28; *Filippo Buonarroti*, 1, 1-36, 252-79; 11, 238-43. Very important in Buonarroti's development were the months he spent as the agent of the Revolutionary Government at Oneglia, a territory belonging to the King of Sardinia, during the military operations of 1794. (See, in addition to Saitta, Pia Onnis, "Filippo Buonarroti, commissario rivoluzionario a Oneglia," *Nuova Rivista Storica*, 1939, 353-79 and 477-500.) At Oneglia, Buonarroti made the acquaintance of Augustin Robespierre and Bonaparte, became a rallying point for Italian refugees and patriots from various parts of Italy, supervised policies of requisition, confiscation, price controls, military supply, and delivered an address on the Worship of the Supreme Being (published in full by Saitta, 1, 252-56) which, without mentioning Robespierre by name, echoes the sentiments simultaneously expressed by Robespierre in Paris.

roti had become a convert to "communism," but there is no sign that he cared much about "communism" in 1796; and indeed Saitta suggests that when the Conspiracy of Equals is rightly seen, as a combination of various anti-Directory activists, the "communism" may be no more than an excrescence.[10]

The other group, typified by Babeuf, was composed of men who had been anti-Robespierrist in 1793-1794. Most of them had played no constructive role during the period of the Terror, much of which Babeuf had spent in prison. In the days of the Revolutionary Government they had denounced that government as a dictatorship. They were what Robespierre called ultras or Hébertists. They were not true sans-culottes, but stormy journalists and intellectuals, who had clamored for the Constitution of the Year I as early as the summer of 1793—that is, had tried to overthrow the Revolutionary Government, the Committee of Public Safety and the Convention, as they now in 1796 tried to overthrow the Directory. These men, Thermidorians of the Left, had rejoiced in Robespierre's fall, and called him, once he was dead, an ogre, a monster, a Caligula "justly abhorred," a tyrant crazed by private ambition. Babeuf had even written a book, *Le système de dépopulation*, alleging that it had been Robespierre's studied policy to solve the social problems of France by reducing the population through the guillotining of two million people.[11] In Babeuf, unlike Buonarroti, there was no yearning for an especially moral republic. With Babeuf, but not with Buonarroti, revolutionary ideology had undergone a "sudden mutation" in abruptly departing both from sans-culottisme and from Robespierre.

Both men in 1796, however, felt themselves to be marching in Robespierre's path. Both represented themselves as his successors, bearing the standard that had been struck from his hands. Precisely how they did so is of interest, since it illustrates the kind of continuity that existed between the French Revolution and the later revolutionary movements of which Babouvism was in some ways an anticipation.

What Buonarroti most feared is illustrated by an episode at the house of James Monroe, which occurred on March 12, 1796, the very moment at which the Conspiracy of Equals was being formed. Monroe gave a state dinner, at which various ambassadors and high personages of the French government were present. Toasts were drunk, including one

---

[10] Saitta, I, 27, ". . . ovvero perche il comunismo era una superfetazione sul tronco della cospirazione?"

[11] *Du système de dépopulation, ou la vie et les crimes de Carrier* . . . (Paris, 1795); Dommanget, *Pages choisies*, 178-85.

aux rois amis de la France, which was enthusiastically cheered. The
Prussian ambassador commented on this attitude in the French republicans, who now believed that kings could be their friends.[12]
Buonarroti had just published a pamphlet of directly opposite tendency, *La paix perpetuelle avec les rois.*[13] As an Italian patriot, he was
afraid that the French would sign an armistice with the King of
Sardinia (as they soon did), instead of befriending the Italian republicans who were working to overthrow him. Toward kings, Buonarroti
argued, there was no proper policy except unconditional surrender.
They could never be trusted, they would never negotiate honestly with
the France of the Revolution. France, to protect itself, must make
common cause with all other peoples. "I invite the French government,"
said Buonarroti, "to aid the revolution in Italy by every possible means"
—to assist the Italians in dethroning the kings of Sardinia and Naples,
the archdukes of Tuscany and Milan, and also the Pope, so that
18,000,000 people could enjoy political freedom and the true equality
that Jesus himself had taught. Italy should be remodeled on the lines
of the Batavian Republic. Italian liberty, added to French and Dutch,
would checkmate the monarchs and assure the liberation of mankind.

Buonarroti rightly believed that the Directory was unlikely to take
up any such crusade. He attributed this hesitation in the Directory to
its bourgeois and moderate character, and thought that if true democrats were in power in France, if the real people could only make its
voice heard, if the great days of Robespierre and the Year II could come
again, there would be more support in France for the Italian republicans
and the patriots of all countries. In short, Buonarroti associated democracy with world-revolutionism. It is doubtful whether this belief
had any foundation. The great Committee of Public Safety had always
been skeptical of the foreign revolutionaries; it had in fact suppressed
those in Paris as "ultras"; and Robespierre had never had any faith in
the universal rising of peoples. Probably the Revolutionary Government
of the Year II, had it faced the same situation, would have taken much
the same attitude as the Directory did, asking the same questions of the
Italian revolutionaries of 1796 as it asked of the Batavian revolutionaries
of 1794—whether they were significant enough to be useful, what
resources they could bring to a common war effort, whether they
could control their own countries in a way favorable to the French

[12] P. Bailleu, *Preussen und Frankreich von 1795 bis 1807,* 2 vols. (Leipzig, 1881-1887),
I, 60.
[13] Published in full by Saitta as one of Buonarroti's "unknown or forgotten writings,"
II, 238-43.

Republic.[14] Buonarroti, a faithful Robespierrist, who had served the Revolutionary Government in the distant outpost at Oneglia, had never been privy to its inner counsels. In his hostility to the Directory, he credited the former Revolutionary Government with ideas it had never had. That Robespierre would have deeply concerned himself with revolution in Italy was a myth.

Babeuf's association of himself with Robespierre involved delicate problems. For one thing, he had been anti-Robespierrist in 1793-1794. For another, he had undergone a "mutation." He did not believe in private property, and in that sense was "communist."

Babeuf derived his communism from a widely respected conception of the Enlightenment, *le bonheur commun*, the common welfare or public happiness, which, however, he believed must lead to the *communauté*, or equal sharing, of material goods and other enjoyments—"comfort for all, education for all, equality, liberty and happiness for all." He derived it also from the democratic movement: "Our dogmas are pure democracy, equality without blemish and without reserve."[15] He believed in 1796 that this *bonheur commun* had almost been reached in 1794, and that all that now stood in the way of its realization was the reaction that had set in since Thermidor, perpetuated by the crude and callous republicans of the Directory, "banal republicans" who preached "no more than any kind of republic." In the face of such a regime, and sensing the hopes of 1794 slipping away, he was tormented by the thought of an unmerciful class struggle, "a war declared between patricians and plebeians, between rich and poor."[16] Reproved even by his radical friends for preaching class war, he replied that this war already existed, that the rich had started it by robbing the poor, that it had always gone on, and was perpetual until the general acceptance of his own doctrines.

In this formulation of an everlasting class struggle Babeuf anticipated Marxism, but he offered no analysis that a Marxist could call "scientific." He had no conception of an economic system as a system, and his critique fell less on capitalism, as such, than on the evils produced by uncontrolled inflation, high prices, scarcity, poverty, ignorance, and the luxurious self-indulgence of the idle rich. We hear in him the voice of the outraged victim of circumstances more than the social philosopher. He had none of Marx's interest in the processes of capital formation, or the role of wages and profit in the allocation of

[14] Above, pp. 117-23.
[15] Dommanget, *Pages choisies de Babeuf*, 240, 247.
[16] *Ibid.*, 236.

incomes, or the proletariat and bourgeoisie as classes generated by the relationships of production. Babeuf's enemy was not the "bourgeois" (a term he rarely used) but the "patriciate," the "gilded million," the "rascals," the "bloodsuckers," the "starvers and invaders of the rights of the People."[17] The whole doctrine was non-economic: it saw no problem of production; a kind of natural and automatic plenty was posited, in which equality was upset because, from sheer cupidity, some people stole what others ought to have.

In his *Tribun du peuple*, at the end of 1795, he published a proposed *Plebeian Manifesto*.[18] "It is time," he said, "to speak of democracy itself." We are accused of favoring the "agrarian law." This is ridiculous: we do not propose to divide up property, since no equal division would ever last. We propose to abolish private property altogether. Only thus can true equality be assured. Equality must be understood literally—"a sufficiency for all, but no more than a sufficiency." No one must be allowed to excel others in wealth or knowledge. We must prevent, "as a social scourge," any man from working harder or producing more than another in order to gain more income. No one has a right to take advantage of any special abilities. It is a vulgar prejudice to believe that a watchmaker should have twenty times the income of a plowman, or that tasks requiring intelligence should be more highly compensated than ordinary labor, or that inventors deserve any reward, since it is "society" that really gives birth to inventions and new ideas. "Stomachs are equal." In place of private property we need a "common administration," with each man placing his product in a common store, and receiving from it his perfectly equal share. Babeuf concluded the Manifesto with a resounding call: "Let everything then be confounded together! Let all the elements be confused, jumbled and knocked against one another! Let all return to chaos, and from chaos let a world rise new and regenerated!"[19]

It is impossible to imagine Robespierre (or Marx) using such language. Yet within a few weeks of writing the *Plebeian Manifesto* Babeuf made his great retraction. He declared that he had been mistaken in following Hébert, and that Robespierre had been right all

---

[17] *Ibid.*, 278 and *passim*. It should be pointed out that Dommanget, Georges Lefebvre, and others have shown a higher regard than the present author for the scientific character, or at least the intellectual quality, of Babeuf's analysis.

[18] Published by Dommanget, 250-64.

[19] Dommanget, 264. In the following number of the *Tribun du peuple* Babeuf refuted the charge of being an *anarchiste* or *désorganisateur*, and after his arrest declared that the conspirators had engaged in no more than a philanthropic dream, like those of other *philosophes* of the century.

the time. "We must remember," he said, "that we are only the second Gracchi of the French Revolution." Robespierre and Saint-Just, the first "Gracchi," we are told, had perished for attempting what Babeuf and his friends now meant to do. Hébertism, as Babeuf now saw it, had been only factious, local, Parisian, deviationist. Robespierrism was the true course of the true Revolution. "The reason is simple: it is that Robespierrism is democracy, and that these two words are absolutely identical."[20]

What are we to make of such a body of ideas? Let us try to avoid both the aversion that Babeuf has aroused in conservatives, and the deference with which the modern Left has regarded its Precursor. Let us remember that the best Marxist historians agree that Robespierre was never more than an advanced bourgeois democrat, and that Babouvism was never more than a futile conspiracy, an agitation among intellectuals with few followers, not at all like the true popular up-heaval of sans-culottisme three years before. What, then, is the place of Babeuf and Babouvism in the history of the French Revolution and of modern revolutions in general?

It seems likely, at least to the present author, that Babeuf might have been soon forgotten, or no better remembered than others like Sylvain Maréchal, if the Directory, on suppressing his conspiracy, had merely imprisoned him and then released him under police supervision, as it did with other such *exaggérés*; if it had not brought him to trial, given him a courtroom forum, made his name a by-word and his execution a martyrdom; and if Buonarroti, whose life was spared at the same trial, had not published thirty years later his *Conspiration pour l'Egalité dite de Babeuf*, in which the realities of 1796 were naturally seen through intervening experience, and transformed by the desire to speak to a newly rising revolutionary and socialist generation.

It is only by an effort that Babeuf's rabid equalitarianism can be seen as a form of socialism or communism, since it is hard to find in it

[20] Babeuf's letter to Bodson, in Dommanget, 284-86. For men who claimed to be the "second Gracchi," it is notable that neither Babeuf nor Buonarroti, if we may argue *ex silentio*, had any recollection in the Year IV of the Ventôse laws of the Year II (above, p. 116) in which Saint-Just and Robespierre had proposed to transfer prop-erty from suspects to poor patriots. When Buonarroti wrote his book of 1828, how-ever, doubtless having made discoveries by historical research in such sources as the *Moniteur*, he declared that the Equals of 1796 had wished to carry forward this program of Robespierre's. This became a standard belief in some socialist and some Chartist circles. The political importance of the Ventôse laws, stressed by Mathiez, has been discounted by Soboul and Lefebvre, and the failure of the Babouvists to mention them, only two years later, seems proof that their importance, for the Left at least, was very slight.

any conception of organized society. Nor can it be called democracy if democracy means a form of government, in which he had no interest. It was an extreme form of radical democratism so far as democracy signified a state of equality. His insistence on "real" equality should not be taken lightly; it was an ideal that he shared with Rousseau, Robespierre, and Condorcet, and the modern world has moved in the direction they indicated, toward greater equality of income, education, and living standards, though hardly by the methods that Babeuf proposed. But no society could long live with a principle of equality in which differences of ability were called a "social scourge."

What Babouvism had to offer later revolutionaries was above all the passionate commitment to revolution itself, a perpetual revolution, or revolutionism, drawing its force from the belief in an everlasting and irreconcilable war of classes. "The French Revolution," said Maréchal, in the Manifesto of Equals which the Babeuf group did not actually adopt, "is only the forerunner of another revolution far greater, far more solemn, which will be the last."[21] What Babeuf came to admire in Robespierre, and the reason why he found Robespierre a more useful model than Hébert, was not so much Robespierre's goals or objectives, which were different from Babeuf's, but his skill as a revolutionary theorist and tactician, his prestige as a man who seemingly had almost succeeded, and his prominence as a leader and spokesman of an effective and militant revolutionary dictatorship. To these ideas Babeuf added lessons in the techniques of conspiracy and manipulation, or the notion of producing revolution by handfuls of professional revolutionaries, which would appeal, not indeed to Karl Marx, but to a great many practicing revolutionaries of later times.

In its immediate effect, and perhaps in its longer-range effects in French history, it was an unfortunate consequence of Babouvism to confuse the whole question of political democracy with insurrectionism and social radicalism. One of the main results of the Revolution, the real French Revolution, the one which really happened, was to make France more self-consciously than ever a nation of property-owners. Nowhere else, thanks in part to the Revolution, was real property so widely owned. A movement to abolish private property had no conceivable chance of success. It could only frighten very large numbers of people. Babeuf's writings in the *Tribun du peuple* were public, and the proofs of conspiracy offered at the trial were genuine and convincing. He insisted, at his trial, that he had done no more than belong

[21] Dommanget, *Maréchal*, 311.

to a Society of Democrats, who, he said, were principally concerned to prevent the restoration of the Pretender. If "democrats" were like Babeuf, who would not fear them? He insisted that his views were only the natural outcome of the Enlightenment, no different from those of Diderot or Rousseau and perfectly harmonious with the general principles of the French Revolution. This was precisely the doctrine of the extreme Right, which also held that Enlightenment and Revolution led inevitably to the kinds of things that Babeuf did and said. It was all very discouraging for the growth of moderate political life. It made moderates hesitate to embrace democratic ideas, it weakened political democrats by associating them vaguely with anarchists, and it gave governments an excuse, if not indeed an actual duty, to repress agitation on the Left.

The Throne and the Altar

If from a hypothetical dead center one looked to the Right, the first to be seen would be the moderates and conciliators already described. They included some men of prominence in the regime of the Directory itself, men who did not make republicanism a matter of first principle, who might accept constitutional monarchy if given adequate guarantees, or who would be inclined to listen to the arguments of émigrés like Lally-Tollendal, when he urged that a combination of old and new property-owners should attempt to decide the future of France. Of the same general complexion were Lally-Tollendal's friends among the French émigrés, the Dutch émigrés who agreed more with the Hereditary Prince than with his father, the churchmen who sought to prevent the capture of Christianity by the royalists, and persons in various governments, including William Pitt in 1797, who could entertain the thought of a peace with France that would leave the Directory in being.

Beyond them lay the extreme Right. Here the characteristic doctrines, in the middle years of the 1790's, were that everything about the French Revolution since June 1789 had been bad, that France before 1789 had had an excellent constitution, or at least one that was capable of satisfactory development and should be restored; and that the war should be fought until the republic in France was overthrown. It was increasingly believed also that the assault on older political institutions had gone hand in hand with an attack on religion, that the real source of trouble was a false philosophy and false conception of man and his place in the universe, and that the good society of the future must therefore rest on a mutuality of interest between government and religion, or between "the throne and the altar." The extreme Right, even more than the extreme Left, also saw the Revolution as a universal disturbance overrunning all boundaries in which all established rights and authorities were threatened by the same destructive force.[22]

This intransigent or anti-conciliatory conservatism was not new. It did not arise simply as a reaction against the French Revolution, still less against its violence and extremism. The enthusiasm for the fall of the Bastille expressed throughout Europe was momentary and deceptive. It was briefly shared both by potential revolutionary sympathizers and by others, deeply conservative, who had long resisted the reforming efforts of monarchs and now rejoiced in the embarrassment of kings. In a word, the advocates both of an aristocratic revolution and a democratic revolution welcomed "liberty" in July 1789. Their agreement was soon over. The Italian economist Pietro Verri, who was a moderate until his death in 1797, noted the change at Milan a few weeks after the fall of the Bastille.

"The nobles and ecclesiastics," said Verri, "seeing the French people intent on abolishing all the distinctions of these orders, prefer a decorative slavery to a liberty that admits no distinction except merit, and hence they foment opinion against France and make themselves prophets of that vast kingdom's total ruin. The most essential and palpable principles of government, of human rights and the nature of authority, principles so crude that they are the norms of savages, are now called by some of us 'metaphysical' principles."[23]

Those of the Milanese patriciate who had resisted Joseph II, those in the diets of Hungary and Bohemia who had upheld their ancient constitution as a protection for serfdom, those in Poland who from devotion to "golden liberty" passed on into the party of Targowica, those in Belgium who to defend the Joyous Entry of 1355 had made up the Statist party, those who found "the cause of all legitimate governments" at stake at Geneva in 1782, those in the Parlement of Paris who in 1776 identified the *corvée* with "divine institutions," the "law of the

[22] J. Godechot, *La contre-révolution* (Paris, 1961); Paul H. Beik, *The French Revolution Seen from the Right: Social Theories in Motion, 1789-99*, in *Transactions of the American Philosophical Society*, n.s. vol. XLVI, Feb. 1956. The Right, as treated by Beik, is defined to include only those "whose opinions would not stretch beyond the point of incorporating the Estates General on a regular basis into the political life of the nation" (p. 3).
[23] Quoted by G. Candeloro, *Storia dell'Italia moderna*, 3 vols. (Milan, 1956-), I, 169.

Universe" and the society of the Three Orders, those in England and Ireland who had been alarmed by proposals for electoral reform, and had attributed such proposals to "system-mongers" and to the insufferable arrogance of the human mind—such men now saw in the French Revolution, before the year 1789 was out, a new and incomparably more formidable apparition of what they had been against all the time.[24] They called its principles metaphysical, and predicted, or rather hoped for, France's ruin. This was the audience most warmly receptive to Burke's *Reflections on the French Revolution*, which he published in 1790, expanding the same ideas that he had expressed in 1784 in debates over the character of the House of Commons.

Among the French, the uncompromising conservatives included the Bourbons themselves, Louis XVI until his execution in 1793, and both his brothers, the Counts of Provence and Artois, of whom the former began to style himself Louis XVIII in 1795, on receiving news of his nephew's death in a Paris prison. Louis XVI had never approved of Artois' emigration, and by contrast with him appeared moderate, but in fact Louis XVI continued to adhere to the program that he had announced in June of 1789, and hence to insist on preservation of the three estates, Clergy, Nobles, and Third, as essential to the structure of French government and society. He never accepted the constitution of 1789-1791 or the legitimacy of the Constituent Assembly. His real view on events in France was like that of William V on events in Holland. After his death, and after the death of Robespierre, there was perhaps a chance of moderate settlement under a constitutional monarchy with Louis XVI's son as regent; but the death of the eleven-year-old Dauphin was another blow to moderate expectations. The new king, or pretender, was a source of dismay both to French monarchists and to the British. Not all Frenchmen who thought a king necessary to France accepted Louis XVIII. Though the subject is obscure, some preferred the young Duke of Orleans, the son of Philippe-Egalité and future King Louis-Philippe. A British spy, presumably a monarchist Frenchman in France, reported on the confused pattern of French constitutional monarchism in 1796: "it demands a foreign king, a Protestant king, a king *à la* 1791, a king with two chambers, a king without the return of the émigrés, a king who does not have to avenge a brother's death."[25] He thought that the constitutional monarchists would nevertheless prevail.

But the constitutional Right was repeatedly outflanked by the extreme

[24] One of the main themes of *Age*, I.
[25] J. Godechot, "Le Directoire vu de Londres," in *AHRF*, No. 116 (1949), 329.

Right. French royalism, so far as it was a significant force supported by numbers of people, was far from arising from affection for the French royal family, for which respect had died in the crisis of revolution and war, but rested rather upon dissatisfaction with the republic and the republicans, and was constitutionalist and reformist in relation to the Old Regime. This moderate royalism was weakened by association with extreme royalism and with British or other foreign interests.

The outflanking had occurred at least as early as June 1792, at Frankfurt, when Mallet du Pan had found his proposal for a manifesto to the French people thrust aside, and replaced by the more intransigent Brunswick Manifesto. It occurred again in 1795. At this time the British government and the more liberally minded French émigrés desired the Count of Provence to issue a conciliatory statement, in which, while proclaiming himself as Louis XVIII, he would offer assurances to Frenchmen involved in the Revolution. Grenville, the British Foreign Secretary, gave McCartney, his representative at the Pretender's court, very specific instructions: His Highness was to be persuaded to promise an amnesty, refrain from alarming the sympathizers with the Revolution, and reassure those whose wealth was in former Church lands and in *assignats*, while agreeing to get the French out of Belgium and to make certain colonial concessions to the British. The Pretender, outmaneuvering all such advice, issued instead his Declaration of Verona.[26]

The Declaration of Verona irritated the British, threw the French moderate monarchists into consternation, and delighted those French republicans who paid any attention to it. Avoiding all specific issues, it dwelt on that "masterpiece of wisdom," the "ancient and wise constitution" of France before 1789. It adopted the condescending tone in which Kings in former days had thought it suitable to address their peoples. "You proved faithless to the God of your fathers. . . . Your tyrants have destroyed the altars of your God and the throne of your king." Such fatherly reproof, mixed with ostensibly religious admonitions, was hardly the right accent to strike in the France of 1795.

Moderates were again embarrassed by extremists, in 1795, when an armed force of excited émigrés, urged on by the Count of Artois, financed by the British treasury and supported by the British fleet, attempted to land at Quiberon Bay, intending to proclaim Louis XVIII

[26] Walter, *Comte de Provence*, 234-38. The text of the Declaration seems not to have been published in the French press, but may be found in English in the *Annual Register for 1795*, 254-62. The French text is given in A. Antoine, *Histoire de sa Majesté Louis XVI* (Paris, 1816), 114-36.

in Brittany and raise civil war against the Republic. These émigrés were destroyed by General Hoche's republican army. The Republic appeared, even to many moderates, as the only defender of France and the Revolution. Soon thereafter came the uprising of Vendémiaire in Paris. The leaders were mainly constitutional monarchists, and theirs was the party that the British government preferred to help, financially and otherwise; but the "absolute" royalists, for whom the constitutional royalists were more detestable than the republicans, persuaded the British agent, Wickham, that the constitutionalists were both anti-British and without strong followers in France. Wickham was tricked into backing the wrong horse, paying British money to the "pures," who were hardly more than conspirators, instead of to the moderate monarchists by whom something might have been accomplished. The Vendémiaire uprising was easily crushed. The Republic again seemed to defend France from the vague horrors of counter-revolution and foreign ambitions, both real and imagined.[27]

After the failure of royalist plans at Quiberon and in Vendémiaire, and hence after the Directory began to operate as a government, the partisans of the Right, like those of the Left, took advantage of its initially liberal policies, and began to carry on, in 1796, a great deal of political activity in Paris both open and secret. Constitutional monarchists, in touch with liberal émigrés and with nominal republicans like Boissy d'Anglas, and still enjoying British support, made overtures to the Abbé Brottier, Louis XVIII's secret agent in Paris. They proposed his restoration on the basis of a modernized limited monarchy.

"His Majesty persists in believing," came the reply, "that it is on the basis of our former constitution that the edifice of the monarchy must be re-established." This was almost the language in which William V rebuffed the Dutch liberal émigrés at the same time: "I persist in the idea . . . that I cannot accept the stadtholderate unless the constitution is re-established."[28]

Royalists of various kinds worked busily to prepare for the elections of March 1797. They developed a network which resembled Babeuf's. "Philanthropic institutes" were set up throughout the country, in which there were two kinds of members, the "friends of order" and the "legitimate sons." The "friends of order," who were mainly constitutional monarchists, believed that the only purpose of the organization was to

[27] On Quiberon and Vendémiaire see Godechot, *Contre-révolution*, 273-81; and on the outwitting of Wickham at Vendémiaire, H. Mitchell, "Vendémiaire, a revaluation" in *Journal of Modern History*, xxx (1958), 191-202.

[28] Walter, 291; above, p. 190.

influence the elections by ordinary methods of publicity and discussion. They did not know of the existence of the "legitimate sons." These latter were secretly engaged in preparing for insurrection, to be launched in the event that the elections were judged to be unsatisfactory; and for this purpose they divided France into military districts, some of which were assigned to the future command of the Count of Artois, some to the Prince of Condé, and some to Louis XVIII himself.[29] The Directory discovered this plot early in 1797, and published some of the papers, seeking to alarm the electorate, and win votes for itself, by simultaneous revelations of the counter-revolutionary as well as the Babouvist conspiracy.

Just before the elections Louis XVIII issued another proclamation. It was supposed to be more conciliatory than the one of Verona. He declared that he was misrepresented by republican slanders, but he still avoided concrete commitments, and while dwelling on his intentions of clemency, observed that he meant to bring back the French people "to the holy religion of their fathers and the paternal government that was so long the glory and happiness of France." Again the moderate royalists were dismayed by such renewed proof of the ineptitude and incorrigibility of the Bourbons. Malouet, in London, thought that no sane or patriotic Frenchman could rally to Louis XVIII.[30]

These more or less practical activities were accompanied by a profuse output of extreme counter-revolutionary writing, which enjoyed a kind of classic flowering in the years from 1795 to 1797. Most of it was by French émigrés publishing outside France, but British and German writers also made their contributions. There was the Savoyard-Frenchman Joseph de Maistre, who has been called the French Burke. There was an adventurer named Montgaillard, who thought that all Europe was corroded by revolution, that "the democratic principle spreads even into cabinets," and the French republicans "concoct their poison even in the councils of kings."[31] There was the Count de Ferrand, who thought the moment had come for all conservative governments to form "a holy alliance."[32] There was Montjoie, a prolific royalist pamphleteer, who thought that if Louis XVI had been truly absolute before 1789 there need have been no revolution, and that the Revolutionaries had been fanaticized by a misunderstanding of certain

[29] Godechot, *Contre-révolution*, 307.
[30] Beik, 92; Walter, 397; Malouet, *Mémoires*, 515, 521.
[31] Comte de Montgaillard, *L'an 1795, ou conjectures sur les suites de la Révolution française* (Hamburg, 1795), 5.
[32] Beik, 55, quoting Ferrand, *Des causes qui ont empêché la contre-révolution en France* (Berne, 1795).

words, such as *liberté* and *pouvoir constituant*.[33] J. F. La Harpe also found "fanaticism" a satisfying explanation of the Revolution.[34] In England, Burke's *Letters on a regicide peace* and other pamphlets by other authors gave currency to similar views. In Germany there was much lucubration, in which various elaborate theories were propounded, including the theory that the French Revolution, and other revolutionary disturbances throughout Europe, were the work of highly organized secret conspirators, deriving from the Illuminati of Bavaria of the 1780's.[35] These German findings were taken up by a Scottish chemist of considerable repute (he had received an honorary degree from Princeton College in America in 1790) who in 1797 published his *Proofs of a conspiracy against all the religions and governments of Europe, carried on in the secret meetings of Free Masons, Illuminati and Reading Societies*.[36] The Abbé Barruel also drew on German researches for a similar book published in 1797.

The most important of these works are those of de Maistre and Barruel. De Maistre's fame came after the Restoration of 1814, but his *Considérations sur la Révolution française* was published in 1797. It was very much a part of the controversies of the moment, for he expressed agreement with both Louis XVIII and Babeuf, declaring his full approval of the Declaration of Verona, and quoting Babeuf to argue that the existing republic was an appalling tyranny. The *Considérations*, however, like the polemics of Burke, rose above momentary questions to the level of a theory of knowledge, an ethic, and a philosophy of society. De Maistre distrusted "reason," and especially the reason of individuals. No society, he maintained, could exist with constant carping and criticism and the proliferation of novel ideas by private persons. A *raison nationale*, "political and religious dogmas," were necessary as a protection against the aberration and presumption of the "reason" of particular men. There must be *préjugés conservateurs*. It was impossible to invent institutions out of hand, or to constitute a government by conscious planning, or to give oneself any rights not already defined, de-

---

[33] C. F. de la T. Montjoie, *Eloge historique et funèbre de Louis XVI* (Neuchâtel, 1796), 154; *Nouveau dictionnaire pour servir à l'intelligence des termes mis en vogue par la Révolution* (Paris, 1792).

[34] J. F. La Harpe, *Du fanatisme dans la langue révolutionnaire* (Paris, 1797).

[35] J. Droz, *L'Allemagne et la Révolution française* (Paris, 1949), Part v, chap. i, "La lutte contre l'illuminisme."

[36] Robison's book had at least five editions. According to the records of Princeton University, the *Dictionary of National Biography* is in error in attributing the Princeton degree to the year 1798; the point is of no importance except to show that the college awarded Robison the degree for his scientific attainments, not for his political opinions of 1797, which, however, were certainly agreeable to the college authorities.

veloped, possessed through history and custom. Institutions grow, and government has a life of its own, like men; society is organic. There is no such thing as man-in-general, but only Frenchmen or Russians formed by their several cultures and environments. The French republic is an artificial creation, a monstrosity having no relation to anything real. The French Revolution is "satanic" and God-hating; philosophism is purely destructive; and the truth is that society needs what are too lightly dismissed as "superstitions." The Revolution is the embodiment of radical evil. From real barbarism men can progress. "But studied barbarism, systematic atrocity, calculated corruption, and above all irreligion, have never produced anything."[37]

The Abbé Barruel, born in 1741, had begun his career as a Jesuit, but after the expulsion of the Jesuits from France had spent years in Germany and Bohemia. Returning to France, he had published a critique of the *philosophes* in 1781, his *Lettres Helviennes*, which were several times reprinted into the 1830's. As early as 1789 he attributed the Revolution to "philosophism." In 1792 he emigrated to England, where he met Edmund Burke and Robert Clifford. There he wrote a history of the troubles of the French clergy during the Revolution. In 1797 he published in London the first version of his *Mémoires pour servir à l'histoire du jacobinisme*, of which a translation by Clifford appeared simultaneously in English. It looks as if discussions with English friends, a knowledge of German and the German language obtained many years before, and a familiarity with writings of the *philosophes* acquired at least as early as 1781, had all gone into the preparation of this classic of the counter-revolution, which was published in its final form at Hamburg in five volumes in 1798-1799, with a full German translation the following year, and of which an abridgement appeared in Paris as late as 1911. There is no known explanation of the simultaneous publication of Robison's *Proofs of a conspiracy*, which Barruel himself noted as a pure coincidence.

Barruel is chiefly remembered as the classic formulator of the conspiratorial theory of the causes of the French Revolution. In that revolution, he insisted, nothing happened because of unforeseen circumstances. All was "premeditated, pre-arranged, resolved, and decided upon." A "sect," numbering perhaps 300,000 "adepts," had been deliberately at work for at least twenty years. But, as so often with historians, Barruel

[37] *Considérations sur la France* (London, 1797), 73 ff. and *passim*; Beik, 62-71; Godechot, 94-106. Louis de Bonald, usually mentioned in this same connection, seems to have been little known until several years later. Beik and Godechot treat him and Chateaubriand at some length.

addressed himself as much to the future as to the past. The Revolution, he said, "is only the beginning of a universal dissolution which the sect has in mind."[38]

Though in the last analysis a phantasmagoria, Barruel's work is not without important merits. For one thing, while talking of sects and conspiracies, he develops the framework for a kind of history of ideas, in which schools and styles of thought are seen as more than individual persons, and as having a certain logic, interconnectedness, or development of their own. As he puts it, he is not concerned to tell of Marats and Robespierres, but to describe the systems of thought "which prepare new Marats and Robespierres for every people."[39] He sees three stages. First came the conspiracy against the Christian religion, which he associates with the *philosophes*. Then came the conspiracy against thrones —the Freemasons in their secret lodges. Then, deriving from both, came the Illuminati, "a conspiracy of sophists of impiety and anarchy against all religion and all government, even republics—against all civil society and all property of whatever kind." This was a wild exaggeration of facts relating to the real Illuminati, who had been a handful of enthusiasts suppressed by the Bavarian government in 1786. According to Barruel, one form of audacity led to another: "Condorcet refused to obey God, Brissot refused to obey kings, and Babeuf refused to obey the Republic, or any magistrates or governing officers whatever. And where do all these men come from? From the same cavernous den of the Jacobins ... all have Voltaire and Jean-Jacques for their fathers."[40] So again the extremes of Right and Left join hands, agreeing that everything in the Enlightenment must lead as a natural consequence to Gracchus Babeuf.

It is another merit of Barruel, if it be allowed as one, that he named by name various "adepts" who were in fact revolutionaries of one sort or another. His lists were fragmentary and peculiar. Since his purpose was to be full and specific, it is reasonable to construe his silences as ignorance, and such a construction leads to some curious observations. Of the Babeuf group he knew only what the Directory made public. He apparently had never heard of Buonarroti or any Italian revolutionaries. He knew nothing of Wolfe Tone and the Irish, and among English Jacobins, aside from Thomas Paine, he named only Watt and

[38] *Mémoires pour servir à l'histoire du jacobinisme* (Hamburg, 1798-1799), I, iv-xviii. On the conspiratorial theory of the Revolution see also pp. 51-2 above on the fabricated idea of a Society of Propaganda in 1790-1791, and pp. 453-54, below on the campaign against secret societies in Germany.

[39] *Ibid.*, I, xx.

[40] *Ibid.*, v, 181.

one other, with acknowledgments to Robison. Among the Belgians he listed Van der Noot, the darling of the Belgian Catholics in their revolt against Austria, but he had never heard of Vonck, who was more truly revolutionary and in fact more conspiratorial. Of the Dutch he named no one but Paulus, knowing nothing of the really secret Batavian revolutionaries of 1794. Among the Swiss he named Peter Ochs and a few others, and he knew also of two Frenchmen, Mangourit and Mengaud, who took part in the revolutionizing of Switzerland. Among the Swedes, he considered the noble Ankerstrom, the assassin of Gustavus III, and the regent of Sweden, the Duke of Södermanland, to be Jacobins or Illuminati. Of the Poles, he named no one but Kosciuszko. He knew of Genet's agitations in Russia, but not in the United States. He declared, however, that he knew for a fact, from a letter received from Boston, that the secret societies were at work in America. He correctly named David McLane as a conspiratorial subversive executed at Quebec in 1797. His information was best for the German countries. He named Campe, Mauvillon, Sonnenfels, and Immanuel Kant, who though not conspirators were adepts in his sense of the word. He knew of the more truly conspiratorial Mainz Jacobins of 1792 (Forster, Boehmer, and a mathematician named Metternich, unrelated to the princely house) and of the Cisrhenane republicans of 1797, but not of the intrigues of Poteratz in 1796. For Austria, he knew of persons named Billek, Hackl, Hebenstreit, Hoffman, Riedel, and Wolstein, all of whom were in fact implicated in the conspiracy at Vienna in 1794. He knew nothing of the Martinovics conspiracy in Hungary, merely remarking that the Austrian Jacobins were executed with seven Hungarian gentlemen. In short, his information was sporadic. He had written five volumes, and missed the conspiratorial aspects of agitation in Ireland, Belgium, Holland, Hungary, and Italy. It is obvious that Barruel reflected only a few German sources.

He knew enough, however, and it may be credited to him as a merit, to believe that the revolution was not merely French but universal. Though he included a chapter on Geneva in the 1760's, he concluded that the disturbance had begun in America. "The sect first announced itself in America, with the first elements of its code of equality, liberty and sovereignty of the people." It may be noted that in the English translation, and ensuing American reprint, the words "in America" were simply omitted at this point.[41] We may easily suggest an explana-

---

[41] *Ibid.*, v, 310-11; Eng. trans., IV, 354. The reference to David McLane at Quebec was also deleted from the English translation, which, however, supplemented the original

tion: even for conservative English-speaking persons, it was simply not believable that the American Revolution had been brought on by a sect of adepts, and they might conclude that Barruel's whole thesis was unsound.

He ended his final volume with a chapter on "The universality of successes of the sect, explained by the universality of its plots." At the time of his writing this final chapter, in 1798, the revolution had in fact spread very far, even to "Rome itself." Barruel's message was the same as Burke's: "It is not France extending a foreign empire over other nations; it is a sect aiming at universal empire, and beginning with the conquest of France."[42] Everywhere, in all countries, there were plotters, adepts, lurking initiates of secret societies, Freemasons, Illuminati, and Jacobins in their hidden cells and lodges who were everlastingly and tirelessly working, for no reason except to forward their own misguided philosophy, to undermine all government, property, and religion.

And what was this misguided philosophy? It was man-worship, according to Barruel, the belief that man was lord of the universe, subject to no limitations or restraints. "For Dietrich, Condorcet, Babeuf and other recent adepts of Weishaupt, there need be no moderator except the man-king, who has nowhere anyone but himself for master."[43] It was in short the repudiation of God. The same idea, in more refined form, has been advanced in the twentieth century in condemnation of the Enlightenment and the Revolution. Barruel put the lesson bluntly: to give any aid or sympathy to Jacobinism was an impiety, and only those who firmly resisted the Jacobins would go to Heaven.[44]

That the revolution was "universal," and that good government is somehow related to a good religion, are propositions in which one may certainly concur without agreeing with Barruel. It was preposterous to attribute the revolutionary agitation in Europe, not to mention America, in any significant degree to the machinations of plotters. As for religion, much depends on what one's religion is. For Barruel—as for de Maistre, or Louis XVIII, or indeed Edmund Burke though he did not use the

with an appendix on the political clubs in England and on the Irish rebellion of 1798, both of which it attributed to Jacobins, Freemasons and Illuminati. That the American Revolution had also been caused by secret societies was affirmed in Germany by counter-revolutionaries as early as 1790. F. Valjavec, *Entstehung der politischen Strömungen in Deutschland* (Munich, 1951), 149, n. 15.

[42] *Regicide Peace, Works* (Boston, 1877), v, 345.

[43] *Mémoires*, v, 112. Dietrich was the first mayor of Strasbourg during the Revolution (*Age*, i, 363-64); Adam Weishaupt was a founder of the German Illuminati.

[44] Final conclusion, *Mémoires*, v, 325.

phrase—it was the religion of the throne and the altar. A good religion was one that upheld the established order, or rather the order that had been established in 1789, and had seemingly been (as it seemed to them) unthreatened at that time except by bad ideas. It was a timid religion, fearful of the human mind, nervous at the mention of liberty or equality. It was a complacent religion, which found justice in custom and made institutions into idols. To what extent it was Christian would be invidious to debate, but in any case, as already observed, a great many authorized spokesmen of the Catholic Church, during these same years, refused to make any such equation between counter-revolution and Christianity.

Fructidor and Floréal

These poetic words refer to two unseemly maneuvers, by which the Directory struck out in turn against the Right and Left.[45] By the coup d'état of Fructidor of the Year V (September 1797) it put down the royalists. By the coup d'état of Floréal of the Year VI (May 1798) it did the same to the democrats. In each case it acted from considerations which the preceding pages should help to explain, but also because of certain developments on the international scene which are described in the following chapters, so that no full account of the two coups d'état is attempted here, and they are included only to round out the characterization of the Directory.

It will be recalled that by the two-thirds rule of 1795 two-thirds of the legislative chambers, the Councils of Elders and the Five Hundred, were until the election of March 1797 former members of the Convention. They had duly chosen five other former members of the Convention for the Executive Directory—Reubell, La Révellière, Carnot, Barras, and Le Tourneur. They started out with an actual belief in their own theories. Sitting as a Convention, they had produced a constitution, and they thought that France was, should be, and could be governed as a constitutional republic. Like most genuine constitutionalists of the time, they looked upon party politics as bad, and had no idea of a system in which one party should govern while another led a recognized opposition. In anticipation of the elections of 1797 they raised alarms over conspiracies of the Right and Left, but they took no practical steps at the local level to influence the voters in their favor.

---

[45] Among the many writings bearing on the subject may be cited A. Meynier, *Les coups d'état du Directoire*, 3 vols. (Paris, 1927), and J. Suratteau, "Les élections de l'an V aux conseils du Directoire," in *AHRF*, No. 154 (1958), 21-63.

The awakening was very rude. The election of 1797 proved to be a humiliating defeat for the Directory. The royalists had not been inactive, and in any case the country felt little attachment to its new rulers. The newly elected third of the Elders and Five Hundred, when added to the "free" third elected in 1795 (that is, the third who had not been required to be members of the outgoing Convention), gave a majority of royalists of various kinds, or at least of persons not well affected to the Republic. When the time came, as provided by the constitution, for one of the five Directors to retire, the chambers replaced Le Tourneur with Barthélemy, a well-known moderate with a preference for constitutional monarchy. Of the remaining Directors, Carnot had developed similar inclinations. At least two generals in the army, Pichegru and Moreau, were carrying on secret discussions looking to a monarchist restoration. But the divisions among monarchists, their connections with England, the loud demands of extremists, and the known views of Louis XVIII all made it impossible for the forces arrayed against the Directory to cooperate. Carnot, who had voted for the death of Louis XVI, could never bring himself to entrust his fate even to constitutional monarchists. Pichegru, uncertain of the future, and unable to get any assurances of a moderate restoration from the spokesmen of Louis XVIII, never actually came forward as a Dumouriez, still less as a General Monk.

In 1797 Bonaparte defeated the Austrians and combined with Italian revolutionaries to set up the Cisalpine Republic. The British, with the Austrians obliged to sue for peace, with no remaining ally on the Continent, and afflicted by troubles at home, showed a willingness to negotiate. In the ensuing talks, which took place at Lille, the sticking-point proved to be the French incorporation of Belgium and the relation of France to the Batavian Republic. The British offered to recognize the French Republic and its annexation of Belgium, in return for the cession to England of the Dutch possessions in Ceylon and at the Cape of Good Hope. The French could not consent to give away the Dutch possessions; if they did so they would invite counter-revolution in Holland, or at least lose the good will that they enjoyed in the Batavian Republic, which would be of value in any future trouble with Britain; and they would give offense, by such betrayal of a "sister-republic," to all revolutionary sympathizers in Italy and other countries, who were useful in the contest with Austria. In addition, on grounds of principle or ideology, the most intense republicans and vehement democrats, while not agreeing with Babeuf, took the view which had been expounded by Buonarroti in his *Paix perpetuelle avec les rois*. They favored the creation of sister-republics, like the Batavian and the Cisalpine, and believed that neither true peace nor true republicanism would be safe until Britain and the monarchies of the Continent were humbled if not destroyed.

Bonaparte, now the spectacular young republican general who had brought the Revolution to Italy, had no interest in a peace that he did not make himself. The monarchists in the two chambers had no interest in the career of Bonaparte, or the liberation of Italy, or the maintenance of the Cisalpine or Batavian republics, or the annexation of Belgium. Nor, of course, did they have any respect for the constitution of the French Republic. It became a question of who would violate the constitution first. The monarchists, disorganized and mutually distrustful, made plans for a coup d'état which they were unable to execute and kept postponing. Their opponents acted. The firm republicans in the Directory, Reubell and La Révellière, prevailing on the indifferent Barras, pressed by Bonaparte and by other generals and civilians who were profiting from their activities in occupied countries and satellite republics, and with the strong approval of an enthusiastic republican soldiery excited by its own victories, and of the ardent republicans in France who saw no difference between moderate monarchists and extreme reactionary royalists and political Catholics, drove through the coup d'état of Fructidor of the Year V. Bonaparte sent one of his generals from the Army of Italy, Augereau, who stood by with a force of troops while Reubell, La Révellière, and Barras expelled Carnot and Barthélemy from the Directory. The "triumvirs" then annulled the elections of the preceding spring, so that the two chambers were severely purged of monarchist and moderate elements. Carnot fled from France; Barthélemy and a great many others were shipped off to French Guiana, the "dry guillotine"; and there was a renewal of anti-clerical and anti-Christian persecution and propaganda, the worst since 1794. The altar suffered from its association with the throne.

For a few months the new or "second" Directory—now composed of Reubell, La Révellière, Barras, Merlin de Douai, and François de Neufchateau—seemed to work harmoniously with democrats of the Left. It appointed some of them to office, and it was at this time, in January 1798, that it allowed the Dutch democrats to carry out their coup d'état against the Dutch federalists. In Italy the old aristocratic Republic of Genoa was converted into a revolutionary Ligurian Republic on the model of the Cisalpine, and for various reasons, including the protection of communications between the Cisalpine and France, Switzerland also was transformed into the Helvetic Republic. With expansionist, determined, and fiercely anti-clerical republicans now more influential in the French government than they had been a year before, and with a good deal of willing Italian assistance, even the Papal States began to fall to pieces, and a Roman Republic was proclaimed.

During the winter, however, as it looked forward to the elections of March 1798, the Directory began to feel uneasy at the strength of the Left which the Fructidor coup had done much to reaffirm. "Constitutional circles" were springing up throughout the country, not wholly unlike the former Jacobin clubs of provincial towns and cities. These new "Jacobins"—or "anarchists" as the Directorial republicans also called them—were in effect political democrats. Most of them accepted the existing constitution, but some extolled the merits of the Constitution of the Year I. The most immediate reality in this line of discourse was not that these democrats expected an actual revival of the Constitution of the Year I, or would live under it peaceably if they had it, but that they rejected important features of the Constitution of the Year III. An unknown and imponderable element of the Left was no more loyal to the existing constitution than the monarchists were.

It does not seem that the Directory was fearful for the institution of property.[46] Babeuf's organization had been crushed, and his movement largely forgotten except at the outermost fringes of both Right and Left. But Babeuf himself had talked not only about the abolition of property, but about democrats and a Society of Democrats, the Constitution of the Year I, and the need for firm measures against restoration of the Pretender. The whole democratic wing of the political world was vaguely associated with crazy extremism. In any case the Directory had already become a kind of oligarchy, a "constituted body" which, though originating so recently in the Convention, was not wholly unlike the "constituted bodies" described in the first volume of this book, and against which the discontents of a whole generation had been aimed. The most innocuous democrats were bound to believe that new men should have a part in public life.

Losing no time in learning the less worthy arts of representative government, the Directory made serious efforts to influence the elections of 1798. These were especially important, because not only the usual third of the two chambers was to be elected, but the seats left vacant by

---

[46] Meynier's opinion, *Coups d'état*, II, 35.

the purge of Fructidor were to be filled, so that some three-fifths of the legislature was to be chosen. Like Robespierre, the Directory accused the Left and Right of secret collaboration against it, and although it was not true that they were in alliance, it was true, as it had been in the days of Robespierre, that they both questioned the legitimacy of the government. The Directory made known its preference for certain official candidates, and covered the country with alleged "highway commissioners," whose real business was to prepare favorable elections in local and departmental assemblies.

But the election of March 1798 resulted in a great victory for the democrats. With the broken monarchists largely abstaining, and the partisans of the government unable to keep control, the three-fifths elected to the two chambers included a great many "Jacobins." Again the chambers and the Directory, the legislature and the executive, which were purposely separated by the constitution, were certain to be at odds. The response of the Directory was more speedy than in 1797. Raising an outcry against the revival of Terrorism, the Directory and its supporters in the two chambers quashed 106 of the elections. It thus obtained a legislative body with which it could work—at least for another year, for there was to be another crisis in 1799.

After Fructidor and Floréal no one could pretend that the Directory enjoyed a popular mandate of any accepted kind. It was a kind of dictatorship without the usual advantages of dictators: it had little prestige or "charisma" (Bonaparte was gradually drawing these to himself), and it was still restricted, even after the two coups, by strong vestiges of constitutional scruples.

The Directory had twice violated the constitution on the plea of protecting it. Nor was the plea by any means wholly false. By the coup d'état of Fructidor the Directory had in all probability prevented a restoration of monarchy, and what a restored monarchy would have been in 1797 may be judged from the statements of Louis XVIII and of monarchists themselves. The issue in the coup d'état of Floréal is more unclear. So far as the democrats and neo-Jacobins were constitutionally minded, the crushing of their elections in 1798 may have lessened the chance for a peaceable parliamentary development in the First Republic. So far as they cared nothing for constitutional restraints, or so far as they wanted a new constitution (which would have been the fourth in eight years), their coming into power would have offered little basis for constitutional stabilization. In any event, the Directory, having antagonized the Right in 1797, antagonzied the Left in 1798, and stood alone. A republic could hardly subsist when the most ardent republicans had been alienated.

It seems likely that the chances for a moderate and constitutional settlement in France, in the years after 1795, were virtually nil. For one thing, the war was still going on. Britain broke off the peace talks after Fructidor, and though Austria made peace, its re-entry into the war could be reasonably expected. Even with governments well established, the needs and atmosphere of war are unfavorable to constitutional experimentation and personal and political liberties. The Revolution—or rather the last years of the Old Regime of which the Revolution itself was merely the outcome—had left the country too divided, with too many memories, hopes and fears, hates and attachments, disillusionments and expectations, for men to accept each other with mutual trust or political tolerance. Any conceivable regime would have had to use force to repress intransigent adversaries. There are times when real choices become very restricted, and consist in little more than a choice of evils, when all that one can really decide, short of becoming wholly unworldly, is which side he prefers to embrace and whose repression he will condone.

The French Republic, even under the imperfect regime of the Directory, continued to exert an attraction for many restless people in Europe, who considered it to represent a better way of life than the various regimes in their own countries under which they lived. We turn now to the world outside of France.

THE REVOLUTION COMES TO ITALY

The Italians want to unite and they want a revolution; they want the Emperor to rule in his own house, the Austrians in Germany, the Bourbons in Spain, the Pope in matters of the Gospel; perpetual friendship and gratitude to France; in short, everything in its place. These are the sentiments of the Italians.—GIUSEPPE POGGI, Milan, 1797

THE REVOLUTION COMES TO ITALY

THE year 1796 is chiefly remembered for Napoleon Bonaparte's brilliant victories in North Italy. In this book, however, Bonaparte will remain no more than one of many generals in the service of the French Republic, and his first Italian campaign will be presented, not as the public initiation of his own career, but as a turning point in the larger revolutionary movement of the European world. It was not the first such turning point. Of such grand events, if we consider only those subsequent to the Terror in France, the first had been the Dutch revolution and establishment of the Batavian Republic, with the consequent alliance of Holland and France against Great Britain. The French victories in Italy made possible the creation of the Cisalpine Republic in the Po valley. Milan immediately became, in 1796, a center to which patriots and revolutionaries congregated from all parts of Italy. Other Italian republics were soon set up on the model of the Cisalpine, and in fact, by the turn of 1797-1798, there was a general alarm at the prospect of a "Cisalpinization" of Europe.

The Cisalpine Republic is best understood in a broad perspective. In the present chapter we begin with a view of "world revolution" as seen in 1796 from Paris, then turn to the French attitude to revolution in Italy, then shift the point of observation to Italy itself, in an attempt to describe the sources of revolutionary agitation in that country from an Italian standpoint. The closing section may seem a digression at first sight, being an account of the Kingdom of Corsica. This "kingdom," existing under British auspices from 1794 to 1796, offers an illuminating counterpart to the Cisalpine Republic, which is treated in the chapter that follows.

"World Revolution" as Seen from Paris, 1796

When the Directory came into being, France was still at war with Great Britain on the one hand, and on the other with Austria, Sardinia, and the German states of the Holy Roman Empire south of the River Main. The new regime, having installed itself against royalist opposition, was at first inclined to make itself agreeable to the most determined republicans of the Left. These included the believers in "international" revolution—Frenchmen who demanded war *à outrance* against kings, and patriots of many nationalities who came to Paris to solicit aid for their respective projects. The mood in the new government was at first to give these patriots a receptive hearing.

At the French Foreign Office a good many staff studies were prepared in the various bureaus, some of which, though never officially adopted, breathed the spirit of Philippe Buonarroti and the atmosphere of the Pantheon Club. One of these, unsigned and undated, but written shortly after the Directory took over from the Convention, observed that since counter-revolutionaries sought to subvert the Republic (as at Vendémiaire and Quiberon Bay), it was necessary and proper for the Republic to do the same to its enemies. "If we want quiet at home," according to this memorandum, "if we want to make a peaceable end to our Revolution, we must set fire to Europe with the revolutionary flame, we must raise up rebellion in Hungary, letting the Turks pay the costs, and sow division among the bandits of Serbia and Moldavia, who have been armed by the Russians and Germans." The author went on to observe that the Committee of Public Safety had been very foolish in its attitude to the English refugee patriots, whom it had imprisoned instead of making use of. "But these elements still exist. They are ready to set England ablaze if only the fire is stirred up a little." And he added that, since the French Army of the Alps had had a few successes, uprisings should be promoted in Lombardy and Sicily, and, as a final blow to Austria, the crown of the Holy Roman Empire be transferred to Protestant Prussia.[1]

Such was some of the advice that Charles Delacroix, the new foreign minister, could obtain in his own office. In addition, a wide array of foreign enthusiasts sought him out. There were men in Paris working for revolution in Ireland, Poland, Germany, Switzerland, and Italy, and the Foreign Office had full reports on the signs of disaffection in England, from the Edinburgh Convention of 1792 to the mass demonstration of 1795, in which King George III, caught in an angry swarm of two hundred thousand persons, was assailed in

---

[1] A paper simply headed "Diplomatie" in Archives des affaires étrangères, Mémoires et documents, France et divers états, vol. 655, fol. 262-63. Dated "An 4-1795" in a later hand.

his own state coach in the streets of London.[2] The French government in 1796, until events in Italy determined otherwise, seems to have had more interest in, and information on, the chances of revolution in England than in the Italian states.

But no one except a few in the government could see these various agitations in one view. The "foreign" revolutionaries in Paris had no more than the most sporadic knowledge of each other's existence. International revolutionism, far from being actually international, consisted in the parallel efforts of separate groups of nationals to take advantage of the war by obtaining French support. Each group had secret interviews with Delacroix, or secret meetings with the Directors, not suspecting that others enjoyed the same privilege. The Italians led by Buonarroti were involved with the Babouvists, and hoped by gaining a more "democratic" government in France to promote revolution in Italy. Occasionally a democratic newspaper might contain items on the foreign patriots, as when the *Orateur plébéien*, on April 14, printed a letter from a "Polish republican."[3] But there is no evidence that the Babouvists had any real knowledge of the simultaneous Poteratz conspiracy for a South German republic, or the equally simultaneous activities of the Poles and the Irish in Paris. For the year 1796 we have the detailed diary of Wolfe Tone, a neglected classic of the Revolution. Living in isolation in Paris, befriended only by James Monroe, having frequent private talks with Delacroix and others, Tone knew nothing of the Italians, Poles, or Germans. He heard rumors in March that the "true original Jacobins" might return to power, and thought this might be a good thing, but he was ignorant of the Babeuf conspiracy until the conspirators were arrested, and then disapproved of their plans for insurrection. He was opposed to insurrection because, more than some others among the foreign revolutionaries, he had confidence in the Directory, which had brought him from his exile in America for the explicit purpose of concerting revolution in Ireland.[4]

From the point of view of the Directory there were two theaters, the British and the Austrian or Continental, in which the instigation of revolution might be useful. Revolution seemed not impossible even

---

[2] On England see AAE, Mém. et doc., Angleterre, vol. 19, fols. 388-92, and vol. 53, fols., 187-225; *Annual Register for 1795* (London, 1800). Chronicle, 37-38; S. Maccoby, *English Radicalism, 1786-1832* (London, 1955), 94.

[3] *Orateur plébéien*, 25 Germinal IV.

[4] *Life of Theobald Wolfe Tone*, 2 vols. (Washington, 1826), 110. Among the papers of the Babouvists was found one referring to the Left Bank of the Rhine (Saitta, *Buonarroti*, I, 31) but apparently nothing on the activities of Poteratz.

in England. Tone was dismayed to find the attention of his mentors so easily diverted from the liberation of Ireland to the direct overthrow of the British government itself. General Clarke, a Frenchman of Irish descent, who spoke perfect English, and was close to the Director Carnot, had a pet project for sending agitators to England to stir up a *chouannerie*.[5] In Paris Tone met an American, Colonel William Tate, who had worked with Genet in 1793 and been secretary to the South Carolina Republican Society. Tate hated the British, and under protection of the French fleet actually landed several hundred armed Frenchmen on the coast of Wales in February 1797.[6] Many Dutch democrats were also eager to take part in an invasion of either Britain or Ireland, and the French supported the unitary-democratic party in the Batavian Republic with that in mind. They also, against Britain, maintained relations with the Sultan of Mysore in distant India.

It was possible also to work through Spain, with which the Directory signed a treaty in June, and which declared war on England in November of 1796. One item of business for the French in Spain concerned Louisiana. There were some in the government who hoped to recover Louisiana for France. This might mean Louisiana west of the Mississippi which had belonged to Spain since 1763 and which the French proposed to regain in return for setting up a Spanish Bourbon prince with a new kingdom in North Italy—so far were these elements in the French government from sponsoring a revolutionary Italian republic. Or, "Louisiana" might mean the whole of French Louisiana before 1763, from the Alleghenies to the Rockies. Since the signing of the Jay treaty between the United States and Great Britain the French believed that the Americans were moving toward war with France. They lost whatever interest they had had in maintaining the existing boundaries of the United States, which were, or course, hardly more than a dozen years old. There was talk with the Spanish of a kind of Latin alliance to check the spread of English-speaking influence in America. There was talk of a separate political entity, in which the Western democrats in the United States, sponsored by France, should have a republic of their own. There was even talk, after the Anglo-French peace negotiations began at Lille, of offering the American West to the British, since it would be easier for the French to give away Kentucky and Ohio than the Dutch possessions

[5] Tone, 49-59, 97, 99.
[6] Commander E. H. Stuart Jones, *The Last Invasion of Britain* (Cardiff, 1950), devoted entirely to this episode and to its repercussions in Great Britain.

in South Africa and Ceylon. Never had the American West been so involved in remote foreign developments.[7]

Believing that the Americans were now working for England, Delacroix embarked, in January 1796, on promoting *une heureuse révolution* in the United States, though all he meant by it was to sponsor the election of Jefferson as president and so bring the American "republicans" into power.[8] The American minister, Monroe, kept assuring the French that the people of the United States (as was probably true, on balance) did not support their own government in its policies of appeasement to England. In April Jefferson wrote a letter to his old friend Philip Mazzei, then in Italy, describing the political situation in the United States, where, he said, good republicans opposed a selfish combination of monocrats, aristocrats, and Anglophiles; this letter, when first published in the Paris *Moniteur* a few months later, created a furor in America, and confirmed the French in their belief that the United States was in need of a "revolution."[9] Meanwhile the French General Collot, on an ostensibly scientific expedition, sounded out the separatist sentiments west of the Alleghenies, and George Rogers Clark was for the second time commissioned as a brigadier general in the French army. The well-known firebrand, Mangourit, who had been an aide to Genet in America in 1793, and who had worked at that time with the South Carolina democrats, including Colonel Tate, was transferred in June 1796 from Madrid to Philadelphia. At Madrid he had proved too outspokenly vehement, loudly declaring that the present King of Spain would be the last. He was told, in his instructions as *chargé d'affaires* in America, to favor the election of Jefferson, seek contacts with Madison and Robert Livingston, and discreetly encourage all anti-British, pro-French, democratic, or separatist feeling.[10] In October the French minister, Adet, openly interfered in the presidential election, to the extent of making public speeches in which he intimated the displeasure of the French Republic if John Adams should be elected.[11] From the Hague, at the same time, the American minister, John Quincy Adams, reported that

[7] F. J. Turner, "The Policy of France toward the Mississippi Valley in the Period of Washington and Adams," in *American Historical Review*, X (1905), 249-79; A. P. Whitaker, *The Mississippi Question, 1795-1803* (New York, 1934); R. Guyot, *Le Directoire et la paix de l'Europe* (Paris, 1912), the index under "Louisiane."

[8] A. DeConde, *Entangling Alliance: Politics and Diplomacy under George Washington* (Durham, N.C., 1958), 456.

[9] *Moniteur*, 6 pluviose An V (January 25, 1797).

[10] R. Palmer, "A Revolutionary Republican: M. A. B. Mangourit," in *William and Mary Quarterly*, IX (1952), 483-96.

[11] DeConde, 472-76.

the French design was to favor a separate Western or Southern republic in the United States, "as they are now forming a republic in Italy."[12]

In Austria there was no likelihood of revolution, nor did the French imagine that there was; but after the suppression of the "Jacobins" at Vienna there remained a good deal of discontent in the city, and the chancellor, Thugut, remarked in July 1796, by which time the French had driven the Austrians from Milan, that he was still more afraid of anti-war feeling in Vienna than of the French army.[13]

Against Austria, especially since it enjoyed the backing of Russia, it was useful for the Directory to express sympathy for the Poles, of whom thousands left Poland after the Third Partition, and many converged upon Paris. Receiving certain assurances from Delacroix in March of 1796, these Polish patriots, with French assistance, brought to Paris from his place of refuge in Poland one of the heroes of the uprising of 1794, J. H. Dumbrowsky, to serve as commander of an armed force of Polish exiles. The Directory sent him on to Bonaparte in Italy, where he organized a Polish Legion, which was attached to Bonaparte's army. The Legion was recruited from Polish refugees in France, Venice, and the Ottoman Empire, and from Polish prisoners of war and deserters from the Hapsburg armies. By July 1797 it had 6,000 men, and Dumbrowsky was boasting that his émigré force was larger than either the French or the Dutch émigrés had been able to raise. Dumbrowsky had far-reaching plans, which the French listened to but never allowed him to execute—to carry war and revolution to Eastern Europe, with a grand march through Fiume, Croatia, the Serbian provinces of Turkey, Wallachia, Transylvania, Galicia, and the old center of Poland, rallying everywhere the enemies of the Hapsburgs, and even forcing Russia to withdraw from European affairs. The Polish Legion never made so grand a march, but it did serve with the French in Italy for two years, and occupies a place of importance in the history of the Polish nationalist movement. The national anthem of later times, a kind of Polish Marseillaise, was created in the Polish Legion in Italy.[14]

[12] J. Q. Adams, *Writings*, 7 vols. (New York, 1913-1917), II, 156. The republic in Italy here mentioned, in November 1796, was the Cispadane, the predecessor to the Cisalpine.

[13] E. Wangermann, *From Joseph II to the Jacobin Trials* (Oxford, 1959), 185.

[14] M. Oginski, *Mémoires sur la Pologne et les polonais*, 4 vols. (Paris, 1826), II, 137-38, 206; L. Chodzko, *Histoire des légions polonaises en Italie*, 2 vols. (Paris, 1829), I, 119, 172-84, 217; II, 31. The Poles, it seems from these passages, were also in touch with certain Greeks in Paris and the Ottoman Empire.

On May 4, 1796, the Directory authorized a French adventurer, named Poteratz, working with a few Germans, to conspire against the governments of Baden, Württemberg, and certain lesser states and set up a revolutionary South German or Swabian republic. Poteratz was instructed to work with the French General Moreau in that theater, and to "bring about the disappearance of the petty animosities which may exist between the inhabitants of the different principalities," and "to unite or weld them all into a single political body." Two weeks later, as will be seen, the Directory countermanded this order.[15] It lost interest in using such methods to revolutionize Germany east of the Rhine, and signed armistices with the South German states in July. When, in January 1797, a petition with 1,500 signatures was brought to Paris from this region, asking for French aid in an attempt at revolution there, the petitioners were refused.[16]

In February and March of 1796, to complete the list, Delacroix had talks with Philippe Buonarroti and another Italian named Cerise. These two were in close touch with Italian revolutionaries and refugees who were assembled at Nice, and who hoped—the more so since both Bonaparte and the civil commissioner associated with him, Saliceti, were Italian-speaking natives of Corsica—to bring about revolution in Italy in conjunction with the coming victories of the French army. Plans were already laid to turn the kingdom of Sardinia into a republic. It was the desire of these Sardinian patriots to stage their revolution shortly before the arrival of the French, so that an Italian provisional government would be already in being, to shield the country from direct foreign or military exploitation. They thus echoed the hopes of various Belgians as long ago as 1792, but the model that they had in mind was the Batavian Republic, which contributed to the common cause as a partner and theoretical equal of France and not as a conquered or occupied country. As Wolfe Tone remarked to Delacroix at this same time, the foreign patriots admired the moderation of the French in Holland.[17]

[15] S. Biro, *The German Policy of Revolutionary France*, 2 vols. (Cambridge, Mass., 1957), II, 573, and his whole Chapter VIII, "Poteratz and the Plan of a Republic in Southwestern Germany," where no relation is seen to simultaneous Babouvist, Italian, or other activities. A five-page appendix is devoted to the spelling of this name, whether Potera, Poterat, Poterats, or Poteratz, the last being proved correct by the author; doubtless in French it was pronounced "Potera."

[16] P. Bailleu, *Preussen und Frankreich von 1795 bis 1807*, 2 vols. (Leipzig, 1881-1887), I, 108.

[17] Tone, II, 196. On Italy in this particular connection the main authorities are Saitta and Godechot, cited below. See also R. Soriga, "L'idea nazionale e il ceto dei 'patrioti' avanti il maggio 1796" in Società nazionale per la storia del Risorgimento italiano, *Atti del XIV Congresso* (Trent, 1927), 119-40.

The Beginning of French Action in Italy

Buonarroti made it clear to Delacroix that he desired, and that the French should accept, not merely a revolution in Piedmont but a general revolutionary rising of the people of all Italy—"Piedmontese, Lombard, Roman, Sicilian and Sard"—in which a vast popular and democratic upheaval should sweep aside the artificial units of existing states and merge all Italians into one consolidated republic. Delacroix seemed to agree: he was supporting the unitary party in Holland, and even instructing Poteratz to "weld together" the South Germans. He endorsed these Italian plans, and recommended Buonarroti to the French agent in Italy, Cacault. But in his instructions to Cacault, Delacroix took a more measured position: Cacault and Bonaparte should use the services of the Italian patriots as they saw fit, but only against states with which France was at war. "You understand," wrote Delacroix to Cacault, "that it is the duty of every French agent to refrain from attempts against allied or neutral powers."[18]

So Delacroix, in March 1796, expressed the view that Lebrun had expressed in 1792, and the Committee of Public Safety in 1794, that, whatever grand and enthusiastic language might be in vogue, the provocation of revolution was to be used as a weapon against actual enemies in the war.[19] It was only the more naive foreign patriots, or the few actual international revolutionaries like Buonarroti, or editors of radical newspapers—or spokesmen of the extreme Right, like Burke and Barruel—who imagined that the French government was intent on indiscriminate world revolutionism. Delacroix also remarked of the Italian friends of Liberty (and the same had often been said of the Dutch) that they should be willing to supply the needs of the French army—"to pay, by sharing some of their wealth, for the blood that is to cement their independence."[20]

During these talks between Buonarroti and Delacroix, the Pantheon Club, of which Buonarroti had been president, was closed by order of the Directory and through the action of General Bonaparte, just before

---

[18] See the documents published by Saitta, *Buonarroti*, II, 1-33, especially Buonarroti to Delacroix, 5 Germinal IV (March 25, 1796), 13-15; Delacroix de Cacault, 7 Germinal (March 27), 16-18; and Cacault to Delacroix, 20 Germinal (April 9), 20-24. In effect, France was at war only with Milan and Sardinia among the Italian states. Naples was inactively at war with France until the signing of peace in October 1796; the papal states and Tuscany were non-belligerent but hardly neutral; Venice and Genoa clung to a precarious neutrality subject to demands from both sides.

[19] Above, pp. 59, 122-23.

[20] Saitta, II, 17; above, p. 61.

his departure to take command of the Army of Italy. Buonarroti lost confidence in Bonaparte, and in the usefulness of the existing French government to the cause of the Italian revolution. He and Babeuf organized the Conspiracy of Equals. Meanwhile, as Bonaparte inflicted defeats upon the Sardinian army, the Italian patriots went into action and proclaimed the republic at Alba, some thirty miles from Turin. The republic thus proclaimed was not at all "communistic," but it did envisage the end of seigneurial dues, the nobility and the monarchy; and the Italian revolutionaries intended it to be a first step toward a Sardinian or even a larger Italian republic. Bonaparte, however, acting on his own authority, and without orders from Paris, signed the armistice of Cherasco with the King of Sardinia, and so recognized the continuing existence of the Sardinian monarchy. Buonarroti in Paris had added reason to overthrow the Directory at the earliest possible moment.

Buonarroti and Babeuf were arrested on May 10. With the discovery of their conspiracy, the balance of arguments in the minds of Delacroix and the Directors underwent a change. The conjunction in time between the plot in Paris, the initiative of the Italian republicans at Alba, the agitation in Swabia of which Poteratz seemed to be the agent, and the disturbances in Holland marked by the revolt of the Amsterdam cannoneers—especially in the absence of any clear evidence—created a mystery for the French government, as for historians. It seemed that there might be not only a plot in Paris to overthrow the Directory, which was evident, but a great concerted movement of international revolution. The Directory reacted immediately, ferreted out Babouvists in France, ordered Blauw and Valckenaer out of Paris, rescinded its instructions to Poteratz, and became suspicious of the Italian refugees. The recall of Mangourit from Spain was a move in the same direction.

In general, after the discovery of the Babeuf conspiracy, the Directory, in its attitude to revolution in foreign countries, showed less inclination to deal with refugees and fiery individual patriots and more of a tendency to think in military terms, and to appeal to settled middle-class persons, who, in various countries, would never make a revolution themselves but might accept a revolutionary regime after the arrival of the French army. In the Batavian Republic, the French, while continuing to favor the unitary democrats, tried to avoid offending the more moderate federalists. The Poles were channeled into the organized Polish Legion, under Bonaparte's command. In the plans for Ireland, arranged with Wolfe Tone, internal agitation was subordinated to the great naval expedition which sailed for Bantry Bay in December 1796, and which failed to land 15,000 troops in Ireland only because of unfavorable winds.

As for the Italians, the view prevailed which Cacault had already expressed before the Babeuf-Buonarroti conspiracy was discovered. His view was shared by most French observers in Italy, including Bonaparte. It held that broad segments of Italian opinion were dissatisfied with the existing order, would welcome the French, and collaborate in a revolution under French protection, but that little clusters of visionary exiles, fugitives, conspirators, and radical intellectuals, like Buonarroti, representing no actual forces in their own countries, would do more harm than good.

"It is not to be doubted," wrote Cacault to Delacroix on April 9, "that when our military forces triumph in Piedmont we can rally these [locally resident] patriots and many others; I believe that in working by a reasonable method to Republicanize the conquered areas in Italy we can obtain advantages, and especially inspire fear and terror in the hearts of all the petty Tyrants by whom this fair country is subjected; but I have never proposed this except as secondary to our victories. . . . Let us enter victoriously into Piedmont, the Milanese and all Italy; we shall find a high-spirited people, and can then use the refugees who have any virtues or character—the number is not large. . . . The notes on Italy signed by Buonarroti and Cerise are pitiful. . . ."[21]

It is argued by some historians that the Directory turned against the Italian revolutionaries of the type of Buonarroti because it was afraid of them. Their implication with Babeuf and preference for a united Italy to be achieved by a vast popular rising or *levée révolutionnaire*, are thought to have stirred up in the minds of Delacroix and the Directors a kind of general bourgeois social fear. It is even argued that this fear on the part of the Directory prevented a unification of Italy that was perhaps possible in the 1790's.[22]

---

[21] Saitta, II, 22.

[22] Godechot, *La Grande Nation: l'expansion révolutionnaire de la France dans le monde 1789-99*, 2 vols. (Paris, 1956), I, 284-311, which restates a thesis set forth in numerous articles, especially "Unità batava e unità italiana all'epoca del Direttorio," in *Archivio storico italiano*, CXIII (1955), 335-56. Saitta, Candeloro, and some others of the best recent Italian historians also attributed the turning of the French Directory against the Italian unitarists to the fear of radicalism aroused by discovery of the Babeuf plot. It is a case of the modern preference for attributing political decisions to ideological or class-oriented interests. Godechot, more than the Italians, believes that unification of Italy at this time might have been possible had the Directory been willing to support the unitarists. He has probably read too much nineteenth-century meaning into Delacroix' language. He quotes Delacroix to Cacault, March

It seems at least equally likely that the French government turned against the Italian refugee patriots because it held them in contempt. The Babeuf-Buonarroti conspiracy, once discovered, proved reassuringly easy to repress. Delacroix, Carnot, and the others, who had remained active during the Terror, were not chiefly characterized by timidity. It is reasonable to suppose that they came to believe that the Italian refugees were mere dabblers in revolution, conspirators playing with firecrackers, that revolution in Italy could not be produced by such methods, and that republics in Italy, if such there were to be, and if they were to be of any value to France, must rest upon men of some standing and experience in their own countries, and not on uprooted exiles.

But the French government was unable to hold to any firm position on the Italian question. One group, led by the Director Reubell, an Alsatian, preferred to regard conquests in Italy as mere diplomatic counterweights, to be given away in return for a peace treaty in which Austria should accept the French annexation of Belgium, and perhaps the Left Bank of the Rhine. This school of thought saw no danger or strength in the Italian revolutionaries, but emphasized their weakness and insignificance. As Delacroix wrote to Saliceti, if it should prove that the Milanese "lack the energy to conquer liberty themselves, we should limit our efforts to obtaining our own advantages, and procuring for the Republic a solid and durable peace."[23] On July 25 four of the Directors endorsed a memorandum prepared by Delacroix, in which it was concluded to be against French interests to set up either one or several "democratic republics" in Italy, since there were not enough serious revolutionaries at Milan to support such a program,

---

27, 1796 (Saitta, II, 17): "Let the boundaries separating the various states disappear, so that only one shall be formed, and the peoples forget their mutual animosities . . ." as if these words meant that Cacault should favor the unification of all Italy. Not seeing the Poteratz affair in this connection, he has not noted that Delacroix used similar language to Poteratz, May 4, 1796 (Biro, *German Policy*, II, 572-73): "apply yourself to bringing about the disappearance of the petty animosities which may exist between the inhabitants of the different principalities, to uniting them, to welding them into a single political body." (Biro here cites AAE, Allemagne, vol. 672, fol. 259.) No one would argue from these words that Delacroix favored the unification of Germany. "Unity" meant cooperation of various kinds of revolutionaries, and disregard of local territorial, class, religious, or other structures, whether in parts of Italy, Germany, the Batavian Republic, or Ireland. For example, Noel wrote from the Hague, on June 14, 1796, that unitarists like Valckenaer and Vreede must be supported, "car enfin ce n'est pas à quelques familles de chaque province, mais à la nation entière, sans distinction de patriciens ou de gouvernés, de juifs ou de chrétiens, de catholiques ou de protestants, que les armes françaises ont rendu la liberté." Colenbrander, *Gedenkstukken*, II, 56.
[23] Delacroix to Saliceti, AAE, Mém. et Doc., France, vol. 1965, fol. 93.

but that Austria should nevertheless be expelled from Italy through the reinforcement of war by diplomacy. It was decided that Austria might receive Bavaria, whose Elector might take over Tuscany, while the Milanese went to the Duke of Parma. Thus Austria could accept the cession of Belgium to France.[24] No plan could have been more shocking to the Italian republicans, had they known of it. It reverted to classic principles of compensation and balance of power as the way to peace.

The facts determined otherwise. For one thing, Bonaparte had other ideas; he was getting out of control by the civilian government in Paris, and was intent upon setting up a new republic in the Po valley. For another, it was not true that there was no serious revolutionary sentiment in Italy. "The Italians," reported Cacault, "want the humiliation of the upper classes, the abolition of feudalisms and titles, the exclusion of nobles from office; it is necessary for the 200,000 privileged to be sacrificed to the 16,000,000 of the population."[25] In any case, could the French, once they were in Italy, simply abandon those who agreed with them? As Miot reported in July, even if it were true that the Italian patriots were not ripe for real republicanism, still we French must do *something*: we cannot simply hand them back to Austria, we cannot annex them to France, and we are committed by what we have already done in Holland; we must let them assemble and set up governments of their own choosing, while our presence protects them from counter-revolution both native and foreign.[26]

The French at this time, in July, had been at Milan for two months, and Italian patriots had flocked to that city from all directions. They set up an essay contest, in good eighteenth-century fashion, on the subject, "Which form of free government is best suited to the welfare of Italy?" Fifty-two papers were written. The prize was awarded a year later to the economist Melchiorre Gioia, who argued that the only possible free government for Italy was a republic. Gioia insisted, pointing to the weakness of the American union in the War of Independence, that the only viable republic must be democratic, centralized, and unitary.[27] This was contrary to the decision taken by

[24] "Italie 7 thermidor an IV," in AAE, Mém. et Doc., Italie 1794-1809, vol. 12, fols. 53-63; Guyot, *Directoire et paix de l'Europe*, 193; the document was published by C. Zaghi in *Bonaparte, il Direttorio e il problema politico dell' Italia* (Ferrara, 1938), 83-91.

[25] "Extrait d'une dépêche du Citoyen Cacault," Genoa, 28 Germinal an IV (April 17, 1796), AAE, Mém. et Docs., Italie 1794-1809, vol. 12, fol. 19.

[26] "Extrait d'une dépêche du Citoyen Miot agent francais près du gouvernement de Toscane, Rome le 9 Thermidor an IV (July 27, 1796)," *ibid.*, fol. 64.

[27] M. Gioia, "Dissertazione sul problema: Quale dei governi liberi meglio convenga alla felicità dell' Italia," published at the time, and in *Opere minore* (Lugano, 1833), IV, 99-311. Gioia meant unification in the nineteenth-century sense.

the French Directory at the time when the contest was announced.

So the basis was laid, in the summer of 1796, for the conflicts and misunderstandings that were to trouble the following years. There was the Directory, unable to hold to any positive decisions, yielding before accomplished facts, pursuing incompatible ends—to gain a lasting peace, to manipulate the balance of power, to hold on to Belgium or the Rhine frontier, to keep the support of sympathizers in Italy but to exploit Italian resources in the war against Austria, to liberate Italy but to discourage steps toward Italian unification, to make the war a crusade for freedom while alleviating the financial problems of France. There were the French generals, whom the Directory found it increasingly difficult to control, and who, like Dumouriez in 1792-1793, sought their own glory and riches in republics to be created under their sponsorship, or who indeed actually believed in liberating the peoples among whom the fortunes of war had brought them. There were the Italian partisans of revolution, both moderates whose moderation made them passive, and the more aggressive spirits who already dreamed of a united Italy, who therefore opposed all existing states and authorities in the peninsula, who had no patience with most of the considerations by which the Directory was affected, and who might turn against the French themselves without at all turning against the Revolution. And there was ground for alliance, in a diversity of grievances against the Directory, between some of the adventurous French generals, the extreme Italian patriots, and the advanced French democrats who formed an opposition to the Directory in France itself.

Italy before 1796

Italy in the eighteenth century was very much a part of European civilization, and its revolutionary agitation was indigenous, not an import from France. It is necessary, as we turn from an emphasis on French policy to an account of Italy itself, to begin with such a dogmatic statement, since the derivative character of those Italian developments has so long been a part of the conventional wisdom. The French have characteristically seen the Italian *giacobini* as rather futile imitators of themselves.[28] Of the British and Americans, it is hardly

---

[28] But this older French view is revised by J. Godechot, now the leading French authority on Italy in the Revolutionary era. There is much of great value on Italy in his *Commissaires aux armées sous le Directoire*, 2 vols. (Paris, 1937); for later summaries of his more intensive work see his *Grande Nation: l'expansion révolutionnaire de la France 1789-1799*, 2 vols. (Paris, 1956).

too much to say that there has never been a good book on the subject in the English language.[29] The Italians have of course always shown more interest, but for generations it was believed that the normal outcome of Italian history was in a constitutional monarchy under the House of Savoy; and certain contrary influences associated with Fascism, while unwilling to attribute much to the French, were hardly more favorable to a historical appreciation of Italian republicanism. Since Italy became a republic in 1946, and with the successful assertion of democratic forces against Fascism, there has been a good deal of corresponding activity in historical circles. No country so much as Italy, since the Second World War, has produced such a flow of new materials and new thinking on this period in its own past.

The new studies differ with each other, some preferring to emphasize constitutional and juridical matters,[30] others calling attention to economic development and the contrary purposes of social classes,[31] but they agree in seeing the revolutionary movement as a positive phenomenon arising from serious causes, and in refuting the charges that it was "passive" and "abstract." These charges were not peculiar to Italy. They were made in somewhat the same way against the Batavian

[29] Literally it would be too much to say; we have had, for example, G. B. McClellan, *Venice and Bonaparte* (Princeton, 1931) and Constance Giglioli (née Stocker), *Naples in 1799: an Account of the Revolution of 1799 and the Rise and Fall of the Parthenopean Republic* (London, 1903). These are well worth reading, but the same cannot be said of Angus Heriot, *The French in Italy 1796-99* (London, 1957), which draws on the old French and English memoirs, pays no attention to the recent Italian studies, and does not even mention many Italian revolutionaries of the period, such as Buonarroti and many others who have been studied at least since Croce's work in the 1890's. The void in English is well-illustrated by the translation (London, 1828, Philadelphia, 1829) of Carlo Botta's *Storia d'Italia dal 1789 al 1814* (Paris, 1824). Botta devoted the first three of four volumes to the years 1789-1799, but only the parts in which Napoleon figured were thought sufficiently interesting to the English public to be translated.

[30] Notably C. Ghisalberti, *Le costituzioni "giacobini" 1796-99* (Varese, 1957); G. Vaccarino, *I patriotti "anarchistes" e l'idea dell'unità italiana* (Turin, 1955); and the texts and notes published by A. Aquarone, *Le costituzione italiane* (Milan, 1958). The work of E. Rota, *Le origini del Risorgimento, 1700-1800*, 2 vols. (Milan, 1948), comes toward the end of a career devoted to the subject since 1910. For two excellent discussions of the new Italian literature see Renzo de Felice, "Studi recenti di storia del triennio rivoluzionario in Italia, 1796-99," in *Società*, xi (1955), 498-513, and G. Spini's long review of Cantimori in *Rassegna storica del Risorgimento*, xliii (1956), 792-96.

[31] Notably G. Candeloro, *Storia dell' Italia moderna*, 3 vols. (Milan, 1956-   ), i, 159-288; B. Peroni, "Gli Italiani alla vigilia della dominazione francese, 1793-96," in *Nuova rivista storica*, xxxv (1951), 227-42; A. Saitta, *Filippo Buonarroti*, 2 vols. (Rome, 1950); A. Galante Garrone, *Buonarrot e Babeuf* (Turin, 1948); D. Cantimori, *Giacobini italiani* (Bari, 1956); Renzo de Felice, ed., *I giornali giacobini italiani* (Milan, 1962); and a series of articles by Renzo de Felice in the *Rass. stor. del Risorg.*, of which the one on Giuseppe Ceracchi (xlvii, 1960, 3-32) will be of especial interest to American readers.

Republic, and after 1798 against the Helvetic Republic in Switzerland. No allegation was more common in conservative quarters than that the French Revolution itself was too "abstract," and the same had been said even earlier of British and Irish reform bills. By "abstraction" was meant that the principles invoked in these movements were irrelevant to real problems. By "passivity" was meant, in part, a mere imitativeness, a response to external stimulus, an uncritical enthusiasm for someone else's revolution and for "French" ideas. This charge was also made against British radicals and American republicans, when their critics supposed them to reflect a vogue for French principles but to have no genuine roots within the country. Passivity also meant an inability to precipitate a revolution oneself, a dependency on France—no arrival of the French, no Italian revolution. In this limited sense the Italian revolution was "passive"—more so than that of the Dutch, who had attempted a revolution in the 1780's, and agitated in Paris from 1787 to 1794, forming a Batavian Legion and a revolutionary committee when the war began. But this argument shows only that the pressure for revolution in Italy had not in 1796 reached the point of spontaneous explosion, not that no such pressure existed, or that it was not rising.

The situation in Italy was in some ways distinctive, in others resembled that of other parts of Europe. Special to Italy was its own kind of territorial fragmentation. Less pulverized than Germany, less united than the seven Dutch provinces before 1795, the country supported about a dozen independent and very dissimilar states. There were two royal monarchies, Sardinia-Piedmont and Naples-Sicily, the papal "monarchy" in the middle, and the ducal monarchies of Parma, Modena, Milan, and Tuscany. Milan, along with Mantua, was part of the Hapsburg empire. Tuscany belonged to the Hapsburg family, but was independent in domestic and foreign policy under its own grand duke. There were also the old patrician republics of Lucca, Genoa, and Venice. Lucca was very small, Genoa ran for over a hundred miles along the Ligurian shore, shutting off Piedmont from the sea, while Venice possessed Venetia, Istria, and the Dalmatian coast and islands. The strongest political units, however, at least in the center and north, were the cities. Municipalism, descended from the medieval communalism, was ingrained in institutions and mental habits, setting town against country, and town against town.

There were nobles in Italy, but they generally lived in the cities, and there was less stress between nobility and bourgeoisie than in northern

Europe. With no central royal court to dominate fashionable society as at Versailles (though an attempt might be made at Naples), with no military tradition for several generations and hence no mentality of an aristocratic officer-caste, with nobles living in town and the old urban families owning estates in the country, there was only limited ground on which the nobleman could feel himself to be superior, or on which the wealthy non-noble could resent the noble as a noble. There were many nobles among the leaders of discontent before 1796, and of revolution after that year.

Though Italy had long lost its former leading role in long-distance commerce, it was by no means economically stagnant, and the growth of a money economy, with the habit of purposeful investment for profit, was visible in Italy as elsewhere. In the south it took the form of un-productive acquisition of large tracts of rural land by city men. In the north there was more economic enterprise, with new forms of business activity, new manufactures, new crops and methods in agriculture, new roads and better communications and development of regional markets. There was also a growing number of persons in the professions, such as medicine, law, journalism, and engineering. The Italian universities were more alive than those of France or England, with men of ideas in their faculties of law and theology; they were also distributed about the country, with men going from one to another.

These developments produced geographical and social mobility. It was characteristic of many Italian cities to have, on the one hand, an established in-group, an oligarchy composed of a few families who had been resident for generations and monopolized the offices and the honors, and on the other hand an out-group of persons newly arrived in the city, or whose fathers had settled in it, who had no local involvement with the established interests, and who believed them-selves equally qualified for the conduct of large affairs. What they wanted was less a united Italy than a modern state. A united Italy was an old dream of literary people, proclaimed also in the 1790's by political intellectuals who had little connection with any organized affairs. For most persons interested in public questions, a modern state was more important, one that could go beyond a mere municipal out-look, favor economic development, be large enough to organize a significant territory, promote education, communications, and public enlightenment, introduce a reasonable kind of taxation, combat the ecclesiastical influences, use the resources of church-owned lands for more secular purposes, and overcome the in-breeding and routine-mindedness of the old urban patriciates. Enlightened despotism had already accomplished something in this direction, especially in Tuscany, which probably for that reason was the least disturbed of the Italian states by revolutionary commotion.

The place occupied by the Roman Catholic Church also made the situation in Italy distinctive. Italy had its share of writers of the Enlightenment, most especially in economic and legal studies. There was little opposition to Christianity, and few were concerned to doubt the divine or at least legitimate mission of the church. The more so, perhaps, because the Church seemed to be in the nature of things, to which no alternative was imagined, a great many people were highly critical of its personnel and procedures. They came to be called Jansenists, and they flourished in Italy after Jansenism in France had been reduced to a clandestine and lower-class persuasion.[32] Jansenists taught in the Italian universities and acted as advisors to governments. Considering themselves to be good Catholics, or indeed the best Catholics, they objected to domination by Rome, had little concern for its temporal power, were critical of monastic establishments, believed the Church too wealthy for its own good, advocated a more apostolic simplicity, and approved the confiscation and resale of church-owned property by the state. It is thought also that Jansenism, by its inner moral attitudes, favored the growth of "Jacobinism" in Italy, since on Christian grounds it emphasized principles of brotherhood and equality, and a spark of liberty in the individual soul, given by grace, apart from worldly and ecclesiastical institutions. The Italian revolutionary movement never became as anti-Christian as the French did, with the result that anti-Christian episodes, when they occurred, were more shocking to the public and more disruptive to the revolutionary parties than they had been in France.

The idea that it was possible to create a better state, a purer church, or a more modern society was mainly voiced by the newer middle classes, with much support from many noblemen and men holding some position within the church. The bulk of the population played a negative role, setting limits to effective political action, both for the

---

[32] There is a large literature on Italian Jansenism in its connection with the political revolution and the secularization of Italian society. See M. Vaussard, *Jansénisme et gallicanisme aux origines religieuses du Risorgimento* (Paris, 1959); E. Codignola, *Illuministi, giansenisti e giacobini nell' Italia del Settecento* (Florence, 1947); A. Bersano, *L'abate Francesco Bonardi e i suoi tempi: contributo alla storia delle società segrete* (Turin, 1957); and the fascinating case study by E. Rota, *Giuseppe Poggi e la formazione psicologica del patriota moderno, 1761-1843* (Piacenza, 1923), reprinted from *Nuova rivista storica* of 1922 and 1923.

old governments and for those issuing from the revolution.[33] Cities were large, with Milan, Venice, Rome, Naples, and Palermo all having over 100,000 inhabitants, and being larger than Lyon, the second city of France; but there never was any true popular revolutionism of the sans-culotte kind, nor even as much as in the Dutch cities. The rural areas swarmed with an increasing population, which rose during the century from about eleven to about eighteen millions for Italy as a whole, so that in many places there were crises over land, employment, and subsistence. It is possible that the burden of taxation and seigneurial dues was lighter than north of the Alps, since no Italian state was a great power with the chronic costs of war and large armies, and expensive living habits were perhaps less common among the Italian aristocracy than among the French. In any case, there was no peasant revolution as in France in 1789, directed against government and seigneurs, and less articulate peasant discontent than in Hungary. The peasants saw little to gain in the programs of Italian reformers and revolutionaries as they understood them, and they blamed their troubles, often rightly enough, on the activities of their own neighboring townspeople, and after 1796 on the exactions, requisitions, and pillage that followed military occupation by the French.

The Italian revolution, in short, was an affair of newer and enlightened elements among middle- and upper-class townspeople, impatient at old vested interests, at their own exclusion from power, and at the slow pace with which the foundations of a modern state were being laid. Revolutionary leaders made no appeal for popular support, as they had done in France at moments of exceptional crisis. Nor could much response be aroused in the name of the "nation," whether in the sense of all Italians against all foreigners, or of co-operation of social classes, or of working across territorial and municipal barriers. The revolution was therefore, compared to the French, less massive, less violent, less self-sustaining, and more dependent on outside aid. To say that it was no revolution at all, however, would be to premise that all revolutions must closely resemble the French.

The news from Paris, beginning in 1789, soon divided the Italians, as it did others, into those who feared and those who favored the French Revolution. What this really meant was a division between those who feared and favored the attainment of similar objectives in

---

[33] This is seriously qualified or denied by Peroni, Candeloro, and others, who prefer to believe that there was a potential revolutionism among the Italian popular classes, which could have been brought to life if French policies had been more favorable.

their own countries. Conservative Italians, as Pietro Verri observed in 1789, soon tried to discredit the new ideas as "metaphysical." Italian governments, both those that were native and those that were subordinate to Austria, made efforts to keep out French newspapers like the *Moniteur*, and imposed a strong censorship on their own presses. These measures proved to be difficult and unpopular, since no revolution had ever occurred in such a glare of journalistic publicity, and the number of persons able and eager to read of these events in north Italy was very large. When, with the war of 1792, revolutionary propaganda began to assume larger proportions, it inspired terror in the authorities. It may be recalled that Joel Barlow's *Advice to the People of Piedmont,* in its Italian translation, was so thoroughly repressed by the King of Sardinia that no known copy now exists.

Such negativism on the part of the governments, and harping on the beauties of purely traditional institutions, made many liberally minded and reformist Italians more receptive to the French. Verri, for example, as a writer on economic and fiscal subjects, had in former years been a staunch supporter of the Austrians at Milan, looking to the enlightened monarchy of Maria Theresa and Joseph II to drive through certain reforms in taxation. When Joseph, to carry out his plans, began to cut down the liberties of the Milanese constituted bodies that opposed him, Verri had second thoughts. He became less willing to accept reform at the price of a despotism that crushed the local organs of expression. But he could have no faith in the existing Milanese magistracies, closed, exclusive, self-perpetuating, and overwhelmingly conservative as they were. He came to believe, therefore, that the combination of practical reform with political liberty was possible only in some new kind of state, which would be at first revolutionary, then constitutional. He saw a state of this kind in the French Directory with its Constitution of the Year III, which embodied what many Italian writers and law professors had been saying for many years.[34] When the French reached Milan in 1796, Verri, Melzi d'Eril, and other prominent citizens were willing to work with them, in the hope of using them for their own purposes.[35] Somewhat similarly, when the Pope spoke out against the French church reorganization in 1791,

[34] Ghisalberti (see note 30 above) in particular shows that the Italian republican constitutions of 1796-1799 carried out the thought of the Italian Enlightenment.
[35] *Age,* I, 105, 389; D. Limoli, "Pietro Verri, a Lombard Reformer under Enlightened Despotism and the French Revolution," in *Journal of Central European Affairs,* XVIII (1958); C. Morandi, *Idee e formazioni politiche in Lombardia dal 1748 al 1814* (Turin, 1927).

the Italian Jansenists tended to divide. These Jansenists, to repeat, were often men of importance in the governments and universities. Some now made their peace with Rome. Others, continuing to favor a secularization of church properties, and to admire certain features of the French Civil Constitution of the Clergy, concluded that such aims could be achieved in Italy only through revolution, and hence through co-operation with the French.

Meanwhile, before 1796, all Italy began to vibrate with clubs, conspiracies, and agitations in which unknown and lesser persons were active.[36] Masonic lodges, long condemned by the papacy, and now also frowned upon by governments, in some cases turned into secret revolutionary organizations. They drew assistance from the Masonic lodge at Marseilles. Filippo Buonarroti, a graduate of the University of Pisa, in 1790 passed over to Corsica, which being French was already in the turmoil of revolution, and published his *Giornale patriottico della Corsica*, the first revolutionary journal in the Italian language. The year 1794 found him as agent of the Revolutionary Government at Oneglia, an enclave belonging to the King of Sardinia within the borders of the Republic of Genoa. With the aid of Tilly, the French envoy in neutral Genoa, various Italians congregated at Oneglia and received lessons in revolution from Buonarroti. How Buonarroti subsequently met Babeuf, and developed further plans for revolution, has already been told.

In 1794 revolutionary plots were discovered at Naples, Bologna, and Turin. The one at Naples dated back at least to 1792, when a French naval squadron had visited the city, and after much fraternization between local patriots and French sailors and officers, two revolutionary societies had been formed. Various noblemen, annoyed at the peculiar influence of the British Sir John Acton over the queen, were involved. The arrests and trials of 1794 were followed by a continuing harassment of republicans until the French army itself arrived in 1799. At Bologna, which belonged to the papal states, a young man named Zamboni, who had traveled in Corsica and France, planned an insurrection to obtain independence for Bologna from the Pope's government. The plan was discovered; Zamboni committed suicide in prison, and his father, whom he had drawn into the conspiracy, died in prison after torture.

Turin and the whole Kingdom of Sardinia had been seriously torn by the war which the King entered against France in the summer of

---

[36] A synopsis in Candeloro, *Storia*, i, 180-197; the special studies are numerous.

1792, after rejecting French offers of alliance at that time. There was much sympathy for the French Revolution; indeed, the French-speaking population of Savoy, the oldest part of this miscellaneous monarchy, voted itself into union with the French Republic late in 1792, in a plebiscite whose authenticity was not much questioned. In the next year, while the government managed to stay in the war with a grant of £200,000 from Britain, two revolutionary clubs were organized at Turin, with assistance from Tilly at Genoa. One, more moderate, was formed around a banker named Vinay. The other, more definitely republican, contained a number of medical students and doctors, including Carlo Botta, then a doctor, and later famous as a historian. With the French advances of 1794 (which brought Buonarroti to Oneglia) plans were made for revolt in Turin, but they were discovered by the police, with help from the British agent in Genoa. The plotters fled or were exiled. Two years later, in April 1796, as already noted, some of these same men, in touch with Buonarroti and the Babouvists in Paris, brought on a more successful insurrection and proclaimed the republic at Alba. But Bonaparte, by signing an armistice with the Sardinian king, repudiated these revolutionaries and frustrated the republican movement.

Various other incidents could be recounted. At Rome, where popular demonstrations against the ungodly French were a common occurrence, the French envoy, Hugo de Bassville, in the revolutionary enthusiasm of 1793, was imprudent enough to display an enormous tricolor at the embassy. He was set upon and murdered by angry crowds. The French complained of the poor police protection at Rome, but did no more than to break diplomatic relations for several years. At Palermo a plot was discovered to assassinate the archbishop. In Venetia the cities of the mainland bore the supremacy of Venice with increasing disaffection. At Padua, for example, nobles, priests, and middle-class citizens, reinforced by professors and students at the University, were all hostile to La Dominante, as the city of Venice was called by its mainland subjects.

When the French under Bonaparte in 1796, having defeated Sardinia, poured down into the Lombard plain, driving the Austrians before them, they met everywhere with little or no resistance. As in Belgium, Holland, and the Rhineland in 1794, so in Italy in 1796, the most notable fact seems to have been that no one cared to defend the existing order. As in these northern regions two years before, either the governments were afraid to arm their own peoples, or their feeble attempts to evoke a kind of popular rising against the invaders came to nothing. At Milan, after the Austrians left, the patricians in the Decurionate enrolled a few volunteer defenders, but as one of them remarked, the people could not become very animated without *il nome di patria*, and there was not much for most Milanese to feel patriotic about.[37] When the French soon thereafter passed on into Venetia, the British representative there dreaded the approach of "the absolute Democracy," and remarked to Lord Grenville: "I may add that the Venetian nobles during this whole contest have improvidently distrusted their own subjects, and have been afraid of allowing them the use of arms to protect themselves."[38]

So the Revolution came to Italy. Cacault thought the Italians more receptive to the French and more suited for liberty than "the stupid Belgians or brutalized Germans."[39] It remained to be seen how long the welcome to the French would last.

The Kingdom of Corsica

But what if Counter-Revolution came instead? What happened if not the French, but their enemies, prevailed? What were the issues in this war, which if not ideological in intention was certainly so in its consequences? An answer is suggested by what happened in Corsica, a region which since it belonged to France had been revolutionized since 1789, but which was Italian in language and in many of its cultural contacts (so far as a region still so primitive may be said to have had any) and which experienced a counter-revolution from 1794 to 1796, when the island was occupied by the British. Before proceeding to an account of the Cisalpine Republic, it is more than a mere digression to glance at this Corsican Kingdom.[40]

Corsica was divided by the revolution in France into revolutionary and counter-revolutionary parties. Among locally prominent families favoring the new order were the Bonapartes. The aged patriot Paoli, on the other hand, became a rallying point for the anti-French and anti-revolutionary elements. He made overtures to the British, proposing that Corsica be set up as a semi-autonomous kingdom on the model

[37] C. Montalcini, *Atti delle assemblee costituzionali italiane . . . Republica cisalpina*, 10 vols. (Bologna, 1917-1943), I, xci.

[38] C. Roth, "La caduta della serenissima nei dispacci del residente inglese a Venezia," in *Archivio veneto* (1935), 188, 211.

[39] Quoted by Candeloro, *Storia*, 190.

[40] For somewhat more detail, with references, see my "Kingdom of Corsica and the Science of History," in *Proceedings of the American Philosophical Society*, Vol. 105 (1961), 354-60.

of Ireland. When the British were forced out of Toulon at the end of 1793 they occupied Corsica, hoping to use it as a base for naval power in the Mediterranean, for maintaining resistance in southern France against the Paris government, and for bringing Genoa and Tuscany into the Coalition.

On the arrival of the British a general election was held, which produced an assembly, which in turn adopted a constitution, declared the country a constitutional monarchy, and offered the crown to King George III. The crown was accepted, and Sir Gilbert Elliot became Viceroy of Corsica. The purpose of the new regime, as stated by the Corsicans now in power, was to protect "liberty and religion" against "the tyrannical anarchy of the present republic of France."

The new constitution was intended to resemble that of England. A Parliament was created, with that name. Legislative power rested in King and Parliament together; that is, the Viceroy had a veto, and laws were enacted, following the British formula, "by the king's most excellent Majesty." Each country district or coastal town sent two members to Parliament, as in England. Men could vote who were at least twenty-five years old, and possessed of landed property. To be elected to Parliament, however, the qualifications were rather high; an annual landed revenue of 6,000 lire was required, the equivalent of some £200 sterling. Here again the parallel to England was striking. Members of Parliament served without compensation, as in England. Since persons resembling lords could not be found in Corsica, the Parliament had only a single house. To protect religion, however, the Catholic bishops sat as members of Parliament, like Anglican bishops in the English or Irish House of Lords. Executive power lay with the Viceroy. Courts were instituted, trial by jury was provided for, and various civil rights were promised. Roman Catholicism was declared the national religion, with toleration for others.

We may profitably contrast, with a little anticipation, this Corsican constitution of 1794 with the constitution of the Cisalpine Republic of 1797.[41] The Cisalpine constitution would proclaim the sovereignty of the people. The executive would be chosen by the assembly, itself elected by voters in proportion to population. The Cisalpine constitution would separate church and state; it would put no bishops in positions of government. The figure of 6,000 *lire* would occur in both

[41] For the text of the Corsican constitution in English see the *Annual Register for 1794*, 103-09; for the Corsican and Cisalpine constitutions, A. Aquarone, et al., *Le costituzioni italiane* (Milan, 1959), 87-120, 715-20.

constitutions. In the Cisalpine Republic, deputies would receive an annual salary of this amount. In Corsica, they received no salary, and were required to have an income of this amount from their own property. The Cisalpine Republic would embody the democratic formula that public officers were wage-servants of the people. The Corsican kingdom followed the principle that government should properly be conducted by an upper class enjoying an independent income from land.

The regime set up under this constitution soon came to represent a cross-section of the forces arrayed against French republicanism, briefly gathered in a kind of happy isle of the European Counter-Revolution. Sir Gilbert Elliot took steps to live in a state suitable to a viceroy, making arrangements for a salary of £8,000, which fortunately for the Corsicans was to be paid from British funds, since it was almost half as large as the whole proceeds of taxation in Corsica. It may be remembered that the first British governor in South Africa, the Earl of McCartney, occupying Cape Town in 1795, received a salary of £10,000, a sum half as large as the total revenue of the Cape Colony.

As his administrative secretary, the Viceroy chose Frederick North, a remarkable linguist with a good knowledge of Italian, who, so far as his social origins were concerned, was the third son of the Lord North of the American Revolution, and hence in later years became the fifth Earl of Guilford. Positions as Anglican chaplain, and as aides to the Viceroy, gave employment to other suitable young men from England. There were also British officers from the garrison and from the fleet, including the future Lord Nelson. And there were French émigré noblemen, who had lost their property after their emigration, and who now sought service with the British in the hope of winning back their former position in France. As Lady Elliot wrote to a friend in England, "We have dukes and princes as ensigns and lieutenants who once enjoyed their £10,000 or £15,000 a year."[42]

The Viceroy had more trouble with some of his Corsican associates. Paoli was crotchety, suspicious, impossible to cooperate with, and unable to accept anyone as his superior or even as his equal in the conduct of Corsican affairs. In effect, the Corsican prime minister under the Viceroy was Pozzo di Borgo. Descended from an ancient Corsican landowning family, he was at this time a young man of thirty, just entering upon a long career of half a century of opposition to the France of the Revolution. Twenty years later, in 1814, upon the defeat

---

[42] *Letters of Sir Gilbert Elliot*, 3 vols., 1874, II, 338.

of Napoleon, he was to ride victoriously into Paris with the Russian Tsar.

Such were the more prominent of the persons now active in the Kingdom of Corsica, unless one wishes also to add the Pope, who began to demand an influence in the island which both the French monarchy and the French Revolution had denied him, and which the Protestant Viceroy dismissed as an intrigue. Without further research, it is hardly possible to say who the less prominent supporters of the regime were. Probably Sir Gilbert Elliot's diagnosis was correct. Everything depended, he reported, on how the bulk of the Corsican people read the future. If they thought that the British would certainly stay, they would accept them; if they thought that the British were in the island only temporarily, they would be unwilling or afraid to commit themselves.

The legislation enacted by the Viceroy and Parliament was of course designed for the benefit of the country as understood by those who now governed it. Some of it suggests the less gentle features of British law at the time. Criminal law was severe, with burglary punishable by twelve years in the galleys, except that the stealing of sacred objects in church was punished by twenty, in the galleys. There was also the war to carry on, and France to be defeated; the British Mediterranean fleet was short 2,000 men, and Corsican seamen became subject to impressment into the Royal Navy.

Some legislation was in the strict sense simply reactionary, undoing what had been done during the Revolution. Property confiscated from the church was returned to it, though with provision for compensation to the new owners. Church tithes were reimposed. Violence against the Catholic religion was made punishable by death. The Revolutionary legislation against primogeniture and entails (*fidecommessi*) was repealed. The Revolutionary principle of removing education from church control was repudiated; a university and secondary schools were to be set up, subject to inspection by the bishops. The salt tax of the late French monarchy was restored; it was now to be much heavier than before 1789, since the new regime showed a preference for indirect taxation.

Other enactments were political, intended to protect the persons now in power from those who might overthrow them. Here the Viceroy tried to exercise restraint. He conceived of himself as a reasonable Englishman among temperamental Latins, and he repeatedly advised against vengefulness. He underestimated the internal discord within the country. He could not believe that respectable Corsicans opposed the new order, since he never met any such people. He tried to learn, and made tours about the island, but he was hardly in a position to be in close touch with the full range of opinion.

Resistance against the Anglo-Corsican kingdom soon developed an indigenous republican underground, committed to the overthrow of the regime and to ending the union with England. So far as Corsica had any professional or business people, they seem to have looked with favor on the French Revolution. Of five leaders of the underground whose names are known, three were doctors. The gentry also proved increasingly disappointing to Sir Gilbert. Where at first he had seen "remarkably good specimens" of a country gentleman, he found them, a year later, not "beyond the pitch of a good yeoman in England, or of the humblest squires of our remote counties."[43] The basis of a social and political system like that of England seemed to be lacking.

Threatened with subversion, and despite the Viceroy's pleas for moderation, the Corsican Parliament behaved like the French Convention during the Terror. At least the legislation was much the same. There were laws against traitors and émigrés. There was a law taking their property from them, and promising it to those who had sustained losses in the late disturbances. There was a law prescribing death to émigrés if they returned, and another decreed death for correspondence with the enemies of Corsica and Great Britain. Another required priests to take an oath to the constitution. There was a law forbidding unauthorized public assemblies, as well as spontaneously formed crowds or *attrupamenti*. Another suspended jury trials, and another offered a reward of 5,000 francs for every secret republican emissary from France that could be apprehended.

Constitution or no constitution, freedom of speech disappeared. In August 1796, the administrative secretary, Frederick North, sent instructions to C. B. Buttafoco, the King's attorney at Bastia. It should be remembered that only a few months before, in England itself, Parliament had curbed political discussion by the Seditious Meetings and Treasonable Practices Acts. It is necessary, said North to Buttafoco, to stamp out all signs of the *maladetto republicanismo francese*. "It will be a great advantage to persuade all the most notable patriots [a word used by all parties] to prevent by common accord political discussion of any kind; but if this proves impossible, and if republicanism shows itself in any way, then it will be necessary to arouse to

---

[43] *Ibid.*, ii, 258, 306.

the utmost the patriotism of the well-affected against the guilty, and to put these persons under arrest."[44]

In short, a regime ostensibly conservative adopted the features of the radicalism it denounced. The counter-revolution became the mirror image of the revolution itself. It was not only Robespierre who pursued the "guilty." Moderation failed. Choices were limited. One might choose between monarchy and republicanism, but there was no real choice between revolution and a peaceful rule of law, or between revolution and a calm and orderly conservatism.

In any case Corsica soon became untenable by the British. When the Corsican-born Bonaparte launched into his sensational campaign in north Italy, excitement in the island got beyond control. The French occupied Leghorn, threatening to invade; for preliminary propaganda, they found a Leghorn Jewish merchant who translated into Italian a work on the imminent collapse of British finances, written by Thomas Paine. The British evacuated, and their chief Corsican supporters became émigrés in their turn. That was the end of the Kingdom of Corsica.

It is ironical to be able to add that the British cabinet, a few weeks later, decided to offer the island to the Empress of Russia. King George expressed an especial personal satisfaction at this solution, which was never in fact carried out.

It was the French Republic under whose auspices the innovations of the next few years in Italy were to be made.

[44] M. A. Ambrosi-R., ed. "Gouvernement anglo-corse: correspondance . . . de Frédéric North . . ." in *Bulletin de la Société des sciences historiques et naturelles de la Corse*, Vol. 42 (1922), 191.

THE CISALPINE REPUBLIC

IN THE NAME OF THE CISALPINE REPUBLIC

The Executive Directory, composed of Citizens Serbelloni, Alessandri, Moscati and Paradisi, recently installed by the commanding general, Bonaparte, in the name of the French Republic . . . has decreed that the same general's proclamation of 11 Messidor should be put into its Acts:

PROCLAMATION

Bonaparte, commanding general of the Army of Italy:

The Cisalpine Republic was formerly under the dominion of the House of Austria. The French Republic succeeded by right of conquest. It renounces that right from this day forward. The Cisalpine Republic is free and independent. . . .

It remains for the Cisalpine Republic to demonstrate to the world by its wisdom and energy, and by the good organization of its armies, that modern Italy has not degenerated and is still worthy of liberty.

Signed: BONAPARTE
Milan, June 1797

THE CISALPINE REPUBLIC

THE *triennio* of the Italians began with the irruption of the French in 1796, and ended in 1799 when the French were driven out by the Austrian and Russian armies, with some assistance from the Turks, by whose combined efforts, it was briefly hoped, European civilization in Italy would be saved from the evils of Jacobinism. The *giacobini* called themselves "democrats." Nowhere else at the time, and certainly not in the United States, was the word "democracy" so enthusiastically adopted. Where in France it was the Babeuf group that most freely applied the term to themselves, and the secretive inner core of the Babouvists understood by it an economic equality to follow upon the abolition of property, the Italian democrats, though some of them were in touch with French Babouvists, were democrats of a more purely political and constitutional kind. The most vehement of them, men like Ranza, Custodi, and Salvador, took pains to argue that private property and some degree of economic inequality were desirable. Buonarroti's own companion of 1796, Guglielmo Cerise, died as a baron of the Napoleonic empire.[1]

During the excitement of the *triennio*, even as they became disillusioned with the French themselves, the Italian revolutionaries were agreed in admiring the French constitution of 1795. Discussions such as were heard in France of the respective merits of the constitutions of the Year I and the Year III were of little interest to the Italians, for whom the various French constitutions looked much alike.[2] For the Italy of the Old Regime the constitution of the French Directory was

---

[1] G. Vaccarino, *I patrioti "anarchistes" e l'idea dell'unità italiana 1796-99* (Turin, 1955); C. Ghisalberti, *Le costituzione "giacobine," 1796-99* (Varese, 1957); G. Spini in *Rassegna storica del Risorgimento*, XLIII (1956), 792-96, reviewing D. Cantimori, *Giacobini italiani, Vol. I: Compagnoni, L'Aurora, Ranza, Galdi, Russo* (Bari, 1956), which puts more emphasis on social as distinct from political revolution. On the use of the word "democratic" in Italy see also *Age*, I, 18-19.

[2] Ghisalberti, 87-91; G. Candeloro, *Storia dell'Italia moderna* (Milan, 1956), finds a preference of some Italians for the "Jacobin" constitution of the Year I.

revolutionary and democratic, and was willingly adopted by Italian Jacobins as a model.

By 1799 there were five revolutionary republics in Italy, all but one swept away in the Austro-Russian reaction. They were the Cisalpine, the Ligurian (which alone survived under French protection), the Luccan, the Roman, and the Neapolitan—or Parthenopean as the French called it.[3] There is room to treat only the Cisalpine on the same scale as was used for the Batavian Republic in an earlier chapter. Absorbing the earlier Cispadane Republic of 1796, and evolving, after the battle of Marengo of 1801, into the Italian Republic and the Napoleonic Kingdom of Italy, the Cisalpine stands as a prominent

[3] That it has always been called "Parthenopean" in English, also, shows how much this period in Italian history has been seen through French eyes in England, and derivatively in America. The *Annual Register for 1799* called it the Neapolitan Republic; it would be well to return to this original English usage. Parthenope was the very ancient city on the site of Naples, where Neapolis or the "new city" was built about 600 B.C.

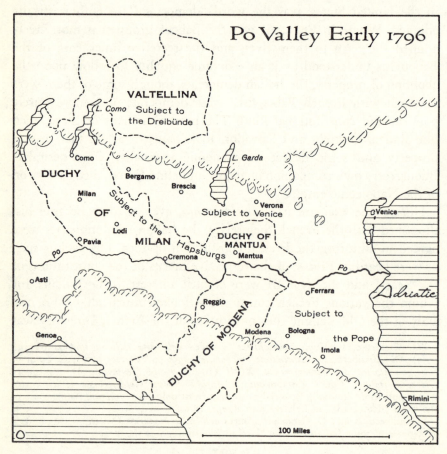

landmark both in the spread of revolution in the 1790's, and in the long process of the modernization of Italy which we know as the Risorgimento.

The Val Padana and the Bridge at Lodi

Reaching over two hundred miles from Turin to the Adriatic, between the Alps to the north and the rough range of the Appenines to the south, lay the open expanse of the Val Padana, the Po valley, the garden of Italy, a land of music and statuary and dramatic emotions, very different from the sober Dutch provinces, but susceptible to much of the same kind of political renovation. The valley, with the changes it underwent between 1796 and 1799, is shown by the accompanying pair of maps. Proceeding downstream from the Kingdom of Sardinia, one passed the region known as Emilia on the right bank, and on the left Lombardy and below it the Terraferma of the Venetian Republic.

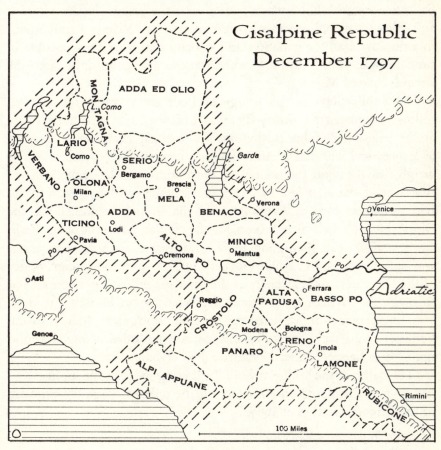

Politically, on the south bank lay the duchies of Parma and Modena, then the "legations" of the Papal States, where the cities of Bologna and Ferrara lived under the rule of papal legates. On the Lombard side were the duchies of Milan and Mantua with their famous cities, and below them the Venetian cities of Verona, Vicenza, Padua, and others. It is well to keep these cities fixed in mind, for it was in them that the Italian revolution mainly took place.

On May 10, 1796, the very day of the arrest of Babeuf and Buonarroti in Paris, there occurred at Lodi, a town on a tributary of the Po not far from Milan, an event of at least equal importance in both actual and symbolic impact. Bonaparte, the new commander of the *Armée d'Italie*, still only twenty-seven years old, so skillfully assembled his divisions that he caught the retreating Austrians at the bridge at Lodi. He himself, against heavy artillery fire from the far bank, put two cannon into position at the bridgehead—"in person, in a hail of grapeshot," as Saliceti reported.[4] The French poured over the bridge, led by Masséna and other divisional generals, with loud cries of "Vive la République," in a display of all the gallantry and bravura that were then possible in time of war. The Austrians were routed, and four days later the French entered Milan.

The implications of the bridge at Lodi set a frame for all that followed. Bonaparte's victory there, and his own feat of courage, were at the beginning of his reputation, his personal charisma or prestige as a successful war-maker, and soon as a peace-maker, which began to weigh heavily upon the politics of the Directory. The republican enthusiasm of the *Armée d'Italie* became legendary. Bonaparte's troops felt more zeal for the Republic than the French armies along the Rhine, but they had little respect for the civilian chatterboxes in Paris, as they would call them, and in fact Bonaparte, with such an army, was able to become virtually independent, to upset the foreign policy of the Directory, and especially at the time of the Fructidor coup d'état to make the civilian government dependent upon himself. In Italy, also, his personal aura suffused the political atmosphere. Italian revolutionaries could act successfully only within the limits of his aims and needs. It so happened that he desired their co-operation.

"The battle of the bridge at Lodi," a leading modern Italian historian has written, "imposed on all actors on the political stage the problem of the democratization of Italy."[5]

---

[4] *Moniteur, réimpression*, XXVIII, 279.
[5] Ghisalberti, 100.

In the following year the whole Po valley came to a boil, but it was for some time uncertain what would be crystallized from the swirling mixture. The irreducible elements were the cities. What happened, characteristically, in city after city, upon the arrival or merely the approach of the French, was that locally dissatisfied persons, who had been agitating since 1789—journalists, lawyers, doctors, university professors and students, merchants in the newer trades, landowners of modern outlook, outsiders and newcomers not ancestrally identified with civic affairs, reinforced by a good many nobles and priests—upset and replaced the older municipal oligarchies, the Senate at Bologna, the Decurions at Milan, the Centumviri at Ferrara. Each new group made its own arrangements with the French army. Many sent their own separate deputations to Paris.

Questions of territory and boundaries became fluid. Only at Venice and Genoa (for by 1797 the revolution spread beyond the valley to these historic centers) did the new provisional governments claim to represent the whole territory of pre-existing states. Elsewhere all was in flux. Padua and Brescia were in revolt against Venice, Bologna and Ferrara against the Pope, Modena and Reggio against their duke, Asti and Novara against the king of Sardinia. In such places the local leaders of revolution, committed to no kind of political unit except their own city, tended to league together for mutual protection. Or from a kind of municipal jealousy, or fear of being overshadowed by immediate neighbors, they imagined a single large Italian state in which all might merge. Thus the idea of a united Italy grew from local roots. But the same purpose might be served by new states of intermediate size. The visible units of the cities, each with its bit of surrounding country, were re-combined into larger entities, though their fates were different. By the end of 1797 Venice and most of the Venetian cities had become a province of Austria, the Sardinian towns remained in that kingdom, and the ancient city-state of Genoa had been revolutionized into the Ligurian Republic. The cities of Lombardy and Emilia, each with its *contado*, had fused into a republic, subdivided into uniform *departimenti*, as in France.

The Italians, like the Dutch, had to pay for their liberation, or rather for the protection of the French army under which they undertook to liberate themselves. For the French, whose immediate problem was the military one against Austria, it would be enough to keep control by a military administration or temporary occupying authority. Such was the preferred program of the Directory in 1796. It was the strength of the native Italian movement that persuaded Bonaparte otherwise. He was a mixture of the dreamer and adventurer, the genuine believer in modernizing principles of the Enlightenment, and the realist accustomed to a careful weighing of political forces as he saw them. He concluded that it was in his own interest, in the interest of France, and of the war against Austria and Great Britain, to let the Italian patriots, within limits, have their way with new republics and constitutions. In return, they had to pay—*liberté et réquisitions*.[6]

The French army was supplied. Bonaparte, a few other officers, and various army contractors made large private fortunes. So abundant was precious metal that the *Armée d'Italie*, alone among French armies, received its wages in hard coin; here was at least one reason for its especial devotion to its commander and to the Republic.[7] By the end of 1796 the French had officially received the equivalent of 45,000,000 francs in Italy in cash and goods, plus some 12,000,000 in gold and silver plate, ingots and jewelry from the *monti di pietà*, which were lending institutions where the owners of such valuables left them as collateral.[8]

It is hard to estimate the real impact on the populations of requisitions expressed in abstract terms of large sums of money. It sounds ominous to hear that the French levied 12,000,000 *lire* on the duchy of Modena, until we learn that the duke quickly raised 24,000,000 and decamped with the whole amount.[9] The "looting" of Italy provided hair-raising

[6] On the contradictions in a policy of *liberté et réquisitions* see especially J. Godechot, *Les commissaires aux armées sous le Directoire: contribution à l'étude des rapports entre les pouvoirs civils et militaires*, 2 vols. (Paris, 1937), I, 284 ff., and his *La Grande Nation*, 2 vols. (Paris, 1956), II, 539-65 and 688-90. Godechot, as a Frenchman trying to be fair and objective, seems if anything more severe than is necessary in judging the behavior of the French at this time. The Italians, like the Dutch, were able to pay for their own "liberation"; the success of their revolutions was entirely dependent on the defeat of the Coalition, and there was no good reason, from their own point of view, why they should not contribute to the common war effort. It was the arbitrary and disorderly character of much requisitioning, and the private corruption and self-enrichment by the French, that were a ground for legitimate complaint. Godechot, while noting the impossibility of a reliable estimate, concludes (*Grande Nation*, II, 565) that in the eight years 1792-1799 the French levied at least 360,000,000 francs in the occupied countries. To give an idea of the meaning of this figure, he remarks that a sum of 360,000,000 was somewhat over half the French annual budget in the 1790's, and compares it to the five billion francs levied by the Germans upon France in 1871, a sum at that time double the French annual budget. He might also have compared it to the 700,000,000 francs levied as an indemnity upon France in 1815. Or the 360,000,000 *taken* by the French may be compared, for size at least, to the £10,000,000 (about 250,000,000 francs) *given* by the British as subsidies to Continental allies from 1793 to 1800. See the references in Chapter VII, note 9, above.

[7] Godechot, *Commissaires*, I, 295.   [8] *Ibid.*, I, 572-73.

[9] *Ibid.*, I, 428. The economist Melchior Gioia, in *I francesi, i tedeschi e i russi in Lom-*

narratives for anti-revolutionaries throughout Europe and the United States. It diminished the need of Italians to feel gratitude to their liberators, but the wiser ones knew that the costs of defeating Austria must be somehow shared, and the faith of democrats was by no means wholly undermined. Since they had not meant to imitate the French anyway, but to have an Italian revolution in which the errors and horrors of the French Revolution were avoided, the faults of the French were hardly relevant to the real questions. Nor did the depredations in Italy seem shocking to the democratically minded in America, who saw Bonaparte at this time as a Republican hero and the campaign in Italy as a Republican crusade. Andrew Jackson, thirty years before the advent of "Jacksonian democracy," hoped that Bonaparte would proceed next to England and set up a free republic there.[10]

It may also be noted that the Italians of the *triennio* felt a strong affinity for the American Revolution.[11] They thought that it had opened an era, leading on to the French Revolution which was now leading to the Italian. Works by Benjamin Franklin were translated and published at both Turin and Venice in 1797. At Venice, his *Poor Richard* was included in the same volume with the Pennsylvania constitution of 1776. The Americans, said the Venetian translator, "were the first to philosophize on the true spirit and advantages of liberty." At Bologna, at the "Circolo costituzionale del Genio democratico," late in 1797, the chairman of the meeting lauded the Americans as predecessors in the search for reason and liberty. Two Italians very active in revolutionary politics of the *triennio*, Carlo Botta and Giuseppe Compagnoni, wrote long histories of America and the American Revolution in their later years. Compagnoni, whose other achievements included the introduction of the Italian tricolor and the first professorship of constitutional law in a European university (at Ferrara in 1797), may indeed have written the longest history of America ever composed by a single man, since his work on the subject extended to twenty-nine volumes.[12]

---

bardia (3rd ed., Milan, 1805) argued that the burden of the thirteen-month Austro-Russian occupation of 1799-1800 was much heavier than that of the Franco-Cisalpine in requisitions, confiscations, tax levies, and public disorder.

[10] Andrew Jackson remarked to James Robertson (Philadelphia, January 11, 1798) that if the French succeeded in an invasion of England "tyranny will be humbled, a throne crushed, and a republic spring from the wreck, and millions of distressed people restored to the rights of man by the conquering arm of Bonaparte." *Correspondence of Andrew Jackson*, 7 vols. (Washington, 1926), I, 42.

[11] L. S. Mayo, *Beniamino Franklin 1706-90* (Florence, n.d.) with the preface by Luigi Rava, "La fortuna di Beniamino Franklin in Italia"; A. Pace, *Benjamin Franklin and Italy* (Philadelphia, 1958) *Memoirs of the American Philosophical Society*, Vol. 47.

[12] G. Compagnoni, *Storia dell'America*, 29 vols. (Milan, 1820-1823), reviewed in *North American Review*, XXVII (1828), 30 ff. The work deals with both North and

The French, as already said, entered Milan four days after the battle of Lodi. Some of the patrician liberals and reformers, Melzi d'Eril, Serbelloni, Pietro Verri, came out to welcome and work with them. Several hundred more middle-class people formed a political club, the Society of Friends of Liberty and Equality, whose troubled existence reflected the changing reactions of the French to Italian revolutionary pressures: soon closed down for its radicalism, it re-opened as the Academy of Literature and Public Instruction, was again closed down, and reappeared again in 1798 as a Constitutional Circle, the name used in France for the revived "Jacobin" clubs of the period between the Fructidor and Floréal coups d'état.[13] Throughout these successive forms the Milan club remained essentially the same, as a center of public debate for the warmest patriots of Lombardy, and for many others from all over the Po valley, with visitors from Rome and Naples.

The French at first tried to rule through a Military Agency, composed of three Frenchmen, re-inforced by a civilian commissioner sent from Paris, named Pinsot, whose task was to supervise the levy of requisitions upon the country. Pinsot, reflecting the opinion then prevailing in Paris, had no desire to create a republic in Lombardy, which he expected to be returned to Austria at the peace table, and hence was unconcerned to build future friendly relations. His aim was to use the resources of Milan as quickly as possible to support the French army and government in its struggle against Austria and the counter-revolution; and he therefore attempted to tap the most mobile and available forms of wealth, which belonged to the professional and business men of the city. Some of these men, however, were the leaders of the democratic or radical party, which as an urban group preferred to have the burden borne by the landowners and rural people, whom Pinsot wished to spare lest they rebel, and by rebelling interfere with the movements of French troops. Bonaparte in this instance supported the Italian democrats against Pinsot.[14]

South America. For a full bibliography on the origins of the Italian tricolor and on the first chair in constitutional law, see C. Zaghi, "Guiseppe Compagnoni deputato al Congresso Cispadano e al General Bonaparte," *Nuovi problemi di politica, storia ed economica*, IV (1933), 3-48. On Compagnoni see also D. Cantimori, *Giacobini italiani: Compagnoni, L'Aurora, Ranza, Galdi, Russo* (Bari, 1956).

[13] The vicissitudes of the club, noted in all the general histories, are conveniently explained by B. Peroni, "La 'società popolare' di Milano, 1796-99" in *Rivista storica italiana*, LXVI (1954), 511-17.

[14] The best account of the disputes centering on Pinsot is in Godechot, *Commissaires*, I, 371-88. Most Italian historians see it as typical of the struggle in Italy of town against country, but Candeloro, *Storia*, I, 211, preferring a class analysis, believes that the

The first weeks of the occupation therefore saw a conflict at Milan which was to characterize all Italy in the next three years. On one side stood the French government and its civilian commissioner, supported by the more moderate of the Italians, who were often owners of rural estates. On the other side stood the more vehement Italians, city men who demanded an independent republic, or even talked of a unified republic of all Italy; they made no effort to conciliate the rural population, but had the sympathy of many French generals. The latter party won out; Pinsot was recalled; and by the end of 1796 the Directory gave up the whole principle of attaching civilian commissioners to the army. The military increasingly prevailed over the civilian authority, in the formation of French foreign policy as in other respects. The Directory, pressed by the generals, and so weakened by the revival of royalist sentiment in France that it could hardly do without the firm republicanism of the Army of Italy, came to accept, at least half-heartedly, the establishment of revolutionary republics south of the Alps.

At Milan the recall of Pinsot marked the triumph of the more advanced Italian democrats. The Military Agency was replaced by a General Administration of Lombardy, composed of Italians. This body worked actively for a Lombard republic and an all-Italian revolution. It sponsored the famous essay contest, which Gioia won, on "Which form of free government is best suited to Italy?" It organized a Lombard Legion, so that within a few months an Italian army (then called Cisalpine) was in the field along with the French. It was in this Lombard Legion that the Italian tricolor—red, white, and green—first appeared. The Italian tricolor and the Polish national anthem of later times (as already explained) were thus generated simultaneously in the Po valley in 1796.

Patriotic feeling ran high at Milan, the more so since the Austrians were not yet really defeated. When Wurmser, regrouping his forces, began a counter-offensive, audiences in the theater sang the Marseillaise. In November there was an uprising in the city, when the patriots, after a great demonstration at a tree of liberty before the cathedral, solemnly proclaimed the independence of Lombardy and demanded elections for "primary assemblies." What they wanted, in short, was a constituent assembly to establish a republic. The uprising was suppressed by the French Army. With military operations still in progress in the

---

Directory and Pinsot, being "moderates," wished to spare the rich and throw the burden on "a greater number of citizens." These "citizens" (*cittadini* or city men), forming the radical party, did include, however, "rich" merchants and financiers.

Milanese, neither Bonaparte nor the Directory was yet ready to countenance a republic north of the Po.

South of the river the situation was different, and the first Italian republic to be constructed along modern lines was therefore the Cispadane.

The Cispadane Republic

The Papal States extended from the mouth of the Po to a point south of Rome, and the men who controlled the affairs of the Church were well aware that the best of Catholics saw nothing sacred in this temporal power. The Austrians or the King of Naples, or both in concert, might someday annex or partition these territories of the Church; but in 1796 the danger seemed most imminent from the French. The Pope maintained no actual army, but after the battle of Lodi the Curia, optimistically expecting a successful counter-attack by the Austrians, took steps to raise a kind of *levée en masse*, in which it had no more success than other governments of the Old Regime. The only effect was to provide the French with another excuse for intervention, and they entered Bologna on June 18, 1796.

At Bologna, it may be recalled, there had been an unsuccessful conspiracy led by Zamboni in 1794. The trial had dragged on, and Zamboni's father had died in prison, and an accomplice had been executed, only two months before the French arrived.[15] There was much restlessness in the city, so that many welcomed the invaders gladly, and complied eagerly with the French demand that Bologna break off from the Papal States. A dispute developed between the Senate of Bologna and those who complained of its closed and oligarchical character. Both were eager to throw off the papal overlordship and restore communal independence, but the Senate took the view that independence, or "liberty," should leave its old position and privileges unimpaired. Somewhat the same question, between constituted bodies and new men, had of course arisen in many other connections—in the Dutch revolt against the House of Orange, the aristocratic revolt against the monarchy in France, and even in the rebellion of Massachusetts against the British Parliament in 1775.[16]

A committee drafted a constitution for a "Bologna republic." It began with a declaration of rights, virtually a translation of the French

---

[15] Candeloro, 187-88; L. Frati, *Il Settecento a Bologna* (n.p., 1923), 246-47. In 1798 the remains of Zamboni and his accomplice, De Rolandis, were placed in a civic urn at the foot of a liberty tree; in 1799 they were scattered to the winds.

[16] *Age*, I, 23, 216, 222, 333-34, 480.

Declaration of 1789. The body of the Constitution, putting sovereignty in the "universality of the citizens," and mapping out legislative, executive, and judiciary powers in quite modern style, was more specifically adapted to the situation at Bologna, since it represented something of a compromise between the two parties in the city. It reflected also the historic municipalism, in the sense of predominance of town over country: the city of Bologna, with a third of the population, was to receive three-quarters of the representation. This Bologna constitution of 1796 is regarded as the first constitution of the Italian Risorgimento, and was in any case the first such written document to be officially drafted in Italy.[17]

There were revolts also at Ferrara in the Papal States, and at Modena and Reggio in the duchy of Modena. The patricians at Ferrara, the Centumviri, tried to keep control, but Bonaparte's civilian associate, Saliceti, out-maneuvered them by setting up a Ferrara Central Administration in which ordinary *borghesi* were included. It was the French also who brought the four towns together, with assistance from the more "radical" or "democratic" of their citizens, those, that is, who were the least identified with the aristocracies of the several municipalities. A congress of the four towns, in October 1796, organized a league for common defense against counter-revolution, not unlike the old leagues of Communes in the Middle Ages. Bonaparte and Saliceti concluded, however, that it would be more practical for them to work through some kind of organized territory; and the more enterprising patriots from the four cities desired more than a mere league to serve the purposes of the French. A second congress met at Reggio in December. It was the first elected assembly of the *triennio*, and its 110 members, many of whom were to serve in later years in the Cisalpine Republic and Napoleonic Empire, came mostly from the business, professional, and landowning middle class, but included several priests and a few nobles. There was also a Jew among them, whose presence signified the new order. After a dispute on vote by head or by *stato* (which in this case meant by city), a problem which both the French Estates General and the Philadelphia Convention had had to face, it was decided that voting should go by head.

The decision favored the democrats, and the Congress proclaimed, un-

---

[17] The Bologna constitution is printed by A. Aquarone, et al., eds., *Le costituzioni italiane* (Milan, 1958), 8-33, as the first modern Italian constitution. The Corsican constitution of 1794 (see above, p. 285), included by the editors in their appendix, was "modern" in a different way, and less truly Italian. For the revolution at Bologna see Candeloro, 220-22, and Ghisalberti, 104-8.

der Bonaparte's urgings, the Cispadane Republic One and Indivisible.[18] "Indivisibility" meant, as in the Batavian Republic, that the new state should not disintegrate into municipal units, since an emphasis on municipalism, federalism, or decentralization would leave the old patriciates in positions of influence. It was therefore the democrats, as elsewhere in Europe but in contrast to the United States, who demanded a homogeneous and unitary state. These men already dreamed of a merger with Lombardy across the Po—some even of an Italian Republic. But the municipal feeling remained strong in the Cispadane. Ferrara, Reggio, and Modena all resisted the ascendancy of Bologna. Bologna, in turn, fearful of subordination to Milan, showed the least enthusiasm for a single republic in the Po valley. The second congress also created an Italian Legion (like the Lombard Legion at Milan) to which it gave the tricolor as a standard, and received with much fanfare an enthusiastic delegation of "Transpadanes" from the Lombard capital.

A third Cispadane congress became a true constituent assembly, the only one to meet in Italy during the *triennio*, since the other Italian republics were to receive their constitutions from the French, or from Italians whom no one had elected for the purpose. The resulting Cispadane constitution, the most unquestionably native to Italy, was of all the constitutions of the years 1796-1799 the most similar to the French constitution of 1795. It was when they were least pressed by the French that the Italian democrats most fully agreed with them on constitutional principles, because they saw in these principles, not "French ideas," but the distillation from a body of thought, the Enlightenment, in which national peculiarity counted for little.[19]

The Cispadane declaration of rights repeated the French even more closely than that of Bologna. A few divergences from the French model, which became characteristic of later such declarations during the

[18] On the formation of the Cispadane see Candeloro, 222-28, and Ghisalberti, 108-12; the latter indicates the sources and special studies. Where older writers of more nationalistic or conservative outlook saw the unification of Italy as a thing-in-itself, or supreme and conscious goal of those who effected it, the modern writers see it more as a by-product of democratic or other revolutionary aims. Local democrats, in this view, having in each case to overcome the opposition of their local oligarchies, reached out to join forces with those of neighboring places, thus building up political communities of increasingly wider scope. As long ago as the Fascist period Carlo Morandi, in an excellent book, *Idee e formazione politiche in Lombardia dal 1748 al 1814* (Turin, 1927), argued that the desire for Italian political unity was thus mainly a result of democratic developments.

[19] For the Cispadane constitution see Aquarone, 42-79; Ghisalberti, 20, and the whole account of Italian constitutional thought before 1796, pp. 23-78.

triennio, may be worthy of a brief comment. Where the French said "nation" (as in "the principle of sovereignty rests essentially in the nation") the Italians said *universalità de' cittadini*, "the citizens as a whole," perhaps because "nation" would suggest a consolidation of all Italy, which would give offense not only to the French, but to many locally rooted Italian interests. The Italians were careful to specify the rights of man "in society," as if to emphasize that "nature" had nothing to do with the question. The Cispadane and later Italian declarations omitted the assurance of consent to taxation, which, however, they said must be reasonable, equitable, and within the bounds of necessity. Equality they explicitly defined as excluding privileges of birth and inheritance. No peaceful citizen was to be disturbed for his religious opinions, but among non-Catholics only the Jews were allowed to have any public signs of their worship. The Cispadane constitution, as if to show its thoroughly "bourgeois" character, not only guaranteed property but offered "special protection to manufacturers, merchants, artists and men of letters of all nations who may wish to come and settle among us."

An Executive Directory of three persons, a Legislative Body in two elected houses, together with machinery for judicial, administrative, financial, military, and electoral functions were set up. The constitution was ratified by a popular vote, 76,382 to 14,259, the size of the minority being large enough to suggest that, though the French urged its adoption, they did not force it on a reluctant or intimidated country. In April 1797 the constitution went into effect, and the new organs of government began to establish themselves.

Few republics of such great significance have been destined to so short a life. The Cispadane, under its constitution, lasted only three months. By the spring of 1797 the military issue was settled. Bonaparte had pursued the Austrians into Carinthia and Styria, and caused panic in Vienna itself, where the Bank of Vienna closed its doors, and crowds demonstrated outside Thugut's house. Thugut and Bonaparte called off the hostilities and signed a preliminary peace at Leoben on April 18, 1797.

Bonaparte was now free to decide what to do about the revolutionary ferment in north Italy. His decision favored the patriots of Lombardy and the Cispadane, to the disadvantage of those of Venetia and Piedmont. With hostilities suspended, he needed no longer to fear the Kingdom of Sardinia in his rear, or to keep it in check by tolerating revolutionary plots against it. He withdrew all pretense of support for the republicans of Piedmont. Toward Austria he would pursue no *guerre à outrance*, nor demand unconditional surrender as favored by French and Italian democrats, but would arrange a negotiated peace, with due regard to balance and compensation, persuading the Austrians to acknowledge the loss of their former possessions at Milan in return for the acquisition of Venice. Where the Directory, in 1796, had wished to gain the old Austrian Netherlands and the Rhine frontier by letting the Austrians keep Milan, Bonaparte in 1797, wanting Milan in addition, would give them Venetia instead.

The Cisalpine Republic, with its capital at Milan, was promulgated in June 1797. The Cispadane was dissolved, and its territories merged into the Cisalpine.

But the exclusion of Venice was the price paid for the birth of the Cisalpine.

The Venetian Revolution and the Treaty of Campo Formio

Venice, founded in the fifth century, was the "eldest child of Liberty," according to Wordsworth's sonnet on the Extinction of the Venetian Republic. It was ruled, however, especially in the eighteenth century, by a group of patricians so exclusive, so tightly knit, so purely hereditary, so secretive, and so few in number that Disraeli, when he entered British politics in the 1840's, could make the term "Venetian oligarchy" a by-word for aristocratic Whiggery of the most exaggerated kind.[20]

The oldest families, whose fortunes had been established in commerce in earlier centuries, now usually lived from the incomes of landed estates on the mainland. The most active men in trade were typically "newcomers," but the word must be understood in a relative sense; in a patrician republic where the last doge, Ludovico Manin, was considered a parvenu because his family had been inscribed in the Golden Book in 1669, a newcomer might be reasonably well established; and the "newcomers" and "outsiders," men of the business, professional, and intellectual classes, who became "democrats" (which to say anti-aristocrats) at Venice as in other Italian cities, were by no means merely transients. There were many such democrats in the city of

---

[20] For Venice *Age*, I, 34; M. Berengo, *La società veneta alla fine del Settecento* (Florence, 1956); M. Pettrocchi, *Il tramonto della repubblica di Venezia e l'assolutismo illuminato* (Venice, 1950); G. B. McClellan, *Venice and Bonaparte* (Princeton, 1931); A. Bozzola, "L'ultimo doge e la caduta della Serenissima" in *Nuova rivista storica*, XVIII (1934), 30-58; for Verona, R. Fasanari, *Gli albori del Risorgimento a Verona, 1785-1801* (Verona, 1950). See also Candeloro, 232-34; Ghisalberti, 112-18.

Venice itself. Since the Republic was organized on the old city-state principle, with the cities of the mainland having no part whatever in its affairs, the mainland cities were somewhat ill-disposed toward the Queen of the Adriatic. In these places also there were "democrats," who might be patricians of their own cities, or middle class people, or priests, or Jews. The actual lower classes, such as servants, water carriers, or gondoliers, and the mass of the rural people, remained either conservative or indifferent.

The rulers of Venice tried desperately to remain neutral in the war that began in 1792. It was difficult for them to get their neutrality respected, especially since they had no armed forces beyond a few Dalmatian mercenaries, whom they did not trust. Any step that they took gave offense to someone, as when they allowed "Louis XVIII" to settle at Verona. The French invasion of the Po valley in 1796 made neutrality even more precarious, since the Austrians could not operate at all, nor the French pursue them, without touching on territory of the Venetian Republic, which reached to within twenty miles of Milan. Indeed the Austrians had already signed with the Russians, before the French invasion, an agreement by which Austria should annex the Most Serene Republic to the Hapsburg empire.

Revolutions against Venice broke out at Brescia and Bergamo as the French approached. Provisional governments were instituted. After a revolt at Verona against the French, and after an unpleasant incident at Venice itself, where the appearance of a French naval vessel at this supposedly neutral port had met with hostile demonstrations, Bonaparte ordered the occupation of all the mainland cities, and sent an ultimatum to Venice, in which he demanded its immediate "democratization." By this he chiefly meant, as did many more genuine democrats, the displacement of the small governing and privileged class.

There were a good many even among the Venetian nobles, as the patricians of the city were called, who had come to believe that there was no future for their venerable republic in its existing form, and who therefore either sank into apathy, or waited with resignation for their fate to be decided by foreigners, or in some cases were excited by the changes that were beginning in the Po valley. "An immense quantity of French cockades" was discovered in the houses of two noblemen who had just returned from a trip to Milan.[21] The formation of the Cispadane Republic was watched with interest. After the

[21] C. Roth, "La caduta della Serenissima nei dispacci del residente inglese a Venezia" in *Archivio Veneto*, 5th ser. (1935), 193.

the revolts at Brescia and Bergamo, which declared themselves to be "republics" independent of Venice, and where the patriots really preferred union with the yet unborn Cisalpine, a Venetian noble spoke up in the Senate for "voluntary democratization." He declared that Venice should at last join with its own mainland dependencies on an equal basis, and that it was impossible to "maintain a pure but discredited Aristocracy in the face of the new democratic Italian government," by which he meant the governments taking form in Lombardy and Emilia.[22] But the Senate refused to admit even the mainland nobility to any role in the government. The doge himself believed reform to be necessary, but impossible; he remarked later, in his memoirs, that the old Republic could bear neither its diseases nor their remedies.

After Bonaparte's ultimatum in May 1797, a Provisional Municipality replaced the old government at Venice.[23] It was never able to exert any authority throughout the territory of the old Republic, for the Austrians occupied Istria and Dalmatia, and in the Venetian cities the patriots, under the French occupation, hoped for union with the Cisalpine. In any case, from the preliminary peace at Leoben in April to the final peace at Campo Formio in October, it remained very uncertain what the future would really bring. The Venetian democrats, less able than those of Bergamo or Padua to accept Milan as a capital, were the more inclined to think along the high level of a united Italian republic, but they could do little more than engage in demonstrations, ceremonies, political festivals, oratory, debates, and some actual attempts at reform. These were in the usual revolutionary direction, and need not be detailed except for one matter in which Venice was a special case.

Among places thus far directly affected by the Revolution, Venice was the one, after Amsterdam, that had the largest Jewish community. Though well received in earlier times, the Jews of Venice had not recently enjoyed very flourishing circumstances, and they lived under various disabilities, including residence in a ghetto. They played a more positive role in the revolution at Venice than at Amsterdam. Many Jews joined with commercial and professional men and with the progressive patricians in support of the Provisional Municipality, in which three Jews sat as members. Jews also joined the new National Guard. In July there was a great public celebration, in which people

[22] Bozzola, 43, quoting a speech of Gabriel Marcello.
[23] Its proceedings have been published by the Accademia nazionale dei Lincei, Commissione per gli atti delle assemblee costituzionali italiane, A. Alberti et al., eds., *Verbali delle sedute della Municipalità provvisoria di Venezia, 1797*, 3 vols. (Bologna, 1928-1940).

of all kinds proceeded to the Jewish quarter, French soldiers and Catholic priests exchanged fraternal embraces, a tree of liberty was set up, and Jews and Christians joined together to tear down the ghetto gates and hack the hinges to pieces. Similar scenes occurred at Padua. At Spalato, however (the modern Split, on the Dalmatian coast), the ghetto was attacked by angry crowds that feared that the Venetian Republic was ceasing to be a Christian state. The Jews lost their newly declared equality of rights when Venice and most of its territory were ceded to Austria at the end of the year.[24]

Meanwhile the fate of Italy was being settled in France. The contrary was indeed equally true: that the fate of the French Republic was being settled in Italy. The French elections of March 1797, as already explained, brought into the legislative councils a majority of moderates and royalists, who favored ending the war on terms acceptable to Austria and Great Britain. Should they gain control of the government, there would be an end to republics in Italy and France alike. Three Directors in Paris—Reubell, LaRévellière, and Barras—appealed for aid to the victorious commanding general of the Army of Italy. Bonaparte, his officers and men, the French civilians who were profiting from the occupation of Italy, and the Italian revolutionaries and democrats (together with the Batavians who feared the outcome of the peace talks then going on between France and England) all depended on the preservation in France of a government firmly committed to the Republic. Bonaparte sent one of his generals, Augereau, who stood by while the three Directors expelled their two colleagues and purged the two chambers.

The coup d'état of Fructidor (September 4, 1797) thus upheld republicanism in France by drawing on strength generated in Italy, and opened the way for the spread of republicanism in Italy by producing a French government more sympathetic to revolutionary expansion. It was in the next few months that republics were set up at Rome and in Switzerland, and the Batavian Republic was democratized. The Fructidorian Directory not only broke off the negotiation with the British, but was not eager for a compromise peace with Austria. Hence for a moment it was receptive to the idea of a democratic republic at Venice. The reviving French democrats, or neo-"Jacobins," also looked with sympathy on the Venetian revolutionaries. Bonaparte, however, now desired a quick and dramatic treaty with Austria. He could then depart from Italy with the prestige of having served as its liberator,

[24] C. Roth, *Venice*, in *Jewish Communities Series* (Philadelphia, 1930), 309-10, 329, 344-69.

and return to France to be enthusiastically hailed as a peacemaker, the military hero who had imposed at least a "land peace," *la paix continentale*, after five years of war.

The result was the treaty of Campo Formio of October 1797. Venice was ceded to Austria, and its territories were divided. France annexed, from Venice, the Ionian Islands off the coast of Greece, which now felt the breath of revolution close at hand. Dalmatia, Istria, and most of Venetia went to Austria. A sizable western segment of the Venetian mainland was added to the Cisalpine Republic.

This arrangement produced general consternation. On the Left, in both Italy and France, there was an outcry against the cold-blooded sacrifice of the Venetian democrats to the greed of Austria and the ambition of Bonaparte. The liberator of Italy seemed an ambiguous character to the Italian republicans. He had, indeed, followed a foreign policy of his own. To the Right, throughout Europe, Bonaparte was a Jacobin. The Cisalpine Republic seemed firmly established. Since other clauses in the treaty allowed France to obtain the Rhine frontier, and provided for the reorganization of Germany at a Congress to convene at Rastadt, it was evident that the Holy Roman Empire was also about to undergo a certain modernization.

The Cisalpine Republic: Sketch of a Modern State

The Cisalpine Republic spread out about equally on the two sides of the Po.[25] It had a population of three and a half million, almost twice as large as the Batavian. It was put together from territories formerly belonging to six different jurisdictions: the duchies of Milan, Mantua and Modena, the northern part of the Papal States, western

[25] The great work is M. Roberti, *Milano capitale napoleonica: la formazione di uno stato moderno*, 3 vols. (Milan, 1946-1947), but only parts of the various topical chapters relate to the Cisalpine Republic before 1799. Roberti gives a briefer statement in his "Politica e amministrazione nell'Italia napoleonica" in E. Rota, ed., *Questioni di storia del risorgimento e dell'unità d'Italia* (Milan, 1951), 75-110. Legislation, etc., was currently published as *Raccolta di tutti gli avvisi, editti e proclami pubblicati nella Lombardia*, 18 vols. (Milan, 1796-1799). The proceedings of the Cisalpine Legislative Body have been published by the Accademia nazionale dei Lincei, Commissione per gli atti delle assemblee costituzionali italiane, C. Montalcini et al., eds., *Assemblee della Reppublica cisalpina*, 11 vols. (Bologna, 1917-1948). Publication is in progress of Melzi's papers, *I carteggi di Francesco Melzi d'Eril, duca di Lodi* (Milan, 1958-), but those for the Cisalpine period have not yet appeared. For the present author two of the most enlightening works ever written on the subject were produced in the 1920's: E. Rota, *Giuseppe Poggi e la formazione psicologica del patriota moderno, 1761-1843* (Piacenza, 1923), available also as a series of articles in *Nuova rivista storica*, 1922 and 1923; and C. Morandi, *Idee e formazione politiche in Lombardia dal 1748 al 1814* (Turin, 1927).

Venetia, and the region known as the Valtellina, the upper valley of the Adda above Lake Como, which had long been dependent on the Dreibünde in Switzerland, and where, as elsewhere, a "revolution" occurred in 1797. The new republic brought together men who had had no habits of working together, and so, like the Cispadane, marked the beginning of a unifying experience. The popular club at Milan became a forum for the most vehement and the most visionary patriots from all Italy. Some five or six hundred from Rome and southern Italy visited Milan in these years. To Milan also came, as refugees, the Venetian revolutionaries who felt they had been betrayed, and others in flight from the Kingdom of Sardinia, where their attempts at revolution, breaking out at Asti, Novara, and elsewhere in 1797, had been ignored by the French and suppressed by the royal Sardinian government. The Cisalpine was a cockpit of republican politics, in which some were satisfied with the new arrangement, others eager to go immediately beyond it, some willing to work constructively with the French, others suspicious of the French as mere self-seeking and cynical moderates.

The Cisalpine constitution, drafted by an Italian committee, was proclaimed by Bonaparte in the name of the French Republic. It resembled the French constitution of 1795, but it also reproduced much of the Cispadane constitution which it replaced, and which had been written by a constituent assembly of Italians working in relative freedom from external pressure; and most of the recent Italian historians, differing from their nineteenth century predecessors who found it important to dwell on national differences, agree that the Cisalpine constitution was not in a meaningful sense "imposed" by the French. If imposed, it was imposed by modern-minded Italians, making use of the occupying authority of the French, upon their own more conservative countrymen.

The document began with the usual declaration of rights, and with a regrouping of the miscellaneous territories into homogeneous "departments," which reached twenty in number by the end of 1797. It set up a legislative body of two elective chambers, which came to be called the Seniori and the Juniori, and an Executive Directory of five persons to be elected by the two chambers. Other clauses dealt with local government, the judiciary, the armed forces, finances, and public instruction. To smooth the transition from provisional to settled rule, and from obvious French control to a regime that was at least in principle independent, Bonaparte himself, upon orders from Paris, appointed the first members of the Cisalpine Directory and of the two chambers. The Italians chosen for these positions included both moderates and democrats, and were purposely drawn from various regions within the new state.[26]

The constitution had a troubled history, as will be seen, and most of what the new Cisalpine authorities attempted was swept away in 1799. It was only in the years after 1801 that their ideas began to be institutionalized, only to be again partly reversed in the reaction after 1814. The legislation of the Cisalpine Republic is therefore to be understood, not as a body of achievements, but as the sketch or design for a new regime, showing what the revolution in Italy during the *triennio* was about.

The Cisalpine period, both before and after the promulgation of the constitution, was a time of rapid development of public opinion and political consciousness, such as Italy had hardly seen since the invention of printing. In contrast to the Old Regime, freedom of the press was at least the rule, and censorship the exception. Ideas made familiar by the Enlightenment were now regarded as matters for action. There were many political journals, which have become very rare even in Italy. Their names suggest the heated political atmosphere in which they were written: the *Termometro politico*, the *Giornale repubblicano di Pubblica Istruzione*, the *Genio democratico*, the *Estensore Cisalpina*, and the *Repubblicano Evangelico* (or "Gospel Republican"), edited by the Parma Jansenist Poggi in refuge at Milan.[27] There were also a good many polemical pamphlets, such as one of 1796 with the revealing title, *Il Risorgimento della oppresa democratia*.[28] Its proposals were moderate and specific: that taxes should be borne by property owners, that measures should be taken to improve agriculture, that international commercial companies should be encouraged, and a "useful" liberty of the press allowed.

Nobility was abolished, with all its titles, ranks, and display of heraldic emblems, along with an array of other practices that had become shocking to enlightened and humane sentiment. Torture disappeared from the law-courts. The opera and the churches were forbidden to use *evirati cantori*, the emasculated tenors that a somewhat baroque taste had made peculiar to Italy.

Steps were taken to create an army.[29] The Italians formerly under

[26] Aquarone, 83-153; Ghisalberti, 116-18, 129-34.
[27] Rota, *Poggi* in *Nuov. riv. st.*, 128. Note the remark of the *Encyclopedia italiana*, XVIII, 185: "Il giornalismo politico italiano ha i suoi inizi nelle reppubliche italo-francesi."
[28] Morandi, 218-19.
[29] In addition to works cited above see C. Cattaneo, *L'antico esercito italiano* (Milan, 1862).

Austria, like those of the former papal legations, had been subject to no military service whatever, but it was a principle of the new order that free citizens must assume responsibility for their own defense. The troops organized in 1796 were at first used to keep the peasants and the counter-revolutionaries under control, but by the end of 1797 there were 15,000 organized Cisalpine troops, who soon thereafter were employed at both Rome and Naples. Conscription was introduced in 1798, in anticipation of the renewal of war; it caused trouble in the rural districts, though it called for a levy of only 9,000 men in a population of three and a half millions. Some Cisalpine soldiers were very enthusiastic; a group of cavalrymen, in 1798, wished to volunteer for the projected Franco-Dutch invasion of England, to attack the "enemy of the human race."[30]

The abolition of gilds, and of many old excises, tolls and internal tariffs, was designed to open the way both for a new fiscal system, with planned budgets and less cumbersome taxation, and for an enlarged and more active trading area in place of the old local and municipal units.

The market for real property was revolutionized by the abolition of *fidecommessi* and by the confiscation and sale of lands belonging to the church. *Fidecommessi* were Italian equivalents to the English primogeniture and entail. They supported landed aristocracy as a social institution, but many nobles as well as middle-class persons in the Italian revolutionary movement desired an end to them. Their abolition allowed younger sons of landed families to inherit land, and individual landowners to sell or borrow at will. Income-producing church properties were confiscated in the Cisalpine as in France. Full studies have yet to be made of the actual consequences, which in any case only began to make themselves felt after 1801, when the new regime became sufficiently stabilized for buyers to take the risk of purchasing land expropriated from the Church. It is known that in the neighborhood of Bologna the proportion of land owned by church bodies dropped from 9 per cent in 1796 to 2 per cent in 1804. The share owned by noblemen fell from 78 per cent to 51 per cent in 1835. The corresponding increase went mostly to middle-class city people, some of whom put the land to more productive use than the former owners.[31]

In Italy the Catholic Church was omnipresent, and disputes over

[30] Montalcini, II, 619-21.
[31] R. Zangheri, *Prime ricerche sulla distribuzione della proprietà fondiaria nella pianura bolognese, 1789-1835* (Bologna, 1957).

ecclesiastical institutions took place as much within it as against it. Church reformers, though without influence at the court of Pius VI, were numerous throughout the peninsula. Some, like Scipione di Ricci, long before 1796, has stressed the power of governments to reorganize and reform the clergy. Others (they were all called "Jansenists") preached a primitive Christian simplicity. Such was Giuseppe Poggi, who edited several different papers at Milan. In Poggi the Jansenist and the Jacobin were completely blended. He argued that true Christian doctrine and the new principles of liberty, brotherhood, and equality of rights were the same. He thought the church should have no authority in the state, and the state none in religion; that there should not even be a civic cult in the manner of Rousseau or Robespierre; and that state and church should simply be separated, with persons of any religion or no religion equally acceptable to the state, and Christianity working upon the state only through the moral consciousness of the individual. "In a well ordered republic," he wrote in his *Repubblicano Evangelico*, "the priest being reduced to a citizen equal to others, deprived of all extrinsic authority and temporal possessions, restricted to a pure administration of the sacraments and preaching of the Gospel . . . will no longer be harmful to the State, but will do his part to making a republican government, such as ours, loved and cultivated as a matter of conscience."[32]

The measures taken by the Cisalpine Legislative Body were not meant to be fundamentally anti-Catholic, but they were inspired in some degree by French Jansenism and Gallicanism, and even had a certain flavor of Protestantism. Secularization of Church property has already been mentioned. Payment of fees to priests for religious services was abolished. Monastic houses and religious vows were prohibited. Civil marriage was provided for, with divorce under certain conditions. Outdoor manifestations of the Catholic cult were severely restricted, images of the Virgin and the saints were to be removed from the streets, streets named for saints were to be re-named for republican worthies, priests were not to offer public blessing to private houses, and no church bells were to toll at night. No ecclesiastical documents originating outside the Cisalpine borders were to be admitted, bishops were to be designated by the government, and parish priests elected by citizens. The Cisalpine (unlike the Batavian or the later Helvetic Republics) even adopted the French republican calendar, without the

---

[32] Rota, *Poggi*, 138; G. Cattana, "Il giansenismo e la legislazione ecclesiastica della Cisalpina" in *Nuova rivista storica* xv (1931), 105-23.

overtones of radical anti-Christianity in which that calendar had originated in 1793. Italian names were invented for the months, and much
of this ecclesiastical legislation was known as the law of 13 Vendem-
miale of the Year VI (13 Vendémiaire, or October 4, 1797).

Many Italians were of course horrified. As Carlo Morandi once remarked, the fact that republicanism and Christianity were closer in
Italy than anywhere else meant that many simple people, especially
in the country, thought that "liberty" was some kind of a heresy, to
be detested accordingly.[33] There were occasional outbursts of violence,
more often in words than in fact, for there was much less real ferocity
in the Cisalpine than in France, or in the Roman Republic of 1798.
Sometimes, however, speakers at the Milan Club worked themselves
into a high pitch of excitement, as when a woman there, in an im-
passioned speech, offered her hand to any man who would bring her
the Pope's head in a basket.[34] Moderate and conservative persons seized
upon and exaggerated such episodes to denounce the irreligion of a
rampant democracy.

It was in this overcharged atmosphere, or in this Jansenistic-Jacobin-
ical uproar, that the man who was to be the next Pope (becoming
Pius VII in 1800) made his first direct and personal acquaintance with
the European revolution.[35] When the French entered Bologna, in June
1796, Cardinal Barnaba Chiaramonti was the bishop of Imola only
twenty miles away. His reception of the French officers was so courte-
ous, and his efforts to keep the peace so consonant with their demands,
that he was already mentioned by some as a "Jacobin." A year later,
with the rest of the Cispadane, the bishop of Imola found his diocese
incorporated into the Cisalpine Republic. He accepted its constitution,
with its abolition of nobility, though like all the cardinals except Maury
he was of noble birth himself. He never conceded the right of the government to appoint churchmen or to exclude papal communications
from the country. But he agreed to waive the title of Monsignor and
be addressed as "Citizen Cardinal." He put Liberty and Equality on his
letterheads, and in between, where the civil authorities put "In the

[33] Morandi, 241.
[34] B. Peroni, "La società popolare di Milano, 1796-99" in *Rivista storica italiana LXVI*
(1954), 511-17.
[35] J. Leflon, *Pie VII: des abbayes bénédictines à la papauté* (Paris, 1958), is not only
an account of Pius VII's career before 1800, but gives a detailed view of the Cisalpine
Republic, pp. 360-531. For a briefer account see Leflon, "Le cardinal Chiaramonti,
évêque d'Imola, et la République cisalpine," in *Rassegna storica del Risorgimento*, XLIII
(1956), 427-33. See also V. Giuntella, "Cristianesimo e democrazia in Italia al tramonto
del Settecento: appunti per una ricerca" in *Rass. st. del Ris.*, XLII (1955), 289-96.

Name of the Cisalpine Republic," he put "The Peace of our Lord Jesus Christ." He gave up the Gregorian calendar in his episcopal documents, and adopted the Republican, in which more recent and more touchy American Catholics have seen a blasphemy against the Incarnation. Late in 1797 the Cisalpine government requested of Chiaramonti, or rather demanded of him, a public declaration that "the spirit of the Gospel is founded on the maxims of liberty, equality and fraternity and in no way in opposition to democracy."

He complied, in his own way, in a Christmas sermon at Imola. His discourse was really a sermon, not a political speech. It abounded in theological references, in quotations from Jesus, St. Paul, and St. Augustine, and in warnings against reliance on merely natural virtues and the dangers of human pride and presumption. Its drift was to argue that democracy was perfectly Christian, but that it needed the Church, since it depended, more than other forms of government, on an unselfishness that only a true religion could instil. He accepted liberty and equality by defining them in his own terms. "The democratic form of government adopted among us, dear brethren, is not in opposition to the maxims I have set before you; it is not contrary to the Gospel. . . . Civil equality, derived from natural law, refined by moral considerations, brings harmony to the political body, when each person co-operates for the good of all to the extent of his own moral and physical faculties, receiving in turn from the protection of society all the advantages which he has a right to expect. . . . Be good Christians and you will be excellent democrats."[36]

This Christmas sermon of 1797 has had a curious and significant history. Bonaparte is supposed to have remarked, with approval, that the Citizen Cardinal "preached like a Jacobin." The event was well remembered for a short time. At the conclave of Venice, during the winter of 1799-1800, when the election of a new Pope was deadlocked for three months, and when Chiaramonti was finally chosen, he was well known to have stood for the conciliation, or Christianization, of the Revolution. Soon thereafter the printed copies of his famous sermon disappeared. Bonaparte, after he turned into Napoleon, wanted no talk of a "Jacobin" pope. Still less after 1814, as the doctrine of the Throne and the Altar came to prevail, or after 1848 and the quarrel between Pius IX and liberal civilization, did the partisans in either camp, Catholic or anti-Catholic, wish it to be known that a Pope had once praised the principles of the Revolution. Only in recent years,

---

[36] Leflon, *Pie VII*, 434.

with the growth in Europe of a Christian Democracy, and with the scholarly work of Giuntella in Italy, and of the Abbé Leflon of the Catholic Institute in Paris, has the Christmas sermon of 1797 been disinterred and expounded.

At the time of his sermon Chiaramonti was regarded as a moderate. There were other Cisalpine bishops who, for whatever reason, accepted the new republic with less reservation than he did, with less insistence on its need of the Church, and less warning against what would now be called naturalism and religious indifferentism. To neutralism in religion the Cisalpine was in fact committed. It did not officially care whether its citizens were Catholic or Christian. Indeed, like the French Republic, it offered a world view that was a kind of alternative religion, with its own ethic, its own sense of regeneration, and its own theory of what had happened in history. It laid great stress on education, and it took education away from the Church.

The whole Cisalpine Republic may be thought of as an educational enterprise. Those who governed it saw in its constitution, not only a structure of government (as such it never worked well) but a vehicle of public enlightenment on the nature of the modern state. They publicized the constitution extensively. They set up, at the universities of Bologna, Pavia, and Ferrara, new chairs in "Cisalpine constitutional law and universal jurisprudence."[37] The constitution, like the French constitution of 1795, specified that the right to vote should in twelve years become dependent on literacy, and it provided that common schools should be maintained at public expense. The Cisalpine legislature spent a good deal of time in the discussion of schools, and was debating this problem when the Russians, under Marshal Suvorov, broke into Lombardy and put an end to the republic.

Politics and Vicissitudes of the Cisalpine

In the Cisalpine, as elsewhere, three kinds of people could be roughly identified: the standard democrats, the moderates, and the reactionaries.[38] The bulk of the people remained passive, for the Italian revolution, unlike the French of 1789, did little or nothing to relieve the

---

[37] Ghisalberti, 190.

[38] On parties and politics in the Cisalpine see C. Zaghi, *Bonaparte e il Direttorio dopo Campoformio* (Naples, 1956), 152-84, and the same author's "Il Direttorio francese e l'Italia: il primo colpo di stato nella Cisalpina" in *Rivista storica italiana* (1950), 218-56; also Godechot, *Commissaires*, II, 34-37, 178-94, and his *Grande nation*, II, 451-77, where a valuable comparative survey of coups d'état in France and the sister-republics is given; Candeloro, 237-43; Ghisalberti, 129-35.

problems of any large number among the rural masses. Complaining of any regime that caused them trouble, victimized by requisitions and pillaging, suspicious of neighboring townspeople, and disliking any change in religion, the rural population remained generally non-political or conservative in a negative way. Among notables, real reactionaries were not much in evidence. A few, from attachment to their former privileges and advantages, became *austriacanti* or "Austrianizers." Of truly reactionary literature the best example was Barzoni's *I Romani nella Grecia*, published, at least ostensibly, at London in 1797. Its message was that the French were like the ancient Romans, the Italians like the ancient Greeks (some Germans at the time thought the same of themselves); the "Greeks" were cultured and flourishing but weak and divided into small states, so that the cruder "Romans" easily conquered them, subjecting them to wanton extortion and plunder, ruthlessly imposing themselves while forever talking of "liberty." When the Austrians returned in 1799 they strongly recommended this work, which was then reprinted in Italy.[39]

Among moderates, there were some who were very conservative. Thus Melzi d'Eril, a liberal patrician who had been among the first to greet Bonaparte after the battle of Lodi, was dubious of the whole republican undertaking. Held back from reaction by his distrust of Austria, which he rightly suspected of wishing to kill the Cisalpine state, he toyed with the thought of a Cisalpine monarchy under a Spanish Bourbon prince. Most moderates did not differ from democrats except in degree. Their "moderation" showed itself in a tendency to federalism, or preference for municipal autonomy as in former times, by their warnings against irreligious excesses, a disinclination to promote revolution throughout Italy as a whole, and a sense of caution against becoming too outspokenly anti-French.

It was the democrats, or *giacobini*, who had the most influence during these years. Some were active in the government, some at the Milan club; and they edited most of the political journals. Advanced democrats talked of vast popular and national upheavals, but had little contact with the actual masses. Those who came from Venice, Sardinia, Rome, or Naples were made radical by the repression from which they had suffered, and by the unteachable immobility of the governments that they opposed. A united Italy was easy for them to conceive, since there was nothing in the country's institutions worth preserving by

[39] Ghisalberti, 170; Morandi, 282-83; *Collezione di proclami avvisi, editti . . . pubblicati dal giorno 28 Aprile 1799*, 5 vols. (Milan, 1799-1800), III, the book notices between pp. 148 and 149.

mere federation. They thought that the French should liberate the human race, or at least the Italian part of it, and were critical of the French Directory for being swayed by military, strategic, or diplomatic considerations. They found friends, therefore, among Frenchmen in Italy who for various reasons were also critical of the Directory—army contractors who resisted sporadic attempts to keep their depredations within bounds; political generals of advanced democratic views, or those who merely strained at the leash of civilian control; or itinerant civilians of one kind and another, whose opinions had been formed during the most radical phases of the Revolution in France. Thus Sylvain Maréchal, who had been a Babouvist, published a diatribe on the French betrayal of Venice. Or there was young Marc-Antoine Jullien, who had worked for Robespierre in 1794, and was working in 1797 for Bonaparte, for whom he published a soldiers' newspaper of enthusiastic republican tone: *Le courrier de l'Armée d'Italie*. At Milan he became involved in propaganda for Theophilanthropy against Christianity, and in plots with secret Italian committees for revolutionizing beyond the borders of the Cisalpine, "to devour the duchies and monarchies that surround it."[40]

For the French Directory, after the peace of Campo Formio, the more excitable of the Italian democrats, with their French friends, became something of a nuisance, causing broils with the Church, preventing the consolidation of the Cisalpine Republic, playing politics with French generals, and making difficult any arrangement with Austria.

The official French attitude toward the "sister" republics was determined in part by ideological factors, which for a few months after the Fructidor coup d'état favored the democrats, and still more by arguments of a military or practical character. We have seen that in Holland a Dutch Fructidor was followed by a Dutch Floréal, that in January 1798, when it seemed that the democrats in the Batavian Republic were more willing than the federalists to co-operate in an attack on England, the French favored a democratic coup d'état in that country; and that five months later, when it seemed that the democrats could not control the Dutch financial and naval power, the French sponsored a coup d'état by their more moderate adversaries. The picture in the Cisalpine Republic was analogous but less clear-cut.

Early in 1798 the French and Cisalpine governments negotiated a

---

[40] G. Vaccarino, *I patrioti "anarchistes" e l'idea dell'unità italiana, 1796-99* (Turin, 1955), 59; A. Aulard, "Bonaparte républicain" in *Etudes et leçons*, IX (Paris, 1924), 82-88.

treaty. By its terms, France recognized the independence of the Cisalpine, while offering it protection; and the Cisalpine, in addition to maintaining its own army of 22,000 men under French higher command, was to keep a French army of 25,000 and pay 18,000,000 lire a year for its expenses. By additional secret articles, it was to engage in no trade with England, and limit its import tariff to six per cent.[41] The treaty, though judged unfavorably by most historians as a sign of the cynicism of the Directory, does not actually seem to have been very unreasonable. The very existence of the Cisalpine Republic depended on the further abasement of Austria, which in turn depended on the defeat of Britain. Despite the treaty of Campo Formio, the Austrians had not yet recognized the new government at Milan. It was known that, not content with annexing Venetia, they aimed at further annexations as the expense of the Cisalpine or the Papal States, and that their real desire was to destroy the Cisalpine altogether, and get the infection of new-style republicanism out of Italy. These aims were made perfectly clear a few weeks later at a secret conference held at Selz.

The Cisalpine Legislature refused to ratify the treaty, which had more support in the Cisalpine Directory. A constitutional stalemate was therefore imminent, as in France before 18 Fructidor of the Year V. In the Cisalpine, as a few weeks earlier in the Batavian Republic, the proposals for a coup d'état originated with the citizens of the state in question, not with the French; the difference was that, where the Dutch coup of January was meant to end a situation in which no constitution was possible at all, the Cisalpine coup, which came in March, did violence to a constitution that seemed not to be satisfactorily working. The Cisalpine minister to Paris was Francesco Visconti. He was of the ancient Milanese patrician family of that name, and a democrat. To the Paris government he submitted a list of men in the Cisalpine legislative chambers and Directory, who he said were aristocrats and Austrianizers, and whom he proposed for expulsion. There would really be no violation of liberty, he said, since the incum-

---

[41] For the treaty see Zaghi, "Direttorio francese," 228-29. In the same year, in India, Lord Mornington made a treaty with the Nizam of Hyderabad, who, as an allied or dependent state, agreed to pay the equivalent of about 4,000,000 francs a year to support a British army of 6,000 men. It was not usual, then or later, to see resemblances between such European and extra-European developments, but parallels can be pointed out in these simultaneous actions of the French in Italy and the British in India. They would include, besides the terms of treaties and creation of dependent states, the self-enrichment of French and British individuals, programs of "reform," and expansion carried out despite reluctance of the home governments.

bents had been appointed, not elected. The situation became very confused, because Bonaparte, who had left Italy in the preceding November, objected to the expulsion of men who were his own appointees. The French Directory, however, agreed with Visconti.

A purge in the Cisalpine was therefore ordered from Paris, and it was carried out, although word arrived, soon after the dispatch of the order to Milan, that the Cisalpine legislature had accepted the treaty. As the diplomatic and constitutional crisis thus abated, the purge at Milan took on more the color of ideology and party strife. General Berthier, Bonaparte's successor in Italy, resisted full compliance with the order from Paris. He was replaced by General Brune.

Brune was the very type of the democratic or firmly republican general. A law student and typesetter in his youth, he had joined one of the volunteer battalions in 1791, and was one of the men (he later became Marshal Brune) for whom the Revolution had most obviously provided careers open to talent. When transferred to Italy in March 1798, he had just been involved in the revolution in Switzerland, where the Helvetic Republic had just been proclaimed. Brune was a believer in international democratization, and he entered with gusto into the purge at Milan. The effect, as in France with the Fructidor coup, and in Holland by the *staatsgreep* of January, was to bring forward the advanced democrats in Italy, where also, through a chain of events to be related later, a Roman Republic was set up at about this same time.

Brune consorted at Milan with the most vociferous revolutionaries, those who looked eagerly to a unification of all Italy, and favored strong language and strong measures against the Church. In France, meanwhile, the democratic revival had shown its strength in the April elections. The French Directory became nervous about the upsurge of "anarchists." By the coup d'état of Floréal it crushed the movement in France. Italian, Dutch and French democrats all denounced this maneuver, accusing the French Directory of moderatism. The Directory therefore decided to "florealize" the two sister-republics also.

Events in the Cisalpine became too complex for lucid narration. The Directory sent a moderate civilian, Trouvé, as minister to Milan to serve as a check upon Brune. He was instructed to work with Italian moderates for a change in the constitution, so that the agitation of democrats, unitarists, and anti-clericals could be allayed. Brune refused the military support necessary for such an action. He went to Paris to plead the Italian democrats' case. The Directory, seeing an issue not only of "sound republicanism" against "anarchy," but of civilian authority against military interference, ordered Brune to uphold Trouvé. Brune returned to Milan but still refused to co-operate. He gave secret information to the Cisalpine democrats on the measures designed against them, while in Paris the democratic press denounced the intimidation of Italy. Trouvé, nevertheless, managed to drive through a new constitution. The one promulgated by Bonaparte a year before was discarded. The new one, dated September 10, 1798, confined the vote to adult males who paid a direct tax, and strengthened the executive with respect to the legislative power.

Trouvé was replaced by Fouché, a man of ambiguous views, still better known as an extremist of the Terror than as the police official that he later became. Fouché sided with Brune. The two together continued to favor the Cisalpine democrats, and by still another coup d'état, the third since March, recalled a great many of them into the government. The French Directory, its orders thus flatly defied, recalled both Fouché and Brune, transferring Brune to Holland. A new set of French agents, dispatched to Milan, ejected Brune's Italian supporters in what amounted to a fourth coup d'état, so that Trouvé's constitution was promulgated in January 1799. Constitutionally speaking, if the word be appropriate, the "Jacobins" had lost out in the Cisalpine, though by this time they were very active at Rome, and had set up a republic at Naples.

The dizzy succession of coups d'état in the Cisalpine made certain general features in the situation very clear. The Cisalpine Republic was not really independent; nor could the French allow it to be, so long as the war was in progress, and so long as the peace of Campo Formio was not really a peace, but a breathing spell before the renewal of war, which occurred at the end of 1798. The Cisalpines naturally resented the domination by France. Anti-French feeling in fact became very strong among Italian revolutionaries and democrats. It is hard, however, to see how, if left really to themselves, they would or could have taken the measures necessary to preserve their independence from Austria. The party conflict in the Cisalpine was native to Italy. The French did not manufacture it. But in the strife between moderates and democrats neither party had any expectation of settling their affairs alone. Each side looked to the French for assistance against the other. They could hardly do otherwise, with the French army present in force within the Cisalpine borders, a situation which in turn could hardly be otherwise so long as no reliable peace existed. It was the

French, in consequence, who controlled the internal politics of the Cisalpine Republic.

As for the French Directory, the affairs of the Cisalpine showed the continuing difficulty of keeping dissident generals in order, and the way in which these generals, reinforced by French "Jacobins" who sympathized with foreign revolutionaries, and by Italian democrats at odds with the French government, formed an opposition that threatened the existence of the Directory itself.

1798: THE HIGH TIDE OF
REVOLUTIONARY DEMOCRACY

*Bonaparte has not yet left [for the Channel].
I had dinner with him here yesterday. He is well
satisfied with the turn of our affairs. He is delighted with the chain of Directories which the
Batavian, French, Helvetic, Cisalpine and Ligurian
Republics are going to form.*—PETER OCHS *at Paris
to* BURGOMASTER PETER BURCKHARDT *at Basel, February* 1, 1798

*Pray assure the Empress from me that . . . I shall
remain here ready to save the sacred persons of
the King and Queen. . . . "Down, down with the
French!" ought to be placed in the Council-room of
every Country in the world.*—ADMIRAL NELSON *at
Naples to* SIR MORTON EDEN *at Vienna, December*
10, 1798

XI

1798: THE HIGH TIDE OF
REVOLUTIONARY DEMOCRACY

THE period of about a year beginning late in 1797 was the high point of the whole decade, and indeed of all European history until 1848, in the matter of international agitation stirred up by the revolutionary-democratic movement. The purpose of this chapter is to try to recapture this moment of excitement, and to offer an impression of the movement as a whole before following it again in separate countries.

Events happened so swiftly, with so little central direction, and yet with so many immediate repercussions over hundreds and thousands of miles, that no plan of exposition can do justice to the reality, which is best seen, though elusively, in any number of chain reactions. For example, in March 1798 the French occupied the Swiss city of Bern and seized its famous "treasure" of some 6,000,000 livres in coin.[1] The money was used to help finance Bonaparte's expedition to Egypt, which in turn was directed in part against the British in India, where the Earl of Mornington, the later Marquess of Wellesley, was at war with Tipu Sultan, who had planted a tree of liberty and considered himself an ally of the French Republic. Mornington was victorious, and while seizing Tipu's treasure at Seringapatam, worth about 25,000,000 livres in gold and jewels, and while setting up satellite states in India, and complaining that his own British subordinates were "vulgar, ignorant, rude, familiar and stupid," remained very much concerned with developments at home.[2] In India he received the weekly *Anti-Jacobin* which the young George Canning, already employed in the Foreign Office, edited for a few months in 1798. He was told by Lord Auckland, in April, that there were secret societies of "United English" committed to the "wildest and bloodiest democracy"; and, as a member of an

[1] J. Godechot, *Les commissaires aux armées sous le Directoire* (Paris, 1937), II, 58.
[2] *The Wellesley Papers*, 2 vols. (London, 1914), I, 83-84; R. A. Majumdar et al., *An Advanced History of India* (London, 1950), 711 ff.; J. W. Fortescue, *History of the British Army*, 13 vols. (London, 1902-1930), IV, 715 ff.

Irish landed family, he knew the gravity of the United Irish rebellion at its height in 1798, in which the Irish, as Lord Mornington learned from Lord Hawkesbury, desired a "democratic republic independent of Great Britain."[3] Actually, the cause of the United Irish had been lost on the day when the French Directory had decided to send Bonaparte to Egypt instead of across the Channel. What the Irish revolutionaries wanted was a republic under the protection of France, like the Helvetic Republic that followed on the French occupation of Bern.

Irish patriots, like many from England, had for some years been emigrating to the United States, where they joined with native republicans to form a growing "Jacobin" party. Never yet in America had the issue of Jacobinism burned so hot as in the first months of 1798, especially since the French Directory, favoring for the moment the spread of international revolution, preparing plans for the invasion of England, and regarding the American government as intolerably pro-British, refused to deal with American emissaries who had come over to adjust the differences between the two countries. Mysterious agents, probably representing Talleyrand and Barras, approached the Americans, in overtures beginning in October 1797, with the suggestion that a treaty might be negotiated if the American envoys would consent to certain financial arrangements, which in effect were bribes. William Pitt himself, in October, was on the point of accepting almost exactly the same proposal, which, as it happened had been made to him through the mediation of an American living in France, probably a Federalist in American politics. It involved the taking of certain "rescripts" of the Batavian Republic in exchange for cash; and Pitt believed it possible to find the necessary £450,000, without the knowledge of Parliament, in certain revenues that came to the British government from India.[4] The Americans, however (and especially the Federalists) were shocked by the disclosure in 1798 of the XYZ affair, as they called it, which led to further maritime hostilities with France, to the Alien and Sedition Acts (supposedly aimed against Irish democrats) and to the Virginia and Kentucky Resolutions by which democracy was to be protected against the encroachments of govern-

---

[3] *Wellesley Papers*, I, 52-53, 80, 281.

[4] Great Britain: Historical Manuscript Commission, *Papers of J. B. Fortescue Preserved at Dropmore*, 10 vols. (London, 1892-1927), III, 356, 360, 369, 378-80; E. Channing, *History of the United States* (New York, 1907-1943), IV, 185-88; R. R. Palmer, "Herman Melville et la Révolution française" in *Annales historiques de la Revolution française*, No. 136 (July-Sept., 1954), 254-56. It appears that the intermediary between the French and Pitt was the uncle of Herman Melville.

ment. In these circumstances, some believed that the best way to allay democratic agitation in the United States was to launch a war of conquest against the American possessions of Spain, then France's ally. This was the view of Alexander Hamilton. The same idea was expressed by General Dumouriez, who was then living in Germany. Appalled by the proliferation of revolutionary republics very different from the one he had envisaged for Belgium in 1792, Dumouriez wrote a book urging all governments to come to the aid of England, and advised the United States to suppress its Jacobins by a war to annex New Orleans, Texas, and trans-Mississippi Louisiana.[5]

The revolutionizing of Switzerland, itself set in motion by the creation of the Cisalpine Republic, aroused the hopes of certain Germans who wished to revolutionize Germany. A group of Germans in Basel, a Swiss town across the Rhine from Baden, revived the agitation for a Swabian Republic that had been briefly favored by the French, working through the adventurer Poteratz, in 1796. From Mainz, occupied by the French, Professor A. J. Hoffman of the University in that city sent agitators into Baden and Württemberg. The professors at the University of Kiel were denounced by Dumouriez for their Jacobinism. At the University of Jena, Professor J. G. Fichte was the favorite of the radically minded students. At the University of Königsberg, Professor I. Kant wrote a "justification" (which he did not publish) of the policy of the French Directory toward England.[6] To the English, in whose own universities such sentiments were unheard of, the behavior of German students and professors seemed most reprehensible. As Hugh Elliot (brother of the Viceroy of Corsica already mentioned in these pages) wrote from Dresden in August 1798 to Lord Grenville, the Foreign Secretary: "The partisans of revolution and innovation have not been more active in any country than in Germany; and, unfortunately, the German universities have been the center of a spirit of

---

[5] Le Général Dumouriez, *Tableau speculatif de l'Europe*, n.p., février 1798, reissued and amplified as the *Nouveau tableau* . . . septembre 1798; see pp. 257-61 of the latter.

[6] K. Obser, "Die revolutionäre Propaganda am Oberrhein in Jahre 1798" in *Zeitschrift für Geschichte des Oberrheins*, new series, xxiv (1909), 199-245 (Obser furnishes no evidence for his remark that the propagandists were "mostly Jews," p. 201); X. Léon, *Fichte et son temps*, 2 vols. (Paris, 1927), i, 518-85; I. Kant, "Rechtfertigung des Direktoriums der französische Republik wegen seines angeblich ungereimten Planes, den Krieg mit England zu ihrem Vorteil zu beendigen. 1798," in *Sämtliche Werke* (1867-1868), viii, 644-45; a memorandum of the Prussian resident at Frankfurt, about February 1798, of which a copy was sent to England, *Dropmore Papers*, iv, 107-108, reporting on "l'influence morale du système révolutionnaire français dans cette partie de l'Allemagne et sur la manière dont les agents démocrates cherchent à agiter les pays de la rive droite du Rhin. . . . Ce ne sont plus actuellement les agents français, mais les clubbistes de l'Allemagne. . . ."

democracy, which has from thence been diffused into all the various classes of what are styled the learned professions."[7]

The Great Nation, the Sister-Republics, and the Wave of Cisalpinization

The year began with the Fructidor coup d'état and the signing of the treaty of Campo Formio. By the first, the French Directory for a few months favored the advanced or democratic republicans in France and elsewhere. By the second, there was "peace on the Continent," or at least the hostilities between organized armies came to a halt; and in effect, if not quite in law, all governments except the British now recognized not only the French Republic, which had incorporated Belgium and was in occupation of the Left Bank of the Rhine, but also the Cisalpine Republic; the Ligurian Republic, which had come into being at Genoa at about the same time; and the Batavian Republic, which dated from 1795.

The French, except for continued British resistance, had clearly won the War of the First Coalition. As one German moderate put it, a war begun to stamp out one revolutionary republic had now resulted in the establishment of four. The French began to call themselves the Great Nation, "not without good reason," as Wolfe Tone remarked in December 1797.[8] The word "nation" was still charged with strong revolutionary significance, implying a people that asserted its sovereignty and its rights against aristocratic, feudal, ecclesiastical, and monarchical adversaries. The term *grande Nation* became widely current, but there was something equivocal in it from the start. For the French it took on overtones of a national self-esteem, from which a contempt for foreigners, including the foreign revolutionaries and republicans, was by no means absent. Republicans outside of France soon came to look on the Great Nation with mixed feelings, respecting it for its power and its principles, but often alienated by its practice, and so turning anti-French while not ceasing to favor the Revolution. For conservatives the expression was always merely ironic.

The Great Nation had its Sister Republics, as they were sometimes called, and these were in fact more sisters than daughters, since in no case had the French government brought them into being by a deliberate or sustained action of revolutionary propagation. The Batavian,

---

[7] *Dropmore Papers*, IV, 281.
[8] *Life of Theobald Wolfe Tone Written by Himself*, 2 vols. (Washington, 1826), II, 455.

Cisalpine, and Ligurian Republics were by-products of military success, of the weakness of the old regime in their respective territories, of the agitations of native patriots, the independent programs of French generals, and the willingness of the French government—the Convention in the case of the Dutch, the pre-Fructidorian Directory in the case of the Cisalpines, and the Ligurians—to accept *de facto* decisions, to recruit allies, or to befriend ideological sympathizers in time of war.

The signing of peace, with its recognition of a new republican order in Western Europe, seemed to open the way to a world of the future— hoped for by some, dreaded by others—in which more such republics might be created in a widening wave of "Cisalpinization." This term, though never current, was in fact used by a counter-revolutionary and émigré writer, the French General Danican, who as a Vendémiairist had tried to block the establishment of the Directory in 1795. In 1798, in a pamphlet sadly entitled *Cassandre*, Danican predicted the progressive Cisalpinization of the whole Continent except Russia.[9]

"The intention of the French," wrote Axel de Fersen in his diary in January 1798, "is clearly to turn all Europe into republics."[10] The German journalist, K. J. Lange, who was warmly hostile to England, which he blamed for the continuation of the war and hence for the spread of revolution, was not so much friendly to the French as ambivalent toward them. He reflected philosophically, after the peace of Campo Formio, that the French had always favored "freedom" for others: Henry IV had helped the Dutch, Mazarin had helped Cromwell, Louis XVI had helped the Americans, and by the Westphalia system the French had assured the liberties of princes and cities in the Holy Roman Empire—and now that France was a republic it would republicanize or "municipalize" all Europe.[11]

"To municipalize," said Dumouriez in February 1798, "to divide up into departments, to establish a provisional Executive Directory and a National Guard, to form primary assemblies to elect representatives to two Chambers, to seize the public funds and the estates of the clergy, to confiscate the property of all kinds of aristocrats, that is of the rich, to demand the protection of France, which has offered it to all peoples

---

[9] Quoted by A. Meynier, *Les coups d'état du Directoire*, 3 vols. (Paris, 1927-1928), II, 279, from *Cassandre*, 152.

[10] *Axel von Fersens dagbok*, 4 vols. (Stockholm, 1925-1936), III, 173, 222-23. I am indebted to Dr. H. A. Barton for translation of this and other Swedish materials, incorporated in his doctoral dissertation at Princeton on the career of Fersen. French and English versions of Fersen's diary are much abridged.

[11] *Deutsche Reichs- und Staatszeitung für den Geschäfts- und Weltmann* (Bayreuth, Nov. 3, 1797), 1,399-1,401.

aspiring to liberty: it is all very easy, quick and alarming for the various peoples." Since Dumouriez believed it entirely possible for England to be invaded, as was generally expected in February 1798, he called upon all the European monarchies to re-enter the war at once. If they did not, he warned, the "fall of all thrones and the destruction of all political, civil and religious constitutions would be the terrible result. Democracy would devour Europe, and end by devouring itself."[12]

In the older "sister republics" there were coups d'état of Fructidorian type, by which the more ardent democrats came into power, in January among the Dutch, in April at Milan. In the Batavian and Cisalpine republics, as in France, political clubs of neo-Jacobin type, now often called "constitutional circles," enjoyed a period of lively activity; a law of February 24, 1798, created such a *circolo costituzionale* in each of the Cisalpine departments.

Newer "sister-republics" now sprang up also, in time of peace or apparent peace, as the older ones had sprung up in time of war. In the summer of 1797 a group of Rhineland Germans, working with the French General Hoche—both of them inspired by Bonaparte and the Cisalpine Republic—organized a movement for a Cisrhenane Republic to comprise the Left Bank of the Rhine. One of their spokesmen, Rebmann, saw a "heavenly dream in which the Batavian, Cisrhenane, Helvetic, Cisalpine and Ligurian Republics" should be joined.[13] The French soon decided, however, merely to "municipalize" and "departmentalize" the Left Bank, and later to annex it, not to countenance a separate republic there. The effect was the same so far as destruction of the old order was concerned. The agitation for a Swabian Republic on the Right Bank flared up at the same time, in mysterious conjunction with General Augereau, who replaced Hoche in October, and had been one of Bonaparte's aides in the Cisalpine. Meanwhile the Irish exiles worked for similar liberation, and Wolfe Tone, who spent a good deal of time in the Batavian Republic on plans for the Franco-Dutch invasion of Britain, and was present at Bonn in September 1797 at the abortive proclamation of the Cisrhenane, pursued his dream for a Republic of Ireland. The Swiss cantons fell into turmoil, and from a welter of short-lived "republics," Lemanic and Rhodanic, a unified Helvetic Republic emerged in March 1798. After the death of the French General Duphot in a street riot at Rome, the papal city was

---

[12] *Tableau speculatif*, 131; *Nouveau tableau*, 279.
[13] J. Hansen, *Quellen zur Geschichte des Rheinlandes im Zeitalter der französischen Revolution*, 4 vols. (Bonn, 1931-1938), IV, 308. On the Cisrhenane movement see below, pp. 440-43.

occupied by units of the French army, supplemented by troops of the new Cisalpine army and of the Polish Legion. A Roman Republic followed. At the end of the year the French occupied Turin, where the end of the Sardinian monarchy could be envisaged, and also Naples, where the most insubstantial of the sister-republics, the Neapolitan or Parthenopean, was proclaimed.[14]

The wave of enthusiasm made itself felt beyond the zone of the satellite republics. At Berlin the Abbé Sieyès made a point of treating the royal court with republican disdain. Asked, upon his arrival as ambassador, whether "His Excellency was clothed with a civil or military character, and was a count or a baron," he replied haughtily that in France there were only citizens, and all citizens were soldiers. When he requested to be excused from wearing a sword at his presentation at court, the king shrugged and the queen laughed, but they let him have his way, since it was Prussian policy to remain neutral between France and its enemies.[15] At Vienna, at about the same time, the French envoy, General Bernadotte, provoked a serious riot by displaying a huge tricolor flag from his balcony. As Fersen remarked of this future king of Sweden, he was "one of the raging Jacobins" (nor was Fersen mistaken) who wished to push the Directory into a more aggressively revolutionary program toward Europe.[16] Fersen himself, newly installed as chancellor of the University of Upsala, was combatting the Jacobinism of Swedish students. "As to the Swedes," wrote Lord Grenville in 1798, "more than half the people there, particularly in trade, are as great Jacobins as Rewbell or Talleyrand, and the Government is little better."[17] (It must be admitted that Grenville's category of Jacobins

---

[14] No less than eight tricolors had been devised by 1798, of which five were then officially in use. The five were the French; the Cisalpine of green, white, and blue; a gray, white, and red for the Roman Republic; a Dutch or Batavian red, white, and blue with horizontal stripes authorized in 1795; and a Swiss or Helvetic tricolor of red, green, and yellow adopted on April 14, 1798. Two others had been ventured but had disappeared: the Belgian red, yellow, and black of 1789; and a Cisrhenane red, blue, and green of 1797. A Greek tricolor of red, white, and black had also been proposed in 1797. Of these, the French, Italian (Cisalpine), Dutch, and Belgian are in use today. The German republican colors of black, red, and gold, used today in the German Federal Republic, date from the revolutionary movement of 1848.

On the Dutch and Belgian tricolors see the *Algemene Winkler Prins Encyclopedie*, art. "Vlag"; on the Helvetic, J. Strickler, *Actensammlung aus der Zeit der Helvetischen Republik, 1798-1803*, I, 644; on the Cisalpine, above, p. 300; on the Roman, A. Dufourcq, *Le régime jacobin en Italie: étude sur la République romaine* (Paris, 1900), III; on the Cisrhenane, J. Venedey, *Die deutschen Republikaner unter der französischer Republik* (Leipzig, 1870), 269; on the Greek, A. Dascalakis, *Oeuvres de Rhigas Velestinlis* (Paris, 1937), 123.

[15] P. Bastid, *Sieyès et sa pensée* (Paris, 1939), 204.

[16] *Dagbok*, III, 223-26, 229.

[17] *Dropmore Papers*, IV, 349.

was fairly ample.) In Spain, now allied to France, the "Jansenist" Jovellanos was in office, and a flurry was created in official and ecclesiastical circles, early in 1798, by a letter written by Bishop Grégoire of the French constitutional church. Thousands of copies were disseminated in Spain and Spanish America. Grégoire called the Inquisition a disgrace to the Catholic world, and urged enlightened Spaniards to get rid of it, at a time when "the cry of liberty sounds in both hemispheres" and "the revolutions begin now in Europe."[18]

Alarms and rumors filled the air when it became known that Bonaparte, transferred from his command of the *Armée d'Angleterre*, had embarked with a huge fleet at Toulon. Not only Wolfe Tone, but Pitt and Grenville, believed him to be headed for Ireland. Fersen was told by Jacobi, a Prussian diplomat, that the French were really going to the Crimea, "to support Poland and revolutionize Europe by stealing in at the back door."[19] It was true that a final uprising of the Poles against the partitioning powers had occurred only the year before, that Kosciuszko passed through Paris in 1798, and that the Polish Legion in Italy, despite the peace with Austria, still hoped to press on into Eastern Europe.

The French landed in Egypt in July 1798, and the modern period of Egyptian and Ottoman history is often dated from that event. The French Revolution, as Bernard Lewis has said, was the first European movement to exert a strong influence on the Moslem world, precisely because it did not appear to be Christian.[20] At the same time the Christian, Greek, and Balkan parts of the Ottoman Empire were thrown more open to revolutionary influence from another direction.

By the treaty of Campo Formio France annexed the Ionian Islands, formerly a possession of Venice. They were Greek-speaking communities, lying close to the western coast of Greece. In these "Gallo-Greek departments" the processes of "municipalization" and "departmentalization" soon began to work; that is, the old institutions began to disintegrate, and members of the old ruling families (including in this case Count Capodistrias of later fame) fled from the country, seeking aid from Britain or Russia. On the Greek mainland, late in 1797, patriots from Athens, Macedonia, Epirus, and Crete, meeting secretly in the Peloponnesus, appealed to Bonaparte to send troops to liberate them from the Turks. In June 1798 Rhigas Velestinlis, who had written a

[18] R. Herr, *The Eighteenth-Century Revolution in Spain* (Princeton, 1958), 417.
[19] *Dagbok*, May 15, 1798.
[20] B. Lewis, "The Impact of the French Revolution in Turkey," in *Journal of World History: Cahiers de l'histoire mondiale*, 1 (1953), 105-15.

constitution for a Hellenic Republic, was executed with seven accomplices by the Ottoman authorities at Belgrade.[21] A few months
later, at Ancona, an Adriatic town in the Roman Republic, the French
Directory set up a "commercial agency" which was in fact, as Talleyrand admitted, "an insurrectionary committee for the Greeks of
Albania and the Morea against the Ottoman Porte."[22] The much
traveled militant, Mangourit, who had shown his revolutionary sentiments in America, Switzerland, and Spain, was put in charge at Ancona. The Roman Catholic bishop of Scutari offered his help, and a
Spanish ex-Jesuit born at Oran contributed his knowledge of Near
Eastern affairs. But the most useful member of the secret committee
was Constantine Stamati, a Greek who had gone to Paris in 1787 as a
medical student and who had worked for the Revolution ever since.
He had been a secret emissary of the Committee of Public Safety to the
hospidars of Moldavia and Wallachia, and now, at the turn of 1798-1799,
from the base at Ancona, he despatched shipments of muskets and
ammunition into Greece and Rumelia. Provision was also made for
more peaceful penetration; or at least Talleyrand, still Foreign Minister,
directed his agents at Rome and Corfu to send fonts of Greek and
Turkish type to Ancona. The type never arrived, nor did the Directory
ever supply the Ancona mission with any money. The enterprise collapsed in 1799, when the French were driven by the Russians, Austrians,
and Turks from the Gallo-Greek departments and from Italy.

Nor, on the opposite side of Western Civilization, was the English-
speaking world unaffected by these excitements of 1798. England itself,
threatened by invasion, was not immune. A secret committee of the
House of Commons, appointed to look into such matters, could find no
evidence, by name, of a single Frenchman or other foreign agent in
concerted action in England with the English clubs. The committee
believed, however (the belief is not shared by later historians), that the
naval mutinies of 1797 had been precipitated and given a political
character by subversives and spies. It believed also that there were, in
1798, in and near Manchester, some eighty local units of United
Englishmen, who in fact included a great many Irish drawn as working
people to that city. The committee seized certain documents of the

---

[21] A. Dascalakis, *Rhigas Velestinlis, la Révolution française et les préludes de l'indépendance hellénique* (Paris, 1937); M. Mangourit, *Défense d'Ancône et des départements romains . . . aux années VII et VIII*, 2 vols. (Paris, 1802); S. Pappas, "L'agence
du commerce français d'Ancône 1798-99" in *Acropole*, VII (1932), 124; J. Lair and E.
Legrand, *Documents inédits . . . Correspondance de Paris, Vienne, Berlin, Varsovie,
Constantinople* (Paris, 1872), 21. On southeast Europe see Chapter V above.
[22] Pappas, 124.

United Englishmen, and when one of their leaders, an Irish priest named O'Coigly, was arrested in February on his way to France, he was found to be bearing a letter to the Directory. In this letter, the United English tried to persuade the Directory that England would rise in revolution at the moment of French invasion.[23]

Among the United Irish in Ireland, as among the Irish exiles in France, there were high hopes for a French landing in either one of the British Isles. As for the Greek patriots or for Thomas Jefferson (who was impressed by "that wonderful man Bonaparte") or Andrew Jackson (who hoped that Bonaparte would liberate England), the twenty-nine-year-old French general exerted a fascination for the Irish. A street ballad went:

> Oh! may the wind of Freedom
> Soon send young Boney o'er,
> And we'll plant the Tree of Liberty
> Upon our Irish Shore![24]

But Bonaparte went to Egypt. The United Irish rose and were repressed, in what Robert Stewart (the future Lord Castlereagh) called "a Jacobinical conspiracy throughout the kingdom, pursuing its object chiefly with Popish instruments."[25] The French, too late, landed a few hundred soldiers on the west coast under General Humbert, who was soon obliged to surrender. Lord Grenville thought that if the French had arrived in force two months sooner the outcome would have been very different.[26]

Canada also had a brief shudder over Cisalpinization. Conspiracies involving handfuls of Canadians and Vermonters (whose trade outlets were easier through the St. Lawrence River than through the New England mountains) were rather trifling in themselves, but they were enough to keep the British authorities in a state of alarm, so much so that one of the conspirators, David McLane, had not only been executed in 1797, but executed with all the ancient public solemnity, by hanging, drawing, and quartering.[27] There is in the French Foreign

---

[23] House of Commons, *Report of the Committee of Secrecy*, 1799; printed also in the *Annual Register for 1799* (London, 1801), 150-82, and in Mallet du Pan's *British Mercury*, 11.

[24] Jefferson to Madison, June 4, 1797, quoted by S. Kurtz, *Presidency of John Adams* (Philadelphia, 1957), 288; Jackson to James Robertson, Jan. 11, 1798, in *Correspondence of Andrew Jackson* (Washington, 1926), I, 42; R. Hayes, *Ireland and Irishmen in the French Revolution* (London, 1932), 4.

[25] Castlereagh to Wickham, Dublin Castle, June 12, 1798, in *Memoirs and Correspondence of Viscount Castlereagh*, 12 vols. (London, 1848-1853), I, 219.

[26] Grenville to Rufus King, *Dropmore Papers*, IV, 288.

[27] On McLane see below, p. 518.

Office Archives an unidentifiable memorandum sent from America in February 1798. It declared that many Canadians were restless, that they preferred an independent republic to re-annexation to France, that an independent Canada would be useful in checking the expansion of the United States, and that two American citizens (probably the Allen brothers from Vermont) were willing to start a revolution, if provided by France with a mere $2,000 with which to begin bribing the Canadian garrisons. Apparently the French took no action on this proposal for a Canadian Republic.[28]

In the United States, though the country was on the verge of war with France, there was less internal interference by France in 1798 than in the preceding years. George Rogers Clark, indeed, using his commission as a general in the French army, made another attempt, as in 1793, to rally followers to invade and "revolutionize" Louisiana; but he received no encouragement from Paris on this occasion, and being blocked also by the American government, fled to St. Louis, then a French village of about a thousand people under the Spanish crown. Between the Alleghenies and the Mississippi there was a good deal of separatist and democratic sentiment, and much hostility to the "aristocratic" East and to the British, but little or no interest in Europe. A separate Western republic, had one ever come into existence, would have been less welcome to the French than to the British and the English-speaking Canadians, who were at this time almost all Loyalists born in the Thirteen Colonies, very much out of sympathy with the American union.

Democracy itself was the great political issue in the United States in 1798, as it was in Europe; and in the United States, possibly even more than in England, Holland, Germany, or Italy, conservatives believed that ideas of popular government were brought in by foreign malcontents and subversives. The young Philadelphia lawyer, Joseph Hopkinson, for example, to arouse his countrymen for war, wrote *Hail Columbia* in 1798. It became the first national anthem. Hopkinson's ideas were expressed, not in the words of the song, which dwelt only on American liberty and the greatness of General Washington, but in a pamphlet which he wrote at about the same time.[29] The French,

[28] Translation of a memorandum written in English, entitled "Moyen d'une insurrection dans le Canada," sent to Paris with a despatch of Létombe, French consul at Philadelphia, in Archives des Affaires Etrangères, Corr. Pol., Etats-Unis, Vol. 49.

[29] Joseph Hopkinson, *What is our situation? and what our Prospects? A few pages for Americans.* (Philadelphia, 1798.) Reprinted in London as *What is our situation? and What our prospects, or a Demonstration of the Insidious views of Republican France. By an American.* (London, 1799.)

he here said, having in mind the wave of Cisalpinization, were out to plunder the world. He then called for stricter laws of naturalization, since Jacobinism in America was due to the inrush of riff-raff from Europe, who came to America howling for Liberty and Equality— "fortune-hunting foreigners . . . imported patriots from England, Ireland and Scotland . . . gangs of discontented and factious emigrants." If it remained a little unclear, in Hopkinson's view, whether the trouble was due to the dreadful French, or to persons whose native language was English, it was perfectly evident that democracy in America was foreign and unwanted, a mere poison diffused by a European revolution.

In Brazil also, in 1798, a republican conspiracy was discovered in the city of Bahia. Four free mulattoes were hanged and quartered. They had declared that they favored, to quote the official sentence, "the imaginary advantages of a Democratic Republic, in which all should be equal."[30] It was the island of Haiti, however, the former French colony of Saint-Domingue, that saw, in the 1790's, "the first great shock between the ideals of white supremacy and race equality."[31] And here, in the latter part of the decade, before insurmountable internal and external forces closed in upon him, Toussaint l'Ouverture seemed almost to be succeeding in founding a free republic of a kind that some European republicans of 1798, though hardly those of the United States, might accept as akin to their own.

A Comparative View of the New
Republican Order

In the rest of this chapter some observations will be assembled, such as are made elsewhere in the book in connection with particular countries, to show what was common to the revolutionary-democratic movement as a whole, which, as Dumouriez said, seemed in 1798 to threaten "all political, civil and religious constitutions."

The class or kind of people to whom the French Directory meant to appeal, and the images and symbols by which it was believed that this appeal might be made effective, are suggested in two grand public events staged in Paris in 1798. In this interval of peace on the continent it was hoped to show what a victory of republicanism would bring.

---

[30] A. Ruy, *A primeira revolução social brasileira* (Rio de Janeiro, 1942), 227. I am indebted to Mr. and Mrs. Stanley J. Stein for assistance in Portuguese.

[31] The phrase is T. Lothrop Stoddard's, *The French Revolution in San Domingo* (Boston, 1914), vii.

It is in the triumphant Republic of 1798, as much as in the harried Republic of 1794, that one should look for the climax of the Enlightenment.

On 9 Thermidor of the Year VI, or July 27, 1798, a long procession in Paris paid honor to Liberty. A troop of cavalry was followed by professors and students from the newly reorganized Museum of Natural History, marching beside triumphal cars bearing exotic plants and minerals and accompanied by a bear from the zoo at Bern, lions from Africa, and camels from Egypt. Next came delegates from the printers and public libraries of the city, and professors from the new Polytechnique and the old College de France. Prize pupils carried manuscripts and rare books. Artists walked beside works of art which had been captured in Italy, and which, it was believed, could be better appreciated and cared for in the capital of the civilized world than in a land of superstition—paintings by Titian and Raphael, and ancient sculpture including the Discus Thrower and the Apollo Belvidere. Also included were the famous Corinthian bronze horses, which the Byzantines had long ago taken from Corinth, and the Venetians from Constantinople. The French now brought them from Venice to Paris, "to rest at last upon free soil." Of various inscriptions carried in the procession one was a quotation from Seneca: "To live ignorant is to be dead."[32] It was indeed a great moment for French science; Laplace, Lamarck, and Cuvier could all have been working in Paris on that day; and Frenchmen then disembarking with Bonaparte at Alexandria were about to become the founders of Egyptology.

A few weeks later an industrial exposition was put on in the Champ de Mars. It was the first of a kind which the Crystal Palace of 1851 was to make more famous. The Minister of the Interior, François de Neufchateau, opened it with a speech. Our French manufacturers, he said in effect, will abundantly demonstrate the superiority of a free people in matters economic; genius and ingenuity are now liberated from gilds and monopolies and from ancient regulations and routines; the day foreseen in the *Encyclopédie*, the day of systematic and public sponsorship of the practical arts, has at last arrived. While the wonders of science were displayed by the illumination of the exhibition halls at night, and by a balloon from which a fire was ignited on the ground, the main business was the viewing and judging of exhibits submitted by 110 French manufacturers and *artistes*. A prize was awarded to

---

[32] *Moniteur*, 9 and 11 Thermidor, VI; other newspaper reports reprinted by A. Aulard, *Paris pendant la réaction thermidorienne et sous le Directoire*, 5 vols. (Paris, 1898-1902), v, 6-9.

one of the Didot family for book design. (Even typography was revolutionized in these years, since the type-face still called "modern" was introduced by Didot and his Italian contemporary Bodoni.) Another prize went to Nicolas Conté for the invention of the lead pencil. A better symbol of a middle-class and "enlightened" world would be hard to find.[33]

In the French view of the new republican order, as conceived under the Directory, the French were definitely to be dominant. There was little thought of equality or mutuality between the French Republic and its satellites, none of which had more than an eighth of the population of France within its old frontiers. It seemed natural to the French—as indeed to many eighteenth-century Europeans—that the learned and artistic worlds should converge upon Paris. It seemed natural that the allied republics should accept the lead of French foreign policy, and contribute money, supplies, and soldiers to armed forces that remained at the highest levels under French command. It seemed natural to favor France in commercial policy, as in the Treaty of 1798 with the Cisalpine; to prevent the importation of British goods throughout the new republican order, and to promote the sale of French manufactures in allied states, while refusing to give equal access for Dutch or Italian products into France.

This clear insistence on putting French interests first, which in some ways merely continued the habits of the Old Regime, and in others anticipated those of the Napoleonic empire, was probably unavoidable, and even necessary. The maintenance of revolution in all countries depended entirely on the strength of France. The Cisalpine, Batavian, and other republics, threatened by their own counter-revolutionaries and by foreign powers, would rise or fall with the French Republic. But the French pursuit of their own national interest, carried to a point of actual exploitation of weaker allies, began very soon to confuse the new republican order. It divided the revolutionary or progressive forces in Europe. Men who remained committed to revolutionary changes in their own countries came to disagree on the extent of collaboration that should be accepted with France; some tried dealing with conservative forces instead; some rebelled against French interference; some accepted the French and hoped to make use of them in a way as calculating or disillusioned as that of the French Directory toward them.

---

[33] *Moniteur*, 5 and 12 Vendémiaire, VII; G. Gérault, *Les expositions universelles au point de vue economique* (Paris, 1901), 24-25.

Nevertheless, the surprising and notable fact, at the time of the Directory as later under Napoleon—a fact which the following nationalistic generations tended to minimize, and which twentieth-century developments in Europe may make more acceptable and more visible—is the degree to which many Europeans looked on the new order with favor.

In a class analysis, as already observed, the international revolutionary and democratic republicanism was above all a movement of the middle ranks of society. Upper-class persons were by no means absent; nobles and prelates were especially prominent in the revolutions at Rome and Naples, and individual "Jacobins" of aristocratic birth could be found in all countries. One has the impression that they were rarest in Germany. The lowest classes outside France, and in France after 1795, were generally apathetic or hostile. Here the great exception was furnished by Ireland, where the mass of the rural population, led by a good many priests, was in active revolt against the English and the Anglo-Irish ascendancy, and for that reason sympathetic to France, the more so since they did not experience the burdens of a French occupation. Elsewhere, and notably in Belgium and Italy, peasants were in a state of insurrection before the year 1798 was over.

Middle-class persons were themselves divided. It has been observed of South Germany that republican propaganda was most successful among the *wohlhabendere Klasse*, while the solidly established old burgher families remained largely impervious.[34] Similar divisions existed within the Batavian and Helvetic republics, where almost everyone of importance was middle-class by general European standards. Men whose habitual business connections were with English firms, or who either invested or borrowed in England, were likely to be on the conservative side ideologically; yet even in these cases a resentment against the "modern Carthage," which had been growing throughout the century, might induce a willingness, at least temporarily, to experiment with new arrangements. In the United States, where commercial contacts with England were reinforced by strong cultural ties, the mercantile community was predominantly Federalist and pro-British, and it was among small farmers and landed gentry, remote from the cities, that one found sympathy for republicanism and for France. In this respect the United States stood in contrast to the European Continent. One result was that Americans never understood how "bourgeois" the

[34] K. Obser, "Die revolutionäre Propaganda am Oberrhein in Jahre 1798," in *Zeitschrift für die Geschichte des Oberrheins*, n.s. xxiv (1909), 230.

European revolution was.[35] A list of North of Ireland radicals in 1798 included Presbyterian ministers, schoolteachers, merchants, shopkeepers, innkeepers, a miller, a land steward, and a watchmaker. A list of Italian revolutionaries in Piedmont, at the same time, for about two thousand whose occupations are known, included many lawyers, Catholic clergy, merchants, doctors and government employees, but hardly any peasants or city laborers.[36]

The friends of the Great Nation, and the warmest citizens of the Sister Republics, were therefore middle-class people of certain kinds. As Mallet du Pan scornfully said in 1796, they were "those foresighted people with their little investments, those sagacious men of business, those second-hand shopkeepers of every description who in most of the commercial cities of Europe continue to show themselves as auxiliaries of the French Revolution."[37] They were lawyers, doctors, journalists, writers, professors and students, middling property-owners and *rentiers*; persons prospering in towns but not belonging to the established inner circles; those hoping to gain from the purchase of church land, as happened in Belgium and Italy, but not in Holland, and not much in Switzerland; those profiting from business with the republican armies; members of religious minorities; Jews who desired a fuller acceptance in the general community, and who obtained it in all the republics except the Helvetic; and enterprising men of affairs, who chafed under the older restraints of gild and town, and could see a place for themselves in a new European economy, dominated by France, in which they would have more freedom in the recruitment of labor and the development of new enterprises or new inventions.

Throughout Western Europe, and by no means confined to the new revolutionary republics, there was a universal phenomenon of politicization. In Poland somewhat the same development had been suppressed. It became manifest in two ways, in political clubs and in the rapid growth of a political press. It would seem that every city of Central and Western Europe must have had its "club," in some cases simply continuing the reading societies and discussion groups that had flourished for years before 1789, in other cases introduced by French soldiers or even by French generals during military occupation after

[35] See Chapter xvi below.

[36] R. B. McDowell, *Irish Public Opinion 1750-1800* (London, 1944), 196; G. Vaccarino, *Storia del Piemonte* (Turin, 1960), 245-71, as cited by J. Godechot in *Revue historique*, Vol. 228, p. 185.

[37] J. Mallet du Pan, *Correspondance politique pour servir à l'histoire du républicanisme français* (Hamburg, 1796), p. 5.

1792.[38] The word "club," of English origin, spread throughout Europe. To designate a busy patriot of republicans views in a derogatory sense, the word "clubbist," *clubbiste*, etc., sprang up in English, French, German, Spanish, and Italian, and so on to *klubista* in Polish. Usually the clubs were open, since publicity was their aim, but even open clubs might develop secret activities, as in Holland in 1794, or turn from an open to a secret existence when forbidden by governments, as with the United Irish groups at the same time. In America the democratic clubs that sprang up in 1793 or 1794 turned into ordinary units of party organization; in England after 1794 the more vulnerable middle-class members ceased to come to meetings; in Continental monarchies they became clandestine; in France after the closing of the Jacobin Club late in 1794 they were prohibited, but soon rose again; so that in France, as in the Sister Republics, in the late 1790's, the democratic clubs and "circles," while often disliked even by republican governments as too radical and too turbulent, managed to remain open as centers of political discussion.

The world of clubs shaded off into a wonderland of secret societies, on which it is almost impossible to obtain satisfactory evidence or to form any rational judgment. A club of a kind that in another country would be open might be secret for local reasons, as at Naples in 1792. The secret societies seem to have been quite distinct from Masonic lodges, though membership might be overlapping. A secret society differed from a club in being organized for action, with no pretense of discussion, since the views of the members were assumed to be firmly formed. A secret society might preserve a certain democratic character, with power flowing up from the membership, through election of delegates by local units to higher levels, as with the United Irish; but it was more usual for secret societies to be controlled tightly at the top, with the members themselves excluded from the secrets. There were organizations of this kind of both revolutionary and counter-revolutionary purpose, such as the Martinovicz conspiracy in Hungary and the Babeuf conspiracy in France, or, at the extreme Right, the Eudaemonists of Germany from 1794 to 1798, the "philanthropic institutes" in France in 1797, or a peculiar organization which the Swedish Fersen learned of from a French émigré at the German city of Rastadt in 1798.

Members of clubs, in some cases more or less clandestine, were usually among the first to welcome the French army in many places

---

[38] See the chapter, "Les clubs" in J. Godechot, *La Grande Nation* (Paris, 1956), I, 317-55.

from Amsterdam to Naples, and to try to take part in setting up a revolutionary republic. But there is no case in which any serious revolutionary disturbance can be attributed to the machinations of a secret society, again with the exception of Ireland, where the United Irish were certainly more than a secret society in any ordinary sense of the word. The books of John Robison and the Abbé Barruel have already been analyzed. They purported to expose a universal secret plot against all governments and religions. They were written in 1797, before the actual height of revolutionary expansion, of which both authors had really very little knowledge. Both drew heavily on German sources, and it seems likely (such an opinion being inevitably impressionistic) that there was in fact more proliferation of secret societies in Germany in the 1790's than in other countries. But Germany was also, along with Spain and Portugal, the part of Europe in which truly revolutionary activity or successful republican agitation could least be found.

It cannot be too often repeated that publicity, not secrecy, was the moving force in the revolutionary-republican movement. Or, to put it more accurately, the desire for publicity was the moving force, for in most countries a politically articulate periodical press did not exist under the old order, but was one of the immediate consequences and manifestations of the new.[39] Political journalism was oldest, most firmly established and most free in England and the United States, but even in England it was only since the 1770's that newspapers had been allowed to report speeches in Parliament. In the old Dutch provinces, the bishopric of Liége, and some of the German states and cities, the periodical press had for some time been relatively free and very voluminous, but even in Holland the editors were not free to report or comment on local affairs, especially after the Orange restoration of 1787. At most, such papers criticized the governments of their political neighbors. In France, the Mediterranean countries, and Eastern Europe there were no politically minded newspapers at all under the old regime.

What happened was therefore in some countries the marked politicization of a press already well established, and in others the creation of a political press as a new thing. A few editors were supported by governments, revolutionary or counter-revolutionary as the case might be; but the economics of publishing were so simple that political journalism was an easy field for private and individual enterprise. Few papers had the gravity or the dimensions of the Paris *Moniteur*. Never

---

[39] See the chapter, "L'essor de la presse politique," in Godechot, *op.cit.*, II, 367-417.

"official" in the 1790's, the *Moniteur* was established late in 1789, and appeared daily in four or more folio pages eighteen inches high. It was filled with despatches from foreign countries, local news, and full texts of legislation and speeches in the assembly. The name was widely copied, as in the *Monitore Cisalpino* of 1798 and the *Monitore Napoletano* of 1799. But most newspapers were small in size, crudely printed, weekly or semi-weekly or simply irregular, limited to a few hundreds or at most a few thousands in circulation, and frequently quite ephemeral. They were short on news and long on opinion, and usually polemical in the extreme. Venom, recrimination, name-calling, and wild accusations were common in all political camps. It is well known what the American Founding Fathers had to suffer at the hands of newspaper writers. The indignation of conservatives at the excesses of the new democratic press would have been justified, had not the conservative papers been equally bad.

In the United States the newspapers multiplied as the democratic movement developed, and most of the persons indicted under the Sedition Act of 1798 were newspaper editors. In Ireland the press had been very lively during the political agitation of 1780-1784, but was thereafter held under restraint, though it managed to express a good deal of enthusiasm for the French Revolution in 1789. The Irishman John Daly Burk, after getting into trouble for his newspaper writings in Dublin, and hence emigrating to America, got into further trouble with his *New York Time Piece* in 1798. In England there was more freedom, and as late as 1798, five years after the war with France had begun, there were three London newspapers that disapproved of the government and its foreign policy, and were called "Jacobin" by their opponents. They were the *Morning Chronicle*, the *Morning Post*, and the *Courier*. The editor of the *Morning Chronicle* was the favorite target of Canning's *Anti-Jacobin*, which nicknamed him Père du Chène, "the name assumed by the Atheist Hébert, the friend and confidant"— so Canning claimed—"of Robespierre."[40]

In France the press was very active under the Directory. There were journals of royalist tone, but normally the government was most apprehensive about those of the most advanced democrats. When it closed them down they appeared under new titles, so that a fitful liberty was in fact enjoyed. Between 1792 and 1800, for example, there were half a dozen successive titles for the paper most commonly known as the *Journal des hommes libres de tous les pays*. This title alone suggests

---

[40] *Anti-Jacobin*, June 11, 1798, II, 471, and *passim*.

one ground for the Directors' concern, the affinity between the French militant democrats and "world revolution."

For the rest of the Continent—or more exactly, for Holland, Belgium, the Rhineland, Switzerland, and Italy—Jacques Godechot, in a remarkable survey, cites about a hundred newspapers by name for these years of revolution. The Dutch press was quite free under the Batavian Republic, even after the democratic coup d'état of January 1798, when opposition in other ways was silenced. On the Left Bank of the Rhine, which had not shared in the journalistic development of the rest of Germany in preceding years, there was a great outburst of newspapers during the French occupation. The Belgians, now "departmentalized" within the French Republic, had more newspapers than they had had in the Austrian Netherlands. The Swiss cantons had been very inhospitable to newspaper editors, and Bern had even forbidden the importation of the *Moniteur*, so that the Helvetic Republic brought about a journalistic as well as a political revolution. The famous educator, Pestalozzi, in September 1798 began publication of *Das Helvetische Volksblatt* under the sponsorship of the new government. In Italy, except in Venice after its transfer to Austria, the story was the same; each new republic had its variety of political journals; and even in Piedmont and Tuscany, which were not republicanized, the spring of 1799 saw a *Repubblicano piemontese* at Turin, and *Il Democratico* at Florence. Journals edited in French at Malta and in Egypt, during the French occupation, began the transmission of new ideas to the Arab world. It is said also that the first newspaper to be printed in Arabic appeared in Egypt at this time.

It is evident that this eruption of journalistic activity, partisan though it was and limited in number of readers, carried with it a revolution in political consciousness, until repressed in the various compromises which the Napoleonic order, and the opposition to it, imposed upon most of Europe.

The Republican Constitutions

Ten constitutions were written for the Sister Republics between the end of 1796 and the spring of 1799. In a survey of their provisions one may consider also the constitution drafted by Rhigas Velestinlis for a Hellenic Republic, and some of the demands of democrats in Britain, Ireland, and the United States belonged within the same school of constitutional thinking. The German journalist Lange expressed a fundamental idea very well, if in somewhat Kantian fashion.

In Germany, he said regretfully, there were rulers and subjects, but no citizens. "A man without citizenship is out of his element, like a fish out of water. He is unawakened to the feeling of his own independence, because he is kept in the perpetual status of a minor and is treated as a Thing, not as an End."[41]

Of the ten constitutions there were some in which native inspiration and authorship were very strong (the Bolognese, Cispadane, Ligurian, Neapolitan, and Batavian), others in which Frenchmen predominated in the drafting (the two Cisalpine constitutions, the Helvetic, and a document prepared for Lucca in 1799), and one, the constitution of the Roman Republic, which was simply written in Rome by four French commissioners. The constitutions were nevertheless all much alike, and all strongly resembled the French constitution of the Year III, both because the French would not have tolerated any wide departures, and because the revolutionaries from Holland to Naples drew on the same fund of ideas, and faced the same problems of "feudalism," oligarchy, church questions, and privileged classes. Even in France, where a revolutionary vanguard continued to favor the constitution of the Year I, most ordinary democrats accepted the structure of the Directory and criticized only its politics and its personnel. In the Sister Republics the constitution of the Year III was accepted without argument as "democratic."

All the constitutions began with declarations of rights, with which all but the Batavian and Helvetic incorporated declarations of civic duties, following the French model.[42] All stated the basic rights to be liberty, equality, security, and property. Equality meant equality in the eyes of the law. As the Greek draft curiously put it: "All men, Christians and Turks, are equal by the natural order." All declared sovereignty to reside in the "citizenry as a whole," which meant, as the Swiss said, that "no part or right of sovereignty could be detached and

---

[41] See the chapter, "Les constitutions," in Godechot, *op.cit.*, II, 418-50; K. J. Lange, *Deutsche Reichs- und Staatszeitung*, April 23, 1799.

[42] For the texts of the Italian constitutions see A. Aquarone, *Le costituzioni italiane* (Milan, 1958); for the Batavian constitution in French translation, D. Verhagen, *L'influence de la Révolution française sur la première constitution hollandaise du 23 avril 1798* (Paris, 1949), 59-99; for the Helvetic constitution in German and French, J. Strickler, *Actensammlung aus der Zeit der helvetischen Republik*, Bern, 1886-1940, I, 567-87; for Velestinlis' proposed draft, in Greek and French, A. Dascalakis, *Oeuvres de Rhighas Velestinlis* (Paris, 1937), 76-125. See also the discussion of the Batavian constitution in Chapter VI of the present book, and of the Bolognese, Cispadane, and Cisalpine in Chapter X. C. Ghisalberti, *Le costituzioni "giacobine" 1796-99* (Varese, 1957), gives an incomparably more substantial discussion of the Italian constitutions than does Verhagen of the Dutch.

become a private property." Native-born men became citizens at a certain age, generally twenty-one. Little encouragement was given to foreigners in these revolutionary republics. Where by the French constitution it was possible to be naturalized after seven years' residence, in the Cisalpine the requirement was raised from seven years in the first constitution to fourteen in the second. The Ligurian constitution required ten years, the Roman fourteen. The Batavians would grant citizenship to persons of foreign birth only if they had resided in the republic for ten years and could read and write Dutch. The impenetrable Swiss, in their revolutionary constitution of 1798, demanded twenty years for naturalization. It may be noted in passing that the American Federalists, in the Naturalization Act of 1798, denounced by the democrats because it raised the requirement for naturalization to fourteen years, only attempted what revolutionary democrats in Europe regarded as normal.

The Batavian, Helvetic, and first Cisalpine constitutions were more liberal than the French in granting the vote to all male citizens, though the Dutch excluded servants and bankrupts. The Cisalpine (like the French) provided for a literacy requirement to take effect twelve years in the future, and the Helvetic stipulated five years of local residence in the commune in which one voted. All the constitutions provided for voting in "primary assemblies," in which two or three hundred voters chose delegates to electoral assemblies, which in turn chose the Legislative Body and certain local officials. All this machinery went back to the first French constitution of 1789-1791. Qualifications to sit in electoral assemblies or in the legislature of the republic varied from one republic to another, but were in no case prohibitively high. Against the older aristocratic tradition of uncompensated public service all the new constitutions except the Helvetic specified salaries for both Legislators and Directors. The Batavian legislator received 4,000 florins a year, the Ligurian ten lire a day; elsewhere, as in France by the constitution of the Year III, given the uncertainty of the currency, salaries were made dependent on the price of wheat.

All the constitutions provided for a legislature in two houses, and for an executive board of five Directors, called "consuls" at Rome and "archons" at Naples. To this pattern there was no exception (since the Cispadane constitution with its three directors had never really been in effect); and even Rhigas' constitution for a Greek Republic reproduced these features. All the constitutions made much of the doctrine of the separation of powers, and contained careful provisions on the judiciary, armed forces, taxation, and management of the public finances. All except the Swiss and Dutch provided for juries in criminal cases. All gave toleration, and were essentially secular, but they varied in religious provisions; the Batavian granted complete religious equality, while the Cisalpine and Ligurian recognized a certain "predominance" of the Catholic Church.

All the Italian constitutions called for common schools of reading and writing, with teachers to be paid from the funds of the several republics. In general, when the constitutions are set in chronological order, a trend is seen toward a strengthening of the executive; and since the later constitutions were in general more dictated by the French than the earlier, a trend in French constitutional thought has been detected suggesting that, if Bonaparte had not taken power in November 1799, a stronger but less military kind of executive might have been created in France.[43] On this point there can be no certainty; and in any case the political machinery of the Sister Republics, as of France itself in these years, never worked very well, and is not the element of major interest in these new governments.

Each constitution (except those for Bologna and Lucca) began by declaring its republic to be "one and indivisible." Each then immediately proceeded to the "division of the territory." Indivisibility and division, to paraphrase Talleyrand, were two words for much the same thing. They reflected the basic structure of a unitary democratic republic. As the French constitution of the Year III, in its first article, divided the area of France into eighty-nine departments, which it listed by name, so did the constitutions of the Sister Republics. The Batavian and Roman constitutions each created and named eight departments, adopting the names of rivers or other natural features; the Cisalpine, eleven, which expansion raised to twenty; the Neapolitan, seventeen. The Ligurian constitution left the names and the exact number for subsequent legislation. The Helvetic created twenty-two "cantons," soon reduced to eighteen; the historic names were used, but boundaries were redrawn to obtain more equality between cantons, and to admit the former subject districts to cantonal status. In each republic the Legislative Body possessed the power to alter the boundaries and number of the departments. Each department, in each republic, had an elected council and a single executive officer appointed by the central government, usually called a "commissioner," as in France, but

---

[43] This was the argument of R. Guyot, "Du Directoire au Consulat," in *Revue historique*, Vol. III (1912), 11-31.

known as a "prefect" in the Roman and Helvetic republics, in anticipation of the later French usage. Within each department there were to be municipalities organized on a uniform pattern according to new legislation.

It was these features of "departmentalization" and "municipalization," as contemporaries saw, that marked the cutting edge of the revolutionary process, mowing down the dense growth of feudal, manorial, aristocratic, patrician, and old-fashioned burgher influences on the immediate local scene. It was these features also, more than the higher levels of government structure, that anticipated the political organization which in later times was to become characteristic of Continental Europe. And it was in these features that European constitutional principles in the 1790's most widely departed from those in the United States.

Nowhere is the difference between American and European "democracy" more evident. In the American union it was Alexander Hamilton who could conceive of abolishing the pre-existing states, or of dividing a big state like Virginia into several small ones so that all might be more equal. In America it was the democrats who in such matters favored the inherited order. In America, to use European terms (in which "federal" was opposite to the American "Federalist"), both the unitary and the federal principle could be accepted. The unitary principle prevailed, at the national level, in the direct election of members of the House of Representatives by electoral districts equally populous, and in the direct authority of the national courts and executive over individual citizens in certain spheres. The "federal" principle prevailed in the equal representation of states in the national Senate, regardless of size, and in the theory that the states were themselves emanations from the sovereign people, and so were not subject, like European departments, to redefinition or reshaping by any higher organs of government. In America the possessors of local power were not thought of as obstacles to democratization. Indeed, it was in the traditional township or county meeting, or in the farmhouse and the village store, that liberty and equality were believed to be most firmly rooted.

In Europe the opposite situation prevailed, with local power and influence reposing in manorial landowners, seigneurial judges, ancestrally prominent families, gild notables, and closely knit urban patriciates, all enmeshed in a variety of localized laws, customs, concessions, and privileges, and all generally reinforced by an officially recognized parish clergy, whether Protestant or Catholic as the case might be. These were the people who generally had the most influence with the mass of the population, which looked to them, rather than to upholders of new ideas, for cues as to their opinions or conduct and for initiative in public affairs.

In Europe, therefore, as already observed in preceding chapters, the democratic movement had to be unitary and centralizing, because it had to destroy before it could construct. It was in Switzerland that the greatest concession was made to the federal principle, for reasons analogous to those in America, namely the popular character of some pre-existing institutions. By the Helvetic constitution, each canton sent four delegates to the senate, regardless of size, while the lower house was ultimately to be elected in proportion to population. Elsewhere the revolutionary movement swept pre-existing collectivities into the discard. It attempted to break up and transform the local leadership structures, the local centers of influence and loyalty, the local habits of deference and subordination. It proclaimed the existence of a "people," not necessarily any pre-existing unit of human beings, and not necessarily a "nation" in the later meaning of the word—a "Cisalpine" people, a "Helvetic" people, the "people between the Meuse, Rhine and Moselle"—of which the first two declared themselves to be independent republics, the third used its newly declared sovereignty to join itself to the French Republic, within which it was organized in departments.[44] In each such case, by the declaration of sovereignty, the claims to sovereignty made by older corporate entities were denied. The change was to be deep, chemical, and molecular. Or, as in a meat chopper, the tissues and sinews of the old order were to be ground up until nothing remained but the individual particles, or citizens, who, if the figure can be tolerated, might then be re-arranged into patties (or "departments") of similar content and equal size.

The same points are illustrated, at the level of pure ideas, by Rhigas Velestinlis' proposed statute for a Greek Republic, which of course never went into effect and has remained virtually unknown. The uncertainty of meaning of both "Greek" and "people" in this document is very clear. On the one hand, Greeks are "the descendants of the Hellenes, living in Rumelia, Asia Minor, the Mediterranean islands and Moldo-Wallachia." On the other hand, the Greek people is a kind of necessary constitutional postulate, "the universality of inhabit-

---

[44] For the "people between the Meuse, Rhine and Moselle" see numerous documents in J. Hansen, *Quellen zur Geschichte des Rheinlandes im Zeitalter der französichen Revolution*, and especially iv, 315-26.

ants of the State, without distinction of religion or language, Greeks, Albanians, Vlachs, Armenians, Turks and all other races." All are equal, but Greek is the official language, because it is easiest to learn. The republic is one and indivisible, but is divided into eparchies and toparchies. These replace the existing collectivities in the Ottoman Empire. The "nation" itself is the basis of representation, *"not simply the rich and the great"* (italics in the original); the people meet in primary assemblies of from 200 to 600 voters, and elect a member of the Legislative Body for every 40,000 of the population. By such means, even more than by the Directory and other organs that the constitution then described, it was hoped that the complex realities of the Greek world, or Ottoman Empire in Europe and Asia Minor, could be dissolved or distilled into a democratic republic.

In Britain, Ireland, and America a process akin to departmentalization took the milder form of the demand for representation according to numbers, that is, of election of representatives by something approaching universal suffrage in equal electoral districts. In England this demand had accompanied the parliamentary reform movement since the 1770's; the purpose was to undercut borough-owners, entrenched town corporations, and other such entities of the English old regime. In America the principle of numerical representation was incorporated in the state constitutions issuing from the Revolution, and in the federal constitution of 1787. In Ireland in 1794, before they turned revolutionary, the United Irish drew up a proposal for parliamentary reform. By this plan "the nation, for the purposes of representation solely," that is, for election to the Irish House of Commons, "should be divided into 300 electorates . . . as nearly as possible equal in point of population." It was hoped thus to break "the vassalage of tenant to landlord," and in the long run, by overcoming the vested interests, to get rid of tithes paid to the Anglican church, reform the taxes, and make it legal for newspapers to be sold for a half-penny.[45]

In France and the states associated with it in 1798 the changes at the concrete local level, in departments and municipalities, proved more permanent than the short-lived republics within which they were first projected. After 1800 the Napoleonic administrators continued to develop and strengthen these local arrangements, which also survived the Restoration of 1814, in different degree in different countries, and so became part of the fabric of modern Europe.

[45] E. Curtis and R. B. McDowell, *Irish Historical Documents 1172-1922* (London, 1943), 237-38; McDowell, *Irish Public Opinion*, 197-98.

At the more general level of democratic constitutional doctrines a difference between Europe and the United States was already apparent. It may be recalled, from the first volume of the present book, that the American state constitutions, when they became known in Europe in the 1780's, had been the subject of much eager discussion. It does not seem (though the matter has not been thoroughly studied) that the American practice was much cited in the constitutional discussions that went on in Holland, Switzerland, or Italy after 1795. The French example had in the intervening years thoroughly overlaid the American, but in any case the American example did not meet the needs in Europe, where democratization required the building up of a central authority by which the territory could be "departmentalized." The point is borne out by a rare publication which appeared in Paris in 1798.[46] It presented in four languages—French, Italian, German and English—the constitutions of the French, Cisalpine, and Ligurian Republics, and the Declaration of Independence of the United States. Perhaps the publisher hoped to circulate it widely as a handbook throughout the new republican order. If so, its rarity today suggests that he was unsuccessful. In any case, it is to be noted that, though he did not forget the Americans, he included no American constitution.

Religion and Revolution: Christianity and Democracy

It was somewhat inconsistently observed by Tocqueville, in his great classic a century ago, both that the Revolution became a kind of religion in itself, and that in the most fundamental sense, despite appearances, it was not directed against the religion of Christianity. In calling the Revolution a religion Tocqueville did not mean, like J. F. LaHarpe in 1797, or numerous more recent historians, to stress its psychology of fanaticism or to see in it a fiercely unreasoning "faith." That it took on these qualities Tocqueville was far from doubting, but it was not in such qualities that he saw the distinctive essence of religion. It was the peculiarity of a religion, he thought, and he was thinking of Christianity, to look upon man in an abstract light, apart from the incidental peculiarity of race, class, nationality, culture, environment, or conditioning, apart from every kind of institutional framework,

[46] *Constitutions des républiques française, cisalpine et ligurienne, avec l'acte d'indépendance des Etats-Unis d'Amérique, dans les quatre langues française, anglaise, allemande et italienne* (Paris An VII). This title was advertised in the *Moniteur*, 2 Vendemiaire VII (September 23, 1798). A copy with a variant title, *Acte d'indépendance des Etats-Unis d'Amérique, et constitutions . . .* , without place or date, is at the New York Public Library.

simply as "man" in relation to other men and to the world as a whole, with all men subject to the same judgment and working out their destiny under the same higher law. It was in this universality, and the corresponding sense of an underlying equality of all human beings, that Tocqueville found the French Revolution to be like a religion, and for that reason to spread rapidly, as Christianity had spread, beyond the boundaries of any one people or country.

The evidence that Tocqueville was unable to gather confirms his insight. The religion of revolutionary republicanism spread beyond France, beyond the Sister Republics, beyond Western Europe. When Rhigas Velestinlis declared Greek and Turk to be equal in the "natural order," he echoed not only the eighteenth-century revolution of Europe but the first-century revolution of St. Paul, who had said that in Christ is neither Jew nor Greek.

With institutional Christianity in the 1790's, revolutionary republicanism or democracy collided violently in all countries. It is true that in France, between 1795 and 1801, church and state were legally "separated," since the connections set up earlier in the Revolution had been repealed; and that the new republics in Italy formally recognized Catholicism as the prevailing religion. Many Catholics nevertheless opposed the new republics as un-Christian. The new states took the view that religion was a purely private and individual matter; they generally forbade church processions and the display of religious images in the streets; they admitted non-Catholics to office; and they granted the church no powers of censorship, political representation, or other instruments of social control. There were many journalists, pamphleteers, writers of books, and speakers in the clubs who criticized or ridiculed the traditional faith; the authorities in the new republics might deplore such outbursts as impolitic, but could hardly restrain them, either in fact, or in accord with the new principles of free expression. Whatever the law, the actual state of feeling was highly inflamed. The situation was comparable, if less acute, in Protestant countries, in all of which some form of Christianity had long been established, with exceptions for most states in the United States.

The collision of republicanism with organized Christianity can be explained in large part, yet only in part, by the reasons that were apparent to Tocqueville, namely that the churches had become identified with institutions of government and social class. That the churches were dominated by worldly elites was enough to explain why revolutionaries attacked them. But it was not the whole explanation, for the

conflict went beyond the merely sociological. The Revolution represented the Enlightenment in militant form, and the Enlightenment,
popularizing and disseminating the effects of the scientific revolution,
offered no less than a new view of man and the cosmos. It was, in the
plain sense of the word, profane; it meant to "desacralize" man, as
Marcel Reinhard has said.[47] It offered a new theory of the source of
reliable knowledge, new methods of verification and certitude, a new
logos for a meaningful universe, a new picture of what had happened
in the past and would happen in the future, a new ethics in which
ideas of liberty and equality received a new application, a new idea of a
new man in a new era, a new set of the truths that should make men
free. In the churches, on the other hand, as human institutions, a good
deal of traditional human lore and learning had accumulated alongside
a more purely spiritual message. The churches had not yet come to
terms with the most indubitable findings of science. They expected
belief in matters which persons touched by the Enlightenment simply
could not accept. And they had not, in their treatment of questions of
right and wrong, made a clear distinction between what they regarded
as religious truth and what were only cultural, social, or utilitarian
values. Conflict was therefore fundamental. Between "enlightenment"
and "superstition" or between "divine truth" and "bad books," it was
hard to see any possible basis of agreement.

The whole question is difficult to deal with beyond a merely descrip-
tive level, since it involves a judgment on what constitutes a "real"
religion, and an assessment of the genuineness of inner motives and
attitudes. Whether the conflict was between religion and irreligion, or
between competing religions, or between doctrines in which the religious appearance was equally specious, is to some extent a matter of
terms.

To follow Reinhard again, the distinctive thing in religion is to
regard something as sacred; the "sacred" is that which is considered
untouchable, above any criticism, questioning, or levity, the object to
which feelings of awe and reverence are addressed. In this sense the
Revolution became in fact for many people a religion, for its most
intense partisans did regard something as sacred: the Revolution itself,
or the Republic, for some in France in 1793, or "humanity" or the
"rights of man," *les droits sacrés de l'homme*, as they were called in

---

[47] M. Reinhard, *Religion, Révolution et Contre-Révolution*, Centre de documentation
universitaire (Paris, 1960), 141. This is by far the best discussion of the whole subject. On the connection between the Revolution and religion see also the present
volume, above, pp. 127-28 and 249-55, and below, pp. 375-76.

French and other languages throughout the decade. As in any religion, the sacred object had the power to evoke self-sacrifice. It could also induce fanaticism and ruthlessness. It could preach a morality in which anything was justified by the sacred cause. In all this Reinhard, a Catholic himself, sees no difference between the Revolution and the Counter-Revolution. Indeed he finds that the displaced forces of the Old Regime were the first to identify their cause with "religion" in their theory of the throne and the altar, and that the outrages of counter-revolutionary terror were if anything worse than those of the Terror proper.[48]

Zealous republicans favored a form of deism or natural religion, professing a belief in a Supreme Being and in immortality of the soul, and in a "natural" code of moral law, in which equality and fraternity were highly esteemed. Attempts were made to organize religious services for the expression of these principles, from Robespierre's Worship of the Supreme Being on through the movement of Theophilanthropy for several years after his death. Under the sponsorship of LaRevéllière-Lépeaux, who was one of the French Directors for the unusually long period of four years, the Theophilanthropists enjoyed a measure of success in Paris, where they were allowed the use of some of the church buildings. Theophilanthropy also attracted a few temporary congregations in the Batavian Republic. It was introduced at Milan without success. There was a group calling itself Theophilanthropist in Philadelphia, led by the well-known American deist, Elihu Palmer. Probably the feeling in these movements was genuine enough, if only because new religions and optional cults are less likely to be troubled with hypocrites. But it was a feeling in which the religious element could hardly be separated from the political. Theophilanthropy, in Reinhard's words, was more anthropophile than theophile. As the Abbé Barruel bluntly put it, the religion of the Revolution was Man-Worship, and the abbé gave more food for thought as a theologian than as a historian of the Revolution. There were many Revolutionary hymns and prayers, in which, however, God was not so much invoked or implored as called upon to witness the mighty actions of the day. Far from expressing any sense of humility, or of man's littleness and dependence, they struck a note of defiance and grandeur, of pride in the Revolution and confidence in the new republican order.[49]

[48] Reinhard, 96-97, 163-85, 220.

[49] *Ibid.*, 193; on Barruel see above, pp. 251-54; on Theophilanthropy in France, A. Mathiez, *La théophanthropie et le culte décadaire* (Paris, 1903); in Holland and Italy, Godechot, *Grande nation*, II, 511, 527; in the United States, G. A. Koch, *Republican Religion: the American Revolution and the Cult of Reason* (New York, 1933).

In the use made of Christianity by many conservatives there was much the same subordination of a religious to an essentially political message. There was nothing "religious," as most people understand the word, about the future kings Louis XVIII and Charles X and many other doctrinaires of the throne and the altar. In England the *Anti-Jacobin* was very free with the epithet "atheist," but it was hardly a journal of religious concern. Its real philosophy appeared in a quatrain:

> Let France in savage accents sing
> Her bloody Revolution;
> We prize our Country, love our King,
> Adore our Constitution.[50]

It is hard to believe that some of the most insistently professing church people, at the close of the eighteenth century, saw any more meaning in the Incarnation or Crucifixion than did Maximilien Robespierre or the Theophilanthropists. At St. Paul's cathedral in London, at Holy Communion at Easter in 1800, only six persons presented themselves as communicants.[51] "Of all the pretences," said Thomas Erskine in 1797, "by which the abused zeal of the people of England has been hurried on to a blind support of ministers, this alarm for the Christian religion is the most impudent and preposterous. . . . Before this discovery of the present ministers, who had ever heard of the Christianity of the French court and its surrounding nobles?"[52]

The organized and responsible church or churches, since the days of the Roman Empire, had always called for civil peace, obedience to law, and acceptance of the civil authorities. The peculiarity now was that they continued to do so with so little compunction. Idealizing stability at a time when society had in fact become unstable, they had not yet digested the new idea of social change, and largely ignored the unsettling aspects of Christianity which had been well known in earlier times. The price paid was that, for over a century, much of the most significant moral development in European civilization, with its chang-

[50] *Anti-Jacobin*, or *Weekly Examiner*, November 30, 1797, p. 104. Note that when Canning and his friends ceased publication of their somewhat playful *Anti-Jacobin* in July 1798, another and entirely different group used the same title in publishing a journal more intentionally religious, *The Anti-Jacobin Review and Magazine*, which appeared monthly from 1798 to 1821, changing its title in 1810 to *Anti-Jacobin Review and True Churchman's Magazine*, and adding *Protestant Advocate* in 1816.

[51] H. Davies, *Worship and Theology in England . . . 1690-1850* (Princeton, 1961), 280.

[52] T. Erskine, *A View of the Causes and Consequences of the Present War with France* (33rd ed., London, 1797), 55. At least thirty-five editions in 1797.

ing sense of justice and humanity, went on outside the pale of institutional religion.

Some ideas that seem recognizably Christian were more frequently expressed by persons who did not call themselves Christians, or were in fact called atheists by their enemies. There are more Biblical echoes in Thomas Paine than in Edmund Burke, appeals to Genesis and St. Paul to argue for human equality and the unity of mankind, to prove that "every child born into the world must be considered as deriving its existence from God."[53] The idea that Jesus had been a good sans-culotte was common enough in France in 1793. The situations and the style of language often appear comical, but what seems incongruous in one set of circumstances is less so in another. Filippo Buonarroti, for example, when he was French representative at Oneglia in 1794, delivered a harangue on the occasion of the Worship of the Supreme Being. It was a long outpouring of Robespierrist and Rousseauist religious feeling. It included an apostrophe to Jesus Christ: "Philosopher-Founder of Christianity, the day of fulfilment of your wishes is not far removed. Your doctrine, disfigured by tyrants, is ours. The time has now come when, following your prediction, science and nature will join all men into a single flock. Brothers and friends, let us give thanks to the Eternal; the Revolution, new proof of his existence, is his work."[54] There are similar overtones in the writings of the radical German republican, Rebmann. When the Dutch, who as already noted were the first to do so, adopted "liberty, equality, fraternity" as a national motto, there were many who regarded it as an expression of Christian doctrine. In Switzerland, Pestalozzi attributed modern ideas of freedom and equality to the "Christian revolution" by which paganism had been superseded in ages past. "Jesus was the most fervent democrat and the most excellent philanthropist," said a Polish Jacobin in 1794.[55]

That the clergy, especially the established clergy in various countries, Catholic or Protestant, were among the chief opponents of the Revolution there can be no doubt. They had good reason, since the Revolution threatened them with the loss of their corporate status, their role in conjunction with governments, their property and tithes. Especially in France, it attacked the religion of which they were ministers, and

---

[53] *Rights of Man*, Everyman ed., 42.

[54] A. Saitta, *Filippo Buonarroti*, 2 vols. (Rome, 1950), I, 255.

[55] On Rebmann, see Hansen, *Quellen*, IV, 1004 n.; on the Dutch, J. Hazeu, *Historie der omwentelingen in vaderlandsche gesprekken voor kinderen* (Amsterdam, 1796), *passim*; on the Swiss, P. Wernle, *Der schweitzerische Protestantismus im 18 Jahrhundert*, 3 vols. (Tübingen, 1925), III, 511-12; on the Poles, B. Lesnodorski, *Polscy Jakobini* (Warsaw, 1960), 246.

exposed them to exile, insult, and persecution, which in 1798 were at their highest point since 1794. Since at the same time the clergy retained their influence with large segments of the population, the result was a fatal weakening of the revolutionary-republican movement, and a conflict between democracy and the churches that was to last for at least a hundred years. The Enlightenment, especially in its Voltairean aspect, and not without reason, had coupled a strong anti-Christianism with the prospect of worldly improvement. No fact was more damaging to the democratic revolution.

All this is so well understood, however, and so true as far as it goes, that a more exact picture must call attention to the opposite fact, that a great many Christian clergy did accept or sympathize with the Revolution, or at least with its goals and its principles. The Revolution caused differences among the clergy, as among men of other kinds. It is necessary to proceed with caution, especially in the absence of detailed studies of the Protestant clergy of northern Europe of the kind that have been made of the Catholic clergy in France and Italy. As when we find business men sympathetic to the Revolution, the question arises whether they were engaged in "legitimate" business or were merely adventurers, in an account of the clergy it is important to know (and it is often impossible) whether in favoring the Revolution they did so as Christians, as apostates, or as de-Christianized humanitarians. Thousands of French clergy accepted the constitutional church. Some became what Burke called "atheistic buffoons";[56] but of men like Grégoire, while they were clearly in a state of schism with respect to Rome, it is hard to deny that they continued to be Christians.

In Holland and Ireland the Roman Catholics and many of their clergy, having long lived under a Protestant ascendancy, were well-disposed toward revolutionary change. A great many Polish clergy supported Kosciuszko. Most of the French émigré bishops, even under the pressures of exile, refused formally to identify the cause of Catholicism in France with the restoration of Louis XVIII. In all the Italian revolutions priests played a role, nor were they all Jansenists by any means. It has already been seen how the future Pius VII accepted "democracy" in the Cisalpine Republic. Two cardinals accepted the Roman Republic of 1798, and the Archbishop of Naples accepted the Neapolitan Republic of 1799. The Archbishop of Scutari was willing to assist in revolutionary agitation in Greece. The German Catholic clergy produced a number of revolutionary enthusiasts, of whom one

[56] Burke, *Remarks on the Policy of the Allies* (1793) in *Works* (Boston, 1839), IV, 114.

of the most notorious, and probably the most thoroughly de-Christianized, was Eulogius Schneider, the terrorist of Alsace. One of the great mysteries of the period is the activity of the ex-Jesuits, men now middle-aged or older, living in various countries as individual clerics, who had belonged to the Society of Jesus before its dissolution by the Pope in 1774. Most ex-Jesuits were apparently counter-revolutionary, like Feller in Belgium, Barruel among French émigrés, or the ex-Jesuits at Augsburg who were a center of anti-revolutionary propaganda in Germany. Others went a different way: the ex-Jesuit Cérutti was a political leader and newspaper editor in the French Revolution until his death in 1792; the Polish ex-Jesuit Switkowski hailed the revolution in both France and Poland; the ex-Jesuit Bolgeni, at Rome in 1798, favored democratization of Italy; and we have mentioned the unknown ex-Jesuit from Oran, who figured in the Greek agitation.

As for the Protestant world, little seems to be known in accessible form about the views of the Dutch Reformed clergy. A significant minority of Swiss pastors showed sympathy for the Revolution in France, and welcomed the Helvetic Republic. It is always said that German Lutheran pastors were very conservative, but one hears of cases among them of sympathizers with republicanism. No bishop of the Church of England or of Ireland is remembered for anything said in favor of the Revolution across the channel, or of parliamentary reform in either island. In England, the inclination to "republicanism" was found among the Dissenting clergy, many of whom favored Unitarianism, or persons in Anglican orders who had turned Unitarian, like Thomas Fyshe Palmer, who was convicted of subversive activity in Scotland in 1793. In Scotland there were various Presbyterians outside the established Presbyterian Church—"seceders," New Lights, and others—who often belonged to democratic political clubs. It was against such people, in large part, that Professor Robison at Edinburgh, in 1797, wrote his *Proofs of a Conspiracy against all the Religions and Governments of Europe*. These New Lights in Scotland, like the Methodists in England, might or might not sympathize with the Revolution in France, but they sympathized with the upper levels of British society even less; and in their demands for itinerant preaching and for Sunday Schools, as a means of improving the condition of the people, their movement was a competitor rather than an antithesis to political radicalism. In Ireland, there were Presbyterian ministers as well as Catholic priests in the ranks of the United Irish.

In the United States the Congregationalist ministers of New England

and the Presbyterians of the Middle States expressed a good deal of tolerance for the French Revolution as late as 1795. Even Jedidiah Morse, who in 1798 raised up a scare by spreading Robison's ideas of revolutionary conspiracy, spoke well of the French Revolution in his Thanksgiving Day sermon of November 1794. As for French guillotinings and atheism, he thought that such "irregularities" should "neither be justified, nor yet too severely censured," but in the last analysis, in a great measure, "excused."[57] In short, contrary to the idea perpetuated by most historians, the American clergy were not unduly shocked by the Reign of Terror. In the French Dechristianization of 1793, which was not unlike the original Protestantism in its smashing of images and repudiation of vestments, the American ministers tended to see another awful judgment on the errors of popery. What turned them more conservative, and to more of a belief that Christianity was itself in danger from democratic excesses, was rather, it seems, the furor raised by Paine's *Age of Reason*, the spread in America of unitarianism, deism, and movements like the Philadelphia Theophilanthropy, and probably also the collapse of the customary order in such respected Protestant countries as Holland and Switzerland after 1795. In America, dependent on England for news and interpretation, these developments were seen purely as cases of French aggression, of the French Revolution degenerating into cynical conquest and exploitation; no native democratic or revolutionary impulse among the Dutch or Swiss was perceived. By the end of the decade, it was more common among the American clergy to look upon the whole European revolution of the past ten years as a sad mistake.

In many countries, however, there was enough sympathy for the new republican order on the part of contemporary Christian ecclesiastics to make it possible for some modern writers, looking back from the middle of the twentieth century, to find anticipations of Christian democracy at that time. Books of this tenor have appeared in France, Italy, Belgium, and Germany.[58]

---

[57] Morse quotes from his own sermon in his *Present Situation of Other Nations of the World Contrasted with Our Own* (Boston, 1795), 15 n. I am indebted for this item, and for the general findings here expressed, to a paper in my seminar by Mr. Gary B. Nash, "The American Clergy and the French Revolution," based on a wide reading of the sermons and writings of American clergy in the Middle and New England states.

[58] For France, the works by Reinhard, J. Leflon, A. Latreille; for Italy, V. Giuntella, "Cristianesimo et democrazia in Italia al tramonto del Settecento: appunti per una ricerca" in *Rassegna storica del Risorgimento*, XLII (1955), 289-96; for Belgium, H. Haag, *Origines du Catholicisme libéral en Belgique, 1789-1839* (Louvain, 1950); for Germany, H. Maier, *Revolution und Kirche: Studien zur Frühgeschichte der christ-*

But with the French occupation of Rome in 1798, the promulgation of the Roman Republic, and the ensuing fate of Pope Pius VI, the relations of religion and the Revolution took another downward step, which further embroiled the conflict between Christianity and democracy.

---

lichen Demokratie 1789-1850 (Freiburg, 1959). J. N. Moody et al., *Church and Society: Catholic Social Thought and Movement 1789-1950* (New York, 1953), is very slight on the earlier years.

THE REPUBLICS AT ROME AND NAPLES

Before going further in the discussion allow me to support my opinion against yours on the affairs of Italy. What you call the force of things, this general tendency towards a republican order, which you think we are unduly opposing in that country —does it exist there really? We have proof to the contrary on every side. At Milan and Rome liberty has struck feeble roots. . . . If at Naples, and especially at Turin, there is a party that calls for the Revolution, it is unfortunately only too true that a more numerous party is working to restore tyranny in the Republics already formed. . . . But even suppose that all Italy were free and united under a single government, do you think we should have nothing to fear from a nation still swayed by prejudice and exasperated against us . . . ? I persist in believing so. We would have much to gain at the moment if we could get a guarantee of the status quo *in Italy.*—TALLEYRAND TO SIEYÈS, *Paris, October* 1798

XII

THE REPUBLICS AT ROME AND NAPLES

PEACE prevailed on the Continent from the signing of the treaty of Campo Formio in October 1797 to the attack on Rome by the King of Naples in November 1798, which proved to be the opening episode in the War of the Second Coalition, and hence of the grand climax or confrontation in 1799 between the Old Regime and the New Republican Order.

But the peace was no more than a semi-peace. On the one hand, neither France nor Austria could accept the terms of Campo Formio with any finality. Each looked for bastions against the other in Switzerland and Italy. On the other hand, France with its Dutch ally remained at war with Great Britain. While British diplomacy worked to bring Continental armies back into the field against France, the French first threatened to invade England and support revolution in Ireland (while carrying on the "half-war" against American trade with Britain), then redirected their fleet and army into the expedition to Egypt, from which it was hoped that Bonaparte could counteract the growth of British power in the Indian Ocean, where both French and Dutch interests were at stake. The Egyptian campaign transferred the Anglo-French conflict to the Mediterranean and the Near East. This in turn simplified the British problem in Ireland, and gave the Bourbon Kingdom of Naples and the Russian Empire a more definite interest in the outcome of the Anglo-French war, so that the British, especially after Nelson's destruction of the French fleet at Aboukir, and the isolation of Bonaparte and his army, found it easier to recruit Continental allies, and to form the Second Coalition early in 1799.

The Politics of the Semi-Peace

In 1798 the French Directory wished to keep the peace on the Continent, the better to concentrate against England.[1] It saw in peace

[1] This section draws heavily on C. Zaghi, *Bonaparte e il Direttorio dopo Campoformio* (Naples, 1956).

also a means to build up a much needed popularity for itself, and to prevent the further growth of military glory and reputations, of which Bonaparte had already given an alarming example, and which were well understood to be a menace to the Republic. That the Directory wanted peace was agreed upon by informed observers, including some who saw in the very desire of the French for peace a good opportunity to attack them. "We want war all the more positively because the enemy persists obstinately in wanting peace."[2] So the French could read in a letter which they intercepted, written in October 1798 by a British agent at Naples to a correspondent employed by the King of Sardinia.

What made peace impossible, at the moment, was the Revolution. It was not that the French government, despite allegations to the contrary, had any set plan of revolutionary expansion. The men of the Fructidorian Directory, having dominated the Right and checked the royalist resurgence in the coup d'état of September, would have liked nothing better than to dominate, extirpate, or at least win the confidence of the revolutionary and democratic Left. They were unable to do so. The five Directors after Fructidor were Reubell, who exercised the main influence in foreign policy; Barras, whose importance was exaggerated by his ill repute; La Révellière-Lépeaux, of Theophilanthropic fame; Merlin de Douai; and François de Neufchateau. Their foreign minister was Talleyrand, whose actual influence in these years hardly went beyond the writing of magisterial memoranda. All would have preferred to subordinate the energies of revolution to the needs of government, to use the idealism of others as means to ends defined by themselves, to be able to turn revolutionary enthusiasm off and on, as an instrument of policy which they themselves determined in Paris. For such to occur, there would have to be some single centralized and disciplined party closely tied to the state, with a cohesive apparatus, both national and international, responsive to manipulation by those in authority. But this was precisely what was lacking, and not even thought of.

The Revolution in 1798, as Carlo Zaghi has said, had ceased to be the organ of a revolutionary government and had become a thing in itself. It had a life and force of its own, as threatening to the permanence of the French Directory as to the governments of the old order. In France the democrats remained very vociferous, were indignant when the Directory referred to them as "anarchists," expressed sympathy in

[2] Letter published in appendix to *Mémoires de LaRévellière-Lépeaux*, 3 vols. (Paris, 1895), III, 197.

their newspapers for democrats in other countries, and criticized the Directors for failing to support "world revolution." Had the revolutionary disturbance been French alone it would have been easier for a French government to control it. It would also have been easier to maintain the advantages of a victorious peace. But the revolutionary movement in Italy in 1798 (as in Switzerland or Ireland) was native, genuine, and significant. Patriots in those countries did not intend to serve merely as tools of French policy, to turn hot or cold as the French Directory might desire.

Many French generals, especially those in Italy, thought of themselves as representatives less of a government than of an international revolutionary movement. They were flattered and excited by the solicitations of the native patriots in the various theaters of war. Since Dumouriez' campaign in Belgium, in 1792, the problem of civilian-military relations had thrown its shadow over the French Republic. Dumouriez, in seeking to please the Belgian Statists, had been reactionary from the French point of view of 1792. The case of Bonaparte in north Italy was more equivocal. In his armistice with the King of Sardinia and repudiation of the Sardinian republicans and in the peace that he dictated to Austria at Campo Formio, involving the cession of Venice and abandonment of the Venetian revolution, Bonaparte outraged the wishes of the most vehement French and Italian democrats, who like Buonarroti believed that there could be no peace with kings. Yet it was to Bonaparte, among the French, that the Cisalpine Republic mainly owed its existence. Bonaparte had befriended Italian revolutionaries in Lombardy, and such was his prestige that the French Directory received most of the blame for not befriending them elsewhere, while the hero of the Lodi bridge was hailed as the liberator of Italy. After his departure from Italy, Italian patriots flocked about other French generals, notably Brune, Joubert and Championnet.

The persistent question, in its crudest form, was: who was to benefit from the wealth which military occupation and local revolution made available? There were requisitions to be levied, and property confiscated from former governments and from the church. Here again the question had existed since 1792. There were various possible answers. The French government might regard the occupied areas simply as temporarily conquered countries, exploiting their resources during the period of occupation for its own purposes in time of war, and keeping power in its own hands and those of its civilian emissaries. This policy required the maintenance of firm civilian control over the military, and of French control over the patriots of occupied countries—neither of which proved possible. A second course was for the French generals in the field to make fortunes for themselves (as Bonaparte had done, and Brune and others did on a lesser scale), by taking the control of army supply away from civilian commissioners from Paris, and lodging it in their own headquarters. In pursuing this line the French military commanders in Italy sought support among the most enthusiastic Italian Jacobins, with whom they combined to resist and discredit French civilians and the French Directory. At the same time, the Italian revolutionaries (like the Dutch a few years before) wanted to enjoy the fruits of revolution themselves; to set up new republics, not be exploited as conquered peoples; and while conceding a certain right of orderly requisition to the French, or agreeing to make payments under treaty, to protest against arbitrary extortion and looting, and to keep the proceeds of the sale of confiscated properties for their own purposes.[3]

Peace was made impossible by revolutionary movements beyond the French borders which the Directory could neither prevent before they happened nor repudiate afterwards. Among the Swiss there were many —Ochs at Basel, La Harpe in the Vaud, Usteri at Zurich—who wished to seize the opportunity to transform the institutions of Switzerland. In addition, Bonaparte desired French control in the upper Rhone valley (the Valais) to secure the communications between France and the Cisalpine Republic. The conservative Swiss élites looked for support to Great Britain and Austria. The Directory could not ignore the Swiss revolutionaries without favoring its own enemies. It told the Swiss, in effect, at the turn of 1797-1798 (as the Committee of Public Safety had told the Dutch in 1794) that it would be best for them to stage their own revolution; but it also ordered General Brune to stand by with French troops; and since the Swiss revolutionaries were mild men who abhorred violence and discouraged mobs, their revolution was in fact effectuated by French intervention, and the Helvetic Republic was proclaimed in March. It is discussed in the next chapter.

Meanwhile trouble brewed at Rome. Some of the Italian democrats from all parts of Italy, who for two years had congregated at Milan, moved on to Rome after the Cisalpine was established. They formed an extreme fringe to a group of permanent inhabitants of the city who desired changes in the Pope's temporal and ecclesiastical government. It is very doubtful what action the French would have taken except for one incident. It seems clear that both the Directory and the Pope,

---

[3] J. Godechot, *Les commissaires aux armées sous le Directoire*, 2 vols. (Paris, 1938).

until this incident, saw their advantage in remaining at peace with each other, the Directory because it wished to keep Austria quiet, the Pope because he knew that his territories were threatened as much by the Austrians as by the French, and as much by the King of Naples as by the revolutionary Italians. The papal government was unable, however, to keep order in the turbulent city, and on December 28, 1797, the French General Duphot was killed in a political demonstration near the French embassy. The death of Duphot seemed the more intolerable to the French because it recalled the death of Hugo de Bassville under similar conditions five years before. In the ensuing uproar it was politically impossible for the Directory to excuse the papal government. French troops from Milan occupied the city. In February the Roman Republic was proclaimed. And soon the peripatetic Italian revolutionaries, now gathered at Rome, were demanding the republicanization of Naples, which, however, was resisted by the Directory and did not occur until a year later, when a combination of a French general with Italian Jacobins brought it about.

The appearance of two more revolutionary republics in peacetime, within three months of the treaty of Campo Formio, made the preservation of peace far more precarious. The new situation was entirely unacceptable to the Austrians. It was the French hope that, by secularization and transfer of the ecclesiastical states of the Holy Roman Empire, currently under discussion at the Congress of Rastadt, the Austrians might receive German territory (as eventually they did, in the archbishopric of Salzburg and elsewhere) in sufficient amount to give up not only their claims in Belgium but their ambitions in Italy. But the Hapsburg government, willing enough to accept a radical transformation of Germany so long as it was effectuated by ordinary diplomatic means, could not accept transformations brought by revolutionary action. It could view without excessive scruple the end of the thousand-year Holy Roman Empire, the Kingdom of Poland, the ancient Venetian Republic, or the temporal sovereignty of the Pope. It could not accept anything done in the name of the Revolution reinforced by the French. The ideological issue was basic, however realistic the motives on all sides, and however much more territory, power, or strategic advantage were in the forefront.

On the one hand, so long as only a semi-peace prevailed, and so long as the French were strong, however much the Directory desired peace, and however "moderate" it might seem to the radicals, revolutionary republicanism could be expected to spread. On the other hand, Austria was already committed to the reactionary position for which it was to remain famous. Frightened by the plots discovered in Vienna and in Hungary in 1794 (and by the Greek plot of 1797, for Rhigas Velestinlis was discovered and arrested in Austrian territory, though executed by the Turks at Belgrade); facing the problem of holding down revolutionaries both in Galicia, annexed from Poland in 1795, and in Venice and Venetia, annexed late in 1797; and having in addition to tolerate the Cisalpine Republic on its own borders, the Austrians were in no mood to accept revolutionary republicanism in the Papal States, which almost adjoined Venetia, or in Switzerland, which adjoined Austria itself. Nor were the British, committed to the overthrow at least of the Batavian Republic, more inclined to accept such republicanization of Europe, which in the nature of the case would mean the ascendancy of France.

The Directory wanted peace, but peace was impossible because the French could not repudiate the revolutions in other countries, and the conservative powers could not accept them. Peace was impossible, as Zaghi puts it, "because the revolution and the fear of revolution were not in the Directory in and of itself, or in the men who composed it, but in the very existence of the Cisalpine, the Roman, the Batavian and the Helvetic Republics. As long as these republics stood, Europe could expect no peace."[4]

If in the French government there was at first some enthusiasm for the birth of new sister republics, or some belief in their usefulness, it was an enthusiasm that as the months passed was increasingly tempered by doubt. The spread of revolution to other countries excited the advanced democrats in France. The revival of democratic demands in France, the "neo-Jacobinism" which was very marked in the spring of 1798 and which in fact won a majority in the French elections at that time, gave encouragement, in turn, to the revolutionaries abroad. The French Directors quashed these democratic elections by the Floréal coup d'état in May. They did so because, like other governments, including the American government in 1798, they objected to public criticism by "democrats." They also feared the association of democracy with Babouvism. And they disliked the predilection always shown by the French extreme democrats for crusading war and foreign revolution. The pacifying of Austria was necessary to a victory over Great Britain, and to pacify Austria the extremists both of France and the sister republics had to be held in check. Such was the turbulence in these republics that Talleyrand argued, in a state paper of July, that

[4] Zaghi, 183.

except for the Batavian, which had a strength of its own and was useful against England, the sister republics were more trouble to France than they were worth, draining off French military resources for their protection, and making peace on the Continent impossible.[5] It must never be forgotten, according to another unusually candid French document, that the sister republics existed for the advantage of France, that they could not be regarded as equals, and that France wished them to possess only a certain measure of "liberty"—enough to make them dependent on France, but not enough to allow them to be hostile or neutral.[6] The realistic Directory had no faith in a mere ideological tie of republicanism to hold other peoples within its orbit.

The British government seems actually to have believed that in continuing the war with France it was working for the liberation of "Europe." No more able to brook neutrality in third parties than the French were, the British considered the conduct of Austria in making peace disgraceful, and the Prussian insistence on non-alignment extremely short-sighted. When the British sent a fleet into the Mediterranean in April they demanded its reception in the ports of powers not then at war, notably at Naples and Leghorn, and at Venice which was now Austrian. They required that Naples and Austria each furnish at least 3,000 seamen to man British warships.[7] They anticipated that the reception of the British fleet at Naples would provoke the French to attack the Neapolitan kingdom for its breach of neutrality; and that this in turn would draw Austria back into the war, so that a Second Coalition could be formed.[8] Actually, when Nelson landed at Naples, after defeating the French fleet in Egypt, the French Directory refused to be provoked, and it was the King of Naples, urged on by Nelson and other British advisers, who took the initiative in attacking the French in Rome. By this time, at the end of 1798, British hopes for

[5] See Talleyrand's long memoir of July 10, 1798 (22 Messidor An VI) in G. Pallain, *Le ministère de Talleyrand sous le Directoire* (Paris, 1891), 243-346, especially the conclusion, 345.

[6] See the "Instructions pour le citoyen ambassadeur . . . près de la République romaine," Paris, 26 Pluviose An VII (February 14, 1799), published by V. Giuntella in *Rassegna storica del Risorgimento*, xxxix (1952), 25-29.

[7] Despatches by Grenville, April 1798, printed in appendix to *Cambridge History of British Foreign Policy*, 3 vols. (N.Y., 1923), i, 580 ff.

[8] See, for example, the letter of Grenville to the American minister to Britain, Rufus King, August 3, 1798, predicting the renewal of war on the Continent when Naples received British naval ships, and remarking that all would be well if only the Continental powers showed "half the energy of the British and American people" against France. (The "quasi-war" between France and the United States was at its height at this time.) Great Britain, Historical Manuscripts Commission, *Report on the Manuscripts of J. B. Fortescue Preserved at Dropmore*, 10 vols., 1892-1927, iv, 272-73.

the liberation of Europe were fastened upon Russia. But the British, to quote a document as candid as the French one just cited, meant to serve their own interests: "to subsidize an army of Russians for British purposes . . . for a vigorous attack on Holland, for the recapture of Malta, the defense of Switzerland, the opening of the markets of South America, the capture of Brest."[9]

It is well to insist on this "realism" or traditional self-interest of the Powers. Not much wisdom is to be gained, however, from a continued emphasis on the point made by Albert Sorel, that the conflict was an evolutionary phase in the ancient rivalry of France with the Hapsburgs, or of the "Second Hundred Years' War" between France and England. Considering the kinds of friends and admirers that each Power was then able to attract, the war had a strong ideological character. The form of European institutions depended on which side should win, or on the nature of the compromises in which the conflict might be resolved. It was a war of democrats and republicans against monarchists and aristocrats.

The Roman Republic

Discontent and disorder had long been endemic in the Papal States and at Rome.[10] In this city of 150,000 governed by ecclesiastics, there had been 4,000 murders in the years from 1758 to 1769, and even before the arrival of the French army the annual number of abandoned babies was about a thousand. Since church affairs were the only industry, along with the fine arts and the training of art students, as in the French Academy at Rome, there was very little of a middle class of the kind found in northern Italy and northern Europe. After the loss of the northern legations—that is, after the revolt of Bologna and Ferrara against Rome, and their absorption into the Cisalpine Republic—the papal territories were limited to some of the most unproductive country in Italy. The rural areas were chronically distressed. A peasant

[9] Dundas to Pitt, December 9, 1798, *ibid.*, IV, 435.
[10] For the Roman Republic: V. Giuntella, *Bibliografia della Repubblica romana del 1798-99* (Rome, 1957); *id., La giacobina Repubblica romana* in *Archivio della Società romana di storia patria*, LXXIII (1950), 1-213; writings by Renzo de Felice cited below; A. Dufourcq, *Régime jacobin en Italie: Etude sur la République romaine* (Paris, 1900); L. von Pastor, *History of the Popes from the Close of the Middle Ages*, Eng. trans., 40 vols. (London, 1891-1953), XL. Pastor's account of the revolution at Rome is the fullest available in English (XL, 213-60, 289-348), but despite its merits, the original German having been published in 1933, it does not take account of the recent work of Godechot and the Italians on the subject. See also E. E. Y. Hales, *Revolution and Papacy* (New York, 1960), 91-129.

revolt broke out in 1791 near Fano on the Adriatic. The bishop reported that "complaint against the government is universal, and there are people who talk in public of the French as liberators and even go so far as to conspire for their arrival."[11] In fact, when the French did arrive, or even approach, the peasants were horrified. At Rome the poverty contrasted with the showy wealth of a few rich families, whose incomes came mostly from rural land, which they owned in such vast amounts that even a backward agriculture could support them in luxury in the city.

"There is nothing to be seen between the ranks of princes and shoemakers, and the houses are palaces or hovels."[12] Sir Gilbert Elliot, in thus describing Rome in 1794, thought that revolution was imminent, held down only by power and bigotry. He was of the school that believed revolution to be caused by ignorant and desperate men. Actually, given the relative absence of a middle class enjoying some independence from church and state (which at Rome were the same), the surprising thing is that there could be any revolutionary movement at all.

Pius VI had tried, in preceding years, to carry out reforms of the kind associated with enlightened despotism in other countries, working especially through his minister Ruffo, who, however, had made enemies among the great landowning interests, so that the Pope had had to dismiss him. In 1797 Pius authorized the sale of church-owned rural land to raise money for public purposes. Financial reform proved unsuccessful. Paper money, inflation, debt, and deficit took their toll. Historians well-disposed to the papacy agree that conditions in both state and church needed much reform. The Pope's nephew, the Duke of Braschi, involved in the grain trade by which the city was provisioned, and having in fact made a somewhat questionable fortune, was attacked in the streets by a mob; his carriage window was broken, his lackey was manhandled, and a plot to blow up his house was announced by the police.[13] Violence at Rome was frequent enough, but it was elemental and undirected.

For a revolution on the European model, there seemed to have been little intellectual preparation. At Naples and at Milan, in the preceding half-century, there had been active-minded Italian "philosophers," but hardly at Rome. Jansenism, so strong in Tuscany and in the universities of the Po Valley, had little following in the pontifical city. The influx of French clerical émigrés in the 1790's hardly favored

[11] Giuntella, *Bibliografia*, xx.
[12] *Life and Letters of Sir Gilbert Elliot first Earl of Minto*, 3 vols. (London, 1874), II, 246.
[13] Pastor, XL, 259.

an understanding of recent events in Europe. Nowhere was there a greater dread of Freemasonry, which had been prohibited to Catholics as a secret society since the days of Benedict XIV. The French Academy at Rome, which continued to be a center for Frenchmen in the city during the years of the Revolution in France, was thought of as a nest of Masonic conspirators. The famous Cagliostro, impostor, alchemist, medical quack, and self-styled founder of a new branch of Masonry (whose successes, it must be admitted, had been obtained north of the Alps), was tried and convicted at Rome in 1789, and died in a Roman prison in 1795. To conservatives there seemed to be something "revolutionary" about Cagliostro, and revolution was but another form of charlatanism. Since at Rome, as elsewhere, one of the first steps of the innovators was to break down the ghetto, and engage in fraternization with Jews, it was also believed, by some, that the Revolution was Jewish.

Nevertheless, there was a revolution at Rome in 1798, and a significant number of Romans took part in it. A detachment of the French *armée d'Italie*, now commanded by Alexander Berthier as Bonaparte's successor, arrived on February 10. The Pope was ordered out of the city, and the papal government was dissolved. On February 15, in the still unexcavated field of the ancient Forum, where a few time-worn Roman columns thrust themselves up among wandering cattle, a gathering of a few hundred patriots, assembled by Berthier, shouted its acclamations to an Act of the Sovereign People. This act asserted the independence of the Roman People, and their dedication to "truth, justice, liberty and equality"; and while specifying that the "spiritual authority of the Pope should subsist intact," abolished his temporal power.[14] A few weeks later the constitution was proclaimed. It was written, as already noted, by four Frenchmen; and it included, as article 369, a provision that, until a future contingency which never came, no law of the new republic could take effect until signed by the French military commandant. It is a curious fact, worth mentioning in passing, that no foreign government ever recognized the Roman Republic, except, in a sense, that of the United States, which was represented at Rome by an Italian who acted as American consul. Having been accredited to the "city of Rome" (not to the Pope) he decided to remain.[15]

[14] Giuntella, *Giacobina repubblica*, 2; Dufourcq, 105.
[15] Giuntella, *Giacobina repubblica*, 72, quoting Timothy Pickering's despatch of June 11, 1799, to Giovanni Batista Sartori, United States consul. Pickering refused formal recognition on the ground that the Roman Republic was not really an independent state.

Who were the Roman "Jacobins"? Some were nobles—dukes and princes—including Prince Borghese and two others of that family. Doctors were even more prominent than among "Jacobins" elsewhere; one doctor, Angelucci, became a consul or Director of the Republic. Lawyers were active as usual, including *curiali* who practiced in the papal courts. Laymen with careers in the papal administration, whose advancement was blocked by a system in which higher positions were always held by churchmen, were also numerous in the revolutionary ranks. So were persons hoping to buy at low prices properties confiscated from church bodies—a practice for which Pius VI had already set a kind of precedent. There were also various artists, including the younger Piranesi and the sculptor Ceracchi, who had twice been to America, where he had mixed with democrats in Philadelphia, been elected to the American Philosophical Society, and done the busts, still famous, of Washington, Hamilton, Jefferson, and Adams. Among the Jews of Rome, who threw off the ghetto badges on the day Berthier entered the city, there were a few who were able and willing to go into public life; several joined the new National Guard, and one was elected a senator. The Jews were, of course, at Rome, the only religious minority. The most astonishing thing about the Roman Republic is the number of Catholic churchmen who accepted it.[16]

Fourteen cardinals (of twenty-six then in the city) took part in a Te Deum at St. Peter's in February to express thanks for "liberty regained." It is true that, as the revolution grew more radical, most of these dignitaries left the scene. Nevertheless two cardinals, Antici and Altieri, reached the point of actually resigning from the Sacred College, for reasons that remain unclear, but in which a reluctance either to go into exile or to suffer from anticlerical persecution seems to have figured. Granted that opportunists and cynics were not absent from the hierarchy of the day, it is not necessary, and would probably be false, to attribute such acceptance of the republic—with its corollary, the end of the Pope's temporal sovereignty—to mere opportunism or timidity. Cardinal Chiaramonti, the later Pius VII, it should be recalled, had accepted the Cisalpine Republic in his diocese near Bologna,

<hr />

[16] On Ceracchi see Renzo de Felice, "Ricerche storiche sul 'giacobinismo' italiano: Giuseppe Ceracchi," in *Rass. st. del Risorgimento*, XLVII (1960), 3-32; on the Jews, H. Vogelstein, *Rome: Jewish Communities Series* (Philadelphia, 1940); on the Catholic clergy accepting the republic, Giuntella, *Giacobina repubblica*, 17, and R. de Felice, "L'evangelismo giacobino e l'abate Claudio della Valle" in *Rivista storica italiana*, III (1957), 196-249, 378-410. It is significant how fully de Felice agrees with Giuntella, the two being the chief experts on the subject, in a long review of Giuntella's ideas in *Rass. st. del Risorgimento*, XLIV (1957), 830-32.

itself recently detached from the papal states. He had delivered his famous Christmas homily, on Christianity and democracy, only a few weeks before his fellow-cardinals gave their blessing to the new order at Rome.

From the cathedral chapter of St. Peter's itself came a finance minister and various other officers for the new government. Various parish priests became known for "republican" sermons. Two friars put on uniforms as battalion commanders. A Dominican joined the new *Istituto Nazionale.* Most inclined of all clerics to republicanism were those called *scolopi,* an order of regulars who conducted a system of schools. Catholics who felt strongly that the church was too wealthy for its own good, or that some of its property could be better used for other purposes, or that governmental power should be wielded by laymen, had no reason, in principle, to oppose the Republic. The extent of such "Jansenist" ideas in Rome is uncertain (common as they were elsewhere in Italy), but such ideas did not have to be Jansenist. The ex-Jesuit Bolgeni was already well known for anti-Jansenist writings. He rejected in Jansenism the idea that the Church should return to an original purity. Arguing, instead, that it should change with the times and accommodate itself to modern conditions, and that spiritual and temporal power could be separated, he took the oath to the Republic, and wrote a pamphlet to explain why good Catholics could be equally loyal to the exiled Pope and to the new Republic at the same time.[17]

It is agreed, by the two best recent authorities on the subject, that the desire for church reform and for political and administrative modernization were both fundamental in the revolution of 1798. It is agreed that the "Jacobin" clergy, while surprisingly numerous, were a minority among ecclesiastics in Rome. To what extent they were early "Catholic Democrats," to what extent the "Jacobin Evangelicals," the *evangelici giacobini,* in whom deism and Theophilanthropy were often mixed with appeals to the Bible, were or were not "in the bosom of the Church," or were or were not Jansenists, or even influenced by Calvin, are matters best left to Italians to discuss and to Catholics to define. It is clear that some of their ideas waited a long time for realization. In particular, the Roman Question, or question posed by the temporal sovereignty of the Pope, while first presented in actual politics by the Republic of 1798, was not settled until the twentieth century.

[17] A. Quacquarelli, *La teologia antigiansenista di G. V. Bolgeni, 1733-1811* (Mazara, n.d., about 1950), 85-93.

The Republic, in its life of a little over a year, never took on even the degree of solidity enjoyed by the Cisalpine. It was never more than a project, and even the zealot Mangourit, when he passed through, reported that it had organized nothing but anarchy. It lived in the shadow of imminent, and later actual, war. It was divided from the beginning by incurable fissures, between French and Italians, between Romans and revolutionaries from other Italian states, between civilian and military authorities, between governing personnel and journalistic extremists, between Rome and the outlying parts of the former papal dominions. Territorial consistency was minimal; an abortive "Ancona Republic" had to be brought in by force, and the "departments," as drawn by the constitution, proved recalcitrant village republics, when they were revolutionary at all.

Hardly had the French arrived, and begun to requisition housing, jewelry, cash, and miscellaneous property, when a mutiny broke out against the troop commander, Masséna. The men and their lesser officers objected to being unpaid, and to lacking lodging and proper rations, while the military higher-ups, by abuse of the requisitions, lived at ease or laid by little fortunes for themselves. (There was a saying at Rome that nothing was so honest as a French soldier, from private to captain inclusive.[18]) While the troops were out of control, revolt broke out among the populace on the right bank of the Tiber, who hated the French, loved the Pope, and engaged in anti-Semitic outbursts. Discipline was restored to the army, and obedience to the population, when a few of the latter were shot by a firing squad. A few weeks later the rural areas fell into insurrection and "brigandage," especially in the most civilized regions along the main road from Rome to the north, where the repeated passage of soldiers made the requisition and pillage especially burdensome. It is estimated that in the end the French levied some 70,000,000 francs in the Roman Republic. They used these sums (apart from illicit private enrichment) in part to support the troops in Rome, in part to supply and pay the main body of the army at Milan, and in part to finance the expedition to Egypt.

When the government was set up the five Consuls, or executive, tended to take sides with the French civilian commissioners, while the two legislative chambers, and especially the lower house or Tribunate, found friends among the French soldiers and generals. The latter were also favored by most of the journalists, many of whom were not Romans, but migrants from the Cisalpine or refugees from Naples,

18 Godechot, *Commissaires*, II, 189.

like Vincenzo Russo, the editor of the *Monitore di Roma*.[19] Patriots divided between moderates and extremists. Disillusionment set in very soon, with the moderates aghast at radical demands, and the radicals impatient that so little progress was being made.

"I am tired of politics," wrote a moderate as early as March 29. "I would like to go somewhere where I could hate men in peace, and die." The more ardent democrats were well aware that democracy had not yet been gained. "When people tell me that Rome is democratized," wrote one of them in the *Monitore*, "I answer that the horses are more democratized than the people. These poor beasts, which were accustomed to the grave, majestic pace of the empurpled tyrants [the cardinals] or the Roman matrons, must now run at a brisk trot or furious gallop, with the plainest harness, under the democratic whip of the French warriors."[20]

The more advanced Jacobins, especially in the clubs and the newspapers, called for revolution in Naples, or wanted all Italy consolidated into one unified republic. Many were from other parts of the country, and they wanted all Italian states of the Old Regime to be dissolved. Consuls and other officials, put by the French in the government, were by contrast moderate Jacobins. Natives of Rome, by the Revolution they meant certain practical reforms in taxation, administration, and tenure of office in their own city. As in other revolutionary republics, primogeniture and entail (*fidecommessi*) were abolished, and there were serious discussions of the penal code and of public education. But the governing personnel had no interest in a big, vague unified Italy in which they would be politically lost. The French Directory were positively set against the idea of a unified Italy, which, if established successfully, would become independent of, or even hostile to, France. The Directory and its civilian commissioners therefore sided with the Roman moderate Jacobins, and were attacked by the radicals for betraying the Revolution.

Advanced Jacobins denounced the rich absentee landowners, and called for a system of more equal property in the hands of small owner-farmers. Vincenzo Russo, in his *Monitore,* gained a reputation for utopian radicalism by demanding what is now called land reform. Some of the French could see the wisdom of such a program, for the small owner-farmer was common enough in France; but fear of the agrarian law or of Babouvism (which had proposed to abolish prop-

---

[19] Russo's *Pensieri politici* and other writings from the *Monitore di Roma* are reprinted in D. Cantimori, *Giacobini italiani* (Bari, 1956), 255-398.

[20] Giuntella, *Giacobina repubblica*, 8 and 20.

erty, not divide it) made it hard for the French to sympathize very warmly. The matter reached the stage of serious discussion in the Tribunate but was blocked by the moderate Jacobins of the Senate and the Consulate. The latter were in many cases landowners themselves, and were buying up land confiscated from the Church. It has been found that, of the 400 known purchasers of Church land in the Roman Republic, about 70 were persons occupying a place in its government. Most others were of the agricultural or mercantile possessing classes; and the total effect of the land redistribution was to produce more, rather than less, concentration of land ownership.[21] It is conceivable, and has been argued, that a serious land reform might have attached the peasantry to the Revolution; but it seems very doubtful that legislation of this kind, with the accompanying legalisms, delays, and confusion, could have overcome the hatreds aroused in the countryside by requisition and looting, and by attacks on religion.

At first, to repeat, persons feeling themselves to be good Catholics had accepted the Republic. Nothing in the constitution or the official republican philosophy questioned the spiritual authority of the Pope. Some Jacobins were religious, some not. In May, some of the French troops were relieved by the Polish Legion sent down from Milan. The Poles, fierce republicans in other respects, were also very positive Catholics. They swarmed to the shrines of the city with cries of devotion to the saints and the Holy Father. These exhibitions of piety aroused the disgust of advanced Jacobins and Jacobin Evangelicals. Efforts were renewed to wipe out superstition. In July there was a great demonstration that recalled scenes in France in 1793. Before an altar of Liberty a miscellany of cardinals' hats, titles of nobility, minutes of the Inquisition, and the golden book of the Capitol were committed to flames; and an architect named Barberi, in addition to breaking a cross and throwing it in the fire, went on to debaptize himself by the simple expedient of washing his hair.[22]

In this overcharged atmosphere, as the advanced wing of the Italian Jacobins loudly threatened the Kingdom of Naples, the governments of Naples and Austria bided their time until all the revolutionary republics in Italy might be destroyed. For a while it seemed that Austria would recognize the Roman Republic (taking Bologna and Ferrara for itself), if only the French would abandon the Cisalpine. Even the most moderate and upper-class Italian republicans, even Melzi d'Eril,

---

[21] R. de Felice, *La vendita dei beni nazionali nella Repubblica romana del 1798-99* (Rome, 1960).
[22] Dufourcq, 241.

the Cisalpine representative at the Congress of Rastadt, were dismayed by signs of conservatism in the French Directory (as in the Floréal coup d'état), and alarmed by the thought that the French, to prevent a renewal of war on the Continent, might abandon them to the Hapsburgs. The minister of the Ligurian Republic in Paris, on hearing of the riotous demonstration against Bernadotte in Vienna, believed that Austria planned an early attack in Italy. He drew the only conclusion possible even for a moderate: "We and all the other democratic republics," he reported to Genoa, "will be unable to avoid making common cause with France against the common enemy."[23]

In September it was learned in Italy that the British had destroyed the French fleet at the mouth of the Nile. Bonaparte with the best of the French army was cut off. Nelson docked at Naples on September 23. He was a pronounced anti-Jacobin, and his enthusiastic monarchism made him a warm advocate even of the Bourbon monarchy at Naples. He was hailed as a saviour, and his officers enjoyed a series of fetes and triumphs. Nelson's arrival reinforced other British influences by which the royal court had long been surrounded, since the king's chief minister was an English expatriate, Acton, and the queen's confidante was the famous English adventuress, Emma Hamilton, wife of the British ambassador. While both the British and the Austrian governments warned against premature action, and preferred to wait until the French attacked Naples, which they stubbornly refused to do, Nelson and the English colony persuaded King Ferdinand to force the issue. The chaos at Rome, and peasant insurrection in the Roman departments, seemed to offer an irresistible opportunity, especially since, as Sir William Hamilton wrote to Grenville, Rome was defended by "not more than 3,000 Poles and French."[24] The Neapolitan troops were commanded by an expert borrowed from Austria, General Mack—a soldier much dogged by misfortune, who had been worsted in Belgium in 1794, and was to surrender to Napoleon in 1805 at the famous capitulation of Ulm.

Mack with his Neapolitans invaded the Roman Republic on November 23. Pushing through without opposition to Rome itself, they tore up the trees of liberty, and King Ferdinand appeared in person to promise the restoration of order and true religion. While panic and consternation gripped the Roman republicans, the French general, Championnet, gathering a force much smaller than Mack's, soon turned

[23] Zaghi, 106, 180, 236.
[24] Camb. Hist. Br. For. Policy, I, 583.

the tables. By a movement equally speedy in the reverse direction, he put Mack to flight, and in January 1799 the French, along with Polish and Cisalpine forces, entered the city of Naples, against the fierce but unorganized opposition of the *lazzaroni*, or populace. The king and queen fled abruptly to Sicily, taking off with 50,000,000 gold francs' worth of valuables and their English friends in Nelson's ships to Palermo. The Neapolitan Bourbons, like the House of Orange, made themselves unabashedly into wards of the British government.

Meanwhile the British signed a treaty with Russia. The Ottoman Empire, at war with France since the invasion of Egypt, prepared to send Turkish forces to Italy. The Austrians, protesting that the time was not ripe, nevertheless soon joined in. The Second Coalition had been formed. The general crisis of 1799 will be described at the end of this book.

At Rome, the invasion, the renewal of war, and the elation of momentary victory all contributed to radicalize the republic. There were forced loans and attempts at economic controls. Since the allied powers claimed to be fighting a crusade for Christianity and the papacy, the handfuls of violent anti-Christians came to the fore as the firmest defenders of the Roman Republic. Their attempts to make political use of a church in which they did not believe only turned Christians against them. The argument that Christianity was democratic, or democracy Christian, began to sound very hollow. Catholic democrats, believers in the separation of church and state, who had at first favored the Roman Republic, were appalled at the treatment accorded the Pope by his captors, especially after the war began—moved at the age of eighty-two from city to city in Italy, increasingly forbidden to see subordinates or advisers, taken through the snows of the Alpine passes to France, and dying there in seclusion. On the other hand there were those, more numerous among the French than the Italians, who could view these events with a positive satisfaction, believing that with the death of Pius VI there would never be another Pope of Rome at all. They found it eminently fitting that in 1799, as the eighteenth century came to a close, in which so much else that was ancient and benighted had disappeared, an end should also be put to the Catholic Church. It seemed that the *infâme* had at last been crushed.

The occupation of Naples raised a new crisis between the French Directory and its own generals supported by the Italian patriots. The Directory was averse to the establishment of another republic in Italy. It estimated that, by direct military occupation, it might raise as much as 200,000,000 francs in the Kingdom of Naples, and at the same time be free of troublesome commitments at a future peace conference.[25] Championnet resisted his orders, refused to deal with the civilian commissioners from Paris, and consorted with Italian patriots who followed him from Rome to Naples, and with those at Naples who welcomed him upon his arrival. In exploiting the resources of Naples, he meant to favor the Italian revolutionaries, his own soldiers, and himself. Remembering Bonaparte and the founding of the Cisalpine, he declared that he had overthrown the Neapolitan monarchy, not to serve the ends of civilian graft and corruption, but to advance the liberation of Italy and mankind.

A Neapolitan Republic was thus proclaimed in January 1799.

The Neapolitan Republic

The Neapolitan Republic lasted less than six months. Farthest out and most briefly seen of all the satellites of Paris, it was by no means the dimmest, since it has always shone with some magnitude in historical literature. It produced the best remembered book to come out of the Italian *triennio*, Vincenzo Cuoco's *Saggio storico*, of which more will be said. At the end of the nineteenth century Benedetto Croce, before turning to the philosophy of history, began his career by writing history itself, and chose the *Rivoluzione napoletana* for his subject. The idyl of Lord Nelson and Lady Hamilton, dallying in Mediterranean palaces while war raged about them, kept an interest in these events alive in England. Of all the sister-republics the Neapolitan is apparently the only one on which a book has ever been written in the English language.[26]

The Kingdom of Naples, embracing the southern half of the Italian peninsula and the island of Sicily, had belonged since 1735 to a branch of the Spanish Bourbon family, represented at the end of the century by King Ferdinand IV. His queen, Maria Carolina, was a Hapsburg,

[25] On this matter, and the conduct of Championnet, see Godechot, *Commissaires*, II, 254-74.

[26] V. Cuoco, *Saggio storico sulla Rivoluzione napoletana del 1799* (Milan, 1801), reprinted at Bari, 1913, from the second edition of 1806; B. Croce, *La Rivoluzione napoletana del 1799* (Bari, 1926), first published about 1895; C. Giglioli, *Naples in 1799: an Account of the Revolution of 1799 and the Rise and Fall of the Parthenopean Republic* (London, 1903). For somewhat more recent works see N. Rodolico, *Il popolo agli inizi del Risorgimento nell'Italia meridionale, 1792-1801* (Florence, 1925); A. Lucarelli, *La Puglia nel Risorgimento; II, La Rivoluzione del 1799* in Commissione provinciale di archeologia e storia patria di Bari, *Documenti e monografie*, XIX (Bari, 1934); C. Cingari, *Giacobini e Sanfedisti in Calabria nel 1799* (Messina, 1957).

one of the many royal offspring of the Empress Maria Theresa, and hence a sister to the late Marie Antoinette of France, and an aunt to the reigning Austrian Emperor, Francis II. The loathing of the royal pair for the French Revolution was implacable, and exceeded if possible only by their dislike of republicans in their own country.

Naples and Palermo were among the largest cities in Europe, huge aggregations of the underemployed and the wretchedly poor, locally called *lazzaroni*, for whom the future held no promise since population was far out of proportion to economic development. Many small and ancient cities dotted the kingdom. As in the Papal States, and in contrast to northern Italy, the rural land was worked by primitive methods, but it was owned in large tracts by men who lived in Naples or the smaller cities, of which they formed the hereditary patriciates. Something remained of the manorial and seigneurial systems, but the condition of the kingdom was not especially "feudal." In the landowning classes, along with an older nobility, were numerous persons who in recent generations had applied the profits gained in the law, government office, or trade, to the acquisition of rural estates, which they used for income without troubling to develop them. Between peasants and townspeople, or between the lower and upper classes in the towns, there was less contact than in northern Italy or western Europe. Peasants and *lazzaroni* were not only illiterate, but spoke no language except dialects which varied from place to place, so that they were shut off from the great world, and even from each other. From the outside world they were reached only by their priests, to whom they were likely to be devoted without actually being very religious. Isolation, poverty, and social disorganization were so great, according to the most recent historian of Calabria, that the peasants had little awareness of belonging either to the Kingdom of Naples or even to the Catholic Church.

The educated classes—those of the higher clergy, the professions of law and medicine, and the circles of the newer Enlightenment which was well represented in the cities—were drawn from the landowning families, among whom the divisions between old nobility and newer gentility were somewhat blurred. With a good deal of leisure and few nagging problems, many of these people favored the most altruistic principles of the day. Nowhere was the sympathy for revolution more disinterested or more idealistic. Given the social realities in the Kingdom of Naples, there was little ground for a self-admiring conservatism, and under a dynasty of such recent date and unedifying deportment the upper classes were not fervidly royalist.

Revolutionary agitation began at least as early as 1792. At that time a French naval squadron had visited the Bay of Naples, and there had been much excited fraternization between French officers and sailors and inhabitants of the city. Two clubs had been formed, and it was in this case a fact that Masonic lodges became conspiratorial centers. The government, which as recently as 1789 had attempted, in recognition of the *lumi del secolo*, to break up the privileged oligarchy at Brindisi by making all its citizens "equally subject to the laws and taxes,"[27] now became fearful of anything suggesting modern enlightenment. Government and clergy combined to keep out a knowledge of French newspapers, French books, French ideas, and French events. Repression became more severe after the dethronement and execution of the French king and queen, and after Naples entered the First Coalition. Large elements of the educated classes, disapproving in Naples as elsewhere of the war against France, became increasingly contemptuous of a government that lived in terror of any public discussion, and even of what its subjects might be privately reading or thinking in their houses. Official prohibitions were countered by secret organizations, which in turn led to arrests and imprisonments. In the years from 1794 to 1798 in Calabria alone, the "toe" of Italy, 493 persons were prosecuted for "crimes of opinion." Hundreds of Neapolitan patriots went into exile, first to France, then in 1796 to the Cisalpine Republic and in 1798 to Rome, which they regarded as a final stage in their return.

When Championnet entered Naples he brought a band of these exiles with him, and was joyously welcomed by patriots who had suffered at home in the preceding years. With the king's ignominious abandonment of the mainland, and the breakdown of the royal government, a great many others who were not really "Jacobins" rallied to the Republic. Thus the eighty-eight-year-old Archbishop of Naples, Cardinal Zurlo, despite all that had happened by this time at Rome, advised acceptance of the new order; and when the miraculous liquefaction of the blood of St. Januarius took place at the cathedral with only minor irregularity, it was given out that God favored the new regime.

Neapolitan republicanism was indigenous and predominantly upperclass. It was indigenous in the sense that hardly any "outsiders," from

[27] Rodolico, 20, quoting an official document of 1789.

other parts of Italy, took part in the Neapolitan Republic, as they had done in the Cisalpine and the Roman. Except for returned exiles like Vincenzo Russo, who had been active in the disturbances elsewhere in Italy, and except for a few intellectuals of enlarged outlook, the South Italian "Jacobins" had little idea of a unitary all-Italian state or nation. The Cisalpine troops who came in with the French were regarded as foreign. North Italian interference or co-operation was not desired.

The high social standing of the republicans is beyond question. Two princes, Caracciolo and Pignatelli, four marquises, a count and a bishop were among the 119 executed as Jacobins in the Bay of Naples before the year was out.[28] To observers like Lord Nelson and Cardinal Maury this infection of the aristocracy by republican principles was the most intolerable and disgusting aspect of the whole affair, and was in fact taken by them as another sign of Italian degeneracy.[29] Very active in the revolution also, after the French arrived and the royal authority crumbled in the provinces, were the town-dwelling rural landowners of the cities of Calabria and Apulia, a *borghesia* that performed few functions of a "bourgeoisie," but which made up most of the educated class outside the capital. To these were added the intellectual and professional elites—doctors, lawyers, pharmacists, university graduates, professors, students, writers, and a surprising number of the clergy. In Apulia, the "heel" of the peninsula, the bishops at first accepted the republic; if they did so primarily to keep the peace, and in deference to "established" authority, they were at least not yet deterred by any systematic conservatism or ideology of the throne and the altar. In southern as in northern Italy there were Jansenists who welcomed a chance for church reform, or even for a kind of spiritual renewal on whose desirability Christians and secular humanitarians could agree.

The weakness of the Republic, which was as apparent to the philosophical idealism of Croce as it has been to more sociologically minded historians, lay precisely in this élite character of its leadership, and in the fact that the leadership never had enough support either from the French or among the mass of its own people. The French Directory

---

[28] Names and occupations of the 119 are listed in Cuoco, 369-75.

[29] On Nelson, see below; Maury wrote in October 1799 to Louis XVIII that "not eight noble families preserved themselves from the revolutionary contagion" and that "revolutionary fanaticism [in Naples] has been more ardent, atrocious and universal among the clergy and nobility than in France itself, so that we are at least under the unexpected obligation to this horde of cannibals of now no longer being the lowest among civilized nations. . . . Ninety-year-old priests, on being hanged, have preached democracy and invoked the French at the steps of the gallows." *Correspondance et mémoires du Cardinal Maury* (Lille, 1891), i, 206 and 233.

did not favor the Republic; Championnet was soon recalled to Paris; there were never more than a few thousand French soldiers in Naples, and most of these, by May 1799, were recalled to the Po Valley to meet the threat of Austrian invasion in the War of the Second Coalition. Left thus to themselves after three months, the Neapolitan republicans, unable to recruit an army of their own, had to face a population which at worst was in armed rebellion and at best had no understanding of what they were trying to do.

The best of the republicans genuinely desired to improve the lot of the common people, to give them schooling and education, to endow them with the benefits of liberty and equality, to impart to them the dignity of citizenship in a decent country and some share in the advantages of European civilization. Typical of these attitudes was Eleonora de Fonseca Pimentel, soon to be remembered as one of two women executed at Naples for republicanism, a high-minded and generous soul who edited the *Monitore napoletano*. Her view was that "the people distrust the patriots because they do not understand them."[30] She proposed, therefore, that civic missionaries be sent into the countryside, and that writings be made available to the people in dialect, to explain the true nature and aims of democracy; and this was in fact done when, for example, a certain priest published, in dialect, *The Republic Justified by the Holy Gospel*. But, as Croce observed, the good Eleonora was in fact mistaken; the people understood only too well, and refused to agree with the patriots because they distrusted them. They distrusted them in part as coming from a distant and pretentious class of society, like modern slum dwellers viewing volunteer settlement workers with suspicion. They associated them with Frenchmen, civilian and military, who were draining the meagre resources of the country. Ignorant and superstitious though they were, they understood that these well-dressed patriots, with their cultured ways, were in many cases precisely those absentee owners of rural land, living in cities and holding country life in contempt, who had for years been encroaching on village commons and building up vast estates to be worked by an agricultural proletariat. Vincenzo Russo, who had called for a division of great estates in the Roman Republic, could get even less attention for this idea in Naples than in Rome. It is true that he befogged the issue with other sentiments then favored by democrats in all countries, such as that public officials should serve for little or no pay. The Neapolitan legislators enacted "the abolition of feudalism," and they did away with primo-

[30] Croce, 36.

geniture and entail, though the Republic did not last long enough for these measures to take effect. Basically, they did nothing about the land question. Abject poverty remained the main social problem; the mass of the people were hardly mistaken in seeing no advantage to themselves in the fine ideals of political liberty, freedom of thought, and strict equality before the law with which the republicans sought to attract them.

The fall of the Italian republics in 1799 was part of the general European counter-revolutionary offensive described below in Chapter XVII. It is appropriate to note here some distinctive elements in the débâcle at Naples—the constructive efforts of the man by whom Naples was recovered for the monarchy, Cardinal Ruffo; his repudiation by the anti-republican extremists; and the consequent fate of the leading Neapolitan "Jacobins," who were not the only Jacobins in Europe to be summarily disposed of in 1799, but who were subjected to an especially dramatic end.

Ruffo, who came from a noble Neapolitan family, had been a reforming minister of Pius VI in the Papal States in the 1780's, and though not a priest had been made a cardinal in token of his services at the time of his dismissal from office. He had tried in the Papal States, without success, to find means by which the peasants might obtain secure tenures of small plots of land. He had more of a sense of the actual social problems of the country, as well as more experience and capacity in administration, than the republicans of either Rome or Naples. In January 1799 he had advised Ferdinand IV not to desert the mainland, but had nevertheless followed him to Sicily. In February he landed in Calabria with only eight companions, and was soon able to combine the armed insurrectionary bands, which he found already in existence, into a half-organized host called the Christian and Royal Army. Since this host was sometimes also called the Army of the Holy Faith (San Fede) the ensuing movement has been known as San Fedism, and represented as an outbreak of religious fanaticism. That it was basically a religious movement is open to question; at least Cardinal Zurlo expressed disapproval at the invasion by Cardinal Ruffo, and many priests were later punished for resistance to the *Armata Cristiana*.[31] Nor was the movement a peasant uprising only, since upperclass townspeople sometimes assumed command of local troops, using the occasion to seize the property of fellow-towns-

---

[31] Fifteen clerics were among the 119 executed at Naples and listed by name in Cuoco; Lucarelli, p. 37, names twelve more for Apulia, as a mere sample from the official register.

men who could be discredited as "Jacobins." It was upon the peasants, nevertheless, that Ruffo was able to rely for a mass following, and he rallied them the more easily because he gave ear to their grievances. He allowed them to reoccupy common lands, abolished certain taxes and unpopular local offices, and declared the "abolition of feudalism." When he requisitioned food for his army he tried to pass the burden to the absentee landlords, and he issued a good many pardons to broaden the basis of his support. But the swarm that swept over the country was under no control, and it descended with fury on cities where the republicans had come into power; at Paola in Calabria numerous Jacobins were killed, and all the upper-class homes, noble and bourgeois, were looted. In May Ruffo reoccupied the city of Naples, and besieged some of the last and most prominent of the republicans in the fortress of St. Elmo. Ferdinand IV had instructed Ruffo to offer no terms. "We wish no mercy shown to any rebel against God and me."[32] Ruffo, nevertheless, in the king's name, gave his promise to the republicans at St. Elmo that if they surrendered their lives would be spared. They surrendered on this understanding.

Ferdinand IV and Maria Carolina considered Ruffo entirely too indulgent to traitors. The English at their court were of the same opinion. Nelson, whose fleet now re-occupied the Bay, believed that countries should be governed like a British warship—by rewards and by punishments. The queen was consumed by feelings of vengefulness toward her own capital. *"Enfin ma chère Milady,"* as she wrote to Lady Hamilton in her international French, *"je recommande à Milord Nelson de traiter Naples comme si ce fut une ville rebelle en Irlande."*[33] Nelson pressed for severity, and if there was any odium in the execution of Jacobins the king and queen were willing enough to let him bear it. The king, still at Palermo, gave orders that the recognition of Ruffo's terms of surrender should be left to Nelson's judgment. A man of stern duty, like Captain Vere in *Billy Budd*, Nelson also believed that the saving of civilization from Ireland to the Straits of Messina required the condign and conspicuous execution of Jacobins. Discussing the terms of the surrender with Ruffo, "that swelled up priest," he was shocked when Ruffo referred to the rebels as "patriots"—"what a prostitution of the word!"[34] To his own subordinate, Foote, he observed: "Your news of

[32] Ferdinand IV to Ruffo, Palermo, April 11, 1799, quoted at length in H. C. Gutteridge, *Nelson and the Neapolitan Jacobins: Documents Relating to the Suppression of the Jacobin Revolution at Naples*. Printed for the Navy Records Society (London?, 1903), 38.

[33] *Ibid.*, 213.

[34] *Dispatches and Letters of Vice Admiral Lord Viscount Nelson*, 7 Vols. (London, 1845), III, 334, 387.

the hanging of thirteen Jacobins gave us great pleasure; and the three priests, I hope [will] dangle on the tree best adapted to the weight of their sins."[35] Nelson, in short, carried out King Ferdinand's wishes with complete personal satisfaction. The prince and former admiral, Caracciolo, was hanged by his order from the yardarm of the warship *Minerva.* He was one of 119 republicans put to death at Naples in the following months.

The Neapolitan Republic expired in an anarchy which in some parts of the country sank into habitual brigandage. The Bourbon monarchy was restored at a ruinous cost: the intellectual élite had been wiped out or silenced, a monarchy once enlightened became notorious for its imbecility, and the king boasted that he would henceforth rely on his faithful *lazzaroni*, the most ignorant and destitute among his people. Loudly complaining that republicans were tools of the French, the monarchy at Naples depended, until its final collapse in 1860, on British, Austrian, or any other foreign support that it could obtain against its own subjects.

One of the survivors of the Neapolitan revolution was Vincenzo Cuoco. He had played a minor role, but was condemned to twenty years' exile and went to France, from which he returned to Italy in 1801 to enjoy a career of some prominence in the Napoleonic states. In 1801 he published his *Saggio storico sulla Rivoluzione napoletana.* It was less a history than a series of reflections on history. Its message was that the revolution at Naples had failed because it was "passive" and "abstract." He extended the same criticism to the whole Italian movement of the 1790's, and, pursuing his reflections, attributed the quality of excessive "abstraction" to the French Revolution itself. His work thus came to represent in Italy, in a mild way, the kind of thinking that Burke expressed in England and which the emergence of the historical school of jurisprudence was soon to express in Germany. Indeed, the *Saggio* was translated into German in 1805. "Abstraction" in this case meant the argument, already long familiar in 1801, that the ideas of the

---

[35] *Ibid.*, 376. The role of Nelson at Naples in 1799 has been much debated. Croce in 1896 (*Rivoluzione napoletana*, xxi) called for an intensive study, which was supplied by F. Lemmi, *Nelson e Caracciolo e la Repubblica napoletana, 1799* (Florence, 1898). Lemmi concluded, 89, that "while many causes may have worked together to push Nelson into the iniquities by which he stained himself at Naples in 1799, the principal cause must be sought in his education, in his proud and imperious temperament and in his political passions and convictions." Gutteridge, *op.cit.*, 1903, reached a more favorable judgment, but though publishing and reprinting many documents, he refrained from including many in which Nelson's "political passions" were apparent, and which had already been published in the *Dispatches* of 1845, from which a few examples are quoted above.

patriots were too general, involving conceptions of a universal liberty or equality, or humanity, or constitutionalism, or asserted rights, that had no relation to practical issues or circumstances, or to the differences among nationalities and national cultures. By the "passivity" of the Italian revolution Cuoco meant that it had been brought in by the French, or at least that the Italian republicans had been hardly more than enthusiasts responding to a French stimulus and entirely dependent on French decisions. Under nineteenth-century conditions Cuoco's view became part of the conventional wisdom.

Italian historians of all schools, for the last half-century, while differing with each other, have found it necessary to refute Cuoco. They have argued that the Revolution of the *triennio* was neither as passive nor as abstract as it seemed to the disillusioned exile. The reader of the preceding chapters of this book can judge for himself. It would seem that the Italians, far from being passive, often pushed the French further than they wished to go. Passive the Italian republics were in the sense of dependency on French power; it was the French defeat of 1799 that destroyed them, and Napoleon's victory at Marengo in 1801 by which, in north Italy, republicanism was restored. But the Italian republicans were not so "passive," or so merely pro-French, as to be incapable of revolt against the French in 1799, as will be seen. The anti-French movement in Italy, by 1799, was confused by the fact that counter-revolutionaries and revolutionaries, while detesting each other, could agree in opposing the French Directory. As for "abstraction," it must be said that something of this quality must enter into any conception of law and justice, and that the ideas of Italian republicans, given the real conditions of the Italian old regime, had enough concrete relevancy to be very uncomfortable to partisans of the old order.

At least three causes for the failure of the Italian republics can be seen, more important than their alleged passivity and abstraction. Most important was the lack of common ground between town and country, arising from the old Italian tradition of urbanism and the city-state. Lack of rapport between townsman and peasant weakened republicanism in north Italy; positive hostility between them made it impossible in the center and south. Secondly, there was the religious question. Enough has been said to show that there was no simple conflict between the Church and the Revolution. Many good Catholics were democrats and republicans; but their efforts were discredited by the extremists of both sides, by a political religiosity which denounced the Revolution as wicked (a view not unknown in Protestant countries) and by the much publicized insults and onslaughts of those who thought the whole Christian religion ridiculous. Thirdly, the French, still engaged in a war for the preservation of their own republic, had more interest in exploiting the wealth of the Italians than in sharing republicanism with them. There was nothing new in the exploitation of countries occupied in time of war, but the French conducted it with thoroughness and persistency, through agents sometimes lacking in personal honesty, in a turmoil enlivened by much talk of liberty and democracy. If they created in Italy not friends but dependents, it was because they themselves saw the Italian republicans in this light.

It is in the *triennio* that many Italians today see the first step in the Risorgimento. To the old dream of a regenerated Italy, and to the writings and labors of eighteenth-century reformers, there had now been added something new. Action had followed upon words. Italians had sat in elected assemblies, adopted constitutions, debated and enacted laws, engaged in politics and diplomacy in the name of the people. New classes of men had come into public life. In a country noted for secretiveness in matters of state, a sphere of public life and of political publicity had been created. And there was in some circles a cult of the martyrs of 1799, like Vincenzo Russo, who was said to have shouted from the scaffold, "I die for liberty. *Viva la Repubblica!*"[36]

[36] Croce, 111.

THE HELVETIC REPUBLIC

To preserve the independence and welfare of Switzerland is our highest goal. Both are threatened by the present internal and external relations of the country. These are due in part to the troubles of the day, but mostly to the deficiencies of our governments. . . . Our governments should do now what they should have done long ago—give Switzerland a constitution which, while granting equal rights and equal liberties to all, endows all with a single interest, and so creates a total community endowed with a new force of life, which can stand against threats both present and future.—PAULUS USTERI TO PETER OCHS, Zurich, January 8, 1798

THE HELVETIC REPUBLIC

ALL Switzerland is only twice as large as the American state of New Jersey, but until 1798, small as it was, it was an incredibly complex mosaic of dissimilar pieces. Nowhere else was the impact of certain principles of the Revolution more apparent and more lasting—especially of the principles of legal equality and of the unity and indivisibility of the Republic. If in New Jersey, with the passage of a few generations, there has grown up a jungle of adjoining boroughs, townships, cities, planning boards, boards of education, and joint districts and authorities of many kinds, they at least exist within a single state and under a comprehensive system of law. In Switzerland, over a millennium, there had grown up an indefinite number of small communities—from cities like Zurich to remote clusters of pastoral families in Alpine valleys—which no longer belonged to the Holy Roman Empire, and did not yet belong politically to anything else.

Switzerland before 1798

Today Switzerland is composed of twenty-two cantons. There were only thirteen at the beginning of 1798, and the thirteen embraced only parts of the region called Switzerland. They were associated for external defense in a perpetual "oath-fellowship" or *Eidgenossenschaft*; not until the eighteenth century did the term come to signify a territory as well as merely a league. All the oath-fellows were German-speaking. They were bound to certain "allied districts" by arrangements which varied in each case. The largest of the allied districts were the Bishopric of Basel (from which the city of Basel had separated when it turned Protestant in the sixteenth century); the Abbey of St. Gallen; the Valais (or German Wallis), which was in the upper Rhone valley above Lake Geneva; and the eastern part of Switzerland which is now the canton of Graubunden, but was then called the Drei Bünde, or Three Leagues, one of which was in turn composed of the Ten Jurisdictions. There was a third general category, called the "subject districts." These were areas conquered in past centuries from the dukes of Savoy or Burgundy by one, several or all the cantons together. Thus the French-speaking Pays de Vaud, north and east of Lake Geneva, belonged to the German-speaking canton and city of Bern. Among the subject districts were also the "common lordships," which belonged to the cantons as a group, or to two or more of them, or to the Drei Bünde. The largest were Thurgau, east of Zurich, and various Italian-speaking regions, such as the area about Locarno and the part of the Adda valley called the Valtellina. After a revolt against the Drei Bünde in 1797, the Valtellina was incorporated into the Cisalpine Republic. To add to the variety, the present French-speaking cantons of Geneva and Neuchâtel did not belong to the confederation at all; Neuchâtel was a principality of the King of Prussia, and Geneva was an independent republic, connected with the cantons only by treaties of specific import.

Local liberties flourished. In the "democratic" cantons of the high valleys, Uri, Schwyz, Zug, and Unterwalden—isolated, small, rural, and Catholic—there was a good deal of local direct democracy, which the inhabitants preferred to keep as local as possible. (These four democratic cantons, however, despite a popular idea current even then, accounted for less than a twentieth of the population of Switzerland.) In the city-cantons, Zurich, Bern, and Basel (as in Geneva), which were busy, Protestant, and fully in touch with Europe, local liberties meant a corporate independence in the councils and constituted bodies described in the first volume. Their citizenship was a tightly held privilege. "An inhabitant of Zurich who has the right of citizenship," said the Russian traveler Karamzin, "is as proud of this as a king of his crown."[1] Certain families enjoyed a hereditary monopoly in the powers of government. There were local liberties of a kind even in the subject districts, which, however, were actually governed, taxed and in fact exploited by members of the ruling families sent out from the dominant cantons. Local liberties and privileges were everywhere, for this or that kind of people, but as Peter Ochs remarked in 1796: "To be born in Switzerland gives no rights whatsoever."[2]

There was no Swiss state, Swiss citizenship, Swiss law, or even Swiss government except for some purposes in foreign relations. Each canton lived "like a snail in its shell."[3] There was religious variety from place

[1] N. M. Karamzin, *Letters of a Russian Traveler, 1789-1790* (New York, 1957), 131.
[2] *Korrespondenz des Peter Ochs*, 3 vols. (Basel, 1927-1937), II, 36.
[3] E. Chapuisat, *La Suisse et la Révolution française* (Geneva, c. 1946), 262. This is a popular summary by a man who devoted many scholarly monographs to the same and

to place, but no religious freedom for individual persons. There were no uniform coinage, weights, or measures. Defendants in criminal cases were liable to torture, and newspaper editors to intimidation and censorship. Transportation was rudimentary, even in the lowlands. There were about a hundred "internal" tariffs. Business and labor in the towns were regulated by conservative gilds, of which there were some thirty in Zurich alone. In many places the rural people were subject, even more than in more modernized monarchies, to heavy manorial dues and to seigneurial jurisdiction. There was certainly none of the equality among language groups for which modern Switzerland is famed. If the Swiss ruling classes spoke French, as they did, it was because French was then spoken by all ruling classes of central Europe. The country was uniformly republican in having no king, nor did it have much of a titled nobility; but with its burghers and patricians, its gilds and seigneuries and locally established churches, it was a picture-book example of what the eighteenth century, still unused to the word "medieval," simply called "Gothic."

That the Swiss remained independent, and had so long managed to stay out of European wars, was due more to the balance of power between France and the Hapsburgs, and to the small size of the neighboring German and Italian states, than to any power or wisdom in the town oligarchs and rural notables of the thirteen cantons with their allied and subject districts. Swiss independence was threatened by the French Revolution and the ensuing war. So was the territorial integrity of the country, especially since the marginal zones on all sides except the north were only loosely attached, enjoying no equality with the inner centers. In the Drei Bünde there was always an Austrian influence. In 1797 the Valtellina went to the new Italy, to which it still belongs. The French occupied the Bishopric of Basel in 1792, and at the same time took over, from the King of Sardinia, the region of Savoy which adjoined and resembled French Switzerland. Geneva had always been

---

related subjects. See also the book-length article on the Helvetic Republic by Arnold Rufer in *Dictionnaire historique et biographique de la Suisse*, 7 vols. (Neuchâtel, 1921-1933); or the same in German, *Hist. biog. Lexicon* . . . (Neurenburg, 1921-1934). Rufer and Chapuisat are the two outstanding authorities of the past generation on eighteenth-century Switzerland. The principal source collections are the Ochs correspondence and J. Strickler, *Actensammlung aus der Zeit der helvetischen Republik, 1798-1803*, 12 vols. (Bern, 1886-1940), of which A. Rufer took over the editorship on Strickler's death. See Rufer's account in *Zeits. für schw. Gesch.* (1952), 261-63. Very full also of information and documents on the subject are several chapters of J. Godechot, *Commissaires aux armées sous le Directoire*, 2 vols. (Paris, 1938).

separate. Disaffection against Bern was very active in the Vaud and the Valais.

A partition of Switzerland was a clear possibility in these years. Under pressure of war and revolution, Switzerland would either fall to pieces or emerge more solid than before. For the fact that it emerged more solid at least two reasons can be given. There was, in all the institutional pulverization, a certain consciousness of common culture and common identity as Swiss, arising from memories of a shared defense of local liberties against outside powers. Secondly, there was the political revolution that produced the Helvetic Republic. The borders of this republic, like those of the Batavian, and unlike those of the Cisalpine or Roman, coincided with the borders of a group of people who had some sense of identity as a nation. The idea of a Swiss people was in the realm of the possible. Much that was durable was accomplished in the Helvetic Republic, whose main features were confirmed in the Napoleonic Act of Mediation of 1803, and reconfirmed at the Congress of Vienna. It is universally agreed that modern Switzerland dates from 1798.

Geneva: Revolution and Annexation

Although it never belonged either to the old confederation or to the Helvetic Republic, it is well to say something first of Geneva, because its fate, annexation to France in 1798, pointed up the dangers to which much of Switzerland was exposed.

At Geneva, when the Revolution broke out in France, there were still at least four different levels of persons: the *citoyens*, the *bourgeois* and the *natifs* of the city, and the *sujets* who lived in the few square miles of its rural territory. The *natifs*, "natives" for several generations, had no political rights, but could live and work in the city. A few were well-to-do, but mostly they formed the lowest economic class. The *sujets* were an inert peasantry. As already related, the preceding quarter-century had re-echoed to the clashes of *citoyens* and *bourgeois*, with the *natifs* playing a minor role and occasionally receiving a few concessions. Since 1763 there had been two opposed parties, one called the *Négatifs*, representing the old principle of government by a closed corporation of self-co-opting governing families, the other called the *Représentants*, not because they favored "representative" government (which was still unknown at Geneva) but because, by making "representations" or complaints against the government, they had come to espouse a democratic or at least anti-aristocratic position. There had been an abrupt counter-revolution in 1782, followed by an "aristocratic resurgence." The patrician *Négatifs*, supported by the intervention of France, Zurich, and Bern, had managed to undo the changes made since the 1760's. Their Edict of Pacification, guaranteed by France, Zurich, and Bern, was called the Black Code by the defeated *Représentant* or democratic party, some of whom were banished from the city, while others went into voluntary exile, mostly in France.[4]

The Revolution in France radically transformed the state of affairs in Geneva.[5] For one thing, the aristocratic party had repeatedly depended on intervention by the French monarchy, along with Zurich and Bern, to protect itself against Genevese opposition. From no government in France after 1789 could the Geneva patricians expect so much sympathy. On the contrary, French official action was now more likely to favor the Genevese democrats. The exiles favored such pressure, and one of them, the banker Etienne Clavière, was even thought to favor the annexation of Geneva to France as early as 1789. The fact that Protestants and Catholics in France now had the same rights, and that the French state no longer defined itself as Catholic, made it possible for a few Genevese, despite their Calvinist background, to see in annexation at least a tolerable idea. In addition, the French agrarian revolution of 1789 had immediate effects in the territory of Geneva. The frontier at its nearest point was no more than a mile from the city. The *sujets* of Geneva, the rural people who had never had any political rights, and who had taken no part in the civic struggles of the past, were aroused to a new political consciousness, not by propaganda but by facts, when they saw peasants a few miles away throwing off their old obligations, and knew that French villagers were receiving newspapers from Paris, talking to returned deputies, setting up new municipalities, and electing local officers under legislation of the Constituent Assembly. In 1792 Savoy was annexed to France, and received the new agrarian and municipal institutions. Within revolutionary France, which now reached both shores of the lake, Geneva was no more than a tiny enclave.

The coming to political life of the rural *sujets* was the new feature in the civil struggles at Geneva after 1789. A certain Jacques Grenus, himself of the old ruling citizen class, having been banished in the counter-

---

[4] *Age of the Democratic Revolution*, I, 127-39, 358-61.
[5] For the following paragraphs see *Histoire de Genève des origines à 1798 publiée per la Société d'histoire et d'archéologie de Genève* (Geneva, c. 1950), in which the pages by E. Chapuisat and F. Barbey, 495-538, review the years from 1789 to 1798. There is a large literature.

revolution of 1782, and having developed an intense animosity toward the aristocratic party, set himself up as leader and spokesman for the *sujets*. What was lacking in Italy became apparent in Geneva (as in Switzerland proper, especially in the subject districts) : namely that rural people could see an advantage to themselves in the Revolution, and that there were city men who were able and willing to make use of rural discontent, and in whose promises the country people could feel some interest and confidence.

The *natifs* also were aroused by the Revolution in France. The greatest concession hitherto made to them (in 1768) had been the right by which some of them, if sufficiently wealthy, could obtain promotion to the rank of *bourgeois* by the payment of a sum of money. Additional efforts to extend rights to the *natifs* had been blocked by the counter-revolution of 1782. Now the *natifs* and *sujets*, under Grenus' leadership, combined into a new party of protest called the *égalisateurs*, determined to abolish the old distinctions altogether. Against this truly popular menace the two traditional adversaries tended to come together. Making peace with each other they introduced a few reforms, but not enough to satisfy the new opposition. They again banished Grenus and annulled his citizenship. When the war began, in 1792, the exiled Grenus was encouraged by the French occupation of Savoy, while the Geneva government brought in troops from Zurich and Bern to protect its neutrality—against objections not only by France, but in the Swiss confederation itself, for it is not to be supposed that the cantons, especially the conservative rural Catholic cantons, were eager to have Geneva as a member of their league, or to be responsible for its protection. Troops of both sides were withdrawn from the neighborhood of the city after negotiations, but in the heat engendered by these proceedings, in December 1792, at a moment when French revolutionary republicanism was streaming into Savoy, Belgium, and the Rhineland, the *égalisateurs* rose up at Geneva, displaced the old government, and effected a "revolution."

The Edict of December 1792 ended the old regime at Geneva. Legal and civil equality was declared for all inhabitants of the territory. The call went out for a National Assembly for the Genevese "nation," some 27,000 persons in the city plus a few thousands of peasants. Political clubs became very active. In part they merely continued the old assemblies called "circles," but some of the clubs modeled themselves on those in France, now at the height of its own Revolution, even calling themselves *clubs de la Montagne*.

The Assembly produced a constitution in 1794, which was duly submitted to popular vote, and ratified clause by clause, by majorities which differed for each clause, but were of the order of 4,300 to 200. In such figures a very high percentage of adult males was represented. In one way the Geneva constitution of 1794 adhered firmly to Genevese tradition: it gave full political equality only to persons of the Reformed Religion. In other respects, while meeting demands that were genuinely indigenous, it resembled the French constitution of 1793. It was very "democratic," for, while it introduced at Geneva the principle of representative government, that is the enactment of laws by a legislature chosen for the purpose, it allowed for a great deal of direct initiative on the part of the citizens in legislation, which it also made subject to a popular referendum.

Meanwhile the economic situation had gravely deteriorated. The war, though Geneva remained neutral, was ruinous to its trade; the export of watches declined drastically. Men out of work frequented the revolutionary clubs. The city was even cut off from its own agricultural districts, most of which did not adjoin it, but were enclaves within France or Savoy several miles away. The city itself, as noted, was an enclave after 1792. With a few boats on the lake, the French could shut it off even from the neighboring Pays de Vaud. The French complained that Geneva, by its neutrality and independence, became a nest of smugglers, spies, and speculators in French paper money. They subjected it repeatedly to blockade and to strict controls in the movement of goods and persons.

Unemployment, food shortage, and high prices thus afflicted the city, and the Geneva revolution therefore ran a somewhat parallel course to the French in economic as well as constitutional matters. The poor turned against the rich. The working class revolutionaries of the radical clubs demanded confiscations and price controls, progressive income taxes, taxes on inheritances and on rents. In July 1794 they revolted again, disarmed and arrested their opponents, and installed a Revolutionary Tribunal. The Tribunal, under armed popular pressure, decreed banishment for 94 persons, and the death sentence for 37, of whom, however, 26 were *in absentia*. The accused were charged, not incorrectly, with resistance to the popular will as far back as the "Black Code" of 1782, and with bringing in foreign intervention at that time. A few months later a second tribunal, the political wind having changed, condemned several others to death, both "aristocrats" and "anarchists," and including some extremists charged with conspiring with France against the independence of the republic.

In 1795 there was a return to regular government under the new constitution. Despite all that had happened, despite the intense hatreds aroused over many years in a small inbred community, the chance for harmony and stabilization looked promising, if only Geneva could be let alone by outsiders. It was not easy, however, for the French to let it alone. Geneva was not, after all, an insignificant place like San Marino, which the French allowed to retain its independence in 1798 on the border between the Cisalpine and the Roman republics. Geneva was an enclave in France, or rather a cluster of enclaves, not claimed with any enthusiasm by the Swiss. Under modern conditions as they were developing, with uniform territorial organization on an expanding scale, it was hard to see how a city as important as Geneva could live encysted in a larger body. In any case the French Directory had no intention of leaving it alone. After a series of protests and counter-protests, with imposition, removal, or reimposition of blockade, the French Directory annexed Geneva in 1798 as part of its general plan of that year for the reorganization of all Switzerland.

Geneva became the *chef-lieu* of a new French department, the Léman. To make it big enough for a department, the Directory added bits of French and of former Savoyard territory to its jurisdiction. Only a few Genevese, irritated to the point of desperation by their own internal conflicts, welcomed the annexation as a solution to problems that they had not solved themselves. The Genevese were never content with membership in the French Republic and Empire, which, however, proved to be not without its reward. When Geneva became a Swiss canton in 1815 it retained some of the former French and Savoyard territory which the French Republic had bestowed upon it. That is why the canton of Geneva today, though one of the smallest in Switzerland, is a good deal larger than the old republic of Rousseau and Calvin.

The Swiss Revolutionaries

It has never been easy in the English-speaking world to see that along with French military intervention in Switzerland there went a good deal of native Swiss revolutionism and willing collaboration on the part of the Swiss themselves. Especially among political reformers and in romantic literary circles in England, where a tendency to sympathize with foreign revolutionary efforts could be found, there had come to be an image of Switzerland as a land of peaceful and innocent liberty, in which no internal revolutionary disturbance was to be expected. The legend of William Tell, for example, was appealed to by conservatives as well as revolutionaries in both Switzerland and other countries.[6] Or (to take another symbol) Lord Byron in 1816 visited the famous chateau at the water's edge in the Pays de Vaud at the eastern end of Lake Geneva. He was so appalled by its dungeons that he wrote his famous poem *The Prisoner of Chillon* on the horrors of prolonged solitary confinement. The poem referred to a sixteenth-century episode. It was not generally realized in England or America that Chillon was used as a state prison until 1798.

Another "prisoner of Chillon" attracted little attention when he turned up as a refugee in Philadelphia in 1794. This was F. A. Rosset, of a prominent Lausanne family, who had taken part in a political banquet held at Lausanne in July 1791 to celebrate the fall of the Bastille. In discoursing on the liberation of France and of mankind, the banqueters had really meant to voice their dissatisfaction at the subjection of Vaud to Bern. Bern reacted accordingly, sensing sedition. Several Protestant pastors who had expressed patriot views at the same banquet were removed from their churches; one was sentenced to prison for four years. Rosset was condemned to twenty-five years' confinement at Chillon. Rescued from the Château by audacious friends, he fled to America, where he was joined by another Vaudois patriot, J. J. Cart. John Adams saw them in Philadelphia, and mentioned them to Jefferson. Adams was amazed that the "canton of Bern could have been so tyrannical," but the two Americans thought little more about such matters.[7] Four years later, in the Helvetic Republic, Americans could see nothing but French aggression.

[6] Cf. R. Labhart, *Wilhelm Tell als Patriot und Revolutionär, 1700-1800. Wandlungen der Tell-Tradition im Zeitalter des Absolutismus und der französische Revolution* (Basel, 1947).

[7] L. J. Cappon, ed., *The Adams-Jefferson Letters*, 2 vols. (Chapel Hill, N.C., 1959), I, 253 ff.; on Rosset and the Vaudois banquets, C. Burnier, *La vie vaudoise et la Révolution* (Lausanne, 1902), 212-38; on the arrest of the pastors, P. Wernle, *Der schweizerische Protestantismus im XVIII Jahrhundert*, 3 vols. (Tübingen, 1925), III, 517. There is a large specialized literature on the Vaudois revolution, much of it published by the Société Vaudoise d'histoire et d'archéologie. That Americans saw only French aggression in the Helvetic Republic seems substantially true, but can be qualified. The American traveler, Joseph Sansom, who inclined to Federalism in American politics, visited Switzerland in 1801, and, upon learning of the Swiss old regime, remarked: "Yet a free and *equal* Citizen of the American Republic, whether *naturalized* or native born, can see but little to regret in the exchange of a *despotic Oligarchy* for a Foreign Dictator—of *oppressive prescriptions* for forced loans—of *National Independence* for Individual emancipation." *Letters from Europe during a Tour through Switzerland*

The Swiss revolutionaries were in truth a mild group of men, the easier to overlook for that reason. Neither then nor by their historians were they often called "Jacobins." Radical tendencies, with adoption of a natural-rights philosophy in criticism of the old order, were more common in the French-speaking than the German-speaking wing of the Helvetic movement, as shown for example in F. C. La Harpe of the Vaud in contrast to Paulus Usteri of Zurich. The fact that before 1798 no French-speaking area enjoyed cantonal status would be enough to explain the sharper demand for liberty and equality, which in any case the closer ties with French thought and culture would reinforce. The German Swiss were less differentiated from the Germans than they later became, if only because Germany itself was not yet the Germany of Bismarck. Valuing their historic traditions, they shared with the Germans a tendency to historicist theories of law and constitutionalism, and saw in a Swiss revolution a need mainly to amplify and extend things already excellent in themselves. Like many Germans, the German Swiss also took a somewhat moralizing view of revolution, deploring all violence as unseemly, believing that the state existed to make men good rather than happy, and holding that only men of elevated character and high ideals should have an influence in politics. Like good Germans, they could look on the French with a certain condescension. The Swiss republican party, one of them wrote, "would wed what is great and true in the maxims of the French Revolution to the results of German morality and higher philosophical culture."[8]

The revolution of 1798 was for most of the Helvetic republicans a brief and not even especially memorable episode in their lives. In no sense did the revolution represent the intrusion and subsequent overthrow of new or unknown persons. Most of the leaders were men of standing before 1798, though only Peter Ochs, the most patrician of all, was at the head of a cantonal government. La Harpe came from the aristocracy of the Vaud, but the Vaudois aristocracy was excluded from the ruling oligarchies of Switzerland. Generally the innovators were men who had traveled widely or developed extensive contacts outside

---

and Italy in the Years 1801 and 1802, Written by a native of Pennsylvania, 2 vols. (Philadelphia, 1805), I, 106.

[8] Quoted by E. His, *Geschichte des neuern schweizerischen staatsrechts*, 3 vols. (Basel, 1920-1938), I, 679, n. 13. On Germanic-Kantian and French-natural-rights attitudes in Switzerland see also W. von Wartburg, "Zur Weltanschauung und Staatslehre des frühen schweizerische Liberalismus" in *Schw. Zeits. f. Gesch.* (1959), 1-40, and H. Büchi, "Die politischen Parteien im ersten schweizerischen Parlament (12 Apr. 1798 to 7 Aug. 1800): Die Begründung des Gegensatzes zwischen deutschen und welscher Schweitz" in *Politisches Jahrbuch der schw. Eidgenossenschaft*, XXXI (1917), 153-428.

Switzerland, so that, while remaining well aware of the advantages of their own country, they were free from the provincialism of self-adulation. Usteri, a medical doctor of Zurich, was active also as a journalist in Leipzig and Augsburg. La Harpe had been tutor to the Russian grand-dukes Alexander and Constantine, until ejected from Russia for sympathy with the French Revolution. His fellow Vaudois, P. M. Glayre (who like La Harpe and Ochs became a Director of the Helvetic Republic), had served as adviser to the King of Poland during the Four Years' Diet, and had long been active in international Free-masonry. Peter Ochs owned property in France; his sister had married the man who became the first Revolutionary mayor of Strasbourg. It was in his sister's house that the music of the Marseillaise had been composed, and in his own house that the treaties of Basel of 1795, by which France made peace with Prussia and Spain, had been signed.[9]

Most of the leaders enjoyed long and successful later careers, not discredited by their experiment with revolution in 1798. Peter Ochs emerged the most stigmatized as a collaborator with the French (so much so that his two sons changed their name to His in 1818); but even Ochs was respected by many persons in the Switzerland set up by Napoleon's Act of Mediation, and served as vice-burgomaster of his native Basel in 1816. La Harpe, the most nearly "Jacobin" of the leaders, went into retirement under Napoleon, but came forward in 1814 to defend the liberty of Vaud against the claims of Bern at the Congress of Vienna, and spent another two decades as leader of the Swiss liberal party until his death in 1838. Usteri, being a doctor, served as a federal sanitary commissioner after 1800, and then, after 1814, was active in the liberal party and press until he died in 1831. J. J. Cart, the fugitive of 1794 in Philadelphia, served for fifteen years after 1798 as senator and appellate judge in the Helvetic Republic. The Zurich educator, Heinrich Pestalozzi, who received his first opportunity to try out his ideas when given charge of war orphans by the Helvetic Directory in 1798, and who played a role as a republican journalist at that time, went on writing, teaching, and observing child development until 1827. Pesta-lozzi's benefactor among the Directors of 1798, J. L. Legrand from Basel, lived on as a cotton spinner and philanthropist until 1836 in Alsace, where he worked on religious and school problems with the pastor J. F. Oberlin, after whom Oberlin, Ohio, was named.

The Helvetic revolution had its similarities and its differences to

[9] On Ochs before 1798 see *Age*, I, 362-64; on the careers of all persons mentioned here, *Dict. hist. et biog. de la Suisse*.

those that produced the other sister republics. Dutch and Italian revolutionaries, to advance their aims, had relied on the war between France and its enemies; the Swiss thought their cause best advanced by peace, and hardly even saw a chance for Swiss revolution until the treaty of Campo Formio brought peace to the continent. The more ardent Batavians and Cisalpines, once their new republics were established, were eager to fight Britain and Austria respectively; most Helvetic republicans tried to remain neutral in the War of the Second Coalition, expecting the French to protect them. The Swiss produced no such apostles of international revolution as Filippo Buonarroti, who believed that no peace could be made with kings. In Switzerland, as in the Dutch provinces and in Italy, once the new republic was established, an intense struggle followed between unitarists and federalists, the former being the democrats, the latter the moderates. Territorial uniformity, the equalization of rights between town and country, between *Stadt* and *Land*, or burgher and peasant, a basic issue in all the sister republics, and in the French Revolution itself, was most especially of the essence of the Helvetic revolution. We hear more of peasant uprisings in Switzerland than in Holland or Italy. The Swiss rural people were in fact radically divided. Those of the democratic Alpine cantons or *Urkantone*, such as Schwyz, Uri, and Unterwalden, were strongly opposed to the Helvetic movement, wishing to keep their ancient liberties unaltered by such modern developments; but the peasants of the subject districts (like the *sujets* of Geneva) put on revolutionary demonstrations in 1798; and it must be remembered that one such subject district, the Thurgau which belonged to Zurich, had almost as many people as Schwyz, Uri, and Unterwalden combined. A degree of cooperation between rebellious peasants and urban leaders is a characteristic of the Helvetic revolution which we miss in the revolutions of the Italian *triennio*. Finally, to complete this comparison, Switzerland suffered, less than the Italians but more than the Dutch, from the burdens and problems imposed by French requisitions, levies, and pillaging, and by the disputes between French civilian commissioners and military commanders in its territory.

Swiss Unity vs. External Pressures

Crises of internal and of external origin combined at the end of 1797 to threaten the Swiss confederation, as the treaty of Campo Formio between France and Austria, following upon the establishment of the Cisalpine Republic, seemed to open the prospect of a new political order in Europe. As elsewhere, the internal and the external were inseparable. Swiss partisans of the old ways hoped that Austria and Great Britain would remain strong; those who desired change looked with a mixture of hope and fear to France. Reformers were alarmed by the discussions between France and Austria initiated in November at the Congress of Rastadt. They feared that these two powers, the better to digest their respective gains under the treaty, would agree upon a guarantee of the existing order in Switzerland. If so, the opportunity for a new course in Switzerland would be missed.

Internal stresses had accumulated to the point where the leading innovators had to make decisions. Resentment against Bern continued in the French-speaking areas of Vaud and Valais. Peter Ochs and his circle at Basel, including men both inside and outside the governing group, were convinced that the existing order in Switzerland was no longer viable and that the rural areas and subject districts must somehow be allowed to participate in a common life along with the old ruling cantons. They too were annoyed at Bern, where the council tried to use its influence with the other cantons to prevent discussion of the French Revolution and of new ideas for Switzerland.

The situation at Zurich was explosive, thanks to what the Swiss call the Stäfa affair. Stäfa is a village about a dozen miles from Zurich, to which it was then subject. It had a reading society, four of whose members drew up a memorial in 1794 addressed to the city, requesting an equalization of rights between town and country, more freedom of entrance into occupations and schools, and the buying up of certain seigneurial dues. Against the appeals for moderation by various notables of the city, such as Pestalozzi, Usteri, and the physiognomist Lavater, the Zurich government dispatched 2,000 troops to Stäfa, and punished no fewer than 260 persons by fine or imprisonment. The ruling elements, to quote a modern Swiss, proved immovable to the point "where even contact with their subject people had been entirely lost."[10] As with Bern and the Lausanne banquet of 1791, so with Zurich and Stäfa, the obstinacy of the authorities, and the extreme disproportion between the punishment and the offence, left a great many people profoundly disaffected. They were to prove in 1798, not essentially pro-French, but in favor of some kind of radical change and unwilling to defend their own governments against French intervention.

Bonaparte, returning to Paris from Italy, was determined to secure

---

[10] The reviewer in *Schweizerische Zeitschrift für Geschichte* (1957), 400, commenting on W. von Wartburg, *Zürich und die französischen Revolution* (Basel, 1956).

the communications of France with the Cisalpine Republic, through control of the upper Rhone valley and the Simplon pass. This meant extending French influence in Vaud and Valais, the very heart of French-speaking Switzerland in which discontent with the Bern oligarchy was so strong. La Harpe, the chief spokesman for the discontented French Swiss, had been established as an exile in Paris for some years, and now began to work closely with Bonaparte. At the moment he was not eager to merge his countrymen with the German Swiss, to be swallowed up in a "German ocean," as he put it, and he proposed to the French Directory, in September 1797, that France intervene to obtain the independence, under French protection, of the Pays de Vaud and adjoining areas. He entered also into correspondence with Peter Ochs, who, though himself bilingual, was the recognized leader among German Swiss who desired a transformation of their country. For both Ochs and La Harpe the main problem was to overcome the resistance of the conservative oligarchies at Bern, Zurich, and elsewhere.

Ochs feared also that the city of Basel was in danger of being annexed to France, as the territory of the bishopric of Basel had been annexed already; and one of his reasons for desiring a quick revolution was that the overthrow of conservative and pro-Austrian elements would remove the excuses for French intervention. Ochs and La Harpe, at the end of 1797, while remaining for two years the principal figures, and even colleagues, in the Swiss revolution, entered upon curiously divergent lines of development, in which the problems of the small political satellite are well illustrated.

It was Ochs, at first, who objected to French intervention, and put his faith in spontaneous Swiss uprisings by which the old order in the several cantons would be displaced, and a Swiss National Assembly be convened to enact a constitution. It was La Harpe, at first, who welcomed the French army into Switzerland, and even believed that the Swiss were so divided that the new constitution should be drafted and imposed by the French.[11] Thereafter the two men moved in opposite

---

[11] See the discussion by G. Steiner, ed., *Korrespondenz des Peter Ochs*, II, clxxxiii-ccviii; and the letter of La Harpe to General Brune, Paris, March 8, 1798, in Strickler, *Actensammlung*, I, 499-500: "The Executive Directory will put the finishing touch to its favor to us, if it persists in replacing the Gothic Swiss constitution, mother of all evils, with an indivisible republic that will unite the various peoples of Switzerland. . . . The minions of oligarchy will doubtless redouble their efforts to prevent the execution of this salutary measure. . . . Ah! Citizen General, preserve us from the double scourge of federalist oligarchy and delirious demagoguery. You have the force needed to render us this signal service . . . for you yourself to give us a constitution that would cost us

directions. Invited to Paris in December 1797, Ochs sat in conferences with La Harpe, Bonaparte, and the French Directors, at which it was decided that France should sponsor revolution in Switzerland. To Ochs was assigned the task of preparing a constitution, and he did so, believing that his draft would be discussed and amended by a future Swiss convention; but in fact Bonaparte and La Harpe vetoed the idea of such a convention, and the Directors Reubell and Merlin de Douai made numerous changes in Ochs' draft.

Ochs was persuaded, nevertheless, to lend his name to the constitution (which the Swiss call the "Paris constitution" of 1798), so that it might seem more acceptable in Switzerland. Once the Helvetic Republic was promulgated, Ochs found himself repeatedly taking the French point of view, urging compliance with French demands for men and money, finding excuses for the most arbitrary actions of the French government and its agents, and persuading his countrymen to accept the needs of French foreign policy, all on the ground that no other defense against Swiss reactionaries and Austrian influence was possible, until the name of Ochs, who was certainly a man of great personal integrity, became identified with the most unpleasant forms of collaborationism. La Harpe, on the other hand, once the new republic was set up, increasingly resisted the French demands, criticized the more extortionate practices of the French occupation, and tried to avoid signing a treaty that would subordinate the Helvetic Republic to French foreign policy, while at the same time tending to a more radical position in Swiss internal affairs, looking to a rapid extinction of seigneurial rights, to special taxes on the wealthy, and to the confiscation and sale of church and émigré properties, so that a Switzerland energized by its own revolution would be the less dependent on France. The result was that by a coup d'état of 1799 La Harpe drove Ochs out of the Helvetic government, only to be driven out himself in 1800.

Only at Basel, in January 1798, did events follow Ochs' original formula. The country people rose up, burned a few chateaux, and lent aid to revolutionary bourgeois in the city, so that the conservatives yielded, equality of town and country was proclaimed, French intervention was forestalled, and an assembly met to write a constitution. In the following weeks there were revolts in other cantons and subject districts. In the Vaud a party of patriots captured the chateau

---

years of labor and torrents of blood if we undertook to do it ourselves." There seems to be a critical misprint here of *vous* for *nous* in line 2 of p. 500.

of Chillon, and proclaimed a Lemanic Republic independent of Bern. Elsewhere the violence met with more resistance. The situation was especially turbulent at Zurich, where the rural subjects of the city, and the large population of the adjoining district of the Thurgau, many of whom were normally employed in weaving and other household crafts under management by Zurich business men, rose in a revolt that had strong economic as well as political implications.[12]

The French, who at first hoped that the Swiss would stage their own revolution, soon concluded, and were pressed by La Harpe to believe, that the Swiss oligarchies would not yield without a struggle. It was decided to finish off quickly—to get a decision of some kind. The Directory in February ordered General Brune, one of the most ardent republicans among French commanders, to occupy the city of Bern. Brune, modeling himself on Bonaparte in Italy, sent an ultimatum to Bern, demanding a *changement démocratique* within three hours.[13] He occupied and "revolutionized" the city in March, ordering the abolition of such titles as *baron* and *bailli*, elections in primary assemblies open to all resident men over twenty, and an end to tithes and manorial dues, on terms to be considered in a future Helvetic Republic. Meanwhile the civilian commissioner Mangourit superintended revolution in the Valais, where there was a good deal of intestine conflict which Mangourit's own intransigence did nothing to pacify. On one occasion the French and the revolutionary Valaisins killed 400 "insurgents," at least according to Mangourit's perhaps boastful report. "Almost 400 enemies have been bayoneted," he wrote to Paris. "These fanatics fought like tigers; they died without a sigh, clutching their rosaries and their relics. . . . Eight priests bit the dust (*ont mordu la poussière*)."[14] And he proposed to send the bishop of Sion to Paris "in the same cage with the bears from the Bern zoo." The Directory soon transferred Mangourit to Naples.

The Directors in Paris could neither agree with each other on the disposition of Switzerland, nor find out what the Swiss themselves

---

[12] On the actually revolutionary uprisings of 1798 see, in addition to basic works already cited: W. von Wartburg, *Zürich und die französischen Revolution* (Basel, 1956); A. Custer, *Die Zürcher Untertanen und die französischen Revolution* (Zurich, 1942); F. Brullmann, *Die Befreiung des Thurgaus* (Weinfelden, 1948); M. Salamin, *Histoire politique du Valais sous la République helvétique*, chez l'auter (Sierre, 1957); Soc. vaudoise d'hist. et d'arch., *Documents inédits sur la Révolution vaudoise de 1798* (Lausanne, 1948).

[13] The correspondence of Brune in this connection is published in *Archiv für schw. Gesch.*, XII (1858), 233-496. See p. 265.

[14] Quoted by Godechot, *Commissaires*, II, 115.

might agree on. Nor, if all the subject districts and common lordships were to become "independent" of the formerly dominant cantons, was it at all obvious what political configuration should ensue. By March 1798 there were some parts of Switzerland in which revolutionary leaders preferred the constitution drafted at Basel, which allowed for a measure of "direct democracy" and cantonal or local autonomy, and others where the revolutionaries said they wanted the Paris constitution, which provided for "representative democracy" in a unitary republic.

In March General Brune, upon orders from Paris, proclaimed a Rhodanic or Rhone Republic under the Paris constitution, and a Helvetic Republic under the Basel constitution, with a third entity, the Tellgau, named for William Tell, where the regime was yet to be determined. The Rhone Republic, in this plan, was to embrace the non-German parts of the old confederation, in general from Lausanne to Locarno.[15] The Helvetic would be essentially the northern region of the German-speaking cities. The Tellgau would be the region of the "primitive" and old-fashioned democratic and Catholic cantons of the high mountains. Since the whole eastern area of the Grisons (Dreibünde or Graubunden) was not occupied by the French, and might fall to Austria, and since Neuchâtel and Geneva were at no time under consideration, it is evident that by this plan what the world thinks of as Switzerland would have been dissolved. Nevertheless, there were forces in Switzerland to which the plan might appeal, or at least seem preferable to any alternative then in sight. The conservative old cantons might prefer to be let alone in an Alpine Tellgau, and the Latin and Germanic peoples of Switzerland had never yet lived together on a plane of equality.

La Harpe, overcoming his fears of a German majority, now threw his influence in Paris against such a partition and in favor of a unified Switzerland. Swiss patriots and revolutionaries generally took the same view, even if the new order had to be imposed on the conservative cantons by force, through the action of a far more centralized government than Switzerland had ever known. For the French, there was an obvious advantage in a unified Switzerland in which their influence might exclude that of other outside powers. The Directory therefore sent new instructions to Brune, who on March 22 proclaimed a single unitary Helvetic Republic under the Paris constitution. This was the

---

[15] E. Mottaz, "La République rhodanique" in *Zeits. f. schw. Gesch.* (1947), 61-79, in addition to more general accounts.

constitution which Ochs had drafted, which the French had amended, which the Swiss now accepted as the price of preserving their territorial integrity, and which, being unitary and consolidationist, gave the Swiss revolutionary leaders, and the French commissioners sent to work with them, the means to restrain aristocratic, oligarchical, counter-revolutionary, federalist, and secessionist tendencies. A Helvetic legislature began to sit at Aarau, with Peter Ochs as president of the Senate; and a Helvetic Directory of five members, chosen by this legislature, assumed the executive power.

The new constitution introduced a legal homogeneity, or equality of rights between town and country and between region and region. The entire territory was laid out in legally equal cantons. To the thirteen already existing, among which Bern and Zurich were reduced in size, were now added a number of others: the German-speaking Thurgau, Aargau, and St. Gallen; the mixed French and German Valais; the French Léman (the old Pays de Vaud); and for the old Italian-speaking *baillages* or *Vogteien* two new cantons, Bellinzona and Lugano, which were combined into the single canton of Ticino in 1803.[16] The constitution also "invited" the eastern region (the Grisons or Dreibünde) to enter the Helvetic Republic as a new canton of Rhaetia or Graubunden. Here, however, internal dissension was very great. Conservatives and Catholics of eastern Switzerland would have nothing to do with the Helvetic Republic; they preferred Austria; and Austrian troops entered this part of Switzerland in October 1798, a few weeks before Mack's attack on Rome opened the War of the Second Coalition. During this war the French under Masséna pushed the Austrians out of the Grisons, where the local patriots, in March 1799, proclaimed the canton of Rhaetia as part of the Helvetic Republic. With this action, the essential outlines of modern Switzerland were delineated.

Partition or dissolution had been avoided. Neutrality was difficult or impossible. The history of the Helvetic Republic, as one Swiss writer has remarked, cannot be understood except as a phase of the European conflict between revolution and counter-revolution.[17] The French

---

[16] The fact is that all the modern Swiss cantons whose date of entrance into the confederation is officially listed as 1803 or 1815 (the Act of Mediation or the Congress of Vienna), with the exception of Geneva and Neuchâtel, and with some modification of boundaries, really date from the revolution of 1798. It is somewhat as if the United States chose to date its independence from the lawful treaty of 1783 instead of from the revolutionary action of 1776.

[17] Steiner in Ochs, *Korrespondenz*, II, ccxxix.

needed their ideological sympathizers in power in Switzerland. As Reubell said in 1801 (after Suvorov's campaign of 1799), his decision to sponsor revolution in Switzerland had kept the Russians out of Paris.[18] By the same token, the powers of the Second Coalition much preferred the Swiss old regime. Conversely, the parties in Switzerland depended on foreign support against each other.

"Switzerland today must be either Austrian or French," wrote Talley-rand to Ochs in August 1798; "I do not suppose it will hesitate in this choice."[19] The view was the same, *mutatis mutandis*, on the other side. William Wickham, the British emissary to Switzerland, worked strenuously to restore the old order there. He did not suppose that the country could remain neutral or truly independent. The old cantons in their old form, he wrote to Grenville in August 1799, "must be delivered, *bound hand and foot*—they cannot have any will of their own. . . . The great Powers of Europe, if they are unanimous, may make of these states what they please."[20]

The French influence lasted long enough for Swiss revolutionaries to proceed with internal changes.

Internal Stresses in the Helvetic Republic

There is room only to mention some of these changes, which in any case resembled those undertaken in other countries touched by the Revolution, and which, while launched in 1798, were generally carried out, with various compromises, in the years when Switzerland, like the rest of western Europe, was protected by the famous Emperor of the French.

[18] Reubell, who did not get along with Bonaparte during the Consulate, made a private note, printed in the appendix to the Ochs *Korrespondenz* (II, 562), and worth quoting at length: "Every day I hear the E(xecutive) D(irectory) blamed for having revolutionized Switzerland, and strangely enough the present government is one of the first to blame it.

"It was after a dinner for Bonaparte and Ochs that Bonaparte pressed Ochs, in my presence, to hurry up with the revolution. The conference took place in my drawing room, shortly after Bonaparte returned from Italy, and it is no doubt to remove all suspicion of his own complicity in this revolution that he now affects to disavow it.

"But far from disavowing it myself I think that I never deserved better of the country than in pressing for it with all my strength. If we had not occupied Switzerland Suvorov would have been in Paris and Bonaparte could not have won the battle of Marengo. I can see that brutes . . . wild beasts and imbeciles . . . who would desire to see Suvorov in Paris would continue to find fault with the Swiss revolution. Intelligent and sensible patriots will keep silent. . . . Look at what this Switzerland was: a crazy formless assemblage of governments without any connection, some oligarchic, others democratic, all despotic and all enemies of the French Republic."

[19] Ochs, *Korrespondenz*, II, 439.

[20] *Dropmore Papers*, v, 218.

From the beginning of the Helvetic legislature two parties developed. One, that of the moderate revolutionaries, was led by Usteri of Zurich and other men from the cities, who advised against haste and violence, thought that action should be taken for the people but not by them, and imagined themselves to be walking in the footsteps of the French Girondists. The other and more radical party drew its strength from rural areas, where the inhabitants, having so lately been subjected to the cities, still harbored suspicions against them. The tendency for peasants to be more revolutionary than townspeople was a peculiarity of the Swiss situation, hardly paralleled either in France or the other sister-republics. The two parties differed on much, especially on the liquidation of tithes and manorial dues. Only a fifth of the tithe at the end of the eighteenth century was owned by church bodies or clerical persons; much of it had become simply a secular property; and most of it had passed into the hands of the former cantonal governments, and so in effect constituted a kind of tax, but a tax that was paid only by rural people, especially in the lowlands. That the tithe had already disappeared from the high valleys suggests one reason why the people there were little drawn to the revolution. Since the tithe was largely a tax, to abolish it was to raise hard questions of public finance and of new forms of revenue. Nor could either the tithe or the manorial dues be liquidated without threatening the incomes of many middle-class revolutionaries. The result was delay, confusion, and frustration; after 1800, when Usteri's party drove out La Harpe and won out over the radicals, various complex adjustments were introduced.

The Republic simmered in what Brune called a "ferment of organization": abolition of gilds, new freedom of occupation and enterprise, new laws of purchase and sale; rationalization of tolls and tariffs— abolition of torture and reform of the courts—proliferation of pamphlets and journals under new press laws—religious liberty and separation of church and state; closing of convents and monasteries and confiscation of their property, with pensions to former inmates; transfer of birth registration from parishes to municipalities; provision for civil marriage, transfer of matrimonial cases to civil courts, and authorization of mixed marriages between Protestants and Catholics—projects to codify the laws—plans to develop higher education and public schools, in which uniform standards should be prescribed, compulsory religious instruction eliminated, and bright boys from poor families given financial aid; along with programs for the training of teachers, for which Pestalozzi received a grant from the Republic to operate a normal school at Burgdorf near Bern.

All this went on during military occupation by the French, while the French were at war with Britain and foreseeing renewed war with Austria. The French made heavy demands on the country, beginning with Brune's removal of the 6,000,000-livre "treasure" of Bern, and continuing with requisitions to support the French forces in Switzerland, to help finance the expedition to Egypt, and for other purposes. Various civilian commissioners arrived from Paris. It was their task, while attempting to control the French military and to repress individual pillage, to produce a lucrative flow of money and provisions. The best-remembered of these commissioners was Rapinat, a man who made jokes about his own name, telling the Swiss with a hearty laugh that he "loved rapine." He seems to have been guilty of no more than excessive zeal in the discharge of his duties, but was lastingly pilloried by a quatrain famous in its day:

> Le pauvre Suisse qu'on ruine
> Demandait qu'on examinât
> Si Rapinat vient de rapine,
> Ou rapine de Rapinat.[21]

The exactions of the French, the irrepressible individual pillaging, the imposition of the new constitution and the initiation of all kinds of structural reforms, naturally combined to create a wide array of enemies to the new regime. Active opposition, as distinct from apathy and resentment, came on the whole from two quarters—the former elites and privileged classes, and the old democratic cantons.

Among the former privileged classes two men stood out as leaders of a wave of Swiss émigrés, who came to number 5,000 or more, and who, like the Orange émigrés from Holland in 1795, or the French émigrés, appealed to the Austrian and other governments for armed intervention, and received British money to foment resistance in their home countries. One of these was N. F. von Steiger, the last *schultheiss* (or chief magistrate) of Bern, a member of one of the families which had flourished for generations by the government of subject districts. The other was the abbot of St. Gallen, who as temporal ruler of some 100,000 people had been an ally of the thirteen cantons, and had nothing to gain by the conversion of his territory to a cantonal status.

The rural, upland, "primitive," and "democratic" cantons, of which

[21] Godechot, *Commissaires*, II, 73.

six were Catholic and two Protestant, likewise opposed the Paris constitution and the Helvetic Republic. They too, in a way, had been privileged under the old order, in which, as original oath-fellows, they were full members in the Eidgenossenschaft, and shared in the suzerainty over various subject districts and common lordships. They were accustomed to sovereignty in their own local affairs, which were very simple. They governed themselves through folk-meetings attended by all grown men. Nowhere in Europe was the antithesis so clearly posed between the old and the new conception of democracy. Against a new conception of national citizenship, and of organized government deriving powers from an extensive people, the older conception reflected a dislike for government itself, so far as it was distant, or possessed of significant powers, or conducted by strangers.

The point is illustrated by a letter to Ochs from K. H. Gschwend, *landespräsident* of the upper Rheinthal, protesting against the new order. (That much the same letter could have been written in America should be evident.) Ochs, said Gschwend, "does not understand the democratic cantons." For centuries they have chosen their own officers "under the open sky." In each canton there is a simple folk whose combined wealth is less than a Basel burgher's. "Where will people find the money to pay for a Directory, two Councils, a Supreme Court, cantonal judges, a standing army and a host of secretaries and clerks?" A despot would be no worse. "Our people have never paid taxes. They will be crushed to the ground if so many taxes are levied now." All these government functionaries will become a new aristocracy. "Do you suppose that free people, sons of the Alps, will bow under such a yoke?"[22]

It is clear that when the Helvetic constitution, the only constitution of the period to do so, explicitly affirmed the new regime to be a "representative democracy," its purpose was to counter the arguments for direct democracy which could be expected from parts of Switzerland. Robespierre, five years before, had likewise upheld representative democracy against the direct democracy of Paris sans-culottes in their local clubs and assemblies. To insist upon representative democracy was to insist upon the authority of a central government, without which no revolution could be made to prevail against its opponents, or any reforms carried out in practice.

The constitution, out of consideration for the small "primitive" cantons, departed from the generally accepted new principle of repre-

[22] Strickler, *Actensammlung*, I, 530.

sentation according to numbers and gave equal representation in the legislative councils, for the immediate future, to the small and large cantons alike. Thus Zug with 20,000 inhabitants had as many representatives as Zurich with over 150,000. In the small cantons there seem, to be sure, to have been a few persons open to modern ideas—"too many false brothers and evil-minded new-fangled people," as one observer expressed it.[23] On the whole, despite the concessions made to them, the small cantons detested the new Helvetic Republic, disliking the thought of subordination to any government beyond their own mountains. They called the constitution the *Höllenbuchlein*—the little hell-book—because, in the words of the community of Nidwalden, "it seeks to rob us of our holy religion, our freedom enjoyed undisturbed for hundreds of years, and our democratic constitution inherited from our blessed ancestors."[24]

The democratic cantons therefore rebelled. The new democratic Republic found itself in the awkward posture of repressing, by force of arms, little groups of simple people who insisted that theirs was the truly democratic way of life. The situation was much relished by the Swiss émigrés, and by the Austrians and the British, all of whom did what they could to prolong it. On the other hand, it was only to the French army that the new Helvetic government, which had no armed force of its own, could look for the means to enforce its authority. It also, only a few weeks after the new constitution went into effect, decreed the dissolution of four "primitive" cantons, Uri, Schwyz, Zug, and Unterwalden, and their combination into a single new canton of Waldstätten. The new republic thus strongly affirmed the unitary principle, by which local districts were only changeable subdivisions of the political community as a whole. The people of the abolished cantons remained in a state of armed insurrection, insisting on the federal principle, or the indissolubility of pre-existing units, the better to protect their traditional customs and outlook.

In these circumstances the French army remained in Switzerland, and was even reinforced. The burden of levies and requisitions mounted. Agents like Rapinat and others could not be controlled by the Paris government. Even in the Helvetic Directory and legislative councils a strong anti-French sentiment soon developed. There were official protests against the French exactions, and pleas that the Helvetic authorities be given more freedom to manage the resources of

[23] A Catholic priest of Schwyz, J. T. Fassbind, in Ochs, *Korrespondenz*, II, 622.
[24] Strickler, *Actensammlung*, I, 608-9.

their own country. Yet the continuing dependence on France could not be denied. Peter Ochs, in particular, took the view that, with the regime of representative democracy threatened in its very existence by enemies both internal and foreign, it would be ruinous to allow anti-French sentiment to go too far; that criticism of the French must remain private and prudent; that public complaint, or exaggeration of regrettable episodes, would only give arguments to the British and Austrians, and to Swiss oligarchy and parochialism.

The history of the Helvetic Republic, like that of the Batavian and the Cisalpine, was therefore punctuated by abrupt coups d'état. Ochs joined forces with Rapinat to prepare a change of government, Ochs acting secretly without the knowledge of his Swiss colleagues, and Rapinat without instructions from Paris. Both wished to get men into the Helvetic government who would work more willingly with the French in the matter of requisitions, and be prompt and decisive in employing French troops against the insurgent cantons. Rapinat forced two members of the Helvetic Directory to resign. The French Directory, as usual, accepted the accomplished fact. The Helvetic councils then proceeded to elect two new Directors, Ochs and La Harpe. They elected Ochs in order to placate the French, and La Harpe in a gesture of independence against them. Ochs and La Harpe agreed on fundamentals, so that the revolutionary legislation outlined above continued to go forward, and French troops were used to suppress a new and more serious outbreak in the high Alpine districts. They differed in the policy to be adopted toward the Great Nation and the European war. The French demanded an offensive and defensive alliance. Ochs, supported by one other Director, Viktor Oberlin, favored such an alliance, arguing that the Helvetic Republic should do its share in a war on whose outcome the existence of all modern republics seemed to depend. La Harpe, two other Directors, and most other Swiss revolutionaries preferred either that the Helvetic Republic should remain neutral, or that its citizens should fight only within their own frontiers if attacked. The French forced Swiss acceptance of the treaty nevertheless.

After the Austrian army occupied the Grisons in October, and the war of the Second Coalition began, the French pressed their demand that the Swiss organize an army of their own (in addition to the old militia) to the extent of 18,000 men, as an auxiliary force to operate with the French army, and to be maintained and equipped at French expense. A good many people in Switzerland, including Pestalozzi as well as Ochs, believed this proposal to be altogether reasonable.

The Helvetic army, however, never developed the strength of the Batavian, or even the Cisalpine, and its weaknesses revealed the weakness of the Helvetic revolution itself.[25] There were too many who wished for the advantages of the revolution without having to fight for them, or who complained of the French yet were content to remain dependent upon them. Many others, of course, objected to the new regime altogether. It was said that the country could not possibly supply 18,000 men, though at least 11,000 Swiss mercenaries had been in the French service in 1789. It was said that Switzerland, already drained by French requisitions, could not afford such an army, even at French expense, which might only take the form of renewed French requisitions. The French asked the Swiss to introduce conscription, on the model of the new French conscription law of 1798. "Nothing would better suit the kings," said Ochs, "than for republics to renounce compulsory service."[26] The Helvetic Directory, after a delay, proposed conscription to the legislative councils, which, on the eve of invasion by the Austrians and Russians in 1799, flatly refused it. Voluntary enlistment proceeded slowly. In some places, notably the former Pays de Vaud, there was an enthusiasm to join; and within limits the new army served as a school of new republican citizenship. The officers, for example, came from various social classes. They included professional soldiers who had seen service with European monarchies in former times, but they also included a former monk of St. Gallen, a butcher, and an impecunious landowner whose income had disappeared when the Helvetic government abolished seigneurial dues. Some of these officers were later to be with Napoleon in Russia, and one lieutenant of 1799 lived to become commander-in-chief of the Swiss Federal Army in 1830. In the overall view, however, for an army planned for 18,000, only 469 officers and 3,587 men were actually incorporated in the six demi-brigades of which the force was composed. And these units suffered heavily from desertion.

On the other hand, attempts to raise a Swiss counter-revolutionary armed force at British expense were even less successful. The most vociferously reactionary districts contributed the least. Supposedly, by September 1799, there were 2,800 men in such units, but hardly two-thirds were in the field. The Genevese Mallet du Pan, who was editing the *British Mercury* in London at this time, and who regarded all partisans of the Helvetic Republic as traitors, reported with disgust, or

[25] See F. Bernoulli, *Die helvetischen Halbbrigaden im Dienste Frankreichs, 1798-1805* (Bern, 1934).
[26] *Korrespondenz*, II, 486.

perhaps with deliberate exaggeration to terrify the conservative powers into action, that far more Swiss, including even a few women, were fighting on the French side than on the side of the Coalition.[27] On the whole, to quote a Swiss historian, "there was as little enthusiasm in Switzerland for military service in English pay, which might lead to a campaign against France, as there was willingness to fight for the French."[28] The predominant feeling in Switzerland, even with Russian, Austrian, and French troops operating in the country, seems to have been one of innocent neutrality violated by outsiders, as if Swiss destinies were uninvolved.

In fact, however, when Marshal Suvorov and his Russians, in July 1799, crossed the St. Gotthard pass from Italy, where they had just overthrown the Cisalpine Republic, into Switzerland, where they meant to destroy the Helvetic Republic, the action was part of a widespread anti-republican movement, with an Anglo-Russian force simultaneously preparing to expunge the Batavian Republic in Holland, and to converge with Suvorov against the French Republic and the supposed source of the whole disturbance—Paris. This grand confrontation is described in a later chapter. In Switzerland, as the Russians entered from the south, the Austrians came in from the east. The Swiss émigrés returned. Some of them, whose views were expressed by the former *schultheiss* of Bern and abbot of St. Gallen, and strongly insisted on by William Wickham, demanded the total restoration in Switzerland of the situation of 1797. Even moderate conservatives wished to restore the system of subject districts with domination by ruling cantons. The Helvetic Republic was kept in being by Masséna's victory at the second battle of Zurich in September 1799; and the exclusion of the old regime from Switzerland, north Italy, Holland, and France itself was further settled by Bonaparte's victory in 1800 at Marengo, which, according to Reubell, could never have happened without the Swiss revolution two years before.

The Helvetic Republic, or at least the Paris constitution of 1798, proved to be more unitary and centralized than the Swiss would tolerate. Other constitutions were to follow, and many compromises made, but they modified without repudiating the principles of the Revolution. The Helvetic constitution of 1798 had the kind of permanence that the exactly contemporary Dutch constitution also enjoyed. It

[27] *British Mercury*, III (July 1799), 341-43.
[28] F. Burckhardt, *Die schweizerische Emigration, 1798-1801* (Basel, 1908), 287. This is excellent also on the incipient restoration of 1799.

was not itself permanent, but its principles of territorial uniformity, legal equality, assured civil rights, and modern citizenship proved to be lasting. In 1920 an important three-volume history of modern Swiss public law began to be published at Basel. Its author, a member of the university there, was Eduard His. He was the great-great-grandson of Peter Ochs. It was not family attachment, but the nature of the subject itself, that made him begin his history with the revolution of 1798, and devote the entire first volume to the fifteen years thereafter.

GERMANY: THE REVOLUTION OF
THE MIND

In republicanism it is rightly accepted that all men as rational beings are free and have equal rights. . . . If power is usurped, abused and oppressive, no objection can be made, it seems, to the justice of a revolution by which it is done away with. For man must not be aggrieved in his rights. But since the abolition of one form of government and introduction of another, if it occurs by force, necessarily involves a state of anarchy in between, which is in itself contrary to reason and opens the way to a thousand wrongs, the rationality of revolution certainly seems to have much against it.—"WHAT SHOULD THE JUST MAN DO IN TIMES LIKE OURS?" in *Deutsches Magazin,* 1798

GERMANY: THE REVOLUTION OF
THE MIND

THE position of Germany was intermediate in more than a geographical sense. When we take a comparative view, we find in this heartland of Europe neither a triumph of counter-revolution as in the East, nor yet the setting up of revolutionary assemblies and republics as in the West. Not wholly content with the place of their own country in the world, the Germans could not enjoy the self-congratulating conservatism of the English, but on the other hand, since they retained a high respect for their existing authorities, they had none of the aversion to their own past that characterized the revolutionary French. It so happened, also, that these years of political change coincided with the supreme efflorescence of German thought and culture. It was the age of Goethe and Schiller, of Mozart and Beethoven, of Kant, Fichte, Hegel, Herder, Schleiermacher, and the Humboldts. Under the influence of such masters, and at this moment of upheaval, a new German national consciousness was beginning to take form. An ambivalent attitude to revolution entered into the national outlook. The Germans neither rejected revolution in the abstract, nor accepted it in its actual manifestations. Nothing was more characteristic, in Germany before 1800, than to continue to hail the principles and goals of the French Revolution with enthusiasm, and to believe that in French hands, thanks to French faults, these principles had miscarried.

The problem of its nationality, and later its nationalism, was for a long time the compelling theme in historical thinking about Germany; but since the Second World War, as in other countries, interest has attached to other matters, accentuated in Germany by the actual division of the country. The question, crudely simplified, is whether Germany really belongs to the world of Western constitutionalism and democracy. For one's view on this question the years of the 1790's are of importance. The Mainz "Jacobins" of 1792, for example, have been variously interpreted as traitors who in collaborating with the French betrayed the true spirit of their country, as simpletons whose ineffectual antics showed the political immaturity of the Germans only too well, and as predecessors of a later democracy of either Eastern or Western type. "German Marxists," wrote an East Berlin historian in 1957, "consider the Mainz Commune and the Rhine Convention as the first democratic republic on German soil." But such German republicans can be seen as forming part of a background to Western democracy also. Recently the tendency in West Germany, breaking with an older tradition that put high value on the special peculiarity of *Deutschtum*, has been to argue that Germany in the 1790's, while of course different, shared in the common experience of Western Europe.[1]

The Ambiguous Revolution

There was no revolution in Germany before 1800. The great changes came in the following decade, when the Holy Roman Empire was converted into some twenty modern states; and these changes were brought about by German governments themselves, when the rulers

[1] The huge literature on Germany at the time of the French Revolution is currently dominated by two outstanding works, F. Valjavec, *Die Entstehung der politischen strömungen in Deutschland, 1770-1815* (Munich, 1951), and J. Droz, *L'Allemagne et la Révolution française* (Paris, 1949), of which Droz gave a compact preview in the *Revue historique*, Vol. 198 (1947), 161-77. Valjavec and Droz in a way supersede the older books by G. P. Gooch and A. Stern, which drew heavily on memoirs and literary materials. Recent East German works, more assertively Marxist than those written elsewhere in Eastern Europe, in the present author's experience, include W. Markov and F. Donath, *Kampf um Freiheit: Dokumente zur Zeit der nationalen Erhebung 1785-1815*, Verlag der Nation [East Berlin, 1954]; H. Voegt, *Die jakobinische Literatur und Publizistik 1789-1800* (Berlin, 1955), which reprints many extracts from the publicist Rebmann; and P. Stulz and A. Opitz, *Volksbewegungen in Kursachsen zur Zeit der französischen Revolution* (Berlin, 1956). The West German school, arguing for an affinity between Germany and the West, is chiefly represented by Valjavec, mentioned above; see also W. Groote, *Die Entstehung des Nationalbewustseins in nordwest Deutschland 1790-1830* (Göttingen, 1955); an article by W. Stammler, "Politische Schlagworte in der Zeit der Aufklärung," in *Lebenskräfte in der abendländischen Geistesgeschichte: Dank- und Erinnerungsgabe an Walter Goetz* (Marburg, 1948), 199-259, where it is argued that the words for liberty, tyranny, equality, humanity, and natural rights were used in Germany as in the West; and the significant older work of E. Hölzle, *Das alte Recht und die Revolution: Eine politische Geschichte Württembergs in der Revolutionszeit, 1789-1805* (Munich, 1931). The work of the American S. S. Biro, *The German Policy of Revolutionary France: A Study in French Diplomacy during the War of the First Coalition, 1792-97*, 2 vols. (Cambridge, Mass., 1957), suffers from the author's unconcealed distaste and hence impoverished understanding for his own subject. For the minutely fragmented political geography of Germany, with both textual explanation and large-scale folding map, see G. Franz, *Deutschland 1789*, Frankfurt, 1952. The quotation from Markov in the paragraph above is from *Annales historiques de la Révolution française*, No. 148 (1957), 285.

of Baden, Württemberg, Bavaria, Saxony, and other domains, in co-operation with Napoleon and with their own reforming civil servants, and at the expense of German prince-bishops, imperial knights, the patricians of free cities, and miscellaneous lesser lordly beings, effected a territorial and legal transformation that wiped out many aspects of the Old Regime. The Revolution from Above, checkmated in the Hapsburg lands, swept over the rest of Germany with astonishing success. Europe offered no other case of structural changes accomplished so rapidly by existing authorities. It was among the princes themselves, in Germany, that the French of the Revolution eventually found their most effective collaborators.

The present chapter, like the whole of the present book, is concerned only with the decade that closed in 1800. It was a decade, in Germany, without great events or dramatic confrontations. Revolution was in the air, but the idea of revolution—and of counter-revolution—was ambiguous.

There was a feeling that "revolution" might be a good thing, if only carried out in due form by the proper persons; and this belief of the 1790's was in a measure confirmed in the following years. The confidence in existing authorities inhibited the growth of a truly revolutionary movement, or even of a critical opposition. There were active groups of radical republicans in the Germany of the 1790's, but they achieved little outside the spheres of journalism and conspiracy. Incipient liberalism was ambivalent, sometimes favoring old estates and constituted bodies as checks upon princely power, sometimes more authoritarian, favoring the princely power against the privileged classes. Conservatism was also inhibited by the fact that so many German governments were not conservative, being committed to policies of progressive change. In Germany, unlike England, conservatism was not the solid philosophy of an active and experienced ruling class. Conservatism itself became an unsettling ideology.[2] To express its disgust with the present, it glorified the medieval, the *altdeutsch* and the *altständisch*, or it asserted the superiority of a pure spirituality over a vulgar world of practical affairs. It found itself opposed, not only to German republicans but in a more insidious way to tendencies in the German governments themselves, and in an unwholesome fashion to the influence of foreigners. It is well known how in the long run the aberrations of Hitlerism built upon pathologically ethnocentric qualities in German conservatism.

[2] This point is developed by Valjavec, *Entstehung*, 310-26.

Distinctive of Germany in the last decades of the Holy Roman Empire was a profound incapacity for collective political action. Divided into some three hundred states, interlaced with fifty free cities and the minuscule acres of a thousand sovereign imperial knights, the German world was one in which any action on the public stage was bound to be local. Waves of political protest or indignation, even if generated, broke against frontiers which were never more than a few miles away. Except for the oligarchic free cities, and for the aristocratic *Reichsritter* or knights, government was conducted by absolutist princes with their officials and experts, so that, even on the local scene, the people outside government had little expectation of participating in it, or even understanding the reasons for its decisions. The prominent elements in the middle class were not lawyers in private practice, nor wealthy men of affairs, with exceptions for trading centers like Hamburg. They were bureaucrats, civil servants, writers, and university professors. In the Protestant states the pastors and men whose fathers were pastors added a strong contribution. But economically the middle class was weak, since commercial enterprises were local and old-fashioned, or else, as in Prussia, dependent for investment capital and management on the state, so that the material base was lacking for vigorous independent initiative. The middle class, in any event, was not estranged from the monarchies under which it lived. Individual burghers might criticize individual noblemen, but there was no deep feeling against nobility or privilege itself, and the belief continued to prevail (contrary to what happened in France in the 1780's) that the government would do what it could to uphold middle-class against noble interests. The fact that German officialdom was reasonably honest, trained, and efficient, whatever its less evident shortcomings, kept criticism of it on a moderate plane.

In these circumstances two kinds of organizations took on more importance in Germany than elsewhere—the universities, and a variety of secret societies. In Germany in the eighteenth century, unlike England and Western Europe, several of the universities were new foundations and others had been recently invigorated with new ideas; they were closely allied to the governments, not in the manner of Oxford and Cambridge, but as training centers for official personnel; at the same time, since professors and students in each institution, such as Jena, came from all over Germany, and indeed from all over Central and Eastern Europe, the universities were places in which the narrow localism of the individual states could be transcended. Beginning about

1770 several new semi-secret student "orders" were established. Modeled somewhat on the lodges of Freemasonry, they aspired to replace the older student societies with their emphasis on drinking and dueling, and they pursued, in the spirit of the Enlightenment, goals of humanitarianism and the self-improvement of youth, which in the 1780's turned to more definitely political interests.[3] The radical journalist, Rebmann, was active in one of these student orders, the *Schwarze Brüder*; and Fichte, when professor of philosophy at Jena, found in them an enthusiastic audience for his message. In general, from some time before the French Revolution until some time after the Revolution of 1848, Germany was characterized by the "radicalism" of students and professors on the one hand; and, on the other, since professors were a species of public officials, and many students became professional government servants, by a certain receptivity in the governments themselves, not indeed to revolution, but to ideas of world-renewal and sweeping change.

Secret societies proliferated in Germany for various reasons, as a protection against censorship and police controls, as a means of overcoming political localism, and as centers for more exciting discussions than were possible in the open reading societies, which sprang up in Germany as in other countries.[4] Freemasonry became more concerned with worldly affairs than in England, and more perversely mysterious than in France. From the 1770's or before, there were secret societies of both progressive and conservative orientation, designed both to advance and to combat the *Aufklärung*. The Rosicrucians were conservative on social questions. The famous Illuminati were radical in their way. Founded in 1778 by Adam Weishaupt, a professor of natural law at Ingolstadt in Bavaria, the Order of Illuminati was apparently modeled on the student associations, but in 1780 it became identified with Masonry and the occultist tradition by A. F. von Knigge of Hanover. It recruited a few hundred members, who were initiated into a private doctrine of world salvation, quasi-religious and quasi-enlightened; but it had no political program, and indeed it spurned mere practical action, while urging its "adepts" to infiltrate the governments and the universities, to acquire power without much thought as to its application. The order was suppressed by the Elector of Bavaria in 1785. Various of its members turned up as individual revolutionary

[3] Valjavec, *Entstehung*, 235.
[4] On secret societies, the Illuminati, etc., see Valjavec, 229-39; Dróz, *Allemagne*, 399-419. There is a large heterogeneous literature.

enthusiasts in the 1790's. The fame of the order, however, is *ex post facto*, a creation of counter-revolutionary propagandists like the Abbé Barruel, who in the 1790's attributed to the Illuminati an importance that they never had. It was true, nevertheless, that secret associations continued to flourish in Germany, of both revolutionary and counter-revolutionary persuasion, mostly quite ineffectual so far as their secrecy permits any judgment of their operations. Examples are the Vienna Jacobins described in Chapter v, and the counter-revolutionary Eudämonists described later in the present chapter.

The habit of mind engendered both in the secret groups and in the much broader spheres of public discussion and journalism was increasingly political in that attention turned more to questions of government and society, but at the same time remained essentially non-political in an important way.[5] There was an eagerness to consider the state in the abstract, but no chance to plan courses of action, assume responsibilities, weigh alternatives and probable consequences, or form alliances with persons of different ideas from one's own. Political thinking became idealistic; it fell not on the contending interests of conflicting groups, nor the actual dilemmas of justice, nor the illogicalities of empirical problems, nor the imperfections that attend the result of all human effort, but on the pure essence of the state itself, or of liberty, right, law, human dignity, perpetual peace, or the general movement of history. The tragedy of Germany, as an acute Frenchman has expressed it, lay in the divorce between politics and intelligence.[6] The intelligence of the Germans went into philosophy; policy was an affair of cabinets, and there was no politics at all.

The Germans themselves at the time, not unaware of this situation, took pride in excelling in the realm of thought. No other people showed such a passion for metaphysics or such a concern for the absolute and the unconditioned. The doctrine of Kant, eventually recognized everywhere as a great step in technical philosophy, was of importance in Germany at the more commonplace level of the history of ideas. The conception of a Categorical Imperative, an absolute sense of duty in general, without much attention to specific duties in day-to-day living, took on momentous overtones as a basis of morality and chief evidence of the existence of God; as such it pervaded the thinking of people in quite ordinary walks of life. There was a feeling that

[5] Valjavec, *passim*, emphasizes the "politicization" of German thought after 1780; Droz, its non-political character; but both can be true according to what is meant by "political."

[6] Droz, *Rev. hist.*, Vol. 198, p. 177, and *passim* in *l'Allemagne*.

with Kant a great intellectual revolution had been effected in Germany, commensurate in its magnitude to the merely external revolution of the French. As an obscure journalist named Geich wrote in 1798: "Our nation has produced a revolution no less glorious, no less rich in consequences than the one from which has come the government of the [French] Republic. This revolution is in the country of the mind."[7]

If a revolution of the mind was a somewhat ambiguous revolution, entirely consistent with inaction on the part of the citizen, the same was true of the Revolution from Above, and indeed of the concept of citizenship itself. In France the language made possible the distinction between a *citoyen* and a *bourgeois*, for both of which the Germans had to use the word *Bürger*. This fact of language alone helps to explain why the German nobility, more than the nobles of France or Italy, looked on "citizenship" with disrelish. Even for the middle classes the old idea of a "burgher" had become archaic. It suggested the jealous localism of the walled town, and a modest acceptance of social inferiority, which the spread of education and enlightenment had rendered intolerable. Burghers came therefore to call themselves *Weltbürger*, which must be translated as cosmopolitans or citizens of the world. The word suggests the absence of national consciousness, and *Weltbürgertum* was long seen by historians as a stage on the way to a more mature and final phase, the *Nationalstaat*.[8] It is not necessary, however, to limit oneself to so negative a view, and it is illuminating to throw the emphasis, not on a *Welt* that was the absence of nationality, but on the *Bürger* who was trying to think of himself as a citizen. As a young diarist at Hamburg confided to himself in 1794: "While inwardly I strive to become a staunch republican, even a democrat, outwardly I admit to being a *Weltbürger*."[9]

Increasingly the German burgher was convinced that, with the broad formation of mind and character which the Germans called *Bildung*, he had claims to recognition that monarchs and noblemen must respect. He believed in natural rights, which he called the rights

---

[7] J. Droz, *La pensée politique et morale des Cisrhenans* (Paris, 1940), 39. Droz quotes at length from various inaccessible journals of the period edited by Geich and others.

[8] Classically set forth by F. Meinecke, *Weltbürgertum und Nationalstaat: Studien zur Genesis des deutschen Nationalstaates* (Berlin, 1908).

[9] From the diary of Ferdinand Beneke (1774-1848), published by Valjavec in the appendix to his *Entstehung*, 445. It is the argument of Groote, *Entstehung des National-bewustseins*, that the *Weltbürger* first tried to reach out to other classes and kinds of people everywhere or anywhere, then developed a national consciousness stressing the similarities between Germans, but not, as in nationalism, glorifying their differences from others.

of humanity, long before the French Revolution. The *Weltbürger* was a potential citizen in search of a country. It must be a country of like-minded persons, a true community, assuring a measure of liberty and equality. Some, in the 1790's, found this country in the French Republic, which they saw more as a human than as a French creation. It was not for them a choice between France and Germany, but between a free and an unfree society, or between an enlightened and a more backward part of Europe or the world. No treason was involved; there was no German national state for them to be traitors to—or citizens of. For the same reason—the existence of hundreds of jurisdictions unrelated except by the ritual of the Holy Empire—there was no arena or forum of collective public action in Germany. In addition, neither the nobleman nor the peasant would work with the burgher, nor he with them. The *Weltbürger*, however excited, was condemned to inaction. His "revolution" was in the mind.

In Prussia the situation was somewhat different because of the prestige of the monarchy. Not typical of Germany as a whole, with a few duchies near the Dutch border but most of its territories lying east of the Elbe (in what are now East Germany and Poland), Prussia was the largest German state other than Austria. Its burghers, in Berlin, Königsberg, and elsewhere, had become rather class-conscious with respect to the agrarian and military *Junker* nobility, but their confidence in the monarchy remained firm. A codification of Prussian law, made public in 1791, was finally promulgated in 1794. The code in fact sanctioned the separation of legal classes in the *Ständestaat*, recognizing a different and unequal status in nobles, burghers, and peasants, and so was in fact contrary to everything in the French Revolution from the Declaration of 1789 to the Code Napoleon of 1804.[10] It was, however, a code—regular, known, predictable, well administered, and, on its own premises, intended to be just. The Prussians took pride in living in a *Rechtstaat*, or state of law.

Sympathy with the French Revolution was widespread in Prussia. The common belief, however, was that the French were only struggling to obtain what the Prussians already enjoyed, and that certainly no popular disturbance was necessary in Prussia, where the monarchy itself would confer all the benefits at which revolution, all too fruitlessly, aimed. Nor was the belief without a tincture of evidence to sustain it. "Jacobins," that is, persons who disapproved of the war with France, or who favored some extension and equalization of civil

---

[10] For the text of parts of the Prussian code see *Age*, I, 509-12.

rights in Prussia, were fairly numerous even in the upper classes. Most exalted among them was Prince Henry, the king's uncle and brother of Frederick the Great. In the Prussian officer corps the British diplomat, Lord Malmesbury, found "a strong taint of democracy," by which he must have meant a reluctance to accept the foreign policy of Great Britain.[11]

There were in fact new stirrings in Prussia, especially after Frederick William III became king in 1797. Serfdom was ended on the crown domain. Studies were made in the General Staff, signalizing the need of reforms which were not instituted until after the collapse of the army at Jena almost ten years later. Thus an officer named Behrenhorst, in 1797, pointing to American, Dutch, and French examples, found that peoples made better soldiers when they felt a positive emotional attachment to their political constitution. A Lieutenant Colonel Karl Ludwig Lecoq proposed that the officer ranks be opened to men of the educated middle classes, and that, for the enlisted ranks, Prussia should cease to rely so much upon "foreigners" (Germans from outside the Prussian dominions) and draw more on "actual citizens," *wirkliche Bürger des Staates*. "An improvement in the soldier's inner spirit," said Lecoq, "is of more real advantage than an increase of numbers." Hermann von Boyen, the later reformer, wrote in 1797 that public floggings and degrading punishments should be abolished. They killed, he said, "a certain self-feeling which must be considered the source of courage." Effective discipline must rest upon the inculcation in the common soldier of a sense of his own honor. All these were lessons drawn in Prussia from the Revolution. But the necessary building up of "spirit" was to be done by the authority of the Prussian government itself, so that no concessions to revolution or to popular clamor need be made. "The salutary revolution which you made from below," the Prussian minister Struensee remarked to a Frenchman in 1799, "will take place gradually here in Prussia. The king is a democrat in his way; he is working constantly to limit the privileges of the nobility. In a few years there will be no more privileged classes in Prussia."[12]

Considered a "Jacobin," and a co-worker of Struensee's, was none

---

[11] Malmesbury to Grenville, Oct. 21, 1794, in *Diaries and Correspondence*, 4 vols. (London, 1845), III, 137-39.

[12] Extracts from various staff studies, either unpublished at the time or published in technical journals, were printed in M. Jähns, *Geschichte der Kriegswissenschaften vornehmlich in Deutschland*, 3 vols. (Munich, 1891); see III, 2127, 2252, 2280. It is curious to find, in 1798, a certain von Ribbentrop warning against admission of Jews into the army (2253). Struensee's statement is quoted by Droz, *Allemagne*, 109.

other than the grandfather of Bismarck, a typical career official named
A. L. Mencken. Accompanying the royal party on the military prom-
enade that ended at Valmy, he was known for French proclivities
even then. In 1796, he was commissioned to plan the organization of
the part of Poland taken in the Third Partition. It was a task looked
forward to with satisfaction by liberals in many parts of Germany,
for whom it seemed a good thing for the cowls and cassocks of Warsaw
to yield to the brisk bearers of a Protestant and modern enlightenment.
Mencken drew up a detailed plan, which was said both to embody
certain lessons of the French Revolution, and to be usable in a reorganization of the Prussian monarchy as a whole. Such, however, are the
ambiguities of authoritarian revolution that no one can say, without
more knowledge, whether the "Jacobin" Mencken and his grandson,
the "red reactionary," would have actually differed in very much.[13]

Both ideological attitudes and considerations of foreign policy produced in Germany a strong current of neutralism. It became manifest
even in Hanover, which belonged to the King of England, and where
there was an attempt in the diet of Calenberg to summon a National
Assembly of the "Calenberg Nation" to declare neutrality in the quarrel
between George III and the French Republic.[14] Here also, in Northwest
Germany, Malmesbury reported "a great Jacobin party" in 1795. The
German diplomatic historian, Bailleu, writing a hundred years later,
concluded that the war of 1792 was the most unpopular war that
Prussia had ever fought.[15] It was widely believed that the war was
England's war, waged by the modern Carthage to enlarge its control
of overseas trade and shipping. Such was the view not only of excited
German republicans, or of the kind of liberals who did not see in the
British parliament a model for imitation. It could be heard even at the
card-tables in royal courts.[16] Prussia made peace in 1795, taking with it
Germany north of the Main in a policy of neutrality in which it stubbornly persisted for eleven years. An ideological and class explanation
of Prussian neutrality was even then offered. "The unfortunate neutrality system," wrote a contemporary, "is the fruit of the rivalry be-

---

[13] There is an account of Mencken in the *Deutsche Allgemeine Biographie*.
[14] G. S. Ford, *Hanover and Prussia, 1795-1803: A Study in Neutrality* (New York,
1903), 46; Droz, *Allemagne*, 131. Calenberg was the part of the electorate that included
the city of Hanover.
[15] P. Bailleu, "König Friedrich Wilhelm II und die Genesis des Friedens von Basel,"
in *Hist. Zeitschrift*, Vol. 75 (1895), 237-75.
[16] See the indignant report of Grenville's agent, de Luc, Berlin, March 13, 1798,
in Gt. Brit.: Hist. MSS Commission, *Manuscripts of J. B. Fortescue Preserved at Dropmore*, IV, 128.

tween the nobility and the Third Estate. The former, partly for personal reasons, and partly because it gets better prices for its raw products from the English, wanted a war against France. The latter, composed of the industrious and literary classes, wanted an alliance with France. The government, forever beset by both parties, now takes the middle course and remains neutral."[17]

Mainz Jacobins and Cisrhenane Republicans

For Germany it is even less possible than for Switzerland or Italy to trace the agitations that occurred in a multitude of places without any central focus. It was in the Rhineland and Southwest Germany that revolutionary republicanism became most apparent. But two other places must be mentioned.

The nearest thing to a mass upheaval occurred among the peasants of Electoral Saxony in 1790.[18] Here, as in neighboring Bohemia, the rural people showed a surprising interest in newspapers, and made positive efforts to learn about the peasant rebellion in France; they were also aroused, as in Bohemia, by unorthodox religious prophets, as when a certain deacon of Döbeln saw signs of the second coming of Christ in the French and Belgian revolutions. The peasants revolted against the servile and seigneurial system. The noble landowners took refuge in Dresden. For a few weeks the unorganized insurgents were in control of some 5,000 square kilometers of the Electorate. The rebellion has been called the most significant such movement in Germany since the Peasant War of Luther's time, and as such has attracted the attention of a recent East German historian, who finds that its importance has been gravely understated in bourgeois historiography. His conclusion, however, confirms the established view. The Saxon insurrectionaries were soon put down by the Elector's troops. Their uprising was an almost unarmed outbreak of simultaneous but unconnected local disturbances; and although the towns of the Electorate were themselves full of unrest, there was no cooperation between town and country. The peasants were isolated, and the net effect, as in Bohemia, was to strengthen the propaganda of counter-revolution. Similar troubles, though less violent, appeared in the following years in the

---

[17] G. F. W. von Cölln, *Vertraute Briefe über die innern Verhältnisse an preussischen Hofe seit dem Tode Friedrichs II*, 2 vols. (Amsterdam and Cologne, 1807), I, 141-42.
[18] Stulz and Opitz, *Volksbewegungen*; Stulz treats the peasants, Opitz the townspeople, of Electoral Saxony. For Bohemia and Poland see Chapter v above.

adjacent territory of Silesia. The protests of the rural weavers grew into a general agrarian restlessness, which reached its height in the summer of 1794, when a rumor spread among the peasantry, probably inspired by Kosciuszko's proclamation at Polaniec, that the new Prussian code would abolish forced labor on the lords' estates.[19] The rumor was of course false, and order was restored. The French had had nothing to do with the Saxon and Silesian agitations, except by the power of their example.

At the other extreme was the free city of Hamburg, the chief overseas port of Germany, a very bourgeois community where the merchant class ruled and no nobles existed, and of all the cities of Germany the most well-disposed to the French Revolution.[20] It was estimated to have no less than forty-one millionaires. Leader of the Francophile group was Heinrich Sieveking, one of the wealthiest and most active commercial magnates. His house became virtually a political club, in which French, Dutch, German, Irish, and American patriots often assembled. Such a mixed group, for example, celebrated American independence on July 4, 1796, at Sieveking's home. A. G. F. Rebmann, the most significant German exponent at this time of advanced revolutionary ideas, was also admired and befriended in these circles when he passed through Hamburg. In 1797 a few Batavian and Hamburg patriots founded a new association, the Philanthropic Society, which worked to promote Theophilanthropy and republicanism. It sent congratulations to Peter Ochs on the Swiss revolution, and it attracted the attention of an investigating committee of the British House of Commons.[21] On the whole, however, the Hamburg republicans had no idea that much change was needed in Hamburg, or even in Germany. For France they simply had a warm fellow-feeling, reinforced by a general belief that the principles of the Revolution were a good thing for the world.

As in Holland, Switzerland, and Italy, so in Germany it took the

[19] Donath and Markov, *Kampf um Freiheit*, 26-27; Valjavec, 201. Here again, the idea that the French of the Directory had lost their appeal to the working classes must be classified, in some measure, as a popular fallacy, or rather a learned cliché. A shoemaker at Giessen was reported to say in 1798 that the rich were "so harsh with the poor people hereabouts that it would be no wonder if they threw the gates open to the French, if they came this far." Valjavec, 227.

[20] P. Rudolf, *Frankreich im Urteil der Hamburger Zeitschriften in den Jahren 1789-1810* (Hamburg, 1933); Droz, *Allemagne*, 135-54; P. Schramm, *Hamburg, Deutschland und die Welt* (Munich, 1943), 25-29; Beneke's diary in Valjavec, 437-54.

[21] *Korrespondenz des Peter Ochs*, 3 vols. (Basel, 1927-1937), ii, 360; Gt. Brit., Parliament, House of Commons, *Report of the Committee of Secrecy* (London, 1799), xli. Droz, *Allemagne*, 143, says that the Philanthropic Society was closed in November 1798, before the Parliamentary committee published its apprehensions.

actual arrival of the French army to precipitate local democrats into open defiance. This happened in the Rhineland beginning in 1792.

The Left Bank of the Rhine was the most microscopically pulverized region in the Holy Roman Empire. Between Alsace and the Dutch frontier there were about a hundred and fifty states. Some of the largest of these were church-states, where the bishop governed as temporal prince. The large bishopric of Liége has already been mentioned in connection with Belgium. There were also the three great archiepiscopal sees, Mainz, Trier, and Cologne. The three cities so named, together with others in the archbishoprics, such as Coblenz and Bonn, were far from being cities on the order of Hamburg. Commercial development in the Rhineland had long been at a standstill. The towns were cathedral towns, or university towns, or courtly and governmental centers, in which the leading persons of economic importance were old-fashioned and conservative gild members. As a result, there was very little bourgeois development, but a large supply of middle-class intellectuals—Catholic ecclesiastics, university professors, librarians, doctors, journalists, booksellers, writers, and employees of government.

The Rhineland had been under strong French influence at least since the time of Louis XIV, and news of the French Revolution produced an immediate impact.[22] As early as 1790 there were cases of peasants, who were not serfs as in eastern Germany, refusing to pay taxes and seigneurial dues. Many purely indigenous disputes were re-vivified by the French example. In the diets of the territories of Trier and Cologne there were demands for tax equality between Third Estate, nobles, and clergy. The privileged classes made no concession. The arrival of French émigrés, who congregated especially at Coblenz, had contrary effects. Their accounts of the Revolution increased the conservatism of some, while their aristocratic behavior sharpened the radicalism of others. The local rulers became more conservative, adopt-

[22] The great published source collection is J. Hansen, *Quellen zur Geschichte des Rheinlandes im Zeitalter der französischen Revolution*, 4 vols. (Bonn, 1931-1938). Useful also for the sources it incorporates is the work of a German republican of 1848, drawing on the papers of his father, a Cisrhenane of 1797: Jakob Venedey, *Die deutsche Republikaner unter der französischen Republik* (Leipzig, 1870). For a contemporary account in English see Ann Radcliffe, *A journey made in the summer of 1794 through Holland and the western frontier of Germany*, 2 vols. (London, 1795). The best historical treatment is by Droz, *Allemagne*, 187-247, 439-50, and the whole of his *Cisrhenans*. Droz holds that German national consciousness took form around a sense of cultural and moral mission, which in the Rhineland in these years expressed itself in the belief (exquisitely ironical to a Frenchman) that Rhineland Germans should be annexed to the Republic for France's good. There is much illuminating material on the French occupation of the Rhineland in J. Godechot, *Les commissaires aux armées sous le Directoire*, 2 vols. (Paris, 1938).

ing, among other measures, a stricter control over the universities. Two university professors who had taken priestly orders, and who had in fact become very unorthodox, may be mentioned. One, A. J. Dorsch, professor of philosophy at Mainz, and one of the rare individuals who had actually belonged to the order of the Illuminati, was deprived of his position in 1791 for Kantian opinions. He spent the following years collaborating with the French in the Rhineland. Eulogius Schneider, a highly successful professor at Bonn, was removed in 1791 for the liberality of his views in the divinity of Christ. He went to Alsace, plunged into the Revolution in France itself, became increasingly violent, and was executed in Strasbourg in 1794 by Saint-Just as an extremist.

There was also Georg Forster, librarian of the University of Mainz, a man of about forty, well known for a variety of publications on science and literature. A cosmopolitan and peripatetic intellectual, born German but of Scottish background, brought up near Danzig, where he had formed Polish connections (he was at one time professor at the University of Vilna), he had, in his youth, accompanied Captain Cook around the world. At Mainz in 1792 he formed a political club, like the clubs so common all over Europe. At Mainz in the summer of 1792 such a club was unavoidably secret. The East German historian, Walter Markov, calls it "a secret democratic party on the model of the Jacobin club,"[23] though how a secret association could resemble the Paris Jacobins is impossible to understand. In October 1792, a month after Valmy, the French general Custine occupied the city of Mainz. Looking about for inhabitants to employ in a provisional government, and finding the gildsmen and town councillors uncooperative, Custine turned to Forster and his group, since they welcomed the French with enthusiasm. The group included a doctor, G. C. Wedekind; a director of the Protestant school at Worms, G. W. Böhmer; and four professors at the University of Mainz, including A. J. Hoffmann, who was to attempt revolution in Swabia and live to see the Revolution of 1848, and Matthias Metternich, a mathematician unrelated to the noble house of the same name.

The Mainz "Jacobins" found hundreds of like-minded persons in the neighboring cities and principalities. The French were at first well received throughout the Rhineland. The peasants favored the agrarian, fiscal, and property reforms of the Revolution. In the towns, the

---

[23] *Kampf um Freiheit*, 11. There is a large mass of writing by and about Georg Forster.

Weltbürger had long been thinking of liberty, equality, and the *Rechte der Menschheit*; and there was little in the crazy-quilt of political geography—free cities, duchies, bishoprics and territories of imperial knights, some of them no bigger than any well-to-do gentleman's private estates—to which a person of enlarged views could feel much positive political loyalty. For everyone who greeted the French with enthusiasm there were a dozen who saw nothing in their own situation to defend. At Aachen, for example, Protestants were annoyed at their failure to receive toleration from the Catholic council of that free city; and since the city possessed rural "subjects" who had begun to object to their inferior status, the peasants offered no resistance to the French. "The spirit in these countries could not be worse," as Freiherr von Stein, the future reformer of Prussia, reported to his government in Berlin. "The magistrates of Worms sent a deputation to meet the French, to give them the keys to the city; and I have no doubt that the burghers here will do the same as soon as the enemy appears before the gates."[24]

A basis existed, therefore, for some kind of democratic movement. The problem in some ways resembled that at Liége, which the modern mind thinks of as Belgian, but which in 1792 was a state of the Holy Roman Empire like any other. The difference was that the bishopric of Liége, relatively industrialized, had already had an indigenous revolution in 1789. It was explained in Chapter II how the Liége democrats, having no desire or reason to combine with the adjoining "Belgian" provinces at a time when they were under conservatively aristocratic domination, took the initiative, in January 1793, in requesting annexation to France. Similarly, in the principalities of the Left Bank, there was no reason why persons who favored change should wish to combine with a "Germany" which had no more existence than "Belgium." Nor was there any special tie among the Left Bank territories themselves, from which the notion of a separate Rhineland Republic could derive any strength.

In March 1793 Forster assembled at Mainz a gathering of patriots from other clubs in the neighborhood, the "Rhenish-German National Convention." It declared the independence of a new state, which could

---

[24] Hansen, *Quellen*, II, 378. Hansen prints many other similar sources. Edmund Burke wrote in 1791 that a "great revolution is preparing in Germany" and that the Rhineland was particularly infected with the *droit de l'homme*; he thought the Westphalia settlement should be maintained in Germany, to preserve the balance of power in Europe, whether the Germans liked it or not. See his *Thoughts on French Affairs* (1791) in *Writings* (Boston, 1901), IV, 328-34.

not be otherwise described than as the "region from Landau to Bingen." This area, which had no identity whatsoever, reached from the Alsatian border about fifty miles north to the bend in the Rhine. The only sovereign was declared to be *das freie Volk*. In the abolition of former sovereignties it was necessary to specify no less than twenty-three jurisdictions, not including the imperial knights nor all the church bodies and free cities which had territorial powers. Three days later the Convention declared for incorporation in the French Republic. At a time when language and culture were not felt to be divisive, the "free people" of the new phantom state, or at least their spokesmen, expected to enjoy more freedom in the great Republic than outside it.[25]

The tide of war turned at this very moment with Dumouriez' defeat at Neerwinden. The Coalition reoccupied Mainz and the zone around it. But the French returned in a few years, and by 1797 another movement of revolutionary character developed. It took the form of demands for a Cisrhenane Republic. The leadership included the former Mainz Jacobins, Wedekind, Dorsch, A. J. Hoffmann, and Professor Metternich (Forster had died), but was now amplified by other groups, by men who had been in trouble during the imperial restoration, those who had formed habits of working with the French occupation authorities, and still others, often disinterested patriots and progressives, who were excited by the spread of revolution since 1793, as now manifested in the Batavian and the Cisalpine Republics. The most famous was Joseph Görres, now a youth in his early twenties, later famous as a Catholic social thinker. But the Cisrhenanes seem never to have numbered more than two or three thousand.

"Citizens!" cried the Cisrhenanes at Bonn to their city council. "Italy is ahead of us; it has proclaimed the Rights of Man and become a free and independent state. We wish valiantly to follow their lofty example. The power of France protects us, so that the revolution of humanity that has become necessary for us will cost no tears."[26] Dutch, Swiss, and Italians had all used this same argument. All hoped to have a peaceable revolution in which the French army would be the substitute for "tears," or mob violence and civil discord.

In newspapers, pamphlets, speeches, and meetings there was demand for a Cisrhenane Republic, to embrace the whole area from Alsace to Holland. The French general Hoche favored the idea. In later generations, in the heyday of nationalism, it was argued by many Germans, including those of radical outlook, that the Cisrhenanes had been good

[25] Hansen, *Quellen*, ii, 798-801.   [26] Hansen, iv, 67; Venedey, 292.

German patriots, warmly insistent on a Rhineland Republic, who had accepted annexation to France only under French pressure. It has more recently been shown by Jacques Droz that the Cisrhenanes were at least ambivalent on this matter, and that, far from demanding a formal independence, many of them really preferred, like the Mainz Jacobins, annexation to France from the beginning.[27] In any event, the Directory decided against a Cisrhenane Republic late in 1797, and initiated the steps which led to complete annexation by 1800. Petitions requesting annexation circulated throughout the Rhineland. Thousands of signatures were collected. Most of the population undoubtedly had no desire for incorporation with France (which now included Belgium also); on the other hand there was little resistance, since there was no alternative that had much appeal. Not only were the French in military occupation, but Rhinelanders themselves as a whole lacked positive faith in the peculiarities of their Old Regime. Across the Rhine lay no political Germany for them to join, but only a Gothic wonderland of incongruous principalities, verging off in the East to the land of *Junker* and serf. It was neither surprising nor discreditable, given such choices, for the Rhinelanders to accept union with France and Belgium. Annexed until 1814, they proved very amenable citizens, and they benefited from various reforms which the Napoleonic empire mediated to them from the Revolution.

Like so much else in Germany, the Cisrhenane movement was ambiguous, and if a revolution at all it was a revolution of the mind. Many Cisrhenanes, a handful of youngsters, doctrinaires, and professors, had the presumption to conceive of themselves as equals to the French in the matter of revolution. They hoped, in becoming French citizens, to make a moral contribution to the Republic which was sorely needed. "In the last ten years," wrote Görres, "we have seen in Germany a revolution which has done no less good for mankind in matters of theory than that of France in matters of practice—I mean the reforms of Kant in philosophy." Or as another Cisrhenane, Wyttenbach, put it: "What a blessing for humanity that the two revolutions, the French and the German, have occurred at the same

---

[27] Droz, *Cisrhenans*, 17-19. Venedey, *Deutsche Republikaner*, 308, writing as a "radical" in 1870, insists upon the anti-French national patriotism of the German republicans of the 1790's. Of the thousands who signed petitions for annexation to France, one of the more curious and obscure cases was that of Cornelius de Pauw, whose *Recherches philosophiques sur les Américains*, published in 1768, had been well known for its thesis of the degeneration of the flora and fauna, including man, in America. De Pauw, an uncle of Anacharsis Cloots, and of equally unidentifiable nationality, signed the petition for annexation at Xanten in 1798. Hansen, IV, 699.

time! May the one raise up what the other has destroyed!"[28] To Latin vivacity would now be added a German earnestness in one great commonwealth. The Swiss, too, it may be remembered, had expressed a similar idea: they would fortify the principles of the French Revolution with "German morality and higher philosophical culture."[29] There were two revolutions, which were of similar force; and to the Declaration of the Rights of Man and Citizen would be added the equally emancipating and stirring doctrine of inward freedom and unconditional duty, the Categorical Imperative.

The case of Rebmann, a prolific radical journalist, is very illuminating. Born in 1768 in central Germany, and educated for the law, he turned to writing, and by 1792 was established at Leipzig in Saxony, where memories of popular rebellion were much alive. He exposed the misery of the stocking-workers at Erlangen, and set forth a socialist idea that the government should purchase and own the stocking-frames, so as to give work to the needy. He likewise, in 1794, translated certain speeches of Robespierre. Forced to move on, he went to Erfurt, a Saxon city which belonged to the distant Archbishop of Mainz. At this time some of the Mainz Jacobins were imprisoned at the citadel of Erfurt, so that Rebmann came to know something of their revolutionary efforts of the year before. He also, in his paper, saluted the Negro revolution in Haiti, and denounced the evils of European colonialism. Again driven away, he went to Hamburg, where he was well received by Sieveking's group; passed on through Holland, where he mixed with the Batavian revolutionaries; and arrived in Paris in 1796, shortly after the arrest of Babeuf. In Paris he published a journal in German (estimating that there were four thousand German workers in the city), in which he seems to have shown little or no knowledge of Babeuf—so limited, apparently, was the impact of Babouvism even in radical circles. He was now very critical not only of the Directory but even of Hébert and Robespierre; he thought the French Revolution had failed "for the fundamental reason that it was lacking in morality." "Paradoxical as it may seem," he complacently wrote, "the truly republican spirit, enlightenment and sound philosophy are infinitely more widespread in Germany than in France."[30]

Rebmann joined in the demand for a Cisrhenane Republic, which he hoped would be the first step toward a great unified democratic republic for all Germany. More than other Cisrhenanes, he resisted the

[28] Quoted by Droz, *Cisrhenans*, 38-39.   [29] See above, p. 404.
[30] Droz, *Allemagne*, 254-58.

idea of annexation, on the ground that the French did not understand true moral freedom; but he abruptly changed his mind, influenced by the Director Reubell, and in November 1798 accepted not only annexation but appointment as a judge in the newly organizing department of Donnersberg or Mont-Tonnerre. Obliged, as he explained, to abandon the beautiful dream, the *schöne Traum*, of making "Germany a republic and the Germans a nation," he was glad that at least some Germans, those west of the Rhine, could be free citizens of a free country.[31] Rebmann, giving up his writing, continued to serve in the judiciary of the Rhineland throughout the Napoleonic years, and even retained a similar post after the Restoration, when some of the territory passed to the crown of Bavaria. Rebmann was of course not the only advanced democrat of the 1790's who held office under the Consulate and Empire. There were many similar cases among the French, Dutch, Poles, and Italians. Some democrats accepted Napoleon, some did not; and both had their reasons.[32]

Southwest Germany, east of the Rhine, was also the scene of considerable unrest during the years from 1796 to 1800.[33] Here it was the well-to-do non-noble class that was most disaffected—doctors, lawyers, merchants, government servants, and men of independent income. They formed clubs and read the numerous papers, such as Posselt's

[31] Hansen, *Quellen*, IV, 793, n. 4.
[32] The *Rebmannfrage* seems to be in need of clarification. Hedwig Voegt's complaint that Rebmann has been shamefully belittled by bourgeois historiography seems hardly fair, since the French bourgeois Droz devotes a whole chapter to him, and the West German bourgeois, Valjavec (218-23) calls him the most important revolutionary journalist in Germany before 1848. Voegt (*Jakobinische Literatur*, 112-30) praises him for his views on class war, but she also emphasizes his attack on "colonialism." It is Valjavec who gives attention to his socialist ideas, and his defense of the Erlangen stocking-workers, of which Voegt seems not to have heard. Voegt, Valjavec, and the *Deutsche Allgemeine Biographie* are all silent on Rebmann's Cisrhenane period, which, however, is abundantly documented in Hansen's source collection, where he may be traced through the copious index. Droz thinks Rebmann the most important German republican propagandist of the 1790's, and notes his Cisrhenane phase, but as a Frenchman is a little impatient of his claims to German moral superiority, and as a good neo-Jacobin feels that Rebmann's ideas on revolution were nebulous, unrealistic, moralizing, and basically not very "radical." One would not suppose that these three writers are talking about the same person. The discrepancies can be attributed to the fact that Rebmann's writings are numerous, rare, scattered, and inaccessible; but Voegt's ignoring of Valjavec and the Hansen documents is hard to explain on this ground. The statement in the *Deutsche Allg. Biog.* that Rebmann became a member of the Legion of Honor in 1804 is not borne out by published membership lists.
[33] K. Obser, "Der marquis von Poterat und die revolutionäre Propaganda am Oberrhein, 1796," in *Zeitschrift für die Geschichte des Oberrheins*, VII (1892), 385-444; *id.*, "Die revolutionäre Propaganda am Oberrhein im Jahre 1798," *ibid.*, XXIV (1909), 199-258; Biro, *German Policy*, II, 568-86; Droz, *Allemagne*, 126-30; Valjavec, *Entsethung*, 43, 203.

Annalen, that favored the new order in Europe. Some of them secretly worked with the French emissary, Poteratz, sent by the Directory in 1796. The Directory cancelled Poteratz' mission, and matters quieted down; but A. J. Hoffmann and others of the original Mainz Jacobins continued to agitate across the Rhine, reinforced by Rebmann in 1798, by which time the Helvetic Republic added a strong stimulus also. At the very moment of the Basel revolution, in January 1798, there was a small *putsch* of Germans from Basel into Baden. In Württemberg there was a long history of parliamentary disputation between the reigning duke and the estates, which had preserved their powers to a degree unusual in Germany. The old quarrels broke out afresh in 1798, but this time with a more modern note; a deputy in the estates, named Baz, actively sought French intervention, and projects were even drawn up for a Swabian or Danubian Republic, under a constitution to be modeled on the French constitution of the Year III. In 1800 a republican plot was brought to light in Bavaria. None of these movements was ever supported by the French government. Their failure illustrates the general truth that nowhere, except temporarily in Poland, did revolutionaries or radical democrats accomplish anything without French aid. The agitation subsided after 1800. Probably a good many south-German "Jacobins" were pacified by the active reformism, with "abolition of feudalism," equalization of civil rights, and rationalization of territory, that prevailed in Baden, Württemberg, and Bavaria in the time of Napoleon.

The Colossi of the "Goethezeit"

Above the busy level of journalists, pamphleteers, publicists, and professors rose the solemn peaks of the great authors of the Age of Goethe, on whom the little that can be said here must be trifling in comparison to what has been said before.

Goethe himself was among the various civilian spectators, like A. L. Mencken, who were present at the cannonade of Valmy. In a phrase often quoted, he later remembered having said, when asked by a companion what he thought of it: "Here and on this day begins a new era of world history, and you can say that you were there." The young poet, Tieck, longed to fight alongside Dumouriez, whose republican army he compared to the Greeks at Thermopylae. Klopstock penned an Ode to the French Revolution when the war began in April 1792.[34]

---

[34] Excerpts from Goethe, Tieck, and Klopstock are given by Markov, *Kampf um Freiheit,* 39-47.

Schiller's Ode to Joy, written several years earlier, was a favorite with German republicans of the 1790's:

> Seid umschlungen, Millionen,
> Diesen Kuss der ganzen Welt!

Sometimes the words were sung to the same tune as the Marseillaise.[35] Schiller, however, whose early dramas had upheld a stormy idea of freedom, turned against the violence of the French Revolution and what seemed to him to be the low level of its aims as revealed in practice. By 1801 he found true liberty to be not of this world:

> Edler Freund: Wo öffnet sich dem Frieden,
> Wo der Freiheit sich ein Zufluchtsort?

Viewing the struggle between France and Britain as a detached observer, he washed his hands of both. No liberty could be at stake in such a contest:

> Freiheit ist nur in dem Reich der Träume
> Und das Schöne blüht nur im Gesang.[36]

The temptation to flee to a dream-world of true liberty led on into the peculiarities of German romanticism, and the idea that the beautiful could flower only in works of art, *im Gesang*, contributed to the serenities of classical Weimar. Both represented a form of withdrawal or an aesthetic attitude for which the interest of events lay in the kind of appeal they made to a spectator, who, while remaining essentially unexcited and uninvolved, could enjoy a succession of somewhat literary emotions—admiration, inspiration, indignation, or disgust. They were part of what Droz characterizes as the humanist reaction to the French Revolution, shared by Goethe, Schiller, Wieland, and Wilhelm von Humboldt.[37] These men did not explicitly oppose the Revolution; they entered into no noisy counter-revolutionary polemics; but they were troubled by the violence and fanaticism that were engendered,

---

[35] Venedey, *Deutsche Republikaner*, 3-4; Schiller, *Werke* (Leipzig, 1895), I, 61. The verses may be translated: "Be embracèd, O ye Millions, Here's a kiss for all the world!"

[36] "Der Antritt des neuen Jahrhunderts" (1801), *ibid.*, 264-65. In translation: "Noble friend: Where opens there for peace, Or where for freedom now a place of refuge?" And: "Freedom is only in the realm of dreams, And the beautiful blooms only in song."

[37] Droz, *Allemagne*, 297-336. For the argument that the lack of an outlet for action, together with certain social and career frustrations, led many into the "way of the dream," or the expectation of a "miracle" (i.e., solutions without effort or understanding), see the brilliant book by H. Brunschwig, *La crise de l'état prussien à la fin du XVIII*e *siècle et la genèse de la mentalité romantique* (Paris, 1947).

and feared that so much obsession with politics would have a bad effect on higher civilization. Deeply non-political, preoccupied with the problems of an elite, concerned for the cultivation of mind and taste, they were too much interested in making room for romantic genius on the one hand, or for classically rounded personalities on the other, to care much about popular doctrines of liberty and equality, by which so many irreplaceable human values and achievements might be threatened. For this "humanist" school, while their critique fell on the betrayals of liberty, it was essentially the doctrine of equality—whether interpreted to mean more equality of wealth, political participation, legal rights, career opportunities, or education—that they found incomprehensible or distasteful.

The thought of Herder, as of Wilhelm von Humboldt, while not expressed in belligerent terms, exerted an influence in an anti-French and anti-Revolutionary direction, since it represented human affairs as moving forward—not by taking thought, nor by setting up the abstract goals of justice, and still less by learning from foreign countries—but by a process of organic or plant-like growth, in which each people or culture went through an experience of which the germ was somehow inherent in itself. A similar insistence on national peculiarity, and on unconscious historic growth as preferable to deliberate planning, could be found in Burke, who was widely read in the 1790's in Germany. At the level of disputatious journalism these ideas were developed by others, many of them Hanoverians, and so especially susceptible to English influence, such as Ernst Brandes and A. G. Rehberg.[38] The ultimate tenor of such a position was to argue that Germany was altogether different from France, and indeed from the whole of Western Civilization, by whose influence its true and deeper character might be corrupted. It was not until later, however, with the development of German nationalism in the nineteenth century, that these implications made themselves evident, superseding the eager cosmopolitanism of the *Weltbürger*.

Kant, Fichte, and Hegel were all warmly sympathetic to revolutionary republicanism. Of Kant, it has been said[39] that he understood the French Revolution better than any other German philosopher, both on its everyday level, since he assiduously read the newspapers while living quietly as professor at Königsberg, and on the more abstract level

---

[38] On Brandes and Rehberg see Droz, *Allemagne*, 348-70. Droz also has chapters or sections on the more eminent thinkers. See also parts of W. H. Bruford, *Culture and Society in Classical Weimar, 1775-1806* (Cambridge, Eng., 1962).

[39] Droz, *Allemagne*, 155.

where his own thought moved. Acknowledging a deep indebtedness to Rousseau, he saw the Revolution as a moral act, an attempt to create a society in which the worth and freedom of the human personality could be unobstructed. There was a strong note of equality in his famous ethical maxim, that each man should so live that the principle of his action might become a universal law. Kant was distrustful of the English, to whom, like many others in Germany, he mainly attributed the continuation of the war. His project for *Perpetual Peace*, written in 1795, was used in Prussia to support the argument for neutrality. In his insistence on the need of moral education for a free society Kant was not altogether different from Robespierre, and Kant himself never ceased to explain the violence of the Terror by the threats of the counter-revolution; but his philosophy became so widely accepted that conservatives in Germany made use of it also. In its conservative form, the argument held that no great improvement in society could occur, and surely no "revolution" should be undertaken, except under the guidance of high-minded and unselfish leaders, and after moral education of the whole citizenry was well-advanced—a simplified "moral" interpretation that Kant himself did not maintain. The criticism to be made of Kant, in which the French historian Droz is seconded by a recent American writer, is that, despite his undoubted knowledge of current events, his philosophy left too impassable a gulf between the ideas of liberty and political action on the one hand, and the domains of empirical knowledge and the actual thinking of individual persons on the other.[40]

Fichte and Hegel, born respectively in 1762 and 1770, were young enough for the upheaval of the revolutionary decade to have a formative effect on their innermost thought and feeling.[41] The same, indeed, has been said of Beethoven, also born in 1770, of whom it may be true that the grand movement for human liberation entered somehow into his music; but it is the nature of music to make such speculations controversial.[42] Since they dealt in words, the impact of the Revolution on Hegel and Fichte is easily documented.

[40] Droz, *ibid.*, 155-71; L. Krieger, *The German Idea of Freedom* (Boston, 1957), 124-25.

[41] See the special number, entitled "La Révolution de 1789 et la pensée moderne," Vol. 128 (1939) of the *Revue philosophique de la France et de l'Etranger*, where M. Guéroult writes on "Fichte et la Révolution française" and J. Hyppolite on "La signification de la Révolution française dans la Phénoménologie de Hegel." The same number is memorable for Ernest Barker's views on Edmund Burke.

[42] See the erratic little book by Bishop F. S. Noli, *Beethoven and the French Revolution* (New York, 1947).

The young Hegel found himself at Bern for four years, from 1792 to 1796, during which he observed the ruling oligarchy of the Swiss old regime at close hand, and sympathized strongly with the revolutionary agitation in the Pays de Vaud. In 1797 he went to Stuttgart in Württemberg, where he could watch the conflict between the duke and the diet. He wrote in 1797 (but did not publish) a pamphlet marked by a vehement radicalism, which he dedicated to "the people of Württemberg," and in which he attacked both the duke for his absolutism and the diet as no more than a selfish privileged oligarchy.[43] It was of course the great French Revolution of 1789 that most profoundly impressed him. At the practical level, he could agree that it had been brought on because the monarchy had proved incompetent, and "the Court, the Clergy, the Nobility, the Parliaments themselves were unwilling to surrender the privileges they possessed." In the larger view, the Revolution embodied the Concept of Right. "Never since the sun has stood in the heavens and the planets moved about it," as he later wrote in his *Philosophy of History*, "had it been seen that man relies on his head, that is on thought, and builds reality correspondingly." If it be the chief characteristic of Hegel's philosophy to see the world as a succession of historical stages, each moving on to a higher degree of freedom, each representing the imprint of mind on outer reality, and each exhibiting an interconnectedness among all aspects of culture and society at a given moment in a common *Zeitgeist*, then this philosophy seems to have been confirmed in him, in his youth, by the acute consciousness of living at a great historical turning point, the grand upheaval of revolutionary republicanism by which everything in the world of human relations was permeated and affected. In 1802, in his *Constitution of Germany*, he called for a revolutionary modernization of the outmoded Holy Roman Empire. In later years, as is well known, Hegel became a convinced monarchist, and held that the Prussian monarchy embodied a higher if not final stage in the evolution of freedom. He never turned against the French Revolution. He did not have to, since his dialectic allowed him to see it conveniently in retrospect as a "stage," which, even though now superseded, had been necessary and right in its own time and conditions. When he delivered his Lectures on the Philosophy of History in the 1820's he made the French Revolution in a broad sense their con-

---

[43] Droz, *Allemagne*, 125.

clusion and climax—finding that "world history is nothing else but the development of the concept of freedom."[44]

Fichte, more of a firebrand than Hegel, owed his general philosophical orientation to Kant, but was inspired by the French Revolution in his most essential metaphysical insight. His doctrine was one of absolute liberty, of a liberty unrestricted by outer reality or by the Thing-in-Itself, since it was the task of the self to employ the Not-Self in the building up of a distinctive universe of its own. It was a doctrine long admired for its stern view of self-reliance, but which in the twentieth century may seem open to debate on both social and psychiatric grounds, not to mention those of theology, and which in any case hardly reflected the civic emphasis of the French Declaration of 1789. In 1793 Fichte wrote a long tract defending the French Republic against hostile criticism at the very moment when it was moving into its period of Virtue and Terror.[45] A year later he published his *Theory of Knowledge*, or *Wissenschaftslehre*. In his own mind the two books were closely connected. The French Revolution and the Fichtean Revolution were, for him, two manifestations of a common impulse, two battles in the one war for freedom. "My system," he wrote in 1795, "is the first system of liberty. As that nation [France] liberated man from external chains, my system liberates him from the chains of the Thing-in-Itself, or of external influence, and sets him forth in his first principle as a self-sufficient being. It was in the years when the French were fighting for political liberty against external forces . . . when I was writing a book on the Revolution, that there came to me as a compensation the first inklings and intimations of my system. Hence the system belongs in a way to the [French] Nation, and the question is whether that Nation wishes to adopt it openly and officially as its own, by giving me the wherewithal to develop it further."[46]

It was not to France, but to the University of Jena, that Fichte was called as professor of philosophy in 1794. He proved to be a sensational lecturer, attracting streams of students who became his personal de-

[44] See the last chapter of the *Philosophy of History* in any translation, or the *Sämtliche Werke*, Vol. xi, *Vorlesungen über die Philosophie der Geschichte* (Stuttgart, 1928), 557, 568.
[45] *Beitrag zur Berechtigung der Urteile des Publikums über die französische Revolution* (1793) in *Werke* (Berlin, 1845), vi, 39-288. Translated into French in 1859, but never into English.
[46] H. Schulz, ed., *J. G. Fichte: Briefwechsel*, 2 vols. (Leipzig, 1925), i, 449-50. See the discussion in Droz, *Allemagne*, 260-73; Guéroult, *op.cit.*; X. Léon, *Fichte et son temps*, 2 vols. (Paris, 1922-1927).

votees. He eloquently preached the liberty and equality of all men, lectured on Sundays, became involved in the affairs of the student orders, and engaged in journalistic controversy on the nature of God. The extreme counter-revolutionary paper, *Eudämonia*, of which more will be said shortly, mounted a press campaign against him; and parents began to complain of the atheism and democratic radicalism to which their sons were exposed. The University of Jena, even then, strongly upheld the principle of *Lehrfreiheit*, or freedom of teaching. The university was in the grand duchy of Weimar, and it happened that the grand duke's minister for cultural affairs was none other than Goethe. The memoranda of Goethe on the Fichte case make curious reading. Goethe was well aware of Fichte's Jacobin principles at the moment of appointment; he hoped he would be discreet; he understood that the new professor espoused democracy only in a theoretical sense, with no actual intent of subversion, etc. Fichte, however, would not be silent, and was loudly accused of atheism by his critics. Since there were many German professors who taught Fichte's views on the divine nature with impunity, it seems that the objection against him was really aimed at his politics. "I have never believed," he wrote, "that they are pursuing my so-called atheism; they are pursuing in me the freethinker who begins to make himself understood (Kant's good fortune was his obscurity)—and an infamous democrat. They are terrified as if by a ghost by the independence that my philosophy awakens."[47] Goethe and the grand-duke tried to protect him, but were finally forced to yield. He was allowed to submit a presumably voluntary resignation. *Lehrfreiheit* and everyone's dignity were technically preserved, but many outraged students departed when Fichte left, and the enrollment at Jena suffered for several years. It was a sign that the youth were not gained for the counter-revolution.

Fichte, who had been eager in 1795 to be accepted as a kind of official philosopher of the French Republic, was made even more pro-French by this experience at Jena. In the spring of 1799, as the War of the Second Coalition began, he thought that "only the French Republic can be considered by a just man as his true country . . . on its victory depend the dearest hopes and even the existence of humanity. . . . The present war is a war of principles. . . . If the French do not obtain

---

[47] *Briefwechsel*, ii, 105; Droz, *Allemagne*, 272; Fichte exhibited a certain caution in his *Appellation an das Publikum gegen die Anklage des Atheismus* (1799) in *Werke* (Berlin, 1845), v, 193-332. The whole episode of Fichte at Jena, and the state of the university at the time, are examined at length in Léon, i, 269-629.

an overwhelming predominance, and if they do not bring about a transformation in Germany, or at least in a considerable part of it, there will be no peaceful place for any man in Germany who is known to have had a free thought in his life."[48] Fichte, like the Cisrhenanes, believed that the Republic was too great and too universal an enterprise to be left to the French alone.

He began to put his hopes also in Prussia, where signs of reform were stirring, and it was to the Prussian minister, Struensee (the one who told a Frenchman that the King of Prussia was really a democrat) that Fichte dedicated his next book, *The Closed Commercial State*, published in 1800. The book drew in part on the Kantian doctrine that the purpose of the state was to improve the moral character of its citizens, and partly on what Fichte recalled of the French Republic in the Year II, when France, because of the war, had in fact been a "closed" state governed by a revolutionary dictatorship. The general idea of the book was to restrict individual liberty, and avoid dependence on foreigners outside one's own control, as a means to building a more just and desirable civil community. How Fichte became an extreme German nationalist some ten years later need not be told. In conclusion, one may agree with Leonard Krieger on both Fichte and Hegel: that they separated the idea of liberty from actual individual persons, and lodged it in a collective group, which in later years, after their revolutionary-republican period was over, became for Hegel the rational state of the Prussian monarchy, and for Fichte the cultural-linguistic-kinship community of the German people.[49]

Counter-Revolutionary Cross Currents

A conscious and controversial conservatism, deliberately aimed at discrediting the new ideas, was neither adopted by the leading thinkers and literary figures of Germany, nor sponsored by the governments of the German states. It was carried on, as was the pro-revolutionary propaganda, by writers of a lesser kind: journalists, publicists, and pamphleteers. Eventually, Friedrich Gentz became the best known of these writers. He translated Burke in 1793, and in 1799 he published at Berlin his *Historisches Journal*, which was designed to combat the whole revolutionary movement in Europe; but it is to be noted that Gentz received his emoluments not from the Prussian government but

[48] *Briefwechsel*, II, 100-101, 104; Droz, *Allemagne*, 279.
[49] *German Idea of Freedom*, 125-38, 179-92.

from the British, from which, beginning in 1800, he sometimes drew as much as £1,000 a year.[50]

Conservatism in Germany antedated the French Revolution, having first taken form as a campaign against secret societies, and against the rationalism, the alleged aridity, and the abstract ideas of the Enlightenment.[51] It was less political than in England, since it did not serve, like Burke's ideas as expressed in 1784, to protect a Parliamentary governing class against the perils of new modes of election.[52] In Germany conservatism sometimes justified the peculiarities of the small states, as in the thought of Justus Möser. Often it arose from religious sources, both Protestant and Catholic. The fact that many Lutheran pastors and Catholic priests thought of themselves as vehicles of the Enlightenment—the fact, that is, that the problems posed by rationalism were internal to the churches themselves—only made the argument the more vehement.

Among Protestants, the most notable anti-revolutionary editor was H. M. Koester, who was also a professor at the University of Giessen, where he taught history and political science. In 1777 he launched the *Neuesten Religionsbegebenheiten*, directing it against the critical and freethinking tendencies of the day, and carrying on in the 1790's with a denunciation of revolution and secret societies.[53] Protestant Germany had also long been affected by the movement of Pietism, which, so far as it taught that Christian satisfaction was to be found in subjective religious feelings, was generally conservative in its implications. Thus the Pietist Jung-Stilling remarked in 1793 that a pure and obedient Christianity, "not the spirit of revolt and revolution," was the best way "to do away with all abuses."[54] Pietism was hardly to be equated with social class, but there was an important group of Pietists among the nobles of Holstein, where they defended the privileges of the noble estates, resisted the reformist absolutism of the King of Denmark, and denounced the faculty at the University of Kiel, including the theologians there, as no better than Jacobins.[55]

Among Catholics, a group of ex-Jesuits established at Augsburg took the lead in denouncing the Enlightenment as a menace to re-

[50] Golo Mann, *Secretary of Europe; the Life of Friedrich Gentz* (New Haven, 1946), 50.
[51] One of the leading arguments of Valjavec, *passim*, but see 5, 11, 255-302.
[52] See *Age*, I, 308-17.
[53] Valjavec, 305.
[54] Quoted by Droz, *Allemagne*, 422.
[55] *Ibid.*, 423-38. The ex-revolutionary, Dumouriez, in Holstein in 1798, also denounced the Kiel faculty for Jacobinism. See above, p. 329.

ligious faith and to civil society. Augsburg was a free city enclosed in Bavaria, where the Illuminati were founded in 1778, and to combat the Jesuits, while using the clandestine methods with which they were credited, seems to have been one of the aims of the Illuminati; at any rate, it is among the Augsburg Jesuits, as early as 1784, that the first deliberate formulation of the "plot theory" of the eighteenth-century revolution is to be found. The theory grew out of earlier attacks on the Freemasons, but the Illuminati made a more sensational target. It was from these somewhat intramural disputes among Catholics, mediated by Protestant Germans, as well as by the Scotch Presbyterian Robison and in America by a stalwart of Congregationalism, Jedediah Morse, that the world was asked to believe, in 1798, that the Revolution of Western Civilization was due to the machinations of a secret society. The Augsburg Jesuits continued to issue a number of periodicals into the 1790's, aimed at the lower clergy and at the mass of the Catholic faithful, to whom they offered an absolute acceptance of the church as the only defense against the horrors of irreligion and anarchy.[56]

In Vienna, L. A. Hoffman, in his *Wiener Zeitschrift*, took up the same crusade against secret societies. How Hoffman himself, in conjunction with Leopold II, had organized a secret "Association," to combat both aristocratism and democratism, has already been explained.[57] The *Wiener Zeitschrift* was shut down in 1793 by the government of Francis II, which wanted no discussion of revolution pro or con, and which, far from subsidizing a conservative ideology, preferred to have no ideology at all. More widely read than the *Wiener Zeitschrift* was the *Revolutions-Almanach* of H. A. O. Reichard, librarian to the duke of Saxe-Gotha. As early as 1790, at the time of the peasant rebellion in Saxony, Reichardt had been asked by the government of the Electorate to publish a counter-revolutionary journal at the popular level. He had apparently done so, declaring that some "fine passages from Dr. Martin Luther and the writings of other pious men" should serve this purpose very well.[58] In 1793 he began to issue his *Revolutions-Almanach* at Göttingen. It was aimed at a more

[56] Valjavec, 290, 292, 305-307. On Robison and Barruel see above, pp. 250-54 and 360; on Morse, below, p. 542. See also Droz' *Allemagne*, and his article, "La légende du complot illuministe et les origines du romantisme politique en Allemagne," in *Revue historique*, Vol. 226 (1961), 313-38.
[57] On Hoffman and the *Wiener Zeitschrift*, Valjavec, 308; Droz, 409-11; D. Silagi, *Ungarn und der geheime Mitarbeiterkreis Kaiser Leopolds II* (Munich, 1960), 105-16; and see above, p. 162.
[58] Stulz, *Volksbewegungen*, 101.

sophisticated audience, and lasted until 1801. At Göttingen, in Hanover, much was known about England; and one of the early articles in the *Revolutions-Almanach* was a long and laudatory account of an English society, founded in 1792, the Association for the Protection of Freedom and Property against Republicans and Levellers. "Levellers" significantly became *Aufklärer* in German.[59]

Reichardt and others, in 1794, formed a secret alliance which they called the "Association A-M," since each member was given a letter of the alphabet as a code name. They published a journal, *Eudämonia*, and so were known as the Eudämonists. The Eudämonists offered the best example in Germany of the 1790's of what a later generation would call the Radical Right. They included the editors Reichardt and Koester, already mentioned; G. B. Schirach, editor of the Hamburg *Politisches Journal*; two conservative booksellers at Frankfurt and Leipzig; the court preacher at Darmstadt; and J. G. R. Zimmermann of Hanover, who was physician to King George III, and who, it may be recalled, had been recruited by Hoffmann into Leopold II's secret Association. They were a Protestant group, but reached out to join with like-minded Catholics, notably Hoffmann, soon after his *Wiener Zeitschrift* was suppressed in Vienna. Organized secretly, concealing their operations, composed in part of men who were former or disillusioned Freemasons, and claimed personal knowledge of conspiratorial societies over the past dozen years, they busily corresponded and exchanged information, using a cypher in which "44" meant the Illuminati and "43" the Jacobins, and they accused, denounced, exposed, and reported upon various persons in government or the universities as crypto-Jacobins or unregenerate Illuminati in disguise. Their journal, *Eudämonia*, was for three years the most influential counter-revolutionary organ in Germany. It was the repeated attacks in its pages, and the campaign of complaint and letter-writing which the Eudämonists organized, which, more than anything else, forced the grand-duke of Weimar to accept Fichte's resignation at Jena. Wild charges finally defeated their own purpose. When the imperial censor at Vienna found himself accused of Illuminism he forbade the paper in Austria. Silenced or discouraged as a nuisance in various of the German states, *Eudämonia* ceased publication in 1798.[60]

Such extreme counter-revolutionaries, though voluble and articulate,

[59] *Revolutions-Almanach von 1794* (Goettingen, 1794), 323-33.
[60] Valjavec, 304-5; Droz, *Allemagne*, 414-16; Léon, *Fichte*, I, 536-49; G. Krüger, "Die Eudämonisten," in *Hist. Zeitschrift*, Vol. 143 (1931), 467-500.

were not numerous, and it is difficult to assess their significance. Their polemics, however, at the least—like so much that was non-polemical in Germany—contributed little, and indeed set up a barrier, to the intelligent understanding of the French Revolution and the European upheaval that accompanied it. A movement fundamental to Western Civilization was trivialized into the doings of plotters. As one of the future Eudämonists said to another, on first hearing of the fall of the Bastille: "It is the work of the 44!"[61]

On the other hand, much in the counter-revolutionary campaign—like much in what German sympathizers with the Revolution also said—inflated and ballooned up the Revolution beyond rational measure. It was more in Germany than in France, more among those who watched it as spectators than among those who were active participants, that the idea grew up of revolution as a vast force with a life of its own.[62] In an empirical view, the Revolution could be seen as an episode, a crisis in affairs, momentous indeed, but still within the pale of comprehensible politics, arising from a breakdown of the old government, involving understandable conflicts of interest, aiming at a future state of society that could at least be foreseen and described in words, subject to criticism for its success or failure, for the wisdom or unwisdom of its measures, or for the moral implications of the means adopted in the pursuit of ends. Among the real revolutionaries of France, including Robespierre, some such view prevailed on the whole, though in France also there were some who glorified revolution for its own sake. Such was not the view taken in Germany either by excited but frustrated revolutionaries without a revolution, or by counter-revolutionaries desiring to argue that revolution was aimless chaos.

"The lava of revolution flows majestically on, sparing nothing. Who can resist it?"[63] It was the Mainz Jacobin Georg Forster who wrote these words. Longing for revolution, he was pleased by the thought of its "irresistibility," though Robespierre, as a real revolutionary, found much to resist, such as the "ultras," in a real revolution. The image of flowing lava, since it made the Revolution seem mindless and inhuman, could appeal to counter-revolutionaries as well as to merely potential, incipient, frustrated, or spectator-type revolutionaries. There is no

---

[61] Krüger, 474.
[62] The argument of K. Griewank, *Der neuzeitliche Revolutionsbegriff* (Weimar, 1955), in the chapter on "Der dynamische Revolutionsbegrift und die Gegenrevolution," 240-59.
[63] Quoted by Griewank, 243.

room here to go into the arcana of German romanticism, in which men like Schlegel and Novalis, while rejecting revolutionary republicanism, looked for a vast outburst of vitalistic and creative life forces to regenerate the world. The rational and politically minded Friederich Gentz, no romantic, began in 1793 to characterize events in France as *eine Total-Revolution*. Repeatedly he contrasted the American Revolution, constructive and rational, with the French Revolution, which he saw as a vast, boundless, all-consuming, blind force, aiming at unrealizable goals, or with no goals except violence and upheaval. The French revolutionaries imagined that when their revolution was over, civil peace would follow. It was Gentz and the counter-revolution that thought otherwise, who saw in France a destructive force that would "favor other revolutions into infinity . . . lead to a succession of revolutions, and turn human society into a theater of never ending civil war."[64]

The accuracy of this interpretation is a matter of judgment. It was at least a way of taking attention from the announced goals of the movement, such as liberty and equality. The irony is that the idea of a dynamic, continuing, and perpetual revolution, of revolution as an elemental or historic force rather than as a political expedient to be rarely used, arose at least as much in Germany as in France, and at least as much among conservatives as among revolutionary democrats and republicans.

[64] *Ibid.*, 248-49.

BRITAIN: REPUBLICANISM AND THE ESTABLISHMENT

I disapprove of monarchical and aristocratical governments, however modified. Hereditary distinctions, and privileged orders of every species, I think must necessarily counteract the progress of human improvement; hence it follows that I am not amongst the admirers of the British Constitution.—WILLIAM WORDSWORTH, 1794

Lord Malmesbury and I have made a large circuit on horseback today. . . . The cottages picturesque; the inhabitants thriving, but preserving a sylvan *sort of character. . . . Everything is in the highest possible order, and this country affords a specimen of general prosperity and comfort which should make even a* Sans-culotte *think twice before tearing off the breeches of the world, and making us sit bare under the Tree of Liberty, instead of on a good, broad, well clothed, aristocratic basis, as they do in Hampshire.*—SIR GILBERT ELLIOT, later Earl of Minto, 1793

BRITAIN: REPUBLICANISM AND
THE ESTABLISHMENT

UNTIL late in 1792 the British government expected to remain at peace, but once engaged in the war with France it became the most persistent adversary of the New Republican Order. In the British official view, at least after 1797, there could be no lasting settlement, nor would British interests be secure, except by a liquidation not only of the French Revolution but of the new regimes in Holland and elsewhere. And it seems true that Britain, which if not fighting for its life was fighting for the freedom to grow, could never have enjoyed its great Victorian and Edwardian imperial age without the destruction of the new order of the 1790's, and the Napoleonic system which succeeded it. The greatest single champion of the European counter-revolution was England, which supplied conservative Europe with an example of perseverance, with a philosophy either traditionalist or constitutionalist as one chose, and with a good deal of money to pay for Continental armies, in sums which reached £10,000,000 by 1800 and £57,000,000 by 1815.

In England itself, however, and more so in Scotland and Ireland, there was a good deal of opposition to the war and sympathy for republican France. On the extent and significance of this "Jacobinism," especially for England itself, there has been considerable difference of opinion. Its importance was stressed half a century ago by the appearance of several books within a single decade.[1] Since then the subject

[1] G. S. Veitch, *The Genesis of Parliamentary Reform* (London, 1913); W. T. Laprade, *England and the French Revolution* (Baltimore, 1909); W. P. Hall, *British Radicalism, 1789-97* (New York, 1912); H. W. Meikle, *Scotland and the French Revolution* (Glasgow, 1912); P. A. Brown, *The French Revolution in English History* (London, 1918). The most accessible printed sources, aside from pamphlets and the *Annual Register*, are T. B. and T. S. Howell, *Cobbett's Complete Collection of State Trials . . .*, 33 vols. (London, 1809-1826); and the many documents of the popular clubs printed by order of Parliament: Gt. Brit., Parl., Committee of Secrecy, *Fire Report . . .* and *Second Report . . .*, London, 1794, and *Report . . .*, London, 1799.

has been in abeyance. In recent years, at a time when German, Italian, Austrian, Hungarian, Polish, and Russian "Jacobins" have all had their several historians, hardly anything has been written on those of Britain, except for one book by a Frenchman which leaves an exaggerated impression of revolutionary agitation in England, and except for a few specialized articles by British writers, some of which, to be sure, are extremely illuminating.[2] On the whole, British historians now warn against an over-estimation of the importance of the British Jacobins, and against attempts to see parallels between British and Continental developments. One writer, a British expert on the French sans-culottes, affirms that the English Jacobins were of no significance, that they were strangers in their own country, and that any war against Frenchmen was well liked by the popular classes. These views seem hardly to coincide with the evidence, and they reflect about what a proper English gentleman might have thought in 1797.[3]

The question is not whether any groups in England desired a revolution in the French sense, or whether revolution was possible in England in any case. The only good answer to these questions has always been "No." The question is rather to examine the kind and degree of disaffection that existed in England and Scotland (the issues in Ireland being somewhat different); to find out who was disaffected, and why; to explain why, except in Ireland, the disaffection could not reach revolutionary proportions; and to set forth the way in which disaffection was dealt with and overcome by the Establishment, to use a modern term, which then referred only to the establishment of religion in the Anglican Church. As for the disaffected, they were variously known by their enemies as Jacobins, Levellers, "clubbists," or "anarchy men." They had no name for themselves, but might occasionally confess to "republican" sentiments. It was not that they proposed to do away with

[2] J. Dechamps, *Les Iles britanniques et la Révolution française 1789-1803* (Brussels, 1949). For the articles mentioned here see below. About a fourth of S. Maccoby, *English Radicalism, 1786-1832* (London, 1955) is devoted to the years before 1800. There has been some good work by Americans: R. T. Oliver, *Four Who Spoke Out: Burke, Fox, Sheridan, Pitt* (Syracuse, 1946); L. S. Marshall, *The Development of Public Opinion in Manchester, 1780-1820* (Syracuse, 1946); D. V. Erdman, *Blake: Prophet against Empire* (Princeton, 1954). Since writing the above I have seen the American edition of E. P. Thompson, *The Making of the English Working Class* (New York, 1964), which puts great stress on English "Jacobinism."

[3] R. C. Cobb, "Les jacobins anglais et la Révolution française," in *Bulletin de la Société d'histoire moderne*, No. 3 for 1960. The warning against exaggeration of the significance of English "Jacobinism" seems to be shared by A. Cobban, *The Debate on the French Revolution* (London, 1950), and by J. Steven Watson, *The Reign of George III* (Oxford, 1960), which is Vol. XII of the *Oxford History of England*.

the monarchy; but they were critical of the kinds of men and institutions by which the monarchy was surrounded, they thought that church and state were controlled by aristocrats, and they regarded more equality as desirable.

In Britain and Ireland, as in Eastern Europe, it was counter-revolution that prevailed. The net effect of the revolutionary decade was to demonstrate, or to consolidate, the strength of the established order. The very lengths to which the established order went, however, in dealing with disaffection (or what was called "sedition") offer a measure of the magnitude of the discontents. The men who ruled England were not the sort to be frightened by witches. The British governing class was neither timid, foolish, intolerant, nor especially ruthless when unprovoked. That Englishmen of this class became fearful of unrest at home, intolerant of ideas or organizations suggesting those of the French Revolution, repressive in Britain, and deliberately terroristic in Ireland can be taken as evidence of the reality of something of which, from their own point of view, they had reason to be afraid. In England as elsewhere there was a contest between democrats and aristocrats.

British Radicalism and Continental Revolution

Situated on an island, commanding the sea, trading with all the world, possessing a highly developed national unity, rejoicing in its liberty, its constitutional monarchy, its common law, and its Parliament, England was in truth very different from the rest of Europe. Of "feudalism" in its many senses nothing remained, or what remained had been transformed into a sort of landowners' rule; the country was politically more homogeneous than France before 1789, or the Dutch provinces before 1795, with the landed class providing a central direction through Parliament and the Crown, while as individuals they retained a good deal of local initiative in the counties. Landownership was highly concentrated, and in process of becoming more so; there was no peasantry, as on the Continent, either of small free proprietors as in Western Europe, or of serfs as in the East; the mass of the rural population worked as wage laborers for farmers who paid rents to the landowners, or in such household manufactures as cutlery and weaving. Freed of peasant conservatism, British agriculture had become innovating and productive, and since the country was also a commercial and financial center, well launched on the process of industrialization,

England was the most wealthy region in Europe, or indeed the world. In a population of nine millions in 1800 there were perhaps ten thousand families that could be called rich, having £1,500 (or over 30,000 French *livres*) of annual revenues. Land was still the chief source of wealth. In Patrick Colquhoun's estimates for 1801, the category of titled persons, "esquires" and "gentlemen and ladies living on incomes," with 27,000 families, was almost twice as large as that of "eminent merchants" and "lesser merchants by sea." In the same estimates there were two million persons in the families of artisans and mechanics, and almost 400,000 in those of tradesmen and shopkeepers. A million persons were habitually on poor relief. Extremes of wealth and poverty were very great.[4]

England had pioneered in many of the developments described in preceding chapters as characteristic of the revolutionary decade on the Continent. The "politicization" of opinion was an old story, dating back to the Puritan Revolution and before. Clubs and coffee houses served the function of reading societies elsewhere. Pamphleteering had long been a national custom, and the periodical press was both highly developed and relatively free. It is thought that the literacy rate about 1780, before the new Sunday School movement sought to extend it, was no higher than in the reign of Elizabeth, since the intervening years had not been as favorable to the lower classes as to the upper. In the 1780's the number of persons able to read began to mount, and in any case, thanks largely to interest in the French Revolution, the number who desired to read the papers, or to listen while others read them, appears to have increased. Nine new dailies were established in London in the 1780's, four of these in the year 1789 alone.

Newspapers in England, however, like books, were expensive. There was a stamp tax to be paid on every copy, raised from 1½ to 2 d. in 1789, and to 3½ d. in 1797. The famous daily generated in Paris by the Revolution, the *Moniteur*, without advertising or government subsidy, was able to sell by subscription for 18 livres a quarter, raised to 20 in 1797. This amounted to two English pence per copy. In France such a price was thought too high for most people, for whom other papers, weekly or semi-weekly, were provided after 1789 for a penny a copy. In England the dailies sold for four pence in 1789 and sixpence in 1797. By the latter year they were three times as expensive as the *Moniteur*. The enthusiasm of French Revolutionaries for cheap popular news-

---

[4] Colquhoun's tabulations may be found in his *Treatise on Indigence* (London, 1806), following p. 23.

papers was not shared by the British government. Little is known of circulation; the *Times* by 1800 was selling about 4,800 a day, but there were a dozen other London dailies; the circulation of the *Moniteur* is unknown, but the *Journal de Paris* had 12,000 paid subscribers.[5]

England was distinguished above all by its Parliament, and the traditions, claims, powers, and prestige of Parliament were so overwhelming that issues of many kinds, including religious, economic, and social, presented themselves in terms of Parliament and its "reform." The Parliament was one of those constituted bodies, described in Volume 1, against which much of the revolutionary impetus in eighteenth-century Europe was directed. The British House of Lords in the 1790's consisted of about three hundred temporal peers and twenty-six bishops. The House of Commons consisted of 558 members sent from boroughs and counties by a variety of methods. Most "burgesses" sitting for boroughs were in fact country gentlemen, as were the "knights of the shire." The law, though sometimes circumvented, still required an income from landed property of £300 a year for the burgesses, and of £600 a year for the knights, that is the members who sat for counties. In the House of Commons elected in 1790 (and the one elected in 1796 was much the same) there were 85 baronets and 121 peers (of Ireland) or sons of peers. Three-fifths of the 558 had had fathers or other close relatives previously in the House. No less than 278 had been educated at Oxford or Cambridge, and 115 at Eton. Eighty-five were career officers in the army or navy, and 41 others held temporary commissions. Over a fifth, that is, while essentially gentry, could be thought of as military personages, while there were 72 lawyers, 27 bankers, and another half hundred whose economic interests were primarily commercial.[6]

It was a point of strength in the British system, in Parliament and elsewhere, that men of agricultural and commercial wealth could meet and act together, and that both forms of wealth were often possessed by the same individuals. There was less tension than on the Continent between elites of different kinds. The elites of birth, rank, wealth, and fashion, of government, the church, and the army and navy, of the uni-

---

[5] R. D. Altick, *The English Common Reader: a Social History of the Mass Reading Public 1800-1900* (Chicago, 1957), 35-77, 322-24; R. L. Haig, *The Gazetteer, 1735-1797: a Study of the Eighteenth-Century English Newspaper* (Carbondale, Ill., 1960); L. Werkmeister, *The London Daily Press, 1772-92* (Lincoln, Nebr.), 1963. For France see E. Hatin, *Bibliographie de la presse périodique française* (Paris, 1866); J. Godechot, *Institutions de la France sous la Rév. et l'Emp.* (Paris, 1951), 57-61.

[6] G. P. Judd, *Members of Parliament 1734-1832* (New Haven, 1955), 79-89.

versities, the law and the learned professions, if not actually all drawn from the same circles, all merged into a generalized upper class. The upper class was not rigidly exclusive; capable persons of modest origins could occasionally reach high positions, in return for acceptance of the upper-class scheme of values. The result was to strengthen the aristocracy, and to deprive the truly common people of an effectual leadership. Precisely because it had avoided the crude dualism of *noblesse* and *roture*, England was of all countries the most successfully aristocratic. If the idea of equality seemed in England especially shocking and nonsensical, it was because what some called inequality, and others a due subordination of ranks and orders, was seen not merely as social necessity, but as an adornment of civilized society, interesting and warmly attractive in itself.

England was the only one of the leading European monarchies, before 1792, which had for a dozen years been a republic itself, and in which a king had been tried and executed, and a significant democratic movement had once developed. Resemblances between the French Revolution and the Puritan Revolution and Commonwealth are evident enough to twentieth-century historians. In the 1790's they were mainly perceived by conservatives, especially those who were not English; Mallet du Pan saw, in the "doctrines" of the French Revolution, a lot of "stories drawn by Rousseau from the filth of the English republic."[7] In England these events had disappeared from the center of consciousness. The name of Cromwell stood as a sign of evil ambition, and the word "Leveller" survived as a term of reproach. The names of Milton and Algernon Sydney might be invoked as symbols of classical republicanism and antique virtue, as in Wordsworth's great sonnets of 1802. But the actual politics of the Puritan Revolution had been put out of mind. It was not for the Dissenters, in their unsuccessful efforts to obtain equality of political rights, to revive memories of a regicide past. Few English "Jacobins," in all probability, had ever heard of John Lilburne. Their historical imagination, like that of Thomas Jefferson, dwelt by preference on King Alfred or even Hengist and Horsa, in a remote age of Saxon liberty before the Norman Conquest. In a country so conscious of its own history this phenomenon is of psychological interest; English Jacobinism was to suffer a similar eclipse or oblivion for a hundred years.

---

[7] J. Mallet du Pan, *Corr. pol. pour servir à l'hist. du républicanisme français* (Hamburg, 1796), XIX.

What was remembered was the revolution of 1688, which had been peaceable enough in England itself. The centennial produced a certain activity on the part of various Revolution Societies, some of which greeted the beginnings of the French Revolution with approval, since in England, as in Prussia for different reasons, it was at first supposed that the French were only seeking to obtain what the English already enjoyed. It was to members of such a Revolution Society that Richard Price, in 1789, delivered his famous discourse on the love of country, which provoked Edmund Burke's *Reflections on the French Revolution*, with its indignant denial that the English in 1688 had "cashiered a king," or ever made laws of their own choosing. On the whole, the dis-affection of the 1790's had little to do with the Revolution Societies, and it had no conscious relationship to "the filth of the English republic."

Disaffection in England, though it may have forgotten its past, was national and indigenous. It was a plant with native roots, which the sudden blaze of light across the Channel brought luxuriantly into blossom. Something has been said in the preceding volume of moves for the democratization of Parliament that had begun in the 1760's, of the agitations led by John Wilkes, of the proposals of the Westminster committee in which the six points of Chartism were already fore-shadowed, of Pitt's repeated failure to obtain Parliamentary reform, and of the similar failures to obtain removal of the disabilities upon Protestant Dissenters. Something has been said also of the formation, before 1789, of a philosophy of conservatism, which held that the British constitution was in no need of change, and indeed could not be modified without risk of anarchy and collapse—a conservatism which is not at all to be understood as a reaction against the "excesses" of the French Revolution.[8] In these earlier movements, except for groups in London and for the Dissenters, the main strength had come from landowners meeting in county associations. Many of the leaders had been of the upper and Parliamentary classes. Persons of this kind remained active after 1789, notably those Whigs who developed in the direction of Charles James Fox. Some of them in 1792 founded a society called the Friends of the People. They continued for years to oppose the war, enjoying a freedom of speech, as members of the upper classes, which would probably have been tolerated in no other country in wartime. They continued also, though with declining con-viction, to talk of a reform of the House of Commons. As late as 1797, after years of war and domestic turmoil, a reform bill was introduced

[8] *Age,* I, 164-73, 179-80, 285-320, 364-70.

by Charles Grey; it failed, but the same Grey was to obtain passage of the First Reform Bill thirty-five years later. As in other countries, so in England, there were upper-class "Jacobins," men who sometimes from conviction, sometimes from eccentricity, and sometimes from factiousness, set themselves in opposition to the views of the government, and the predilections of the established order. In general, however, their contacts with popular discontent were desultory at best. The Whig Friends of the People had no desire to mix with men of lower station, and the true radicals felt for them neither confidence nor respect.

On the Continent the professional classes, including the clergy, furnished many sympathizers with the French Revolution and sponsors of change in their own countries. The same was much less true in England. A church whose bishops were administrators sitting in Parliament, whose parsons hobnobbed with squires, whose ranks were recruited from yeoman and gentry families, and which in any case had lost touch with the newer forms of the laboring population, was in no mood to be critical of the social order. "Individuals have nothing to do with the laws but to obey them," said the Bishop of Rochester in the House of Lords.[9] Dissenting and Unitarian clergy were more susceptible to republicanism. In Scotland, where a system of patronage to church livings, on the English model, had been introduced into the established Presbyterian Church after the Union, and where, partly in protest against this system, various other Presbyterians had broken away, the established clergy were generally satisfied, feeling close to the government and the landowners, but the "seceders," "New Lights," etc., were rightly suspected of political radicalism. Methodist clergy in England tried to be officially neutral on political questions. The effects of Methodism, however, were by no means conservative. Men taught to read in Methodist Sunday Schools, or to speak up in Wesleyan meetings, often figured as leaders in radical clubs.[10] Home missions, Bible reading, and itinerant preaching, in both England and Scotland, offered a kind of competing program to that of the French Revolution as a force calling the established order into question.

On the Continent, eastward from France itself, university professors and students were prominent among partisans of the new ideas. At the two English universities, assimilated to the aristocracy since the

---

[9] *Parliamentary History*, XXXII, 267.

[10] See the report on an unpublished dissertation by R. F. Wearmouth, "Methodism and the Working Classes of England, 1800-1850," in the *Bulletin of the Institute of Historical Research of the University of London*, No. 41 (1936), p. 121. The same point is made for Manchester by L. S. Marshall, *op.cit.*, 122. For Scotland see Meikle, *op.cit.*, 34-40, 194-213.

Restoration, and at a low point in their intellectual history, the same was not so. Even in Scotland, where the universities were more alive, but attached to the Presbyterian establishment, a "Jacobin" professor was a rarity. In Europe, professional government employees, sometimes trained in the universities in subjects corresponding to modern economics and political science, might favor reforms or even collaborate with the French. The same was not true in England, which had no professional class of this kind. In Europe, and also in America, the new groups usually included a contingent of doctors. We hear little of doctors in the English radical clubs. In Europe, the lawyers were everywhere divided, but few types were more common than the radical lawyer. In England the radical lawyer was less in evidence. Causes for these differences can only be suggested, in the absence of more detailed investigation; they might range from the class structure of the professions in England to the empirical habits of the English mind. As for the lawyers, their division into a hierarchy of barristers, solicitors, and attorneys, the fact that legal counsel was associated with large property rather than small, the location of legal study, and the formation of lawyers in the Inns of Court, with nothing like the atmosphere of a Continental university, the steeping of the youthful mind in the mysterious lore described by Blackstone, the disregard of Roman law as taught on the Continent, which was more likely to raise questions of principle concerning the state, public authority and justice, may all help to explain the incredible conservatism for which English law was to remain famous until the days of Dickens.

In Europe it was usual enough to find business men favorable to the main aims of the Revolution, and in this matter the same was true, to a degree, of England also. Commercial men were already more integrated into accepted society than in the other monarchical states of Europe. It has just been observed that 27 bankers sat in Parliament, in which the interests of trade were far from being unrepresented. The knighting of Richard Arkwright in 1786, and the granting of a baronetcy to the elder Robert Peel in 1800, suggest the transition of the factory-builders into higher social circles. Peel himself, however, at first felt enthusiasm for the French Revolution, as did various other men of affairs, the more so if they were outside the established church, or lived in the newer and politically unrepresented industrial towns. Such men often looked on the aristocracy as arrogant social drones, unbroken to useful work, who wasted their own money on racing, gambling, and large entertainments, and the people's money in lucrative but idle jobs and appointments. Both partners of the famous firm of Watt and Boulton were strongly of this opinion, and even talked, not very seriously, of emigrating to America. Their sons, before settling down in the firm's business, were notorious "Jacobins."[11] The fate of Thomas Walker of Manchester will be mentioned later. The most curious case, in a way, was that of the ironmaster, John Wilkinson, the man who had first successfully used coal in place of charcoal in the smelting of iron ore, and had designed and cast the first iron bridge in Britain. A Dissenter and a friend of Priestley's, he was irritated at the failure, which became "final" in 1790, to obtain equal rights for non-Anglican Protestants. He was so outraged and alarmed by the church-and-king mobs that attacked Priestley in 1791 that he protected his ironworks with howitzers and swivel-guns against similar attentions. "Manufacture and commerce," he wrote, "will always flourish most where Church and King interfere least." A man of sixty, who had made a large fortune, he bought £10,000 worth of French Revolutionary public bonds. Late in 1792, only a few weeks before England and France went to war, needing a scrip with which to meet his payrolls, he had his cashier endorse French *assignats* and circulate them as money. Since his workers were mostly Dissenters full of the ideas of Thomas Paine, this device, in December 1792, was inflammatory to say the least. Wilkinson would have agreed with the "clubbists" of Norfolk: "Surely the interests of all the industrious, from the richest merchant to the poorest mechanic, are in every community the same: to lessen the numbers of the unproductive, to whose maintenance they contribute."[12] By the "unproductive," such men meant the leisure class, not the unemployed.

Well-to-do business men in England, however, had too much to lose to persist indefinitely in opposition. They were close enough to some segments of the upper class to be sensitive to its scorn, ridicule, or hostility. Men in their position, after the war began, could not remain obstinately unpatriotic; even so, many of them disapproved of the continuation of the French war, which interfered with their ex-

[11] On the Watts and Boultons of both generations see E. Robinson, "An English Jacobin: James Watt, Jr.," in *Cambridge Historical Journal*, XI (1955), 349-55.

[12] W. H. Chaloner, "Dr. Joseph Priestley, John Wilkinson and the French Revolution, 1789-1802," in *Transactions of the Royal Historical Society*, 5th ser., VIII (1958), 21-40; E. Robinson, "New Light on the Priestley Riots," in *Historical Journal*, III (1960), 73-75. The quotation from the Norfolk society is from H. Butterfield, "Charles James Fox and the Whig Opposition in 1792," in *Cambridge Historical Journal*, IX (1949), 293-330.

port trade. A group of textile manufacturers at Manchester signed a petition for peace in 1795.[13] Among the signers were Robert Peel and Robert Owen, who were no merely passive conservatives, since Peel a few years later obtained passage of the first English factory act, and Owen became famous in the annals of socialism. By this time, however, whatever their views on the war (Peel resoundingly changed his mind in 1798 with a free gift to the government of £10,000), they had ceased to feel any sympathy for the French Revolution, or to have anything to do with the English radical clubs. As the years passed, the business men joined with the professional classes in repudiating republican sentiments. And as these upper middle-class groups made their peace with the established order, the English "Jacobins," those who felt most strongly in 1792, and who continued to feel so, were characteristically of a lower occupational status, neither the paupers nor the agricultural laborers of whom the lower third of the English people consisted, but the industrious, skilled and self-respecting men of good habits and limited income, strongly resembling, in their socio-economic level but hardly in their psychology or their actions, the Paris sans-culottes as described by M. Albert Soboul.

It is a question whether England had, as a class, any such people as "intellectuals," since thinking and writing were neither unduly admired on the one hand, nor unduly looked down on by the active classes on the other. The establishment had its intellectuals, as in Archdeacon Paley; Hannah More and others rallied to it vigorously after 1793. Jeremy Bentham approved neither of the British Constitution nor of the Rights of Man. Various newspaper editors, such as the Joseph Gales who published at Sheffield before going to America, were democratic radicals of a type familiar both on the Continent and in the United States. Thomas Paine (though considered somewhat American), with his *Rights of Man* of 1791, Mary Wollstonecraft with her *Vindication of the Rights of Woman* of 1792, and William Godwin with his *Political Justice* of 1793, all showed contemptuous impatience of the established order, and of the kind of arguments marshaled in its defense. Mary Wollstonecraft's retort to Burke deserves perpetuation: "It is, Sir, *possible*, to render the poor happier in this world without depriving them of the consolation which you gratuitously grant them in the next."[14] She and Paine had ideas on the division of large landed estates, but Godwin, a more purely specu-

[13] Marshall, *Public Opinion at Manchester*, 126.
[14] Quoted by Veitch, *Genesis*, 169.

lative thinker, had little interest in persons who could not afford the three guineas charged for his book.

The poets, Wordsworth, Coleridge, Southey, Campbell, Blake, and Burns, all resonated excitedly to the message for human rights..All except Blake and Burns were still quite young men in the 1790's. Burns, the most humble in origin, was the first to lose sympathy for the French Revolution. Blake lived as an engraver in London, and mixed in the political clubs of the city. It was Blake who helped Thomas Paine escape to France when he was indicted in 1792. It is argued that Blake's enigmatic style, both in his poems and in his engravings, was a defense against threats to which men of his kind were exposed; that, in short, had he felt more free, he would have expressed his republican sympathies more plainly. He is remembered for his brooding dread of "these dark Satanic mills." The phrase has usually been understood to signify a poet's fear of the degrading effects of long hours of factory employment. It would seem, however, that Blake, an artisan in London, had not yet heard that an Industrial Revolution was in progress, and really felt horror for the shops in which weapons to destroy the French Republic, and human liberty, were being made.[15] Wordsworth perhaps felt the whole drama most deeply. It is possible that his poetry, like Fichte's metaphysics, was in some sense the product of a profound feeling for liberty and equality. He himself, in his theory of poetic diction, favored a forthright and easy simplicity which he liked to believe was the language of the common people. Wordsworth grew away from his first exaltation very slowly. The English poets, in fact, seem not to have turned against France until the winter of 1797-1798.[16] It was not the Terror nor Thermidor that made them change their minds, so much as Fructidor, Campo Formio, and the transfer of Venice to Austria. Since they saw Italy, Switzerland, and Holland in an unrealistic glow, with no knowledge of their contemporary political problems, the setting up of new-style republics in these countries seemed to be no more than the conquest and cheap collusion that conservative propaganda said it was. Coleridge eventually turned into one of the more weighty philosophers of the organic society, and Wordsworth into the poet of the church. Since their con-

---

[15] Erdman, *Blake*, vii and *passim*. For Wordsworth, F. M. Todd, *Politics and the Poet: a Study of Wordsworth* (London, 1957), is the most recent of many relevant works.

[16] J. Voisine, *Jean-Jacques Rousseau et l'Angleterre à l'époque romantique: les écrits autobiographiques et la légende* (Paris, 1956), 150-52.

tacts were with the gentle classes, they had never been "clubbists" even in their youth.

In a different category may be put true working-class bards, such as the Paisley weaver, Alexander Wilson, and the Sheffield file-maker, Joseph Mather. Their songs and ballads, at first printed ephemerally only in broadsides for their own neighbors, were not published in book-form until a half-century later. Both sang the merits of Paine and his *Rights of Man*. Both raged against the king and court. According to Alexander Wilson:

> For British boys are in a fiz,
> Their heads like bees are humming,
> And their rights and liberties,
> They're mad upon reforming
> The court this day.

Mather, whose style was more solemn, wrote on the war with France:

> Facts are seditious things,
> When they touch courts and kings,
> Armies are raised.

Some of Robert Burns' poems, before his change of sentiment, were of the same character, as in his "a man's a man for a' that." How much such verses circulated locally and orally is not known.[17]

The English radicalism of the 1790's, to summarize, so far as it was represented by the popular clubs, was largely a disturbance among what must be called the lower middle class, since for one reason or another persons above this level either took little part, or ceased to take part, after 1793. It is this more genuinely popular character of organized discontent that distinguishes the reform movement of the 1790's from the agitations of the days of Wilkes and the American Revolution.

In Scotland the disaffection was more broadly based. For example, when the Whig Club of Dundee sent an address of greeting to the French Assembly, seventy-six persons signed it, virtually all of whose occupations were also given.[18] There were eleven "esquires" and eleven members of the clergy. There were one doctor and three surgeons. There were two "writers"—a word used in Scotland to mean a kind

[17] On Wilson see Meikle, *Scotland*, 121; on Mather, W. H. G. Armitage, "Joseph Mather: Poet of the Filesmiths," in *Notes and Queries*, Vol. 195 (1950), 320-22.
[18] The address, dated June 10, 1790, is printed in full in the appendix to Veitch, *Genesis*, 359-62. See also Meikle, *Scotland*.

of lawyer. There were thirty-three merchants. With them were the rector of a school, a teacher of English and a teacher of mathematics—also a watchmaker, an architect, a dyer, a stationer, and a baker. It is a list of the sort that one might expect from Ireland or parts of the Continent, but not from England. The Scottish Society of Friends of the People likewise had a mixed membership, where the English society of the same name, with its dues of two-and-a-half guineas, was limited to the well-to-do. A lingering feeling against England, a sense of exclusion from public life (there were only about 1,300 actual freehold voters in a population of a million), a Presbyterian habit of participation in common affairs, the repeated splits and disputes among Presbyterians since the Union, the connection between church and state, the existence of severe poverty along with a widespread literacy, the sermons of itinerant and unauthorized preachers, who were frowned upon by established Presbyterians, and much inclined to anti-aristo-cratic outbursts, combined to spread discontent in Scotland, especially as the American and French Revolutions, over the period of a genera-tion, began to arouse a new political consciousness.

One other feature of the radicalism of the day—English, Scottish, and Irish—may be mentioned as of more than incidental importance. Many troublemarkers left the country, not like Dutch or Italian refugees fleeing to France and hoping soon to return, but to places so distant as to make them thereafter inoffensive to the established order. This exodus took the form both of more or less voluntary emigration to America, and of involuntary transportation to Botany Bay. The number of those going to America in the decade before 1800 is not known, but it included Joseph Priestley, Benjamin Vaughan, Thomas Cooper, John Binns, and Joseph Gales from England; James Callender from Scotland; William Duane and John Daly Burk, and for a few years Wolfe Tone, Napper Tandy, and Hamilton Rowan, from Ireland. Australia had received a heterogeneous lot of some 8,000 convicts by 1799. Some of these were vicious characters; but at a time when there were over a hundred capital offenses in English law many others were hardly guilty of serious misbehavior. From England and Scotland not many were deported on political charges—indeed the "Scotch martyrs," Muir, Palmer, Skirving, Gerrald, and Margarot, may have been the only ones. Many deported as criminals, however, were probably "democrats" also. In 1800 there were two thousand Irish political offenders in New South Wales. Mutinous soldiers and sailors were also sent there. On the whole, and with exceptions, these off-scourings from the "Pitt terror" proved to be useful citizens in both

America and Australia. Vaughan received an honorary degree from Harvard, and Cooper became president of a college. One of the founders of the hospital at Sydney was a young medical officer involved in the mutiny of the Nore. The first Presbyterian service held in Australia was conducted by Thomas Muir, deported from Scotland in 1793 for sedition.[19]

Clubs and Conventions

A popular democratic movement appeared quite suddenly in Britain in the course of the year 1792. Clubs sprang up all over the country, sometimes called "popular societies," as in France, consisting of neighbors who met in taverns to talk about the meaning of the French Revolution, the war beginning on the Continent, the policy of the British government, and the vices of the idle rich. Two clubs came especially into prominence in London. There was the Society for Constitutional Information, to which Thomas Paine gave £1,000 received as royalty for his *Rights of Man*. More important, and more popular, was the London Corresponding Society. It was founded by Thomas Hardy, a master shoemaker who owned a shop employing half-a-dozen skilled craftsmen. By his own account, Hardy, having been interested in the American Revolution, and having observed the failure of upper-class efforts to obtain Parliamentary reform a dozen years earlier, deliberately decided to organize a more purely popular movement, to be carried on by "tradesmen, shopkeepers and mechanics." The immediate aim was to change the mode of election to the House of Commons, but the impulse and the ultimate goal were more broadly social, reflecting the deep resentments of "an industrious class of men." As he wrote to a correspondent in Scotland, explaining the origin of the London society, with the rambling syntax of one unused to writing: he and his friends had discussed "the low and miserable conditions the people of this nation were reduced to by the avaricious extortions of that haughty, voluptuous and luxurious class of beings who wanted us to possess no more knowledge than to believe all things were created for the use of that small group of worthless individuals."[20]

[19] For those going to America see the biographical dictionaries; for Australia, E. O'Brien, *The Foundation of Australia, 1786-1800: a Study of English Criminal Practice and Penal Colonisation in the Eighteenth Century* (London, 1937), 282-93, 321, 384; M. Roe, "Maurice Margarot: A Radical in Two Hemispheres 1792-1815," in *Bulletin of the Inst. of Hist. Res. of Univ. of London*, XXXI (1958), 68-79.

[20] See the Manuscripts of Francis Place, British Museum, Add. MSS, 27,814 fol. 178. The fairly sudden appearance of a popular radicalism in 1792 is evident in H. Butterfield, "Fox and the Whig Opposition," *loc.cit.*

Charging dues of only a penny a week, the London Corresponding Society within a few months had a membership of about 2,000, divided into neighborhood units that held their own local meetings. It took its name from the intention to correspond with similar societies that were being organized throughout the country, with a view to bringing a concerted pressure of the literate working classes upon Parliament. Its enemies tried to fix in the public mind the idea that it was established to correspond with the French Jacobins. There was never much more than an exchange of compliments between the Jacobins and the British clubs, in whose activities, when later closely studied by Parliament, no Frenchman was ever detected. The London Corresponding Society was like the Paris Jacobins in that it was not at all secret; it differed altogether from them in its primarily working-class membership.

It was one of the chief activities of the popular clubs to distribute propaganda, or, as they would say, to instruct the public on the real circumstances of the country. Most especially, they reprinted the works of Thomas Paine, the Second Part of whose *Rights of Man* appeared in February 1792. In it, Paine went beyond ideas that were merely political. He denounced in detail the fiscal system by which taxes were thrown heavily onto articles of common consumption. He proposed a progressive inheritance tax, so designed that income in the bracket between £12,000 and £13,000 would be taxed at 50 percent, and all income above £22,000 a year would be confiscated *in toto*. His purpose was not to give land to the poor, nor even to take it away from the rich as a group, but to oblige the wealthiest families to divide their landed estates among their heirs—to do away, in short, with primogeniture and "aristocracy." The point, in fact, was to force the rich to live on their own incomes, instead of being obliged to find emoluments for younger sons in church and state. Such ideas threatened the social system at its foundation. Before much could be accomplished, however, it was necessary to alter the way in which the Commons were chosen. In the First Part of the *Rights of Man* readers could find a comparison, or rather a contrast, between the British and the French Constitutions. In the latter, Paine pointed out, every man who paid 2s. 6d. in taxes had a vote, and each member of the French parliament represented an equal number of persons, counted as persons—not boroughs, counties or corporations of absurdly various size and importance. This was what was called "universal representation."

In May, faced with these tracts of Paine's, and with a swelling volume of similar literature, much of it written in angry refutation of Burke, the government issued a proclamation against seditious writings. The effect, if anything, was to extend their circulation. While Paine, indicted for his Part Two, escaped to Calais, the clubs remained relatively quiet during the summer, in breathless expectation of what would follow upon the Austro-Prussian invasion of France. Then came the fall of the French monarchy in August, and the September Massacres. These events further estranged the British upper classes from the French Revolution. They had no such effect on the democratic clubs. After Valmy and the French invasion of Belgium, as it seemed that the newly born Republic would triumph, the clubs reached a feverish height of excitement. Bonfires at Sheffield in October celebrated the Prussian retreat. At Dundee, in November, a thousand people rioted, and burnt in effigy "two gentlemen who were obnoxious to them."[21] Scotch peasants, according to an informant of the Duke of Buccleuch, cared nothing for Parliamentary reform, but would like to get ten acres apiece in a division of land, and were all reading Thomas Paine. In London, also in November, hundreds of persons trying to hold a mass meeting in Kensington Common were dispersed by dragoons. English clubs took steps to send muskets and shoes to French soldiers. Five of them—the London Corresponding Society, the Manchester Constitution Society, the Manchester Reformation Society, the Norwich Revolution Society, and the London Constitutional Whigs and Friends of the People—combined to convey a joint address to the French Convention, expressing the hope that Great Britain would enter the war against "tyrants" on the side of France, or at least remain neutral. An English-speaking group in Paris—English, Scotch, Irish, and American—presented a similar declaration to the Convention in November.[22]

On December 11, 1792, just as the government was ordering up the militia, mainly to preserve internal order, but in expectation also of war with France, an assembly met at Edinburgh. Delegates attended

[21] The quotation is from the *Annual Register for 1792*, Chronicle, 44.

[22] The addresses of English clubs to the French Convention sounded more revolutionary when put into French, presented in an atmosphere of public excitement in the Convention and published in the *Moniteur*, which was read all over Europe. The London Friends of the Revolution of 1688, claiming to represent "plusieurs milliers de négociants, d'artisans, de manufacturiers et d'ouvriers," declared that they would regard war against France as "une déclaration de guerre contre nos propres libertés." The spokesman for the Society for Constitutional Information, in his speech preceding presentation of the address, observed that with the French example "les révolutions vont devenir faciles," and that there might soon be "une Convention nationale d'Angleterre." The spokesman for the English-speaking residents of Paris called all existing governments *prétendus*. *Moniteur, réimpression*, XIV, 543, 592-94.

from eighty societies in sixty-five Scottish towns and villages, mostly in the zone of handicraft manufacture from Glasgow to Dundee, an area in which there were now tens of thousands of club members. Delegates addressed each other as "citizens," and there was an alarming connotation in the word "convention" itself, which had come into use in France only three months before. It was not that the word signified what it did in France or America; there was no thought of a convention as a body empowered to draft a new and written constitution of government; the dangerous idea was that a collection of men brought together by clubs and societies, by claiming to represent the people, should question the adequacy or legitimacy of the House of Commons. The Convention, which met for three days, overruled but did not silence its more militant members: it voted against officially receiving an address from the United Irish; it professed its attachment, to which some took exception, to King and Lords as well as Commons; and it declined even to petition Parliament, on the legal ground that petitions would be received only from such constituted bodies as counties and boroughs, or from individuals. It passed a resolution, however, for a more equal representation in Parliament, it published its minutes, and it made arrangements to meet again. On disbanding, the members took the French oath "to live free or die."[23]

As Britain and France went to war, in February 1793, the radical agitation became more intense. The Society for Constitutional Information voted honorary membership for several members of the French National Convention including Jeanbon Saint-André, a former Protestant pastor. By 1793 some 200,000 copies of the *Rights of Man* had been sold; the total a few years later was put at the unbelievable figure of 1,500,000, which, however reduced by skepticism or caution, remains well above the 30,000 estimated for Burke's *Reflections*. In 1793 petitions for reform poured in upon Parliament. Those from Scotland outnumbered the ones from England. The one from Edinburgh stretched "the whole length of the floor of the house." In England the movement was lively, with new societies forming in various towns. A petition from Norwich had 3,700 signatures, one from London and Westminster 6,000, one from Sheffield 8,000. The House of Commons refused even to receive the Sheffield petition, finding it "disrespectful." It was true that the thought in these petitions was not so much to reform the House as to transform it. What was wanted was not simply an extension of what existed, but the replacement of one theory by

[23] The proceedings are printed in full by Meikle, *Scotland*, 239-73.

another, with respect to what the House of Commons and its relations to the country ought to be.

The Dundee Society, composed largely of weavers, since its petition had had no effect, prepared and published an *Address*. It was written by George Mealmaker, and submitted for improvement of language to Thomas Fyshe Palmer, an Englishman who was a graduate of Eton and Cambridge, and had gone to Scotland after developing Unitarian ideas. He had played a prominent role in the militant minority at the Edinburgh Convention, becoming what Robert Dundas called "the most determined rebel in Scotland." He nevertheless advised the Dundee society against publication of its manifesto, in which the war was denounced in very strong language as the scheme of a wicked ministry to enslave the people.[24] Palmer was arrested, tried, and sentenced to seven years in Australia for his part in the Dundee affair. His case followed that of Thomas Muir, also prominent in the Edinburgh convention, who was sentenced to fourteen years.

These Braxfield trials left an unpleasant impression on many persons not sympathetic to the militant radicals, since Justice Braxfield had made a political commotion in his own courtroom and offered a variety of emphatic *dicta*: such as that "in this country . . . the landed interest alone has a right to be represented," and that he "never was an admirer of the French," but could "now only consider them as monsters of human nature."[25]

Undeterred by the fate of Muir and Palmer, the Scotch clubs persisted in their idea of a Convention. A second Convention met in April, and a third, this time a British Convention, planned in conjunction with the London Corresponding Society, met at Edinburgh in November 1793. Hamilton Rowan came from Ireland, and the London and Sheffield societies sent delegates from England. Among the Scotch, fewer of the educated or substantial classes attended than at the first Convention a year before. The British Convention was very vehement in its language. When the Lord Advocate of Scotland accused it of desiring "not a reform but a subversion of Parliament," he was far from being mistaken, though he greatly exaggerated the degree to which it accepted violence as a means of introducing "a republic or democracy."[26] Thirty constables sufficed to break the Convention up. Three leaders, Maurice Margarot, William Skirving, and Joseph Ger-

---

[24] Extracts are printed by Maccoby, *English Radicalism*, 71.
[25] Brown, *Fr. Rev. in Eng. Hist.*, 97, quoting from *State Trials*, XXIII, 231.
[26] Meikle, 142.

rald were sentenced by Braxfield to terms in Australia. In 1794 most of the clubs in Scotland ceased to meet.

In England, however, the repression of the Scotch clubs and conventions, and the sentencing of the "Scotch martyrs" to deportation, had inflammatory effects: The London Corresponding Society held a general meeting on January 20, 1794. It protested against the proceedings in Scotland, denounced the war to restore despotism in France, and declared that, if the government sought to crush liberty in England, the Society should "issue summonses . . . to the different societies affiliated and corresponding with this society, forthwith to call a General Convention of the People."[27] Feeling ran high at Sheffield, where thousands of toolmakers, cutlery workers, and other skilled mechanics read a variety of radical literature, including the *Register* edited by Joseph Gales. A great public meeting took place on April 7, of which the general theme was that everything else having failed, and the petition of a year before having not even been received, some other (but unspecified) course of action must be found. One speaker darkly hinted that the voice of the people would soon "recommend the 558 gentlemen in St. Stephen's Chapel to go about their business." Resolutions were passed, demanding "universal representation" as a right. An "Address to the British Nation" was adopted, probably composed by Joseph Gales.[28] One of the best statements of British radicalism of the day, this Sheffield *Address* made no reference to France but refuted the argument for "virtual representation," as the Americans had refuted it a quarter of a century before. It declared that petitioning had been proved useless and a "complete revolution of sentiment" must come about. It complained that plain mechanics could get no attention from "gentlemen," and that the common man in England was not free or secure in his property. "What is the constitution to us, if we are nothing to it? The constitution of Britain, indeed, is highly

[27] While the fear of a "convention" is noted in all works on the subject, the quotation is from a printed leaflet in the Wentworth Woodhouse collection at the Central Library in Sheffield, headed "At a General Meeting of the London Corresponding Society, held at the Globe Tavern Strand, on Monday 20th of January 1794, Citizen John Martin in the Chair, the following Address to the People of Great Britain and Ireland was read and agreed to."

[28] The Address is printed with *Proceedings of the Public Meeting . . . at Sheffield . . . of April 1794* in the Wentworth Woodhouse collection. On Joseph Gales' years in England see W. H. G. Armytage, "The Editorial Experience of Joseph Gales, 1786-94" in *North Carolina Historical Review* (1951), 332-61. For Sheffield, an important center of radicalism, see also G. P. Jones, "The Political Reform Movement at Sheffield," in *Transactions of the Hunter Archaeological Society* (Sheffield), iv (1937), 57-68, and J. Taylor, "The Sheffield Constitutional Society," *ibid.*, v (1943), 133-46.

extolled as the greatest effort of human wisdom—so is the constitution of Turkey at Constantinople." The Sheffield mechanics went on to explain what they meant by equality.

"Yes, countrymen, we demand Equality of Rights, in which is included Equality of Representation, without which terror is law, and the obligations of justice are weakened, because unsanctioned by the sacred voice of the people. We are not speaking of that visionary Equality of Property, the practical assertion of which would desolate the world . . . but that Equality we claim is to make the Slave a Man, the Man a Citizen, and the Citizen an integral part of the State, to make him a joint Sovereign, and not a Subject." At Sheffield, the Address continued, people wanted a state in which rich plunderers would not go unscathed—where the same law would apply to all. Joseph Gales, the probable author, soon fled to Hamburg, from which he passed on to America. Here he astonished the natives by producing a verbatim record of speeches in Congress, having brought with him the Old World art of shorthand; he lived many years as a democratic journalist in North Carolina.

In 1794 the government struck back against radicalism in England, as in Scotland in 1793. The talk of a Convention amounted to talk of an Anti-Parliament, of a body claiming more representative validity and more rightful authority than Parliament itself. In addition, so much agitation against the war was undesirable after a year of hostilities. The war against France would seem more necessary, and become more popular, if it could be proved that seditious Britons, in conjunction with the French, meant to revolutionize Britain itself. Conservatives would be mollified by the prosecution of persons bold enough to desire change in the institutions of England.

Pitt's government therefore put on the State Trials of 1794. Indictments for treason were issued against various persons—Thomas Hardy as head of the London Corresponding Society, Horne Tooke and John Thelwall as radicals and clubbists over many years, Thomas Walker of Manchester, and others. Beginning in September 1794, the trials were simultaneous with the last operations of the Revolutionary Tribunal of Paris and with the initiation of the Jacobin trials in Vienna, to both of which they offered a refreshing contrast; for, though the government tried hard to obtain the conviction of men whom it regarded as enemies of the state, as it had successfully done in Scotland, it had now to go through the procedures of English law, which meant that the proceedings were public, the jury was independent, and competent counsel was available to the accused. Hardy and the others were defended by Thomas Erskine, who had defended Paine *in absentia* in 1792. He showed that some of the evidence brought in by the government was fabricated. No serious intent of armed rebellion, or of collusion with the French, could be proved. The jury, composed of substantial London business men, such as brewers and wholesale grocers, acquitted Thomas Hardy after only two hours of deliberation. All the other defendants were acquitted also. The prosecution of these critics of the established order, though legally unsuccessful, was not without effects of the kind intended. The fear of similar proceedings, with the disgrace and the expense that they involved, helped to drive men of standing out of the radical movement, which became more clearly identified than ever with certain elements of the working classes. The state trials also hastened the process, evident since 1792, by which, in the Parliamentary classes, the Whig Party fell to pieces. It is indeed from early in 1792 that the pre-history of what became the Conservative and Liberal parties half a century later can first be traced. Some Whigs, such as Fox, Sheridan, Erskine, and the Earl of Lauderdale, had held firm for neutrality, advised against domestic repression, thought that a little Parliamentary reform might prevent radicalism, and while uninvolved in the popular clubs generally felt for them a tolerant attitude. Others, led by the Duke of Portland, and including Burke, William Windham, and Sir Gilbert Elliot, had urged Pitt to control seditious writings and associations, and even, in November 1792, to go to war against France. What the British ministry needed, said Burke, was a "basis in the strong permanent Aristocratical interests of the country."[29] A third group of Whigs, conservative in home affairs, who could not go along with Fox, or "with men who call on 40,000 weavers to dictate political measures," had nevertheless been afraid, six weeks before the war began, that public opinion would not support it. The aristocratic Whigs joined Pitt's government in a coalition in 1794. The Duke of Portland became Home Secretary, Windham Secretary at War, and Elliot, as explained in Chapter IX, Viceroy of Corsica at £8,000 a year. It was the coming of these Whigs, as Keith Feiling once said, that made the Tory party conservative.

The acquittals of 1794 gave encouragement to the London Corresponding Society, whose minutes show increasing attendance at its general meetings through 1795. In England as in France the war produced food shortages and rising prices, so that immediate economic

[29] Quoted by Butterfield, "Fox and the Whig Opposition," 319.

grievances were now added to a general social malaise and a bitter class consciousness as sources of discontent. The society had perhaps as many as 5,000 members in London in 1795. It served as a nucleus for mass meetings and public demonstrations, usually orderly, for, as a recent British writer has put it, plebeian politics had come a long way since the days of Wilkes and the hooliganism of No Popery mobs. In October 1795 the most enormous crowd that anyone could remember, estimated at 200,000 persons, swarmed in the streets to watch the procession for the opening of Parliament. With hoots for the dukes and earls, and with cries of "Bread! Bread! Peace! Peace!" the populace pressed closely about the king's own coach, in which "a small pebble, or marble or bullet broke one of the windows."[30] The king was extricated with difficulty amid the hisses of his subjects.

The government, now reinforced by the Portland Whigs, and with popular agitation after three years showing little sign of abatement, proceeded at once to severer measures. Parliament passed two bills: the Treasonable Practices Act, which greatly enlarged the definition of treason, and the Seditious Meetings Act, which made it unlawful for gatherings to assemble to hear "lectures" except in the presence of some kind of officer of the law. Fox, Erskine, and some seventy others voted against the two bills in the Commons. They argued that the London Corresponding Society had had nothing to do with the assault on the king, that to deny lawful means of expression would produce more revolutionary sentiment rather than less, and that the government was concocting imaginary dangers, which was doubtful, in order to persist in an unpopular war, which was more nearly true. The sponsors of the two bills were in a great majority. The state trials, they said, had proved that some people wanted "representative government." The young Lord Mornington, not yet off to his conquests in India, complained of books designed "to excite the poor to seize the landed property of the kingdom." William Windham asked gentlemen of the house to remember that "there was such a thing as the French Revolution." There was a French party in Holland, he said, and there was one in America. "Was there a country in Europe," he demanded rhetorically, "safe from the poison of these principles, or which had not felt the effect of this great democracy?"[31]

As the Two Acts went into operation, the membership of the London Corresponding Society, and of similar radical clubs throughout

---

[30] *Annual Register for 1795*, Chronicle, p. 38; Maccoby, *Eng. Radicalism*, 93-94.
[31] *Parliamentary History*, XXXII, 274-363.

the country, began to decline. Cautious spirits, or respectable young men aspiring to rise in trade, like Francis Place, ceased to be active. Under the new conditions the management of club affairs fell to the adventurous and the bold. Where in 1793 the London Corresponding Society had voted against the use of the word "citizen" as a term of address by its members, the word was commonly used in the society in 1796, and by its correspondents in Leeds and other northern towns, who also closed their letters with "Health and Fraternity"—the *salut et fraternité* of the revolutionary French.[32] In November 1796 there was enough life in the radical movement for five hundred persons to sit down to an eight-shilling dinner, at the Crown and Anchor Tavern in London, with the radical Earl of Stanhope, who praised the "80,000 incorrigible Citizens" despised by Edmund Burke.[33] Under pressure, the London society became more secret. It established contacts, difficult to unravel, with the United Irish, who broke into full rebellion in 1798, and with the nebulous groups called the United English, who were fairly numerous among the old "clubbists" in the neighborhood of Sheffield and Manchester. Some clubbists began to drill and arm. In 1797 there were mutinies in the Navy—in the Channel fleet at Spithead, in the North Sea fleet at Nore, in the South Atlantic squadron near Cape Town—and indeed the very ship that carried the "Scotch martyrs" to Australia in 1795 was troubled by a mutiny in which the convicts were joined by the soldiers who guarded them. The mutineers complained against abuses of treatment and in the receipt of their pay. No connection with radical clubs was ever discovered, and historians have agreed in dissociating the outbreaks from any revolutionary intentions; but the investigating committee of the House of Commons believed (as seems likely enough) that what might have been a mere "breach of subordination and discipline" was made far more serious by the persistent agitation of the political clubs against the form of government and the governing class.[34] In 1798 there was still enough disaffection for Pitt, expecting invasion by the French at any moment, to have *habeas corpus* suspended. Various organizers and agitators went to prison without trial. In 1799 the London Corresponding Society and certain other clubs were proscribed by name,

[32] British Museum, Add. MSS., 27,814, fol. 126 for August 1, 1793, and Add. MSS. 27,815 for materials of 1796ff.

[33] Add. MSS. 27,817, fol. 44.

[34] *Report of the Committee of Secrecy of the House of Commons, Ordered to be Printed 15 March 1799*, p. 18.

and ceased to exist. The government had succeeded in crushing the popular radical movement—at least until after Waterloo.

The "Levée en masse" of the People of Quality

But the government did not have to do it alone. If the liberty of England was shown in the latitude, all things considered, so long allowed to the voices of disaffection, it was shown also in the alacrity with which the upper classes, on their own estates and in towns and villages far from the capital, rushed on their own initiative to uphold their way of life. "The hands of Government must be strengthened if the country is to be saved," wrote Lord Grenville, the Foreign Secretary, to his brother the Marquis of Buckingham during the crisis of November 1792; "but, above all, the work must not be left to the hands of Government, but every man must put his shoulder to it, according to his rank and station in life, or it will not be done."[35]

On the Continent, from Holland to Naples, the conservative elements, when they faced domestic agitation and foreign threats, showed little but helplessness and bewilderment, or, indeed, counted on Great Britain for protection. One German journalist, dreading Cisalpinization in 1797, could think of nothing to recommend to his readers except to keep calm and trust the authorities. In England matters were different. Here the government could call for an arming of the people without serious trepidation. England, with the possible exception of Catalonia, was the one country that saw a kind of spontaneous mass rising of conservative character. The aristocracy showed its powers of self-help.

There were four things that England must do, wrote William Eden, Lord Auckland, from his post at The Hague, in November, as Dumouriez' republican hordes swept over the Low Countries. It must work for a pacification in Europe. It must prepare its navy. It must put down internal sedition. And it must bring Englishmen of all classes to a due sense of "the blessings which they are risking in pursuit of a bubble."[36] This should be done, he said, by proclamations to the people, by speeches in Parliament and discourses in the pulpit. Many other methods were soon found.

We must do something, said the Marquis of Buckingham, "to reconcile the lower ranks of people to our Constitution, and to their situation

---

[35] *Memoirs of the Courts and Cabinets of George III . . . by the Duke of Buckingham and Chandos,* 2 vols. (London, 1853), I, 228.

[36] Gt. Brit., Hist. MSS. Comm., *Manuscripts of J. B. Fortescue Preserved at Dropmore,* 10 vols. (London, 1892-1927), II, 342.

under it."[37] Here, implicitly, was a recognition of the deep social alienation expressed by the working people of Sheffield, when they said that the Constitution was nothing to them since they were nothing to it. There was not much, however, that the marquis had to propose, beyond the lightening of certain taxes, the repeal of the law of 1773 requiring laborers to work six days a year on the roads, and an amendment of those features of the Poor Laws which prevented laboring people, if it seemed that they might become public charges, from moving about freely from place to place in search of work. In effect, with one notable exception, nothing was done in the way of actual concessions to allay popular discontent. In 1793 a few concessions were made to property-owners among the Catholic Irish, in the hope of preventing their drift in the direction of "Jacobinism." In England it was not possible even to modify the game laws. By these laws, only landowners possessing estates worth £100 a year were legally allowed to shoot as much as a partridge. A bill was introduced in 1796, and the Foxite Whigs made their usual speeches, arguing that both modest farmers and "opulent merchants" were injured by the game laws; but a majority in the Commons held that even the game laws were part of the fabric of the constitution, devised by the wisdom of ancestors, and not to be tampered with without danger to existing ranks and orders.[38]

The one notable exception was the "Speenhamland system" in the administration of poor relief. It arose, characteristically enough, outside the circles of Parliament and the government, when the justices of the peace in Berkshire, in 1795, taking note of the rise of prices, ruled that wages of the laboring poor should be supplemented by grants from the poor funds. The practice soon spread to other counties throughout much of England. It was criticized for holding down wages, and for pauperizing much of the laboring class; but it did something to relieve the worst cases of destitution, and it did so at the expense of the landowners who paid the poor rates. The annual cost of poor relief for all England in the 1790's rose from about £2,000,000 to about £4,000,000. Whether the upper classes took up this burden for political reasons, out

---

[37] *Ibid.*, 327.

[38] *Parl. Hist.*, xxxii, 838-54. Sir Richard Sutton remarked (p. 848) that "in these times of democratical doctrines, he did not hesitate to utter the aristocratical opinion that the game laws of this country were founded on good principles, and secured to the landed proprietors that superiority of privilege and enjoyment which they could best exercise without injuring themselves, or interfering with other pursuits." So little was the interest in the matter, or likelihood of passage, that only 82 members were present, or at least took the trouble to vote: 65 Noes to 17 Ayes.

of social fear, is very uncertain; it was not "the poor," but the next higher classes that were most vocal in their disaffection. Frederick Eden, the nephew of Lord Auckland, also prompted by the rise of prices after 1794, made detailed studies of how families contrived to live on £20 a year, and in 1797 published a famous book, *The State of the Poor*, which Karl Marx later praised for its exact and factual content. Nowhere in the book did Eden show any actual fear of the people whom he was studying. He remarked, however, that it was not the agricultural laborers so much as the rural "manufacturers" that were most often on relief. So far as the increase of relief payments, under the Speenhamland system, went to weavers and other rural household workers, it may have reduced their interest in radical clubs and propaganda.

The propertied classes, in short, to a degree that one would not find in many parts of the Continent, were willing to lay taxes upon themselves in return for their domination in government and society. In 1799 Pitt was even able to introduce a new income tax. Exempting persons with less than £60 a year, and containing a progressive feature from £60 to £200, it imposed a flat ten percent on incomes above £200, so that the rich paid at the same rate as the broad middle class. It is not clear whether the landowners paid any more under the new income tax than under the old land tax which it supplanted. The public revenues continued to come largely from indirect taxes, of which the stamp tax on newspapers, already mentioned, was but a small example. But in principle the English governing class, in its war with France and with its own adversaries at home, accepted its liability to taxation.[39]

The conservative *levée* took the form mainly of counter-organization and counter-propaganda. As early as 1791, in the Birmingham riots, a mob more or less spontaneously formed had attacked the home of Joseph Priestley, popularly disliked as a Unitarian and a reformer; his house and scientific equipment had been destroyed; and the sequel had shown the solidarity that existed between the local gentry, the Anglican clergy, and some of the less enlightened popular strata. Priestley's

---

[39] The Speenhamland system, set forth in all the general histories, is noted as one of the means used to "blanket discontent" by A. Mitchell, "The Association Movement of 1792-93," in *Historical Journal*, IV (1961), 77. French historians, such as Mathiez, who made so much of the Ventôse laws of 1794 as Robespierrist projects to assist the poor, seem not to have known that the British upper class did somewhat the same, more effectively. For the income tax see A. Farnsworth, *Addington, Author of the Modern Income Tax* (London, 1951). Addington in 1803 maintained the yield on Pitt's tax while reducing the rate to 5%. The war-time rate on the old land tax had gone as high as 4s. in the pound of income, i.e., nominally 20 percent.

friends—Wilkinson, Watt, and Boulton—had been outraged, but were made more cautious. Priestley himself continued to speak out, and was listened to by the radical clubs that began to spring up, according to a letter written by Horatio Nelson to the Duke of Clarence in December 1792. At this time, as the government called up the militia, and set guards at the Bank of England and the Tower of London, more organized methods of checking "sedition" were adopted.

In November there met at the Crown and Anchor Tavern in London, as a group of private citizens, but with encouragement from the government in the background, a gathering of gentlemen who organized themselves as the Association for Preserving Liberty and Property against Republicans and Levellers. Its chairman was John Reeves, a writer on English law, and on its executive committee was John Bowles, a barrister, who was provided with secret service money and wrote a number of highly conservative pamphlets in the next few years. The new Association printed thousands of copies of its *Proceedings*, which it sold for three shillings a hundred, so that they could be given away for a halfpenny, or for nothing. Within a few weeks hundreds of other such associations were formed throughout the country, under the auspices of gentlemen and the clergy. Only in a few places, notably Sheffield, was discontent so nearly universal as to deter their formation. The associations called the attention of government to booksellers who kept radical literature in their shops. They threatened innkeepers with suspension of licenses if they allowed radical gatherings to meet on their premises. They got up petitions for which signatures of the "lower orders" were solicited. Thomas Paine was burnt in effigy in many places. A few of the associations took to secret methods, a bit like the Eudämonists in Germany, putting spies into the democratic clubs, and spreading defamatory rumors about persons of contrary opinions. Often they received large contributions from wealthy donors, of which they spent the proceeds on circulating books and pamphlets in praise of church, state, and constitution, and in derogation of France.[40]

Except in places like Manchester, where feeling ran high on both sides, the associations went out of existence as organized bodies in 1793. They had done much to impose silence on merely moderate critics of the existing order, and to confine radicalism to persons willing to take the consequences of open defiance. From Birmingham the London Association heard that loyalists outnumbered the malcontents six to

[40] Mitchell, "Association Movement"; *Proceedings of the Association for Preserving Liberty and Property against Republicans and Levellers* (London, n.d.).

one; confidence grew, though a situation in which, in wartime, the loyalty of a seventh of the population was uncertain would appear to be little to boast of. When Lord Auckland returned from Holland he found, "with concern," in November 1793, "that all the lower classes are more or less affected by the execrable doctrines of the day. But the main body of the kingdom is still sound."[41] It is not possible to say what a man in Auckland's position meant by "lower."

As the Associations against Republicans and Levellers became inactive, they were succeeded by armed and uniformed companies of volunteers, organized by men of local prominence after the war began. It must be remembered that England had next to no regular army; that what army there was, in 1793, was on the Continent and in Ireland; and that the English, in any case, would not tolerate the presence of regular troops in their neighborhood. The volunteer companies, ostensibly organized to repel French invasion, were mainly engaged in combatting internal disaffection. In some places, landowners recruited their tenants; in others, factory owners of the new type, enjoying a closer contact with their workers than was possible under the old system of dispersed rural industry, drew on reliable employees to build volunteer units. The companies were of course officered by the upper classes, and largely filled by the middle, but efforts were made to obtain a representation of the lower classes also in their ranks. At their drills, parades, and assemblies the right ideas were inculcated and publicized. The companies taught, as Auckland had put it, the blessings that Britons had the good fortune to enjoy. A lieutenant in Renfrewshire called them "a principal means of crushing that seditious and democratic spirit which has so much prevailed." At Chiswick, near London, it was found that the volunteers "encouraged and restored a due principle of subordination amongst the different classes of the people."[42]

The impact of all this self-generated but well-organized activity could be illustrated from many specific cases. Thomas Walker, for example, was a textile manufacturer at Manchester, a man of inherited means, an Anglican of sufficient social station to have had his portrait painted by Romney. He had even once been elected boroughreeve, as the chief public officer was called at Manchester, which though already a town of 75,000 had no municipal organization except for its old manorial institutions. Walker developed an interest in radical politics

---

[41] *Dropmore Papers*, ii, 455.
[42] J. R. Western, "The Volunteer Movement as an Anti-Revolutionary Force, 1793-1801," in *English Historical Review*, LXXI (1956).

and parliamentary reform. He was the friend and employer of James Watt, Jr., and the sponsor of Thomas Cooper, who founded the democratic *Manchester Herald*. He was attacked by the local branch of the Society against Republicans and Levellers, caught up in the treason trials of 1794, victimized by false testimony, and, though acquitted, obliged to spend thousands of pounds on his defense, and to suffer a besmirchment of character from which his public reputation never recovered. To take another example, in 1797 about fourteen hundred Frenchmen landed on the coast of Wales under the command of an American adventurer in the French service, William Tate, a "democrat" from South Carolina. The invasion was a fiasco; the Welsh did not rise in the insurrection to which they were invited; the enemy was soon disarmed and captured by volunteer companies that rushed to the scene. It was the events that followed that were significant—more treason trials, false evidence, and local persecution, not of the coal workers and rural laborers of whom no one was afraid, but of the Dissenters and Methodists who were detested by upholders of the establishment, and of farmers and tradesmen who, especially in Wales, remained obstinately outside the Church of England.[43]

Meanwhile the country was flooded with reading matter. John Bowles, of the Association against Republicans and Levellers, published early in 1793 his *Real Grounds for the Present War with France*. It went through several editions, and it introduced into historiography, since many historians continued to repeat it, the idea that the French Convention, in offering aid "to all peoples wishing to recover their Liberty" on November 19, 1792, had actually intended to subvert and revolutionize all governments, including the British. John Reeves, of the same Association, wrote his *Thoughts on the English Government Addressed to the Quiet Good Sense of the People of England*. It found the French Jacobins to be much like the old English Puritans, and propounded the theory that the French Revolution and the Protestant Reformation were the twin sources of the evils of modern times. William Playfair, in 1795, published his *History of Jacobinism, Its Crimes, Cruelties, and Perfidies*, in which he neglected to mention that he had once been involved in Paris in the French Revolution himself. At Edinburgh, where Playfair's brother was an eminent scientist at the university, there was a good deal of apprehension, since the faculty

[43] F. Knight, *The Strange Case of Thomas Walker: Ten Years in the Life of a Manchester Radical* (London, 1957); Commander E. H. Stuart Jones, R.N., *The Last Invasion of Britain* (Cardiff, 1950); A. Davies, "La Révolution française et le Pays des Galles," in *Annales historiques de la Révolution française* No. 140 (1955), 202-12.

was alarmed by the radical sentiments and democratic preaching of Presbyterians outside the official Church. John Robison of Edinburgh University, as already mentioned several times, gave warning to the public in his *Proofs of a Conspiracy against All Governments and Religions*. Edmund Burke, when it seemed that Pitt might sign a treaty with the French Directory, wrote his uncompromising *Letters on a Regicide Peace*. George Canning edited the *Anti-Jacobin Review*. Writings of French émigrés were translated; indeed the English edition of Barruel antedated the French. Mallet du Pan's pamphlets were also translated; in 1799 he set up in England, with a government subsidy, and published his *British Mercury* to attack the French Revolution. An obscure tract by the Italian Barzoni came out in English, the *Romans in Greece*. It held that the French in Italy were nothing but plunderers. Someone found and translated a shocking work by the German Count von Soden, who had left the Prussian civil service because he disapproved of the Prussian policy of neutrality. It was a tale of French atrocities in Franconia. The republican soldiers (called Huns) were said to frequent "Jew taverns"; they seized women and violated them in the streets, against the resistance of fathers and brothers who were "inhumanly mangled"; when remonstrances were made to the French Commander, General Bernadotte (the future king of Sweden), he replied airily that "these are trifles, which in time of war must be overlooked."[44]

Malthus' *Essay on Population*, a more creditable work, first published in 1798, also formed part of the campaign of dissuasion against the new ideas. Malthus, though in Anglican orders, was more the type of the French *abbé*. He came to feel, like Frederick Eden, a deep and sympathetic interest in the problems of the poor. He thought, however, that the ideas of Godwin, which he attributed also to the French Revolution, offered only a treacherous and deceptive hope to the poor themselves; and his *Essay on Population* was designed explicitly as an answer to Condorcet's *Progress of the Human Mind*. Malthus, like Eden, had the merit of emphasizing that the best way to relieve the poor was to raise the productivity of their labor. He agreed, in 1798, that the existing extremes of inequality of wealth were bad, that the rich had a greater "facility of combination" than the poor, and that the poor could live on a seven-hour working day, if only they could "agree."

---

[44] *Anecdotes and characteristic traits respecting the incursion of the French republicans into Franconia in the year 1796. By an eye-witness. Translated from the German* (London, 1798), 20-21, 65. A translation of *Die französen in Franken 1796* (Nuremberg, 1797).

These observations disappeared from later editions of the *Essay*, in which Malthus, aiming at a clinical objectivity, and harping more on "abstinence" as a check on overpopulation, produced a classic of the dismal science. Even in 1798, however, what he had to offer the laboring classes was mostly a lesson in patience. It was simply a fact, he said, that in the lottery of life some people must draw a blank.[45]

The books and pamphlets just mentioned were aimed at persons of at least a moderate degree of education. This was the first generation, however, of what may be called the true common reader. The Sunday School movement for a dozen years had with difficulty been spreading some knowledge of reading among the actual lower classes. In 1797 there were some 1,086 such schools with 69,000 pupils. The sponsors of the movement were generally devout people, Evangelicals or Methodists, who, against the skepticism or indifference of the more satisfied clergy, had hoped to spread an acquaintance with the Bible. They were shocked to find their pupils devouring Thomas Paine. Archdeacon Paley's *Reasons for Contentment* was abundantly distributed in reply. Hannah More, a good lady who had done much for the lower classes, resolved to put the spread of literacy to better use. Beginning in 1795, she wrote a series called the "Cheap Repository Tracts." Funds contributed by well-wishers, from the Evangelicals of the Clapham Sect to the Bishop of London and the king's brother, the Duke of Gloucester, made it possible to sell them for less than a penny. By March 1796 no less than two million were in circulation. Thomas Paine was engaged on his own ground; perhaps he had even met his match, though no one can tell what effect these efforts really had. One of Miss More's more successful compositions was *Village Politics*, written in the form of a dialogue in twenty-four pages. It was a bit different from the *Feuille villageoise*, one of the most successful papers of the French Revolution. She published it anonymously, and, when found out, apologized for it as intended only for "the vulgar." Its tone and message may be judged from the following excerpt:

"*Tom*. Pooh! I want freedom and happiness the same as they have got in France.

"*Jack*. What, Tom, we imitate them? . . . Why. I'd sooner go to the Negers to get learning, or to the Turks to get religion, than to the French for freedom and happiness. . . . Instead of indulging in discon-

[45] T. R. Malthus, *First Essay on Population, 1798, with Notes by James Bonar* (London, 1926).

tent . . . (for envy is at the bottom of your equality works), I read my Bible, go to Church, and think of a treasure in Heaven.

"*Tom.* Aye, but the French have got it in *this* world.

"*Jack.* 'Tis all a lie, Tom. Sir John's butler says, his master gets letters which *say* 'tis all a lie."[46]

The Abortive Irish Revolution of 1798

Whether the Irish rebellion of 1798 should be thought of as an unsuccessful revolution is perhaps optional. As Wolfe Tone said shortly before his suicide in prison, in such matters it is success that counts: "Washington succeeded, and Kosciuszko failed."[47] In any case the Irish uprising was of significant magnitude, involving a population equal to that of the United States, and half that of England. The discontents were put down by force, and a good deal of force proved to be necessary. Late in 1798 there were 140,000 British troops in Ireland, of whom half could be called regulars; and this half, or 70,000, was twice as many as the number of British soldiers that ever fought on the Continent against the French Republic and Empire from 1793 through the battle of Waterloo.[48]

To recall briefly the well-known tribulations of eighteenth-century Ireland, it seems safe to say that the contrasts between poverty and

[46] *Village politics, addressed to all the mechanics, journeymen and day labourers in Great Britain, by Will Chip, a country carpenter,* 3rd ed. (London, 1793), 5, 18; Altick, *English Common Reader,* 67-77.

[47] *Life of Theobald Wolfe Tone,* 2 vols. (Washington, 1826), II, 531. Tone's diary and autobiography, especially in this first edition with its large appendix of other documents, remains a principal source for the United Irish movement. For sources and older studies see S. Simms, "A Select Bibliography of the United Irishmen," in *Irish Historical Studies,* I (1938), 158-80. For more recent work: R. Jacob, *The Rise of the United Irishmen, 1791-94* (London, 1937); R. Hayes, *Biographical Dictionary of Irishmen in France* (Dublin, 1949); R. B. McDowell, *Irish Public Opinion 1750-1800* (London, 1944); H. Nicolson, *The Desire to Please; A Story of Hamilton Rowan and the United Irishmen* (New York, 1943); B. Inglis, *The Freedom of the Press in Ireland, 1784-1841* (London, 1954); C. Dickson, *The Wexford Rising in 1798* (Tralee, 1956); and the studies by two Americans: H. L. Calkin, "La propagande en Irlande des idées de la Révolution française," in *Annales historiques de la Révolution française,* No. 139 (1955), 143-60, and *Les invasions d'Irlande pendant la Rév. fr.* (Paris, 1956); and J. H. Stewart, "The French Revolution on the Dublin Stage," in *Journal of the Royal Society of Antiquaries of Ireland,* XCI (1961), 183-92; "*Burke's Reflections* in the Irish Press," in *French Historical Studies,* II (1962), 376-90, and "The Irish Press during the French Revolution," in *Journalism Quarterly,* XXXIX (1962), 507-18.

[48] Buckingham to Grenville, Dublin, November 5, 1798: communications are "almost stopped" despite "71,000 *effective regulars* and 47,000 yeomanry" (plus some militia), *Dropmore Papers,* IV, 362. Not counting Hanoverians and other Germans in the British army, the British had about 36,000 troops in the Anglo-Russian invasion of Holland in 1799; 26,000 at Salamanca in 1812; and 26,000 at Waterloo. See J. Fortescue, *History of the British Army,* 13 vols. (London, 1910-1930), IV, 666; VIII, 630; X, 430.

great wealth, and between discrimination and privilege, were more pronounced than in any country of Western Europe before the French Revolution. There were three religious communities that had little to do with each other. A tenth of the population was Anglican. This tenth, the "ascendancy," owned five-sixths of the land, and received such benefits as the established Church of Ireland was able to confer; its members occupied the government offices and enjoyed an array of pensions and sinecures; a few hundred of them controlled the Irish Parliament at Dublin; and they included the families of various British notables of the next generation, such as Castlereagh, Palmerston, and the two Wellesleys, that is the Earl of Mornington and the Duke of Wellington. A fifth of the population were Presbyterians. In eastern Ulster they lived as a compact majority group; they were predominantly middle-class, or at least they had no aristocracy; many were merchants, tradesmen, linen weavers, and artisans, but many also were tenant farmers; and, thanks to their lively interest in America, to which there had been much recent emigration, and to their Dissenters' dislike of bishops and landed gentility, they were peculiarly susceptible to republican sentiments.

Almost three-quarters of the people were Roman Catholics. The Catholics had been largely expropriated in the seventeenth century, through seizures by Anglican landlords and the mass settlement of Scottish and English Presbyterians. The Catholic Irish had joined with the French on a famous occasion, when the French landed an army of 6,000 men in Ireland to support James II; it was upon the defeat of the Irish and French in 1690, at the battle of the Boyne, that the eighteenth-century regime in both Britain and Ireland was constructed. The Irish Catholics long suffered the consequences by deprivation of almost all legal rights. By 1790 the most severe features of the penal code had been removed. No Catholic could yet hold office or vote for a member of the Irish House of Commons, but normal property rights had been restored, though the number of Catholic gentry and freeholders was in fact very small. A Catholic episcopate was tolerated, a shadowy group alongside the Protestant prelates of the Church of Ireland, who, though often absentees, held the ancient sees, titles, and revenues—Armagh brought £8,000 a year. The Catholic bishops of Ireland, accepting the inferior status of their people, proved in the 1790's to be far more conservative than those of France or Italy. Since the middle of the century an important class of Catholic merchants and business men had grown up, as among French Protestants before the Revolution, and for similar reasons—since they were kept legally out of the government and the armed forces and were restricted in the professions, the universities, and remunerative church appointments, they could advance themselves only in trade.

Catholics and Presbyterians had long held each other in mutual aversion and horror, but by the end of the century the old religious animosities had begun to fade, and leaders of the two out-groups came to feel that they shared the same grievances, suffering alike from the insecurities of farm tenancy, from the expense of paying tithes to an alien church, and from exclusion from politics. The coming together of Catholics and Dissenters was correspondingly feared by the ascendancy and by the British government. The failure of the two groups to cooperate in 1783, a failure due both to themselves and to the manipulations of Anglicans, had been a main cause of the collapse of the movement for Parliamentary reform at the time of the American Revolution.[49] From the upheavals of those years somewhat opposite results had ensued. The Irish Parliament enjoyed a little more freedom with respect to Great Britain after 1782. But as the instrument of an entrenched and hereditary minority, the Irish Parliament firmly refused any extension of political rights. The governing class, anticipating that the granting of power to the "native" Irish would undermine the whole system in church and state, and undo the whole seventeenth-century settlement of law and property (as eventually it did), stood fast against what was called reform, and would indeed mean revolution. The troubles of Ireland were thus primarily internal, though the Anglicans could maintain their position only through the connection with England. As so often in the history of the empire, however, the central government at Westminster was sometimes more willing than the local rulers to listen to popular discontents. William Pitt, as early as 1791, was coming to feel that the only solution might be in an abolition of the Irish Parliament and a union with England, as happened in 1801. Only thus, he reasoned, could the obstinacy of the Irish ascendancy be overcome, and the causes of revolutionary ferment alleviated; only thus, by merging the Irish Catholics, along with the Dissenters, into a larger United Kingdom in which they would be a minority, could they be given political rights without danger to Great Britain. Pitt's views on union with England, in short, while unwelcome to the Irish Parliament, were not unfriendly to the Irish people.

[49] For Ireland, 1778-1784, see *Age*, I, 287-94, 302-308.

Unrest in Ireland was endemic. Agricultural workers, made desperate by poverty or by loss of land through eviction, or stirred up when landlords replaced Catholic with Protestant tenants, or vice versa, formed secret associations to offer threats and retaliation. Such, in the last decades of the century, were the Defenders, who were mostly Catholic, and the Protestant Peep-of-Day Boys in Ulster. Very different were the middle-class organizations, public and avowed, such as the armed Volunteer companies which had formed about 1778, and worked without success for a reformation of Parliament. Discouraged and inactive after 1784, the members of these companies were still in possession of their weapons, especially among the Presbyterians of the north. In 1789 they were reawakened to politics by news of the French Revolution. The press and the theaters of Dublin, Cork, Belfast, and other towns re-echoed with enthusiastic praises for the new order in France.

In Ireland, however, as in England and Scotland, organized disaffection came to a head in 1792, in the very months that preceded the outbreak of war between France and Britain. The new feature, distinguishing it from the agitation of a decade before, was a more determined resolution to overcome the old Catholic-Protestant differences. The Catholic Committee, a kind of self-help organization formed many years before, fell into new hands in 1792, when the Catholic bishops and gentry were outvoted by a more militant group of Catholic laity. "What prevents you," asked a certain Dr. Ryan in the Committee, "from coalescing with your Protestant brethren? Nothing! Not religion. It is the spirit of the present times to let religion make its own way by its own merits. . . . Let us lay down the little character of a sect, and take up the character of a people."[50] The Catholic Committee of Dublin developed a network of similar committees throughout the island. It employed as its agent a young lawyer named Theobald Wolfe Tone, who had been born an Anglican. Tone helped also to found at Belfast, late in 1791, a group that called itself the Society of United Irishmen, composed mainly of Presbyterian merchants and professional men, who, by the word "United," meant to express their willingness to work with Anglicans and Catholics. In 1792 a United Irish club was established at Dublin. It included 130 Protestant and 140 Catholic members, among whom there were 67 "cloth merchants," 32 other "merchants," 30 attorneys, 26 barristers, 16 physicians, 15 grocers, and

[50] Minutes of the meetings as published in Tone, I, 266.

so on down through a list of solid occupations.[51] United Irish lodges spread rapidly through the country. They were at first perfectly open and orderly, resembling the political clubs that were common on the Continent and in the United States, aiming at a reform of the Irish Parliament as a first step toward further social changes, but already inclined, in view of the frustrations of a decade before, to be radical in their ideas. The Belfast group, in 1792, established one of the most significant democratic newspapers of the English-speaking world at this time—the *Northern Star*. Published twice a week, it sold by subscription for less than twopence a copy. In December 1792, simultaneously with the first convention in Edinburgh, and with the triumph of the militants in the Catholic Committee at Dublin, a few Ulstermen formed a society called "The Irish Jacobins of Belfast."[52] It was possibly the only such group, in any country except France itself, that openly adopted and acknowledged the name "Jacobin" for itself; it was soon closed down by the government.

The United Irishmen pressed for parliamentary reform, denounced the war against France, circulated Paine's *Rights of Man*, and demanded the calling of an Irish "convention," of the kind that had met in Ireland in 1783, and which the example of the French Convention now made far more fearsome. The Catholic Committee, which even when radicalized was more moderate than most United Irish clubs, drew up a petition to the king in December 1792. Deliberately avoiding the inflammatory phrase, "rights of citizens," and modestly requesting only the restoration of ancient privileges, the petition begged for relief from discrimination, and was in fact graciously received by King George III.[53]

The authorities reacted in 1793 with a mixture of concessions and new controls. On the one hand all "conventions" claiming any representative character were prohibited. On the other, the Irish Parliament under strong pressure from the British ministry, enacted certain measures of Catholic relief. Catholics (if they met the usual requirements, such as the forty-shilling freehold) were now allowed to vote for the Irish House of Commons—though not to be elected to it. They could now become members of municipal corporations and take degrees from Dublin University. It was hoped thus to prevent the union of Catholics and Dissenters against the establishment, but the number

[51] R. B. McDowell, "The Personnel of the Dublin Society of United Irishmen," in *Irish Historical Studies*, II (1941), 12-53.
[52] Jacob, 180.
[53] Tone, I, 227, 451-61.

of Catholics benefited by the concessions of 1793 was not great, and the agitation continued. A small group of Whigs in the Parliament introduced a reform bill, hoping to deflect the forces of radicalism. It was a moderate bill, but it soon collapsed before the immovable self-satisfaction of the Irish Commons, expressed, as in 1783, by that strong man of the established order, and friend of Burke, Sir Hercules Langrishe, who now reinforced his former arguments by pointing to the horrors of the Revolution in France, which proved, he said, that a mere breath of change would lead to convulsions.

The United Irish Society of Dublin, early in 1794, produced and publicized a draft for a reform bill of its own. To undercut the vested interests lodged in boroughs and counties, and to push aside differences arising from religion, it adopted the new principle of personal, individual, and numerical representation. It proposed that 300 electoral districts, equal in population, should each send one représentative to the House of Commons. All domiciled men over twenty-one were to vote. The House should be newly elected once a year. Members were to receive pay, and be under no requirement to own property. Except in rejecting the secret ballot, the program anticipated the Chartism of the 1830's, and it shared in the theory of representation which the American and French revolutions had developed, and which the "sister republics" to France were soon also to adopt. Such theory, however, was contrary to the theory of the British and Irish constitutions; and would also, if acted upon, become an actual menace to the existing social order. The United Irishmen of Dublin, far from being merely or naively political, saw their program as a step toward other changes— toward the abolition of tithes and primogeniture, and a transformation of taxes and tariffs, upon which the socio-economic-ecclesiastical institutions of the country so largely rested.[54]

Meanwhile many of the Irish radical leaders, both Catholic and Protestant, came to believe that the welfare of most of the Irish people required a severance of the British connection, without which the ascendancy in Ireland could not survive. Their case was not unlike that of the Dutch patriots who also had made serious efforts for constitutional change in the 1780's, run up against an uncompromising refusal on the part of Dutch conservatives, and had reason to believe that the Orange regime, as restored in 1787, was wholly dependent on the support of England. Like the embittered Dutch patriots, the

---

[54] McDowell, *Public Opinion*, 197-99, and "Select Documents: United Irish Plans for Parliamentary Reform," in *Irish Historical Studies*, III (1942), 39-59.

frustrated Irish felt neither loyalty to their own government nor sympathy for its war with France. Irish and Dutch both entered into secret correspondence with the French in 1794. The Committee of Public Safety sent over an agent to inquire into the strength of a revolutionary movement in Ireland. This agent was William Jackson. It may be noted, as a suggestion of the role of America in these events, that it was this Jackson who had edited, back in 1783, the London edition of the American state constitutions and state papers of the American Revolution. Jackson was caught in Dublin by the Anglo-Irish authorities, who now had evidence against various English and Irish conspirators. Benjamin Vaughan, Hamilton Rowan, and Wolfe Tone all fled, by different routes, to America.

The authorities, detecting collusion with the enemy in wartime, and regarding the United Irish program as subversive in any case, declared the United Irish societies to be illegal. Driven underground, they became more positively revolutionary. They began to accumulate arms, impose secret oaths, hold clandestine meetings, and plan rebellion, counting on French aid. They aspired to set up a republic, and after 1795 took the Batavian Republic as their model. To Wolfe Tone, at least, when he was in Paris in 1796 (assisted by money given privately by the American minister, James Monroe), it seemed that the "moderation" of the French in Holland was an inspiration to the Irish.[55]

The French, from 1796 to 1798, along with their Dutch allies, made three attempts at invasion of the British Isles. The first two were of large scale, but unsuccessful; the third was successful, but the force put ashore was too little and too late. The French Directory could never commit itself wholeheartedly to an invasion of Ireland. It was not only that the hazards of the sea and the British fleet had to be faced, and that the war required, until late in 1797, the concentration of French forces in Italy. There was a feeling in Paris, among those willing to venture on an amphibious operation, that if an overseas attack were to be launched it should be launched directly against England itself. The public tumults in England and Scotland, the outcries in the British press, the state trials, the alarm loudly voiced by conservatives, the messages brought to Paris from English clubs, reinforced in 1797 by the naval mutinies and the suspension of gold payments by the Bank of England, gave a kind of credibility to the reports of a tiny handful of British visionaries, that revolution would break out in England if only a French army could be brought in. By the French Directory these reports were

[55] Tone, II, 164, 169, 173, 196, 203.

relished rather than believed. It seemed likely enough, however, that if a few tens of thousands of veteran French troops could set foot in England, the British army would be too small and ineffectual to prevent their marching into London. The idea of invading England directly, or at least of stirring up an inverse Vendée in the West (as in Colonel Tate's raid in Wales), was a source of consternation to the Irish in Paris, who believed it to be a diversion and a delusion, ruinous to Irish hopes.

In 1796 a force of 15,000 French soldiers, commanded by Hoche, and with Wolfe Tone in a French uniform as his aide, reached Bantry Bay, on the southwest coast of Ireland, without interception by the British fleet. The site was a poor one in that the United Irish were not yet organized in the southwest, so that no preparations had been made to receive them. Stormy weather in any case made disembarkation impossible, and after sixteen days of agonizing uncertainty the fleet withdrew. In 1797 the Dutch prepared an invasion. The Batavian leaders were strongly hostile to England, remembering the events of the 1780's, the flight of William V to England in 1795, and the constant British threats to the Dutch colonial empire. Among the shifting plans there was one for landing in Scotland, crossing that country, and ferrying over to Ulster, where the United Irish plans for revolution were well advanced in 1797. An expedition of almost 15,000 troops was organized with a minimum of French aid, and a Dutch fleet ready to escort them stood at the Texel. Weeks of dead calm, broken only by contrary winds, held the expedition in total immobility while the British fleet recovered from the mutinies at Spithead and the Nore. It was not British sea power that prevented invasion in 1796 and 1797.[56] England, as Tone remarked, had had its greatest escape since the Spanish Armada, which also had been defeated by the wind.

In October 1797 the British inflicted severe damage on the Dutch naval power at Camperdown, reducing the escort available to prospective invaders, though not enough to make them give up their plans. Early in 1798 an even more imposing force was assembled, the famous if shadowy *Armée d'Angleterre*, composed of both French and Dutch units, and with Bonaparte, just returned from Italy, assigned to command it. It was commonly believed in the British government that

[56] The judgment of Commander E. H. Stuart Jones, R. N., *An Invasion that Failed: The French Expedition to Ireland, 1796* (Oxford, 1950). See Tone's diary, *Life*, II, 205-447, for the Bantry Bay and the Dutch expeditions, with the allusion to the Spanish Armada on p. 266.

the enemy was about to attack either England or Ireland. No moment in Ireland could be more propitious, for the United Irish preparations were as well developed as they ever became. The Directory, however, advised by Bonaparte and Talleyrand, decided at the last moment against the risk of a channel crossing. Bonaparte with an army of 38,000 men sailed for Egypt instead. It is possible that this was one of the worst strategic blunders ever made.[57] The French started for Egypt on May 19, 1798, just as the Irish rebellion, having broken out in April, was raging at its height. So far as the Egyptian expedition was part of an intelligible strategy, it was designed as an alternative means of weakening the power of England—this time by threatening the Indian sources of British wealth. The campaign in Egypt and the Levant, however, instead of weakening England, the only European power with which France was then at war, reactivated war in the Mediterranean and opened the way to the Second Coalition. An invasion of Ireland in 1798 might have been no more costly than the invasion of Egypt, in which, eventually, the French lost both a fleet and an army. Supposing that a French army were to land in Ireland at all, which was not impossible—the French had landed there in 1689, and spent sixteen days in Bantry Bay in 1796—such an army, even if its communications were cut off, would be more embarrassing to the British than the French army isolated in Egypt, which surrendered in 1801. Had the French occupied Ireland for any length of time, it may be doubtful that a viable Irish Republic would have resulted. The Directory might even have traded Ireland away at the peace table, as Venice had been traded away to the Austrians. But the British might have been obliged to make peace on terms favorable to the French Republic; and if the French had had troops in Ireland and not in Egypt, and if Nelson's fleet had been on the coasts of Ireland and not of Naples, the Continental powers, which were hardly likely to come to the rescue of England, would have formed no Second Coalition. To pursue speculation even further, the Directory, by making a relatively lasting peace, might have established itself as a relatively lasting regime.

As it turned out, the French went to Egypt, and all that happened, so far as invasion of Ireland was concerned, or French aid to an Irish revolution, was that General Humbert with a thousand men landed

[57] The point is developed in an unpublished doctoral dissertation at Princeton University (1963), by Steven T. Ross, "The War of the Second Coalition."

on the western coast, at Killala, in August 1798.[58] Another 10,000 French troops were ready to follow, should Humbert have enough initial success. By this time, however, the strength of the United Irish uprising had already been broken. Although the extreme western part of the island, where the people still largely spoke Gaelic, was the least affected by the United Irish organization, Humbert found several hundred Irish who were willing to join him. The astonished Anglican bishop of Killala found his palace swarming with Frenchmen and native Irish. The Franco-Irish force repelled a party of cavalry sent against them, and penetrated the country for some fifty miles. Excitement ran high for a moment; songs of liberation were composed:

> Ireland's sons, be not faint hearted,
> Welcome, sing them *Ça Ira*.
> From Killala they are marching
> To the tune of *Vive la*.
> *Vive la*, United heroes,
> Triumphant always may they be,
> *Vive la*, our brave French brethren
> That have come to set us free.

Humbert was soon obliged to surrender; there were, after all, 140,000 British troops in the island. Exchanged and returned to France, he was too much of a republican to suit Napoleon a few years later, and withdrew to America. He had the pleasure of fighting the British again in the War of 1812, was mentioned in despatches by Andrew Jackson, and died at New Orleans in 1823.

To recur to the Irish themselves. As they proceeded after 1796 secretly to accumulate arms, the British proceeded to disarm them; and as they built up an organization, from the local to the national level, the British arrested their leaders. The "British," it must always be understood in this connection, included those Irish who either upheld the established order, or who, whatever their doubts, were opposed to armed insurrection or to separation from England. Almost half the British troops in Ireland were Irish yeomanry or militia of various degrees of reliability. Presbyterian Ulster was a hotbed of the United Irish movement and of democratic republicanism, but it produced also in 1795 the Orange lodges, ultra-Protestant, violently anti-Catholic, and determined to crush the United Irish at any price. The

---

[58] R. Hayes, *The Last Invasion of Ireland: When Connacht Rose* (Dublin, 1939). The verses quoted here are from Hayes, the page preceding the table of contents.

troubles rekindled the religious hatreds that had slowly been burning out. In the worst of the atrocities that followed, it was often Irish against Irish.

The United Irish armed themselves by accumulating pikes and pitchforks, or fitting up the weapons they had had since 1780, or stealing firearms from military depots. The French Republic seems to have done less in the way of surreptitious arming of potential revolutionaries in Ireland than the French monarchy had done for those in America in 1776. After the French showed their intentions, however, at Bantry Bay in December 1796, the mass recruitment of United Irish went rapidly forward, until there were 100,000 in Ulster alone. Local societies chose delegates to form regional bodies, which culminated in an Executive Directory, ready to take over, at the proper moment, as a government for an Irish Republic. The contrast has already been noted between the truly popular and relatively democratic though "underground" United Irish, and the conspiracy formed in 1796 by Babeuf in Paris, with its Directory in which power flowed from the top, and which remained shrouded in secrecy from its own handful of followers.

The British countered by reinforcing their garrison in Ireland against both insurrection and invasion, by searching homes and hiding places for concealed weapons, and by infiltrating the United Irish lodges with spies. Command was entrusted to an officer chosen for his willingness to be ruthless, General Lake, who wrote to his superiors, in 1797, that "nothing but terror will keep them in order."[59] The terror took the form of quartering troops on the inhabitants, searches, seizures, burnings, hangings, "half-hangings," tortures, deportations without trial, and condoning the barbarities of Orangemen and bands of yeomanry that wandered about the country under no control. The United Irish and their sympathizers replied in kind so far as possible. The appalling struggle was not between Catholic and Protestant, and still less between Anglo-Saxon and Celt; it was a struggle of political type, for and against an independent Irish republic.

The measures taken by the government, or taken in its name, were so effective that the United Irish, like Kosciuszko in 1794, had to act before they were ready, and before it should be too late. The insurrection began in Ulster in April 1798. It soon spread to other parts of the island, with all sorts of people, such as the agrarian Defenders, and those who had hitherto belonged to nothing, joining in as the

[59] Quoted by Jones, *Invasion that Failed*, 197.

moment of decision seemed to present itself. The most serious fighting was in the southeast, in Wexford. Here a certain Father John Murphy, who had hitherto been politically inactive, but was maddened by the recent acts of repression coming on top of the chronic misery of his people, emerged as a military leader of some talent, guiding a host of poorly armed peasants into battle. Other priests, while their bishops deplored the whole proceeding, also appeared in the ranks of the rebels—enough for Castlereagh, who was then chief secretary to the Lord Lieutenant, to call the uprising "a Jacobinical conspiracy pursuing its object chiefly with Popish instruments." These rebel priests, said a conservative Catholic, were "the very faeces of the Church." Twelve Presbyterian ministers are also known to have been involved in the rebellion, of whom three were executed.[60]

The insurrection, however, was doomed from the start. Its higher leaders were either on the Continent or in British jails. There was widespread participation, but no central direction; no one knew what was happening beyond his own locality; nothing could be synchronized, momentary successes could not be consolidated, nor local defeats of the British turned to advantage. The hope of French armed intervention gradually faded; it remained faintly alive for weeks, while Bonaparte and his army were at sea, until the news came, stupefying to the Irish, that the French were in the most incredible of all places, at the far opposite end of the world of Europe and of republican revolution, contending in the desert with the Mamelukes of Egypt. Humbert's landing in August was for the United Irish only a tragic reminder of what might have been.

It was clear by July that the revolt had failed, but sporadic fighting continued, and the repressive measures used to prevent rebellion before it came were continued with a new intensity after the worst of the danger was over. Many Englishmen were disgusted by what they saw. Cornwallis, who had commanded in America and who was sent to Ireland in 1798, thought the conversation of officers at his own table too extreme: it was all about "hanging, shooting, burning, etc., etc., and if a priest is put to death the greatest joy is expressed by the whole company."[61] One is reminded of Nelson and his officers at

---

[60] Dickson, *Wexford Rising; Memoirs and Correspondence of Viscount Castlereagh, Second Marquess of Londonderry,* 8 vols. (London, 1848), i, 219; McDowell, *Public Opinion,* 241; W. Fitzpatrick, *Secret Service under Pitt* (London, 1892), 290.

[61] *Correspondence of Charles, First Marquis Cornwallis,* 3 vols. (London, 1859), ii, 369, his letter from Dublin Castle, July 24, 1798: "Except in the instances of the six

Naples a year later. The Marquis of Buckingham thought Cornwallis' generals "the worst in Europe"; the "rapine and cruelties" of his troops were "atrocious"; rebels were afraid to surrender; and with forty-three generals the government forces were undisciplined and "licentious."[62]

No estimate of the number who died in the rebellion and in its repression has ever been possible. Many were sent to Australia. Various leaders were executed for treason; and Wolfe Tone, who had slipped into Ireland from France during the fighting, and who was captured and faced certain hanging, cut his throat in prison. The time was far distant when inmates of British prisons could emerge as heads of independent states on good terms with their former rulers.

The rebellion was followed by the Act of Union of Great Britain and Ireland. The union, which lasted until the First World War, was clearly one of the diverse products of the revolutionary era. There were at least three good reasons for it. It was strategically necessary to Great Britain; the French had threatened an invasion of Ireland in every war since the days of William III, and this time they had come uncomfortably close to causing real trouble by their efforts. The union was intended also, by Pitt, Buckingham and others, as a system within which Irish Catholics could safely be granted political rights. How this intention came to nothing is a fact well known and requiring no elaboration here. Finally, and more often forgotten, the union was a phase in the general movement of counter-revolution, or anti-republicanism, throughout the British Isles and the Continent. It was a device for suppressing Jacobinism in Ireland.

In 1799, during the debates on the union, one of the new peers, Lord Minto, the former Sir Gilbert Elliot, delivered a long speech in the British House of Lords. He gave a good many reasons for a union of Ireland with Great Britain. One of them was that "an Irish democratic republic, or rather anarchy, must be the first and instant consequence of our separation." Such a republic, allied to France, he said, would bring chaos not to Ireland only, but to England. "It is part of

---

state trials that are going on here, there is no law either in town or country but martial law . . . conducted by Irishmen heated with passion and revenge. But this is trifling compared to the numberless murders that are hourly committed by our people without any process or examination whatever. The yeomanry are in the style of the Loyalists in America, only much more numerous and powerful, and a thousand times more ferocious."

[62] *Dropmore Papers*, IV, 264, 266.

our own tenement which is in flames, and we come in absolute contact with this pestilent contagion." Even in England, in 1799, "internal discontent, or speculative error, or the secret machinations of French corruption and English treason, or popular hope" would all be aroused and amplified if both an Irish and a French republic lay across the narrow seas. The old order in Ireland, in its old form, could not be maintained. But the Anglican supremacy in the smaller country, together with the existing order in Britain itself, would emerge safer and more secure, reconfirmed and reinvigorated by their union.[63]

So republicanism in both islands succumbed to the forces or persuasions of the establishment. The movement was not only defeated, but in a way almost forgotten. The United Irish attempt at a revolution fell into the category of lost causes, its memory kept alive by circles of devotees, but its once living significance generally disregarded. A historian of the United Irish found herself unable even to make a list of towns in which lodges had existed, since records had been destroyed, and local annalists had drawn a discreet veil over these embarrassing forebears.[64] In Great Britain, when a democratic radicalism gathered strength again after 1830, there was a certain hesitation, even by men who had lived through both phases, to refer back to the days of the London Corresponding Society, to a time when democratic ideas had been tainted by sympathy for another country's revolution, and for a government with which Britain was at war. It came to be believed in some quarters that the disaffected had been not very numerous, and not very reputable. Here was another victory for the *levée en masse* of the people of quality.

It is tempting to look once more into the mail pouches by which the far-flung members of the British aristocracy were held together. Late in 1798 Lord Mornington, as he made his preparations against the Sultan of Mysore, and fretted about Jacobinism in his native Ireland, and the future of his own large estates there, received a communication sent to him months before by William Eden, Lord Auckland. It was the same Auckland who had urged upon Grenville, in 1792, the need of making Britons aware of their special blessings. Writing in April, Auckland had to admit that the news from Ireland was very bad. But in England the outlook was better. "With respect to this good old island," said Auckland, "I can say with extreme pleasure and confidence that I have never seen it so rightly disposed.

[63] *Parliamentary History*, xxxiv, 771-72.   [64] Jacob, 5.

There certainly exist in London, Manchester and other places, clubs and secret societies of men connected and affiliated as 'United English' on grounds of the wildest and bloodiest democracy. But they are few in number, and composed of the refuse of mankind."[65]

Vae victis!

[65] *The Wellesley Papers: The Life and Correspondence of Richard Colley Wellesley, Marquess Wellesley* . . . , 2 vols. (London, 1914), I, 52-53.

AMERICA: DEMOCRACY NATIVE AND IMPORTED

Beware, ye American aristocrats! Your principles and efforts are leading you to a precipice. . . . If the cause of France, which is the cause of human nature, should succeed, then farewell kings, aristocrats and the long catalogue of clerical impositions.— ELIHU PALMER, 1793

The cursed foul contagion of French principles has infected us. . . . If she fails the world will be free. I have the highest confidence in the success of England.— GEORGE CABOT, 1798

I see how the thing is going. At the next election England will set up Jay or Hamilton, and France, Jefferson, and all the corruption of Poland will be introduced; unless the American spirit should rise and say, we will have neither John Bull nor Louis Baboon.— PRESIDENT JOHN ADAMS TO HIS WIFE, 1797

AMERICA: DEMOCRACY NATIVE AND IMPORTED

It was the Americans who had first given the example of rebellion, proclaimed the rights of man and the sovereignty of the people, and established a new public authority in their state constitutions by recognizing a constituent power in bodies called conventions. They had attracted the lively notice and admiration of dissatisfied persons in many parts of Europe. A mere fifteen years later the American image had already faded in a more blinding light on the screen of the world's opinion, and the mild accents of the heralds of liberty had been succeeded by a more ringing and compelling voice. If an influence had passed from America to Europe before 1789, after that year the direction was reversed. If, as Barruel said, the "sect" had first shown itself in America, within two decades the United States was in the worthy position of a kind of Israel, and the ecumenical church, as embodied in the New Republican Order, had its center—complete with power, doctrines, and abuses—in Paris.

Like other countries, the United States felt the strong impact of the French Revolution. As elsewhere, the development was twofold. On the one hand, there was an acceleration of indigenous movements. On the other, there was an influence that was unquestionably foreign. The latter presented itself especially with the war that began in Europe in 1792, and with the clash of armed ideologies that the war brought with it. The warring powers in Europe, which for Americans meant the governments of France and Great Britain, attempted to make use of the United States for their own advantage. Different groups of Americans, for their own domestic purposes, were likewise eager to exploit the power and prestige of either England or France. Some Americans saw the future of the United States best secured by a victory of the French Republic; others saw no hope for their own country except in a triumph by Great Britain. Political thought was also sharpened, heated emotionally, and broadened to the all-embracing dimensions that the word "ideology" suggests. American democracy, as expressed in the new Republican party, was shaped in part by the revolution in Europe; and American conservatism, as it came to be expressed by High Federalists, shared in some of the ideas of the European counter-revolution, especially as transmitted in books imported from England. The indigenous and the foreign became indistinguishable. In the way in which internal dissension passed into favoritism for foreign powers, the United States did not differ from the countries described in preceding chapters, from Ireland to Poland and from Scotland to Naples.

At the same time the case of the United States was very special. Despite the war of words, the domestic conflicts were for most people not deeply bitter. Between social classes there was less fear and hostility than in Europe, less deference, and less contempt. "Aristocrats" in America had less to lose, and "democrats" less to complain against. There was always, however buried and overgrown, a truth at the bottom of the famous aphorism of Tocqueville, that the Americans had been born equal, and so needed no revolution to become so. There was an underlying bent toward equality in the customs of the people, of the kind that perplexed the Venezuelan revolutionary, Miranda, in 1784, when he was travelling in the United States to seek aid for a revolution in Spanish America, and found it difficult to arrange for his servant to eat alone. One notable of the New England "establishment" was the clergyman Jedediah Morse, who in 1798 was an extreme Federalist. He had recently received an honorary degree from Edinburgh University. In 1798 the established Presbyterians of Scotland would have thought him suspiciously radical, since he not only wanted to do something for Negroes, but actively sponsored Sunday Schools, a popular religious press, frontier missionaries, and itinerant preaching.

Most especially, the United States had already had its revolution. New forms and new principles had been introduced into government, an older colonial aristocracy had been displaced, and an ideal of equality as well as of liberty had been affirmed. The great question in the 1790's was how the American Revolution would turn out. After 1789, when the new federal constitution went into effect, it was also a question of whether the constitution would become implanted and, if so, to what kinds of people and classes of the population the government of the new republic should mainly look for support. The United States was unique also in the grand reckoning with which the century ended. In 1801, after a generation of democratic agitation and counter-agitation throughout the area of Western Civilization, the American republic was the only country in which a peaceable transfer of power took place in a democratic direction, when, without use of a coup d'état, and without armed rebellion against him, a man denounced hysterically in some quarters as a Jacobin calmly assumed the highest executive office.

In a book of this kind, it may be illuminating first to glance briefly at the "other" Americas.

The "Other" Americas, Latin and British

For Latin America, where revolution against Spain broke out somewhat later, the years before 1800 were a time of precursors and preparations.[1] Contact with Europe north of the Pyrenees was infrequent, and with the United States even more so. Jefferson, when in Paris in 1787, was approached by both a Mexican and a Brazilian interested in "revolution," but he gave them no reason to expect his aid; and in fact, for a long time thereafter, Latin Americans with new ideas looked more to France than to the United States. Ironically enough, in the light of world revolution, it was from very different sources that aid for Latin American independence was most forthcoming. Miranda, after seeking support in vain in the United States and in France, found it in England. The break-up of the Spanish empire, opening its possessions to world trade, was one "revolution" for which Pitt's government could feel a positive sympathy; and Alexander Hamilton in 1799 talked more of liberating Latin America than Thomas Jefferson ever did.

Latin America then began at the Mississippi. At St. Louis, where Frenchmen lived under Spanish rule, a society calling itself the Sansculottes serenaded the priest on 1 Vendémaire of the Year V, to wish him a republican New Year. At New Orleans the *Moniteur de la Louisiane*, set up in 1794, was one of the first newspapers in Spanish

[1] See H. D. Barbagelata, *La Révolution française et l'Amérique latine* (Paris, 1936); R. R. Caillet-Bois, *Ensayo sobre el Rio de la Plata y la Revolucion francesa* (Buenos Aires, 1929); A. Ruy, *A primeira revoluçao social brasileira, 1798* (Rio, 1942); E. Clavéry, *Trois précurseurs de l'indépendance des démocraties sud-américaines: Miranda, 1756-1816; Nariño, 1765-1823; Espejo, 1747-1795* (Paris, 1932); A. Montalvo, *Francisco Javier Eugenio de Santa Cruz y Espejo* (Quito, 1947). I am indebted to both Professor and Mrs. Stanley J. Stein for assistance with the languages and for findings they have made in Brazilian and Mexican archives.

America; there was also some kind of political club, and six persons were deported to Havana for expressing republican sentiments.[2]

Various conspiracies were discovered further south, all purely local and momentary. There was one at Quito in 1794, at Buenos Aires in the same year, at Caracas, La Paz, and remote Potosí in 1797, and at Bahia, in Brazil, in 1798. Generally the conspirators were found to be using French terminology (such as "citizen" and "republic"); at La Paz part of the evidence consisted in copper engravings showing the death of Louis XVI. Distance, censorship, and the absence of any systematic French propaganda meant that French writings, as found in South American conspiratorial circles, were of a highly random character. At Bogotá, in 1793, Antonio Nariño printed a hundred copies of the Declaration of the Rights of Man and Citizen. At Rio, after a visit by a French ship in 1792, a translation of the French constitution was made into Portuguese. Otherwise, the French works that we hear of were extremely sporadic. For some reason, both at Mexico City and at Bahia, about five thousand miles apart, the authorities were alarmed to find handwritten copies of speeches made in the French convention by Boissy d'Anglas, who was certainly one of the most sedate men of the French Revolution. *The Orateur des Etats-généraux de 1789*, attributed to J. L. Carra, was found in the hands of a Brazilian mulatto—as in the bookshops of Moscow. Worried officials also found copies of Volney's *Ruines*, with its disconcerting subtitle, *Méditations sur les révolutions des empires*.

The Latin American disturbances, even at this early date, are of interest in that they raised racial issues in a way that had no parallel in Europe or the United States. Many persons of Indian or Negro descent were already better off than in English-speaking America. At Quito the leading figure was Espejo, a pure-blooded Indian, a medical doctor, who was also head of the first public library at Quito. In 1792 he began to publish a periodical, and founded a patriotic society of some fifty members, in the best European style. His group secretly obtained copies of Nariño's edition of the Declaration of Rights, and in 1794, possibly on hearing news of the French invasion of Catalonia, put up placards in the streets. It is not clear to whom they were addressed, since at least one of them was written in Latin. Espejo was imprisoned, tortured, and died thereafter. Nariño was transported to Spanish Africa.

[2] A. P. Whitaker, *The Mississippi Question, 1795-1803* (New York, 1934), 39, 155; A. Fortier, *History of Louisiana*, 4 vols. (New York, 1904), I, 152-56.

At Buenos Aires and Bahia the plots involved mulattoes and Negro slaves. At Buenos Aires certain French merchants were alleged to have offered freedom to Negroes in return for joining in a revolt against the Spanish crown. At Bahia the conspiracy was more substantial. A French frigate had stopped at Bahia in 1797, and a number of local teachers, doctors, and clergy had thereupon had the idea of forming a literary society. About the same time a company of mulatto soldiers petitioned for equality of treatment with a company of white soldiers at Bahia. A handful of whites, mulattoes, and slaves formed secret links with each other. Most of the mulattoes were soldiers, but one was some kind of minor official or notary. Of the whites, one was a Latin teacher from a local planter family, and one was a surgeon educated in Portugal. However hopeless as a revolutionary movement, their efforts suggest the social discontents, the thinking, and the knowledge of the outside world in a town on the Brazilian coast at the time. The conspirators probably had heard that the French had abolished slavery; whether they knew of the revolution in Haiti is not clear from the evidence. By the middle of 1798 they had learned that the Pope had been ejected from Rome, and that the French were about to invade England. Some thought that the French would soon reach Brazil.

On August 12, 1798, proclamations appeared in public places, addressed to the people of the *Citade da Bahia Republicana*. They denounced the oppressiveness of government and taxes, urged that the yoke of Europe be thrown off, demanded freedom to trade with countries other than Portugal, and specifically with France, and issued warnings to priests who preached "fanaticism." They called upon all soldiers, both white and colored, to work together, as "brothers and equals," for Popular Liberty. The outburst was easily put down, and thirty-four persons were arrested. They were accused of sedition and impiety, and of wanting "the imaginary advantages of a Democratic Republic in which all should be equal, with access to public office and representative positions without difference of color or condition . . . following the example of the unfortunate and disgraced people of France."[3] Four persons, all free mulattoes, were hanged and quartered, and several others transported to Africa.

Brazil, as it turned out, was the last American country to abolish slavery. Haiti was the first. It was here, in the wealthy French sugar colony of Saint-Domingue, where 30,000 whites lived among almost half a million slaves, along with some 25,000 free Negroes and mulat-

[3] Ruy, 236.

toes, that the repercussions of the French Revolution in America were the most immediate and the most violent. From early in the Revolution, over protests of the planters, the French had given equal civil rights to free colored persons in their colonies. When the slaves also were aroused, and began to rebel, the Convention, in 1794, abolished slavery in all possessions of the Republic. Most of the whites left the island, and Toussaint l'Ouverture, a Negro, emerged as the local leader. He worked for several years to maintain the tie with France, in whose army he was commissioned as a general officer by both the Convention and the Directory. Struggling against chaos, against breakdown in labor, production, and government, in a turmoil of strife between rivals, and between mulattoes and Negroes, with threats of Spanish and British intervention, and in fear of a reimposition of slavery, Toussaint managed to maintain a regime whose stated ideals at least were those of the European revolution, at the cost of atrocities that were worse than those of the Vendée or Ireland. In 1802 Bonaparte tried to regain control for France, capturing Toussaint in the process, and to return the ex-slaves to the old conditions. The French army perished of disease. Toussaint's successors declared independence.[4]

It is hard to estimate the effects in the United States of the revolution in Haiti. The French consul at Philadelphia estimated in 1797 that there were over 20,000 French refugees in the country. Almost all must have come from San Domingo and other French West Indian colonies. Such men, if not exactly fervent republicans, were no lovers of England either; and their presence, especially in places like Philadelphia, where they congregated, added fuel to the flame of American political agitation. In a larger sense, the famous Cotton Kingdom of the American South, if it be dated from Eli Whitney's invention, was born simultaneously with an increased dread of slave rebellion. The number of known slave revolts in the United States rapidly rose in the decade of the 1790's, culminating in the one called Gabriel's rebellion in 1800. The heightening of the tempo would seem to reflect the growth of republicanism, with its demands for "liberty," among American whites and especially Southern whites. American slaves must also have overheard conversations about what had happened in San Domingo.

[4] There have been many books on the revolution in Haiti, of which two of the best are by T. L. Stoddard (the later racist or Anglo-Saxonist) *The French Revolution in San Domingo* (Boston, 1914), and by an American Negro, C. L. R. James, *The Black Jacobins: Toussaint Louverture and the San Domingo Revolution* (New York, 1938). On French refugees, largely from Haiti, see F. Childs, *French Refugee Life in the United States 1790-1800: An American Chapter of the French Revolution* (Baltimore, 1940).

American Negroes, like those of Brazil, or like the serfs of Hungary and Bohemia, were not wholly impervious to news from the outside world.[5]

British North America was in a way as much a product of the American Revolution as was the United States. The Canada Act, passed by the British Parliament in 1791, was designed, in the words of a Canadian-born historian, as a defense against both the French and American revolutions.[6] It expressed the idea that the troubles in the old thirteen colonies had been due to an excess of democracy. The act created two provinces, Lower and Upper Canada (Quebec and Ontario), with similar structures of government. Each received an appointed governor, an appointed upper house which it was hoped might become hereditary, and endowments for an established church. In Lower Canada the British favored the old French seigneurial land law; and in the development of Upper Canada, in which émigrés from the United States had settled, they granted land in extensive tracts, hoping that a good solid landed aristocracy would grow up. Adequate provision was made also to support the dignity of officers of state. For example, William Smith, a native of New York and a Yale graduate, who had been chief justice of New York before the Revolution, went to Canada as a Loyalist, declaring that "all America was abandoned to democracy." He became chief justice of the new province, where he received a larger salary than the chief justice of the United States. The same was true for the new office of chief justice of Upper Canada, which still had practically no population. Upper Canada, though a frontier community, was deeply conservative, because peopled by refugees from the American Revolution. In Lower Canada the French were more restless, having no affection for the British authorities; but they lacked sympathy also for the anti-Catholic New Englanders with whom they had often been at war, and the arrival of some fifty émigré priests from France, reinforcing the views of the British governor and such

[5] H. Aptheker, *American Negro Slave Revolts* (New York, 1943), 209-34.

[6] J. B. Brebner, *North Atlantic Triangle: The Interplay of Canada, the United States and Great Britain* (New Haven and Toronto, 1945), 66-67. See also Mason Wade, *The French Canadians* (London, 1955), 97-101, and his "Quebec and the French Revolution of 1799: the Missions of Henri Mezière," in *Canadian Historical Review*, XXXI (1950), 345-68. An unpublished dissertation at the University of Chicago (1950) by H. L. Vernon, "The Impact of the French Revolution on Lower Canada, 1789-95," stops short in the middle of the story. There is a good deal of detail in the older works by the British Canadian, W. Kingsford, *History of Canada*, 10 vols. (Toronto, 1887-98), VII, 337-454, and the French Canadian, F. X. Garneau, *Histoire du Canada*, 5th ed., 2 vols. (Paris, 1913), II, 431-54.

Loyalists as William Smith, helped to inoculate the *Canadiens* against sympathy for the new France.

The two countries, representing the losers and the winners of the American Revolution, remained in an odd conjunction in the 1790's. Both were involved in the war between France and England, and in the agitations of Genet; both had their furor over Jacobinism, and their alien and sedition laws. The difference was that there was as yet no significant indigenous democratic movement in Canada.

Neither France nor Great Britain yet quite accepted the boundaries in the North American interior as really final. For both, it might seem reasonable for the United States to remain confined east of the Appalachians. The French had plans, never of high priority, for a possible recovery of the whole of the former Louisiana, of which the part east of the Mississippi now belonged to the United States, and the part west of the Mississippi to Spain. When Genet was minister to Philadelphia in 1793, at a time when France was at war with both Spain and England, he tried to organize expeditions against the possessions of both these powers. In these designs he found many Americans eager to participate—South Carolinians against the Spanish in Florida (William Tate, who later led the French raid into Wales, was one of the moving spirits here); George Rogers Clark and his Kentuckians against St. Louis and the lower Mississippi; Vermonters against the British in Lower Canada. Genet and a certain French Canadian, Mezière, prepared a revolutionary pamphlet, *Les Français libres à leurs frères canadiens*. It called for Canadian independence, and for abolition of seigneurial dues, compulsory road work, and privileged trading companies. It was circulated by hand, and read aloud at the door of a church in Montreal. Next to nothing happened, but enough happened to alarm the British authorities. Lord Dorchester, the governor of Lower Canada, feared disaffection among the French-speaking people of his province. An act was passed for the expulsion of aliens. Loyalty Associations were formed, as in England. The governor in Upper Canada, J. G. Simcoe, who until the Jay treaty considered much of the Great Lakes and Illinois country to be part of his territory, was sure that the woods were full of "Jacobin emissaries" far into the back country. In what must surely be one of the earliest references to the politics of Chicago and St. Louis, Simcoe, in 1794, named both places as centers of agitation against England. He was particularly annoyed at a "Black Chief" at Chicago, whom he believed to be in the pay of the United States.[7] This individual

[7] *The Correspondence of Lt. Gov. John Graves Simcoe*, 5 vols. (Toronto, 1923-31), II, 222.

must have been Baptiste Point du Sable, a French-speaking Negro remembered as the first "white man" to live permanently at the site of Chicago, a mysterious figure of whom nothing is really known, but who was said to be—as if to show the long interconnections in this wilderness—an escaped slave from San Domingo.

The agitations went on for several years. In 1796 the French general, Victor Collot, on the pretense of a scientific expedition, made a western tour as far as the Mississippi. He found the French at St. Louis to be "excellent patriots," and the spot well suited as a base from which to end "the usurpations of England"; but the British, in consequence of the Jay treaty, were now beginning to withdraw from the region south of the Lakes, and the drift of Collot's secret plans was to detach the country west of the Alleghenies from the United States.[8] Meanwhile George Rogers Clark, the conqueror of the Illinois country, the hero of Kentucky republicans, and the co-worker of Genet, concluded that the United States was controlled by a British faction which he detested. He went to St. Louis, and there, among its French population, hoped for a time, in 1798, that Louisiana would come under the control of France.

At the same time there were mysterious contacts between Lower Canada and Vermont. In 1796 the Vermonter, Ira Allen, was captured by the British at sea, aboard a vessel, the *Olive Branch*, carrying 20,000 muskets bought in France, presumably for use in a Canadian revolution. Létombe, left as French consul at Philadelphia after Adet's recall, received approaches from conspirators, including two Americans who offered to revolutionize Canada and set up a republic there.[9] There were some Vermonters who, if given the option, would prefer to be joined with an independent Canadian Republic rather than with the United States, since the only easy mode of communication of Vermont with the outside world was by the Richelieu and St. Lawrence rivers. In view of such plots the government of Lower Canada passed a

---

[8] Collot's travels were published in 1826 in Paris in both French and English; both are rare, and the present reference is to the edition in English, *A Journey in North America*, 247-51. See also D. Echeverria, "General Collot's Plan for a Reconnaissance of the Ohio and Mississippi Valleys, 1796," in *William and Mary Quarterly*, 3rd ser., IX (1952), 512-20. Also A. DeConde, *Entangling Alliance: Politics and Diplomacy under George Washington* (Durham, N.C., 1958), 446-49.

[9] *The Correspondence of the French Ministers to the United States 1791-97*, edited by Frederick J. Turner for the *Annual Report of the American Historical Association for 1903*, includes the dispatches of Létombe only to the end of 1797; the series continued into 1798, and includes a memorandum of February 1798 in which two American citizens are said to be ready to instigate a revolution in Canada if supplied by the French with some $40,000. Archives des Affaires Etrangères, M. et D., Angleterre, vol. 47, fols. 349-52.

sedition act in 1797. Its most spectacular victim was David McLane, who was in fact guilty of subversion, and who was hanged at Quebec in 1797.[10] It has already been remarked how the Abbé Barruel included McLane in his list of "adepts" of the international revolution, and how the British edition of his work, and hence the American, simply deleted his name, as if to suggest that such things—except in France—should best be forgotten.

It would be wrong to suggest that any possibility of revolution existed in British or in Latin America, Haiti excepted, before 1800. It is clear, however, that pockets of discontent could be found, and that there were conspirators who hoped to imitate or benefit from the French Revolution. Persons were executed for sedition from Quebec and Quito to Bahia and Buenos Aires. In the United States no one was executed under the Sedition Act of 1798, and in that respect the politics of the United States exhibited a certain moderation. The hanging of numerous rebel slaves was regarded as a police action, of no political consequence; just as the desire of slaves for liberty, having nothing to do with American politics, was not even to be dignified by the epithet of Jacobinism.

Which Way the New Republic?

There has been a recent trend toward seeing the problems of the United States in the 1790's as those of a "new nation," of the same general kind as the "new nations" of the twentieth century.[11] In many ways the parallel does not hold. Though the first people to break away from a European colonial empire, the Americans had never lived under colonialism in its more recent sense. They themselves, most of them, were transplanted Europeans by racial stock, and their only culture was that of Europe, however modified or diluted. Some of the more difficult problems of adjustment to Western Civilization, as faced by new nations of the twentieth century, therefore did not exist in the

[10] See Garneau, II, 449; Kingsford, VII, 444-51. It appears that the body, after hanging, was decapitated and "drawn" but not "quartered." The head of a "traitor" was then held up to public view, in the traditional manner. See also Timothy Pickering to Rufus King, June 20, 1797, in *Life and Correspondence of Rufus King*, 6 vols. (New York, 1895-1900), II, 192. It does not occur to the Federalist Secretary of State, Pickering, writing to his minister in London, to doubt that American citizens, of whom he mentions McLane and two others, should be accused of "treason" to the British crown.

[11] See W. N. Chambers, *Political Parties in a New Nation: The American Experience 1776-1809* (New York, 1963); R. L. Ketcham, "France and American Politics, 1763-93," in *Political Science Quarterly*, LXXVIII (1963), 198-223; and forthcoming studies by S. M. Lipset.

United States. In addition, the Americans had enjoyed a good deal of self-rule in the old British empire; and, except at the extremes, among the upper classes and among the slaves, the level of wealth was higher than among corresponding classes in Europe. The Americans in colonial times had not suffered from exploitation, and in their first years of independence they did not suffer from poverty. Only in some respects was the country a "new nation" at all; it had announced some new ideas that had proved exciting in Europe, and it was already modern in its lack of feudal, dynastic, and churchly attachments; but in some ways it was actually old-fashioned, having shared less than Europe in the scientific, literary, capitalistic, governmental, and bureaucratic development of the preceding two hundred years. American English, with its neologisms and it archaisms, was characteristic of the state of society.

Nevertheless, the United States faced some typical problems of a new nation. It had to create a viable government, avoid domination by foreign powers, and prevent its territory from falling to pieces. It had to follow up its revolution by developing a new principle of legitimacy or authority. The leadership had somehow to enlist the interest of the whole people in a new enterprise, and build up their loyalty to a new regime. It was necessary also to develop roads, communications, public opinion, and group spirit or national identity. There was the general problem of economic development, and hence of access to foreign capital and the technical skills of older and more civilized countries; or, at least, decisions had to be made on whether or not such development was desirable.

It happened also, as for new nations in the twentieth century, that the United States found itself in a world agitated by revolution, with all forces tending to gather around opposite poles, each of which represented something ultra-modern. England, while conservative socially, led in industrial, commercial, and financial development, and in its network of relationships with the transoceanic world. France, by no means economically backward, had become through the Revolution more modern than England in other important respects: it now represented a society in which tradition had been rejected, planning for the future was thought to be possible, government was detached from an institutional church and from legally defined social classes, land law and local government had lost their old seigneurial features, careers were to be open to talent, promotions made by merit, and schools and higher education developed by the state in the interests of public utility. Where older societies, to obtain general acceptance, stressed the duties of social subordination and religious faith, the newer society stressed the duties of citizenship and the advantages of modern enlightenment. In the test of war the new order in France, with its citizen army and its popular patriotic enthusiasm, had proved itself stronger than the old regimes which opposed it. The announced principles of the new order, liberty, equality, and the recognition of human and civic rights—originally developed as weapons against the older society, and still far from being realized in the new—proved to have a strong appeal in all countries to which news of them came. Indeed, they had their own roots in many parts of Europe and in the United States. To call them "French ideas" was a mere allegation of their opponents.

In the United States, hardly had the new federal constitution gone into effect, when differences of opinion began to show themselves on the course which the new republic ought to take. One view held that the country needed economic development, along the lines in which Western Europe was then more advanced. The other view held that the older, simpler, and in a way more native ways in America were better and should be adhered to. The former view held that the country needed more banking, credit, shipping, transportation, and manufactures, both as things desirable in themselves and as a means of consolidating national independence, and that the central government should have enough power to plan and sponsor such innovations. In the other view it was better to favor the existing agricultural character of the country, keeping trade in an auxiliary position; a central government with minimum powers would suffice. In the former view, the new central government should associate itself with men of means, persons who had capital of their own to invest, or who could borrow it abroad, and who in any case might make trouble for the new regime if they withheld their support; in the opposing view, such a policy smacked of favoritism or privilege for the rich. Finally, in the one view it was necessary to seek good relations with an advanced European country, which for Americans could only be England, in view of the familiarity of the language and methods of doing business, the availability of long-term credit, and the British predominance at sea; while in the opposing view it was distasteful to try to conciliate England, whose government had not yet accepted the American Revolution very gracefully, and against which there remained a good deal of popular hostility, generated by the still recent War of Independence.

It need hardly be said that the first of these views was Alexander

Hamilton's, and the second, that of the men who came gradually to look to Thomas Jefferson as their leader. Hamilton managed to enact his program during the first years under the new constitution. The assumption of pre-existing state debts by the national government, the paying off at par of all public securities however depreciated, the establishment of a bank under federal charter, the introduction of excises and import duties to produce revenue for debt service, the encouragement of foreign trade to provide customs revenues at a high level, were all designed to serve his political as well as economic ends— to build up the power and credit of the new central government, and to encourage men of wealth to lend, invest, or speculate with their money.

If such purely internal questions had been the only sources of disagreement, it is possible that the fortunes of the new republic would have been worse than they proved to be. Hamilton's program lacked popular appeal. It was not easy to understand, and it offered nothing for the ordinary citizen to become enthusiastic about. It emphasized the differences of class interest. However national in design, it was highly regional in the feelings which it elicited; it made most of its friends in the northeast, and most of its enemies in the south and west. Division of opinion and interest there was bound to be; the question, in a "new nation," was what form such a division should take. Quarrels between élites without popular following might be ruinous, especially if geographically localized. They might lead to a disintegration of the existing union into a plurality of smaller republics, as happened in the great vice-royalties of the Spanish empire a generation later. They might lead to demands for a new constitution, and replacement of one constitution by another, as happened in France, until no constitution commanded enough respect to enjoy the advantages of legitimacy and authority. Or the divisions might take the form of political parties, each having members scattered throughout the country, each offering a means of connection between leaders and popular following, each providing symbols that could arouse enthusiasm and serve as a basis of organized if not always very informed opinion, and each willing, in the last analysis, to surrender the powers of government into the hands of the other without rebellion, revolution and violence.

The remarkable thing is that the divisions in the United States took this latter form, the form of political parties, and in particular the form of a two-party system. In producing the two parties, as in the constitutional convention of 1787 and the Revolution before it, the Americans displayed a good deal of political originality, since there had never been parties of this kind before, simultaneously popular and governmental, at work both in the national capital and in local taverns and clubs, and brought into existence to take part in really contested elections.[12] The parties made possible a mass participation in the exercise of public powers as laid down in the constitution. They made it possible also for a free government to function successfully, if a free government be defined as one which can tolerate opponents, and presumptive successors in office, without fears for its own existence.

It is widely agreed, among those who have most studied the matter, that the two American parties, and hence the beginnings of a two-party system, were produced in the United States by reactions to the European war and the French Revolution. The paradox, therefore, is that the ideological differences aroused in the United States, which became very heated, and the actual dangers of subservience to foreign powers, which were very real, may have contributed, by creating national parties to debate national issues and elect candidates to national office in an atmosphere of public involvement, to the solidarity of the union, the maintenance of the constitution, and the survival of the republic.

There was, to be sure, something peculiar in the entire phenomenon. Hamilton, who loathed the French Revolution, was more of a revolutionary than Jefferson both in temperament and in the policies that he espoused. He was more impatient of the compromises on which the federal constitution rested, he wanted to make over the country, and he would have liked, if he could, to abolish the states (especially Virginia) and replace them with small *départements* created by a national government, as in the French and other revolutionary republics in Europe. Jefferson, who sympathized with the French Revolution, was actually a good deal of a moderate, both in personality and in his ideas of what should be done. He spoke for a kind of liberty and equality that had long existed in America, and did not have to be fought for as in Europe, a liberty that meant freedom from government, and an equality of the kind that obtained among yeoman farmers—a way of life that had been threatened by British policy before 1775, and was threatened by Hamiltonian policy after 1790, in each case with the support of American "aristocrats" or persons aspiring to become such. Because of their different views on the need of change, it was Hamilton who

[12] The theme of Chambers, *op.cit.*, to which I am much indebted.

was the "unitarist," and Jefferson the "federalist," in the sense then current in Europe, where, as has been seen, the radical democrats were unitarists, and the moderates inclined to the decentralization of power. The unitarist and "revolutionary" Hamilton was certainly no Jacobin, but he was the nearest that the United States ever produced to a Bonaparte.

On a more general plane, also, the kinds of people who in the United States favored the French Revolution were not the same as in Europe. Nor were conservatives in America socially akin to those of Europe. There was a curious reversal or transposition. In Europe, on the whole, those who favored the French Revolution were middle-class people living in towns, including a good many bankers and businessmen, especially those interested in the newer forms of economic enterprise and development. Among the rural population, on the Continent, it was the landowners and property-owning farmers living nearest to the cities, most involved in a market economy, and enjoying the best communications with the outside world, who were most receptive to the Revolutionary ideas. In America the opposite was more nearly true. The business and mercantile community, and the farmers who lived nearest to the towns, or along the rivers and arteries of traffic and communication, were generally Federalist, and they became anti-French and anti-Republican. The same inversion holds for the counterrevolution, which in Europe was essentially agrarian. It drew its strength from the landed aristocracy, and from peasants who were politically apathetic, or looked upon cities as the abodes of their enemies. In the United States the Virginia gentry, and the farmers farthest from towns, along the frontier from Vermont through western Pennsylvania into Kentucky, were strongly Jeffersonian, Republican, anti-British, and partisan to the French Revolution. To this broad generalization various exceptions must be recognized, since in America (as in Europe) many urban "mechanics" and many of the professional classes, notably doctors, favored the newly forming republicanism; but the cities in America were still small compared with those of Europe in any case; and the broad features of the transposition would appear to be valid.[13]

This reversal of roles can best be explained by the differences between the United States and Europe, differences which Louis Hartz has

[13] For comparisons of Europe and America, both explicit and allusive, see above, pp. 3-4, 26-27, 55, 124-25, 299, 336-38, 345, 350-53, 374-75, 403, 416, 456, 472-73, 500, and below, pp. 541-42, 567, 569-75.

summed up as the lack of the "feudal factor" in America.[14] It was due also to a certain failure on the part of Americans, because of these very differences, to understand the Revolution beyond the Atlantic. In Europe the revolutionary movement, though it carried aristocratic liberalism and Babouvist communism at its fringes, was most especially a middle-class or "bourgeois" affair, aimed at the reconstruction of an old order, and at the overthrow of aristocracies, nobilities, patriciates, and other privileged classes. It is hard to see how Jefferson, who so much disliked cities with their moneyed men and their mobs, could have been so sympathetic to the French Revolution had he seen it in an altogether realistic light. The same is true of American democrats generally. But Hamilton and the Federalists were if anything even more mistaken. They imagined that men like themselves, in Europe, were as hostile to the Revolution as they were. Or rather, in their own self-definition, they failed to identify with the European urban middle classes, which they really resembled, and preferred to associate themselves with the British and European aristocracies, which they hardly resembled at all. Hamilton was a self-made man, a parvenu; even George Cabot, who became a very "high" Federalist, and whose family later became prominent, was the author of his own fortune, largely made in privateering during the War of Independence. These men could not see, and probably did not even know, that many men of business in Europe—the Watts and Boultons, Walker and Wilkinson, Gogel, Sieveking and the Bohemian banker, J. F. Opiz, to name only those mentioned in preceding pages— were willing enough to sympathize with the ideas of the French Revolution in principle.

Hamilton began in 1790 to borrow money in Europe, to pay off the debt to France incurred during the American Revolution. For this purpose it was awkward to obtain funds in England, and he turned to Holland. The principal Dutch banker in these transactions was Nicolaas van Staphorst, who with his associates provided the United States with 23,500,000 guilders between 1787 and 1794. Staphorst, an old Patriot of the 1780's, accepted the Dutch revolution of 1795 and was active in the early months of the Batavian Republic. He worked on American affairs through a leading Antwerp banker, Joseph de Broeta. Broeta was very pro-French; he welcomed the opening of the Scheldt river, collaborated with Dumouriez, and, at some personal risk during the Austrian restoration of 1793, concealed 267,000 livres due to the French,

[14] L. Hartz, *The Liberal Tradition in America: An Interpretation of American Political Thought since the Revolution* (New York, 1955).

which he paid over to them on their return to Belgium in 1794. Yet Alexander Hamilton preferred to believe that the Revolution in Europe was the outbreak of an unruly and ignorant populace.[15]

The point is, of course, that both parties in America, far from being interested in an exact understanding of events, were using the current ideological arguments for their own purposes. Nor, for all the reversal of roles, were those arguments irrelevant to American issues. The bankers, merchants and shipping magnates who supported the Federalist party would not have been considered really high-class in Europe. In the class structure of America, however, they were upper crust; and the fact that there was no higher or older aristocracy for them to rebel against is what made it possible for them to be so conservative. The High Federalists seem to have thought (John Adams and merely moderate Federalists were not so sure) that the upper classes of the United States and Great Britain had a great deal in common. Aspiring to be aristocrats, they made themselves into legitimate targets for democrats. Appropriating the language of the European counter-revolution, they naturally found "republicans" arrayed against them. The great dispute in America was no mere comedy of errors, nor incongruous shadow-boxing; it was, as in Europe, a contest between different views on right and justice, on the form of the good society, and on the direction in which the world in general, and the new United States in particular, ought to move.

The Impact of the Outside World

Before more is said on internal divisions, it is important to point to a few ways in which there was no division at all.[16] There was no revolutionary extremism in America. Not only did no one propose "communism"; no one had even officially proposed, as in France, a comprehensive system of public schools. Truly counter-revolutionary opinion was equally absent. No one called for a restoration of King

[15] On Staphorst see P. van Winter's account in *Nieuw Nederlandsch Biografisch Woordenboek*, VIII, 1285-86; on de Broeta, E. Discailles, "Un négociant anversois à la fin du XVIIIe siècle," in Académie royale de Belgique, *Bulletin de la classe des lettres* (Brussels, 1901), 505-58.

[16] For the present section it is hardly necessary to cite the abundant bibliography, of which a good recent summary is given by Chambers, *op.cit.*, 209-16. I have drawn especially on Chambers; on J. Charles, *Origins of the American Party System* (Williamsburg, 1956); A. DeConde, *Entangling Alliance: Politics and Diplomacy under George Washington* (Durham, N.C., 1958); D. Malone, *Jefferson and the Ordeal of Liberty* (Boston, 1962); J. C. Miller, *Alexander Hamilton, Portrait in Paradox* (New York, 1959); and have attempted to point up what is commonly known with observations arising from a comparative view of Europe and America.

George, or a return to subordination under the Parliament of Great Britain. No American of any importance would have accepted the Canada Act of 1791. Natives of the old colonies who preferred such arrangements had departed; those who returned either changed their minds or kept silent. The United States had no party of returned émigrés. Such "counter-revolution" as had occurred was purely relative. The Pennsylvania constitution of 1776, with its resemblances to the French Jacobin constitution of the Year I, was replaced by a new one in 1790; but the new Pennsylvania plan, in which the governor, senate, and lower house were all directly elected by a wide suffrage, was exceedingly democratic, not only by European standards of the 1790's, but also in the light of American experience before 1776. The federal constitution was "conservative" in that it created a national government, in place of a league of states; but it created also, for the first time in America, a theater for popular politics on a national stage.

To the constitution itself there was no basic opposition. Those who had argued against it in 1787, while the argument was open, accepted it in good faith after its ratification, and after adoption of the first ten amendments to protect individual and state rights. Here again the difference from France and its sister-republics was pronounced. The divisions that formed in the 1790's did not prolong earlier differences over the constitution itself. That the anti-Federalists were unfriendly to the new constitution was an empty accusation; the chief founder of the Republican party, James Madison, was himself one of the authors of the new federal document, and co-author with Hamilton of the *Federalist* papers. If Madison and Jefferson, in 1798, toyed with ideas of "nullification," it was Hamilton and the High Federalists who, under pressure, were tempted by the thought of scrapping the constitution altogether. As the constitution itself was not a party issue, neither was "democracy" in the mere sense of the extent of the suffrage. The issue, as it developed, was the activation of voters whose right to the suffrage was not in question. As the decade passed, more men already qualified to vote actually voted.

At first, in 1790 and 1791, there was only Hamilton's program, and the opposition to it. Or rather, there were Hamilton's various measures, and sporadic critiques in which different individuals, in the new Congress and outside it, objected to some of these measures while accepting others. Hamilton, supported by Washington, took the view that the opposition was opposition to government itself. Since no parties of modern kind yet existed, nor was the idea or need of them even recognized, the issues soon took on larger dimensions, becoming a question of the propriety of opposition itself, or the right of citizens to disagree with, criticize, and work against public officials. In addition, Hamilton's plans required good relations with England. It may be that at this time, in the aftermath of the American Revolution, a dislike of England, or rather of its government and social institutions, was a more positive and more popular sentiment in America than was affection for France. With France the alliance of 1778 was still in effect, and there were memories of French aid in the late war with England; but what aroused fellow-feeling in America was the French Revolution, since the French declaration of rights, the new constitution, and the vocabulary of debate, vindicating liberty against tyrants, and equality against privilege, echoed what had been heard in America for some time. When Adams and Hamilton spoke out against the French Revolution, they aroused others all the more fiercely to its defense. A feeling spread that the French Revolution was a continuation of the American, and that the American Revolution itself was endangered, or unfinished.

In America, as in England and Europe, the year 1792 was a turning point. The war was seen by some as an outburst of militant and destructive revolutionary crusading, and by others, probably far more numerous, as a defense against a brutal intervention in French affairs by a league of aristocrats and despots. The proclamation of the French Republic was seen by some as a piece of madness and violence, and by others, far more numerous, as the dawn in Europe of a light first seen in America. The French victories at Valmy and Jemappes were enthusiastically hailed. On February 1, 1793, the French declared war against England; they were now fighting that old bugbear of Americans, King George III. News of this development came almost simultaneously with the arrival of the first minister of the French Republic, Edmond Genet, who disembarked at Charleston, South Carolina, on April 8, 1793.[17]

Genet had spent several years in Russia, where he had formed a low opinion of those who raged against the French Revolution while crushing the new order in Poland. He had found signs of potential revolutionary disturbance even in Russia. He had been present in

[17] On Genet see above, pp. 62-64, 90, 144; W. Blackwell, "Citizen Genet and the Revolution in Russia, 1789-92," in *French Historical Studies*, iii (1963), 72-92; M. Minnigerode, *Jefferson, Friend of France 1793: the Career of Edmond Charles Genet* (New York, 1928); E. P. Link, *Democratic-Republican Societies* (New York, 1942); and works cited in the preceding note.

Paris when English-speaking delegations, including the American Joel Barlow, came to offer greetings to the Convention. Late in 1792 he had been to Geneva, and he had worked in Paris with Dutch revolutionaries who urged the French to invade and liberate their country. Genet, from experience, sensed an international struggle of momentous scope. He was prepared to see the American critics of France as another species of the same old aristocrats, and American democrats as another branch of the forces of world liberation. He would have enjoyed the toast made at Oeller's Hotel in Philadelphia, in 1795, long after his departure: to the emancipation of Holland and the revival of Poland— "may the Russian she-bear [Catherine II] be made to dance to the tune of Ça Ira!"[18]

Genet received a series of ovations on his long journey from Charleston to Philadelphia. He was told that in America relations were strained between government and people. He went about his business, counting on the United States as an ally under the treaty of 1778, devising expeditions against the British and Spanish possessions, issuing French military commissions to Americans, seeking accelerated payment on the debt, arranging to get shipments to France through the British blockade, and using American seaports as bases for French privateering. President Washington meanwhile issued his Proclamation of Neutrality. That the United States should remain neutral, or uninvolved in actual hostilities, was agreed to by everyone in the government, including Jefferson as Secretary of State; and indeed Genet himself, and his home government, believed that the United States could be more useful to France if technically neutral. It was the proclamation that caused trouble, since sentiment in the country was not neutral at all. To announce neutrality in formal terms seemed, to the opposition, to be an insult to an ally, a rejection of a sister republic, and an unnecessary concession to arbitrary demands by the British. As for the British, now at war with France, they began to strengthen their alliances with Indians in the West, to stop American vessels bound for Europe, and to impress American seamen into the British fleet.

Genet plunged also into American politics. He sponsored the political clubs that were forming quite independently of his arrival. He mixed familiarly with the opposition, by which he was feted and lionized. Many Americans thought that Genet and the French represented their interests better than their own government. They thus

[18] M. Haiman, *The Fall of Poland in Contemporary American Opinion* (Chicago, 1935), 215.

resembled many Dutch, Irish, and others. There was a widespread feeling, especially in the West, where the operations of men like Simcoe had their most immediate impact, that if Britain and the coalition defeated the French Republic the American Republic would collapse also. "If kings combine to support kings," asked Hugh Brackenridge, novelist, Princeton graduate, and Western Pennsylvania landowner, "why not republics to support republics?" "A breach between us and France," said the *Pittsburgh Gazette*, "would infallibly bring the English again on our backs; and yet we have some wild beasts among our own countrymen who are endeavoring to weaken that connection."[19]

Genet naturally encouraged such sentiments. Jefferson as the warmest friend of France in the government was distressed that Genet went so far as to weaken his own cause. It was from the French government, however, that Genet received his first rebuke, on the basis of information that must have left America less than three months after he stepped ashore in Charleston. In France he had been associated with Dumouriez and Brissot, who in the spring of 1793 were replaced in power by the new party of the Mountain. On July 30 the French foreign minister, under the newly forming Robespierrist Committee of Public Safety, in a sharp reprimand to Genet, reminded him that he was accredited "to treat with the *government* and not with a *portion of the people*," and that the American President and Congress were the only legal authority in the United States, according to the constitutional principles of the French Revolution itself.[20] In short, the most Jacobin of all French governments agreed with the American Federalists, when they accused Genet of appealing to the people over the head of the government. At the request of the United States, Genet was recalled a few months later. Finding more admiration among American democrats than among French ones, he remained in America, married the daughter of a New York Republican, and lived in the United States for forty years.

During the months of Genet's ministry new political clubs began to form, the democratic or republican societies. While active Federalists had met in each other's living rooms, or the public rooms of the better hotels, people of a plainer sort now began to meet in more modest quarters, in taverns or country stores. Over forty such clubs are known

[19] Link, 54-55.
[20] F. J. Turner, ed., *Correspondence of the French Ministers to the United States*, in *Annual Report of the American Historical Association for 1903*, II, 228-29.

to have existed, beginning in March 1793, chiefly in the seaboard towns and along the frontier. According to Oliver Wolcott they were composed of "the lowest order of mechanics, laborers and draymen"; and Timothy Dwight, perhaps recalling a famous remark of Burke's, thought that democracy, like the devil, was entering into "a herd of swine."[21] It is true that the societies had numerous members of inferior station, but about half the membership was middle-class, consisting of merchants, lawyers, larger landowners, and a good many doctors. They somewhat resembled the Sons of Liberty of the 1760's, or the radical clubs that sprang up in England and Scotland in 1792, or similar groups in Holland, or the provincial Jacobin clubs of France. They hardly resembled the Paris Jacobin club, which, especially in 1793, was full of men active in the government. Men in the American government of republican opinions, such as Madison and Jefferson, did not belong to these clubs, which were of local, spontaneous, and popular origin. They were not yet a political party but only a step in that direction; most of them disappeared within two or three years, as a more organized Republican party came into being. Some of the clubs did take part locally in elections, and it was these clubs, apparently, that inspired the older Tammany societies with political interests. Their attitude was one of suspicion of government and of office-holders, an anti-élitism, a class consciousness of a general sort pitting the "many" against the "few." The tone was suggested by the Ulster Democratic Club in the Catskills of New York, which stood "on guard against designing men in office and affluent circumstances, who are forever combining against the rights of all but themselves."[22] The clubs were opposed to Hamilton's policies, to British influence, and to fine gentlemen who used hair-powder or wore silk stockings. At a time when the newspapers carried more foreign than local news, they were fascinated by the great spectacle of the war in Europe. They were unanimously and excitedly pro-French. On the success of the French Revolution against its armed enemies, according to the prospectus of the Massachusetts Constitutional Society, in January 1794, depended the happiness of "the *whole world of Mankind*."[23]

To men who still conceived themselves as the proper guardians of society, suited by wisdom, experience, and position to form a governing

[21] Link, 94.
[22] *Ibid.*, 95.
[23] C. D. Hazen, *Contemporary American Opinion of the French Revolution* (Baltimore, 1897), 194.

class—that is, to most of the more articulate Federalists—this sprouting up of popular clubs, whose stock in trade was the criticism of government, seemed novel and alarming, if not revolutionary. When the farmers of Western Pennsylvania demonstrated against the new federal tax on spirits (in the so-called Whiskey Rebellion of 1794), it was charged that the clubs promoted insurrection, which was not true; but it was true that both the formation of clubs and the resistance to taxes expressed an antipathy to Hamilton's program, and indeed to government itself. President Washington called the clubs "self-created." He meant that they were extra-legal, and that only duly constituted bodies and duly elected representatives should deliberate or exert pressure on public issues; the phrase recalled what the British authorities had said of American correspondence committees twenty years before, and were saying of the London Corresponding Society at precisely this moment. So far as the Federalists found themselves denying the legitimacy of any opposition to government arising outside government circles, the emerging Republicans could rightly accuse them of betraying the American Revolution.

The Federalists thought also that the clubs, since they appeared simultaneously with Genet, were the result of his machinations. "Genet's clubs," the British minister called them contemptuously in reporting to Grenville; and American Federalists agreed. Many likewise insisted that "democracy" was a foreign and imported idea. The bulldog of the Federalist press, William Cobbett, himself a foreigner lately arrived from England, was especially emphatic in this opinion. The Pennsylvania Democratic Society organized itself in the middle of 1793. According to Cobbett, it was Genet who proposed the word "Democratic" for its title.[24] Two-thirds of the democrats in America, said Cobbett, were foreigners who had landed since the war. Their very language had an alien flavor: "The word citizen, that stalking-horse of modern liberty men, became almost as common in America as in France."[25] Others took up the cry; the altogether native American, Joseph Hopkinson, declared it to be a "notorious" fact, in 1798, that "the bulk of opposition to our government," by which he meant the Republican party, "is composed of these fortune hunting foreigners."[26]

[24] Link accepts this as a fact, citing Minnigerode, who gave no reference, but probably drew on Cobbett, *History of the American Jacobins Commonly Denominated Democrats* (Philadelphia, 1796), 16. Cobbett's word cannot be accepted as evidence.
[25] *Ibid.*, 22, 25.
[26] *What is our situation? and what our prospects? A few pages for Americans* (Philadelphia, 1798), 22.

The Republicans were also "vile organs of a foreign democracy."[27] The word democracy became so controversial that Jefferson preferred to avoid it, and the opposition adopted the less offensive name of Republicans.

That either the clubs or the word "democracy" were a foreign growth in America was untrue. It was as false as Cobbett's preposterous allegation that Genet had spent 20,000 *louis d'ors* to set up the Pennsylvania Democratic Society. The democratic societies arose from native causes, and the word itself, in a favorable sense, was used in America before Genet arrived. Patrick Henry had so used it in the Virginia ratifying convention. At another center of indigenous traditions, Plymouth, Massachusetts, on January 24, 1793, there was a public meeting "to celebrate the victories of the French Republic." The Congregationalist minister, Chandler Robbins, who was considered to be a fairly strict Calvinist, pronounced a eulogy on the French Revolution, with copious quotations from the Bible. An ode was written for the occasion by Mr. Joseph Coswell in four stanzas one of which read:

> See the bright flame arise
> In yonder eastern skies,
>> Spreading in veins.
> 'Tis pure Democracy
> Setting all nations free,
>> Melting our chains.[28]

Genet, as the vivacious young envoy of an embattled republic, probably had a stimulating effect on American democrats; but it was not Genet, nor foreign intrigue, that brought a democratic movement into consciousness of itself at this time.

The American popular democrats, though not Jefferson and the Republican leaders, might if left to themselves have welcomed, or even forced, another war with England (as in 1812), especially in view of the uncompromising demands of the British, which at times filled even Hamilton with dismay. John Jay went to England to negotiate a treaty. At the same time James Monroe went as minister to Paris, to maintain good relations with France while Jay tried to deal with England. Monroe, an enthusiastic republican, arriving just after the death of

---

[27] Quoted by J. C. Miller, *Crisis in Freedom: The Alien and Sedition Acts* (Boston, 1951), 32, from the *Pennsylvania Gazette* for October 18, 1797.
[28] Coswell's Ode to Liberty is bound with Chandler Robbins, *An Address Delivered at Plymouth on the 24th day of January, 1793, to the inhabitants of That Town, Assembled to Celebrate the Victories of the French Republic Over its Invaders* (Boston, 1793).

Robespierre, was very partial to the French Convention and to the Directory after it. Well disposed to democrats everywhere, he befriended Thomas Paine and Wolfe Tone in Paris. He was so eager to please the French that he sometimes failed to put the policies of his own government in their proper light. He believed that Jay in London was betraying him; he was so opposed to an American rapprochement with England that the French thought he must be deceiving them; and he seems not to have known, or to have been unconcerned, about French designs on the region west of the Alleghenies. Washington finally recalled him, and the ensuing uproar formed another stage in the differentiation of Federalists and Republicans. Meanwhile Jay negotiated his famous treaty, with Alexander Hamilton secretly working, through the British minister in Philadelphia, to satisfy the British in a way that even Jay thought too extreme. The British conceded practically nothing except evacuation of the Northwest Territory. They refused to moderate their position on the impressment of sailors, or on matters of contraband, search, and seizure at sea in wartime; they refused to pay for American slaves taken off during the War of Independence (a sensitive matter to southern Republicans); and they refused to open their West Indian islands in a useful way to American commerce. The best that could be said in America for the treaty was that it prevented war with England. Undoubtedly such a war at this time would have been ruinous to the new republic, both from the impact of British power, and the effects of internal dispute and break-up within the United States. Politically, however, the argument was not a strong one; it sounded too much like appeasement.

It was in the controversy over the Jay treaty that the democratic movement grew into a Republican party, and that the Federalists closed ranks to obtain the goodwill of Britain, which was necessary both to their practical program and to their view of life and society. When Washington and the Senate ratified the treaty, debate raged in the House on measures for putting it into effect. The treaty became a question between government and opposition, or Federalists and Republicans. It raised also, above the prosaic problems of debt and taxation, and above localized grievances such as the excise on spirits, a question on which people of all kinds, throughout the country, could form an opinion and become emotionally aroused. The question was seen, and strongly felt, as a choice between England and France, between two sides in an ideological war, between the old forces and the new in a contest without geographical boundaries, between monarchy and republicanism, Anglomen and Gallomen, men of substance and Jacobins —and between those who wished to move forward with a continuing American Revolution, and those who wished to restrain or qualify the implications of that event. On this basis the treaty was attacked and defended in the newspapers. Political leaders had an issue on which they could ignite public opinion, form connections with interested local groups, bring out the vote, and offer candidates for election on a basis of continuing principle, not merely of momentary issues or personal or passing factional groupings. The decisive bill to implement the treaty passed the House in April 1796 by a narrow margin, 51 to 48, on a clear party division. The two parties, Federalist and Republican, then girded for the presidential election of that year, which, with the retirement of Washington, was the first contested presidential election.

Both contenders for the office of President of the United States, in 1796, were denounced as the tools of foreign ideologies and foreign powers. Both parties presented themselves, their candidates, their opponents, and the issues in terms of the struggle raging in Europe. For Federalists, Jefferson was a Jacobin, an atheist, a libertine, a leveller, and almost a Frenchman. Adams was the friend of order, talent, and rational liberty. For the Republicans, Adams was a monocrat and an aristocrat who longed to mix with English lords and ladies; and Jefferson the upholder of republican principles. An electoral circular put out by the Republican Committee of Pennsylvania explained the choice. It was "between the uniform advocate of equal rights among citizens, or the champion of rank, titles and hereditary distinctions; . . . the steady supporter of our present republican constitution; or the warm panegyrist of the British Monarchical form of Government."[29] That the bland Virginian was a Jacobin, or the irritable Boston lawyer an Anglomaniac, were about equally fantastic; but such was the atmosphere of debate.

The "Corruption of Poland"

The French Directory took the Jay treaty, along with Monroe's ambiguities and his recall, to mean that the United States was now virtually allied to Great Britain.[30] Indeed the British were of somewhat the same

[29] A facsimile of the election circular is included in N. E. Cunningham, *The Jeffersonian Republicans, 1789-1801* (Chapel Hill, 1957), 112.

[30] For the present section, in addition to works previously cited: S. Kurtz, *The Presidency of John Adams: The Collapse of Federalism, 1795-1800* (Philadelphia, 1957); M. J. Dauer, *The Adams Federalists* (Baltimore, 1953); E. W. Lyon, "The Directory and the United States," in *American Historical Review*, XLIII (1938), 514-

opinion; the new treaty with the United States, as already noted, was one of the few matters for encouragement mentioned in the address opening Parliament in 1795. As Grenville remarked to Rufus King a little later, in 1798, at a time when Britain had no allies on the Continent, he wished that Europe had shown "half the energy" of the Americans against "the infernal spirit of atheism and modern philosophy."[31] The French also concluded from the debate over the Jay treaty, not without evidence, that the United States government did not enjoy the entire confidence of its own people. The Directory began to do more officially what Genet had done so largely on his own initiative. Secretly, with Collot's mission, it explored the possibilities for a separate republic west of the Alleghenies. Publicly, the new minister to Philadelphia, Adet, under instructions from Paris, interfered in American political affairs; as the election of 1796 approached, Adet made speeches advising the Americans to avoid the displeasure of France by electing a true patriot and friend of the great Republic—Thomas Jefferson. With reason, and counselled by Hamilton, Washington at this moment reshaped his Farewell Address; he urged Western Americans to remain in the Union, and all Americans to keep enthusiasm for foreign powers out of their domestic politics.[32]

Adams was elected, but only by 71 electoral votes to Jefferson's 68. Jefferson became vice-president, but the Federalists remained in power, especially since Adams retained Washington's cabinet, which was composed of a group of strong Hamiltonians. In January 1797 the Paris *Moniteur* somehow obtained and published a copy of Jefferson's "Mazzei letter," written some months before at the height of the agitation over the Jay treaty. It caused an uproar on becoming known in America, but it was of course read in Paris also. The Frenchman could read, in his paper for 6 Pluviôse of the Year V, on the authority of the new American vice-president, that, though the American people remained soundly republican, the government was controlled by *un parti anglican-monarchico-aristocratique*. The editor remarked that the French Directory, by breaking relations with a government so perversely submissive to the English, would serve the cause of republicanism in the United States. It was now possible for the French,

32; J. M. Smith, *Freedom's Fetters: The Alien and Sedition Laws and American Civil Liberties* (Ithaca, 1956).

[31] See above, p. 371; and Great Britain: Hist. MSS. Comm., *Manuscripts of J. B. Fortescue Preserved at Dropmore*, 10 vols. (London, 1892-1927), IV, 272-73.

[32] F. Gilbert, *To the Farewell Address: Ideas of Early American Foreign Policy* (Princeton, 1961), 123-34.

in their relations with the United States (as later for Americans in their relations to other countries) to feel that they could be hostile to its government while remaining friendly to its people.

In the following months, having imposed peace on Austria, the French hoped to do the same with England, and went to work on their plans for invasion. American Republicans, including Jefferson and the still unknown Andrew Jackson, looked forward with satisfaction to a French landing in England. "Nothing," wrote Jefferson, "can establish firmly the republican principles of our government but an establishment of them in England. France will be the apostle for this."[33] For other Americans such an event would signify the collapse of civilization.

The French began to attack American shipping, which since the Jay treaty was far more useful to Great Britain than to France. An American commission went to France to attempt a settlement. Someone in the French government, probably Talleyrand or Barras, made to these Americans a proposal that had almost been accepted by the British; they could have peace, for a price, the price being payment in cash for certain "rescriptions" of the Batavian Republic of uncertain value. The Americans refused the bribe; and Adams, under Federalist pressure to discredit the French and their American sympathizers, published the documents on this episode, the "XYZ papers," in April 1798. Had the Federalists known that Pitt, in his need for peace, had almost accepted a similar proposal, made to him through the respectable mediation of a Boston merchant then in France, Thomas Melville, they would surely have been disconcerted;[34] but this secret was well kept, and the Federalists complacently seized on the XYZ papers as proof of the incorrigible corruption of the French Directory, which, officially, had had nothing to do with the matter. Jefferson and the Republicans, having somewhat idealized the French anyway, reacted with shock and dismay to these unfortunate revelations; and since clashes at sea continued between American merchant ships and French privateers in an undeclared quasi-war, a great many people found their admiration of the French suddenly cooling. Others, as in all such ideological conflicts, remained unshaken in their previous sympathies, and blamed the trouble with France on the British orientation of American policy. As for the French, in these early months of 1798,

[33] A. Lipscomb and A. Bergh, *Writings of Thomas Jefferson*, 20 vols. (Washington, 1903), IX, 412. On Jackson see above, p. 299.

[34] *Dropmore Papers*, III, 356-69; above, p. 328.

at the height of the wave of revolutionary democracy in Europe, with revolution in Switzerland and Rome and insurrection expected in Ireland, they were in no mood to be patient with an American government which its own people called Anglophile and aristocratic. A little later, with the renewal of the European coalition against them, Talleyrand and the Directory became more willing to deal with the United States.

Against the possibility of real war with France, and over Republican objections, Adams created a Navy Department and began to build a fleet. Hamilton and the Federalist militants pressed also for an army. Taxes were raised, the small regular army was enlarged, and generals were appointed, with Hamilton as commander under Washington's nominal leadership. What use such an army could be against the French neither Adams nor the Republicans could understand; but Hamilton and his followers began to call war with France inevitable and even desirable, and to dream of campaigns in which, allied with Great Britain, they might invade and liberate Latin America, in regions unspecified—perhaps Florida, the West Indies, New Orleans, Texas, or Mexico—an ambition at other times most alive among "democrats." There was ground also to suppose that Hamilton, whose dislike of Virginia was well known, and who had shown his taste for using martial methods to teach respect for government in the Whiskey Rebellion, might employ his new army against the agrarian Republicans in the south, or even to bring in what he would consider a more workable constitution.

Matters were further inflamed by the Naturalization Act, the Alien Act, and the Sedition Act, passed by Federalist majorities against Republican resistance in 1798. The first two reflected the belief that democratic ideas were an importation from Europe. And, indeed, as noted in the last chapter, a remarkable number of British and Irish radicals had come recently to the United States, and several were editing very vociferous Republican newspapers. There were also thousands of Frenchmen in the country. At a time when hostilities with France were actually in progress, and when the French had shown their willingness to interfere in American politics, and enjoyed a large American following, a reasonable argument for precautionary measures could have been made; but in truth the three Acts, like the war spirit which they reflected, were conceived and executed for domestic political purposes. No one was ever deported under the Alien Act, though many French refugees were frightened away. About fifteen persons were indicted under the Sedition Act, and eleven convicted. There was no "sedition" in the United States, except possibly for certain intrigues in the west which never came into the question. At Quebec, Bahia, Vienna, Budapest, and Dublin the persons put to death for sedition had in fact conspired against the state. The same was true of many counter-revolutionaries executed in France during the Terror. In the state trials in England and Scotland, the accused had at least favored ideas incompatible with the British constitution as then understood. The same was not true of those convicted of sedition in the United States. None of them had taken part in any conspiracy, and they all accepted the form of government and the constitution. They differed with the Federalists on how the government should develop, and they criticized its personnel and its policies, often in extravagant and abusive terms. The Federalists, however, had not yet accepted the propriety of criticism of government. Opposition to their policies, or even to their persons, was what they meant by sedition. The repression on which they embarked, astoundingly enough in view of American "moderation," had less actual justification, if only by *raison d'état*, than the repression conducted by either conservative or revolutionary regimes in Europe and the rest of America. All eleven persons convicted under the Sedition Act were active Republicans, and six of them were newspaper editors. The Federalists, it seemed, really meant to crush a party which had arisen in opposition to government, even if they destroyed freedom of the press as well. The Republicans naturally took alarm, since the existence of their newly formed party was what most obviously was at stake. In the south they responded, through Madison and Jefferson, with the Virginia and Kentucky Resolutions, in which state legislatures took it upon themselves to declare federal laws, in this case the Alien and Sedition Acts, to be unconstitutional and of no effect. The remedy would have proved as fatal as the disease, had matters gone further, so far as the creation of a viable national government was concerned.

At the same time the polemics in print came to a climax. Over the decade, it is possible to distinguish two periods, an early one in which writings favorable to the French Revolution seemed to preponderate, and a later one, beginning about 1795, when the tide, in words at least, turned more in favor of England. The Americans were not yet a book-writing people. Books, often enough, like the *Federalist*, were reprints of articles written for newspapers. Adams' *Defense of the Constitutions of the United States* had been written in England; since it drew heavily on works which did not then exist in American libraries, it could not have been written in America. Paine's *Rights of Man* was also written in England. Strongly identifying the French and American revolutions, it was reprinted at least nineteen times in the United States between 1791 and 1796. The first American printings of some of Rousseau's works, including the *Social Contract*, were made also at this time. On the whole, most books in the United States, as in colonial times, were still imported; and this fact gave an advantage to Great Britain.

Newspapers and pamphlets, and printed sermons and Fourth of July orations, were the more usual native media of expression. The newspapers, having no reporters, copied from each other, and from the papers which every arriving ship unloaded on the docks from Europe. Here again the British had the advantage. As early as 1790, Thomas Jefferson, having just returned from France, and finding Fenno's *Gazette of the United States* full of British accounts of the French Revolution, reached an agreement with him to supply extracts from the *Leyden Gazette*, published in French in Holland by the old Patriot, John Luzac.[35] In the following years, as controversy mounted, native-born editors were joined by others from Britain and Ireland. The Federalists won William Cobbett to their side; but most of the newcomers found the Republicans more congenial, and brought to the American political scene some of the animus that they had formed against the Establishment in England and Ireland. John Daly Burk edited the Boston *Polar Star*, and later the New York *Timepiece*; Joseph Gales moved from the Sheffield *Register* to a paper in North Carolina; and Thomas Cooper, formerly of the Manchester *Herald*, wrote pamphlets for which he was convicted under the Sedition Act in 1800. There was in truth, as the Federalists said, a certain foreign influence conveyed through American newspapers, both in their clamorous emphasis on war and revolution in Europe, and in the personal backgrounds of some of the editors. Even the native-born firebrand, Benjamin Franklin Bache, irrepressible editor of the Republican *Aurora*, had spent, as the grandson of Benjamin Franklin, eight years of his boyhood in Paris and Geneva.

More purely American was the Fourth of July oration, a new *genre* already well developed, and most American of all, the long and meaty sermon. The surprising thing about many Fourth of July orations was the way in which many of them subordinated the American Revolu-

[35] J. P. Boyd and others, *Papers of Thomas Jefferson*, XVI (Princeton, 1961), 237-47.

tion to the French. In 1793 someone printed and bound together two such orations, one delivered by Elihu Palmer at Philadelphia and one by Hugh Brackenridge in western Pennsylvania, along with extracts from one of Robespierre's speeches, containing sentiments that would appeal to American democrats, such as that government caused more evil than "anarchy" did, and that the farmer should have the same vote as the grain merchant.[36] And according to a patriotic oration at Boston, a year after Robespierre's death, the struggles of Americans in their revolution, compared to those of the French, "were but as the first achievement of Hercules in his cradle to the wonderful labors that were reserved for his manhood."[37]

The clergy included, until 1795 or later, a good many who spoke sympathetically of the French Revolution from the pulpit. It was usual to attribute the signs of irreligion in France to the impostures of Roman Catholicism, and the violence of the Terror to the horrors of the Old Regime and the arrogance of European aristocrats. As Chandler Robbins said at Plymouth, quoting Solomon, oppression makes men mad. In the fall of the old system in France, Samuel Stillman saw "the judgment of God." Even the president of Yale, Ezra Stiles, hailed the execution of Louis XVI as a sign that European monarchs would soon be "tamed." The clergyman and geographer, Jedidiah Morse, as late as 1795, declared that the "irregularities" in France, including the atheism, were temporary and should be excused.[38]

A change came about in 1795. For the clergy, and those who followed their lead, the publication of Paine's widely read *Age of Reason*, and the development of Elihu Palmer into a deistic lecturer who reached popular audiences, caused great consternation. It was realized that Christianity itself and not merely Roman Catholicism was being called into question. The French invasion of Holland and Switzerland, two Protestant countries highly regarded in America, made an

[36] *Political Miscellany* (New York, 1793).

[37] George Blake, *An Oration Pronounced July 4, 1795, at the Request of the Inhabitants of the Town of Boston* (Boston, 1795), 27. The historian David Ramsay delivered a similar oration, praising France, at Charleston, S.C., on July 4, 1794.

[38] Chandler Robbins in the Address cited in n. 28 above; S. Stillman, *Thoughts on the French Revolution* (Boston, 1795), 12-14; *Literary Diary of Ezra Stiles*, 3 vols. (New York, 1901), III, 428; J. Morse, *Present Situation of Other Nations of the World Contrasted with our Own* (Boston, 1794), quoting from his Thanksgiving Day sermon of 1794. I am indebted for this information on the clergy to my former student, Mr. Gary B. Nash, who reports finding only one case of opposition to the French Revolution among American clergy before 1794, and that this one case is the only one cited by various historians who think that the American clergy soon turned against the French revolutionaries.

unfavorable impression. In addition, by 1795 and 1796, party lines were being sharply drawn over the Jay treaty. Federalists became more committed to England than ever, and one way to expose and refute Republicans in America was to circulate increasing numbers of English books.

The waves of British writing against the French Revolution, as described in the last chapter, now began to wash over the United States. Of books actually imported there can now be little trace. It is possible, however, to identify reprintings made and sold by American booksellers, some of whom made a specialty of literature of this kind.[39] One of these was William Cobbett; another was Paul Nancrède, a Frenchman who had been in America since 1785, detested the French Revolution, taught French at Harvard, and sold books in Boston.

Burke's *Reflections* had two American printings in the 1790's, one at New York in 1791, and one at Philadelphia in 1792. There were none thereafter; it is hardly surprising that the book had little appeal for Americans at that time. In 1795 Cobbett reprinted Playfair's book on the "crimes and perfidies" of Jacobinism, to which he added an appendix of his own on American democrats. Cobbett likewise, with associates in New York, brought out an American edition of Robison's *Proofs of a Conspiracy* in 1798. The English translation of Barruel, in four volumes, appeared in 1799 at Elizabeth, New Jersey. Works by Mallet du Pan were printed in New York as early as 1795. Nancrède reprinted the English versions of Barzoni's *Romans in Greece*, and Mallet du Pan's *History of the destruction of the Helvetic union and liberty*.[40] A short work called *Cannibals' progress, or the dreadful horrors of French Invasion*, brought out in England but apparently not very successful there, was printed in 1798 in at least fourteen different American towns, mostly in New England, and obviously by prearrangement. Five thousand had been sold at Philadelphia in a few days, according to the New Haven *Gazette*, which perhaps exaggerated in order to sell it in New Haven. "The despots of France," said the American introduction to *Cannibals' Progress*, after enslaving France and desolating all European republics, "have insulted America and demanded of her a tribute." The reference was to the XYZ affair; and foolish American republicans were to learn from the horrors in Germany, where there had at first been many sympathizers with the

---

[39] See C. Evans, *American Bibliography: A Chronological Dictionary of All Books, Pamphlets and Periodical Publications Printed in the United States of America* [from 1639 to 1800], 14 vols. (Chicago, 1903-1959).
[40] For these books see above, pp. 222, 250-54, 318, 488-89.

French Revolution, what fiends the French republicans really were—they tied women to trees for wholesale rape, and butchered civilians without mercy.[41] Cobbett sold this tract for $3.50 a hundred. Another Philadelphian, Joseph Hopkinson, who wrote *Hail Columbia* in preparation for war with France, made a contribution toward restoring the balance of trade in this kind of commodity. One of his efforts was reprinted in London 1799: *What is our situation? and What our prospects, or a demonstration of the insidious views of Republican France, By an American.* In the next year, on a more honest and dignified level, John Quincy Adams, American minister to Berlin, reading Friedrich Gentz's new *Historisches Journal*, came upon his comparison of the French and American revolutions. Gentz, a professional counter-revolutionary polemicist, declared that the American Revolution had been a good thing because it was only a conservative protest against innovation, the French Revolution a bad thing because it had attempted systematic change. This was what John Quincy Adams wanted to hear; he translated it and published it in America in 1800, no doubt hoping to assist in the re-election of his father against the Jacobin Jefferson. It was reprinted in America in 1955 as a study in revolution.[42]

Meanwhile Jedidiah Morse had stirred up a furor of his own. As late as 1795 he had sympathized with the French Revolution, but he learned from his correspondents in Edinburgh, in 1797, that Professor Robison was preparing a book showing the real causes of that upheaval, and he managed to obtain a pre-publication copy of Robison's work in Philadelphia. In 1798, just at the height of the XYZ excitement, Morse delivered two "fast day" sermons. He solemnly announced that the world was in the grip of a secret revolutionary conspiracy, engineered by the Order of the Illuminati—that Genet's clubs of five

[41] Anthony Aufrere, *The cannibals' progress; or the dreadful horrors of French invasion, as displayed by Republican officers and soldiers, in their perfidy, rapacity, ferociousness and brutality, exercised towards the innocent inhabitants of Germany. Translated from the German.* (London, 1798.) The British Museum lists only one English edition. It is not clear whether Aufrere, an English antiquarian, really translated this work or wrote it himself. References here are to the Albany edition (1798), 3-4, 23.

[42] First edition, F. von Gentz, *Origin and principles of the American Revolution, compared with the origin and principles of the French Revolution* (Philadelphia, 1800). Reprinted in paperback by Henry Regnery, with an introduction by Russell Kirk (Chicago, 1955). Gentz's work also, at this time, far from reflecting the dominant sentiment in neutral Prussia, was of British inspiration. "In short, the *Historisches Journal* for 1800 took the tone of an English propaganda sheet. Nothing betrayed its Prussian origin except its language, its author and its place of publication." P. R. Sweet, *Friedrich von Gentz: Defender of the Old Order* (Madison, 1941), 49.

years before had been surface manifestations of this underground plot, and that the Republicans in America, recently so much in evidence, were the dupes or accomplices of this same pernicious organization, which labored everywhere, at all times, patiently, implacably, and behind the scenes, to overthrow all government and all religion. The publication of Robison's and Barruel's books served to confirm these allegations. An enormous outcry arose in the press. The Republicans were indignant. There were many skeptics, even among the New England clergy. For the Federalists such disclosures were welcome if not altogether believable; some odor of disreputability might be expected to cling to the democrats; and in any case, following the usual psychology of such affairs, to wish to doubt or examine the charges might in itself be grounds for suspicion. On the whole, the scare soon blew over. The hostilities that it reflected were more lasting and more real.[43]

Such was the state of the country during the presidency of John Adams—divided by interminable contention, bewildered by accusation and counter-accusation, flooded by propaganda, with its citizens appealing to foreigners in their disputes with each other, beset by laws against sedition and by their partisan enforcement, threatened by counter-resolutions putting the states above the federal government, carrying on actual hostilities with France at sea, and with important men clamoring for all-out war against that infidel republic, for which armies were being raised, American citizens prosecuted as if they were traitors, and alliance solicited with Great Britain.

As John Adams expressed it to Abigail, it was the corruption of Poland, with the roles of Russia and Prussia played by John Bull and Louis Baboon. He was captivated by neither.

Democracy in America

That the United States not only survived intact, but saw the Republicans come peaceably into office, and within three years even acquired Louisiana, so that the old European ambitions in the heart of the continent were at last removed, was due to a combination of factors, some of which can be credited to the wisdom of the Americans, and some simply to their good fortune. The British by 1799 were so preoccupied with restoring their rule in Ireland, and the French found the restoration of their rule in Haiti so hopeless, while both

[43] V. Stauffer, *New England and the Bavarian Illuminati* (New York, 1918.)

became so involved in the renewal of hostilities on the Continent, that they both relieved their pressure on the United States, which, being on the other side of the ocean, they could not in any case really quite treat as a "Poland." Adams reasserted Washington's policy of governmental neutrality, however unneutral the country itself might be. He decided early in 1799 to negotiate with France. Since he was doubtful of French intentions, his chief aim was to combat the war spirit of the Hamiltonians, which was running very high. Russian victories in Italy, mediated through the British Foreign Office, convinced Hamilton that the hour had come to strike. The High Federalists, like counter-revolutionaries in Europe, believed for several months in 1799 that the French Revolution was at last over, that the Bourbons would be restored, that Britain was about to triumph, and that the moment was therefore opportune for an Anglo-American liberation of Spanish America. Adams scoffed at the notion; the French Revolution, he said, would go on for years.

Against the loud protests of the most intransigent Federalists, Adams sent over a peace commission. French attacks on American shipping soon came to a halt. The High Federalists, robbed of their war and their dreams of glory, in which some of them had hoped to snuff out American "Jacobinism," disowned their own president as hardly better than a Jacobin himself. Adams, in making peace, probably expressed the wishes of the rank and file of his party, but he ruined himself in the eyes of its leaders, who, detesting him as a traitor, would not exert themselves for his re-election.

In the election of 1800 the Republicans, Jefferson and Burr, won 73 electoral votes against 65 for Adams and Pinckney. After the crisis produced by the tie between Jefferson and Burr, which had to be resolved by the House of Representatives, the transfer of power took place to what, until then, had been an organized opposition. Adams yielded his office rather ungracefully; Hamilton refrained from the coup d'état of which, in another environment, he might have been capable; and Jefferson proved to be entirely conciliatory, happily free of any spirit of retaliation. No doubt the special conditions in America, in contrast to Europe, made it possible to practice these irenic virtues. The fact that the central government had little power anyway, in contrast to Europe, likewise made its transfer to new hands less alarming.

The "Revolution of 1800" hardly lay in the acts of the new administration, which repealed the war taxes of 1798, reduced the army, allowed the Alien and Sedition Acts to expire, effected a few changes in the judiciary, and made it easier for small farmers to acquire land in the West, where Ohio became a state in 1803, and the whole of the former *Louisiane* soon stood open to settlement. The "revolution" consisted in the repudiation of pretensions to which the Federalist chieftains had become victims.

The Federalists had fallen from a precipice of their own making, as Elihu Palmer had somewhat floridly predicted in 1793. A party which had begun with constructive economic and fiscal ideas wound up ten years later crying for military demonstrations. A party that had at first stood for national unity in ten years brought the country to the brink of civil war. Men who claimed to be the best friends of the constitution, and to be consolidating the American Revolution, now disparaged the sovereignty of the people and denounced liberty and equality as delusions. Gentlemen hardly known for their own piety called republicanism atheistic. Those who happened to be manning the government identified themselves with government itself. The prominent Federalists, at least in their own estimation and their attitudes, became, under stress of the world ideological conflict, so much like the privileged classes of Europe that Americans turned against them in disgust. Plain farmers who had voted Federalist in 1796 voted Republican in 1800. Many who had never voted before now came to the polls. The Federalists never again elected a president or had a majority in Congress. That was the Revolution of 1800. It was, in its way, a considerable "revolution," for it gave answers to two of the great questions posed during the decade. It showed that the constitution was becoming authoritative, generally accepted above the strife of parties. And it showed the direction in which the new nation would develop.

In this vindication of democracy in America it is hard to disentangle what was indigenous and what was owing to influences from abroad. It is clear that the foreign influence was very great. The division into Federalists and Republicans was itself the consequence of war and revolution in Europe. Federalism suffered from too close an association with the European counter-revolution. Republicanism, or the ideology of American democracy, gained in range and drive from association with the European revolutionary forces. Never again could American democratic ideas be ethnocentric or backward-looking, dwelling on good old Saxon liberties in the far-off days of King Alfred, nor predominantly defensive, complaining of innovations and protecting simple farmer folk from the wiles of cities. Henceforth, there would be a belief, more than in 1776, that democracy was a matter of concern to the world as a whole, that it was a thing of the future, that while it was blocked in other countries the United States should be its refuge and its example, that Americans had a kind of duty meanwhile to develop it and to promote it, so that peoples of other nations, old and new, might someday move in the same direction. Both the successes and the reverses of the Revolution in Europe helped to fix this attitude in the American mind. There is something in the paradox propounded by a third party, the German historian Otto Vossler, who thought that the "American mission," like the Statue of Liberty, was the gift of the French Republic.[44]

[44] *Die amerikanischen Revolutionsideale in ihrem Verhältnis zu den europäischen: Untersucht an Thomas Jefferson* (Berlin, 1929); and see my summary of this work in *William and Mary Quarterly,* 3rd ser., XII (1955), 462-71.

CLIMAX AND DÉNOUEMENT

*And where shall we find this Dramatic Monarch
who shall have the courage to allow himself to be
installed by Regicides and Democrats, and to brave
the shame, the instability and the dangers of his
dignity? In one of the Courts of Europe? . . . Will
France herself furnish this borrowed Monarch from
the filth of the Revolution, to succeed to the Throne
of Charlemagne?*—MALLET DU PAN, London, 1799

*The French can no longer be governed except
by me. I am persuaded that no one but myself,
were it Louis XVIII or even Louis XIV, could
govern France at this time.*—BONAPARTE, Paris, 1800

*Do you call this a Republic? . . . I know of no
Republic in the world, except America, which is
the only country for such men as you and I. It is my
intention to get away from this place as soon as
possible. . . . I have done with Europe and its
slavish politics.*—THOMAS PAINE, Paris, 1802

CLIMAX AND DÉNOUEMENT

IN THE year 1799, with the War of the Second Coalition, there took place a gathering and confrontation of the forces separately described in preceding chapters—a confrontation in which the matter in question was the survival of the New Republican Order in Europe, as in 1793 it had been the survival of the Republic in France itself. Neither side can be said to have won. Or rather, the Counter-Revolution was certainly defeated, but the New Order prevailed only by being transmuted into something else, the authoritarian, innovating, dynamic, and yet compromising semi-monarchism or semi-republicanism represented by Bonaparte.

As the year began it was clear that revolutionary, democratic, radical, or republican movements (the appropriate word varying from place to place) had been extirpated in Poland and Eastern Europe, crushed in Ireland, and silenced in Great Britain, while even in the United States the continued existence of Republicanism as a political party was not yet certain. On the continent of Europe, on the face of things, or as seen on a map, with the installation of a republic at Naples in January, and the addition of the Grisons to the new Switzerland in March, the zone of the new-style republics now reached its furthest extension. The *République française,* including Belgium and the German left bank of the Rhine, adjoined the Batavian Republic on the north and the Helvetic on the east. Its troops were in occupation of Turin, from which the King of Sardinia had withdrawn to the island half of his kingdom. The French also occupied Tuscany with the renewal of war. The rest of the Italian mainland (except for Venetia) was laid out in republics to which the names Cisalpine, Ligurian, Roman, and Neapolitan had been given. A short sail from Brindisi lay the "Gallo-Greek departments," or Ionian Islands, now annexed to France and undergoing the usual changes. Farther overseas, in Egypt, though cut off by Nelson's victory, was the already fabulous hero of the Lodi bridge, who, with his soldiers and his corps of civilian administrators and scientific experts, was giving the Arab world its first injection of Western modernity.

On the surface, it all looked imposing, and it horrified the conservative in all countries. In fact, the situation in the New Republican Order was very precarious.

The Still Receding Mirage of the Moderates

The struggle went on because compromise was impossible, and compromise was impossible because so few people were ready to occupy a middle ground, and because so many, on both sides, feared that any advantage gained by their adversaries would be ruinous to themselves. "Moderation," as remarked in Chapter vii, could have two meanings, not necessarily related. It could mean a preference for a middle way, and it could mean a desire to avoid violence, in the sense either of war against other states, or forcible repression of dissent within, or abuse of constitutional law by the resort to coups d'état. Given the facts of war and revolution, it was a question whether even a middle way could preserve itself without violence.

The French Directory, early in 1799, was a moderate regime in many respects. It had little interest in revolutionary expansion. It had done less than it might have for the United Irish. It disapproved of the establishment of the Neapolitan Republic, and it recalled General Championnet, by whose action that republic had been created. By coups d'état at the Hague and Milan, during the preceding year, it had supported Batavian and Cisalpine moderates against democratic elements in those countries, and it had discouraged those Italians who aspired to Italian unification. Distrusting their own generals, fearing military dictatorship, and satisfied with the republican cordon that extended from the Texel to the Tiber, the civilian Directors of France— who in early 1799 were Reubell, LaRévellière, Barras, Merlin de Douai, and Treilhard, along with their foreign minister Talleyrand—would greatly prefer to remain at peace on the Continent. Peace was made impossible, however, as explained in Chapter xii, by the very existence of the sister-republics, among which the Batavian was intolerable to Great Britain, and the Cisalpine to Austria. The astounding decision to send an army to Egypt, made at the instigation of Bonaparte and Talleyrand against the judgment of Reubell, was designed to finish off the maritime war with England, but resulted instead in the renewal of hostilities on the Continent. The French invasion of Egypt brought Turkey and Russia into the war, while the French reverses in the East, and the consequent appearance of Nelson at Naples, tempted the King of Naples into attacking the Roman Republic, in what proved to be the opening move in the War of the Second Coalition. To this extent, the foreign policy of the Directory had proved a failure.

Domestically, the Directory sought to hold a middle position between restoration of the monarchy with features of the old regime on the one hand, and a revival of the popular revolutionism and aggressive equalitarianism of the Year II on the other. The course pursued had been zig-zag rather than middling. It had also been unconstitutional and immoderate in its methods. Twice the Directory had annulled the results of lawful elections. In 1797, by the Fructidor coup, it had probably prevented a restoration of the monarchy under Louis XVIII. In 1798, by the Floréal coup, it prevented the "Jacobins" from enjoying the majority in the two Councils to which the election of the Year VI entitled them.

This *floréalisation* of the democrats preceded by only a few days Bonaparte's departure for Egypt, and, like it, marked a point of no return for the First French Republic. That the Directory should have used violence against royalists and clericals was at least understandable; most of them were irreconcilable to the Republic on any terms. To do the same for the most eager republicans was more clearly fatal to republican institutions. The truth seems to be that the "official" republicans, those enjoying office or influence, from the Directory itself down through the several branches of government and locally into the departments—mostly men of some means, standing or prominence, born in the upper strata of the former Third Estate—seem already to have come to see themselves as a natural ruling class, and to regard any criticism of government, or avowed opposition, as improper. Jacobins themselves in the eyes of William Pitt and Alexander Hamilton, these official French Republicans, like English gentlefolk and American Federalists, denounced other republicans as Jacobins, anarchists, *énergumènes*, and *désorganisateurs*. The "Jacobins" of 1798 were not, however, the militant Jacobins of 1793. Still less were they the old sans-culottes, who had been crushed since 1795. Their very numbers, sufficient to win elections in many parts of the country by constitutional and open methods, suggest that they were more than a small minority of extremists. They were, in a sense, the predecessors of the Radical party of a century later, predominantly middle-class persons of various levels of income and occupation, men who had developed a strong political consciousness, were committed to the Revolution and the Enlightenment, detested priests, émigrés, aristocrats, and "the rich," wanted a more general participation in public affairs, and claimed a right to be elected to office without being selected by those already in power. Probably in France at this time, torn by war and revolution, no party development such as occurred in America could take place. If it could, the Jacobins of 1798 might have become a kind of French Jeffersonian party. In any case, the Directory itself killed the experiment.

The Directory, in short, with its middle way, had no friends. Among the French, the regime by its very nature repelled both the former privileged orders and the former sans-culottes and the working classes, and after Floréal it no longer appealed to the large body of democrats and republicans that the Revolution had brought into being. French generals in occupied areas, even those who were firmly republican, were disaffected toward the Directory as then constituted, if only because the Directors had tried to assert civilian authority over their operations, military, political, and financial. Generals who favored the more revolutionary elements in the sister-republics, like Championnet at Rome and Naples, and Brune at Milan and later in Holland, accused the Paris government of moderatism and sympathized with the French Jacobin opposition, by which in turn they were regarded as heroes. In the sister-republics the most pronounced patriots had turned anti-French. Still adhering to the aims of the Revolution, in Italy and elsewhere, they believed that the interests of their new republics were sacrificed to those of France, they objected to the coups d'état and to the looting and pillage, and they complained of the more orderly requisitions which, not unreasonably in the circumstances, were designed to support the French armies.

It was widely agreed, in France and in Europe, that the regime in France was about to undergo another abrupt mutation. The royal pretender, "Louis XVIII"—largely forgotten in his own country, and unrecognized even by the Powers as a king-in-exile—felt renewed hopes for his restoration. He had become more moderate than in 1797. Evolving toward the mood for which he would be known in 1814, he now conceded, in 1799, that it would be necessary to deal with men involved in the Revolution—that, as he wrote to his royal brother in July, "there can be services which oblige us to close our eyes on the greatest crimes."[1] But he made no public promises or offer of guar-

---

[1] Quoted by G. Walter, *Le comte de Provence* (Paris, 1950), 335.

antees, and he aroused no confidence or enthusiasm in France. Among the French émigrés his stock had risen. With the young Duke of Orleans (the future Louis-Philippe) severely compromised by the Revolution, and far off on a tour of America in any case, the idea of a restoration of monarchical authority pointed straight at the "legitimate" candidate. Even Malouet, who as a moderate and liberal émigré had thought in 1797 that no good Frenchman could rally to Louis XVIII, rallied to him two years later, with or without any constitution, charter, or prior statement of program or policy. It was necessary, said Malouet, simply to rely on the new king's discretion.[2] Even Mallet du Pan, who was "moderate" at least in believing a total counter-revolution to be impossible, believed that Louis XVIII offered the only solution. Yet he was still the Cassandra, darkly declaring to be essential what he knew to be out of the question. Thus he said, in 1799 (as in 1793), that the Coalition needed the firm central control of a kind of Committee of Public Safety. And as for the necessary new ruler of France, as he sarcastically asked, who would accept a throne from "regicides and democrats," with the shame and instability that would ensue?[3] The question of course was soon answered by Bonaparte.

The difficulties in an intermediate course were illustrated also by the Dutch. It may be remembered from Chapter vi that the émigré Stadholder, William V, relying wholly on the British, was opposed by his own son (the future King William I of the Netherlands), who resented the loss of Dutch shipping and colonies to the British, believed that the former Dutch regime had suffered from serious weaknesses, and advised some kind of concession to the new forces in the Batavian Republic. There were men high up in that republic who secretly favored a moderate Orange restoration, preferably under the ex-stadholder's son. The Hereditary Prince had a painful scene with two Orangist émigrés at a meeting at Yarmouth in England in March 1800. British policy at this time, as in 1787, required an almost unconditional restoration of William V and the old Union of Utrecht. The Hereditary Prince was told by his two friends that he must choose between England and France—that the English were his benefactors, and the French robbers and rebels. The prince, losing his temper, shocked his companions by shouting that the British had long wanted a "dictature" over Holland and that his own ancestor, William the Silent, had after all been a rebel. "It was hard," said this future King

---

[2] *Mémoires de Malouet*, 2 vols. (Paris, 1874), II, 529-30.
[3] For this and other quotations used at the head of this chapter see Appendix.

of the Netherlands, "that a man could not declare his own opinion, if it went against the [British] ministers, without being declared a Jacobin."

His friends immediately reported this distressing episode to Lord Grenville.[4]

The Conservative Counter-Offensive of 1799

Never between Valmy and Waterloo did the Counter-Revolution come so near to success as in 1799—as may be seen, for example, in the fact that the Russian armies, operating in Italy, Switzerland, and Holland, had never until that time, and have never since, been seen so far westward in Europe in conditions of actual combat. Russian power, absent from the First Coalition, was essential to the Second. Subsidized by the wealth of England, at a rate of £850,000 for 45,000 men, the Russian troops were greeted in conservative quarters as the hope of civilization, to effect the "deliverance of Europe," as Pitt said in the House of Commons.[5] Without the Russians, said Mallet du Pan (who was now drawing £100 a month from the British government), there would be an "end to Christianity, Royalty, Property, Liberty and the whole structure of society" in central Europe.[6] And Cardinal Maury, writing at length and repeatedly to Louis XVIII from the supposed privacy of the conclave of Venice, during the long stalemate of the papal election, reported that this august Christian assemblage hoped devoutly for a prolongation of the war and an invasion of France by the Russians.[7]

It was the British who took the lead in bringing together the Second Coalition, and in setting its aims. In the years 1799 and 1800 they granted subsidies of almost £3,500,000 to Russia and various German states. The Prussian king remained obstinately neutral, while the Spanish were still more afraid of England than of France. Russia came into the war by the decision of the new Tsar Paul, who was disturbed by the continuing unrest in Russian Poland, the agitation of Polish émigrés in the French service, and conspiracies of Poles and others in the Moldavian border zone, as well as by the French invasion of Egypt; and who also, though not a Catholic, had been

---

[4] H. T. Colenbrander, *Gedenkstukken der algemeene geschiedenis van Nederland* (The Hague, 1907), IV, 1102-05.

[5] *Parliamentary History*, XXXIV, 1044.

[6] *British Mercury*, 5 vols. (London, 1799-1800), II, 207.

[7] *Correspondance diplomatique et mémoires inédits du Cardinal Maury*, 2 vols. (Lille, 1891), I, 253, 256, 268, 275, 318, 347.

elected grand-master of their order by the Knights of Malta, in the hope that by his influence they might get back their island from the French. It was the Austrians who gave the British the most concern, for the Hapsburg government lacked enthusiasm for having its territories crossed by the Russian army, nor, intent on getting the French out of Italy, did it much care who or what kind of people governed in Paris. The British were haunted by the thought in 1799 (as in 1813) that Austria and France might make a separate peace, by which Austria would recognize the French government and its possessions in return for the destruction of the Italian republics and a hegemony of Austria in the peninsula.

Pitt was now convinced, after years of experience, that no lasting peace could be made with the French Republic. For this view there was indeed some reason, for it was the peculiarity of the Directory that it could not control its own generals, that revolutions sprang up, as at Naples, which the Directory itself did not desire; that, as Carlo Zaghi has said, the Revolution had become a thing quite independent of the French government, which, seldom actually pressing for revolutions in other countries, could not repudiate them once they occurred, without playing into the hands of its own most implacable enemies.[8]

To restore the Bourbon monarchy in France was therefore one of the British aims in the war of 1799. For the rest of the revolutionized region the formula was much the same. Externally, there might be changes: Belgium and Holland might be joined under the House of Orange; and the Dutch possessions in Cochin, Ceylon, and South Africa were to remain British. Internally, the several old regimes in these countries were to be revived. For Switzerland, the British offered £30,000 a month to raise a force of Swiss against the Helvetic Republic, and recommended the "re-establishment of the ancient order of things in that country" as demanded by N. F. von Steiger, the former *schultheiss* of Bern and leader of the most intransigent of the Swiss émigrés.[9] For Belgium, the British considered themselves the guarantors of the old provincial constitutions, violated not only by the Belgian and the French Revolutions, but by "the Emperor Joseph, the first Jacobin of his time."[10] For the Dutch, Lord Grenville, speak-

<hr/>

[8] See Chapter XII above and C. Zaghi, *Bonaparte e il Direttorio dopo Campoformio* (Naples, 1956), 69, 183-84.

[9] See the documents published in the appendix to F. Burckhardt, *Die schweizerische Emigration, 1798-1801* (Basel, 1908), 432-35.

[10] Great Britain: Historical MSS Commission, *Report on the Manuscripts of J. B. Fortescue Preserved at Dropmore*, 10 vols. (London, 1892-1927), V, 199.

ing as British foreign secretary, explicitly rejected the proposals of the Dutch moderates. He agreed that nothing quite like the British constitution would work in Holland, since the Dutch had no "great body of landed proprietors," of the kind that, in Britain and Ireland, filled the Parliament and the "magistracy of the country." He insisted that the Dutch abandon the kind of unity introduced by the Batavian Republic, and replace it with a degree of provincial sovereignty as under the Union of Utrecht. Explaining what he meant, Grenville allowed himself a rare flight of ideological generalization, which may stand as a programmatic statement for the counter-offensive of 1799.[11]

"The reasons," said Grenville, "which have induced H.M. to incline towards a different arrangement [from that proposed by Dutch and Batavian moderates] . . . are founded principally in an opinion that such is probably the wish of the best and soundest part of the people of the United Provinces, and also in a desire to avoid as much as possible the appearance of innovations proceeding on general and abstract principles of equality, in opposition to institutions grounded on ancient usages and conformable to the old and established distinctions and classes of that people." He might have said the same of Belgium and Switzerland, Italy and France.

The plan for the overthrow of revolutionary republicanism was essentially military, but involved also the expectation that native elements would rise against their republican governments as soon as the armies of the Coalition appeared. There was in fact, throughout the New Republican Order, a good deal of peasant discontent and rebelliousness in 1798 and 1799. Rural unrest persisted in western France since the days of the Vendéan disturbance, and rural insurrection was chronic in Belgium. In Switzerland the small rural "primitive" cantons were held in the Helvetic Republic by force. In Italy the peasants had never favored the new movements, and by February and March of 1799 the whole of southern Italy was in a state of revolt. We have seen how Cardinal Ruffo gathered a host of Neapolitan peasants by the promise of reforms. It has been seen repeatedly, in the preceding pages, how in Europe, in contrast to America, revolutionary republicanism was a movement of townspeople, and conservative attitudes largely agrarian in their origin. Mass rural discontent throughout the New Republican Order offered a force, a social reality already in existence, to which leaders of the Counter-Revolution might have appealed to heighten their own strength.

[11] Colenbrander, *Gedenkstukken*, III, 410-12.

The notable fact, however, remarked upon by Jacques Godechot, was the lack of any contact between conservative doctrine, as expressed by Burke, Mallet du Pan, Joseph de Maistre, and others, and the realities of anti-Revolutionary sentiment and insurrectionism among the common people.[12] Conservative ideology, if "agrarian," was agrarian in that it looked with suspicion on cities, and expressed a view of life in which large landownership, along with manorial or seigneurial institutions, was very important. It was not agrarian in reflecting the outlook of rural laborers or small farmers. Peasants often had ideas of their own for which the philosophy of conservatism made no more allowance than did democratic republicanism. Peasants complained of poverty, under-employment, lack of land, unfair taxes, unjust law courts, and much else. To recruit and hold mass rural support against the New Order it would have been necessary, as Ruffo attempted to do in Naples, to offer some positive expectations about the future. It was not enough to praise ancient ways, or inveigh against city people and abstract ideas, or raise alarms about the state of the Christian religion. But to deal adequately with real agrarian grievances would have been to propose another kind of revolution, and this was what the conservative ideology, and the international conservative leadership, could not do. In the great anti-republican campaign of 1799 the one actual source of popular anti-republicanism was not used.

The Coalition, therefore, and most notably the British government, in its plans for fomenting and using discontents within France and its sister-republics, looked less to the desires of the rural masses than to those of the former aristocracies and privileged classes. Royalists in France, and old regents or patricians or other disaffected persons in the Helvetic and Batavian Republics, worked busily and secretly with their respective émigrés and with various British agents, such as the mysterious Colonel Crauford and the acknowledged envoy, William Wickham. In France the royalist "agency" in Paris and the secret "philanthropic institutes" in the provinces again became active, as before Fructidor. In southern France the strength of "Jacobinism" at Toulouse made the royalist reaction in the surrounding area all the more intense. Almost ten thousand insurgents besieged Toulouse in August 1799; the republicans of the city with difficulty drove them away. The plan was for such revolts to coincide with one another, and with the invasion of France by the Coalition. But as underground and

---

[12] J. Godechot, *La Contre-révolution* (Paris, 1961), 407. See pp. 347-90 for *le grand assaut contre-révolutionnaire* throughout Europe in 1799.

conspiratorial movements they could not be coordinated or synchronized. Occurring one by one, they were suppressed in turn; and, as it happened, the Second Coalition never entered France at all.

The military plan envisaged a far-flung deployment. "From the Zuyder Zee to the Tiber," said Mallet du Pan, "Europe is now covered with armies, almost contiguous, embracing one of the most extensive circles ever heard of in the history of wars ancient or modern."[13] Indeed, the Coalition reached beyond the Tiber, for Nelson reigned at Naples, the Russians soon occupied the Ionian Islands, hoping to do the same at Malta; a force of British and Turks obliged Bonaparte to retreat from Acre in Palestine, and in India Mornington disposed of Tipu, subjugated his kingdom, and put an end to French Jacobinism in that country.

On the European continent the armies were in three parts. One Russian force, under Marshal Suvorov, along with the Austrians, and with Turkish assistance, operated in Italy. Another Austro-Russian force had Switzerland for its immediate object. An Anglo-Russian expedition was preparing to land in Holland. The three were then to converge upon France, with the main blow delivered by the Austro-Russians from Switzerland, who were to enter by way of Lyon to the acclaim of the royalists.

It was in Italy that the conservative counter-offensive enjoyed its greatest successes. Suvorov began to defeat the French, with their Cisalpine and Polish auxiliaries, in the Po valley in April. Except at Genoa, all the Italian republics fell. When Pius VI died in France, to which he had been removed at the outbreak of the war, the victories of the Coalition made it possible for the cardinals to meet for the election of a new pope. This fact alone was significant, since the most determined free-thinking and Voltairean republicans had hoped that with the Roman Republic the papacy itself might become extinct. The collapse of the republic at Rome left the city in a state of confusion, so that the cardinals met for their conclave at Venice under the protection of Austria.

They assembled in the belief that the Revolution was at last about to expire. Cardinal Rohan, of Diamond Necklace fame, the *ci-devant* Bishop of Strasbourg, once the richest prelate in France, with over 400,000 livres a year of church revenues, was so confident of his imminent restoration that he refused to attend the conclave at all. He hovered about south Germany, ready to proclaim himself in his diocese

[13] *British Mercury*, IV, 117.

upon arrival of the Austro-Russian armies. The conclave proved to be a long one, since the Austrian party among the cardinals could not elect their candidate, it being known that Austria wished to annex portions of the Papal States. After several months, in March 1800, when it seemed that the new regime in France would be more tolerant of Catholicism, and in opposition to the ambitions of Austria, the Spanish government used its influence to support those cardinals who were least uncompromising toward the Revolution. The result was the election of Cardinal Chiaramonti, the Bishop of Imola, who had in his way welcomed democracy and accepted the Cisalpine Republic in 1797, and who, as Pius VII, soon negotiated a concordat with the French Republic.

Meanwhile, in 1799, the anti-republican forces were triumphant. At Naples 119 republicans, including fifteen clerics, were put to death; and the restored monarchs gave classic expression to the most extreme sentiments of counter-revolution, when Queen Maria Carolina told Nelson to treat Naples "like a rebel Irish town," and King Ferdinand ordered no mercy for "these rebels against God and Me." Reactionary insurrectionism using religious slogans spread from south to north. What was called San Fedism in Naples was called the Viva Maria in Tuscany, and a good deal of violence broke out against persons not sufficiently Christian. Enraged country people invaded the town of Siena, sacked its ghetto, killed over a dozen Jews, and burned three of them alive along with the tree of liberty in the *piazza*. Jews were also brutally manhandled at Ancona, in the Roman Republic, after its surrender by the French. Further north, with the collapse of the Cisalpine Republic, the *triennio* was followed by the *tredici mesi*, or thirteen months, known also as the Austro-Russian Reaction.[14]

What happened in the now defunct Cisalpine Republic is worth amplification, since it suggests the kind of thing that might have happened in France and elsewhere if the Coalition had won the war. At first, in April 1799, the Austro-Russians were welcomed, especially in the countryside. Even at Milan, like the French in 1796, they met with a friendly reception, signalized by public festivals and poems written for the occasion. This good feeling did not last long.

---

[14] For the phrases quoted from the King and Queen of Naples see p. 388 above. For confirmation of the incidents at Siena my former student, Mr. R. B. Litchfield, has made a study in the libraries of Florence; he concludes that at least three Jews were actually burned, but that the archbishop's remark, *furor populi, furor Dei*, was the embellishment of an anti-clerical writer about 1880. For Ancona see M. Mangourit, *Défense d'Ancone et des départements romains . . . aux années VII et VIII*, 2 vols. (Paris, 1802), I, 207.

The military victory was due mainly to the Russians, but the Austrians assumed the dominant role in the occupation. It was only in certain ways, chiefly internal, that the Austrians wished to restore the old order. Having obtained Venetia from Bonaparte in 1797, they now wished not merely to regain the old Milanese but to expand it, and they therefore preferred the enlarged boundaries of the Cisalpine Republic, which gave them a foothold in the papal territories across the Po. In Piedmont, for which they had ideas of their own, they forbade the King of Sardinia to return. In the Cisalpine they continued to collect taxes as levied by the late *intruso governo democratico*; and (being still "Josephist" at least in this respect) they did not restore to the Church the property confiscated by the Republic, though they took it away from persons who had begun to buy it. In other ways the work of the revolution was supposedly undone. "All laws," according to a proclamation of the Emperor Francis, "published in the time of anarchy of the so-called republic are totally abrogated." *Austriacanti* replaced Cisalpines in office. Eight hundred *giacobini* were deported to Austria, other hundreds having fled to France. The school for teaching the German language at Milan was reopened. Other schools and universities were closed, notably the University of Pavia; Jansenists were hunted out; Jews and other non-Catholics lost their recently gained civil rights. Observance of religious holidays was made compulsory. A strong censorship was imposed on the press, and the Archbishop of Milan issued a pastoral warning against bad books, "the fruits of unrestrained liberty," which sometimes taught that hell was an invention of priests, and in any case conveyed "the malignity of the black conspiracy against the Altar and the Throne." Book-burnings took place in public squares. For more edifying reading, Mallet du Pan's *British Mercury* appeared in Italian. Hunting rights, seigneurial courts, and *fidecommessi* were restored; but even the Lombard nobles disputed with men sent down from Vienna. Meanwhile the Austrian and Russian armies, as formerly the French, lived by requisition upon the country, and although the Austrians within a few months obtained the removal of Suvorov and his Russians to Switzerland, the burden of military occupation remained heavy, and the complaints against arbitrary pillage and looting remained at least as numerous as under the French. Moderates, and even former *austriacanti*, soon turned against Austria. The economist Melchior Gioia, a year or two later, wrote a book to show that, for agriculture, commerce, and taxation, not to mention ordinary freedom from censorship and the police, the Austro-Russian "liberation" had been incomparably worse than the French. The feeling grew that what northern Italy really needed was independence, but when the French returned in 1800 there were many Italians who, in the circumstances, were delighted to see the restoration of the Cisalpine Republic.[15]

In May 1799, soon after the Austro-Russian victory in Italy, the Austrian commander at Milan, who somewhat incongruously was the Count of Hohenzollern, expecting to make an early entrance into France, issued a manifesto. It was addressed to the soldiers in the French army, and it told them that their Directory were a pack of despots, hated in France itself, who had enslaved Italy for their own advantage. It urged them not to resist their true friends, and pointed to the vast array of armed forces poised "from the Tiber to the Rhine"—Austrian, Russian, British, Turkish, aided by the outraged victims of the countries oppressed by France. "But," the Count of Hohenzollern continued, still addressing himself to the French (for something had been learned since the Brunswick Manifesto seven years before), "it is not a war of the Sovereigns who govern those mighty States. It is a war of Peoples, who no longer tremble before your armies and who have ceased to worship your principles."[16]

It remained to be seen whether the peoples would rise in answer to such a call.

The Revolutionary Re-arousal and Victory

The débacle in Italy precipitated a crisis in France. In part the trouble was parliamentary and constitutional. In mid-April the voters met in their assemblies for the elections of the Year VII, by which a third of the two legislative councils was to be renewed. News of Suvorov's victories was just coming in. The republics had collapsed at Naples, Rome, and Milan. In April, also, near Rastadt, two French delegates to the diplomatic conference at that city were waylayed and murdered. Invasion of France was expected, with which royalist conspirators and insurgents were known to be in collusion. Zealous republicans threw the blame for these conditions on the Directory, which they accused not only of inefficiency but of venality, immorality, cyni-

---

[15] *Collezione di proclami, avisi . . . pubbicati dal giorno 28 aprile 1799 in avanti, epoca memorabile del fausto ingresso fatto in Milano dalla Vittoriosa Armata di sua Maesta l'Imperatore Franceso II*, 5 vols. (Milan, 1799-1800), I, 247; IV, 148-53; V, 87. See also M. Roberti, *Milano capitale napoleonica: la formazione di uno stato moderno*, 3 vols. (Milan, 1946-1947), I, 54-56, 234-36. For Gioia's work see p. 299 above.
[16] *Collezione*, I, 128. (May 26, 1799.)

cism, and corruption, exaggerating as much as the royalists the short-comings of a regime that no one loved. In the elections the candidates sponsored by the Directory did very poorly. The independent candidates, democrats and "Jacobins," won most of the seats, so that the incoming third, when added to the *jacobins non-floréalisés*, or democrats in the two councils who had survived the purge of 1798, produced almost a democratic majority in the legislative branch of the government, composed of the Five Hundred and the Elders. Since even many moderates had long objected to the way in which the Directory had abused the constitutional equality of the Legislative Body, the road was open for a legislative retaliation against the executive.

The military crisis made the Republic more dependent than ever on the army. The Directory, however, had alienated the generals. It had consented to send Bonaparte to Egypt in part to get him off the political stage. It was about to try Championnet for insubordination. Bernadotte, Brune, Masséna, and Joubert had all shown their lack of respect, in one way or another, for civilian superiors in Paris and for civilian commissioners in the field. They now added their contribution to the discrediting of the Directory, declaring that the civilians sent to Italy and other occupied areas in the past years were guilty of dishonesty, pillaging, exploitation, and fortune-hunting, the very offenses of which most of the generals were guilty themselves, and which the Directory had tried to regularize or prevent. The democrats in the two councils, in their dislike of the Directory, gladly believed the indictment that the military men drew up.[17]

A coalition of democrats and generals rapidly formed. In May, as provided by law, the five Directors drew lots to see which of them should retire; the lot fell to Reubell, who for almost four years had strongly insisted on civilian control over the military. To replace Reubell the Council of Five Hundred nominated a firmly republican general, Lefebvre; but the Council of Elders still resisted the drift toward military solutions; and the two councils agreed on electing Sieyès to Reubell's place. Sieyès, then minister to Prussia, had been known since 1789 as a constitutional expert, and was to take the lead in bringing in Bonaparte and a new constitution a few months later. No one, probably not even himself, knew in May what course he might adopt for the internal reorganization of France; but he had at times thought

---

[17] J. Godechot, *Les commissaires aux armées sous le Directoire: contribution à l'étude des rapports entre les pouvoirs civils et militaires*, 2 vols. (Paris, 1938), II, 369-91.

the Directory too moderate in its attitude to revolutionaries in Italy and Poland, and to that extent was acceptable to the more vehement democrats and the generals who favored revolutionary activity abroad.

Not content with the constitutional replacement of Reubell by Sieyès, the democratic-military coalition, in retaliation for Floréal, and in a mood of urgency in the face of invasion, arbitrarily reorganized the rest of the executive also. Though not wholly illegal, this operation came to be known as the coup d'état of Prairial of the Year VII. The election of Treilhard as Director a year before was annulled on a technicality. Threats of investigation and outlawry induced Merlin de Douai and LaRévellière to resign. The one Director who was unquestionably corrupt was now the only one left, Barras, who, not to mention the scandal of his private life, was intriguing with the democrats, the royalists, and the British at the same time. In place of Treilhard, Merlin, and LaRévellière, the Five Hundred proposed a list wholly composed of generals and admirals, but the Elders again demurred; and three mild, ineffectual, and honest men were in fact chosen—Ducos, Gohier, and Moulins. As for the generals, Bernadotte became war minister, Joubert the military commandant in Paris, Championnet received the newly reactivated *Armée des Alpes*, and Masséna and Brune were confirmed in their commands in Switzerland and Holland.

What had happened, in a way, and continued to happen throughout the summer of 1799, was a kind of revival and breakthrough, against the Directory, of the popular and the international revolutionism described in Chapter II above. Yet the difference from 1792 or 1794 was very great. There was no sans-culottisme, no truly popular revolutionism in the streets. International revolutionism was now represented, not by foreign exiles congregated in Paris, but by French army commanders who had worked with native democrats in the sister-republics. French democrats found these generals ideologically sympathetic, and necessary as allies against both the Directory and the Coalition. The French neo-Jacobins of 1799, who represented a kind of popular movement at least in opposing the Republican oligarchy, were sensitive also to revolution and counter-revolution in other countries. They had been aroused by the fall of the Cisalpine Republic, and the fate of Poland was not far from their minds. In Puy-de-Dôme, for example, when the departmental officials gave a patriotic address to the new auxiliary battalions being raised for the war, they pointed to the contrasting precedents of Poland and the United States. "Let this contrast awaken your courage! If victors, we shall have the good fortune of the United Americans; if vanquished, the fate of Poland will be ours."[18]

The "foreign" or "international" revolutionaries themselves, that is those Italian, Swiss, and Dutch who most warmly upheld the new-style republics in their own countries, shared the dislike of French neo-Jacobins and generals for the French Directory as it was constituted before Prairial, and had indeed become skeptical of France itself. In Italy the Milanese La Hoz, an officer in the Cisalpine army, working through a secret society called the *Raggi*, or "rays" (the first secret society of the Risorgimento), fought for republicanism and independence in north Italy, and became so anti-French that for a time he aided the Austrians. In Switzerland, where the Helvetic Republic faced the same threat of invasion and dissolution as the French and the Cisalpine, the more militant party overcame the moderates in June 1799, when La Harpe drove Ochs out of the Helvetic Directory. La Harpe, more "Jacobin" than Ochs, was also more hostile to the French. In Holland, where it was known or suspected that moderates in the Batavian Directory were in touch with Dutch émigrés, the democratic groups sought to undermine the moderates and looked for support from the sympathetic General Brune. Here also a neo-Jacobin movement might have occurred had not the coup d'état of Brumaire, in Paris in November, changed the whole situation.

In France the two councils, having subordinated the Executive Directory to themselves, began to take on the attributes of a Convention, that is of a body possessing unlimited public powers, and in particular of the Convention of 1793, which had used drastic measures to cope with a supreme emergency.

The mood was as in 1793, yet noticeably different. Despite all appearances, a spirit of law-abidingness and constitutional routine had developed. The cry of *la patrie en danger* was again heard, but it was not officially proclaimed. There were demands for the death of the ex-Directors, but they were not acted upon. All annual classes of conscripts were called up, as in the *levée en masse* of 1793; but they were called up in more methodical fashion, under the Conscription Act of 1798. A forced loan of a hundred million francs was levied upon the rich; what came out, in practice, was a progressive income tax developed in orderly fashion in the legislation of 19 Thermidor of the

---

[18] G. Bonnefoy, ed., *Histoire de l'administration civile dans la province d'Auvergne et le département du Puy-de-Dôme* (Paris, 1900), II, 306, as cited by my former student, Mr. Isser Woloch, who in a study of the "Jacobin revival" of 1799 found references to Poland fairly frequent.

Year VII. It was, to be sure, incomparably more "progressive" than Pitt's income tax of the same year. Where the very richest persons in England paid only ten per cent by the law of 1799, those in France might lose as much as three-quarters of their annual revenue. Most ominously recalling the Terror was the Law of Hostages of July. It was enacted to deal with counter-revolutionary conspiracy, insurrection and collusion with enemy powers, of the kind which, as already mentioned, threatened Toulouse in August. By this legislation, in any region declared by its local authorities to be troubled, the relatives of émigrés, ex-nobles, and "brigands" were to be put under arrest. For each patriot killed by political violence, four "hostages" would be deported. For each act of pillage, the hostages would raise a sum to indemnify the victim. The emergency passed before much enforcement of this law began.

A sign also of revived revolutionary enthusiasm, outside the ranks of government itself, was the reopening of political clubs, on the model of the true Jacobins of five years before, in Paris and other cities through the country. The Constitution of the Year III, like George Washington, frowned upon "self-created" societies. It put the formation and operation of political clubs under close restriction. The Pantheon Club had been closed in 1796, and the constitutional circles of 1798 had found it hard to develop beyond the status of local discussion groups. In the summer of 1799, facing much the same situation as in 1792, upholders of the new order again rushed to its defense. On July 6 a group met in Paris that called itself the Reunion of the Friends of Liberty and Equality—the very name that the Jacobins had officially adopted in 1792. Several of its members had played prominent roles during the Year II; one, Prieur of the Marne, had been a member of the great Committee of Public Safety. Speakers called for a return of that exalted spirit that had stopped the First Coalition; they denounced suspects, conspirators, profiteers, royalists, and aristocrats; they praised various figures of the past, even the "virtuous martyr" Babeuf; and they demanded that the Republic save itself by using the money of the rich and the enthusiasm of the common man. The Paris club voted to restore "the democratic spirit" in government, to establish "equal and common education," to provide work for the needy, and property for veterans who had risked themselves in defense of the country. The notable point, however, is that this revived Jacobin club proved very ephemeral. The Directory itself, which now reflected the wishes of the democratized councils, closed the club down on August 13. It had lasted only thirty-eight days.

Enough happened in the summer of 1799 to raise a specter of social revolution, "agrarian law," division of property, and confiscatory taxation of the rich. All this made it easier for Bonaparte a few months later to present himself not only as the defender of the New Order against the Coalition and the Bourbons, but as the savior of society itself from dissolution and anarchy. Yet it seems clear, on balance, that the neo-Jacobinism of 1799 was not an actual renewal of real revolution, so much as the excited reaction of an abortive democracy, half-formed and ill-formed by four troubled years of very imperfect constitutional government, to a threat posed by internal subversion and foreign invasion, on the part of men and powers whose intention to destroy "democratic" institutions was unconcealed. It is very doubtful that the neo-Jacobin or quasi-democratized regime in France in 1799 was a viable government. But its non-viability was due as much to the strength of its enemies as to its own weaknesses.

On the other hand, the enemy also had his weaknesses, and if the New Order survived in France in 1799 (somewhat transmuted) it did so in part, as in 1793, because its enemies could not agree, and shared no true common purpose against it. Each of the Coalition powers had its own interests. The British could presumably have assembled more strength against France on the Continent, had they been less involved in India and in Ireland, and if their overseas and commercial ambitions had not made both the Dutch and the Spanish fearful for their own colonial empires. They might have produced wider fissures in the Continental republics if they had had more appeal for the moderates in those countries, if they had not in 1799, as at Quiberon and Vendémiaire in 1795, become identified with the ultra-conservatism of intransigent émigrés. In 1799 the Austrians and Russians could agree neither with each other nor with the British, whom they regarded with the air of a lord toward his banker as hardly more than a source of funds to finance their armies. The Russians, after Suvorov's conquests in Italy, were annoyed that the Austrians so soon maneuvered to get them out.

North of the Alps, as in Italy, the Austrian designs were more territorial than ideological. At the critical moment in the summer of 1799, as the Austro-Russian campaign was about to open in Switzerland, the Vienna government, instead of carrying through with this main blow which was to lead to a direct invasion of central France, ordered its army to move in the direction of Mainz, so that Austrian influence might prevail in a future disposition of the Rhineland, Liége, and the former Austrian Netherlands. The Russians were left to carry on the Swiss campaign alone. For this purpose Suvorov moved up from Italy to join Korsakov, taking his army through the St. Gotthard Pass in a memorable operation, and very much irritated at the Austrian betrayal of Russia in both Italy and central Europe. The Austrians, said Lord Grenville, cared nothing about overthrowing the government in France, "the real root and origin of its wickedness." Pitt called Austrian policy "atrocious and perhaps fatal."[19]

It was among the crags of Switzerland and in the watery lowlands of north Holland that the Second Coalition came to grief. In Switzerland, after the main Austrian force had departed, the Russian general Korsakov faced the French Masséna, whose French army was supported by a few thousand Swiss in the new demi-brigades of the Helvetic Republic. The expected rising of Swiss against the French never materialized. The Swiss did not find the "Cossacks" congenial. To William Wickham, who had said that Switzerland could not be neutral, that it must be dominated and made over either by France or by the Coalition, the rough indiscipline of the Russian soldiers was a cause of infinite dismay, since it made the Swiss more tolerant of the French. The Russians, said Wickham of these indispensable allies, were "shag all over," and he quoted Voltaire: *ôtez seulement l'habit et vous sentirez le poil.*[20] Masséna defeated Korsakov in a three-day battle, on September 25-27, called the Second Battle of Zurich. Suvorov, struggling through the passes from Italy, arrived too late, since without Korsakov he was too weak to challenge Masséna alone. The great Russian commander, the hero of Odessa, the counter-revolutionary by whose orders the dummies used in bayonet practice were called "French republicans," and who was remembered in Poland as the butcher of Praga, was obliged to retire with his Russian host into the Hapsburg dominions. Far away in America, on the northernmost frontier of New York State, the settlers learned of this news with such pleasure that they named one of their new towns Massena.

Meanwhile, late in August, in an unopposed amphibious operation, a combined force of British and Russians, under the Duke of York,

---

[19] *Dropmore Papers*, v, 147, 404.
[20] *Ibid.*, 485: "just remove the clothing and you will feel the hair." See also, on the Russians in Holland and Switzerland, *ibid.*, 449, 455-56; but on October 24, 1799, Dundas was still telling Pitt that "a Russian army as large as can be got, and as large as you can afford to pay, is an essential ingredient to every purpose," *ibid.*, 498.

landed on the tongue of land between the North Sea and the Zuyder Zee. Against them, on a line across the middle of the peninsula, stood a force of French, with several thousand Dutch troops under General Daendels, all commanded by the French General Brune. The strategy of the invaders depended on a rising of the Dutch against the Batavian Republic. The Orangist émigrés, though never numerous, had excellent connections with the British government and royal family, so that their accounts of Dutch restlessness under French tyranny had been well received in England; Grenville had thought, on July 30, that the country "unanimously" favored the British, as he imagined that it had done in 1787. It is true that Henry Dundas was more skeptical, reminding his colleague of the false hopes once put in the American Loyalists.[21] In any case, no rising took place in the Batavian Republic. The Russians were no more welcome to the Dutch than to the Swiss, especially since, far more poorly supplied than the British, they did a great deal of pillaging in the small territory that they occupied. The country remained calm. A party of Orangist émigrés, entering from the German side, was easily put to flight by the National Guard of Arnhem. The main invasion force, floundering in useless maneuvers among the polders, hemmed in by Brune and Daendels, waited for weeks for news of an insurrection that never came. Sir Ralph Abercrombie, the chief actual commander under the Duke of York, suffered a gradual disillusionment. Two weeks after the landing, while still hopeful, he remarked that "the Prince [of Orange] has been deceived in thinking he had more friends than enemies in this country." The truth dawned on him a month later, just before the final collapse: "The grounds on which this great undertaking were founded have failed. We have found no cooperation in the country."[22] On October 10 Brune, thinking it best to get the invaders off the Continent while preserving his own forces intact for employment elsewhere, signed the Convention of Alkmaar with the Duke of York. The Anglo-Russians returned to their ships, and departed. They had captured some of what remained of the Dutch navy; that was all.

The Tsar Paul, much displeased at the fortunes of his armies in Western Europe, where they had been so unsuccessful against the enemy and so little appreciated by their friends, recalled Suvorov and refused to take any further part in the war. Except in Italy, it was clear by October that the conservative counter-offensive had been

---

[21] *Ibid.*, 208, 215.   [22] *Ibid.*, 387; Colenbrander, *Gedenkstukken*, III, 429.

repulsed by the New Republican Order, in a kind of ideological show-down that was evident in the social origins of the leading antagonists. Brune, a provincial lawyer's son who had once been a printer's apprentice, had forced the brother of the King of England to sign a humiliating agreement and beat an ignominious retreat. Masséna, who had begun life as a cabin boy at sea, and then been an army sergeant, with further promotion impossible under the conditions of aristocratic resurgence in the 1780's, had discomfited a Russian nobleman, the "Prince of Italy," Marshal Suvorov, who himself was the son of a general and senator of the Tsarist Empire. The facts did not escape contemporaries. Mallet du Pan commented on the failure of "oppressed nations" to show sympathy for the Allies. Country people, he thought, had not behaved too badly. But people in the towns "have everywhere but too plainly discovered the degeneracy to which they were sunk by luxury, selfishness and the love of pleasure."[23] Those who could not defeat the bourgeoisie could at least insult it.

With the battle of Zurich in September, and the Convention of Alkmaar in October, the threat of an invasion of France was alleviated, and the neo-Jacobin agitation began to subside. Brune and Masséna, the real victors of the moment, had no political following, at least outside the ranks of militant democrats, and no political ambitions. On October 9 Bonaparte stepped ashore at Fréjus. A Republic which had in any case become dependent on generals, and in which the democrats most especially wished to have army commanders in office, now succumbed to the fascination of the youthful general who since the bridge of Lodi had outshone them all. A month of rapid and secret machinations, involving Sieyès, Bonaparte, and his brother Lucien and others, and with strong resistance from a good many democrats, who had never forgotten the betrayal of Venice, and preferred a general with a more unswervingly republican record, eventuated in the final coup d'état under the Directory, that of 18 Brumaire of the Year VIII—or November 9, 1799—by which the Republic underwent its expected mutation, and emerged as the Consulate. Its disillusioned philosophy was expressed by the new First Consul: "The French can no longer be governed except by me."

Two Men on Horseback

In the end we retreat into symbolism. Revolutions, agitations, social movements, and glacially slow readjustments in a democratic direc-

---

[23] *British Mercury*, III, 332; see also 341-43.

tion were to go on for a long time, but a historical period came to a close with the century itself, and the Age of the Democratic Revolution may be thought of as ending in a final scene of two men on horseback.

On the first day of the new century, January 1, 1801, the vice-president of the United States, Thomas Jefferson, soon to be president, left the boarding-house in which he resided with a few colleagues among vacant lots and half-finished buildings, on an unpaved and untidy thoroughfare known as C Street, in the new Federal City. The vice-president was hardly an inexperienced provincial, for he had known the court of Versailles well enough in former days, and been present in Paris at the time of the fall of the Bastille; but he accepted the peculiarities of life in America. Going down from C Street, he took the public ferry across the Potomac, and at Alexandria hired a horse, for which he paid three dollars.[24] He rode for some ten miles to Mount Vernon for a social call on Mrs. George Washington. He had sometimes disagreed with her late husband, but her high-columned establishment overlooking the river already represented a common ground of American politics. He then returned as he had come, a solitary figure on a slow-moving, placid beast, of a kind that anyone was free to ride, or at least anyone who was white and had three dollars.

At about this same time the painter David, an old Jacobin of 1793, was at work on one of his memorable compositions, which may now be seen near the empty royal apartments at the palace of Versailles. He conceived of a horse and rider against a rocky Alpine background, moving steeply uphill, the horse a highstepping, tense, and furious charger, with startled eye and mane flowing in the wind, the rider a uniformed officer seated securely on his restless mount, transfixing the spectator with an imperious gaze, and while lightly holding the reins in one hand, pointing with the other over the mountains and into the future. It was a glorified picture of the master of the New Order in Europe—"Bonaparte crossing the St. Bernard Pass"—just before his descent for the second time into the Po valley, where in June 1800 he defeated the Austrians at Marengo. This victory restored the Cisalpine Republic, and finally broke up the Second Coalition. Democracy in Europe had not exactly succeeded, but the great conservative and aristocratic counter-offensive had utterly failed.

That Bonaparte and Jefferson were very different human beings,

[24] D. Malone, *Jefferson and His Time. Vol. III: Jefferson and the Ordeal of Liberty* (Boston, 1962), 499.

as different as the horses they rode on, hardly needs to be pointed out. Jefferson, like American republicans generally, had once admired Bonaparte; even today there are at least six places in the United States named "Marengo." But Jefferson turned against the increasingly despotic ways and mad egotism of his one-time hero. "Do you call this a Republic?" asked the disgusted Thomas Paine in 1802. The author of the *Rights of Man* had had enough of Europe, and returned to America, and his abandonment of the old continent was also symbolic. As the great republican enthusiasms of the 1790's subsided, and as Europe went on with its chronic wars, there came to prevail for a long time in the United States a feeling of self-chosen and fortunate isolation, a belief that the vices of Europe were incorrigible, and that Americans should be as little involved as possible with an old world where true liberty could not exist. It was hard for the man on the three-dollar horse to understand the man on the charger, to comprehend why decent people could so long uphold Bonaparte, to think in terms of alternatives instead of ideals, to see that some things taken for granted in America, like "equality before the law," might in Europe have to be fought for.

Bonaparte and Jefferson had this much in common: both were detested as "Jacobins" in some quarters, yet under Bonaparte as First Consul and Emperor, and under Jefferson as President, the democratic and republican agitation quieted down. Revolutionary excitement was over. In America republicanism faded off into the general attitude of most people in the country. In Europe, where Bonaparte for a time treated republicans and royalists pretty much alike, giving them jobs if they could be useful, and imprisoning or even executing those who persisted in conspiracy or subversion, the forces making for change were content for a while to operate within an authoritarian framework which he provided. Men of practical bent and modern outlook, freed both from popular demands and from old-noble pretensions, relieved of the fear of both revolution and reaction, and protected by armed force, until 1813, against the inroads of ever-reviving Coalitions, worked together at a liquidation of the Old Regime in various countries, in an area much like that of the New Republican Order of 1798. This area was the Continental heartland of Western Civilization, comprising France and Italy, Switzerland and what are now called the Benelux countries, to which was soon added Germany as far as the Elbe—the sphere of Napoleon's empire, and of the "Europe" of 1960. The very German philosopher Hegel, as he watched the

Emperor of the French ride through the streets of Jena in 1806, just before annihilating the Prussian army, saw the movement of history, of humanity, and of true liberty embodied before his eyes—"the World-Soul sitting on a horse."[25]

In the twentieth century both the World-Soul and the horse have become archaic, and the dialectic of Hegel has become unconvincing. It is not as easy to generalize about the grand sweep of human events as it once was. It is not easy to summarize what happened in the world of Western Civilization in the forty years from 1760 to 1800, or to be certain of the meaning of these years for the subsequent history of mankind. For the ideas set forth at the outset of the first volume of this book a thousand pages of evidence have now been offered. In history, for large ideas, there is no such thing as proof; no view, however much demonstrated, can pretend to be conclusive or final. It is hoped, however, that the reader can now see these events of the eighteenth century as a single movement, revolutionary in character, for which the word "democratic" is appropriate and enlightening; a movement which, however different in different countries, was everywhere aimed against closed élites, self-selecting power groups, hereditary castes, and forms of special advantage or discrimination that no longer served any useful purpose. These were summed up in such terms as feudalism, aristocracy, and privilege, against which the idea of common citizenship in a more centralized state, or of common membership in a free political nation, was offered as a more satisfactory basis for the human community.

What had happened by 1800, even in countries where it was temporarily suppressed, was the assertion of "equality" as a prime social desideratum. It was an equality that meant a wider diffusion of liberty. That the assurance of some liberties meant the curtailment of others was well understood, so that, more on the continent of Europe than elsewhere, the democratic movement brought a consolidation of public authority, or of the state. It was not an equality that could long accept the surrender of liberty; the solution provided by Bonaparte could not prove to be durable. Nor was it an equality that repudiated the power of government; the world of Thomas Jefferson would also pass.

In forty years, from 1760 to 1800, "equality" took on a wealth of meanings, to which few new ones have been added since that time.

[25] J. Hoffmeister, ed., *Briefe von und an Hegel*, 2 vols. (Hamburg, 1952), I, 120.

It could mean an equality between colonials and residents of a mother country, as in America; between nobles and commoners, as in France; patricians and burghers, as at Geneva; ruling townsmen and subject country people, as at Zurich and elsewhere; between Catholic and Protestant, Anglican and Dissenter, Christian and Jew, religionist and unbeliever, or between Greek and Turk in Rhigas Velestinlis' memorable phrase. It might refer to the equal right of gildsmen and outsiders to enter upon a particular kind of trade or manufacture. For some few it included greater equality between men and women. Equality for ex-slaves and between races was not overlooked. For popular democrats, like the Paris sans-culottes, it meant the hope for a more adequate livelihood, more schooling and education, the right to stroll on the boulevards with the upper classes, and for more recognition and more respect; and it passed on to the extreme claim for an exact equality of material circumstances, which was rarely in fact made during the Revolutionary era, but was feared as an ultimate consequence of it by conservatives, and expressed in Babeuf's blunt formula, "stomachs are equal."

Monarchy, religion, the church, the law, and the economic system— along with the British Parliament, the Dutch Union of Utrecht, the old folk-democracies of the upland Swiss, the gentry republic in Poland, and the patrician communes of Italy—were brought into question so far as they upheld inequalities that were thought to be unjust. "Everywhere inequality is a cause of revolution," said Aristotle long ago, and his observation may remain as the last word on the subject. The problem of the historian in deciding upon the causes of revolution, as of rulers in preventing or guiding it, is to identify the sore spots, the political, economic, sociological, or psychological matters which arouse, in a significant number of relatively normal human beings, the embittered sense of inequality which is the sense of injustice.

The present book began with a quotation from Alexis de Tocqueville, and may close with another. For Tocqueville the course of all history revealed a continuing movement toward a greater "equality of conditions." In the introduction to his *Democracy in America*, thinking of both France and the United States, and indeed of all Europe since the Middle Ages, he explained his view of world history, in which he was less oracular than Hegel, and less dogmatic than Marx.

"The gradual trend toward equality of conditions," he said, "is a fact of Providence, of which it bears the principal characteristics: it is universal, it is enduring, it constantly eludes human powers of control; all events and all men contribute to its development.

"Would it be wise to think that a social movement of such remote origin can be suspended by the efforts of one generation? Can it be supposed that democracy, after destroying feudalism and overwhelming kings, will yield before the powers of money and business—*devant les bourgeois et les riches*?

"What then does the future hold? No one can say."[26]

Here was no prediction of revolution to come, no conservative theory, as with Friedrich Gentz, that one revolution must lead endlessly to another, to show what a great evil the French Revolution had been; no neo-revolutionary message, as with Karl Marx, to show that since one revolution that he called "bourgeois" had occurred, another that he called "proletarian" must surely follow. It was only a prediction that the future would see an increasing equality of conditions, brought about in ways that could not be foreseen, and were not prescribed. It was a prediction that even inequalities of wealth and income, like others, would be reduced either by revolution or otherwise. Such has in fact proved to be the case.

For Tocqueville it was a troubled anticipation, in which difficulties and losses were to be expected as well as gains. In substance, however, it was the anticipation that had inspired the last days of Condorcet, who had rejoiced to see, in 1794, at the end of the "Progress of the Human Mind," the vision of a future world in which all invidious differences between human beings would be erased.

All revolutions since 1800, in Europe, Latin America, Asia, and Africa, have learned from the eighteenth-century Revolution of Western Civilization. They have been inspired by its successes, echoed its ideals, used its methods. It does not follow that one revolution need lead to another, or that revolution as such need be glorified as a social process. No revolution need be thought of as inevitable. In the eighteenth century there might have been no revolution, if only the old upper and ruling classes had made more sagacious concessions, if, indeed, the contrary tendencies toward a positive assertion of aristocratic values had not been so strong. What seems to be inevitable, in

[26] *Démocratie en Amérique,* in *Oeuvres* (Paris, 1951), Vol. I, Part I, p. 4. The standard English translation (Reeve-Bradley, New York, 1946, I, 6), by calling *les bourgeois* "tradesmen," betrays its mid-Victorian origin and misses the full relevancy for modern times. The other quotation from Tocqueville alluded to here precedes the title-page of *Age,* I, and is from *L'ancien régime et la Révolution,* Book I, Chapters III and v. The quotation from Aristotle is from the *Politics,* v, I, Jowett translation.

both human affairs and in social science, must be put in contingent form—if x, then y. If a sense of inequality or injustice persists too long untreated, it will produce social disorganization. In a general breakdown, if a constructive doctrine and program are at hand, such as were furnished in the eighteenth century by the European Enlightenment, if the capacities of leaders and followers are adequate to the purpose, and if they are strong enough to prevail over their adversaries, then a revolution may not only occur and survive, but open the way toward a better society. The conditions are hard to meet, but the stakes are high, for the alternative may be worse.

✯ APPENDIX ✯

References for the Quotations at Heads of Chapters

I. J. Mallet du Pan, *Considérations sur la nature de la Révolution de France, et sur les causes qui en prolongent la durée* (London and Brussels, 1793), v.

II. A. von Arneth, ed., *Die Relationen der Botschafter Venedigs über Österreich im achtzehnten Jahrhundert*, in *Fontes rerum austriacarum*, Pt. II, Vol. 22 (Vienna, 1863), 340.

III. This and other letters by "A Calm Observer," first published in the *Morning Chronicle*, were reprinted as a book under the same pseudonym by Benjamin Vaughan as *Letters on the subject of a concert of princes and the dismemberment of Poland and France* (London, 1793); see p. 260 of the second edition.

IV. "Rapport sur les principes du gouvernement révolutionnaire, 5—nivôse An II, 25 décembre 1793" in C. Vellay, *Discours et rapports de Robespierre* (Paris, 1908), 311-12.

V. Letter in Latin from Szulyovsky to Hajnotzy in K. Benda, *A magyar jakobinus mozgalom iratai*, 3 vols. (Budapest, 1952-1957), I, 1066; P. K. Alefirenko in *Istoricheskiye Zapiski* (1947), 236; Thomas Campbell, *The Pleasures of Hope, with Other Poems* (7th ed., London, 1803), 28.

VI. H. T. Colenbrander, ed., *Gedenkstukken der algemeene geschiedenis van Nederland van 1795 tot 1840* (The Hague, 1906), II, 493-94.

VII. Comte Reynaud de Montlosier, *Des effets de la violence et de la modération dans les affaires de la France* (London, 1796), 33.

VIII. J. Mallet du Pan, *Correspondance politique pour servir à l'histoire du républicanisme français* (Hamburg, 1796), p. vi of *avant-propos* and p. xv of text.

IX. Giuseppe Poggi in his paper, the *Estensore cisalpino*, as quoted by E. Rota in *Nuova rivista storica*, VII (1923), 246.

X. *Raccolta degli editti, proclami, avvisi ecc. pubblicati in Milano dal 7 maggio 1796 in avanti*, 18 vols. (Milan, 1796-1799), VII, 475-76.

XI. G. Steiner, ed., *Korrespondenz des Peter Ochs*, 3 vols. (Basel, 1927-1937), II, 275; *The Dispatches and Letters of Vice Admiral Lord Viscount Nelson*, 7 vols. (London, 1845), III, 194.

XII. G. Pallain, ed., *Le ministère de Talleyrand sous le Directoire: correspondance diplomatique* (Paris, 1891), 394.

APPENDIX

XIII. Steiner, *Ochs*, II, 220.

XIV. "Was hat der rechtschaffene Mann in Zeitläufen zu tun wie die unsrigen sind?" von Herrn Professor Rickfels in *Deutsches Magazin*, Altona (January 1798), 10.

XV. W. A. Knight, ed., *Letters of the Wordsworth Family*, 3 vols. (London, 1907), I, 68; Countess of Minto, ed., *Life and Letters of Sir Gilbert Elliot First Earl of Minto*, 3 vols. (London, 1874), II, 129-130.

XVI. "Extracts from an oration delivered by Elihu Palmer, 4 July 1793," in *Political Miscellany* (New York, 1793), 23; H. C. Lodge, ed., *Life and Letters of George Cabot* (Boston, 1877), 173; C. F. Adams, ed., *Letters of John Adams Addressed to his Wife*, 2 vols. (Boston, 1848), II, 252.

XVII. J. Mallet du Pan, *The British Mercury, or Historical and critical views of the events of the present times*, 5 vols. (London, 1799-1800), III, 472-73 (August 15, 1799); *Oeuvres du comte P.-L. Roederer*, 8 vols. (Paris, 1854), III, 332 (conversation with Bonaparte, August 2, 1800); H. R. Yorke, *Letters from France in 1802*, 2 vols. (London, 1804), II, 342 (conversation with Paine).

★ INDEX ★